TRIPOLITANIA

TRIPOLITANIA

D.J. Mattingly

B.T. Batsford Limited · London

To Jenny
with love and thanks

First published 1995

Typeset by
Goodfellow & Egan Ltd,
Cambridge

Printed by
The Bath Press, Bath

Published by
B.T. Batsford Ltd
4 Fitzhardinge Street,
London, W1H 0AH

A catalogue record for this book is
available from the British Library

ISBN 0 7134 5742 2

CONTENTS

LIST OF
FIGURES

LIST OF
PLATES

ACKNOWLEDGEMENTS

This book is the product of many years' study of Roman Tripolitania, commencing with a Ph.D. thesis on the province that I completed in 1984. That it has taken me a further 10 years to revise, expand and develop the thesis into this book can be put down to many things: three job-changes (including a trans-Atlantic move and back again), making habitable several dilapidated houses, numerous switches in computer hardware and software, three children and my own widening research horizons can account for much of that! That it has got done at all I owe to a number of people who have given particular encouragement at vital stages. First mention must go to my Ph.D. supervisor, Barri Jones who introduced me to Roman Africa and who has contributed immensely to my understanding of the region and its archaeology. My father, Harold Mattingly, a wonderful source of knowledge and good sense about the ancient world, has been a much-valued sounding board for my ideas, and over the years has contributed innumerable helpful suggestions. A special word of thanks goes to Anthony Birley who, having read the entire thesis, first encouraged me to publish it with Batsford. The successive Batsford advisory editors for archaeology, Graham Webster and Michael Fulford have also been generous with their time and advice. A massive debt is owed to the patience and persistence of Peter Kemmis Betty who kept me going against all the odds, whilst always remaining sympathetic and polite in the face of several delays.

Parts of the work rely heavily on my knowledge of the pre-desert landscapes explored by the UNESCO Libyan Valleys Survey in which I participated from 1979-84, and I must thank the project's directors, Barri Jones and Graeme Barker, for their generosity in allowing me to refer freely to that material and to utilise a number of illustrations from the project archive. Sections of chapters 8, 10 and 11 are expanded and re-edited versions of text that was originally published as a single article in *Antiquités africaines* 23 (1987). I am grateful to the editorial board of that journal for permission to use the material in this way. The Society for Libyan Studies also gave permission for me to reproduce a small section from an article originally published by me in *Libyan Studies* 19 (1988) as part of chapter 7 and to reproduce a number of figures for which they had the copyright. Figures 6:1, 6:4, 6:6 and 6:8 were drawn for me by Alison Wilkins; figures 2:6, 2.13, 5:6 and 9:2 are the work of Debbie Miles, but most of the other figures and photographs are my own except where sources are acknowledged below. A general word of thanks is offered to all who have helped with providing illustrations or in giving copyright clearance. Specific acknowledgements are as follows: Figs 0:1, 4:2, from Barth 1857; Fig. 2:7, from Bates 1914; Fig. 2:10, from Jones and Barker 1980; Fig. 5:5, from Lyon 1821; Fig. 6:2, from Jones 1989b; Fig. 6:3, from Ward-Perkins 1993; Fig. 6:5, from Lezine 1972; Fig. 6:7, from Kenrick 1985c; Fig. 6:9, from Constans 1916; Figs 7:6, 7:11, 8:5, 11:2, from Jones 1985a; Fig. 7:10, from Hunt *et al.*, 1987; Figs 10:3, 10:4 from Buck, Burns and Mattingly 1983; Figs 10:5, 10:6, from Brogan and Smith 1985; Fig. 11.1, from Welsby 1992; Fig. 11:3 from Welsby 1991; Fig. 8:4 and Plates 2, 3, 6, 10, 11, 35, 38, 39, 41, 46, 47, 48, 52, 53, 54, 55, 56, 57, from the ULVS archive; Plate 5, from Charles Daniels; Plate 30, from Barri Jones; Plates 20, 59, 60, 61, from the Jamahiriya's Museum, Tripoli.

The work could not have been written without the material support and assistance of colleagues in the Institut National du Patrimoine (formerly d'Archéologie et d'Art) (Tunis) and the Department of Antiquities in Tripoli. For the former, particular mention must be made of Mohammed Fantar, Hedi Slim and Nejib Ben Lazreg; for the latter, Ali Khaduri (President) and Giuma Anag in Tripoli, Mohammed Shitewi and Omar Mahjoub (present and past Controller at *Lepcis Magna*) and Abdullah Rheibi (Gar Yunis University, Benghazi).

A host of other scholars have encouraged my studies, by sending off-prints and supplying references and answers to my questions: most notably, Tony Allan, the late Olwen Brogan, Jean-Pierre Brun, David Buck, Rob Burns, Charles Daniels, Antonio di Vita, Ginette di Vita-Evrard, Hazel Dodge, John Dore, Maurice Euzennat, Lisa Fentress, Peter Garnsey, Dave Gilbertson, Bruce Hitchner, John Humphrey, Philip Kenrick, André Laronde, Yann Le Bohec, Phillipe Leveau, John Lloyd, Clementina Panella, René Rebuffat, Joyce Reynolds, Alan Rushworth, Brent Shaw, Isabella Sjöström, Pol Trousset, Hafez Walda, Susan Walker, Derek Welsby, John Wilkes, Dick Whittaker.

I have profited enormously from discussions with colleagues at the Institute of Archaeology, Oxford, at the University of Michigan and, more recently, at Leicester. In the latter stages Bruce Hitchner read the entire typescript and made numerous helpful suggestions and morale-boosting comments. Two Leicester colleagues, Neil Christie and Marijke van der Veen offered valuable criticisms of specific groups of chapters. I alone am responsible for errors of fact or judgement that remain. For Batsford, Charlotte Kilenyi has proved an efficient and speedy editor of the work in press.

Finally, and most importantly, I must acknowledge my debt to my family who have allowed me the time and space to finish this book. I extend a big 'thank you' to Rebecca, Susanna and Douglas (born with impeccable timing the week the typescript was completed). Last mention must go to my wife Jenny, always the most honest and perceptive critic of my work. It is undoubtedly conventional to say that without her support my Ph.D. and this book would never have been written, but it is also entirely true. She is also responsible for the index and more than anyone deserves the dedication of this work.

A NOTE ON THE TRANSLITERATION OF ARABIC PLACE NAMES

The different modern histories of Libya and Tunisia have resulted in rather diverse forms of transliterating modern place names from Arabic. The imposition of a single unitary scheme would have had obvious merits from the point of view of consistency, but would have rendered the names of many well-known sites almost unrecognizable. Accordingly I have generally kept French style transliteration for sites in Tunisia (e.g., Chott Djerid) and Italian style in Libya (Gebel Nefusa). By and large I have tried to render names of sites in the form in which they will be most familiar to modern students of the region (thus Bu Njem rather than Bu Ngem, since the site is now best known through the publications of Rebuffat).

The use of the term Tripolitania in this book refers to the geographical area of northwest Libya and southeast Tunisia, whereas *Tripolitana* is used in reference to the mid-imperial *regio* (region) and the late Roman *provincia* (province).

PREFACE

1
THE HISTORICAL FRAMEWORK

The chronological limits of this study are, at one extreme, Caesar's victory at *Thapsus* which ended the civil war in Africa (46 BC) and, at the other, the conquest of North Africa by the Vandals (which was completed by AD 455). These are no more than convenient *termini* for the study of the Roman province and its frontier and there is, of course, much valuable information on political, military and socio-economic matters in sources on earlier and later periods, notably those relating to the Byzantine reconquest of the region. In the main, though, the discussion centres on the 500 years when the region known as the *Emporia* and later as *Tripolitana* was part of the Roman provinces of Africa. Although the province of *Tripolitana* was the product of Diocletian's reforms *c.* AD 303, the Tripolitanian region had always stood out from the rest of *Africa Proconsularis* and the title of this book requires no special pleading.[1]

The history of Tripolitania (below, chapters 3, 4 and 9) was closely linked to that of its main city, *Lepcis Magna*. The form *Lepcis*, used here in preference to the commonly encountered *Leptis*, is derived from the neo-Punic name *Lpqy*, indicating the Phoenician origin of the settlement. At its apogee *Lepcis Magna* was probably second only to Carthage among the cities of Roman Africa in terms of its size, wealth and munificence.[2] Though originally Phoenician settlements, the three towns, which were known corporately as the *Emporia* and later as the *Tripolis*

(*Lepcis, Oea* and *Sabratha*), came under the controlling influence of Carthage in her heyday. The integration of Phoenician and Libyan ethnic groups probably began at an early date and was accompanied by agricultural development of a deep hinterland zone. Although the territory is notable for the marginality of its agriculture, it became one of the richest areas in early–mid imperial Africa.

2
PREVIOUS WORK

The area of Roman Tripolitania is today split into two by the political division between northwest Libya and southern Tunisia. This has presented an obstacle to modern research, since most antiquarians and scholars have worked on only one side or the other of the modern frontier. A prime objective of this book is to reunite Tripolitania as a geographic entity and to study it as a single unit.

Interest in the Roman history of the region was largely quiescent until the early nineteenth century. Most of the first wave of Europeans to pass through Tripolitania from that date were explorers heading for the Fezzan and beyond, into the Sudan. Setting off on their expeditions, their observations of the countryside and of archaeological features were often precise and enthusiastic (in contrast to the condensed accounts they gave of their return journeys when their senses had been dulled by malaria). Lyon (1818–20), Denham, Clapperton and Oudney (1822–4), Richardson (1845–6), Barth (1849–55), Duveyrier (1860), Nachtigal (1869) and others have left a rich archive of description and

Fig 0:1 Three Romano-Libyan monuments recorded by Barth in 1850s Tripolitania: a) olive press in the Gebel Tarhuna;
b) obelisk mausoleum south of Mizda; c) obelisk mausoleum in the Wadi Tabuniya near Gheriat el-Garbia (from Barth 1857).

drawings, notably of sites close to the main caravan routes of eastern Tripolitania (Fig. 0:1).[3]

Commander Smythe had less ambitious exploration in mind when, in 1817, he made a brief journey into the interior to discover the 'lost city' of Ghirza. He was, however, profoundly disappointed and set the pattern for later archaeological work in the area by subsequently concentrating on exposing (and pilfering) columns and decorated marble at the coastal site of *Lepcis Magna*. Another early expedition was that of the Beechey brothers (1821–2), who followed the Syrtic coastal route from Tripoli to Cyrenaica.[4]

The French conquest of southern Tunisia in the 1880s had important repercussions for the study of that region. The cartographers of the 'brigades topographiques' and off-duty officers, aided by French antiquarians, began the first systematic mapping and study of ancient ruins, as well as carrying out excavations. Although of variable quality, judged by modern standards, this work constitutes a large and invaluable data-base. In Libya, meanwhile, access was made extremely difficult by the Turkish government of the region. Cowper (1895–6) and the Frenchman de Mathuisieulx (1901, 1902, 1904) were exceptions in being granted permisson to explore the Gebel region. Cowper's methodical study of the remains of olive presses is still of great value, despite the fact that he wrongly identified them as prehistoric megaliths.[5]

Italy's seizure of Libya in 1911 was followed by the first systematic archaeological excavations, though mainly concentrated on the coastal cities of *Lepcis Magna* and *Sabratha* and on rich villas, such as Zliten. Because of the unsettled nature of the Gebel and pre-desert hinterland for a protracted period after the initial Italian invasion, little work was carried out there. It was only in the 1930s that the conquest of Fezzan (southern Libya) was finally achieved, allowing major scientific and archaeological expeditions to be sent there.[6] Paradoxically, work in southern Tunisia had tailed off and comparatively little that was new was recorded between the 1930s and the 1960s. But in Libya, following the Second World War, the interim British Military Administration inaugurated a major programme of work on the interior of eastern Tripolitania under the direction of J.B. Ward-Perkins and R.G. Goodchild. Italian and British teams also continued to work on the major coastal sites. Since the independence of Libya in 1951, British, Italian and French teams have continued to work with the Libyan Department of Antiquities on a variety of projects.[7]

Since the 1960s both the Tunisian Institut National d'Art et Archéologie (now, du Patrimoine) and the Libyan Antiquities Department have been increasingly active in the field. In 1964 a small British expedition attempted to follow the Roman *limes* road through both Tunisia and Libya and in 1968 a joint Tunisian and French team inaugurated a phase of renewed fieldwork and publication, including Trousset's important thesis on the western *limes Tripolitanus*. The latest major international project in Libya has been that of the UNESCO Libyan Valleys Survey (hereafter ULVS), a joint Anglo-Libyan and Franco-Libyan venture. This has involved the detailed study of a considerable area of the pre-desert hinterland of eastern Tripolitania.[8]

The amount of material available is substantial and the quality of archaeological preservation at many sites would alone merit the present attempt at synthesis. This synthesis has of necessity also to draw on material from other parts of Roman Africa – for comparison, contrast and for the simple reason that Tripolitania, for much of its history, formed part of broad administrative arrangements that covered a large part of North Africa. This is not intended to be read, therefore, as a proxy history of Roman Africa as seen from Tripolitania, but a study of the latter zone constructed upon my perception of some central themes in the history and archaeology of Roman Africa.

3
CONCEPTUAL FRAMEWORK

The conflict theory

A great deal has been written on Roman Africa starting from the assumption that there was always conflict between 'the desert and the sown', that is, between nomads and sedentary people. Such theories assert that the Romans expelled nomadic tribes from the cultivatable Tell and steppe-lands, forcing them back into the northern Sahara and constructing frontiers to prevent their re-entry into what rapidly became a zone of sedentary agriculture and civilization. The nomads established their dominance in the oases of the northern Sahara and, with the diffusion of the camel in the late Roman empire, were increasingly able to attack the Roman frontiers with impunity. Or so the theory asserts. Variants on this conflict theory have been applied to the study of mountain enclaves within the Roman provinces, such as the Great Kabylie range. Unsubdued nomadic tribes were allegedly penned up in such mountain 'reservations', from where they would break out periodically to pillage sedentary agricultural settlements. In spite of the questionable assumption that nomadic and sedentary people are necessarily antipathetic towards each other, such theories have dominated the literature for over 50 years. This is one of many instances of the Romano-African past being recreated in the light of twentieth-century European experience and aspirations in North Africa. My history of Roman Africa is not dominated by endemic warfare, nor do colonists from overseas feature as major actors.[9]

The *limitanei* theory

This theory arose in response to the need for an explanation of the apparent growth in agricultural settlements at various points along the Roman frontiers in Africa. Carcopino first suggested that much of the new settlement might have been that of army veterans, designed to firm up the frontier zone. The whole case rests upon a possibly spurious reference to land allocation to frontier guards in the 'Life' of Severus Alexander and an entry in the Theodosian Code referring to lands held by a border militia. In consequence there has been a tendency to identify almost all better quality construction work in the frontier zone as being military or paramilitary in origin. The issue became much more complex when Goodchild adapted the idea and applied it to the evidence he had discovered in Libya in the 1940s. There, most of the fortified farms (or *gsur*) seemed to be of third century or later date. He argued that this was a clear vindication of the passage relating to Severus Alexander, and that the men who garrisoned these farms were border militia or *limitanei*. The use of the term *limitanei* was unfortunate as it is, in fact, incorrect in this context. Goodchild's theory has been further undermined by more recent work which has shown that there was extensive settlement in the region of earlier date. Nonetheless it is still an influential hypothesis and one cannot disregard his evidence that some of the frontier settlements do appear to have had official connections just as some individuals bore official military titles (see below, chapter 10).[10]

The minimalist approach

If Goodchild represents the maximalist point of view of Roman involvement in the frontier zones, then the opposite approach has also attracted interest.[11] This argues for minimal Roman influence on, or involvement in, the socio-economic development of the frontier zones. The majority of the *gsur* are to be interpreted as indigenous dwellings which had nothing to do with organized militia. The main problem with this approach, however, is one of terminology. How to define, for instance, what 'Roman influence' constituted in a region such as Tripolitania and how such influence was exerted both actively and passively? Only by studying the Roman and native interaction in the fullest possible detail can we strike a balance between these two opposed viewpoints. Although there is a great deal that should be

described as 'Libyan' or 'African' rather than as 'Roman' in the frontier lands, these regions did not exist in a vacuum and were profoundly affected by imported political, social and economic developments.

The secondary literature on Roman Africa remains a minefield because of the significant role played by the successive conceptual *schema* in influencing interpretation. Whilst many historians and archaeologists of Roman North Africa have modified some of their views, away from the extreme positions of, for example, Gsell or Goodchild, the legacy of the earlier conceptual frameworks lingers on. It will become apparent in the pages to come that I reject the assumptions which underlie the 'conflict theory', and that the '*limitanei* theory' must be abandoned in the light of new evidence. And I have not followed the extreme post-colonial minimalists in shaping my picture of the past. In assembling the detailed evidence for the context and development of the region, some new approaches have emerged which, I hope, provide a valid and coherent alternative perspective. Nevertheless, a considerable debt is owed to the ideas of earlier scholars, who may be out of fashion now, but who were never entirely wrong.

4
TOWARDS A PROVINCIAL CASE STUDY?

Studies of Roman provinces are sometimes constrained by the clichéd formula of the genre, producing a rather bland, stereotypical view of life in the Roman empire. Whilst it is impossible to subvert entirely the structure of such studies, as the chapter headings of this book will indicate, it is my intention to explore in greater detail a number of fundamental themes which differentiated Tripolitania from many other parts of Africa or the empire at large. First, there is the extraordinary and undeniable fact that, in *Lepcis Magna*, one of the least promising environments of the Mediterranean hosted one of the wealthiest Roman provincial towns. This is in part a question of geography (chapter 1) and in part one of politics and economics (chapters 3, 6, 7). The geographical peculiarities of the region are also of prime significance to explanations of its later precipitate decline (chapters 9–12).

Rural economy and settlement trends provide the second major theme. The exploitation of the countryside, and in particular the evidence for massive olive cultivation, is a notable focus in the examination of the ancient economy of the zone and of the close links between town and country (chapter 7). The sedentarization of tribal groups from the pre-desert margins of the Sahara was an important side-effect of the economic and political incorporation of the region in the Roman empire, yet the settlement pattern that emerged was not static and there appear to have been important changes taking place in later antiquity (chapter 11).

The ethnic and cultural character of the people, dwellers in both town and country, is a third dominant theme (chapters 2, 3, 7, 8, 11, 12), particularly in view of the near total lack of evidence of colonization from outside the area during the Roman period. The fourth theme concerns the influence of the Roman frontier on the region. The coastal towns were highly

civilized centres and by the first century AD were becoming well integrated into the Roman empire, but they were separated from the Saharan desert and 'another Africa' by only a thin stretch of territory. In consequence, I believe that military involvement in the region was more important than has normally been recognized and from an earlier date (chapters 3, 4, 5, 9, 10). A final aspect which will reappear at several points concerns the successful breakthrough of the regional elite into the central political structures of the Roman state. As we shall see, the elevation of L. Septimius Severus, a citizen of *Lepcis,* as emperor at the close of the second century had profound implications for the region, further setting it apart from the rest of Roman Africa.

Fig. 0:2 Roman Tripolitania. Map showing locations of principal sites named in the text. Open symbols indicate that the exact location is uncertain. Latin place names are given in italics, where these are reasonably well established; non-italic names are modern place names.

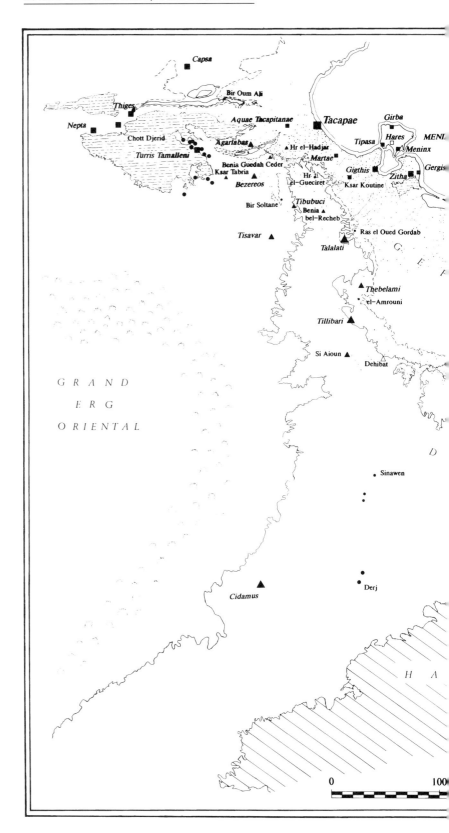

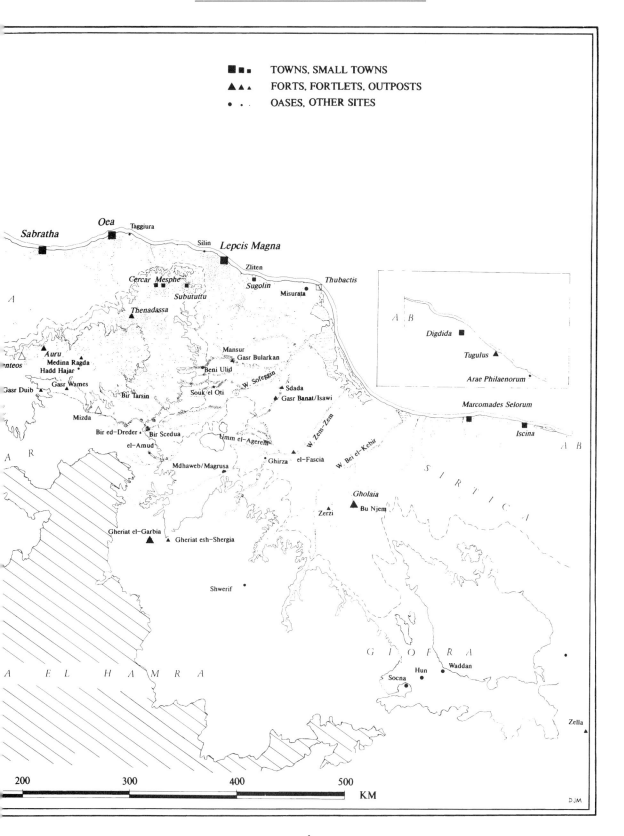

TOWNS, SMALL TOWNS
FORTS, FORTLETS, OUTPOSTS
OASES, OTHER SITES

1
GEOGRAPHY AND CLIMATE

1
INTRODUCTION

Although Tripolitania was administered as part of *Africa Proconsularis* until the third century AD, there were sound geographical reasons for eventually differentiating it as a separate territory. The physical relief and climate of the region distinguish Tripolitania from Rome's other territories in North Africa. It stands apart as a hybrid between Mediterranean and Saharan zones, and may even be considered to lie outside the Maghreb proper, which is characterized by the Atlas mountains (Tell) and high plains (steppe). In terms of structure and climate Tripolitania is more immediately Saharan, although the long littoral imposes certain Mediterranean climatic nuances.[1] The main ecological zones are well defined and have imposed the essential conditions and limitations of settlement in the region.

Early modern explorers noted with astonishment the extensive remains of ancient settlement in zones then almost devoid of population (Plate 1).[2] Similar observations were made in Tunisia, Algeria and Morocco and, perhaps inevitably, there was speculation that major climatic change had occurred in the post-classical period. Modern research, however, suggests that the ancient conditions were much the same as those of today and a good deal of information on the ancient environment can be assembled from a combination of ancient and modern sources. We shall first examine the meagre ancient sources and then consider the comparative value of studies of the modern geography, climate and ecology of the region.

2
ANCIENT EVIDENCE FOR GEOGRAPHY, CLIMATE, FLORA AND FAUNA

The ancient sources relating to the geography and climate of North Africa are the starting point for this brief survey. It is self-evidently important to establish to what extent the ancient environment of Tripolitania was similar to and/or different from that of today.

As we shall see below, modern Tripolitania comprises three fundamental geographic zones: the coastal plain (known as the Gefara in the central sector), a curving chain of hills (the Gebel) and the predesert plateau beyond (Dahar) that shades off into the true desert. This tripartite division is echoed in a number of sources. Strabo describes mountains and plains lying between the coast and the *Garamantes*, and also mentions large lakes (chotts?) and 'rivers which sink beneath the earth and become invisible' (wadis). Pliny described the Gefara as a desert separating the *Emporia* from *Africa Proconsularis*, which it certainly is in its central sector where movable sand dunes extend right up to the coast. South of there, he mentioned forests full of wild beasts, presumably a reference to the then wooded Gebel. Beyond was a desert and then came the land of the *Garamantes*. The sixth-century African poet Corippus gave vivid descriptions of a relatively arid Gefara, a wooded and populous Gebel and desolate desert lands of Dahar and Syrtica.[3]

More commonly Latin and Greek authors only had

1

detailed information on coastal features and described desert lands of the interior without reference to the wooded and fertile Gebel. There are ample references to show that the desert regions had much the same character then as now. The oases of the Sahara are vividly described by Herodotus as spring mounds and by Lucan as isolated, spring-fed 'woods' within the desert. Cato's celebrated crossing of the Syrtic desert with an army of 10,000 in 48 BC was difficult to emulate, even for small groups or individuals, until the construction of the 'Littorea' road in the 1930s. The 'sweltering Syrtes' (*Syrtes … aestuoses*) of Horace and the 'burning sands of a thirsty land' (*calidas terrae sitientis harenas*) of Corippus were not the products of poetic exaggeration, as the number of other examples shows.[4]

Of the coastal features which are described, Strabo's account of the lake of *Zuchis* (Sebkha Taourgha) and the wooded *Cephalea* promontory (Ras Misurata) are particularly evocative. Similarly, Procopius' description of sand dunes covering part of *Lepcis Magna* at the time of the Byzantine reconquest is supported by archaeological evidence and the modern state of the site.

Several sources referred to the perils of navigation along the Syrtic coast. The lack of good anchorages, the unpredictable shallows and the wrecking activities of the coastal-dwelling *Nasamones* tribes all contributed to the number of lost ships and the bad reputation of the inshore waters. As Strabo observed, however, the wrecks were mainly the result of sailors being loath to lose touch with the shoreline in spite of the perils involved.

> The difficulty with this Syrtis and the Little Syrtis is that in many places their deep waters contain shallows and the result is, at the ebb and flow of the tides, that sailors sometimes fall into the shallows and stick there, and that the safe escape of a boat is rare. On this account sailors keep at a distance when voyaging along the coast, taking precautions not to be caught off guard and driven by winds into these gulfs. However, the disposition of man to take risks causes him to try anything in the world and particularly voyaging along coasts.

Sea traffic between Cyrenaica and Tripolitania was not entirely discouraged, but the greater volume of trade and shipping probably moved north and west of *Lepcis* to Carthage and Rome as a consequence.[5]

In spite of its reputation as one of the granaries of Rome, Africa was always a country of low rainfall and of few perennial springs, streams or rivers, a situation neatly summed up in Sallust's phrase, 'impoverished in water from sky and land' (*caelo terraque penuria aquarum*). Periods of drought and crop failures are attested in the sources and Hadrian's visit to Africa in AD 128 coincided with the end of a five-year drought. Consequently he was highly esteemed in Africa afterwards.

Literary and archaeological evidence show that the rain which did fall was carefully utilized by the construction of control walls, dams, terraces and cisterns. Strabo described a 'Carthaginian wall' built in a wadi near *Lepcis*, and Frontinus described dam building as an 'African habit'. In another revealing passage, he contrasted Italian and African attitudes to flood water:

> In Italy a pretty big dispute may flare up in order to keep off flood water. But in Africa the same issue is handled quite differently. Since that is a very dry area, they have no dispute on this score unless someone has stopped rain water flowing on their land. They make embankments and catch and retain the rain water, so that it may be used on the spot rather than flow away.

The well-known *Lamasba* inscription, which gives details of the distribution of irrigation water to landholders, comes from a region of Algeria with over 400 mm rainfall (annual average). The fact that such measures were necessary because of a dispute between landholders over irrigation water, and in an area where commercial dry cultivation of cereals should have been possible in any case, implies that the pattern of rainfall was as unpredictable in the past as it is today. The archaeological remains of ancient hydraulic works are extensive, but much more detailed study is needed for us to understand all the different systems of water management.[6] The evidence seems, nevertheless, to suggest that Roman Africa developed agriculturally not as a result of higher rainfall, but through the careful control and management of the available water resources. Some regions were clearly worse off than others. Strabo described the Greater Syrtes coastline as 'destitute of water' and Africa in general as being like a leopard skin, with spots of dense habitation surrounded by desert. Sallust's description of a semi-arid zone around *Capsa* (Gafsa) also rings true of the steppe today. An inscription from Bu Njem exhorted the soldiers to relax in the baths away from the 'heat beating on these endless sands' and to enjoy a respite from 'the sun and fitful wind's scorching'. The latter remark is evidently a reference to the notorious hot desert wind (*ghibli*), which is also noted in other sources.[7] The available evidence supports the view that rainfall in antiquity was neither abundant, nor reliable.

Referring to *Africa Vetus* and the Numidian kingdom, Sallust described the land as fertile and good for crops and pasture but with relatively few trees. It is likely that the eastern Maghreb was never as well afforested as the Great Atlas ranges further west. But Pliny and Strabo both attest woods and forest on the coast and in the Gebel in Tripolitania. The cultivation of extensive 'forests' of olive trees began at an early date and Pliny was referring snobbishly to quality, and not to quantity, when he said that Africa was not noted for its wine and oil, but only its grain. As observed already, Tripolitania is not suited for commercial cereal cultivation and it is significant that the cash crop *par excellence* in antiquity, as today, was the olive. Although olive cultivation extended well beyond the region now considered economically viable, the evidence again indicates better water management rather than climatic change as the main factor. There is evidence for a wide variety of other fruit trees in Africa and Tripolitania in the Roman period: peaches, pomegranates, nectarines, plums, apples, jujubes, pears, figs (highly rated by Pliny), vines, almonds, pistachios, carobs. The once celebrated lotus tree evidently diminished in importance with the spread of arboriculture in the favoured areas of the coastal plain and Arab folklore remembered a time when Tripoli's orchards ('forest') extended to the Gebel. Evidence for modern cultivation will be discussed below.

Relief carvings from mausolea in Tunisia and Libya and mosaics from *Lepcis* and Zliten illustrate agricultural activities in the region (Plates 59–61). These confirm that, in spite of the low rainfall, cereals were cultivated as a dietary staple. Documentary records from the Roman fort at Bu Njem show that it was supplied with grain and olive oil by small scale cultivators of the pre-desert.[8]

Current research in the Sofeggin and Zem-Zem has produced a wealth of new environmental evidence from ancient middens, from which a detailed picture of the flora is now emerging. Preliminary results show a remarkable range of crops and plants for such a marginal zone (Table 1:1), although it is paralleled by the surviving cultivation at Beni Ulid and from a similar area of the Negev desert in Palestine. It is particularly interesting to note that the list of wild plants (that is the 'natural vegetation') indicates a dry or arid-zone environment much as today. The cultivation of olives, cereals and so on can be related to the archaeological evidence for the development of a run-off farming technology.

The cultivation of date palms and other crops in the oases of the northern Sahara is also attested by the ancient sources. Archaeological survey and excavation in Fezzan has corroborated this. The palaeo-botanical samples obtained from the Garamantian hillfort of Zinchecra are particularly important in attesting the early cultivation of bread wheats, alongside date palms and a range of other irrigated crops. Palms were used extensively in construction work in both fort and *vicus* at Bu Njem.[9]

The faunal record in antiquity reveals a decline in wildlife numbers and species from late prehistoric times onwards. Cave paintings and rock carvings from the north and central Sahara show that at one time it was much less arid than today. The spread of desert necessitated a northward or southward movement of many species and many of those that remained north of the desert in Tripolitania and Maghreb have died out through overkill by man, rather than for climatic reasons (Table 1:2). North Africa was one of the main hunting grounds for the animal displays (*venationes*) in amphitheatres around the Roman empire. Several early sources refer to a

Cultivated Plants	Rating	Timber Samples	Rating	Wild Plants	Rating
Barley	WD*	Olive	WD*	Emex spinosa	DR
Wheat	WD	Bamboo	IR	Zizyphus sp.	DR
Olives	WD*	Palm	IR	Medicago sp.	DR
Grapes	WD	Tamarisk	DR	Chenopodium sp.	DR
Figs	WD	Acacia	DR	Caryophyllaceae	DR
Dates	IR			Malva sp.	DR
Almonds	WD*			Chrysanthemum sp.	DR
Pulses (peas, lentils)	WD			Polygonum sp.	DR
Water Melon	IR			cf. Galium sp.	DR
				cf. Cruciferae	DR
				cf. Bromus	DR
				Fumaria	DR
				Anchusa officinalis	DR
				cf. Compositae	DR
				Spergula cf. arvensis	DR
				Avena fatua	DR

Table 1:1. Evidence for Roman period cultivated and wild plants from the Sofeggin and Zem-Zem area (data from Ghirza, the ULVS (van der Veen 1981; 1985a/b) and personal observation (of timber samples)). Key to water dependency ratings: IR = irrigated conditions needed; WD = water dependent; WD* = water dependent, but some drought resistance; DR = drought resistant.

Animal	Extinct	Ancient sources	Iconographic/faunal evidence
Donkey		Plutarch *Cato Y*, 56	Barker and Jones 1982
Horse		Strabo 17.3.6	Barker and Jones 1982
Camel		Marichal 1979	Demougeot 1960; Brogan 1955; Clarke 1986
Cattle		Herodotus 4.183, Strabo 17.3.19	Barker 1986
Sheep		Strabo 17.3.19	Brogan 1965a; Clarke 1986
Goat		Strabo 17.3.19	Clarke 1986
Elephant	*	Pliny 5.26; 8.32	Bovey 1979; Churcher 1980
Ostrich	*	Synesius *Letter* 134	Paradisi 1963; Rebuffat 1969; Saladin 1902
Gazelle			Churcher 1980; Clarke 1986
Giraffe	*	Pliny 8.69	Barker 1986; Paradisi 1963; de Mathuisieulx 1904
Rhinoceros	*		Bovey 1979; Churcher 1980
Auroch	*		Churcher 1980
Antelope	*	Pliny 10.201	Saladin 1902
Wildcat			Saladin 1902
Leopard	*	Pliny 10.202	Ward-Perkins and Toynbee 1949
Panther	*	Pliny 8.62	
Wolf	*	Pliny 8.80	
Hyena		Pliny 8.108	
Jackal		Pliny 8.108	
Lion	*	Lucan 9.941-47	Aurigemma 1926
Porcupine		Pliny 8.53	
Wild ass	*	Pliny 8.16	
Hartebeast	*		Bovey 1979
Buffalo	*		Bovey 1979
Wild boar	*		Aurigemma 1926
Hunting dog		Pliny 8.143	
Rabbit			Saladin 1902
Snake		Diodorus 3.50.2; Lucan 9.710; Lucian *de dips*	
Scorpion		Strabo 17.3.11	

Table 1:2. Wild and domesticated animals attested in Tripolitania and the northern Sahara in antiquity (this is not intended to be comprehensive. The * denote species now extinct in the region).

Tripolitanian 'wild beast zone' and Pliny specifically mentions elephants in the hinterland of the *Emporia*. The elephant was, moreover, one of the civic symbols of *Lepcis* and of *Sabratha*, perhaps indicating a connection with the trade in wild beasts.

The expansion of agriculture in the Roman period was achieved at the expense of potential predators or competitors in the 'wild beast zone'.[10] The lion survived in the Moroccan Atlas until 1922, the auroch until the 1940s and the ostrich is also recently extinct. Many other species such as the rhinoceros, giraffe and elephant were probably already hunted to the point of extinction during the Roman period.

There is now some information on the pastoral economy of ancient farmers in the Tripolitanian pre-desert zone. The results of faunal analysis of material collected by the ULVS, though based on a small sample, are illuminating. Of 4,225 large mammal bones recovered from midden sampling and small-scale excavation, 1,070 were identifiable to species. No less than 721 were sheep or goat bones, with 200 gazelle (196 from a single site), 40 camel, 30 pig, 29 bovid, 13 canid, 11 equid, 7 human, 2 antelope, 1 cat. On Roman period sites, the vast majority of the sheep/goats were killed in their second year of life, indicating that their primary exploitation was for meat. The unusual concentration of gazelle bones at one site close to the limits of settled agriculture illustrates the way that hunting could supplement the diet of farm-raised meat. On all the sites examined, spanning the Roman and medieval periods, sheep and goat herding was the most intensive form of stock-raising activity.

Of the domestic animals, the long-horned cattle have subsequently died out, but the modern descendants of the stocky, long-necked horses, of the sheep, goats and camels can still be seen today. As with the flora, the basic conditions of the country do not appear to have changed significantly and one must look for reasons other than climatic change for the denudation of once wooded and fertile land and the extinction of entire species of wildlife.[11]

The overall picture from the literary sources is thin, but consistent in portraying Tripolitania as a comparatively arid zone with a mixture of Mediterranean and Saharan characteristics. A deeper understanding of the ancient topography, climate, flora and fauna must depend on modern sources of data and on our judgement of whether or not there has been significant climatic change since the Roman period.

3
PHYSICAL GEOGRAPHY

Because of the accident of modern political geography, recent works tend to deal either with southern Tunisia alone or with northwest Libya. The region which is more properly defined as Tripolitania in the ancient sense extended from *Tacapae* (Gabes) to *Arae Philaenorum* (Ras el-Aàli) and covered approximately 175,000 square kilometres.[12] The greater part of this is techni-

cally pre-desert (true desert lands were excluded from the calculation) and in its wider context Tripolitania may be considered as essentially Saharan. Figures for modern Libya as a whole show that only 9 per cent of the land mass is not desert, and only 3 per cent is used for agriculture.[13] Broadly speaking, the same pattern is true for Roman Tripolitania; there was a restricted, fertile margin near the coast and a vast desert hinterland. If this Saharan hinterland, including Fezzan, is added to the calculation of size, one is dealing with an area in the order of 610,000 square kilometres. Thus Tripolitania is far more closely linked to the Sahara by climate, relief and physical proximity than most regions of the Maghreb.

At its simplest level, the geography of Tripolitania consists of three main zones (Fig.1:1). A broad coastal plain (the Gefara) runs from east of Tripoli (*Oea*) to the gulf of Bou-Ghara (*Gigthis*), where it merges with the coastal plain of the Gabes region (the Arad). A narrow extension of the coastal plain runs eastwards from *Lepcis* around the Syrtic gulf. To the south of the Gefara and curving in a great arc towards Homs (*Lepcis Magna*) at one extreme and Gabes at the other is the mountainous escarpment of the Gebel. To the

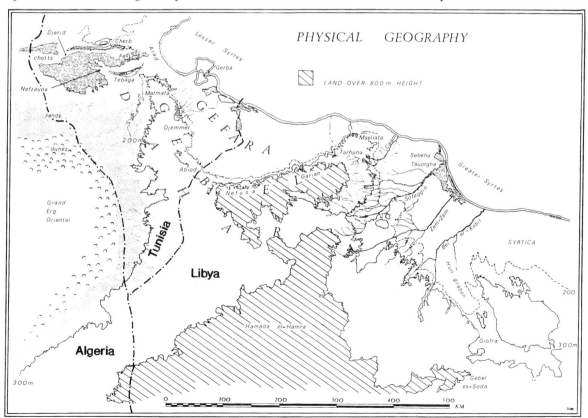

Fig 1:1 The physical geography of Tripolitania and modern political boundaries.

south, the Gebel merges gradually into the Saharan plateau (the Dahar). As we shall see, however, there are important local variations even within these broad categories and a number of other quite distinct physical zones must also be considered.[14]

The Gebel
Together, the Gebel, Gefara and Dahar once constituted a 'dome' of Jurassic and Cretaceous strata (limestones, dolomites, marls and clays). The collapse of the central region created the Gefara basin and the cliff-like face of much of the Gebel along the faulting. Later erosion of the uplifted Gebel has created several contiguous hill groups which are separately referred to as the Gebel Matmata and the Gebel Demmer (Tunisia), the Gebel Nefusa, Gebel Garian, Gebel Tarhuna and Gebel Msellata (Libya).[15] From a minimum width of about 10 km, the Gebel is normally a band of hills about 20–25 km wide. To the south it merges with the Dahar, which emphasizes the essentially Saharan nature of the formation. Its physical characteristics vary considerably between sectors. The highest portion is the Gebel Nefusa/Garian region which attains 800 m plus, whilst those of Tarhuna, Matmata and Demmer rarely reach 500 m.[16] The northern cliff escarpment is also most pronounced in the central section from Nalut to Garian, with access on to the plateau limited to a few routes, following deeply incised wadi beds. In the Libyan sectors generally, it is possible to move parallel to the scarp edge along the undulating plateau. But in the Gebel Demmer the eroded scarp edge is so broken up that movement is restricted either to the foothills or to the Dahar. In some areas lateral movement from the Dahar through the Gebel and into the Gefara is also limited to 'passages obligés'.

South of Garian the limestone plateau is overlain by extensive basalt flows, which are probably late Pliocene or Pleistocene in date. Except in the region of these flows, soils are normally wind-deposited and loess-like, deriving from the limestone plateau. On Garian the soil cover is up to 10 m thick in places. Angular quartz grains coated with a thin film of iron oxide give these soils a characteristic red colour.[17]

The Gefara
The Gefara is the collapsed centre of a Mesozoic anticline. Erosion of the Gebel in the Miocene and later has produced considerable aggradation of parts of the Gefara plain. More recent Quaternary erosion and deposition has been concentrated in the wadi beds which cross the Gefara plain to the sea. Even today, alluvium is being redeposited in places. At the apex of its arc the Gefara is about 150 km wide and east to

west along the coast it extends for over 350 km. The character of this relatively flat plain varies markedly between its extremities and its centre and between the coast and the interior. A large portion of it is technically desert. Setting out for Ghadames in 1848, Richardson was surprised to find that 'the desert reaches to the walls of the city of Tripoli'. Although some of the dune fields are of relatively recent origin, wind-blown sand was also a problem in the coastal plain in antiquity. The eastern Gefara south of Tripoli and the western Gefara south of Bou-Ghara (*Gigthis*) are comparatively well-watered zones, however, as is a narrow strip at the foot of the Gebel. A band of oases along the coast have helped make that a preferred zone of settlement as well. It is incorrect, therefore, to describe the Gefara as entirely arid steppe-lands, but neither should it be assumed to have once all been fertile. The coastal region is the most densely settled part on account of its subterranean aquifers and oases. The chain of oases from Tagiura to Gabes is only broken up by some extensive areas of sebkha near the Tuniso/Libyan border.[18]

The Dahar
The Saharan plateau or Dahar extends up to the Gebel escarpment and it is primarily climatic differences that demarcate them as separate zones. To the southwest the Dahar slopes off into the Great Eastern Erg (see below), to the south it runs into the foot of the Hamada el Hamra and to the southeast it is dissected by the great wadi basin of Sofeggin, Zem-Zem and Bei el-Kebir. This latter zone is marginally less arid than the two former, though none of them is as well-watered as the Gebel (see below).

This Mesozoic plateau formation has been deeply eroded at its eastern extremity by substantial water courses during the Quaternary age. Following initial down-cutting into the limestone strata, soil deposition has occurred and, in spite of the low rainfall, cultivation is possible in the Sofeggin and Zem-Zem wadi systems. But elsewhere the desert character of the Dahar is much more strongly pronounced. The major limiting factor to movement in the Dahar has nothing to do with relief, though; it is the availability of water which dictates settlement and land use in this transitional, pre-desert zone.[19]

Chotts, Erg and Hamada
The north-western limits of Tripolitania are sharply defined by the Chott Djerid and its eastward continuation Chott Fedjedj. These chotts (more correctly sebkhas – seasonal lakes/salt flats) are vast inland drainage basins formed by the Tertiary faulting of the Atlas formation. The cliff-like Gebel Tebaga and Cherb

ranges were the uplifted results of the same incident. The presence of the seasonal lakes and these abrupt mountain barriers imposes limitations on movement between Tripolitania and the rest of northwest Africa. South and south west of the Chott Djerid extends the Great Eastern Erg or sand sea which was practically impassable until modern times. Movement east to west, therefore, is restricted to the far south (Tibesti and Hoggar) or the 'passages obligés' of the Djerid and Arad. For precisely this reason the Axis powers chose the Gabes coastal plain as their main line of defence against the advancing British in the 1940s. This strategic bottle-neck between Tripolitania and the rest of Roman Africa was made doubly important by the existence around the Chott Djerid of two major groups of oases, the Nefzaoua to the south and the Djerid to the north. Only those of the Nefzaoua fall within the geographical zone of Tripolitania, but their links with those of the Djerid (on the northwest side of the Chott) were probably close.[20]

The Saharan character of the Dahar is also reinforced by the imposing form of the Hamada el-Hamra, which separates Tripolitania from Fezzan. This Palaeocene limestone cap, on cretaceous limestone strata, has a reddish-brown tint from which its Arabic name (the Red Desert) is derived. Approached from the north it presents an 80–100 m scarp and in places attains over 900 m in height. Although there are some fine red soils in depressions, the Hamada is a rock desert feature and is almost entirely waterless and barren.[21] To the east of the Hamada lies the basalt extrusion known as the Gebel es-Soda (Black Mountain), which is interposed between the oases of Giofra and Fezzan.

Syrtica and the Hun graben

The Sofeggin, Zem-Zem and Kebir wadi systems, descending from the Dahar, enter the Syrtic coastal plain which extends from Misurata to *Arae Philaenorum* (Ras el-Aàli). The geology is mainly Tertiary (Palaeocene and Miocene) with extensive faulting aligned northwest to southeast. The most important of these fault lines is the Hun-Waddan graben (210 km long, about 25 km wide) which runs from the Bei el-Kebir to the oases of Giofra (Hun, Waddan and Socna). This natural corridor is one of the most important routes between the coast and Fezzan. It is also the area of Tripolitania most susceptible to seismic activity in recent times.

Further east the interior consists of a limestone plateau of Tertiary date, whilst the coastal formations are of the Quaternary age. The area is almost entirely desert in character but the wadi beds contain limited areas of fertile alluvium. The western Syrtic coast is notable for the Sebkha Tauorgha, a seasonal lake (110 by 30 km) into which the wadis Sofeggin and Zem-Zem empty. In antiquity, there was apparently an unsilted exit from the lake into the sea.[22]

The Sahara (including Fezzan)

Some of the Saharan landforms have already been alluded to. The northern limit of the Sahara is conventionally defined as the zone of extension of date palm cultivation producing dates for consumption. Under this definition the whole of Tripolitania lies within the Sahara since dates are grown for food in the coastal oases from Misurata to Gabes, though they are not of high quality because of the relative humidity. It is not always appreciated that only one fifth of the Sahara is sand desert and only one fifteenth covered by dune-fields. The stone plateaux of Dahar, Syrtica and the Hamada el-Hamra are structurally typical of much of the Sahara. The lifting and faulting of the region, in part relating to the period of the Atlas formation, brought artesian nappes to the surface and permitted the development of the characteristic oases of the zone. Between the Hamada el-Hamra and the Great Erg, barren sand and stone desert are alleviated by the few oases of Ghadames, Derj and Sinawen (the latter memorably described by Richardson as 'but a handful of date trees thrown upon the wide waste of the Sahara'). To the east of the Hamada, the Giofra, Zella and Augila oases are links in a chain of oases stretching to the Nile (Fig. 1:2). North/south routes from the coast to Fezzan incorporate the oases of Mizda, Bu Njem and Gheriat el-Garbia *inter alia*. Whilst the oases of the Nefzaoua occupy the key strategic position defining the western/northwestern limits of Tripolitania, the southern and eastern limits were less precise.

South of the Hamada el-Hamra and sandwiched between the Edri and Murzuk sand seas there are three roughly parallel bands of oases, known collectively as Fezzan. These oases formed the heartlands of one of the most formidable Libyan tribes, the *Garamantes* (chapter 2). These oases are of particular importance in that they lie astride the key north/south trans-Saharan routes as well as linking with the east/west chain that bestraddles the northern Sahara.[23]

4
CLIMATE

According to Jean Despois, climate is the most important geographical factor in North Africa and rainfall is the most significant of the climatic variables. The rainfall isohyet map is useful as an indicator of where the

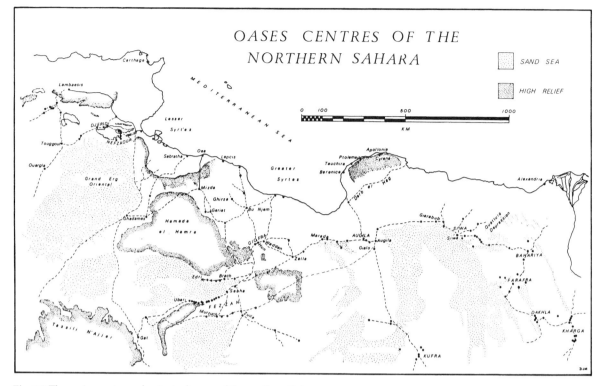

Fig. 1:2 The major routes and principal oases of the northern Sahara.

desert begins (Fig. 1:3).[24] The differences between the North African frontier environments is nowhere clearer. In *Mauretania Tingitana*, the most southerly Roman forts lay in a region receiving 400–600 mm per year. In *Caesariensis*, the Severan frontier (*limes*) also followed this high rainfall band. The *Legio III Augusta* was located at *Lambaesis* in *Numidia* in a 400 mm plus zone. Only in the vicinity of the wadi Djedi and in the *Ad Maiores/Capsa/Tacapae* sector was the Numidian *limes* in a region receiving under 200 mm per year. In stark contrast the Severan frontier zone in Tripolitania lay almost entirely south of the 100 mm isohyet (with the exception of a few Gebel road-stations) (see Fig. 4:4).

Apart from a small section of the eastern Gebel and the coast between Tripoli and Homs which receive an annual average over 300 mm, Tripolitania is poorly served by its rainfall (Fig. 1:3). In agricultural terms, there are no locations suitable for large-scale commercial cereal production (requiring 400 mm per year or more) and about half the Gebel does not even receive the 200 mm theoretically necessary for dry cultivation of cereals. Figures for eastern Tripolitania alone, the most fertile region, show that only 3.6 per cent of the total landmass receives over 250 mm rainfall and only 7.8 per cent over 200 mm annual average. Over 67 per cent receives less than 50 mm per year and over 80 per cent under 100 mm (Table 1:3). Dry cultivation of olives is reckoned to require a minimum of 150 mm rainfall per year, so according to these figures 88.2 per cent of eastern Tripolitania lies outside this limit.[25]

Average Annual Rainfall (mm)	Area (sq. km)	% of total landmass
50 or less	151,700	67.3%
51–100	30,000	13.3%
101–150	17,000	7.6%
151–200	9,000	4.0%
201–250	9,400	4.2%
251 and above	8,200	3.6%
	225,300	100.0%

Table 1:3. Analysis of relationship between rainfall figures and land area in Eastern Tripolitania (northwest Libya). (Data from Polservice 1980, B-6.)

8

Name (and Number on Fig.1.3)	Average (mm)	Max. (mm)	Min. (mm)	Location
1. Zuara	214	–	–	coastal plain
2. Tripoli	340	750	160	coastal plain
3. Homs	265	–	–	coastal plain
4. Misurata	253	433	77	coastal plain
5. Sirte	180	–	–	Syrtic coast
6. Azizia	211	469	83	Eastern Gefara plain
7. Tigi	140	–	–	Southern Gefara plain
8. Cussabat	325	–	–	Eastern Gebel
9. Tarhuna	273	–	–	Eastern Gebel
10. Garian	336	510	64	Central Gebel
11. Jefren	241	449	50	Central Gebel
12. Zintan	170	–	–	Central Gebel
13. Nalut	129	586	41	Central Gebel
14. Mizda	63	234	11	Upper Wadi Sofeggin
15. Beni Ulid	61	200	92	Middle Wadi Sofeggin
16. Shwerif	45	146	13	Upper Wadi Bei el Kebir
17. Gheriat esh Shergia	49	133	7	Upper Wadi Zem-Zem
18. Gerba	207	–	–	Lesser Syrtes island
19. Gabes	138	–	–	Lesser Syrtes coast
20. Medenine	141	–	–	Western Gefara plain
21. Ben Gardane	181	–	–	Western Gefara plain
22. Foum Tatahouine	123	–	–	Western Gebel
23. Matmata	243	–	–	Western Gebel
24. Kebili	86	–	–	Nefzaoua oasis
25. Tozeur	99	–	–	Djerid oasis
26. Gafsa	179	–	–	Steppe to north of Chott Djerid
27. Hun	32	–	–	Giofra oasis
* Sebha	10	30	0	Fezzan oasis
* Murzuk	8	31	0	Fezzan oasis
* Brak	10	19	0	Fezzan oasis
* Gat	13	38	0.1	Oasis to southwest of Fezzan
* Augila	11	42	0.2	Oasis to southeast of Syrtica
* Kufra	1	–	–	Oasis in southern Libyan desert

Table 1:4. Annual average rainfall figures (in mm) for Tripolitania and selected neighbouring locations (to be used in conjunction with Figure 1:3 – the * indicate sites beyond the southern and eastern limits of that map). Where available, maximum and minimum recorded figures are also given.

Table 1:4 above and Figure 1:3 illustrate the distribution of rainfall.[26] The eastern Gebel from Garian to Cussabat (Msellata) and the coastal region between Tripoli and Homs (*Oea* and *Lepcis*) are the most favoured regions. In the Dahar, rainfall falls away rapidly to the south and the Sofeggin and Zem-Zem basins lie in a zone with a range from only 50–100 mm annually.

The western Gebel (with the exception of the Matmata region) lies in a rain-shadow area and receives under 150 mm per year, as does a vast area of the Gefara plain. Only at the western and eastern extremities do the wadis carry flood water to the sea following rains. South of Ghadames and the oases of the Giofra, rainfall drops rapidly below the 25 mm mark and Fezzan receives less than 10 mm.

These annual averages, however, mask two critical variables. The chief problem with the rainfall in North Africa is that it is extremely erratic in its distribution from year to year and within any one year. The maximum and minimum values indicate massive devia-tion from the 'norm' between years of dearth and years of plenty, as in the extreme case of Nalut: annual average 129 mm, maximum recorded 568 mm, minimum 41 mm. Even the better-watered areas reveal the same wild fluctuation as, for instance, Tripoli (340 mm, 750 mm, 160 mm) and Garian (336 mm, 510 mm and 64 mm).

The risk of drought is further increased by the distribution of rainfall through the seasons. There is little or no rain in the summer months (May to August) and most rainfall occurs in the period October to March. The agricultural year starts in September and rains in both autumn and spring are necessary for a successful harvest. Where more detailed figures are available, giving a month by month breakdown, the true extent of the unpredictability becomes apparent (Table 1:5). The figures for Garian, with one of the highest average rainfalls in Tripolitania, indicate that precipitation is very unevenly distributed within any one year and from one year to the next. Indeed, this

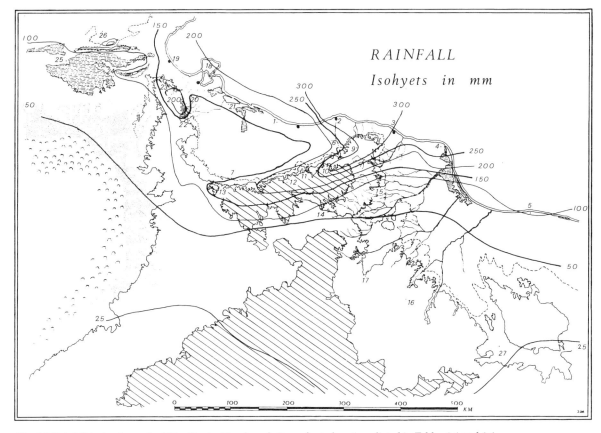

Fig. 1:3 Rainfall isohyet map for Tripolitania. Numbered sites refer to locations listed in Tables 1:4 and 1:6.

Year	January	February	March	September	October	November	December	Total excl. summer
1926	176	133	65	10	0.1	1	44	438
1927	**71**	**26**	79	10	3	0	0	**188**
1928	146	103	**35**	4	3	26	130	447
1929	97	80	93	29	**16**	86	56	457
1930	**29**	**44**	**34**	0	35	36	**44**	221
1931	**63**	**54**	0	29	18	9	75	248
1932	183	**34**	61	18	58	91	58	503
1933	**61**	153	101	0	0	32	110	456
1934	165	72	**19**	12	52	31	**46**	396
1935	**49**	**16**	72	29	**6**	**19**	**2**	**192**
1936	**49**	**3**	**3**	0	**9**	28	110	**202**
1937	**60**	64	**7**	15	43	20	**17**	**225**
1938	133	80	101	0.2	8	69	81	473
1939	81	74	**29**	29	1	23	**30**	**268**
1940	**15**	**0.5**	**15**	64	11	5	?	?
1941	**0**	**12**	**21**	0	0	0	**28**	**62**
1942	**29**	8	**22**	?	?	?	?	–
1943	?	?	?	?	4	87	8	–
1944	149	**31**	47	12	5	77	23	343
1945	**21**	127	**33**	0	83	**18**	99	382
1946	86	79	**18**	24	5	14	22	247
1947	**24**	**3**	**18**	?	?	?	?	–
Maximum	183	155	101	64	83	91	130	503
Minimum	0	0.5	0	0	0	0	0	62
Average	80	57	42	15	18	34	52	319

Table 1:5. Rainfall at Garian 1926–1947 (in mm). Numbers in bold indicate figures below the monthly/annual averages, drought years are thus shown by runs of bold figures in autumn or spring. Summer rainfall (April–August) is not included, but since it averaged only 30 mm for the period, total average annual rainfall equalled 349 mm (Source: BMA 1947, 73)

pattern of erratic variation is the norm and years when the total approximates with the annual average are the exception. In the period 1926–47 (21 agricultural years), autumn rains were late or inadequate on no less than 13 occasions. Spring rains also failed or were poor on five occasions and five years were subject to the sort of drought which leads to large scale crop failure (1935–6, 1939–40, 1940–1, 1941–2, 1946–7). Only six or seven years show the distribution of rainfall needed to produce bumper harvests. Only one year (1944) deviated by less than 10 per cent from the annual average.

Brehony has shown that in the Gebel Tarhuna, also, two in every seven years are seriously affected by drought. For the most marginal zones, such as the Sofeggin and Zem-Zem valleys, this kind of variation is even more critical and droughts of four, five and seven years have been reported at Beni Ulid.[27]

In Tripolitania, then, annual precipitation is not only low but it is also capricious and unpredictable. In many areas the year's rainfall arrives all at once in the space of a few hours and much of the expected benefit can be lost in the subsequent floods. Special agricultural technology was developed to cope with the problems of run-off water in order that these areas of scarce water resources could be brought under cultivation (Plate 2). The viability of human settlement and land-use have depended to an extraordinary degree on this hydraulic technology.[28]

As with rainfall, the temperature figures reflect the combination of Saharan and Mediterranean influences. The long littoral and the Gebel are subject to a varying degree of Mediterranean and Tell climates. To the south the climate becomes first 'continental steppe' and then 'pre-desert' in character. In Syrtica, the desert climate encroaches very close to the coast. Generally, the coastal regions have higher minimum temperatures and lower maximums than the inland area (Table 1:6).

Because of the much lower relative humidity in inland areas there is generally a greater range of temperature there than for the coastal sites. The relative humidity is 51.3 per cent at Remada, for instance, but 68 per cent at Gabes. The aridity of the interior is thus aggravated by greater daytime temperatures and much colder nights. The danger to olive trees in arid lands can come from frost as much as from drought. The lower humidity of the interior is an important factor in the formation of dew and frost. The cold winter temperatures can even lead to snow in the higher reaches of the Gebel, as in 1980 when several thousand sheep were lost as a result. Another associated climatic feature is the high potential evaporation factor, which effects people, vegetation and soils alike.[29] Once again the modifying climatic influences of the Mediterranean benefit only a limited area of coast and Gebel and in the most southerly section of the Greater Syrtes the desert advances right up to the coast.

The effects of scorching winds blowing off the Sahara (the *ghibli*) have often been remarked on. The *ghibli* can ruin crops and kill young plants and livestock, and it increases evaporation. It is essentially a desert feature but its influence is felt in the Gebel and on the coast. The *ghibli* often carries sand with it and such sandstorms also affect the northern zone. De Mathuisieulx lost one of his horses in a six-hour storm near the Zem-Zem and further into the Sahara the results can be even more devastating, as at el Golea in 1947 when 2,000 sheep and 1,500 goats were killed.[30]

5
FLORA AND FAUNA

The catalogue of the modern flora and fauna of Tripolitania compares unfavourably with that of antiquity discussed above. The complex issue of climatic

Name (no. on Fig. 1.3)	Date of observation	Maximum °C	Minimum °C
2. Tripoli	1919–1978	46.0	−0.6
4. Misurata	1945–1978	50.6	+1.1
6. Azizia	1919–1978	57.3	−3.2
11. Jefren	1925–1976	48.6	−1.5
13. Nalut	1944–1978	44.4	−3.9
14. Mizda	1958–1978	49.7	−5.0
15. Beni Ulid	1925–1971	56.8	−1.0
17. Gheriat esh Shergia	1968–1978	45.9	−4.2
* Ghadames	1944–1978	50.6	−5.8
24. Kebili	–	55.0	
* Sebha	1931–1934	45.8	+0.1
* Murzuk	1931–1934	49.0	+0.3
* Gat	1931–1934	51.5	+1.1

Table 1: 6. Temperature range at some Tripolitanian locations (cf. Table 1:2 and Fig. 1:3). (Sources: Despois and Raynal 1967; Polservice 1980; RSGI 1937.)

change is discussed in more detail below and the intention here is simply to establish the nature of the surviving environments and wildlife, as an essential preliminary.[31]

Natural vegetation

There are several different types of surviving natural vegetation but almost all represent types of steppe rather than Mediterranean maquis. The Gefara is a mixture of alpha steppe (in Tunisia), of sandy bush and dwarf shrub steppe and of sterile gravels (in its central regions). The Gebel is characterized as denuded high plains steppe with some potential for tree cover and there has been progress towards reafforestation. Further south into the Dahar, the natural vegetation diminishes both in size and in concentration and it becomes a bush and dwarf-shrub steppe again. The same applies to the Syrtic hinterland, except in the vicinity of the Sebkha Taourgha where the vegetation comprises mainly salt-resistant shrubs (as around the Gefara Sebkhas and the Tunisian chotts). The vegetation is concentrated in the wadi valleys in the Sofeggin and Zem-Zem basins. Although mainly bush and dune shrub today, occasional trees have survived the attentions of nineteenth- and early twentieth-century charcoal burners. These are, notably, acacia

and tamarisk, but batoom trees are also present; cypress, myrtle, lotus and juniper still existed 150 years ago. After rains many of the wadi beds are 'green with herbage and adorned with flowers'. Perhaps surprisingly, the same is true of the normally lifeless and forbidding Hamada el Hamra.[32]

In summary, the surviving vegetation cover is generally sparse and steppe-like. The more Mediterranean steppe cover such as alpha, esparto and jujube is limited in extent by the climate, but much of the degeneration of the natural habitat must be viewed as degradation by human agency. There has undoubtedly been considerable northward encroachment of the pre-desert steppe because of deforestation and defoliation of the Gebel.

Cultivated plants (Fig. 1:4)

Along the coastal strip, at the foot of the Gebel and in sand-free strips at either end, the Gefara is cultivated. In modern times the erratic rainfall has been supplemented by deep-bore artesian wells, with potentially disastrous effects on ground-water reserves. Cereals and fruit trees, notably the olive, are the main cultivars. In the many coastal oases, date palms, olives, figs and other fruits, cereals and vegetables are grown in traditional irrigated gardens. The most important

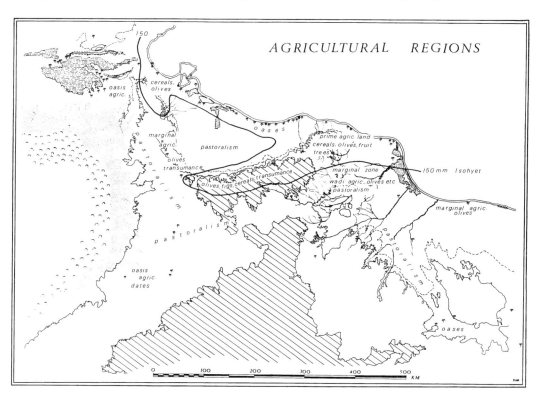

Fig. 1:4 Agricultural regions of Tripolitania and traditional modes of exploitation.

areas of the coastal plains are in the vicinity of Medenine in the western Gefara and in the Msellata foothills, where dry cultivation of cereals and olives has proved possible. The Gebel regions of Msellata, Tarhuna and Garian are the best watered upland areas and *Lepcis* and *Oea* incorporated much of this land in their *territoria*. Cultivation is concentrated on the more temperate, northern edge of the plateau and consists principally of arboriculture (olives, figs, vines, pomegranates, pistachios, almonds, carobs, peaches, apples, pears). Cereals are also grown (wheat and barley), but yields are very low in comparison with other Mediterranean countries. A wide range of vegetables and herbs is grown in small, irrigated gardens. Palms are irrigated in a number of small oases on the Garian and Nefusa plateaux. Economically, olive cultivation is the most important activity, followed by figs and date palms.

In the pre-desert zone, agriculture is now limited mainly to the scratch cultivation of cereals in the wadis. At Beni Ulid, a considerable stretch of the valley bottom is still covered by an orchard of olives, palms, figs, plums and almonds, whilst cereals, vegetables and pulses are grown in plots between the trees.

A similar range of flora is cultivated in the oases of the Nefzaoua, Ghadames, Giofra and Fezzan. Date palms are the principal economic resource, however, as other fruit trees do not always mature properly. The larger oases contain hundreds of thousands of palms. Cereals are also grown, but in too small a quantity to replace dates as the dietary staple of the inhabitants. Most other trees, vegetables and herbs are grown in small, intensively irrigated plots.[33]

Wild animals

In 1947, the wild animals of the region included wild boar, hyena, fox, jackal, oryx, mouflon, gazelle, hare and marmot. Some of these are now extinct and others, such as the gazelle, are seriously endangered. Leopards may have survived as late as the 1930s, but ostriches were extinct much earlier. The surviving fauna represent an ever diminishing proportion of the species present in antiquity, with man the chief culprit in the regrettable record of extinction.[34]

Domesticated animals

In 1960 there were 860,000 sheep, 950,000 goats, 153,000 camels, 80,000 cattle, 92,000 donkeys and 782,000 chickens in Libyan Tripolitania. Along with horses, these are the principal livestock of the Tunisian territory also. An important aspect of these species, especially horses, camels, sheep, goats and donkeys, is that they have undergone adaptation to arid zone conditions. The main breed of sheep is the fat-tailed Libyan Barbary and, along with goats, they are now the chief resource of the pastoralists.

The Tripolitanian camel is the single-humped dromedary and is the animal best adapted to an arid zone environment. It can go for 15 days without water, being extremely resistant to fluid loss and able to replenish its fluid levels within minutes, when water becomes available. The number of camels, horses and donkeys has declined in recent years with the ever-increasing availability of motorized transport, but in the past these three animals (and perhaps horses in particular) were bred on a much greater scale. By no means, then, have sheep and goat herding always been the dominant forms of pastoralism in the region.[35]

6
CLIMATIC CHANGE

It is apparent from the previous sections that the modern climate is probably similar to that of the Roman period. But it is also evident from prehistoric cave and rock pictures in the central Sahara that major climatic change has occurred at some era in the past. The latest thinking is that, following a wetter phase from *c.* 40,000 – 20,000 BC, there was a gradual change towards a drier climate. The last major pluvial phase may have been as late as 6,000 BC, with major climatic change then occurring between 4,000 – 2,000 BC. The latter date certainly marks the beginning of the current arid and desiccating climatic phase. Most geographers and geomorphologists believe that there has not been any significant change since.

There has been a growing realization in classical archaeology that climatic change can no longer be used as a convenient, catch-all explanation for the major changes in settlement patterns and economies in the Roman period. Current geomorphological work in the Libyan Valleys Project supports the view that the Roman period climate was not significantly different from modern conditions.[36]

In 1969 Vita-Finzi published his fundamental, but subsequently much-criticized, thesis on post-classical climatic change and its effects on the Mediterranean valleys. In it he argued for a climatic 'oscillation' between the Roman period and the present. But he agreed that modern conditions are remarkably similar to ancient ones. The postulated wetter phase in the Middle Ages which Vita-Finzi held responsible for major aggradation of valley floors all round the Mediterranean cannot be shown to have existed in the Sofeggin and Zem-Zem region although there is some evidence from the coastal region near *Lepcis*. The ULVS work has traced evidence for landscape change and degradation, but these indices do not seem to correspond to a single event or process and seem rather to represent the normal stresses and hazards of the exploitation of a highly marginal environment. Whilst one cannot rule out the possibility of oscillation between drier and wetter conditions, micro-climatic change on a regional basis or a minor increase in aridity, the likelihood is that the climate of Tripolitania has remained relatively stable from late Neolithic times to the present.[37]

There can be no doubt, however, that landscape changes have taken place. In the Msellata hills and the coastal region there has been deep gullying and blanket erosion of soils, with redeposition at different locations. This erosion need not necessarily indicate a phase of higher rainfall in the past, bearing in mind the normal pattern of heavy downpours and run-off floods of the region. It is more likely to be the result of sheet erosion of soils exposed by vegetation loss, and this could be due to overgrazing, agricultural clearance, timber felling, or the breakdown of dams and water control walls. Even in 1857 Barth suggested that the denuded landscape of parts of the Gebel was the result of neglect, rather than of climatic change and that the process might be reversible. The contrast between past and present was graphically demonstrated by Oates' survey of the Fergian region between Tarhuna and Msellata in the 1950s. He recorded 63 sites which had been equipped with olive presses in the Roman period (126 individual presses in total). There were only about 20 surviving olive trees in the region at that time, though they have now been more extensively and successfully reintroduced. The great success of the olive groves replanted this century in the western Gefara, in the Gefara south of Tripoli and in the Gebel Tarhuna have further demonstrated the viability of these areas after centuries of underexploitation.[38] In some instances, then, the process of denudation of the landscape has proved to be reversible, which would not be possible if climatic change was the cause of deterioration. Until experiments have been carried out in the pre-desert one can only speculate on the probable results of replanting and recultivation of the wadi beds. The extreme marginality of these zones means that they would have been affected by even very minor climatic change, but, more importantly, there may have been ecological changes brought about by the previous periods of exploitation and subsequent neglect.

How significant were these factors? Climatic change and environmental breakdown have been ruled out as unitary explanations for the decline of Roman farming in the Tripolitanian pre-desert zone. There was no single moment of catastrophic breakdown in the system. However, there are indications that the exploitation of these extremely marginal lands was highly vulnerable and the changing environmental conditions may have affected the farming communities in a very piecemeal way across several centuries of struggle, rather than rendering them all unsustainable at a stroke.

7
HUMAN EXPLOITATION: PASTORALISM AND AGRICULTURE

Although it is clear that the ancient environment in Tripolitania bore many similarities to the modern one, literary evidence for farming practice in Roman Tripolitania is rather thin. In subsequent chapters we shall examine in detail the archaeological evidence for ancient settlement and land-use, but this alone cannot fill all the *lacunae*. As Whittaker has stated,

> We shall never be able to reconstruct a portrait of society in North Africa under Roman rule from the ancient sources and archaeology alone. There is more information to be had about the Maghreb from any standard, modern textbook on the subject than from the entire corpus of ancient literature.[39]

Certain insights into the lifestyles of its ancient peoples may be gained from studying the recent history of traditional economic practice in different regions of Tripolitania (Fig. 1:4).

The Gefara
Because of low rainfall and shifting sand dunes most of the central Gefara is unsuitable for settled agriculture. Only the areas immediately north of the Gebel escarpment, a narrow coastal band of oases and portions of the eastern and western Gefara are suitable for unirrigated agriculture. Although the modern tribes of the Gefara are primarily pastoralists (for instance only 1 in 13 of the Siaan tribe are sedentary), they do practise scratch cultivation wherever possible and have tribal centres in the oases. In the foothills of the Gebel and in the western Gefara there are permanent villages and a greater amount of sedentarization.

The western Gebel
The Gebel Matmata (Tunisia) and Gebel Nefusa (Libya) are occupied mainly by relic Berber populations, both

sedentary and semi-nomadic. Both groups normally farm some lands in the Gefara below the escarpment for scratch cereal cultivation. The pre-desert plateau of the Dahar is also exploited as winter pasturage for the flocks. Many of the pastoral tribes actually possess dry-farming lands in the Gebel, orchards of olives, figs and almonds and permanent villages. Such tribes normally leave only a 'core' population in their 'home' village when they transhume with their flocks in summer after the harvest. Both Louis and Despois distinguish these transhuming tribes and their mixed economy from either fully sedentary or 'nomadic' tribes.

The agricultural communities tend to specialize in arboriculture, with cereal cultivation pursued more opportunistically according to the pattern of rainfall in a given year. The principal crops are olives, figs, dates, almonds, vines, pomegranates, barley and wheat. In spite of a trend towards sedentarization (and particularly olive cultivation) in modern times, some tribes remain more exclusively pastoralists. They have traditionally procured their cereals and other agricultural products by a combination of means; scratch cultivation or oasis farming, trade, or as a 'protection' fee exacted from sedentary communities. These protection arrangements also benefited the farmers, since they were not only spared the disruption of raids from their contracted partners, but the latter were obliged to defend their sedentary allies from the raids of others as well. These contracts were supplemented by a regular barter trade in meat, wool and dates against cereals, olives, figs and so on. The economic bases of these groups of people are essentially complementary to each other and give the region a distinctive mixed economy. The agricultural practices in the Gebel involve the use of dams and barrages in a system of run-off agriculture which directly parallels that of the Roman period; much can still be learned here at first hand of the practicalities and problems of these ancient farming methods.[40]

The eastern Gebel

The Gebel Tarhuna and the Msellata regions present similar topographic characteristics to the Gebel Nefusa, but sedentary agriculture had been increasingly limited to the Msellata, prior to the Italian colonization of the Gebel in the 1920–1930s. Brehony has characterized the tribes of the Gebel Tarhuna as having regressed into semi-nomadism. It is clear, however, that his 'semi-nomads' tend towards 'transhumants', with fixed termini, sowing and pasture lands. The shifting cultivation of cereals supplements the pastoral base.

Arboriculture had almost died out in the Tarhuna region in the nineteenth century, but has revived since the creation of the large Italian estates such as Breviglieri. Some progress has been made towards the reafforestation and refoliation of the area, which had been severely denuded by overgrazing and charcoal burning. The Gebel is actually well suited to the dry farming of the olive tree as the numerous ancient ruins testify (Plate 1).

Since the 1930s there has been a significant shift towards sedentarization among the pastoral tribes, partly in response to the agricultural redevelopment just described. The declining importance of pastoralism was exacerbated by the Italian expropriation of over 40,000 hectares of the traditional grazing lands of the Tarhuna tribes, and the catastrophic slaughter of 50–60 per cent of all livestock during the Second World War.

The Gebel Msellata has suffered far less defoliation from overgrazing and settled agriculture, particularly arboriculture, has continued in this region. Prior to the 1930s, the Msellata region provided the semi-nomadic tribes of Tarhuna and the Orfella region (Beni Ulid) with seasonal employment at harvest time. The almond and olive harvest lasted several months from September and participating tribes were paid in kind with up to one seventh what they harvested. The creation of the Italian estate at Breviglieri (El-Khadra) diverted 3,000 of these crop pickers.

In the eastern Gebel, then, we also find that the pastoral and sedentary economies are necessarily interactive.

The Nefzaoua and the western Dahar

The oases of the Nefzaoua and the pre-desert plateau (the Dahar) lying southeast of the Chott Djerid and east of the Great Erg, broadly speaking, comprise a single zone. The region is characterized by two modes of life, sedentary agriculture in the oases and semi-nomadic transhumance elsewhere. All the tribes, however, are part-pastoralists and part-cultivators. Each tribe owns land in one or more oases, which is cultivated in some cases by sharecroppers of a reduced social status (*khammes*). Mostly, though, the sedentary communities are of equal status and the transhuming elements are often involved in the harvest. In the nineteenth century the population of the Nefzaoua was about 18,000 (8,000 semi-nomads and 10,000 sedentary cultivators) at a time when the antique canalizations and *foggaras* were in a state of decay. Since renovation of these the population has increased significantly (22,000 semi-nomads and 28,000 sedentarists in 1963).

As in the Gebel, the Second World War and a series of disastrous droughts in the 1930s and 1940s did untold damage to the pastoral tribes as 80 per cent of their livestock died. Since then there has been an increased tendency towards oasis agriculture.

The transhumance movements of the Dahar tribes extend west to east into Gebel and Gefara as we have seen above. Others transhume over great distances north and south from the Nefzaoua. The northward movements take the tribes into the Bled Segui to the north of the chotts and other areas where run-off or dry farming is possible, and interaction with sedentary groups is necessary. The tribes of the Nefzaoua and Dahar thus have territorial interests in several distinct ecological zones.[41]

Ghadames and Derj depression

A similar pattern of life applies in desert region centred on the oases of Ghadames and Derj. The oases are the only local sources of dates, cereals and vegetable crops. Since the collapse of the caravan traffic, little trading has been conducted with the Gebel tribes, but it was certainly once an important supplement to the range of crops grown (the most important imports were olive oil and grain). The northward transhumance of flocks still extends as far as Remada, the site of one of the Roman frontier forts.

The Sofeggin and Zem-Zem

Although the rainfall figures drop below the minimum levels for dry farming, run-off agriculture of the wadi alluvium is possible in many places. Particularly in the north of the region, where rainfall is highest and more consistent, permanent villages exist and there are trees in the wadis, notably at Beni Ulid (Plates 2 and 37). These village populations include a substantial permanent element along with transhuming groups. However, without some system of water control the wadi agriculture rarely rises above the level of scratch cultivation and so the traditional economic mode has been pastoralism with shifting cereal cultivation. The use of pasture and water catchment cisterns is regulated within each sub-tribe of the Orfella. Some tribes send contingents north to the harvest in the Msellata region as we have noted already. The Orfella also have extensive pasture rights near the Syrtic coast.

Fezzan

Cauneille has shown that many of the major semi-nomadic tribes of western Libya are confederated from sub-tribes. Elements of these sub-tribes transhume across the entire region from Gebel to Fezzan. Most of the tribes own agricultural land either in the Gebel or Fezzan and some have permanent villages in these regions. So once again it is not easy to categorize the tribes as 'nomads' or 'farmers'. The modern culti-

vators of Fezzan still use many of the foggaras, which have been maintained and constructed anew up to recent years. In some tribes oasis cultivators are held in a lower social status (haratin) by a proprietorial class of semi-nomads.

Syrtica

This region is divided into two main zones: a better-watered coastal plain and a pre-desert steppe or interior zone where there are a number of important oasis centres (Zella and the oases of the Giofra). The presence of numerous ancient ruins, including olive presses, in the coastal region show that the area is now underexploited. The tribes are predominantly pastoral, though a certain amount of scratch cereal cultivation is practised. However, the pasture is considered the best in Tripolitania. The oases centres provide a sedentary focus for the interior pastoral tribes, where the usual range of oasis crops is cultivated.[42]

Examination of the modern response to the climatic and geographical limitations imposed on the indigenous populations in different regions suggests several important conclusions. First, the more marginal the ecological zone, the greater the importance of pastoralism. Second, to counterbalance this, it must be reiterated that a pastoral economy cannot exist in isolation from sedentary agricultural communities. By association with oasis cultivators, by trade, by 'protection' arrangements, by working as seasonal labour at harvest time, semi-nomads generally succeed in integrating an element of a mixed economy into their pastoral base. In general the interrelationships between semi-nomads, transhumers and sedentary farmers take the form of symbiosis rather than conflict.

Third, there are indications of the sort of political or economic pressures and opportunities which can lead to increased sedentarization. Sedentary communities have thrived particularly in the Gebel, Fezzan and the many oases centres. The redevelopment of agriculture in the Gebel Tarhuna has illustrated the ability of semi-nomadic tribes to break away from traditional practice and adopt a new modus vivendi.

Summary

The stability of settlement and exploitation in Tripolitania over the last few millennia appears to have been fragile, with successive phases of increased sedentarization or of pastoralism attested or postulated. Ecological factors are not the only ones to be considered in seeking to account for such changes of strategy, but when social and political issues are examined in subsequent chapters it will be important to keep the essential marginality of the region in mind.

2

THE TRIBAL
BACKGROUND

1

THE GRECO-ROMAN VIEW
OF NATIVE AFRICANS

Since the nature of the 'opposition' was bound to have had a profound influence on Roman policy and the history of Roman/native interaction, the study of a Roman frontier province cannot proceed far without considering the indigenous population. The ancient Maghreb was peopled by tribes of Mediterranean character, rather than of negroid stock, and their descendants are the Berbers of today. Before turning to a detailed examination of the tribes of Tripolitania, it is necessary to gain a wider perspective of the general character, organization, lifestyle and culture of the pre-Roman tribal societies of North Africa.

There are three main sources of information on the tribal background. First, there are the primary source references and epigraphic material, but since these are mainly geographical or historical references relatively little concerns the social structures and lifestyles of the native people. There is, however, a greater volume of primary source material than, for instance, for Roman Britain.[1]

The second category of data is archaeological, providing details of settlement sites, burial customs and religious practices. For North Africa this is a comparatively meagre resource, which is a reflection of the almost total emphasis placed, up to now, on the excavation of Roman cities.

Third, there is information of a purely comparative

nature derived from anthropological study of similar societies and communities in the recent past in the Maghreb and elsewhere. Because the Arab invasions brought considerable changes in tribal society in North Africa it is not possible to make direct equations between modern political experiences and the ancient native societies. It is reasonable to assume, however, that useful comparison does exist between traditional Berber rural societies (still using agricultural techniques and equipment of great antiquity) and their forebears.[2] It can be argued that, since modern climatic conditions have a close correlation with ancient ones, such comparanda can illustrate a range of possibilities, whether for social organization or in terms of lifestyle, in a given ecological zone.

In later chapters reference will be made to theories which have presented the history of the African frontiers as a conflict 'between the desert and the sown', that is between nomadic and sedentary people. Rachet is one of the most recent and extreme proponents of the theory, seeing the history of Roman Africa largely in terms of conflict and confrontation. Such an interpretation gained credence because it seemed to match up with problems encountered by the French in their North African territories in the nineteenth and twentieth centuries. This distorted perspective of tribal society has led, therefore, to extremely subjective historical conclusions.[3] Since perspective is all important, considerable space is devoted here to the discussion of a new basis for understanding Libyan tribal society.

There are two fundamental modern works relevant to the study of the tribes in Tripolitania. The catalogue compiled by Jean Desanges from source references for all the known North African tribes in antiquity, remains the starting point for all new research. His comments on the tribes, however, were largely restricted to the question of their geographical locations. In addition, there is the classic study of the eastern Libyan peoples by Oric Bates. His restrained and cautious examination of linguistic, cultural and ethnographic material, in addition to the primary sources and the limited archaeological data then available, provides many insights. However, the overall impression received from these and other secondary works is that the primary sources they followed contained confusions and contradictions.[4]

The main reason for the lack of detailed study of socio-economic aspects of tribal society in North Africa also concerns the primary sources. There are several aspects of the problem. First, the majority of references relate not to the native population in isolation, but in contact with Romans, Greeks or Carthaginians. There are no literary works written in the Libyan language and no single Roman source to compare with the *Germania* of Tacitus. Although there are geographical works, many of these are compilations (and often inexact ones) from earlier works. Comparatively little ethnographic detail was recorded and some such material was clearly repeated anachronistically from earlier sources. Thus both Mela and Pliny reproduced stories from Herodotus and other Greek sources whose validity in the first century AD must be doubted, but all too often has not been. The exact dates of the sources used by Pliny are not always evident and as well as borrowing from other historians, such as Mela, he had access to official documents ranging in age from a few years to centuries old. It is not possible therefore, to say that Pliny's account presents a consistent picture of North Africa in the second half of the first century AD. Indeed far from it; his *Natural History* is an elaborate collage and often lacks geographical and chronological coherence. It is not surprising that occasionally there are geographical blunders or miscomprehensions. Nor does the inclusion of material which is plainly mythical or apocryphal encourage absolute confidence in the veracity of other uncorroborated stories. There is also the danger that an undetected official bias may have distorted certain facts or that the Roman historians and geographers may have introduced their own distortions in order to match their information with their preconceptions. These potential weaknesses are often not detectable, particularly once a passage has been extracted from its full context.

That Pliny did not always understand the significance and geographical indications of his own sources is clear from his account of the campaign of Cornelius Balbus *c.* 20 BC. Pliny was here using two distinct sources of information, from the first of which we learn that Balbus captured three tribal centres of the *Phazanii*, followed by three of the *Garamantes*, including *Garama* (Germa). The second source provided a list of names and effigies carried in Balbus' subsequent triumph. Pliny confessed his bewilderment that few of these names corresponded with those he had already given from his first source, but he could not explain the discrepancy. Consequently many ingenious and sometimes ludicrous proposals have been made by scholars seeking to fit the names to modern locations. However, it seems certain that one group of names relates to southwest Numidia – *Milgis Gemella*, *Tabudium* and *Viscera* being equivalent to the later frontier forts of *Gemellae*, *Thabudeos* and *Vescera*. Balbus, or more likely one of his lieutenants, must have conducted a subsidiary campaign hundreds of kilometres to the west, of which Pliny was clearly unaware.[5]

Another of our most valuable sources, Ptolemy of Alexandria, is equally difficult to assess. Ptolemy is important because he listed a great number of tribes, many being sub-tribes of larger units, and he endeavoured to give precise coordinate locations for many of them. Unfortunately the maps that can be constructed from this information are subject to inaccuracies and some tribes whose positions can be checked independently are completely misplaced.

Even greater problems are encountered, however, when the geographical information from two or more different sources is compared. Although there are some broad similarities, these are outweighed by the discrepancies and contradictions. The efforts of modern commentators to produce maps of tribal locations based either on a particular source or on a historical period illustrate nothing more than the scope for disagreement. Tribal names appear and disappear; traditional lands of tribe X are suddenly occupied by tribe Y, only for X to reappear in the same place at a later date.[6] The implication is that there was either a very unstable tribal society in the Roman period or that there is something wrong with the geographical analysis of either the ancient sources, the modern commentators or both. The solution suggested here is that not all tribal names encountered in the sources were of equal significance and that the existence of a 'hierarchy' of tribal names explains many of the apparent contradictions.

2
TRIBAL HIERARCHY :
GENERAL DISCUSSION

The possibility of a common origin of all the Berber tribes has been much canvassed, but its relevance for the Roman period is dubious. Migration of Berber peoples westwards from the Egyptian Sahara had probably occurred from at least the second millennium BC and by the later centuries BC these people were widely scattered and had evolved distinct regional traditions and dialects. There are still over 40 surviving Berber dialects among the relic Berber populations of the Maghreb and although in antiquity writing was comparatively little used, at least four different alphabets are known from Libyan inscriptions. The prevalence of mythical tales of the origin of ethnic groups among the Libyans from the different contingents making up Hercules' army imply that in historical times there were always broad ethnic divisions. Up to the time of Caesar the most important of these were the *Mauri* of Mauretania, the *Numidae* of the Tell and the *Gaetuli* of the steppe and pre-desert zones.

Pliny stated that there were 516 *populi* in North Africa between the river *Ampsaga* and *Arae Philaenorum*, that is to the exclusion of the Mauretanian provinces and of *Cyrenaica*. This figure included 53 urban *populi*, but the rest were predominately rural tribes. In the succeeding chapters Pliny listed only 25 of these tribes by name. For comparison, Desanges' catalogue contains fewer than 130 names for this region. This represents about two sevenths of Pliny's total. The discrepancy can best be explained as evidence for a tribal hierarchy.

The Numidian kingdom was the most significant African powerblock encountered by the Carthaginians and the Romans in the latter centuries BC and although their heartlands lay mainly in northwestern Tunisia and northeastern Algeria, the Numidians came to control a formidable tribal hegemony. The kingdom resulted from the enforced union of tribes achieved by Massinissa who elevated himself from the rank of *rex Massyliorum* to *rex Numidarum*. From then until the break-up of the Numidian kingdom by Caesar, its constituent tribal names are barely mentioned by Roman sources. Only after the creation of *Africa Nova* were smaller tribal units again referred to in Numidia. In its heyday the Numidian confederation included, by hegemonic links, *Garamantes*, *Gaetuli*, *Nasamones* and *Mazax* from the Tripolitanian lands.

The *Gaetuli* are recorded in several distinct contexts from the Atlantic coast to the vicinity of the Greater Syrtes. The name was to an extent synonymous with the tribes living beyond the fringe of civilization in the pre-desert. The *Gaetuli*, however, often operated as political groupings of tribes, though we do not know the precise size of such confederations. Caesar was aided by *Gaetuli* tribes against Juba I in 46 BC and similar groups featured in later revolts. The *Mauri* are normally identified with the predominantly mountain tribes of the kingdom of *Mauretania*. In these three examples the question must be posed as to whether the ethnic names were used by Roman authors simply in a generic sense for vague groups of tribes or in reference to the highest level of tribal hierarchy encountered in Africa. In at least some of these instances, notably the Mauretanian and Numidian kingdoms, the latter interpretation seems justified.[7]

At a lower level of the tribal hierarchy came large tribes such as the *Musulames* (*Musulamii*). Early in the first century AD this tribe occupied a large territory spanning the modern Algerian/Tunisian border centred around Tebessa. Literary and archaeological evidence suggests that the *Musulames* contained both sedentary and pastoral or semi-nomadic populations. The tribal hierarchy operated at lower levels still and some of the sub-tribes or septs of the *Musulames* are known by name: *tribus Gubul* at *Theveste* (Tebessa), another *tribus* [...] from south of Madauros in the tribal territory and there was a *regio Beguensi* in Musulamian land, which is probably to be associated with the *Begguenses* tribe known from other sources.

Another example of this stratification has been detected in northern Numidia between *Simitthu* (Chemtou) and *Hippo Regius* (Bône). Three inscriptions from this area show the existence of a *tribus Misiciri*. The term *tribus* was at first taken to mean clan, but Camps has argued, on the basis of no less than 62 Libyan inscriptions containing the ethnic MSKRH that they were a tribe or even a confederation occupying a large territory. The Libyan inscriptions seem to show that the *Misiciri* were subdivided into clans or sub-tribes: the NSFH, CRMMH, NNBIBH, NFZIH and NNDRMH. Fentress has rightly observed that the idea of the *Misiciri* being a confederation similar to the *Numidae* is disproved by the fact that one of the deceased tribesmen was presented as being both a Numidian and a member of the *Misiciri*. She proposed instead a three-tier hierarchy, with the *Misiciri* being a tribe within the Numidian ethnic grouping but with the NSFH, CRMMH and so on, being sub-divisions or clans of the tribe. The Libyan texts of the three bilingual inscriptions record the name of the deceased and their filiation and Fentress observed the similarity between these texts and the modern Berber practice of identifying an individual with a family group, an extended family group, a clan, a sub-tribe and a tribe.[8]

The same thing can be shown for the *Zegrenses*, a tribe of *Mauretania Tingitana*. They are referred to on the famous *Tabula Banasitana*, a bronze tablet detailing a grant of Roman citizenship to a tribesman and his son. Both men were called Aurelius Julianus following the grant, which was due to the close associations maintained with Rome by the clan (*familiae*) of the Juliani and especially by their immediate family group (*domus*). It is also significant that the elder Julianus was one of the notables (*populares*) of one of several *gentes* which made up the *gens Zegrensium*.[9]

The mechanics of such a hierarchical structure can only be guessed at – and modern parallels can help shape our guesses; nevertheless the widespread existence of this type of tribal segmentation need not be doubted.

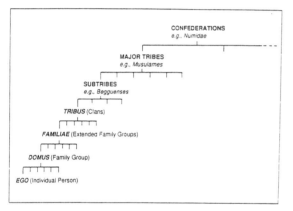

Fig. 2:1 A model of tribal hierarchy for Roman Africa (after Mattingly 1992)

The 'tribal hierarchy' model favoured (Fig. 2:1) is extremely close to the diagrams used by Gellner and other social anthropologists to illustrate what they call 'segmented societies', a feature of surviving Berber tribes in Morocco. In traditional Berber tribes the essential sub-division is the extended family group, the *ikhs* or *thakherroubt*. This includes not only the direct descendants of a tribal elder, but also nephews and cousins, workers and slaves. The reunion of two or three of these family groups creates distinct geographic groupings or clans (*tachdert*). It is the union of groups of *tachdert* that creates a small tribe (*taqbilt, khoms, arch*). Within the tribes each clan has the right to regulate its own affairs, but tribal matters such as defence are discussed and decided upon by an assembly composed of the chiefs of the *ikhs*. There is, therefore, great respect attached to the persons of tribal elders.

As Gellner has observed, the segmentary system is the essential element of most surviving Berber societies. He concluded, however, that the system balances potentially rival groups in a way which can sometimes prevent the efficient functioning of the highest levels of the hierarchy. Although the anarchic tendencies may render a tribe unable to defend itself at a moment of crisis, such incidents are rare and more commonly the latent confederation of forces occurs.[10] In antiquity, large-scale confederation seems to have been even more common and the potential ability of great confederations of tribes to coalesce in opposition to Rome must have affected Roman strategic thinking. Large-scale confederation against Rome in North Africa is reflected in the nomenclature of tribes such as the *Quinquegentiani* of the Great Kabylie and seems to have become more common in the later principate. The same dangerous trend was evident on the northern frontiers of Germany and Britain (as shown by the *Marcomanni*, the *Alamanni* and the events of the so-called Barbarian Conspiracy).[11]

The segmentary levels of the tribal hierarchy cannot unfortunately be strictly related to the use of terms such as *gens, natio* and *tribus* in the primary sources. *Natio* and *gens* were used interchangeably by some of the ancient writers. The problem with the other term, *tribus*, has already been encountered in the case of the *Misiciri*. It could be used to describe fairly substantial tribes as well as sub-tribes and clans.

How does the principle of tribal hierarchy affect our interpretation of the peoples described by Pliny and Ptolemy? In view of the loose terminology employed and the range of sources from which they took their material, it is unlikely that the lists of tribes they gave were all from a single stratum in the hierarchy. Thus one cannot assume that the 25 tribes named by Pliny, out of a total of over 450, were all major groupings. There was doubtless confusion between the reports of different visitors to the same area concerning the name of the tribes encountered since, if asked who they were, the indigenous population had several options, ranging from a close kin group up to a great confederation. Exactly this sort of confusion occurred in the early contacts between white explorers/settlers and native Americans when successive reports on the same areas produced names from different levels of the tribal hierarchy there and many variants in spelling. The problem was hinted at by Pliny himself, who complained that the Libyan names of people and places were absolutely unpronounceable except by natives.[12]

Leadership of modern Berber tribes is decided in various ways. Sometimes a chief with wide powers is elected from amongst the notables to lead the tribe. In particular circumstances, such as when faced with an external threat, groups of tribes may ally together to form confederations (*leff* or *cof*), again with an elected chief who presides over an assembly of the tribal leaders. Another method of electing tribal leaders is described by Gellner as 'election by rotation and comparability'. The basic principle is that if the tribe is comprised of three rival clans A, B and C, then in year one the tribal leader is elected from amongst candidates from clan A by the members of clans B and C. In year two the leader is elected from clan B by clans A and C and so on. The system is structurally democratic, if occasionally anarchic in its results.

The Azgar confederation of the Sahara is another interesting Berber group. They are divided into two grades of tribes, nine noble (*ihaggaren*) and 32 servile tribes (*imghad*). Six of the *ihaggaren* comprise several clans. An *amghar*, chief, is elected by each tribe and these corporately (the *imgharen*) elect a 'king' (*amenukel*) from the available members of a royal family. The king rules with the aid of the *imgharen* and can be deposed by them. In this tribe, as in other Berber societies, tribal leadership is not restricted by primogeniture succession.

Tribal chieftains in the Roman period were described by a variety of terms in the Latin and Greek sources and on inscriptions. The chief Latin ones are *rex, dux, princeps, tyrannus, praefectus* and *magistratus*. It is difficult to understand the political basis for the power of many native rulers. On the one hand, references to *seniores* and *populares* suggest that councils of minor chieftains or elders sometimes played a role. In wartime a commander-in-chief was normally appointed by allied tribes from amongst their tribal chiefs. Ierna and Carcasan in the Byzantine period were clearly in such a position, as Tacfarinas, Aedomon, Faraxen, Firmus and others had been earlier.[13] All we can infer about the processes of selection, election and succession is that they were varied and complex.

The *Zegrenses* tribe of *Mauretania Tingitana*, mentioned on the *Tabula Banasitana*, illustrate the limitations of our understanding. The elder Julianus was one of the *populares* or notables of one of the sub-tribes (*gentes*) which made up the *gens Zegrensium*. His son, the younger Julianus, became chieftain (*princeps*) possibly as a result of his added prestige as a Roman citizen, but one cannot be sure. The leadership does not appear to have been hereditary, but rather elective or selective.

Another important example concerns the *Baquates*, who along with the *Bavares* and *Macennites*, are mentioned on a remarkable series of inscriptions, also from *Mauretania Tingitana*. The 11 altars of peace (*arae pacis*) from the town of *Volubilis* detail ritualistic peace treaty relations between Roman governors and successive tribal leaders.

Only the final two inscriptions (AD 277–80) speak of a king of the *Baquates*. Up to AD 245 at least, the conferences were held between the Roman *procurator* and a native *princeps*. In the earlier period it is clear that the title of *princeps* was not automatically hereditable and presumably the chieftain was elected. A son could succeed his father as in the case of Ilalsene, son of Ureti. However, they were evidently not related closely to Aurelius Canart(h)a, who had been chief 20 years before, when already honoured with Roman citizenship, and one of whose sons had died at Rome.

The operation of tribal hierarchy is evident in these inscriptions. Four mention a *gens Baquatium*, one the *gentes Baquatium* and two mention the *Baquates* in confederation; *gentes Macennitum et Baquatium* and *gens Bavarum et Baquatium*. There were apparently no firm rules governing the use of the term *gens/gentes* by the stonecutter here, perhaps indicating that there was considerable doubt amongst Roman officials as to whether a confederated tribe counted as a single or multiple units. In my model of tribal hierarchy, the *gens Bavarum et Baquatium* is a single stage higher than the *gens Baquatium* which was itself confederated from the *gentium Baquatium*, and so on down.

The obvious importance placed on the dedication of the altars and the making of the peace treaties by Rome, shows that the *Baquates* were a cohesive and significant confederation of tribes. The rarity of family links between the chiefs suggests that the leadership may have been rotated amongst rival sub-tribes or possibly been decided on the grounds of personal strength, power and religious prestige. It is inherently unlikely, however, that the annual rotation of leadership described by Gellner for the modern tribes of the Atlas applied in this case. The death of the son of Aurelius Canartha in Rome, whether he was there as a hostage, to receive schooling, or on a mission, implies a tenure of chiefly office of longer than a single year. The altars seem to have been erected to mark the election of each new chief, his recognition by Rome and the confirmation of peace. The irregular time lapse between altars (even though we may not have a complete sequence) suggests that the *princeps*, once promoted, may have held the position for his lifetime or, alternatively, for as long as his prestige controlled the sub-tribes.[14]

Whilst the strength of the Baquatian confederation may be an atypical example of the hierarchical structure, it is highly significant that even the more loosely confederated major tribal groups possessed the latent potential for united action.

3
TRIBAL HIERARCHY: TRIPOLITANIA

The long littoral of the two Syrtic gulfs provided an important basis for the geographical location of the interior tribes in the ancient sources. In theory we should expect greater precision than for inland areas of *Mauretania* or *Numidia* which were distant from the coast. In reality the sources are not infallible; as we have seen, Ptolemy's coordinate locations are often untrustworthy and Pliny may have confused the two *Syrtes* on at least one occasion.

Whilst some information is acceptable and can be corroborated by archaeological data, as for instance in the case of the *Garamantes*, there is a good deal that is plainly anachronistic or apocryphal. The *Psylli* 'who did battle with the south wind' is an example of the latter. Similarly, the efforts of Roman geographers to locate the *Lotophages*, known from their Greek sources, were increasingly an anachronism in the first century AD (see below).

A more serious defect with the ancient sources was the conceptual framework within which they were written. There was a tendency to categorize tribes within a series of bands moving away from the coast into the interior, with each band representing a stage

Location	Habitation	Example in sources	Characteristics
Mediterranean coast Coastal plain	towns	*Libyphoenices*	relatively civilized, agriculturalists, sedentary
Coastal hinterland Interior hinterland	huts (*mapalia*)	*Proximes Gaetuli Interiores*	Increasingly less civilized, pastoralists, non-sedentary
Interior		*Garamantes Augilae Ethiopes*	Barbaric, promiscuous
Deeper interior	live underground (unnaturally)	*Troglodytae*	Utterly barbaric
Deepest interior		*Blemys Satyres*	Fantastical (no heads etc.)

Table 2:1. Schematic model of progressive barbarism with distance from Mediterranean coast (after Pliny and Mela). Cf. also Shaw 1983.

Desanges' map no.	Date/period	Location assigned to *Macae* by Desanges
4	Hellenistic	From *Arae Philaenorum* to the *Cinyps*, on the Greater Syrtes littoral, in the eastern Gebel and pre-desert hinterland of western Syrtica.
5	Early Principate	Southern littoral of Greater Syrtes only. *Cissipades* now shown as occupying western shore
10	1st–2nd centuries AD (interior tribes after Pliny, Ptolemy)	[*Samamukii* in hinterland of western Syrtes littoral, *Makkoi* in hinterland to southwest of Syrtes]
7	2nd–3rd centuries AD	Central sector of southern littoral of Greater Syrtes. Western shore now occupied by *Elaeones*, southwestern area by *Seli*, *Muducivvi* and *Zamucii*.
8	Byzantine	Along southeastern littoral of Greater Syrtes only. *Laguatan* now on western shore.

Table 2:2. The migrating (or misinterpreted) *Macae* (after Desanges 1962).

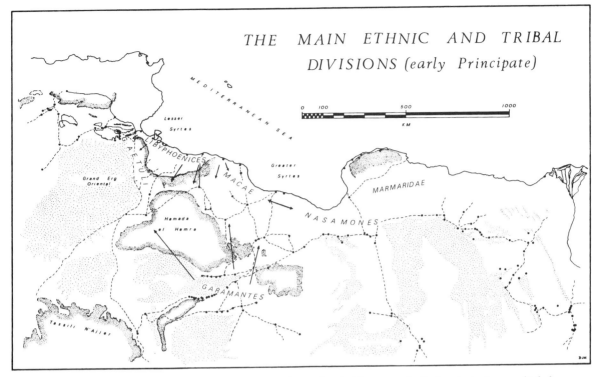

Fig. 2:2 The main ethnic and tribal divisions in early imperial Tripolitania. The arrows indicate principal areas of tribal expansionism or hegemonical relations.

in increasing barbarity and degeneracy (Table 2:1). We now know that the *Garamantes*, for example, were skilful agriculturalists (as well as pastoralists) with large oasis towns' and the same was almost certainly true of the Nasamonian *Augilae*. Yet the perspective of the ancient compilers has distorted the truth through the selection of information which seemed to fit their model. The difficulty is how to spot the authentic information and to see its significance even though it was used within a rigid and artificial framework. Mela, for instance, commented that the interior pastoral tribes were scattered about and neither consulted together nor had fixed rules. He added, however, that they practised polygamy and had many children and thus had relations everywhere. The information was neatly phrased to fit Mela's framework, but there is more than a passing resemblance to the segmented structure of modern Berber tribes based on extended family units. In such communities there is little need for tribal law because intra-familial restraints on conduct are very strong. Although Mela appears to deny the practice of alliance between family groups, his cryptic comment about the existence of extensive family ties is a hint that confederation could occur in specific circumstances on agnate or ethnic grounds.[15]

A similar indication of the mixed subsistence pattern of Libyan tribes may be given by Diodorus Siculus. Describing the *Auschisae, Marmaridae, Nasamones* and *Macae* tribes of *Cyrenaica* and *Syrtica*, he wrote:

> Now of these, those are farmers who possess land which is able to produce abundant crops, while those are pastoralists who get their sustenance from the flocks and herds which they maintain and both these groups have kings and lead life not entirely savage or different from that of civilized man. The third group, however, obeying no king and taking no account of justice makes robbery its constant practice and attacking unexpectedly out of the desert it seizes whatever it has happened upon and quickly withdraws to the place whence it has set out.

Although Diodorus made a tripartite division of the interior peoples, it is significant that it is not done in terms of the large tribal units. The implication is that the *Macae*, for instance, comprised sub-tribes in all three categories, farmers, pastoralists, and tribes living off brigandage. Whatever the defects of his structured framework and his description of the interior tribes as entirely barbaric, he certainly gives evidence for a form of tribal hierarchy. In the remainder of the passage Diodorus related more information on the third group of tribes, which in some ways contradicted his earlier verdict on them. Although their leaders had no cities, they had towers (*pyrgoi*) in the oases. Other tribes were subject to them and submitted to their authority and presumably paid tribute in return for protection. This was still a common form of alliance between semi-nomadic and sedentary people in the Tripolitanian Gebel in the recent past.[16] Agriculture was one of the criteria of civilization used by the ancient writers, but there was no guarantee that sedentary tribes were politically dominant over pastoral ones, and Diodorus implied that the opposite could be the case. Another interesting aspect of this passage is that the alliance between the tribes described by Diodorus was imposed by military force.

The generalized and simplified approach adopted by Pliny, Mela, Diodorus and others to explain the way of life of barbarian peoples was not so much deliberate distortion as a product of their general perspective. Even so there are some clear indications that tribal society was segmented.

There are considerable problems involved in reconciling the geographical data from the various sources to produce maps of tribal settlement. If one takes but one tribal group, the *Macae*, and examines the positions they are mapped in, by Desanges for instance, it is clear that there is something awry (Table 2:2)

The existence of several hierarchical levels of tribal names can explain many of the apparent contradictions but the broad ethnic and political divisions have not normally been distinguished from sub-tribal names in previous work. The basis for the following analysis of the Tripolitanian tribes has been the identification of a number of primary or super-tribal groups or confederations. These include tribal names which appear in several sources, often indicated as numerous people: the *Macae, Nasamones, Garamantes* and *Gaetuli* (Fig. 2:2). There were also some divisions created by Greek and Roman sources to refer to large groups of people in a general way, as for instance the *Lotophages* and *Libyphoenices*, though the ethnic equivalence of these names to the major tribal ones is doubtful.[17]

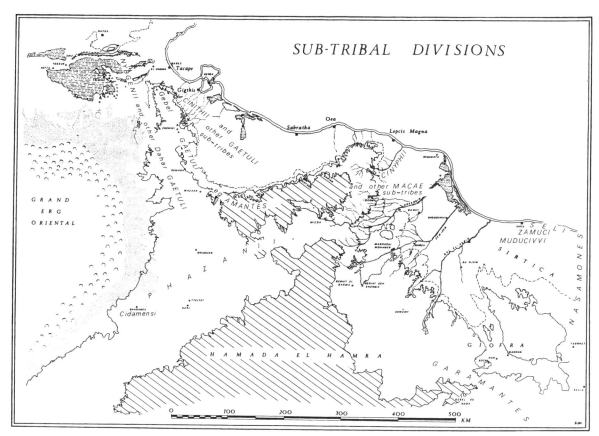

Fig. 2:3 Sub-tribal divisions of the major confederations/groupings in the early imperial period (only groups whose location is secure are marked).

4
TRIBES AND SUB-TRIBES OF TRIPOLITANIA

The discussion above has led us to identify four principal tribal groupings in pre-Roman Tripolitania. It follows that the *Gaetuli*, *Garamantes*, *Macae* and *Nasamones* were each composed of numerous sub-groupings in a hierarchical or segmented structure and that some of these sub-tribes can be identified from the primary sources (Figs 2:2, 2:3). In each case, it would appear that the larger unit included sub-groups of pastoral, sedentary and mixed lifestyles and that the major population centres were frequently located at perennial springs, oases or hillforts. The apparent existence of a fifth large group, the *Lotophages*, is due to a historical anachronism and does not represent the reality of the immediate pre-Roman situation (see below). The coastal towns and their territories were inhabited by people described in a general sense as *Libyphoenices*. But it is doubtful that this designation was a unifying one and each town will have tended to act in its own narrow interests. The Libyan elements of the Libyphoenician populations progressively lost their tribal associations. In late antiquity two new groups can be identified, the *Arzuges* and the *Laguatan*; they will be fully discussed later (chapter 9).

Table 2:3 summarizes the primary source references to the tribes of Tripolitania, Syrtica and Fezzan. Where possible an approximate location is given and an attribution to one of the primary groups (although these are admittedly tenuous and more than one alternative is possible in some cases. Through the operation of hegemonic control a tribe could belong in more than one group at different times).

The *Lotophages*

The primary sources give us several options for the location of the *Lotophages*. The island of Gerba (*Meninx*) was indicated by Polybius and by Strabo, although the latter also referred to the Lesser Syrtes embayment as a whole as *Lotophagitis*. Scylax gave the lotus-eaters an island base as well, but his position is too far east to have been Gerba. Herodotus described a mainland setting on a narrow headland, a reference often identified with the Zarzis peninsula near Gerba. On the other hand, Roman sources were later not entirely confident of where to find them. Ptolemy described Gerba as *Lotophagitis*, but also placed *Lotophages* near the *Cinyps* (east of *Lepcis*). Mela identified them in *Cyrenaica* whilst Pliny related the lotus tree to the Greater Syrtes in particular. When dis-

cussing *Meninx* he did not connect it with the *Lotophages*. The second century *Periegesis* of Dionysius also placed the *Lotophages* east of *Lepcis Magna*. Although the consensus of the Greek sources identify the *Lotophages* with the island of Gerba and the Lesser Syrtic coast, by Roman times it had no geographic or ethnic significance. Later sources evidently applied the term to any communities close to where the lotus tree was found. As Brogan has shrewdly observed, the development of the Phoenician *emporia* into the great Libyphoenician *civitates* must have absorbed most of the Libyan coastal tribes. The identification made by Latin authors between the *Lotophages* and the Greater Syrtes is indicative of the slower speed of social and economic development there than along the Lesser Syrtes coast, where no native people who fitted the image of the *Lotophages* could be found in the first century AD.

All that can be reasonably concluded about the *Lotophages* is that they were coastal or island tribes in regions where the lotus tree flourished. In all probability many of these tribes were absorbed in the expansion of the *Libyphoenices*. Stephanus Byzantinus, quoting Philostos, named the *Erebidae* and *Gindanes* as tribes of the *Lotophages*. Since other references indicate a location in western Tripolitania for these tribes it is possible that they were centred on the littoral of the Lesser Syrtes.[18]

The *Libyphoenices*

Here again the nomenclature is a convenient generalization coined by the Greeks and imitated by the Romans. The apparent coherence of the group name was by no means evident to the *Libyphoenices* themselves. It was used as a general name for the people in the coastal plains between Carthage and *Byzacena*. Strabo more accurately also described Libyphoenician peoples existing round the southern edge of the Lesser Syrtes as far as the promontory of *Cephalae* (near Misurata). In this southern zone the *Libyphoenices* were divided into the individual populations centred on the towns of *Tacapae* (Gabes), *Gigthis* (Bou Ghara), *Sabratha* (Sabrata), *Oea* (Tripoli) and *Lepcis Magna* (Lebda). These towns started life as Phoenician *emporia* established at regular sailing intervals. Carthage had jealously guarded her maritime trading monopolies whilst she also dominated the *emporia* and this had the important effect of diverting the energies of the *emporia* to the exploitation of the land. Dramatic development took place in the last centuries BC, for as well as the spread of agriculture and arboriculture there was intermarriage and integration between Libyans and Phoenician/Punic people. Having passed under the aegis of Rome, these

Tribal name	Sub tribe of	Primary sources	Secondary sources	Location
Akhaemeneis	*Gaetuli*	Ptolemy 4.3.6; 4.6.6	B 64; D 75	S of Lesser Syrtes?
Amantes	*Gaetuli*	Pliny 5.34–35	D 76–77; R 40–41	Gebel to N of *Phazania*
Anacuta	*Laguatan?*	Corippus 2.75	C 348; D 76–77	Tripolitania?
Arzosei	*Gaetuli*	CII 8.22787 / *ILAf*30	D 77–80; Br 280–81	Near Bir Soltane in the Dahar
ARZUGES	–	Orosius *AP* 1.2.90; St Augustine *Lett* 46, 47, 93; Corippus 2,148	B 68; C 93–95; D 77–80; Br 280–81	The S and/or SW frontier regions of Tripolitania in the late Roman period.
Astakoures, Astrikes	*Gaetuli (later Arzuges?)*	Ptolemy 4.3.6; 4.6.6; Corippus 2.75; 6, 391, 404, 431, 451, 464	B 64; Br 280, C 80–81, 348	Western Tripolitania
Austur, Austuriani, Ausuriani	*Laguatan*	Amm. Marc. 26.4.5; 28.6.1-14; Corippus 2.89, 91–96, 209, 345; 5.172; 7.283; Synesius *Lett* 57, 78; *Cat* 1.1568–9, 1572; Priscus Panita *FHG* 4, p. 98.	B 68, 71; Br 282–84; C 102–104, 348; D 82; Mattingly 1983	Desert tribe with bases to E of Tripolitania and to S of Syrtica?
Bubeium (cf. limes Bubensis	*Gaetuli? Garamantes*	Pliny 5.37, *Not, Dig* Occ. 30	B 59; C 77; D 84; Desanges 1957	Unknown
Cinithi	*Gaetuli*	Pliny 5.30; Tacitus *Ann* 2.52; Ptolemy 4.3.6; *CIL* 8.22729	B 58, 64, 68; Br 278; D'86; R 39	South of Lesser Syrtes in vicinity of *Gigthis*, which appears to be their assigned *civitas*
Cinyphi	*Macae*	Silius Ital. 2.60; 3.275; Ptolemy 4.6.3	B 63; D 87	Wadi Caam area (*Cinyps*) to the E and SE of *Lepcis Magna*
Cissipades	*Macae*	Pliny 5.28; *CIL* 16, 39, 46; *CIL* 3.14429	B 57; D 87; R 41	West side of Greater Syrtes
Dolopes	*Gaetuli*	Ptolemy 4.3.6; 4.6.6	B 63; D 88	SW Tripolitania ? transhumant between desert and western Gefara
Elaeones	*Macae (?)*	Ptolemy 4.3.6	B 63; D 88	Region of Greater Syrtes
Erebridae	*Lotophages*	Ptolemy 4.3.6; Stephanus Byz.; *Philostos* 33	B 54, 63; D 89	Western Gefara?
Eropaei	*Gaetuli*	Ptolemy 4.3.6; 4.7.10	B 63; D 89–90	W. Gefara and desert interior to S
Gadabitani	*Gaetuli?*	Procupius *aed* 4.4.12; Corippus 2.117–18	D 91; Br 279–80	Near *Lepcis Magna* or possibly name derived from *Cidamensi*?
GAETULI	–	Strabo 2.5.33; 17.3.2, 3.9, 3.19; Florus 2.31; Tactius *Ann*; Dio 55.28.2–4; Sid. Apoll. *Carm* 5.337; Corippus 5.431.	B 56, 59, 68, 92; D *passim*; R 44–45; Br 277–78; Fentress 1979; 1982, 330–34; Trousset 1982b, 98	General and possibly vague usage for tribes near both Syrtes and in interior to NW of *Garamantes*. No evident close connection with the Gaetuli S of Numidia and well to the W
Gamphasantes	*Gaetuli (?) cf Phazanii*	Herodotus 4.174; Mela 1.23; 1.47; Pliny 5.26, 5.44–45	B 53, 92; Br 279–80; D 91–92	Phazania region?
GARAMANTES	–	Herodotus 4.174; Strabo 2.5.33; 17.3.3, 3.7, 3.19, 3.23; Livy 29.33; Virgil *Aen* 6.791–97; Mela 1.23, 1.45; Pliny 5.26, 36, 38, 6.209; 8.142, 178; 13.111; Florus 2.31; Tacitus *Ann* 3.74; *Hist* 4.39; Ptolemy 1.8.4–5, 10.2; 4.6.3–5, 6.12, 8.2; Solinus 30.2; Isidorus 9.2; Amm. Marc. 22.15.2; Iul. Honorius B. 47, 53, A 48, 54; Orosius 1.2.88, 2.90; Sid. Apoll. 5.36; Corippus 6.198; John of Biclar A569, p. 212	B 49, 53, 56, 58, 91–92, 98, 103; Br 281–82; C 93, 101–02; D 93–96.	Numerous locations in modern Fezzan, notably Wadi el Agial, Wadi esc-Sciatti, Wadi Berguig, the Murzuk depression. The hegemony of this confederation extended at various times a considerable way to N and S along the desert routes
Gindanes	*Lotophagi*	Herodotus 4.176; Stephanus Byz. *Philostos* 33	B 52; 110–11; D 97	Western Gefara? Near Ben Gadane?

Table 2:3. Catalogue of tribal names and ethnic or generic terms used by ancient sources in relation to the native people of Tripolitania (Key to commonly cited secondary sources: B = Bates 1914; Br = Brogan 1975b; C= Courtois 1955; D = Desanges 1962; R = Rachet 1970).

Table 2:3. *cont.*

Tribal name	Sub tribe of	Primary sources	Secondary sources	Location
Ifuraces	*Laguatan*	Corippus 2.113; 3.412; 4.641; 8.490, 648	B 67, C 348; D 99–100	Tripolitania/Syrtica?
Ilaguas *Ilaguatan* *LAGUATAN* *Leuathae* *Lawata*	–	Corippus 1.478; 2.87, 96, 106, 210, 345, 4.374; 5.153; 6.108, 195, 238, 437, 454, 462, 469, 604; 7.383; 8.580, 647, id, 1.144; 467; ; 4.48, 85, 629; 5.171; 6.278, 7.535; 8.434, 474, 501 Procopius *BV* 4.21.2–22; 4.22.13–20; 4.28.47; id, *Aed.* 6.4 Arab sources	B 67; Br 283–86; C 101–04, 344–45; 348–50; D101–02; Jerary 1976; Mattingly 1983; Oates 1954, 110–11.	Great confederation of tribes, initially attested in eastern deserts of Libya and progressively further to the west in late empire/Arab period. Umbrella term for most tribes of Tripolitanian hinterland and desert oases of Tripolitania, Syrtica and Cyrenaica in Byzantine period
LIBYPHOENICES	–	Diod. Siculus 20.55.4; Livy 221.22; 25.40; Strabo 17.3.19; Pliny 5.24; Ptolemy 4.3.6	B 55–57, 64; Br 267–68; D 103, R 38.	Coastal strip and immediate hinterland of *Byzacena* and Tripolitania. Population based on old Phoenician emporia.
LOTOPHAGES	–	Herodotus 4.177; Scylax 110; Polybius 1.39.2; 34.3.12; Strabo 3.4.3; 17.3.17; Mela 1.37; Pliny 13.104; Ptolemy 4.3.6; Dionysius *per.* 206; Stephanus Byz. *Philostos* 33.	B 52, 54–57, 63, 91, 99; Br 278; D 103, 105; R 40.	Gerba and area of Lesser Syrtes, though some sources specify Greater Syrtes and Cyrenaica also. References of Roman date probably anachronistic.
Macares	*Macae?*	Corippus 2.62	C 348; D105	Mountains and wooded area. Tripolitanian Gebel?
MACAE *Maces* *Makae*		Herodotus 4.42, 175; Diodorus 3.49.1, Silius Italicus 2.60; 3.275; 5.194; 9.11, 89, 222; 15.670; Pliny 5.34; Ptolemy 4.3.6; 4.6.6; *Liber gen.* (Frick I, p.20); *Excerpta Barb*, (Frick I, p.202)	B 52, 54–57, 63, 67, 91, 106, 121, 133, 137, 146–48; Br 278–79; D 106–07; R 41; Rebuffat 1982c, 196–99	Western neighbours of *Nasamones* on coast and in western and southern hinterland of the Greater Syrtes, extending as far north as the Wadi Caam (*Cinyps*)
Maklhues *Makhrues*	*Gaetuli*	Herodotus 4.178 (cf. Pliny 7.15); Ptolemy 4.3.6; 4.6.6	B 52, 57–58, 64, 91, D 107; R 40	Western Tripolitania?
Machyles	*Macae?*	Pliny 7.15	B 67; 91	Near *Nasamones*, therefore near Greater Syrtes?
Mamuci (cf. *limes Mamucensis*)	*Macae*	cf. Zamuci. *Notitia Dig Occ* 31.26	B 67; D 133	Tripolitania or Syrtica
MARMARIDAE	–	Scylax 108; Diodorus 3.49.1; Strabo 2.5.33, 17.1.13; 17.3.22; Pliny 5.32, 39; Florus 2.31; *AE* 1934, 257	B 54–57, 62, 66; C 280; D 164–65	Major group of tribes of eastern Libyan desert and margins of Cyrenaica and Syrtica.
Mazices *Mazax*	?	*Liber gen* p. 167; Aethicus (GLM 88); Philostorgius 11.8; Nestorius 1.7; Nicephorus Callistus 14. 36; Synesius *Lett* 24; Vegetius 3.23; Corippus 1.549; 5.80, 376, 6.44, 167, 450, 600; 8.305	B 66, 71, C 100, 120, 125, 348; Br 285; D 112–13.	Late Roman tribal designation (covers wide geographical area from Egypt to Mauretania.) Status of the name unclear (may be generic)
Mecales *Imaclas*	*Laguatan*	Corippus 2.75; 3.410	B 64, 68; D 113–14	Tripolitania
Moukthousii cf. *Muctuniana manus*	*Gaetuli?*	Ptolemy 4.3.6 Corippus 2.116, 120	B 64; D 116–17	Near Lesser Syrtes/western Gebel?
Moutougoures	*Gaetuli*	Ptolemy 4.3.6	B 64; D 116–17	Near Lesser Syrtes
Muducivvi	*Macae*	*IRT* 854	Br 279; D 117; R 154.	Vicinity of Sirte on Greater Syrtes
M.S.Li (cf. *N.GL.Bi* or *T.GL.Bi*)	*Macae?* *Libyphoenices?*	Levi della Via 1964a, 60	Br 280–81; Brogan 1964, 47–56; Levi della Vida 1964a, 57–63	Wadi el-Amud, middle Wadi Sofeggin, Tripolitanian pre-desert

Table 2:3. *cont.*

Tribal name	Sub tribe of	Primary sources	Secondary sources	Location
NASAMONES	–	Herodotus 4.172; Diodorus 2.17.50; Strabo 2.5.33; 17.3.20; Lucan 4.679; 9.439–44, 458–59; Silius Italicus 1.408; 3.320; 13.481; Pliny 5.33–34; Ptolemy 4.5.12; 4.5.13; Zonaras 11.19; *IRT* 854: Corippus 6.198, 552, 589, 593, 692; 7.465, 510; 8.95, 177, 234, 248, 274, 423, 428, 446, 639 (cf. same late sources as for Macae)	B 52–57, 62, 64–66, 71, 91, 98, 100, 105–06, 157, 166–68, 174, 179; Br 279; C 102–03, 348; D 152–54; R 39–41, 153–54, 159–60.	E and SE littoral of Greater Syrtes and deep desert hinterland extending to oasis of Augila and other oases.
Nathabres cf. *Nabathrae* cf. *Niteris/Nitiebies*	*Gaetuli*	Orosius 1.2.43–45 Ptolemy 4.6.6 Pliny 5.37	B 68; C 93, 102; D 122–23	South of Tripolitania
Nigitimi	*Gaetuli*	Ptolemy 4.3.6; 4.6.6; *Tab. Peut.*	B 63; D 125	South of Lesser Syrtes? Western Gefara?
NUMIDAE	–	Caesar *BAf* 97–2; Sallust 77.1–4	Br 277	Numidian confederacy/hegemony extended into Tripolitania in 2nd–1st century BC.
Nybgenii	*Gaetuli*	Ptolemy 4.3.6; 4.6.6; *Liber Gen* p. 109 (211); *Chr. Alex* p. 109 (182); *Chron. Pasch* I, o 59; *CIL* 8.11051; 22786–88; *ILAf* 655	B 63; D 129; R 163–64; Trousset 1974: 43–46; 1978, 164–69	Centre in Nefzaoua oases of Kebili and Telmine. Lands included the Chott Fedjedj and N Dahar.
Phazanii	*Gaetuli*	Pliny 5.26–35; Ptolemy 4.7.10	B 53, 98, 100; Br 279–80; D 16, 130–316; R 37; Desanges 1957, 19	Centred on oasis of *Cidamus* (Ghadames) in SW Tripolitania, their territory probably included the zone N of the Hamada el Hamra and the S Dahar
Psylli cf. *Seli*	*Macae?* *Nasamones?*	Herodotus 4.173; Pliny 5.27; 7.14; Strabo 17.4.6.	B 52, 55, 58, 63, 66; Br 279; D 155–56	Greek Sources give a location near the *Nasamones* on the Greater Syrtes.
Samamuki cf. *Zamucci*	*Macae*	Ptolemy 4.3.6–4.3.11	D 132	Northeastern Gebel/Gefara?
Seli (see above Psylli)	*Macae?* *Nasamones?*	*Tab Peut.*		The towns of *Digdida municipium Selorum* and *Marcomades Selorum* on the *Tabula Peutingeriana* raise the possibility that there may have been two groupings on the Greater Syrtes, one in *Macae* territory, the other perhaps Nasamonian.
Sigiplonsi	*Gaetuli*	Ptolemy 4.3.6	B 63; D133	Western Gefara?
Silcadenit cf. *Silvacae* cf. *Silvaizan*	?	Corippus 2.52–55, 62.	C 348; D 134	Tripolitania?
Sintae	*Gaetuli?*	Strabo 2.5.33	D 135; R 37, 39	Western Tripolitania, possibly western littoral of Lesser Syrtes
Tautamei	*Macae?*	*Liber Gen.* 145, p. 102; *Chr. Alex* 117, p. 102	D 137	Placed between *Nasamones* and *Macae* in late sources. Perhaps a sub-tribe of one of them on the Syrtic coast or an oasis.
Theriodes	*Gaetuli?*	Iulius Hon, A48, p. 54; Herodotus 4.181	D 138	*Phazania?*
Tidamensii (cf. *Phazanii*)	*Gaetuli?*	Ptolemy 4.3.6	D 138	Perhaps the people of *Cidamus* (Ghadames), chief oasis of the *Phazanii*.
Troglodytes	*Aethiopes*	Herodotus 4.181, 183; Mela 1.23, 44; Pliny 2.228; 5.34, 43; Ptolemy 4.4.6	B 103, 168; D 139–40	S of *Garamantes* and modern Fezzan
Ursiliani Urceliana	*Laguatan*	Vegetius 3.23; Corippus 2.75; 6.390	C 100, 348; D 141–42	Desert bases S of Greater Syrtes?
Zamucci	*Macae*	*IRT* 854	Br 279, D 117	In vicinity of Sirte (*Marcomades*)

independent *civitates* were among the richest communities in North Africa by the early principate. In subsequent decades they continued to expand into the Gebel hinterland of the semi-arid Gefara and one can trace this by the spread of their predominantly Punic culture and architecture.

The expansion of the lands of the urban *civitates* was probably in part achieved by the absorption of elements of the Gebel and pre-desert tribes (technically *Gaetuli* and *Macae* in my classification). The predominance of Libyco-Punic culture and the neo-Punic language in this region indicates that the expansion was accomplished by Libyphoenicians rather than Romans (see chapter 8, below). Unfortunately it is less clear what happened to Libyan tribes whose traditional lands were taken over. One tribe, the *Cinithi*, possibly centred in the western Gefara, was associated with *Gigthis*, which may have been designated its *civitas*. Other information shows that the *Cinithi* were a Gaetulian tribe. The prestigious civil career of *L. Memmius Messius* in the early second century indicates that some of the *Cinithi* were able to participate at the highest levels of municipal life in *Gigthis*. An inscription from a mausoleum near Jefren records the name *Chinitiv* (?) and is presumably another instance of the integration of the elite of the *Cinithi* with the *Libyphoenices*.

Not all levels of Libyan tribal society will have been treated in this manner. Abd el-Hakam, referring to the conquests of the *Lawata* tribe (see chapter 9, *Laguatan* below), stated that they had dispossessed the *Rum* of *Lepcis* and *Sabratha* of their lands. However, the '*Afariq* who were subject to the *Rum* remained paying a tribute which they were accustomed to render to all who occupy their country'. The *Rum* were not Romans, but the Romanized *Libyphoenices*. One may guess that the *Afariq* were some of the original Gaetulian and *Macae* population of the Gebel, who had been transformed into dependent sharecroppers.

The *civitates* of the Libyphoenicians were fiercely independent of each other and it would be mistaken to view the agricultural expansion as a coordinated and agreed 'carve-up' of the interior lands between the different communities. The rivalry between the cities, notably *Lepcis*, *Oea* and *Sabratha* could have disastrous consequences. In AD 69 a disagreement over territory between the *Lepcitani* and *Oeenses* flared up into a war. At other times indiscriminate expansionism of one or other of the coastal cities must have antagonized the Libyan tribes of the Gebel. The support of Tripolitanian tribes for Tacfarinas between AD 17–24 indicates that there was resentment against both Rome and the *Libyphoenices*. Roman frontier policy had, therefore, not only to take account of poten-

tially hostile Libyan tribes, but also of the possibly adverse effects of allowing nominally independent cities too much freedom of action. The importance of delimiting and fixing the territories of tribes and cities alike was illustrated dramatically by the events of AD 69–70 (chapter 3).

Within the *civitates* there is no denying the strength and wealth of the leading *Libyphoenician* families, a point best demonstrated in the case of *Lepcis Magna*. The remarkable building programme of the Julio-Claudian period was achieved with local money by peregrine nobles and not by Italian colonists (see below, chapters 3 and 6).[19]

The *Gaetuli*

Source references to the *Gaetuli* can be divided into three distinct geographic groups. Pliny described *Gaetuli* south of *Mauretania* on the Atlantic seaboard. Separated by deserts from this group were another set of *Gaetuli* who lay south of the main tribes of *Africa*. Other sources link this group closely with the *Numidae*, with whose territory they were adjacent. These *Gaetuli* were once located by modern scholars in the Wadi Djedi area of Algeria, but many indications show that the more northerly *Gaetuli* tribes extended to the Tell, where they were closely linked in the sources to the Numidian kingdom as dependent, allied tribes or as rebellious subjects. In the second century AD, Apuleius described himself as '*semi-Numidam, semi-Gaetulam*', hinting at an ethnic mix in his home town of *Madauros* (whose location he described as lying on the divide between *Gaetuli* and Numidians: *Numidiae at Gaetuliae in ipso confino*). This may be no more than a literary flourish for an educated Roman audience, but it could equally be an echo of a once significant ethnic reality.

The third use of the term was to describe practically all the tribes lying south of *Africa Proconsularis*, but north of the *Garamantes* and the *Aethiopes*, and extending to the region of the two Syrtes. Virgil, Florus and Strabo were all specific on this last point. Orosius mentioned *barbaros Gaetulos Nathabres* south of the *Regio Arzugum* near the *Garamantes*. Finally the *Tabula Peutingeriana* has *Gaetuli* tribes marked at various points between the Aures mountains and a point south of the Greater Syrtes.

Although their combined numbers made them for Strabo the largest Libyan people, there is no evidence for a united Gaetulian kingdom or state. Mela, indeed, described them as a numerous but segmented people (*natio frequens multiplexque Gaetuli*). Confederation was perhaps normally on a comparatively small scale, as, for example, between a grouping of six Gaetulian tribes in Numidia recorded in an inscription.[20]

There are many references to the nomadic way of life and the barbarous and warlike conduct of the *Gaetuli*. It seems likely that '*Gaetuli*' proved a useful blanket term to describe the little-known pastoral tribes of the pre-desert who were assumed to have these characteristics. We shall see in the following discussion that the Tripolitanian tribes which were nominally *Gaetuli* can be subdivided into broad geographical groupings. Whilst I have retained the overall name for convenience, the tribes are dealt with below with reference to these zones. Since the majority of the *Gaetuli* tribes are not firmly located much of what follows is hypothetical.

The tribes of Phazania

Pliny's account of the campaign of Cornelius Balbus mentioned a region known as *Phazania*. In spite of the apparent similarity of name this does not correspond with the area known as Fezzan since the early Islamic era. The latter is equivalent to the land of the *Garamantes*, which according to Pliny lay beyond the Black Mountain and across a stretch of desert from *Phazania*. The names of three *urbes* of the *Phazanii* – *Alele*, *Cilliba* and *Cydamus* – were also recorded and the latter can be identified with the oasis settlement of Ghadames. This defines *Phazania* as the region lying northwest of the modern Fezzan and the Hamada el-Hamra. The western limits were probably defined by the Grand Erg Oriental, whilst the eastern boundary may well have been the Mizda corridor leading to Gheriat and Fezzan. Interestingly, an area of the pre-desert west of Mizda and southwest of Gasr Duib is still called 'Fezzan' on recent maps. The northern limits may well have been close to the Gebel. It is possible that *Alele* and *Cilliba* are commemorated by the names of the Roman frontier forts at *Talalati* and *Tillibari*. Research by Rebuffat has also shown the presence of native fortifications of early Roman date marking the route between Ghadames and Nalut. Finally Ptolemy placed the *Phazanii* as neighbours of the *Nybgenii* which is only possible if both tribes practised transhumance over as extensive distances as is done today. The *Phazanii* may well have controlled oases and wells as far north as modern Dehibat. In all this area permanent settlement is only possible in the Gebel and in the oases (notably Ghadames, those of the Derj depression and Sinaouen).

The political organization of the tribe seems to have been hierarchical, with the *Cidamensi* (=*Tidamensi* of Ptolemy) being the principal subtribe. Other tribal names sometimes linked with the tribe are the *Gamphasantes*, the *Gadabitani* and *Theriodes*. The arguments are not entirely convincing and are best summarized by Desanges.

Fig. 2:4 Relief of a Libyan chieftain from Ghadames (after Brogan and Smith 1985).

We have some evidence which indicates that *Cidamus* (Ghadames) was a prosperous and sizeable centre in antiquity. Roman military occupation is attested in the early third century, but a mass of second-century pottery from a large area of the oasis indicates earlier Roman contacts with this tribal and trading centre. There is an important group of Roman period tombs at Ghadames and these could relate either to native notables, to the known Roman garrison of the third century AD or to both. A fine depiction of a (?) Libyan chieftain from Ghadames (and most likely originating from this cemetery) provides some evidence in favour of the former interpretation (Fig. 2:4). Native fortifications, associated with second century AD pottery, have also been reported by Rebuffat at other minor oases north of Ghadames.[21]

The Dahar and Nefzaoua tribes

The northward curve of the Tunisian Gebel at Dehibat and the sand sea of the Eastern Erg, define a corridor of arid semi-desert plateau running north from *Phazania*. The presence of a number of important wells in this part of the Dahar make it an important transhuming route. Transhumance takes place both north to south from the oases of the Nefzaoua and east to west from centres in the Gebel. The north to south movements tend to be semi-nomadic in nature. Sedentary argiculture is only practised in the Gebel and the oases of the Nefzaoua.

Ptolemy listed certain tribal names twice in different positions in the interior. The first group can be placed in the vicinity of the Lesser Syrtes, the second much deeper into the northern Sahara. It is possible that Ptolemy had simply made an error, but alternatively he may have been trying to indicate the practice of long-range transhumance from the Nefzaoua down the Dahar. The tribes listed were, *Akhaemeneis/ Akhaemae; Astakoures/ Astakouri; Dolopes/Dolopes; Eropaei/ Oreipaei; Nybgenii/Nugbenitae.* Given the weaknesses of Ptolemy's data, no reliable map can be established, but for one of the five tribes, the *Nybgenii*, more information is available.

It should not surprise us that the integration of tribal lands within the Roman provinces brought about a gradual increase in the sedentary component of the tribes. Trousset has described the Roman delimitation of the territory of the *Nybgenii* as a move which turned them from semi-nomads into transhumers.

The main tribal centre of the *Nybgenii* has been established by inscriptions to be the oasis of Telmine in the Nefzaoua. This is one of the group of small but important oases bordering the south and east sides of the Chott Djerid and Roman period remains have been found in many of them.

At Mansoura, a few kilometres northeast of Telmine there is a prominent mound or 'tell' of demolished mud-brick. The modern village of Telmine itself sits on a hillock which looks largely artificial in origin. The development of such tribal centres in the Roman period was swift in some cases and Telmine was promoted to the rank of *municipium* during the reign of Hadrian. The rapid promotion of the tribal centre suggests that it was already of considerable size and political importance when Roman interest in the region increased under the Flavians. The combined population of the Nefzaoua oases could have been considerable. In the last hundred years the total has varied between 18,000 and 50,000 people. A similar picture is emerging of the important oasis settlements on the other side of the Chott Djerid, notably *Nepta* (Nefta), *Tuzuros* (Tozeur) and *Thiges* (Kriz?).

Ptolemy's statement that the *Nugbenitae* and *Oreipaei* were neighbours of the *Phazanii* suggests that transhumance may have been practised in antiquity down the corridor of Dahar. If Ptolemy's other 'doubled' tribes are to be located close to the *Nybgenii*, then it is likely that they also had oasis centres in the Nefzaoua, or even that they were sub-tribes of the *Nybgenii*. The *Nybgenii* were certainly treated as the chief tribe of the Nefzaoua by the Romans. It is possible that Telmine was designated their *civitas* capital because tribal authority was in some way already exercised over the other oases from there. The absence of Ptolemy's doubled tribes in other sources (with the possible exception of the *Astoukoures*, cf. the *Astrikes* of

Corippus) can best be explained if they were part of the tribal hierarchy of the *Nybgenii*.

The Romans delimited the *Nybgenii* tribal territory in relation to that of *Capsa* and *Tacape*. Another boundary stone from the Dahar at Bir Soltane mentions the tribal names *Arzosei* and (...) *maba* (...), one of which may also have been a *Nybgenii* sub-tribe and the other a transhuming tribe from the Gebel. Access to wells is all-important in a region like the Dahar and the boundary stone was presumably regulating the use of those at Bir Soltane.[22]

Gefara and Gebel

A second group of tribes was listed only once by Ptolemy and seems to refer to peoples based near the Syrtes, in the Gefara plain and in the Gebel. These are the *Cinithi, Moukthousii, Moutougoures* and *Sigiplonsi*. To these can be added the *Amantes* of Pliny, who, situated north of *Phazania*, were most likely a Gebel tribe of the Nefusa region.

Florus mentioned an alliance between *Musulames* and *Gaetulos accolas syrtium* in c. AD 6, whilst Tacitus specifically pairs the *Cinithi* with the *Musulames* during the Tacfarinan revolt. As explained already, the *Cinithi* seem to have been the chief Gaetulian tribe of the western Gefara and Lesser Syrtes littoral and were later connected in some way with the *civitas Gigthensium*. Another inscription from *Thysdrus* (El Djem) refers to a *praefectus gentis* of the *Cinithi* but the man involved was not necessarily a native Cinithian himself and no connection between the tribe and the town of *Thysdrus* is implied.[23] The sedentarization and urbanization of the *Cinithi* was not accomplished without a struggle, as references to them participating in the Gaetulian and Tacfarinan revolts show. Nevertheless, by the end of the first century AD, it is probable that many of the *Gaetuli* tribes of the cultivable western Gefara and the coastal plains were being sedentarized either as farmers or as farm labourers.

Similarly for the Gebel tribes, the agricultural opportunities of their lands were good and from an early date they probably practised a mixed economy. The more ample water resources allowed a tribal dispersion over a wider area. With increasing sedentarization, whether imposed or adopted willingly, the ability of these tribes to form alliances and muster large numbers of men may have been weakened. At any rate, once pacified these tribes were more likely to acquiesce than the *Nybgenii* and *Phazanii* of the pre-desert regions. The development of oases in the latter regions enabled substantial populations to grow up around tribal centres. Historically it was the pre-desert and desert *Gaetuli* tribes which posed the greatest threat to the Libyphoenicians and to Rome and a large amount of military activity in the first century AD was directed towards the oases centres of Fezzan, Giofra, Djerid, Nefzaoua and *Phazania*.

The *Macae*

The *Macae* (*Makae, Maces*) appear in many of the sources and we have seen the problems which occur if they are assumed to be a tribe of equal status with all others located in the same area (see above, Table 2:2). The geographic indications make a good deal more sense if the *Macae* are viewed as a major tribal grouping or confederation.

Herodotus and Scylax placed the *Makae* as western neighbours of the *Nasamones*, extending as far as the river *Cinyps* (Wadi Caam). It was the *Makae* who, with the Carthaginians (*Lepcitani?*), evicted the settlement of the interloping Greek Doreius from the *Cinyps* in *c.* 517 BC. Silius Italicus confirmed the association with the *Cinyps*, by describing the *Cinyphii* as a sub-tribe of the *Macae*. Other sources also locate them on the littoral of the Greater Syrtes, west of the *Nasamones*: Diodorus Siculus, Pliny, St Hippolytus. Pliny stated that the *Macae* lay between the *Nasamones* and the *Amantes*, who lived 12 days west of the Greater Syrtes. This implies that the *Macae* extended far back from the coast into the Gebel and the pre-desert zone of the Sofeggin and Zem-Zem wadis. Scylax supports this conclusion by describing the *Macae* as transhumers who moved with their flocks and beasts away from the coast into the interior in summer. Furthermore, Ptolemy gave the *Macae* two positions; first, on the coast where they were described as *Syrtites* and then in the interior near the mountain *Girgiri* where the source of the *Cinyps* lay. The *Macae* were associated, therefore, with a sizeable area of Gebel and pre-desert as well as with the Syrtic coastline, roughly the same as that occupied by the Orfella tribes today. Rebuffat has identified the tribes of the Bu Njem region as *Macae*, which is in accord with my analysis.[24]

According to Strabo the western limit of the *Nasamones* was at *Arae Philaenorum*, but this is demonstrably incorrect (see below). The eastern limits of the *Macae* are not certain, but the absorption of *Psylli* tribes may have created close links between neighbouring *Macae* and *Nasamones* tribes.

Diodorus Siculus described the *Macae* as the most populous of the Libyan peoples and showed that they were an ethnic grouping of sub-tribes rather than a single, united tribe. The following groupings are therefore proposed as *Macae* sub-tribes.

Cinyphii

The *Cinyphii* in Hannibal's army were described by Silius Italicus as *Maces*. Although Ptolemy distinguished them from the *Macae* this may reflect a growing association between the *Cinyphii* and the *Libyphoenices* of *Lepcis* by the later first century AD or be simply an error. The earlier association of the *Macae* with the *Cinyps* is confirmed by Herodotus.

Cissipades

This tribe was located by Pliny close to the western shore of the Syrtic gulf, but is otherwise unattested in North Africa. However, a cohort of *Cissipades* is known from Upper Moesia in AD 93, though the unit may have been raised earlier than the Flavian period. If Pliny's location is correct, then the *Cissipades* are best explained as a sept of the *Macae*.

Elaeones

Situated by Ptolemy between the *Cinyphii* and the *Macae*, but otherwise unknown, one can assume they were a *Macae* sub-tribe and that Ptolemy had misunderstood the status of the names.

Machyles

They were positioned by Pliny inland from the *Nasamones* and should not be confused with the *Maklhues* of Herodotus near the Lesser Syrtes. Pliny gave semi-mythical information on the tribe, but their location and name suggest a connection with the *Macae*.

Samamukii, Mamucii, Zamuci, Muducivvi

The evidence concerning these four sub-tribes is inter-related and can be dealt with together. *Mamuci*, *Samamukii* and *Zamuci* have sometimes been equated with each other on the grounds that these similar names may all indicate the same tribe. The presence in all three names of the stem *-muci* suggests another possibility, that all three are distinct sub-tribes of the *Macae*, an interpretation which might be arrived at from the geographical evidence in any case.

The existence of the *Mamuci* tribe is inferred from the reference to a *limes Mamucensis* in the *Notitia Dignitatum*. The *Samamukii* were assigned two positions by Ptolemy, near the *Cinyphii* and also in the interior north of the *Girgiri* mountain. The *Zamuci* are fairly precisely located by a land boundary stone found 3 km east of Sirte (*Marcomades*), delimiting their land from that of the *Muducivvi*. These two tribes are not otherwise attested and in this region should be *Macae* (or *Seli?*) sub-tribes.

Seli *(cf. Psylli)*

The *Seli* tribe are marked on the Peutinger Table associated with the towns of *Digdiga* and *Marcomades* on the Syrtic gulf. According to Bates, *Seli* is the most likely Libyan form of *Psylli*, a tribe who, according to Roman sources, lost their independence before the Roman period. The re-emergence of the name in Roman times would seem to show that some *Psylli* had become sub-tribes of the *Macae* and *Nasamones*.

Tautamei

This tribe is only known in later Roman sources, where it was placed between the *Nasamones* and the *Macae* on the Syrtic coast. Therefore, it was probably a sub-tribe of one of these major groups.

The *Macae* provide a clear example of the usage of a tribal name to designate a large group of tribes. Unlike the *Nasamones*, the *Garamantes* and the *Gaetuli*, however, the *Macae* confederation seems to have remained largely dormant in the Roman period. The *Macae* tribes were by and large integrated into the Roman provincial structure without major problems.[25]

The *Nasamones*

The *Nasamones* were the other major grouping of tribes of the Greater Syrtes. Herodotus mentioned them as a coastal tribe, who also had control of the *Augila* oasis where they harvested dates in summer. The coastal dwellers were notorious in antiquity as pirates and wreckers. Although Strabo restricted their territory to *Cyrenaica* alone, it is clear from the events of their revolt in AD 85–6 that they spanned the provincial boundary and there was a substantial portion of the tribe in *Africa* as well (chapter 4, below). Although Domitian claimed to have annihilated them in AD 86, the survivors may well have withdrawn for a period to their southern oases and later sources continued to place them on the Syrtic coast.

The evidence for a tribal hierarchy is to be found partly in the split between coastal and oasis dwellers. Some of the possible sub-tribes (*Seli, Tautamei*) have been mentioned above (under *Macae*). The *Augilae*, the inhabitants of the *Augila* group of oases, were treated as a tribe by Mela. The predominant role played by this major oasis implies that it was the tribal centre and the annual date harvest provided a reason for regular reunion of the transhuming sub-tribes with the sedentary oasis dwellers.

Augila lay technically within the Cyrenaican desert but is also important because of its position on the east-to-west chain of oases which linked Egypt and Africa. For instance, the Ammon cult probably spread westwards by this route, with *Augila* being a major cult centre and perhaps second only to *Siwa* as an oracular source. There were certainly many other temples to *Ammon* west of *Siwa* but we know that one

in particular was a centre of prophesy. Procopius described this function of the *Augila* temple and Mela also commented on the renown of the *Augilae* as prophesiers of the future. In the *Iohannid* of Corippus, the *Laguatan* sought an oracle from *Ammon* somewhere in the Syrtic region, and *Augila* was most likely meant. *Augila* was, therefore, both a tribal and a religious centre for the *Nasamones*, which may have been a significant factor in maintaining the cohesiveness of the Nasamonian confederation. There is not enough evidence, however, to be certain of the precise form of tribal leadership, though kingship or chieftainship linked to the religious centre of *Augila* is a possibility.[26]

The history of the Syrtic region in the late Roman period is one of change and tribal upheaval. Although the *Nasamones* were still mentioned in the literature it is unlikely that they continued to constitute an independent confederation. The *Laguatan* tribes, which seem to have moved westwards along the great chain of oases from *Siwa* to *Augila*, emerged to head a new and powerful confederation (chapter 9, below). The *Nasamones* of *Augila* and their other oases centres were thus absorbed by the *Laguatan*. When Corippus used the term *Nasamon* to describe *Laguatan* warriors he was not being entirely anachronistic or 'poetic'. This absorption of the interior *Nasamones* tribes probably began as early as the later third century AD.

The *Garamantes*

The *Garamantes* are practically the only Libyan tribe to have been researched on a broad basis. Not only has the literary evidence been well commented on but pioneering studies have been done in the fields of archaeology and anthropology.

Once again the hierarchical system would seem to have been present and the leading modern authority on the *Garamantes*, C.M. Daniels, has concluded that the tribe was probably a confederation. The archaeological evidence for the *Garamantes* comes from Fezzan, where fieldwork has revealed Garamantian settlement in three bands of oases sandwiched between the Hamada el-Hamra, the sand sea of Urbari and Murzuk. These are the Wadi esc-Sciatti to the north, the Wadi el-Agial and the Wadi Berguig and the Murzuk/Zuila depression to the south (Fig. 2:5).[27] Although extensive evidence for settlement sites, irrigation systems and cemeteries has been found in all of them, the single most important centre (*Garama*) was located in the Wadi el-Agial. *Garama* was described by Pliny and Ptolemy as the capital and as a '*metropolis*' of the tribe. Initial excavations beneath the medieval mud-brick 'caravan town' of Germa, in the centre of the el-Agial plain, revealed

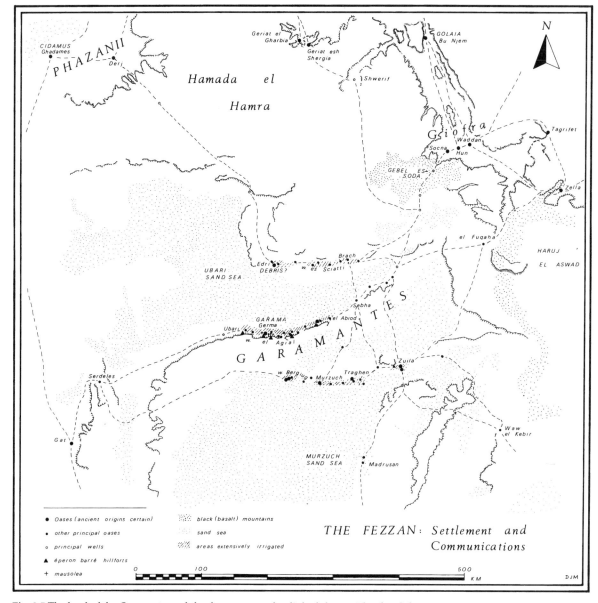

Fig. 2:5 The land of the *Garamantes* and the desert routes that linked them with other Saharan oases.

traces of ancient *Garama*. However, the earliest dating evidence there was only from the fourth century BC and the origins of the *Garamantes* in Fezzan were known to be much earlier. The solution lay in the discovery of an 'éperon barré' site at Zinchecra some 3.5 km to the southwest, where occupation spanned the period from the ninth century BC to the first century AD (Fig. 2:6).

Over 130 km of the Wadi el-Agial was intensively settled and cultivated. Caputo calculated that there were about 60,000 visible burials in the Wadi el-Agial in the 1930s, but Daniels now believes this to be considerably underestimated (Plate 5). A demographic model based on 120,000 graves would suggest a maximum Garamantian population of only 7,000. Instead Daniels suggests that the peak population was probably over 10,000 and sustained at that level for some time. The el-Agial plain was irrigated at numerous points by *foggaras* which tap an artesian nappe at the foot of the southern escarpment of the wadi. The *foggara*, a series of shafts linked by a tunnel at the bottom, is common in the northern Sahara, as well as the

34

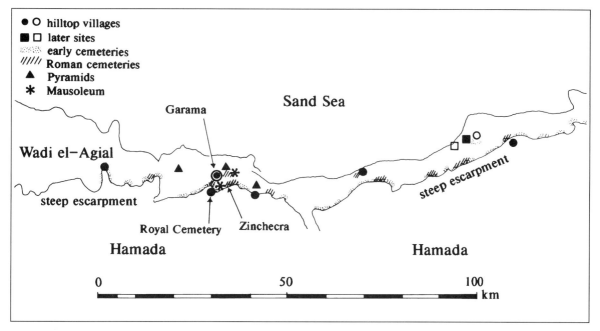

Fig. 2:6 Garamantian settlement geography in the wadi el-Agial depression (after Daniels 1989).

Near East and Persia (where it is called *qanat*). Although these features are commonly assumed to be of post-classical date in the Near East, in Africa some are certainly of Roman date or earlier. None of the examples in Fezzan has been independently dated, but the likelihood must be that the origins of the irrigation systems coincided with the development of cereal cultivation in the area around the ninth century BC. Daniels has recorded 60 *foggaras* in a single 6 km stretch of the el-Agial and another report gives the combined lengths of the *foggaras* in the Germa area as 2,000 km! The same long history of the use of *foggaras* is evident in the Nefzaoua.[28]

Herodotus mentioned both agricultural and pastoral practices among the *Garamantes*, namely the spreading of loam on to the salty soil before cultivating it and the peculiar, backward-grazing cattle. Disappointingly, Mela and Pliny gave no up-to-date information although it must have existed following the campaign of Balbus. Until systematic exploration of Fezzan in the 1930s, considerably more importance was placed, therefore, on the sources which depicted the *Garamantes* as a tent-dwelling (Lucian) or as a warlike and intransigent (Tacitus) tribe. Tribal resistance was interpreted as nomadic antipathy for sedentary peoples and 'civilizing' powers, and little credence was given to the specific reference to oasis agriculture. The archaeological investigation of Fezzan has revealed a very different picture of

Garamantian farming. From the early first millennium BC, the people inhabiting the hillfort at Zinchecra were growing wheat and barley, perhaps also the vine, and making use of the range of products obtainable from the date palm. Other plants seem to have been exploited for medicinal uses or as herbs. Whilst there is also ample evidence for pastoralism, in the form of animal bones and dung deposits at many sites, our perspective has shifted considerably away from the idea that these people were simple herders.[29]

The *Garamantes* had developed into a sophisticated mixed pastoral/agricultural society a long time before their first contacts with Rome. Large segments of the population lived in substantial and permanent mudbrick or stone-built settlements which in some cases merit being viewed as urban or proto-urban centres. Trade is potentially a complicating factor in attempting to reconstruct the Garamantian economy (see chapter 7), but it does not affect the conclusion that, in describing the tribal background here, we must get well away from the nomad and sedentarist dichotomy.

The linear depression of the Wadi el-Agial is seen by Daniels to correspond to the Garamantian *fauces* of Ptolemy. Other evidence, however, suggests that their territory was more extensive than Fezzan alone in the early Roman period. Pliny and Herodotus placed the 'lands of the *Garamantes*' closer to *Augila* than is feasible if modern Fezzan alone was implied. The 10- or 12-day journey by horse or camel would only carry

Fig. 2:7 Libyan tribal leaders from Egyptian art – a possible model for the appearance of the *Garamantes* (from Bates 1914).

deposed king, though there are no other references to the process of succession or limitations to the power of the kings. There was a temple of Ammon at *Garama* and a religious connection with the kings is possible. However, Ayoub's attribution of specific tombs in the Wadi el-Agial to the Garamantian monarchy and his attempt to assign dates and lengths of reign on the basis of grave goods has not been generally accepted.

Examination of a limited number of skeletons has shown that the *Garamantes* were in origin a Berber tribe of Mediterranean type, with a certain admixture of negroid stock. There may have been some social distinctions between different racial types, but much more anthropological work needs to be done before firm conclusions can be reached. Depictions of eastern Libyan tribal leaders from Egypt are thought to give a good impression of the appearance of the *Garamantes* themselves (Fig. 2:7).[30]

The essential features of the Garamantian kingdom were its internal cohesion and its strong links with other Berber tribes further north and east, both through military alliance and the cult of Ammon. Although the *Garamantes* were the dominant native political power in the early principate, they played only a minor role in the later history of the region and may well have been subordinated to the *Laguatan*.

The archaeological work in Fezzan has provided a wealth of new information about the cultural contacts of the *Garamantes*. Finds from the excavations include objects imported from Greece and the Hellenistic world, Egypt, Rome and the Sudan (Table 2:4).

Trade was undoubtedly one way in which these goods could have reached Fezzan, but whatever the arrangement, the reason for their importation was that the *Garamantes* wanted them. The significant quantities of fine pottery and glassware imported must reflect a Garamantian rather than a Roman preference, since the scale of breakages of such fragile goods on the desert tracks would have been a major disincentive to the shippers (merchants or otherwise). The high prestige value of these goods in the Roman world and their use in funerary contexts in Fezzan indicates the way in which indigenous elites often sought outside symbols of high social status to strengthen their own prestige. The point is illustrated in a more recent context by requests made by Sudanese chieftains of early European travellers.

The architecture of the ashlar masonry buildings in *Garama* and of nearby Punico-Roman style mausolea is indicative of another level of this contact between the Garamantian elite and Rome. The buildings are evidence that the *Garamantes* were indeed pacified by the late first century and were given the opportunity to identify with Roman concepts of wealth and

one as far as Zella or possibly the oases of the Giofra. Similarly, Silius Italicus related the story of Asbyte, daughter of the Garamantian Hiarbas, serving under Hannibal with *Gaetuli, Nasamones* and *Macae,* who were subjects or allies of her father. The campaign of Cornelius Balbus may have been a response to joint action by a confederation of *Phazanii* and *Garamantes* and the war between *Lepcis* and *Oea* of AD 69–70 provides another example of the northern outlook and interests of the *Garamantes.* They were brought into the struggle by the *Oenses,* an unlikely alliance if their influence was solely restricted to Fezzan at this date.

There are reasons, though, for seeing this northward extension as hegemonical rather than hierarchical confederacy. Third-century graffiti from Bu Njem show that the local tribes were not *Garamantes* and that the *Garamantes* themselves lived well to the south by that date. The earlier success in this zone of a Garamantian-led confederation need not be doubted.

Unlike the *Macae,* however, the *Garamantes* had a strong, confederated, structure and were ruled by kings. In the late first century AD a Roman expedition was accompanied to the Sudan by a Garamantian king and when Sidi Ocba invaded Fezzan in AD 666–7 there was still a king at Germa. Pliny mentioned a

Source of imported goods	Artifact types	Reference
Egypt	Nubian sandstone Alexandrian glass, faience ware, glass fish beaker Wooden headrest	Ayoub 1967a, 17, 21 Daniels 1973, 39; Ayoub 1967a, 9; Taggart 1982, 81–84 Daniels 1971a, 267
Greece and Greek World	4th century and later Hellenistic Black glaze wares	Daniels 1973, 37
Sudan	Ivory Gold	Ayoub 1967b, 218–19 Ayoub 1967a, 16, 20
Carthage	?	
Roman Africa/ Roman empire	Terra sigillata, Arretine, African Red Slip wares Roman and Tunisian amphorae	Ayoub 1967a, 19–49; Daniels 1973, 38–39; 1975, 251–52 Ayoub 1967a, 20; Daniels 1973, 39; 1975, 252–55

Table 2:4. Imported goods found on Garamantian sites in Fezzan.

prestige. Collaboration of native elites would thus be rewarded by material goods and benefits in cases where the elites showed a receptiveness for cross-cultural borrowing of status symbols.[31]

5
NOMADS AND FARMERS

The ancient sources are disappointingly inexplicit or untrustworthy when dealing with the economic practices of the interior tribes. The schematic vision of progressive barbarization meant that tribes were often presented as crude stereotypes of an expected model. The primary sources are, therefore, of uncertain reliability in relation to the nature of the economic bases of tribes, whether pastoral, sedentary or mixed. The additional problems caused by anachronistic 'borrowed' material have already been dealt with.

The greatest difficulties, however, have been caused by modern commentators through their translation of the primary sources. An appropriate example is the term *nomades*. True nomadism has been rare in North Africa and the movements of flocks and people are normally well regulated. The problem is partly one of semantics and geographers and social anthropologists have yet to agree which of the terms 'nomads', 'semi-nomads' and 'transhumers' are (and which are not) applicable to the Maghreb. In the historical field nomadism has become a term loaded with the connotations of aggressive nomadism attached to it by earlier generations of scholars. The terms semi-nomadism and transhumance are,

therefore, now normally used in reference to the pastoral societies encountered in the region in antiquity.[32]

Two interrelated questions on the nature of nomadism must be examined. First, whether the supposed conflict between 'the desert and the sown' is a necessary condition of the interrelationships between semi-nomadic and sedentary people. Following on from this is the fundamental question of whether the nomads and sedentary farmers dichotomy can be expressed in terms of tribal units. In other words, were some tribes entirely nomadic and others entirely sedentary, or is there a considerable overlap in tribal groupings between these two extremes? Trousset has summarized the development of the theory that the Roman frontiers came to separate two incompatible ways of life and has shown that new archaeological evidence has demanded a reconsideration of this premise. Although there are certainly outbreaks of violence between nomadic and settled communities even in the modern Maghreb, the more normal relationship is symbiotic. Close, and peaceful, coexistence is necessary to both sides since the semi-nomads need grain and agricultural produce and can provide animal products (meat, wool, leather) in exchange. They are also an essential source of seasonal labour for ploughing, harvesting, crop-watching and shepherding. The regulated grazing of the pastoralists' flocks on the stubble fields after harvest also benefits both parties as the farmers get their fields manured in the process.

Even more debatable is the belief that there was a clear line between nomadic and agricultural zones along which the Romans established their frontiers. Nor is the theory of an eviction of semi-nomadic tribes into the north Sahara tenable. Instead we shall see that the allegedly nomadic tribes contained significant sedentary communities in oasis centres and that many 'sedentary' tribes continued to practise transhumance to some extent.[33]

In answer to the second issue, it is evident from a wide range of material that tribes were not composed exclusively of the practitioners of a single economic mode, pastoral or sedentary. Diodorus specifically defined three types of *Macae* sub-tribes, agriculturalists, pastoralists and 'brigands'. Recent work on the *Musulames* tribe shows that at the time of the Tacfarinan revolt, they comprised both sedentary and semi-nomadic sub-groupings. The existence of large hillforts such as Kalaat Senane implies a degree of sedentarization even if the majority of the population still practised transhumance. The example of the *Garamantes* is even more clearcut.

Fentress has collated the evidence for 'nomadism' from the primary sources on North Africa. She observed that it was only in the most interior regions that the existence of agriculture was specifically denied. In order to account for the practice of agriculture in those parts of North Africa where its pre-existence could not be ignored by Greco-Roman writers, a mythical or quasi-historical context was created, involving the Numidian king Massinissa (or alternatively Hercules) as a suitable, non-Roman 'civilizing' agent. The large-scale grain exports made by Massinissa to Rome in the early second century BC are a fair indication that agriculture was in fact well established before his reign began. Even in the more southerly regions, towards *Capsa*, the inhabitants produced enough grain to warrant storing it in fortified places.[34] These examples support the assertion that semi-nomadism and agriculture were not mutually exclusive practices. A tribe which was predominantly pastoral may well have included 'core' sedentary populations in oases, or in villages in more favoured locations where agriculture was possible. Semi-nomadic tribes today still normally practise some scratch cultivation of cereals during their migration cycles. In any case the assumed antipathy between the two groups can be countered by the observation that there were equally strong reasons for them to coexist symbiotically.

The arguments so far are not intended to deny the fundamental importance of pastoralism to tribes operating in the semi-desert region, as much in antiquity as today. In these regions, seasonal transhumance is dictated by geographical and climatological conditions and one can argue that there are broad similarities between recent and ancient transhuming routes. The close correlation between the placing of Roman forts and fortifications and the points of convergence of transhumance corridors has been observed by many modern scholars. However, it is a mistake to believe that sedentary agriculture was foreign to pastoral tribes in antiquity, or detested by them. In fact sedentarization was a continuing process from pre-Roman times and it is evident that in between the two extremes there were transhuming and semi-sedentarized groupings who practised a mixed economy.

6
CULTURE AND RELIGION

When studying the cultural history of the Berber peoples in North Africa one is first struck by the multiplicity of outside influences: Greek, Egyptian/Alexandrian, Phoenician/Punic, Roman, Ethiopian and later Vandal, Byzantine and Arab. Some of these contacts had a lasting impact, others left little long-term indication that syncretism had once occurred. Bates has masterfully illustrated these cultural influences of the eastern Libyans and no exhaustive repetition is necessary here. But an important point, which has sometimes been missed, is the significance of the Libyan cultural dynamic in tailoring the outside influences to fit its requirements. When we talk of Punicization or Romanization from a Libyan point of view it must be as a selective 'cultural assimilation'. Benabou has argued that there was 'cultural' as well as 'military' resistance to Rome in Africa and, certainly, the Romanization of North Africa was 'particular and original'. But Benabou may have overestimated the level of cultural assimilation which the Romans were trying to achieve among the Berbers, for as Garnsey observed acculturation was aimed specifically at existing elites. Moreover, it is difficult to privilege 'African' resistance over other real or supposed opposition, on any level, to Roman rule. The receptiveness of the indigenous elites to the importation of cultural artefacts and behaviour produced a cultural cocktail, whose specific ingredients and proportions are now difficult to distinguish.[35]

The syncretism (identification) of native deities with Punic and Roman gods cannot obscure the underlying Libyan character of the cults. So, for example, Jupiter Ammon was an adaptation of the great Libyan god, Ammon, whose cult originated in the oasis of *Siwa* and spread both into Egypt and westwards across the Libyan deserts. Ammon (or Amon) had many qualities and it is a measure of his importance in the Libyan pantheon that he was conflated with both Zeus and Jupiter. The ram-headed

Ammon had associations with desert tracks (as the guide and protector of travellers), with oases, with the cult of the dead and with prophecy for which the oases of *Siwa* and (later) *Augila* were famed.

The westward spread of the cult of Ammon is particularly significant for Tripolitania as is demonstrated by the many temples (*Ammonia*) for which we have evidence. Ammon worship was a unifying aspect for the Libyan tribes, particularly those of the desert and of the oases. The westward migration of the *Laguatan* in the later Roman empire followed the same chain of oases from *Siwa* to *Augila* that had allowed the original westward dissemination of the Ammon cult. It is hardly surprising, therefore, to find a major revival of Ammon worship amongst the Libyan tribes of sixth-century Tripolitania. Corippus noted on several occasions the importance of the oracles obtained by the *Laguatan* (probably from the *Ammonium* at *Augila*).[36] The oracles were initially used to excite tribal support and unite the confederated forces; secondly, the propaganda value of such prophecies was used to maintain confidence on the eve of battle. The geographical spread of Ammon worship periodically posed a serious threat to Roman attempts at tribal control, particularly from the fourth century onwards when the Christian empire was no longer able to deflect religious opposition by pagan syncretism.

The veneration of the dead has been a common trait in successive North African cultures and was a feature of Ammon worship. This veneration has taken many forms, from ancestor worship to the consultation of their spirits at elaborate ceremonies held at their tombs. Funerary monuments were frequently elaborate and betray a greater than usual respect for the observance of rites at the tomb in future (see below, chapter 11). Even in early Christian times, similar practices continued. The activities of the Circumcellions, during the Donatist schism, are well known. Their name suggests an association with small shrines or tombs and they are known to have venerated martyrs. Such practices undoubtedly have a long history in North Africa; in Islamic times for instance, one can trace the tendency in the creation of saints or *marabouts*.

There is also a form of veneration of the living. Gellner has observed that the institutionalized 'saints' in the Moroccan Atlas must be an Islamic version of an earlier social phenomenon. The essential factor is the possession of *baraka* by an individual, as this marks him out and sanctifies him. *Baraka* is, therefore, an extremely useful and necessarily uncommon commodity, bestowing religious sanctity and rare prestige. It seems certain that the origins of this lie in the tribal society of the Maghreb before the Arab conquest. An association between a form of *baraka* and traditional Libyan religious practice is suggested by certain events in the Byzantine wars. Corippus described in some detail the three great *Laguatan* chiefs, Antalas, Ierna and Carcasan. The rise to prominence of Antalas was the result of a prophecy sought by his father from Ammon. His *baraka* was established by the oracle, which marked him out as a future, unifying leader of the Berber tribes. Antalas then signified his coming of age by the ritual killing of a ram, the sacred beast of Ammon. Ierna, chief of the *Laguatan*, possessed *baraka* through his parallel duties as high priest of Gurzil, the bull-headed son of Ammon. He was also renowned for stage-managing favourable omens. Finally, when in flight after his defeat he refused to relinquish the effigy of Gurzil which he had carried into battle. It was a symbol of his prestige and the guarantor of his *baraka*, but its very weight prevented his escape from the pursuing Byzantine cavalry. Carcasan was elected leader in his place and his first act was to seek an oracle from Ammon. The prophecy foresaw the victorious entry of Carcasan and the *Laguatan* into Carthage and he was immediately able to assemble a new confederation of *Laguatan* and allied tribes on the strength of it.

Similarly, it seems reasonable to credit the kings of *Numidia* and *Mauretania* with a form of *baraka*. The control of disparate tribal groups is easier to understand if some quasi-religious concept underlined their authority. After his death Massinissa was worshipped in a temple at Dougga and later a shrine was set up to another Numidian king, Micipsa, at Cherchel. The authority of other Numidian and Mauretanian kings, Jugurtha, Juba I, Juba II, and Ptolemy, appears in a different light when the concept of *baraka* is suggested. In these monarchies it was possibly institutionalized as an inherited feature of the office. The success of Tacfarinas as leader of a major revolt may likewise have been aided by his being accepted as the leader of multi-tribal groups on account of his *baraka*.

Even though the evidence for an early form of *baraka* is slight, in combination with native religions such as the Ammon cult it may have been a crucial factor in the history of native resistance and revolt.[37] In his analysis of medieval and modern tribal society in the Atlas, Gellner noted that most of the changes of dynasty were initiated by semi-religious crusades which were brought about among the Atlas tribes by the 'rare crystallization of authority by religious charisma'. The latent dangers of a society where tribes may suddenly unite behind a charismatic leader or for the purposes of a religious crusade are unlikely to have been lost on the Romans either.[38]

Hierarchical or segmental tribal structures suffer from several potential weaknesses. Theoretically the hierarchical links between clans, between sub-tribes and between tribes enables large-scale confederation to take place in times of crisis. Problems occur when the latent confederation fails to happen, as in the 1920s Rif rebellion in Morocco. The significance of the cult of Ammon and other Libyan deities (and in more recent times, Islam) is that they provided an additional basis for united action which could trigger the unification process. The potency of a leader possessing religious and social charisma in effecting this has been illustrated. Roman frontier policy had to come to terms with the fact that resistance was latent, even in pacified or semi-pacified areas where Libyan tribal society, culture and religion remained strong.

7
WARFARE

What sort of threat did the *Gaetuli, Garamantes, Macae* and *Nasamones* pose to the Libyphoenician inhabitants of the coastal towns and later to the Roman government in Africa?

There is little direct or wholly reliable evidence for the style of warfare practised among the Libyan tribes of Tripolitania and Fezzan. Herodotus recorded that the *Garamantes* fought from four-horse chariots, a statement corroborated by many discoveries of rock paintings of two- and four-horse light chariots from Fezzan and elsewhere in the northern Sahara. The likely date span of these pictures was *c.* 600–300 BC, with the importance of cavalry becoming paramount by the latter date. As Camps has observed these are prestige vehicles and their use is highly suggestive of the emergence of an elite-dominated tribal society. The Roman accounts of campaigns against the *Garamantes* gave no information about the style of warfare encountered, but there are broad hints in other sources.

If one considers the tribes of North Africa as a whole, the dominant feature of their warfare was the mounted cavalry engagement or skirmish. The Numidian and Moorish cavalry were famed in antiquity for their skill and cunning. Livy, Silius Italicus and others recorded the deeds of Carthage's African allies in the Punic wars and Lucan similarly described the Numidian and allied troops of Juba I. The Numidian king Syphax sought help from Rome in 213 BC because his people were only practised in cavalry engagements and being unable to fight as disciplined infantry had been worsted by the Carthaginian phalanx.[39]

The concentration on horsemanship amongst the Numidian tribes was also applicable to their southern and western neighbours. Lucan and Silius Italicus recorded contingents from the southern tribes fighting alongside the Numidians. Lucan referred to Gaetulian, bare-backed cavalry, Massylian horsemen who controlled their horses with a switch, *Nasamones, Garamantes* and the javelin-throwing *Mazax*. Silius Italicus mentioned a similar mixture of tribal contingents with Hannibal in Spain and Italy: *Garamantes, Macae* and *Cinyphii, Nasamones* and *Gaetuli* (who rode without reins). The descriptions of battles reinforce the impression that the Libyans were recruited mainly as cavalry. A *Macae* sub-tribe (forming the *Cinyphiae turmae*) was in action at Lake Trasimene and at Cannae the Libyan tribes, who were mainly cavalry fighters, made up the left wing of Hannibal's army. Strabo confirmed that horses and horsemanship were essential features of the *Gaetuli* and *Garamantes* tribes. Describing the interior regions occupied by these two broad groups, he wrote,

> Both horses and cattle have longer necks than those of other countries. Horse-breeding is followed with such exceptional interest by the kings that the number of colts each year amount to one hundred thousand.

Even assuming that Strabo exaggerated the figure, the implication is clearly that the southern tribes possessed large numbers of horses. It is apparent therefore that the *Numidae* and *Mauri* were not the only tribal groupings to practise cavalry warfare; the *Garamantes, Nasamones, Macae* and *Gaetuli* also possessed large numbers of horses.[40]

Infantry was not unknown in native warfare and may have increased in importance over time, though its role was normally fairly limited in engagements with Rome, being unsuited to pitched battles. The infantry comprised light-armed skirmishers, mostly employed in hit-and-run attacks or ambushes. They were unsuited to hand-to-hand fighting with disciplined and armoured troops. Their chief weapons indicate their role: javelin, bow and arrow, slings and slingstones. The cavalry also used the throwing spear as the main strike weapon and each man carried two or three of these into battle.

The main difference between cavalry and infantry may have been one of status not numbers. Strabo's reference to the particular interest of kings in horse-breeding suggests some form of social differentiation. Indeed the horse has continued to be an important status symbol in the Maghreb. In the nineteenth century the horse was still the prized possession of a warrior elite and tribesmen who did not own, or could not borrow, horses were organized as infantry whose duty it was to guard the encampment, the camels and the women whilst the cavalry did battle. The horse was essential, in fact, for all three of the main pursuits of the elite: warfare, raiding and hunting. Between such tribes the scale of raiding and warfare is limited not by the available manpower, but by the number of horses. We shall see in a later chapter that tribal warfare was not greatly different in the sixth century AD.

The arms and armour of the Libyan tribes have been well discussed by Bates and others and only a few observations are necessary here. Some of the earliest sources remarked on the shortage of metal for producing weapons. But though mineralogically scarce, metals could be traded and it is likely that most of the interior tribes were in a position to produce metal-tipped spears by the first century AD. Archaeological evidence for metal working in *Garama* proves that the necessary technology existed in the oasis centres. Arms and armour will also have become available to the tribes through contact with and service in the armies of Carthage and Rome. The Libyan warriors encountered by Rome in battle were not, therefore, equipped merely with fire-hardened and sharpened wooden spears.[41]

Body armour was rarely worn by the Libyans, though shields were sometimes carried. These were mostly circular bucklers of wood and leather. The lack of body armour allowed for swift movement of cavalry and infantry, a point noted by Diodorus. In a pitched battle against disciplined infantry, however, it was a grave disadvantage and the result of such engagements almost invariably favoured Rome. Although Tacfarinas trained his troops to fight as a disciplined formation, following the Roman model, the arms and armour of his troops were unsuited to a pitched battle and they were routed by Furius Camillus in AD 17. The future course of that war was notable for the considerable success enjoyed by Tacfarinas when he resorted to a policy of skirmishing and guerrilla warfare. In the same way, Jugurtha had won his victories by surprise attacks or by persistent skirmishing with the advancing or withdrawing Roman columns.[42]

An important tactical advantage open to the tribes of the periphery was their ability to withdraw into their desert or steppe-like confines after a successful raid or attack. The *Garamantes* excelled at this tactic since pursuit was made doubly difficult by the great distance between the coast and their tribal heartland and second by their habit of concealing the desert well-heads under piles of sand as they retreated. Rome's achievement in adapting to desert warfare

should not be underestimated, for the logistics and the risks were enormous. Nevertheless, once an army penetrated the natural defensive screen several factors worked against the defenders and in favour of the attackers. The existence of hillforts and oasis centres presented Rome with targets for her attack. Second, the sub-divisions of tribal society could cause a fragmentation of the wider tribal alliances when the campaign was on home territory and Rome could threaten several sub-tribal centres simultaneously. The resistance to Balbus in 20 BC, for instance, may well have become disunited as his campaigns accounted for seven tribes or sub-tribes split between 23 hillforts or tribal centres.[43]

In summary then, the tribes of Tripolitania and further south possessed two principal military characteristics. First, they fought mainly on horseback as light armed cavalry with javelins. The confederation of sub-tribal groups could reunite substantial cavalry forces, but these were most effective in mounting surprise attacks, as may have happened when the *Nasamones* nearly defeated Flaccus in *c.* AD 86. Pitched battles, or concerted campaigning by the Romans, normally ended in the defeat of the Libyans.

The second point concerns the operation of tribal hierarchy in military matters. Occasional feuds and inter-tribal raiding must have been features of society in pre-Roman times as the occupation of hillfort sites indicates. To some extent the existence of inter- or intra-tribal conflicts will have weakened the chances of major confederations opposing Rome. However, as we have seen in the previous section, the influence of Libyan religion and a leadership cult based on an ancient form of *baraka* could overcome many of the obstacles to large-scale confederation. In any case some of the tribes, such as the *Garamantes* and *Nasamones*, seem to have been more permanently confederated under the strong central authority of kings. The northern hegemony of the *Garamantes* extended well to the north of the modern Fezzan in the heyday of the tribe. The sharpest Roman military response was provoked by such large scale confederation whether hierarchical or hegemonical.

8
TRIBAL CENTRES

A wide range of settlement types were described in the ancient sources which concerned rural and interior Africa: tents (*tecta*), huts or villages (*mapalia*), towers and refuges (*pyrgoi, turres* and *munitiones*), hillfort tribal centres and even urban or proto-urban settlements (*oppida, urbes, castella*). The majority of the more detailed information dealt specifically with the kingdom of *Numidia* and in modern geographic terms it was principally related to the northwestern parts of Tunisia and the extreme northeast of Algeria.

The Numidian kingdom was centred round a group of urban or proto-urban settlements which were recognizable towns prior to the annexation of *Africa Nova* by Caesar in 46 BC, namely *Thugga* (Dougga), *Vaga* (Beja), *Zama Regia* (Zana), *Bulla Regia* (Hammam Djeradj), *Hippo Regia* (Bone), *Sicca* (El Kef) and *Cirta* (Constantine). *Thugga* had achieved a remarkably high level of urban organization by the second century BC, as bilingual Libyan and neo-Punic inscriptions show. Many of the other early urban sites, such as *Zama*, situated in the plains where there was little natural defence, were fortified and garrisoned. In the periphery of the Numidian kingdom, however, hillforts were more common as tribal centres, as is made clear from the detailed account of the Roman capture of a number of these sites in the Jugurthan war at the end of the second century BC.[44]

A second type of tribal centre is also described by Sallust, the oasis *oppidum*. In 107 BC Marius captured *Capsa* (Gafsa) by a bold piece of campaigning across the arid steppe-lands. *Capsa* is described as *oppidum magnum* and was not a hillfort but a fortified centre based around a perennial spring. Whether it could justifiably have been called a town at this stage is debatable; clearly its geographical location and the logistical problems of the campaign caused Marius more trouble than the nature of the defences or the size of the population. It is significant enough that a permanent and defended settlement existed at the oasis which lay outside the dry-farming agricultural zone. The importance of the site survived Marius' massacre of the male population and in the first century AD there was a recognizable town at *Capsa*, whose magistrates were *sufetes*. It is interesting to note that Marius captured other *oppida* in the region of *Capsa*, which is perhaps an indication that other oases had already emerged as population and tribal centres.[45]

The two types of tribal centre in North Africa which are defined above and which were called *oppida* by the Roman sources obviously represent only one aspect of a wider site hierarchy. Population may well have been dispersed in tents, huts, undefended villages, farms and so on for much of the time. However, what we shall examine below is simply the evidence for the tribal centres since these sites are those which will have most immediately concerned the Roman army.

The archaeological evidence for the two types of centre reflects a basic distinction between the two. The oasis sites have generally continued to be occupied from ancient times and the archaeological evidence is often restricted to a few stray finds of Roman period material. On the other hand, the hillforts are remarkably well-preserved in many cases, since few developed into urban centres. Detail of internal buildings can be recovered by air-photography or surface survey, though unfortunately little work of this kind has as yet been done.

Hillforts are a common feature throughout North Africa, from Morocco to Fezzan. The great wind-and-water eroded escarpments of the Maghreb frequently have projecting, flat-topped spurs which are connected to the main escarpment only by narrow isthmuses. Sometimes a spur is left completely detached from the main landmass. These sites are ideal defensive positions on account of their flat tops and steep scree-covered slopes or cliffs (Plate 3). Their chief limitation is the problem of water supply in areas of low rainfall and few springs. Where these promontories were joined to the main escarpment by a land link, the narrow isthmus was often fortified with walls, rock-cut ditches and gates, hence the general name for this type of site, 'éperon barré'. In the case of detached promontories the only access was by zig-zag paths up the escarpment, generally to a single point of entry or gate. In some cases the natural defences were augmented by the construction of solid dry-stone ramparts.

These basic features have often been noted, but little else besides. The interiors were sometimes described with the dismissive phrases 'restes de constructions' or 'constructions berbères' or simply ignored altogether. The irregular lay-out and rough, dry-stone construction of the interiors were no doubt a disappointment to many of the early antiquarians and explorers, who were clearly more inspired by classical architecture. Because of this lack of detailed study of the interiors and the problem of water supply, the hillforts have sometimes been viewed as temporary refuges and little more than that. More detailed archaeological work on this class of site, such as that by Marion in an area southwest of the most westerly fort in *Mauretania Caesariensis*, has shown the need to modify this conclusion.

All the hillforts examined by Marion contained traces of internal buildings or huts. There were no structureless or 'temporary' refuges. The provision of internal buildings suggests regular or seasonal occupation at the very least. The occurrence of grain silos, carbonized grain and quernstones implies a degree of sedentarization or at least a mixed, transhuming economy. There are as yet fewer data for eastern Algeria and Tunisia though there is ample evidence for the existence of the hillforts themselves. One site for which there is a good, published air-photograph confirms the impression that these sites were not temporary refuges. El Krozbet (Fig. 2:11) is a hillfort located near the southwestern end of the El-Kantara pass in Algeria. My drawing is taken from Baradez's air-photograph and produced at an approximate scale (based on the size of the room units). The site is probably between 2 and 3 hectares in size and the complexity of many of the hut-units is reminiscent of the Magrusa site (see below). At some stage there seems to have been an attempt towards 'planning', based on an axial street. As at other sites, considerable open space and enclosures imply that animals could be brought up on to the plateau top. There does not appear to be an enclosing rampart, except perhaps where the steep approach path neared the summit.[46]

Tribal settlements centred on perennial springs or oases in the pre-desert and desert regions can rarely be detected from archaeological evidence alone, since finds of Roman period material are not certain evidence for pre-Roman settlement at these sites. In the absence of excavation in the oases, one must place a greater reliance on the ancient sources. *Capsa* (Gafsa) has already been considered but there are other less

detailed, or less specific cases. Diodorus, in a passage quoted above, referred to the *pyrgoi* (towers) built by the desert tribes at the water sources as store-houses. It is possible that the Greek term *pyrgoi* was used in direct translation of a Libyan term, since the *civitas* capital of the *Nybgenii* was known by the Romans as *Turris Tamalleni*. In any case the implication is that there was some permanent and fortified structure built in the oases and that as well as defending the tribes' water rights, these 'towers' acted as repositories for non-portable valuables. The desirability for semi-nomadic or transhuming herders to produce some grain, dates and vegetables will have encouraged the development of oasis agriculture, as is evident in a source as early as Herodotus and in the specific case of the *Garamantes*. By the first century AD it is likely that fairly substantial oasis settlements existed at many locations.

The campaigns of Balbus, *c.* 20 BC, took his troops to various oasis centres in Fezzan and the Wadi Djedi in Algeria. *Garama, Cidamus,* and probably *Debris,* were oasis centres located on the Fezzan campaign and some of the other ones named, *Cilliba, Alele,*

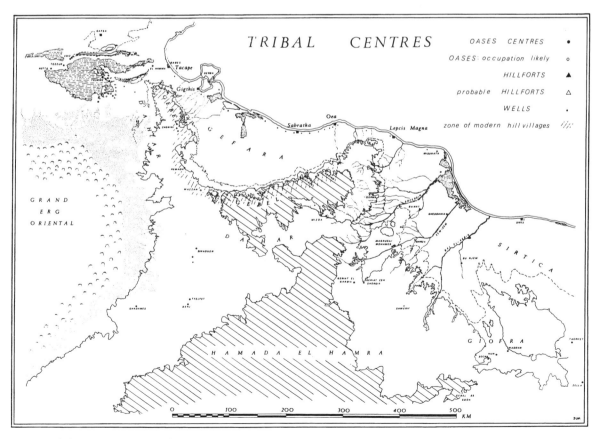

Fig. 2:8 Tribal centres in oases and hillforts in Tripolitania.

Thelgae, for instance, may also have been oasis *oppida.* In Algeria identifications can be proposed for some sites: *Tabudium,* the modern oasis of Thouda; *Milgis Gemella,* the oasis of M'lili; *Viscera,* the oasis of Biskra. Other names listed by Pliny and Ptolemy related to settlements whose location appears to have been in the desert and were most likely, therefore, centred on oases or springs.[47]

So much then for the literary evidence which, though thin, presents a consistent picture of tribal centres in the desert and pre-desert being centred on water sources. Such centres served as a home base for transhuming elements of the tribe, as an agricultural focus where cereal, vegetables and dates could be grown, as a storehouse for these crops and the non-portable goods of the tribe and as a home for a core sedentary population. The development of the irrigated area of the oases by digging new *foggaras* and wells has continued down to modern times.

There are a number of fundamental differences between the two types of tribal centre discussed above. Hillforts seem to have individually catered for populations of a few hundred at the most. The problem of reconciling the superb defensive position of hillforts with the unavailability of water on these sites was a serious and limiting factor in their development. By contrast the oasis centres could expand with successive improvements of the water supply. Some of the major groups of oases, such as the Nefzaoua, and Djerid, those of *Phazania* and of Fezzan or Augila could probably muster populations numbering thousands, even though the majority of these may have spent part of the year transhuming away from their tribal centre. In military terms, this may have given the pre-desert and desert tribes an advantage over the Gebel and hillfort based tribes.

Although the hillfort tribal centres were difficult positions to storm without heavy losses, their small size suggests that tribal organization may have been much more fragmented among tribes whose main settlement centres were hillforts. The sort of tribal grouping which could have assembled around hillforts was almost certainly at a lower level of tribal hierarchy than the tribal units which could gather at a major oasis. The largest and most significant tribal centres of Tripolitania, therefore, were those of the desert confederations, the *Nasamones,* the *Garamantes,* the *Gaetuli* of *Phazania* and the Nefzaoua. It was against these tribes that Rome was obliged to direct her main military effort rather than those of the major zones of hillfort settlement in the Gebel and the great wadi basins (the *Macae*).

The *Macae* sub-tribes occupied both hillfort and oasis centres. Recent work by the ULVS has located a number of hillfort sites (Figs 2:8–2:11). Although the Magrusa/Mdhaweb group is collectively impressive, these are small sites in relative terms, whose populations will have numbered no more than a few hundred souls and in some cases rather less.

The Magrusa/Mdhaweb *oppida*

This complex of sites is situated some 18 km west of Ghirza up the Zem-Zem at a point where two large tributaries join the wadi from the north and where there is an extensive area of cultivable alluvium in the broad wadi floor. The eroded scarps of the area

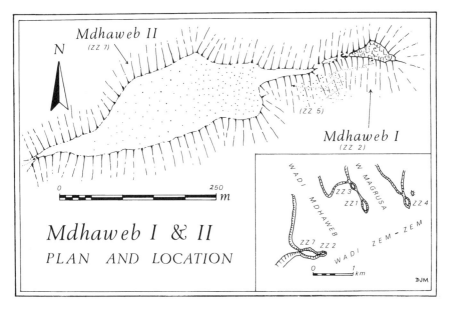

Fig. 2:9 The Mdhaweb and Magrusa complex of hillfort sites (inset) and detailed plan of the Mdhaweb sites.

(All photos taken by the author, unless stated otherwise.)

1 Stone uprights of a Roman olive press in the Gebel Tarhuna near Gasr ed-Daun. Note the denuded appearance of the Gebel landscape in the right background, beyond the limits of the area of successfully reintroduced modern olive plantations (left background).

2 Flash flood following a storm, Wadi Beni Ulid October 1980. The wadi floor is sub-divided by low walls identical to those of Roman date. Note also the cultivation of olive trees on the wadi floor (source: ULVS).

3 The hillfort of Gasr Magrusa, seen from the north overlooking the floodplain of the Wadi Zem-Zem (source: ULVS).

4 (*Top left*) Dry-stone buildings against the rampart of the Banat hillfort, Wadi N'f'd.

5 (*Bottom left*) A well-preserved and densely clustered Garamantian cemetery of Roman date on the southern escarpment of the Wadi el-Agial (source: C.M. Daniels).

6 (*Left*) Gheriat el-Garbia, kite air-photograph of the Roman fort looking northeast towards the well-preserved gate. The line of the defences is particularly clear, including the substantial traces of most of the gates and towers. The interior is mostly overlain with buildings of a later village (source: ULVS).

7 (*Below*) Gheriat el-Garbia from the northeast. Note the presence of the oasis below the escarpment beyond the fort.

8 (*Top left*) Gheriat el-Garbia. The northeast gate, with two of its three arches standing. The left-hand tower is preserved close to its full height.

9 (*Bottom left*) Gheriat el-Garbia. The northwest defences, incorporating two substantially preserved interval towers.

10 (*Above left*) Bu Njem, vertical aerial view of the Roman fort (source: ULVS).

11 (*Above right*) Bu Njem, aerial view showing detail of headquarters building with baths (covered by tin roof) to left (source: ULVS).

12 (*Below*) Gheriat esh-Shergia, Roman fortlet. Detail of southwest corner standing to height of *c.* 7 m. The rebated corner and ashlar construction is exactly paralleled at Gasr Isawi, Wadi N'f'd.

13 (*Top left*) Circular watch-tower (*burgus*) constructed *c.* AD 222–35, 1 km north of the fort of Gheriat el-Garbia.

14 (*Top right*) The *clausura* at Bir Oum Ali looking east. The ancient gate lay just beyond the modern roadway.

15 (*Bottom left*) Detail of the construction of the Bir Oum Ali wall on the west side of the pass.

16 (*Above*) The Tebaga *clausura* looking north (centre rear-ground) and the north chamber of the gate-house (foreground), with detail of blocked doorway.

17 (*Left*) The Skiffa *clausura* from the south, with its gate-house visible just before the point where the earthwork is lost in the area of sand dunes.

18 (*Right*) The Hadd Hajar *clausura* as an earthwork in the central part of the plain, looking west.

19 (*Below*) The Hadd Hajar *clausura* as a stone wall in the eastern side corridor, with preserved gate-house.

provide a series of semi-detached or isolated outliers projecting over the wadi plain. These sites are classic 'éperon barré' positions but it is remarkable that no less than five such sites were utilized in an area of limited water resources (Fig. 2:8).[48]

The site known as Gasr Mdhaweb I (ZZ 2) is the most visually prominent of the group, on account of a standing tower about 6 m high which controls the direct approach to the site from the west (Fig. 2:9). The entire summit of the rocky promontory is surrounded by a wall of dry-stone construction, with a single entrance in the south side approached by a zig-zagging path built up in places on ramps of rubble. The interior of the 1.7 ha site was very densely built up. The dry-stone buildings were regularly coursed and of a reasonably high standard of construction. The pottery and the architecture both suggest that the site as it stands is of comparatively late date (third century AD forward), though traces of earlier structures are probably obscured by this late phase.

Mdhaweb II (ZZ 7) is, at 2.95 ha, the largest of the group and occupation also continued down the scarps (ZZ 5). Although at first sight the plateau top appeared featureless, close inspection revealed traces of demolished walls and shallow depressions, which can be identified on kite air-photographs as traces of huts spread over the greater part of the plateau (approx. 300 by 100 m). These huts ranged from circular to rectangular to linked units, the greatest density of occupation being towards the eastern extremity of the plateau. Almost all the pottery collected came from the eastern 150 m of the wide plateau.

Although there were no perimeter defences, the narrow isthmus connecting the western end of the spur to the main escarpment was fortified at its narrowest point (4 m) by a wall, leaving only a 1.5 m passage at its north side.

Sherds collected from the site included the earliest African Red Slip ware (ARS) forms (later first/early second century AD) as well as some later material. Since the western part of the site is aceramic but is covered with traces of unsophisticated scoop buildings (or hearths) cut into the limestone pavement, it is possible that the greatest extent of the site was achieved in the period before the first contacts with Rome. However, no flint was found and the problems of dating such a site without excavation are obvious.

Gasr Magrusa (ZZ 1) possessed superb natural defences, augmented by a massive stone rampart and monumental gateway and these make it the most striking site of the group (Fig. 2:10–11; Plate 3). The perimeter wall (enclosing approx. 1.23 ha) was constructed using two lines of irregular and massive limestone blocks, set on edge with an infilling of smaller stones. At the narrow northern end of the site, where the rampart overlooks the approach track, it was backed by a parapet walkway to allow for effective downward observation and firepower. The gateway comprised two massive orthostats set on the inside of the inturned rampart terminals. Such inturned terminals are also evident at the Banat village and to a lesser extent at Magrusa north (see below).

The buildings on the top of the plateau occupied the centre of the site; in no case were they built as lean-to structures against the perimeter wall, which suggests that the buildings were constructed first (compare Magrusa north and Banat below). The plan and layout of the site has a certain sophistication since buildings are ranged on either side of a 'street'. There are five main building complexes, each facing away from the accessway and on to the privacy of its yards. Construction was of roughly coursed, irregular limestone blocks, with some crude orthostats being used to reinforce corners, wall junctions and as door posts.

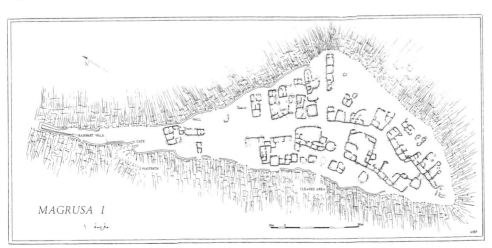

Fig. 2:10 Detailed plan of Gasr Magrusa (from Jones and Barker 1980).

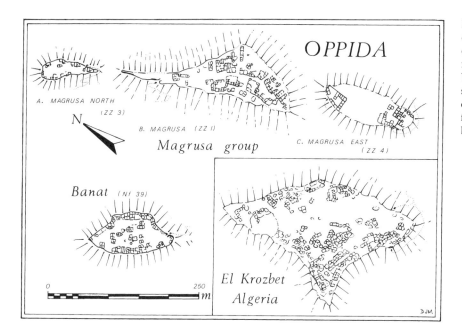

Fig. 2:11 Comparative plans of three of the Magrusa group of hillforts and of one from near Gasr Isawi/Banat in the Wadi N'f'd. The El Krozbet site in Algeria is included for comparison, being traced from an air photograph (in Baradez 1949).

Some areas of the plateau top were empty of structures, perhaps intended for accommodating livestock in an emergency, but a part of the space evidently was used for threshing grain. Very early ARS forms are also present on the site.

Magrusa north (ZZ 3) lies between Magrusa and the main escarpment to the north on another semi-detached spur site. The zig-zag approach track can be traced up the west side before passing directly below the southern defences and up the east side to a gate. The top of the plateau (0.25 ha) is surrounded by a perimeter wall (average thickness 1.2 m, maximum preserved height approx. 2 m). The gate was approximately 1.66 m wide (an attempt had apparently been made to block part of it) flanked to the south by an inturned rampart terminal, with access to the interior necessitating a climb up a ramp.

The buildings of the interior were for the most part erected as lean-to structures against the perimeter wall. In appearance the dry-stone walled huts were inferior to those of Magrusa I, where a single hut complex contains as many rooms as the entire Magrusa north site. It is a possibility that Magrusa north was built to house the same size of sub-tribal, hierarchical unit as utilized each one of the large complexes on Magrusa I. Both would seem suitable to house an extended family group or small clan. Early ARS was also collected from this site.

Magrusa east (ZZ 4), on another detached outlier, most closely resembles Mdhaweb I, both in its architecture and its late Roman date. The spur top (0.64 ha) was only built on at its north and south ends (covering 0.25 ha), with the northern structure apparently having no direct access on to the plateau (its solitary entrance in its west side opened out on to a difficult descent). This building is similar in plan and construction to the late Roman fortified farms (gsur) of the Ghirza region. The southern part of the plateau was occupied by two distinct groups of buildings, one of which was similar to the fortified structure just described. The neat masonry, traces of two external staircases, niches, windows and a stone door lintel clearly show a degree of architectural pretension and the complex was entered through a two-storey 'tower'. It is possible that these two gasr-like buildings were the residence(s) of a sub-tribal chief or chiefs in the later Roman period.

The other buildings were of much rougher construction. One of these was a simple three-room unit; the other formed an L-shape of eight rooms with a long narrow building (21 × 7 m; perhaps a byre) attached to its north side. These are best interpreted as service or subsidiary buildings for the main southern complex. The dating of all the structures on ZZ 4 seems to be broadly in the third to fourth centuries AD.

The Magrusa/Mdhaweb group of sites constituted an extraordinary concentration of people in what is a bleak and inhospitable location (at least in summer). It is worth speculating that it marks a sub-tribal centre of the Macae and was perhaps only occupied in winter, when some cultivation of the wadi alluvium would have been possible. It is unlikely that there was adequate water for year-round occupation and fixed base transhumance of most of the sub-tribe was probably necessary in summer. In this example, then, we seem to have evidence for a sub-tribe numbering hundreds rather than thousands, and practising a mixed economy with a bias towards fixed-base transhuming pastoralism. The dating evidence for the group as a whole suggests a long sequence of occupation, from pre-Roman at ZZ 7 (and possibly other sites), to late Roman at ZZ 2 and ZZ 4.

The Banat Village (Nf 39)

A further example of the 'perched' *oppidum* has been discovered c. 400 m west of Gasr Isawi (Banat) in the Wadi N'f'd (Fig. 2:11).[49] Investigation showed that the original approach path had zig-zagged up the east side of the steep, scree-covered scarp. The site was entered through a gate in its perimeter wall near the southeast corner. The sill stone of the gate was still *in situ* with the pivot hole visible. Beyond the gate, the inturned terminals of the rampart and a slight slope up into the interior parallel defensive features at the Magrusa sites. The 1.5 m thick rampart was erected before the internal buildings as most of those were abutted against it.

The surviving huts, overlying faint traces of an earlier building phase, can be divided morphologically into three- to five-room units, some with small enclosed yards or enclosures attached (Plate 4). The layout falls midway between that of Magrusa and Magrusa north in terms of complexity, but with a similar technique of construction in dry-stone rubble and using crude orthostats at corners and at doorways. There was also a series of small circular features (1–2 m diameter) whose interpretation is uncertain (hearths, grain-stores?).

A mass of pottery was recovered from the site, including large quantities of ARS of the late first, second and third century AD. The close proximity of Gasr Isawi, a probable Roman fortlet (see chapter 5), to the native hillfort is suggestive of Roman policing of a traditional sub-tribal and market centre of the *Macae*.

The dating of these Tripolitanian hillforts is a problem. There were abundant Roman fine wares (ARS, *terra sigillata*) on all the sites but, on the other hand, no flint. The coarse wares are not at present diagnostic, so certain occupation in the pre-Roman Iron Age is difficult to prove. However, the presence on these hillforts of the earliest imported fineware forms suggests that they were important tribal settlements in the first century AD at the time when contact was first firmly established between the pre-desert tribes and Rome.

No doubt many more of these hillfort sites will be discovered when they are looked for. Rebuffat has

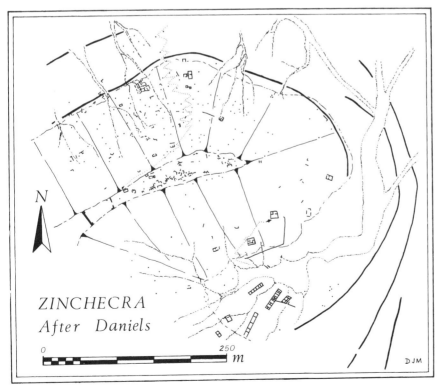

Fig. 2:12 The Zinchecra hillfort, Fezzan – a Garamantian settlement, ninth–fourth century BC, with a few rectangular structures on the south side of the first century AD (after Daniels 1970b).

ZINCHECRA
After Daniels

0   250
                 m

located at least one, at Bir Zayden in the Wadi Bei el-Kebir region. The Gebel region is also dotted with examples, many of recent date but some of undoubted antiquity. Outside *Macae* territory to the west, the Gebel Nefusa and the Tunisian Gebel Demmer and Gebel Matmata are densely covered with fortified villages occupied today by relic Berber populations. The long history of occupation and reoccupation of these sites has obliterated most of the evidence for their earliest antecedents, but some of the defensive positions were certainly occupied in the Roman period.[50]

There were also *Macae* centres at the major oases and wells. The town of *Macomades* (Sirte) may have developed from a *Macae* oasis settlement. Ancient ruins or Roman pottery have been found at Zella, Waddan and the Giofra oases. Roman forts in Tripolitania were normally located at oases which were presumably already native centres, as in the case of Bu Njem and Gheriat el-Garbia, Ghadames, Remada and Ras el-Ain. Other important wells or oases where ancient settlement is known or suspected

are Mizda and the wells of Sceghega and Shwerif.

The tribal centres of the *Garamantes* are well-known following Charles Daniels' research in Fezzan. The earliest sites in the Wadi el-Agial seem to have been spur sites along the southern edge of the wadi depression. From the fourth century BC these sites were increasingly superseded by wadi floor oasis centres. The twinned hillfort/oasis centre at the tribal *metropolis* of *Garama* has already been referred to (cf. Fig. 2:6). The main reason for the migration of the Garamantian centre from scarp edge to wadi centre is apparent from the plan of the Zinchecra hillfort (Fig. 2:12). The area of the plateau top is very restricted at only 0.635 ha and consequently there was a tremendous spread of terraced occupation sites down the steep escarpments, particularly on the north side.

A total area of about 62.5 acres (25 ha) was defined by a series of enclosing banks at the foot of the escarpment and the intensive occupation covered an area of about 12.5 ha (approx 31.25 acres). Each dot on Figure 2:12 represents a habitation site (over 300 being noted), with excavated examples shown in plan. The

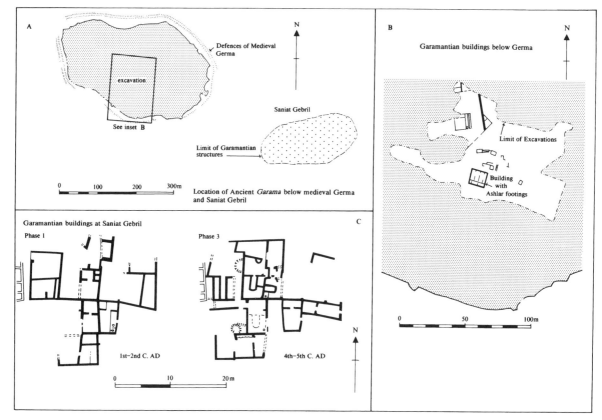

Fig. 2:13 The traces of the Garamantian metropolis of *Garama* below Medieval Germa and Saniat Gebril: a) location of excavations; b) ashlar buildings at centre of settlement; c) mud-brick houses and workshops at Saniat Gebril (after Daniels 1970a; 1977).

agricultural development of the plain and the increasing water requirement, coupled with these cramped conditions of population and flocks on the terrace sites, favoured a move into the plain. Although perhaps initially occupied in tandem, the unfettered development of the wadi centre site soon eclipsed the old hillfort centre.

Daniels discovered other hillfort sites in the Wadi el-Agial (for example at Tinda, Charaig, Fjej, Leksair and Chlef) and has suggested that these may also have been paired with wadi centre oasis sites. Evidence for Garamantian settlement has also been found in the Wadi Berguig to the south and Wadi esc-Sciatti to the north (Fig. 2:5). Pliny's account of the campaign of Balbus implies the existence of regional centres of the *Garamantes*. *Garama* itself and *Debris* (Edri?) with its hot springs were clearly oasis sites. On the other hand an invasion of Garamantian lands should logically have involved the besieging of some of the Garamantian hillforts and *Thelgae* may have been in this category. When Sidi Ocba invaded Fezzan in AD 666–7, he captured the oases and caravan centres of Waddan and Germa and, with more difficulty, the important hillfort of Gaouan. Both types of tribal centre, thus, had a long history in Fezzan.

Most of the wadi centre oasis settlements of the *Garamantes* are unlocated due to poor archaeological visibility on the wadi floor, but the cemeteries that served these major settlements are highly visible at intervals along the lower slopes of the southern scarp of the el-Agial (Plate 5). *Garama* (Old Germa) is thus uniquely important because of the excavations carried out there by Ayoub and Daniels. The site was declared a national monument and the population resettled in New Germa in the 1930s, a far-sighted action which made excavation possible in the 1960s. The walled medieval caravan town of Germa

(10ha/25 acres) overlies the larger site of the Garamantian capital, whose remains may justly be considered those of a town. Surface traces extend 300 m beyond the walls of medieval Germa to the suburb of Saniat Gebril (2 ha/5 acres) (Fig. 2:13). The mud-brick buildings of Saniat Gebril were large and complex with a date span of the first to fifth centuries AD. The biggest surprise, however, was the discovery of ashlar masonry walls and footings in the centre of Old Germa. Overlying several earlier phases of mud-brick construction, these buildings date to the later first century AD and had a long life thereafter. The possible explanations for the presence of these extraordinary buildings are discussed in the next chapter.[51]

SUMMARY

In this chapter, I have established the segmented nature of the ancient tribal societies of the region and their capacity for occasional confederated action on a grand scale. The military potential of different groups has been assessed and their economic and social organization and cultural coherence analysed. The *Garamantes* loom large in the discussion since, although living beyond the southern limits of Tripolitania, they appear to have been the dominant tribal group in pre-Roman times and have been the subjects of the most detailed modern research. Overall, the Garamantian evidence serves not only as a useful corrective to the stereotype of 'barbarian' Libyans promoted by the ancient Roman sources, it also reveals important aspects of the response of the peripheral tribes to the coming of Rome. The sophisticated Romanized buildings at *Garama* were as much a part of the contact situation as were the dramatic incidents of warfare and resistance.

3

HISTORY, ADMINISTRATION AND THE INFRASTRUCTURES OF GOVERNMENT

1
FROM *EMPORIA* TO PROVINCE: AN HISTORICAL OUTLINE

Before Rome

The major towns of the region known as the *Emporia* and later as *Tripolitana* originated as Phoenician trading settlements. The earliest archaeological evidence from *Lepcis* dates to the mid–late seventh century BC, that from *Sabratha* to the end of the sixth century and from *Oea* to the fifth century. Because of the relative inaccessibility of the Phoenician levels at these sites the dates assigned must be considered provisional, but given the early pre-eminence of Carthage (*Qart-Hadasht*) among the western Phoenician sites it is possible that the Tripolitanian settlements were first established as Carthaginian colonies in response to Greek advances in and beyond Cyrenaica. Herodotus relates how the Carthaginians (presumably including the inhabitants of *Lepcis/Lpqy*), in alliance with the *Macae*, expelled a Greek attempt to establish a colony at the mouth of the 'river' *Cinyps* in *c*. 520–517 BC. The earliest material from *Sabratha* (*Sbrt'n*) suggests only temporary occupation and the full-scale development of the site perhaps commenced from the late fifth–early fourth century BC. *Oea* (*Wy't*) is the most difficult to place chronologically because of the dearth of evidence, but the existence of oases and of natural, if rudimentary, harbour features at both *Sabratha* and *Oea* were factors which would have attracted the attention of Carthage. *Lepcis* is believed to have ini-

tially lacked adequate harbour facilities but the cape of Homs just to the west would have provided some shelter to the shoreline and the islands at the mouth of the Wadi Lebda may likewise have afforded protection to shipping beached there. The proximity of *Lepcis* to much of the best agricultural land in the region (Herodotus extolled the productivity of the *Cinyps*/Wadi Caam area) could explain its development at an earlier date than its western neighbours. Pre-Phoenician activity at or near these sites is suggested by the fact that all three names are Libyan rather than Punic. There was certainly considerable intermarriage with the indigenous population, leading to the characterization of the inhabitants of the *Emporia* as *Libyphoenices*.[1]

The subsequent growth and prosperity of the settlements was evidently achieved under Carthaginian domination. In the third century BC *Lepcis* apparently paid a daily tribute to Carthage of one Talent (equivalent to a yearly exaction of almost 9 tonnes of silver). This may have represented a charge on all three towns and not simply *Lepcis* alone, but even so it would have been a heavy burden had not the economic development of the region been well advanced by that date. The wealth of the zone is thought to have been from three sources, agriculture, trans-Saharan trade and maritime commerce (chapter 7). Extensive Carthaginian control in the region is hinted at by the numerous reports of Libyan tribal groups fighting in the Carthaginian armies.[2]

The defeat of the Carthaginians at *Zama* by Scipio Africanus and the end of the second Punic war in 201 BC had major implications for the *Emporia*. For although nominally still subject to Carthage they were to enjoy a far greater measure of freedom thereafter. Massinissa, the Numidian king, had spent a brief period in hiding in the region between 'the *Emporia* and the *Garamantes*' in 204 BC and so was familiar with the economic potential of the zone. In the aftermath of the second Punic war he consistently attempted to wrest control of the *Emporia* away from Carthage. Rome was several times called on to mediate and finally decided in 162–161 BC in favour of the Numidian's claims to the area. Thereafter the *Emporia* paid tribute to Numidia, but no doubt with considerable advantage to their trading activities which had traditionally been closely circumscribed by Carthage. The third Punic war and the destruction of Carthage (149–146 BC) removed the principal commercial rival of the *Emporia* on the southern shores of the Mediterranean and must have had important economic consequences for the Tripolitanian towns. The creation of the first Roman province in 146 did not directly affect the position of the *Emporia* as subjects of the Numidian kingdom, now ruled by Micipsa. However, when the succession arrangements for the kingdom were disrupted by one of Micipsa's beneficiaries, Jugurtha, and Rome became involved in a difficult and lengthy war with the rebel Numidian (112–105 BC), the *Emporia* clearly favoured relations with Rome. In 111 BC an embassy was sent by *Lepcis* to Rome to secure an alliance as a *civitas foederata*. In 109 BC, the pro-Roman faction in the town, fearful of a rival movement led by a certain Hamilcar, requested and was sent a temporary Roman garrison. Even though the *Emporia* were nominally returned to the legitimate Numidian kingdom after the death of Jugurtha these incidents demonstrate the very considerable independence of spirit and action enjoyed by the region, remote as it was from the Numidian heartlands. Indeed, with their commercial outlook on to the Mediterranean, the towns had much common interest in the fortunes of the rapidly expanding Roman empire. Although we lack information in the meagre sources of the first half of the first century BC, it is likely that the *Emporia* maintained very close links throughout this period with Rome. We know of at least one Roman merchant, M. Herennius, who used *Lepcis* as a base for his operations at this time.[3]

Incorporation into empire

The civil war between Caesar and the Pompeians (49–46 BC) had unexpected and serious repercussions in Africa. The conflicting claims of Caesar and his rival to represent the true authority of Rome were not simply ideologically based, but were backed up by force. In some regions the speed of Caesar's advance and victory produced rapid conversion to his cause.

But in Africa the catastrophic defeat in 49 BC of his lieutenant Curio by the Republican forces, amply assisted by the Numidian king Juba, obliged many wavering towns to render material support to the victors under threat of military action against them. It is possible that *Lepcis* was an unwilling or tardy supporter of the Republican cause as Juba evidently had problems with a town called *Leptis* in 49 BC (though this could well be *Leptiminus* in Tunisia rather than *Lepcis Magna*). When Cato crossed the Syrtic desert from Cyrenaica in the winter of 48–47, however, the town welcomed the 10,000 reinforcements for the Republican army. It had little alternative in the circumstances.

The strength of the Republican army in Africa, with its powerful Numidian ally, was a major obstacle to the completion of Caesar's victory and necessitated a hard-fought campaign culminating in the battle of *Thapsus* in 46 BC. As a result of their support for the Republican cause Caesar annexed the Numidian kingdom and severely punished the most clearly implicated African towns. *Lepcis Magna* (rather than *Leptiminus*) was almost certainly the 'Leptis' fined 3 million pounds (about 1,000 tonnes) of olive oil annually. *Lepcis* was also probably reduced in status for a period as a *civitas foederata* or a *stipendiariae*. A new province of *Africa Nova* was created by Caesar from the heartlands of the Numidian kingdom.

It is not clear at what date the *Emporia* were formally added to this unit, but, in spite of the fine attached to *Lepcis* (and perhaps its neighbours also), the towns seem to have enjoyed a continuing high level of independence well into the first century AD. This was no doubt primarily a fact of their remoteness from the administrative bases of the Roman provinces. The essential point here is that by 46 BC the *Emporia* were under Roman suzerainty, although maintaining a considerable level of local autonomy. The scale of Caesar's fine confirms that the region was already rich.[4]

During the principate of Augustus there was a spate of wars and revolts in Africa and the Tripolitanian hinterland was certainly involved on a number of occasions. Triumphs were celebrated *ex Africa* in 34, 33, 28, 21 and 19 BC. We know little about most of the actions involved, but the latter incident was the celebrated campaign of Cornelius Balbus against the *Garamantes* of Fezzan. The two provinces of *Africa Vetus* and *Africa Nova* were united as *Africa Proconsularis* at the latest by 27 BC and governed by a senior senatorial nominee rather than by an imperial appointee. In reality, though, the continuing level of warfare in Africa may have commonly secured the selection of governors known to be acceptable to

Augustus. Indeed, at least one Augustan governor was a specially appointed imperial legate and some proconsuls involved in active campaigning were given extended terms of office.

Some serious incidents affected the region of the *Emporia*. In 3 BC it appears that a Roman proconsul was killed in Africa, perhaps murdered by the *Nasamones*. At an unknown, but possibly similar, date, Quirinius (governor of Cyrenaica or proconsul of Africa?) campaigned against *Marmaridae* and *Garamantes*. There was a major revolt in AD 3–6 in which the *Cinithi* of the coastal region of western Tripolitania were certainly involved and following which the people of *Lepcis* erected a celebratory inscription, commemorating the liberation of the province from the Gaetulian war (*provincia bello gaetulico liberata*). Late in Augustus' reign and in the first year of that of Tiberius, there was major road construction to provide a continuous link between the *Emporia* and the winter quarters of the legion at *Ammaedara* (Haidra, near the modern Tuniso-Algerian border). Tripolitania was evidently seen as a potential, major theatre of warfare. The roads were built through the lands of the *Musulames* and the *Cinithi* tribes and show that some extension of direct Roman territorial control had occurred. During the consequent revolt of the Musulamian chief Tacfarinas (AD 17–24), the *IX Hispana* legion was temporarily posted to *Lepcis* from Pannonia in AD 22. The final Roman victory of AD 24 was celebrated in inscriptions at both *Lepcis* and *Oea*.

These military events are discussed in more detail in the next chapter, but the implication of the record of warfare is that from early in the reign of Augustus the Tripolitanian towns were in the front-line of Roman expansionism in Africa. The archaeological record from *Lepcis Magna* would suggest that the consequences of these wars were ultimately much to the advantage of the towns. Although some land was evidently lost to *Lepcis* for a time during the Tacfarinan revolt, the streets of the town were paved within a decade of the end of the war with the revenues from the land recovered. The record of construction in the town in the first century AD suggests booming prosperity.[5]

As already noted, the fine imposed by Caesar appears to have been lifted at a fairly early date under Augustus and *Lepcis*, *Oea* and *Sabratha* were allowed considerable autonomy as *civitates*, though whether they were *libertae* or governed by a *foedus* is controversial. The three towns all minted coins during the first century BC and continued to do so under Augustus and Tiberius, using the emperor's head on the obverse. There are many other indications of a high

level of local autonomy being maintained, with a notable absence of evidence for colonists or outsiders breaking into the local power structure. This is a singular characteristic of Tripolitania. As Birley has noted, the *Emporia* 'were in a different position to the rest of Punic Africa. They had enjoyed virtual independence for a century and a half, had never been conquered and had not had to surrender land to settlers from Rome.'[6] The towns of the region clearly continued to enjoy favoured status in the early principate and profited from the pacification of the neighbouring tribal peoples and from the delimitation of lands which was beginning in the reign of Tiberius during the proconsulship of Aelius Lamia (AD 15/16). In 8 BC a remarkable building programme had already begun at *Lepcis*. Paid for by local Libyphoenician notables, it was to transform the townscape into one of the earliest and most complete 'Romanized' centres in Africa (chapter 6, below).

Lepcis was also notable for the assiduousness with which it courted imperial favour. Inscriptions show that the imperial cult had unusually early beginnings there, with a temple of Rome and Augustus in the forum and priests (*flamines*) of Caesar Augustus by 8 BC, further reinforced when the *chalcidicum* (a colonnaded market hall) of AD 11/12 was dedicated to the *numen* of the emperor. Although the people of *Lepcis* spoke Punic, from the reign of Augustus inscriptions started to appear in Latin as well as neo-Punic script and these frequently honoured the ruling emperor and his local representative, the proconsul. The importance of the town is also shown by the frequency with which proconsuls were named as patrons of the place.[7]

In AD 39–40 there was an important Roman administrative reform, with control of the legion in Africa being transferred from the proconsul to a legate appointed directly by the emperor. Hereafter the region of the *Emporia* was subject to two branches of government, a civil bureaucracy based at Carthage and a military one based in the headquarters of the Third legion, initially at *Ammaedara*, then at *Theveste* and from the early second century at *Lambaesis* in Numidia. The potential conflict of interests between proconsul and imperial legate came to the fore in the crisis of AD 68–69 when the rival claimants for the purple sought supporters in Africa. Valerius Festus, the legate, was a kinsman and initially a supporter of Vitellius, but, as the balance tipped in favour of Vespasian, he switched allegiance and assassinated the supposedly pro-Vitellian proconsul Piso to prove the point.

The uncertainty surrounding the future form of the central government may have contributed to the outbreak of a war between *Lepcis* and *Oea* in AD 69. Their quarrel was over land ownership and land use along their common boundary, but it escalated into a full-scale military confrontation, with the *Oenses* calling in the *Garamantes* to assist them. The territory of *Lepcis* was overrun and the town besieged before Roman detachments came to its relief. Valerius Festus subsequently conducted a major campaign to the Garamantian heartlands. The incident was a serious breach of civil order by the Tripolitanian cities but it is apparent from the sequel that *Oea* was held largely responsible and *Lepcis* was to benefit as a result. In AD 74 the boundary between the territory of *Lepcis* and *Oea* was resurveyed by a special imperial legate, Rutilius Gallicus, confirming *Lepcis* in possession of much of the best agricultural land in the eastern Gebel. Possibly at the same time, and certainly by AD 77, *Lepcis* was elevated to *municipium* status with Latin rights, conferring Roman citizenship on her aristocracy through their tenure of the town magistracies. Gallicus may personally have promoted the cause of the town as his wife was honoured by a statue erected at the Lepcitanians' expense in Turin, Gallicus' home town. Within a further generation *Lepcis* attained *colonia* status (AD 109) and Roman citizenship to her own citizen body. The promotion of other Tripolitanian cities was a much slower affair. Although we lack certain proof, neither *Sabratha* nor *Oea* seem to have been raised to municipal status before the reign of Antoninus Pius in the mid second century.[8]

The *pax romana*

After further military action in the later first century (involving the *Garamantes* and *Nasamones*) the second century was a period of peace and burgeoning prosperity in the region. All the towns have produced evidence of major investment in public buildings and amenities by their elites. The pacification of the tribal groups of the region was followed up by the delimitation of their lands and large areas of marginal pre-desert were newly brought into cultivation by the indigenous population. Although the region always maintained much of its earlier (and conservative) Punic culture, there is no doubt that from the Flavian period onwards there was overall support for and participation in the Roman system of government by the elites of the region, both urban-based and tribal. The scale of rewards achieved by these notables varied, of course, but the leading citizens of *Lepcis* were clearly operating in the highest levels of the imperial administrative system by the mid-second century AD.

Lepcis was indisputably one of the richest and most exceptional towns in Africa at this date and this wealth was translated into personal political power through the entry into the Roman senate and equestrian order of her leading citizens (see below). The early self-confidence of the Lepcitanians and the existence of influential supporters at Rome are demonstrated in their judicial pursuit of a corrupt proconsul, Marius Priscus, and his legate, Hostilius Firminus at the end of the first century AD. The worst excess had occurred at *Lepcis*, with the two officials having been bribed by a rich citizen, Flavius Marcianus, to eliminate an enemy by judicial murder. The trial of the ex-proconsul and legate at Rome in AD 100 was a minor *cause célèbre*, with Pliny the Younger and Tacitus presenting the case for the prosecution and Trajan himself presiding. Priscus was stripped of his senatorial rank, obliged to repay the bribes and banished from Italy, though Firminus escaped more lightly. *Lepcis* was not adversely affected for having laid such charges against a Roman official, indeed promotion to *colonia* status followed shortly after and the earliest Lepcitanian senator at Rome, a certain Fronto, was adlected sometime early in the second century.

Another courtroom drama took place in the AD 150s involving members of the governing class at *Oea* and Apuleius of *Madauros* (rhetorician, philosopher and author of *The Golden Ass*). After marrying a wealthy widow at *Oea*, Aemilia Pudentilla, he was prosecuted on the sensational charge of witchcraft by some of her kinsfolk and her disappointed local suitors. The trial at *Sabratha* was heard by the proconsul for AD 158, Claudius Maximus, during his annual judicial peregrination. In the course of defending himself against the charges, Apuleius provided many insights into provincial life and the character of the local aristocracy (see chapter 7). There is no doubt that Apuleius was acquitted. But the story is illuminating in other ways for it shows that even in the mid-second century, the aristocracy remained suspicious of outsiders, even to the point of open hostility and litigation. After the trial Apuleius and Pudentilla seem to have removed themselves to Carthage.[9]

By the late second century the region could boast a considerable number of members of the Roman equestrian order and a more select, but significant, body of senators. We know most about those who reached the consulship or who held important governorships (see below). Some at least of them played a decisive historical role in the dramatic events of the years 192–6. When Commodus was assassinated in the last hours of the year AD 192, a train of events was set in motion leading to renewed civil war. Birley has argued that there was a substantial body of African senators in high office in 192 who may have been privy to the plot to replace the unstable Commodus with P. Helvius Pertinax, a senator of comparatively

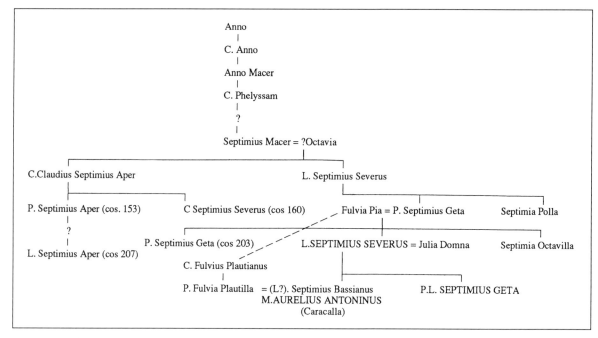

Fig. 3:1 Simplified family tree of L. Septimius Severus, excluding less immediate kin and Julia Domna's Syrian relations (after Birley 1988a).

humble origins. The evidence is circumstantial but the Lepcitanian senator L. Septimius Severus, his brother P. Septimius Geta and Clodius Albinus of *Hadrumentum* were all appointed to major northern military commands (with control of no less than eight legions) due to the influence of the African praetorian prefect and chief conspirator, Laetus. At first all went well for Pertinax but a mutiny amongst the praetorian guard ended his brief reign and triggered civil war. Septimius Severus made the most of his fortunate position as governor of Pannonia, being close to Rome with three legions at his immediate disposal and with a further two commanded by his brother. Septimius was quickly recognized in Rome but he faced two further provincial rivals, Clodius Albinus in Britain and Pescennius Niger in Syria. Three years of fighting was required to reunite the empire under a single authority and the eventual victor was not only an African but a Lepcitanian (Fig. 3:1).[10]

The African emperor

In the course of his reign (AD 193–211) L. Septimius Severus initiated a major phase of frontier expansion in Africa, perhaps as a result of trouble brewing beyond the frontiers at this time. He may even have played an active part in campaigning in Tripolitania, though all too little detail is known of the affair. As a result, though, there was major restructuring of the frontier arrangements in the Tripolitanian region.

He almost certainly revisited his home town in AD 203, conferring on *Lepcis* the coveted status of the *ius Italicum* – a rare honour involving significant tax exemption for a provincial city. A major programme of urban renewal was undertaken at *Lepcis*, undoubtedly with imperial patronage and producing some of the most spectacular monumental architecture of Roman Africa (Plates 20–24). The *quid pro quo* from the town was the promise to supply the city of Rome in perpetuity with a free olive oil donation.

Septimius Severus and his immediate successors instituted a number of significant administrative reforms in Roman Africa. The creation of a province of *Numidia* was a logical solution to the anomaly caused by the overlapping powers and areas of authority of the legionary legate and the proconsul. However, in Tripolitania, the division of the region between proconsular and legatine authority was less clearcut. It seems probable that the concepts of a *limes Tripolitanae* (or *Tripolitanus*) and a *regio Tripolitana* originated at this time in part because of the need to define civil and military spheres. Di Vita-Evrard has argued strongly that the first mention of the *regio Tripolitana* should be assigned to AD 211, though with the origins of the term perhaps slightly earlier. Most of the references to the *regio* involve imperial financial officials and it seems clear that the definition of the territory had administrative utility. The accession of Severus had immediately increased the amount of imperial estates in the region and this was further augmented by confiscations. A procurator for the imperial property in the region (*ratio privata regionae Tripolitanae*) was therefore an entirely logical development. Similarly, the oil donation given by *Lepcis* was presumably the motivation for another new post (though the first attestation perhaps dates to the reign of Severus Alexander) of an official responsible for the oil *annona* (*procurator ad olea conparanda per regionem Tripolitanam*). Third, *curatores* overseeing the finances of the individual towns of the *Emporia* were replaced in the early third century by a *curator rei publicae regionis Tripolitanae*. In all these cases, an expansion of imperial involvement or interference in the financial matters of the area favoured a new and specific name for the region. The first reference to the *limes Tripolitanus* is in the Antonine Itinerary, attributable to the reign of Caracalla (211–17). Di Vita-Evrard suggests that the adjectival form *Tripolitanus* implies the pre-existence of the *regio Tripolitana*. This supposition may be confirmed by her suggested expansion of mid-third-century references to a *praepositus limitis (regionis) Tripolitanae*. The military, political and financial changes in Africa under Septimius Severus thus seem to have favoured the redefinition of the zone previously known as the *Emporia*.[11]

The choice of the name *regio Tripolitana* reflects the pre-eminence of the three eastern cities, *Lepcis*, *Sabratha* and *Oea* and, no doubt, Septimius Severus' own close association with them. At this stage the important town of *Tacapae* (Gabes) may have remained part of *Africa* proper, though it seems to have been included in the fourth-century province of *Tripolitana*, whilst *Gigthis* and the lesser centres of western Tripolitania were clearly overlooked in the choice of the name.

Although the geography of Tripolitania had always kept it somewhat isolated from the rest of *Africa Proconsularis*, it is unnecessary and misleading to see in this Severan measure the development of quasi-provincial structures. The existence of the *regio* as a territorial framework for financial and military appointments did of course provide a convenient module when Diocletian fragmented the provincial structure *c.* AD 303, but we should not try and read too much into Septimius Severus' motives with the benefit of hindsight.

The political ramifications of the period of the Severan dynasty were of great significance to the future of the region. As noted already, in return for the advantages which they received from their compatriot Septimius the Lepcitanian aristocracy offered to contribute towards the new oil dole for the city of Rome. The gift was freely given, but later emperors up to Constantine continued to levy it as a tax. If the reign of Severus marked the pinnacle of success for the Tripolitanian cities (and undoubtedly there was a further influx of people from the region into the senate and equestrian order), it was also the starting point of its decline. Septimius used another prominent Lepcitanian, C. Fulvius Plautianus, as *comes* during his campaigns and by AD 197 as his praetorian prefect. The extent of Plautianus' importance may be gauged by the fact that Septimius' elder son was betrothed to his daughter and that Plautianus was awarded senatorial status and a consulship, whilst still holding the equestrian prefecture. The lavishness of Plautianus' expenditure at the wedding of Antoninus and Fulvia Plautilla caused considerable comment; Dio alleged the dowry would have sufficed for 50 princesses. But in 205 Plautianus abruptly and completely fell from grace and was executed, his estate confiscated and his name subjected to public erasure (*damnatio memoriae*). A special procurator had to be appointed to oversee the incorporation of Plautianus' wealth into imperial ownership and this fortune undoubtedly included major estates in Tripolitania. Other prominent citizens of Tripolitania were executed and their goods confiscated under the rule of Antoninus (Caracalla), starting with his own brother Geta and his cousin L. Septimius Aper. When Caracalla was himself assassinated in AD 217, the greatly augmented imperial estates in Tripolitania passed entirely beyond local control. Coupled with the burden of the oil dole, this significant depletion of the lands of at least two of the town's major families can only have had a negative effect on the local economy.[12]

Local problems were compounded by the larger difficulties of the empire as a whole during the third century. The *legio III Augusta* was disbanded in disgrace in AD 238 because of its role in putting down an African-based revolt against the emperor Maximinus in favour of the provincial governor Gordianus. Although Gordianus and his son were killed almost at the outset, the senate at Rome adopted a grandson of Gordianus as the emperor Gordian III and once his power was secure he took action against the legion responsible for the deaths of his forebears. In consequence of the loss of the sole legion in Africa there was major restructuring of the frontier arrangements in Tripolitania in the middle decades of the third century. An inscription from one of the Tripolitanian forts contains a cryptic reference to a war at this time, though just how widespread the incident is unclear. Although the legion was reformed in the 250s to face mounting military problems in western Numidia it is unlikely that any extra troops were then sent to

Tripolitania. Indeed it is apparent that the military commitment to the area was being scaled down in the later third century, involving redeployment of some units from eastern Tripolitania to positions in the west. By the end of the third century and on the eve of the creation of the province of *Tripolitana*, there are signs that the apparent confidence in the peacefulness of the Tripolitanian frontier had been misplaced.[13]

Small wonder that, compared to the Antonine period, there was comparatively little privately sponsored public building in the post-Severan age. Even when *Lepcis* was made capital of the new province of *Tripolitana* under Diocletian there were few major projects and some of those went unfinished. Lepelley in a recent series of books and articles has suggested that municipal life continued to thrive in North Africa in the late empire. The information from Tripolitania, however, is once again different and supports the older view of a significant, qualitative change in what constituted prosperity (chapter 9 below). But it is also clear that economic decline had begun earlier. Here, then, is the great paradox of Roman Tripolitania: both in its precocious development and in its premature decline it stands out from other regions of Roman Africa.[14]

2
THE STRUCTURES OF CIVIL GOVERNMENT

The civil administration of Africa was centred on the office of proconsul. The proconsulships of Africa and Asia were the most prestigious positions left in the gift of the senate by Augustus and they normally went to senior senatorial figures, in many cases marking the pinnacle of a career in provincial government. When the legate of the *Legio III Augusta* was removed from the proconsul's jurisdiction (AD 39–40), the proconsul was left with two junior legates of praetorian rank, one based at Carthage with him and the other at *Hippo*. The possible existence of a third legate based at *Lepcis* has been canvassed in the past but now seems unlikely. Even though there was no high-ranking official stationed permanently in the region in the early empire, the proconsul and his Carthaginian legate were frequent visitors and patrons of the *Emporia*, as is clear in particular in the rich civic epigraphy of *Lepcis Magna*. Their activity took several forms. First there were the annual assizes held by the proconsuls during a tour of the province, which presumably always involved a visit to at least one of the Tripolitanian towns. Claudius Maximus, for instance,

heard the case against Apuleius in the basilica at *Sabratha*. But judicial matters were neither the sole reason for coming to the region nor the only activity on arrival. The predecessor of Claudius Maximus, Lollianus Avitus had heard Apuleius give a public lecture, presumably in the basilica at *Oea*, and he is also known to have overseen repairs to a fountain in the theatre at *Lepcis*. The proconsul's visit was an occasion for the cities to honour him, by mentioning him (in second place to the emperor) in dedications of buildings, or by erecting statues or bases in his name. As the most important of the Tripolitanian cities, *Lepcis* was particularly active in courting proconsuls and the long list of patrons of exalted rank demonstrates the effectiveness of her tactics. Proconsuls also initiated building projects of their own on occasion. In the early empire, when the proconsuls still had the resources of the legion at their disposal, they were also great road builders, as in the cases of A. Caecina Severus towards AD 12 and of Aelius Lamia in AD 16/17. The latter governor was clearly also involved in the delimitation of the territory of *Lepcis Magna*, and another Tiberian proconsul Vibius Marsus had a similar task surveying tribal territory in western Tripolitania in AD 29/30. Since he dedicated an arch at *Lepcis*, it is possible that his land delimitation work was also directed at the eastern part of the region. On occasion, the proconsul seems to have acted through his legate, as in AD 35–6 when Rubellius Blandus instructed Etrilius Lupercus to oversee the paving of the streets of *Lepcis* and the erection of two arches.[15]

The proconsuls were also responsible in the early empire for financial matters but the growth of the specialized financial secretariat controlled by imperial appointees from the equestrian order (procurators) gradually eroded this during the first century AD. The important imperial estates in Africa had demanded the presence of financial agents of the empire at an early date and the system grew out of that. By the second century AD there was a *procurator provinciae Africae* with an ever-growing staff of junior procurators with specialized functions. We have already noted something of the administrative reforms of the early third century in this context.

Financial officials known as *curatores* of individual towns were appointed with increasing frequency in the second century and later, with responsibility for some fiscal aspects of local government, previously an area of proconsular expertise. Although much local government in the Roman world was devolved on to town councils, governors played an important role in regulating the conduct of regional administration by scrutinizing town finances and by investigating reports of malpractice. Although the appointment of *curatores* is frequently interpreted as a sign that towns were getting into financial difficulties, this was not necessarily the case. It is possible to take the view that they were fulfilling much the same role as the proconsuls had earlier whilst also being part of a general trend towards expansion and fragmentation of the imperial buraucracy. It is undoubtedly true that the Roman administrative staff in Africa had swelled in size many times between the reign of Augustus and the end of the third century.

Local government was conducted through the towns of the region, with the major centres administering large *territoria* and potentially also wider areas and peoples assigned to them. Thus *Lepcis* possessed a delimited territory of several thousand square kilometres, but may well have administered a bigger region still. Several small towns fell within the *territorium* of *Lepcis* and their failure to develop to higher urban status is in marked contrast to the pattern in northern *Africa Proconsularis*, reflecting the strength of the control exercised over them by the coastal cities.[16]

The Punic system of urban-based government was well suited to the needs of Rome through its intrinsic similarities to the Roman model; it was oligarchic, based on two annual magistrates (*sufetes*) and four lower officials (*mahazim*) elected by a council and an assembly. The similarity to the Roman pattern of two senior (*duoviri*) and two junior magistrates (*aediles*) supported by the aristocratic council and citizen body (*senatus populusque* or *ordo et populus*) is self evident. The long established and easy dominance of the Lepcitanian elite within their town would seem to have discouraged Rome from any attempt at excessive interference with arrangements. When the town became a *municipium* in c. AD 74 there was evidently no change to the central organs of local government. Instead of remodelling and renaming the Punic magistracies on Roman lines the town continued to elect annual *sufetes* and the *mahazin* were simply renamed *IIIIviri aedilicia potestate* rather than being reduced in number and called *aediles*. The 'municipium sufetal' is a unique African example of the Roman state accommodating local custom to this extent and will not have been repeated when *Sabratha* and *Oea* became *municipia* at a later date. *Lepcis* relinquished the Punic titles and normalized her magistracies when she became a *colonia* in AD 109. Thereafter the *quattuorviri* system of magistracies applied: two *duoviri* supported by two *aediles* drawn from and supported by an aristocratic curial body of 100. The granting of the Latin right (*ius Latii*) in the AD 70s had the important effect of bestowing Roman citizenship on the annual magistrates. In a short space of time the Punic nomenclature of the leading families was wholly replaced by adopted Roman names. As Birley has shown, however, the choice of names frequently reflects the Libyphoenician background of those involved. From AD 109 all her citizens were also Roman citizens, still further disguising the Libyphoenician character of her population by adopted Roman-style names.[17]

The government of tribal peoples through urban centres is illustrated by several examples from the region. First, the *Nybgenii* tribe of the Nefzaoua and Dahar was administered through the creation of a Roman style *civitas* capital at Telmine (*Turris Tamellini*), which became a *municipium* under Hadrian. Another Gaetulian group, the *Cinithi* were attached to the town of *Gigthis* for administrative purposes, whilst the names of *Marcomades Selorum* and *Digdida municipium Selorum* on the Syrtic gulf indicate links with the *Seli* sub-tribe.[18] This important aspect of the process of pacification and 'Romanization' is considered in more detail in the next chapter.

In many towns of the Roman world the activities of their ruling aristocracies did not extend much beyond the locality. They competed for places on the main town council (*curia*), for the magistracies and priesthoods and for popular approval through individual acts of beneficence (euergetism). They owned or controlled large amounts of land and other resources, and they made marriage alliances with each other. *Lepcis*, *Oea* and *Sabratha* (the latter two to a far lesser extent) were among a select number of towns that became more completely integrated into the imperial system of government. From the early second century at the latest, the top local magistracies (the *duoviri quinquennales* elected every fifth year) were no longer seen in these towns to be the pinnacle of a political career. The wealth and strong ties of patronage established by the Tripolitanian elite gave them an entrée into higher levels of government. During the Flavian period they were appearing in the equestrian order and by the early second century in the senate also. The first senator, Fronto, of *Lepcis* was followed by numerous others. As we have seen, *Lepcis* could claim several consuls and high ranking governors as her own prior to the dramatic achievement of Septimius Severus in AD 193. In the late second- and third-century epigraphy at *Lepcis*, therefore, it is possible to ascribe a Lepcitanian origin to a number of the Roman officials (proconsuls, legates, procurators and curators) commemorated for service in the administration of *Africa Proconsularis*. This neatly illustrates a paradox of Roman provincial government. In allowing a high degree of local autonomy, the Roman state gave opportunities to the governed to govern not simply themselves but others in the empire.[19]

3
THE LOCAL ELITE

The earliest surviving inscription from *Lepcis Magna* is of the late second or early first century BC and was carved in neo-Punic script (a variant on the older Phoenician script developed after the destruction of Carthage). Much of the most important epigraphic records in the first century AD continued to be in neo-Punic, though frequently with a parallel Latin text. From the combination of Latin and neo-Punic epigraphy, quite a lot can be learned about the principal families at *Lepcis* in the late first century BC and first century AD. Foremost among them, at least in terms of epigraphic evidence, were the Tapapii (Punic 'Tabahpi'). Annobal Tapapius Rufus paid for the original market in 8 BC and the theatre in AD 1/2 (Plate 40). The Tapapii seem to have been influential in the promotion of the imperial cult at *Lepcis*. Annobal himself was a *flamen* and another holder of this priesthood, Bodmelqart ben Annobal, was perhaps his son. A *sufes* in the reign of Tiberius called Bodmelqart Tabahpi may have been another linear descendant of Annobal. Bodmelqart's magistracy coincided with the erection of larger than life statues of the Julio-Claudian dynasty in the temple of Rome and Augustus. Another member of the Tapapii family, Iddibal son of Mago, dedicated a shrine in the theatre to the *Di Augusti* in AD 43 and under Nero (61–2) yet another member of the family, Ithymbal Sabinus son of Arish, is recorded as priest of Augustus. The family was still represented among the *sufetes* in the AD 60s and without doubt was ancestor to one of the major Romanized *gentes*, though which one is unclear. Unfortunately it is not possible to equate the leading families of the first century AD with the Latinized nomenclature of the second century. The rapid transplantation of Roman for Punic nomenclature, starting in the last quarter of the first century AD, has obscured the connection between the two groups of names.[20]

In an important article Birley has illustrated the process of Latin name selection which may have gone on at *Lepcis*, drawing attention to three main categories of change. First, there was complete and potentially random replacement of names. In some cases this might involve adopting the names of the emperor or some other important patron (ex-proconsuls seem to have been a favourite at *Lepcis*). Alternatively combinations of names may have been selected for their historical resonance, as in the cases of L. Cassius Longinus and P. Cornelius Balbus from *Lepcis*. Second, some names were selected for the similar sound they had to a Punic original. Thus Aemilius is phonetically similar to Himilis, Macer to M'qr and so on. The third category of names included those which were used as translations or equivalents of Punic originals. The theophoric nature of Phoenician names favoured this style of translation. Muttunbal ('gift of Baal') could become Diodorus in Greek and Saturninus in Latin since Ba'al was equated with Saturn in Roman Africa. In other cases part of the Punic name was rendered by a past participle. Thus the idea behind Punic names compounded with Muttun ('gift, given by'), for instance, could be rendered by Roman names such as Donatus or Datus. All these practices are well attested in the evidence from *Lepcis*.

In many cases the Punic antecedents and pedigrees of the major families just vanish from our sight. Not only did the names change, but the civic epigraphy became universally Latin-based (although Punic remained the vernacular language of the region). T. Claudius Sestius, responsible for further alterations in the theatre in AD 92, gave himself away, however, by including traditional Punic epithets and by erecting his dedication in both Latin and Punic (the last dated public inscription in neo-Punic at *Lepcis*).[21]

Despite the difficulty of tracing the ancestors of the major families of the second and third centuries, Birley has recently sought to identify those of Septimius Severus with a Punic family who used the names Gaius and Macer, both attested in the prosopography of the Septimii (Fig. 3:1). In AD 53–4 Gaius Anno (G'y ben Hn) repaved the forum and erected a portico in his grandson's name, possibly as a means of launching the young man's political career in the town. The grandson, Gaius Phelyssam (son of Anno Macer) was honoured with a separate statue base erected by the people of *Lepcis*. Birley postulates the existence of a member of this family who took the names Septimius Macer on acquiring citizenship, thereby initiating the Septimian *gens* proper.[22]

The rise of the Septimii is simply the most dramatic case amongst an impressive number of success stories involving Lepcitanian families in the second century AD. What is most striking is the prodigious wealth of the *Lepcitani*, which, together with a limited amount of personal patronage by established figures, qualified some of them at an early date for entry into the aristocratic social circle at Rome. The prominent first-century AD philosopher L. Annaeus Cornutus originated from *Lepcis* whilst the emperor Vespasian's wife Flavia Domitilla was reputed to have previously been the mistress of a Sabrathan knight, Statilius Capella. Already in the later first century AD, the Septimii owned lands near Rome as well as in Africa. Lucius Septimius Severus (grandfather of the future emperor) was brought up in Italy and a poem by

Statius stresses the extent to which the Liby-phoenician adolescent had been integrated into Roman culture and manners. Had he chosen to remain at Rome a career in public service, with equestrian rank at least, seems to have been open to him, but instead he returned to *Lepcis* to be its leading citizen at the time of its promotion to colonial status. He was successively one of the last holders of the *sufes* magistracy, a specially appointed *praefectus* during the changeover and one of the first pair of *duoviri* of the new colony. The first Lepcitanians to reach the consulship at Rome were probably his nephews, P. Septimius Aper in 153 and C. Septimius Severus in 160. In AD 174 an arch was dedicated at *Lepcis* by C. Septimius, then proconsul of Africa, and his kinsman and legate, L. Septimius Severus (grandson of the original L. Septimius). As we have seen, in the civil war of AD 193–6 L. Septimius Severus, by then himself holding a major consular governorship, was to become emperor.[23]

Apart from the Septimii there were several other major families from *Lepcis* making an impact in empire-wide politics during the later second century. The Fulvii were in origin a settler family (one of only a handful detectable) of the late first century BC, but were later well intermarried with the other major Lepcitanian *gentes*, including the Septimii. We have already noted the prominence of C. Fulvius Plautianus, whose kinship ties with Severus were established through the latter's mother. In spite of the downfall of Plautianus in AD 205 a C. Fulvius Pius (possibly a descendant of Severus' maternal grandfather) became consul in AD 238. Another prominent Lepcitanian family, the Silii Plautii sent several of its sons to the senate. L. Silius Plautius Haterianus was *quaestor* of the province of Crete and Cyrenaica in *c.* AD 165–6 and a [...] Silius Q. P[lautius] Haterianus was successively legate of the *legio II Augusta* in Britain and governor of Cilicia. In the early third century L. Silius Amicus (Haterianus) was consul, *curator* of *Oea* and proconsul of Asia (the latter post in AD 230). A combination of different strands of evidence suggests that most of the major families of the town (Septimii, Fulvii, Plautii/Silii Plautii, Cornelii, Servilii) were represented in the senate by the early third century. Other important administrative posts went to equestrian *Lepcitani*: Q. Marcius Dioga was prefect of the *annona* at Rome under the Severans; M. Ulpius Cerealis held a procuratorship.[24]

Insofar as the epigraphic evidence from *Sabratha* and *Oea* allows, it seems that the level of attainment of their aristocrats was somewhat lower though a small number of knights and senators is known for the late second and early third century AD. This lesser achievement in part reflects the slower pace of urban promotion; *Oea* had gained colonial status by the 160s and *Sabratha* the same honour by the 180s. L. Aemilius Frontinus of *Oea* reached the proconsulship of Asia in the later second century and his brother was also in the senate. Q. Sicinius Clarus was another senator from the town, being appointed governor of Thrace in AD 202. Both the Aemilii and the Sicini had earlier played prominent roles in the mischievous prosecution of Apuleius. At least one senator is known from *Sabratha*, Messius Rufinus.[25]

4
INFRASTRUCTURE AND GEOPOLITICS

The pattern of ancient settlement in Tripolitania was conditioned in part by the geographic and climatic factors outlined in chapter 1 (Fig. 3:2). Information on Roman period settlement illustrates this well. Rural settlement was particularly subject to environmental factors and limitations. In the next chapter, the development of the Roman frontier is analysed in detail and it will become clear how much that depended on a clear understanding of the physical conditions of life in the region. The frontier security was based on forts and communications and in a parallel way the civil government rested on an infrastructure of towns and roads.

Urban sites

The urban settlements of the region were rather more numerous than the provincial name suggests, with four cities attaining the rank of *coloniae* (*Tacapae* (Gabes), *Sabratha*, *Oea* and *Lepcis*), and a further six towns being recorded as *municipia* (*Turris Tamalleni* (Telmine), *Gigthis* (Bou Ghara), *Zitha* or *Ziza* (Zian), *Pisidia* (Pisida), *Thubactis* (at or near Misurata), *Digdida* (Wadi el-Hariga)).[26] Almost all of these centres were situated on or very close to the Mediterranean coast (the oasis of Telmine is the notable exception) and most of the coastal sites were developed as harbours on what was a vast littoral, perilously under-provided with safe anchorages.[27] Several other coastal sites seem to have been reasonably substantial small towns and may have had at least the status of *civitates* (self-governing communities). These were *Gergis* (Zarzis), effectively the harbour for *Zitha*, *Marcomades Selorum* (Sirte) and *Iscina* (Medina Sultan). A further three settlements in the Arad and western Gefara plains may have had similar status: the oasis with bathing establishment of *Aquae Tacapitanae* (el-Hamma),

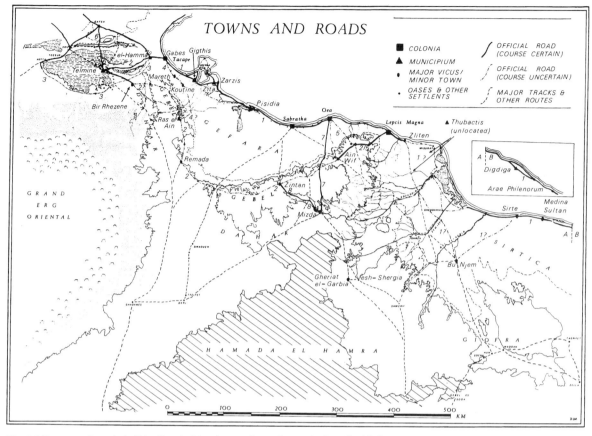

Fig. 3:2 Towns and roads in Tripolitania. Numbers refer to the roads described below.

Martae (Mareth) and *Augarmi* (Ksar Koutine or Hr Kedama?). The island of Gerba, which was attached to the mainland by a causeway at *Ponte Zita*, had at least four urban centres of uncertain status (*Meninx* (el-Kantara), *Tipasa* (Adjim), *Girba* (Gerba) and *Hares* (?)).[28]

There are in addition a number of substantial villages or small towns within the extensive territories of the coastal towns and these were probably subject to administrative control from the major centres throughout the Roman period. *Sugolin* (Zliten), *Subututtu* (Gasr ed-Daun) and *Mesphe* (Medina Doga), for instance, can be related to the territory of *Lepcis Magna*.

There were also sites which to a greater or lesser extent depended for their existence and livelihood on the presence of a military garrison. A number of small towns in the Gebel (which may have also fallen within the territory of one of the major cities) can be seen in this category (*Thenadassa* (Ain Wif) and *Auru* (Ain el-Auenia). Most of the major Roman forts in the frontier zone also had their civilian settlements (*vici*) and these were on occasion extensive.[29]

The archaeology of these various categories of urban sites will be discussed later (chapter 6), but two points need to be established straight away. The level of urban development outside the five major centres of *Lepcis*, *Oea*, *Sabratha*, *Tacapae* and *Gigthis* was low in comparison to many other areas of *Africa Proconsularis*. This is only partly explicable in terms of the relative poverty of the agricultural land, since the wealth which catapaulted the Lepcitanian elite to empire-wide prominence could have supported a good number of towns at a more mundane level of achievement. The failure of many of the small towns of the region, and particularly of the interior, to fulfil their potential of becoming self-governing communities reflects rather the uniquely favoured status of the major cities in local administration. These centres were allowed to control *territoria* of several thousand square kilometres in extent and perhaps to administer local government over even wider zones. In northern Tunisia, the process of urban promotion and administrative restructuring went to the other extreme, with authority fragmented and a density of one self-governing town every 30 square kilometres or so in the most congested areas. The development of extraordinarily large *territoria* for the major towns in Tripolitania was economically desirable in the early empire but it is a remarkable feature that the local power of those cities was sustained into the later empire.[30]

Roads, tracks and milestones

The major roads of Tripolitania are known primarily from surviving Roman itineraries or from finds of milestones. Outside the periphery of the major towns few of the roads seem to have comprised built or paved pistes. The arid climate will have facilitated the cheap maintenance of beaten earth road surfaces. The lack of perennial rivers in the region (with the exception of the Wadi Caam) limited the need for bridge building. The Roman roads thus differed little from their antecedents among the myriad trackways of the region, linking town and country, desert and littoral. The prime distinction will have been that the Roman roads were carefully surveyed to limit gradients and to facilitate the passage of wheeled traffic. Thus we might expect some signs of cuttings at crossing points of the wadis or in mountain passes.[31]

The most effective means of tracing the routes followed are provided by the surviving milestones, where they have been recorded *in situ*. The milestones do not necessarily indicate the date at which roads were constructed, of course, and in Tripolitania as elsewhere the greatest erectors of milestones were the third-century emperors, undoubtedly exploiting the propaganda value of the medium. Of 108 milestones known in the region, 94 (87 per cent) relate to third-century emperors (59 (55 per cent) to Caracalla alone), 7 (6.5 per cent) to the first century, 4 (3.7 per cent) to the second, 1 (0.9 per cent) to the fourth, with 2 (1.9 per cent) uncertain. Considerable importance thus attaches to first-century milestone evidence on the principal routes.[32]

The most important road in Tripolitania throughout its history was the interprovincial, coastal highway, which ultimately ran on to link Carthage and Alexandria (Fig. 3:2). The earliest epigraphic evidence from this road dates to the last years of Augustus, when the proconsul Caecina Severus is recorded on a milestone near *Sabratha*, but the route was undoubtedly in use much earlier. The coast road is known from the two main sources of Roman road itineraries, the Peutinger Table (in origin a map of the later second century AD surviving in a medieval copy, Fig. 3:3) and the Antonine Itinerary (early third century). There are some variations between the route followed by these itineraries and this probably reflects the unbuilt nature of the piste, allowing a number of options to be followed at certain points. For instance, in the sector between *Lepcis* and *Marcomades*, where the Sebkha Tauorgha prevented a truly coastal route the Antonine Itinerary describes a much shorter route. It probably kept much closer to the western edge of the Sebkha. The Peutinger map seems to describe a more inland route and Rebuffat has attempted to identify one of the sites named on this sector, *Chosol*, with Bu Njem (*Gholas, Chol, Gholaia*). The argument is far from conclusive, but clearly this route went some distance inland before turning back to the Syrtic coast. The only milestone from this sector lies on the coast, south of the Sebkha, and presumably relates to the route described in the Antonine Itinerary.[33]

Tables 3:1 and 3:2 compare the information from the Antonine Itinerary and the *Tabula Peutingeriana* with two other itinerary-derived sources, the Ravenna Cosmography and Guido. No attempt is made to correlate the ancient sites with modern locations. Some are self-evident (*Lepcis, Oea, Sabratha*, etc.), but many of the minor sites are by their very nature unlikely to be locatable since there are doubts about many of the precise mileage figures involved (thus *casas villa Aniciorum, Ad cisternas*). Much speculation has been attempted in the past, often employing maps inadequate to the task.

Total distances by stages of coast road	Antonine Itinerary		*Tabula Peutingeriana*	
	m.p.	km	m.p.	km
Tacapae (Gabes) to *Lepcis Magna* (Homs)	338	500	310	459
Lepcis Magna to *Marcomades Selorum* (Sirte)	222	328.5	min. 259 max. 286	383 423
Marcomades to *Arae Philaenorum* (Ras el Aàli)	159+	235+	151+	223.5+
Total distance *Tacapae* to *Arae Philaenorum*	719+	1063.5+	min. 720+ max. 747+	1065.5+ 1105.5+

Table 3:1. *Total distances on the coastal route (route 1, on Fig. 3:2); M. P. = mille passuum (Roman miles).*

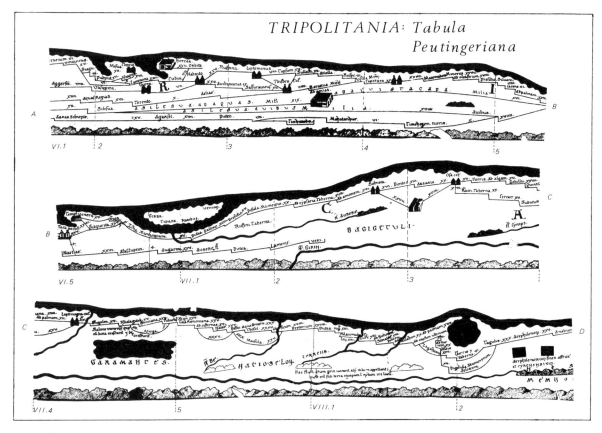

Fig. 3:3 The *Tabula Peutingeriana* for Tripolitania (after Miller 1887).

In the first section between *Tacapae* and *Lepcis* it is apparent that the minor sites along the roads fell into several categories:

a) small/medium towns (*Gigthis, Zita, Pisidia*);
b) large villa estates (*villae Aniciorum, villa Magna, Fulgurita villa, villa Repentina, villa Marci*);
c) wells, bridges, shrines (*putea Pullene, Pontos, Ad Amonem, templum Veneris*);
d) *tabernae* or inns (*Ad Cypsaria, Flacci, Nivirgi*);
e) oases or native settlements (*Ad Palmam; Getullu*).

Basic facilities for travellers may have been available at the various categories of sites but outside the towns these were perhaps of the kind to be avoided if possible. Apuleius was following this route towards Egypt in the 150s when he fell ill and was obliged to stay at *Oea* to recuperate, thus becoming involved with Pudentilla. His friend and Pudentilla's son, Sicinius Pontianus, was less fortunate when he fell ill on the road from Carthage to *Oea* in 158. He died soon after his arrival home.

Beyond *Lepcis* the route began its ever more arduous passage around the Syrtic coast. An increasing number of names evoke the importance of water supplies (*Ad Cisternas, Dissio aqua amara, Putea Nigrorum*) and the relative scarcity of cultivation on some stretches is perhaps revealed by the landmark name *Ad Ficum*. Major settlements were few and far between beyond *Marcomades* (Sirte) and travellers may have had to carry water for several days, camping out in between small towns such as *Iscina, Digdida* and *Tugulus*.

A particular problem relates to the identification of ancient *Thubactis* or *Tubactis municipium*, which has been variously located at the important oasis of Misurata, at two anchorages to the west and east of Misurata or some way south and inland from Misurata. The question is complicated and defies easy answer (see further, chapter 6).[34]

The other major 'route' is the *limes Tripolitanus* road known from the Antonine Itinerary and in certain sectors also by milestones (Fig. 3:2, no. 2; Table 3:3). This route also connected *Tacapae* and *Lepcis*, but by a series of inland deviations. In the process it combined

Antonine Itinerary 59.6–65.6	Tabula Peutingeriana seg. vi.5–vii2		Ravenna Cos. 3.5	Ravenna Cos. 5.5–6	Guido
Tacapas Colonia 25 m.p.	Tacape col 25 m.p.		Tacapas	Tacapa colonia	
Agma sive Fulgurita villa 25 m.p.	Fulgurita 25 m.p.	26 m.p. Templ(um) Veneris			
Giti municipium	Gigti 17 m.p.		Githi	Githit	
35 m.p. Ponte Zita municipium	Ziza municipium 15 m.p.		Zita	Vita	
	Putea Pallene			Putea Balleane	
30 m.p. Villa Magna, villa privata	18 m.p. Praesidium			Praesidium	Praesidium
31 m.p. Fisidia vicus	15 m.p. Pisidia municipium 20 m.p.			Fisidia	Fresidia
26 m.p.	Ad Cypsaria Taberna		Cipsaria	Gipsarea	Gypsarea
Casas villa Anicorium	17 m.p. Ad Amonem			Ammonis	Ammonis
28 m.p. Sabrata Colonia	16 m.p. Sabrata 16 m.p.	27 m.p.	Sabrata	Sabrata	Sabrata
27 m.p. Vax villa Repentina	Pontos 13 m.p.			Pontos	Pontos
	Assaria	[unnamed site]	Poteo	Passaria	Passaria
28 m.p. Ocea Colonia	20 m.p. Ocea col. 12 m.p.	18 m.p. 16 m.p. [inland route]		Oxea	Oxena
25 m.p.	Turris ad Algam	Flacci Taberna		Turris Alba	Turris Alba
Megradi villa Aniciorum	15 m.p.	20 m.p.		Getula	Getua
29 m.p.	Getullu	Cercar			
Minna villa Marci	24 m.p.	15 m.p.			
	Quintiliana 14 m.p.	Subututtu 25 m.p.		Quintiliana	Quintiliana
	Ad Palmam			Civitas Palma *Mata	Palma *Mapta
29 m.p.	12 m.p.				
Leptis Magna Colonia	Leptimagna col		Leptis Magna	Leptis Magna	Paletis Magna
20 m.p. Seggera	20 m.p. Sugolin 15 m.p.			Subgoli	Subgoli
24 m.p. Berge	Nivirgi Taberna 15 m.p.	15 m.p.	Neveri	Nivergi	Nivergi
25 m.p. Base	Simnuana	Virga	Scemadana	Simadana	Simadana
30 m.p. Thebunte (or Tabunte)	22 m.p. Tubactis mun. 25 m.p.	10 m.p.	Thubacis	Thubactis	Thubactis
30 m.p. Auxiqua (or Auziqua)	Casa Rimoniana 25 m.p.			Rusticiana	Rasticiana
30 m.p. Annesel	Ad Cisternas 15 m.p.	35 m.p.	Cisterium	Cisternas	Cisternas
18 m.p. Auxiu (or Auzui)	Nalad 25 m.p.	[short cut]	Nadalus	Nadalus	Nadalas
	Dissio (Vissio) Aqua Amara		Disio	Dision	Dision
	30 m.p.	30 m.p.		*Onulsol	*Onusol
25 m.p. Astiagi (or Stixgi)	Musula 25 m.p.	Chosol 35 m.p.	Musol	Mulsol	Musol
	Ad Ficum 18 m.p.			Ficum	Ficum

	Praetorium		Praetorium	Praetorium	Praetorium
	28 m.p.				
	Putea Nigrorum			Putea Nigra	Putea Nigra
20 m.p.	13 m.p.				
Marcomanibus Sirtis	Marcomades		Sacomadis	Macumades	Macitapades
	Selorum			Maiores	Maiores
	13 m.p.				
	Zure			Zoures	Zures
	13 m.p.				
	Ad Speluncas			Spelunca	Speluncas
30/34 m.p.	13 m.p.				
Iscina	Scina loc. Iudaeor.		Isyri	Isina	Iscina
	Augti.				
	[mileage omitted]				
	Aulazon			Aulazon	Aulazon
	20 m.p				
31 m.p.	Ad Palmam		Palma	Palman	Alma
Tramaricio	18 m.p.				
	Ad Capsam Ultimum			Capsum	Capsultimum
				Ultimum	
	12 m.p.				
	Ad Turrem	[short cut? -		Turris	Turris
		no mileage given]		Lapideum	Lapidum
	20 m.p.				
25 m.p.	Praesidio				
Aubereo	22 m.p.				
	Zagazaena		Zacassama	Zasasma	Zacasama
24 m.p.	12 m.p.	[mileage omitted]			
Digdica	Digdida municipium	Turris et Taberna		Dicdica	Didicca
	Selorum	6 m.p.			
24 m.p.	[mileage omitted]				
Tugulus	Tagulus			Tragulis	Trigulis
25 m.p.					
Banadedari					
	30 m.p.				
	Arephilenorum fines		Arephilenorum	Arepelonorum	Arepoenorum
	Africe et				
	Cyrenensium				

Table 3:2. The Tripolitanian coast roads from *Tacapae to Arae Philaenorum* (comparison of the different routes followed by the Antonine Itinerary and the *Tabula Peutingeriana* and analysis of place-name evidence of the Ravenna Cosmographer and Guido. Entries in the second column under *Tabula Peutingeriana* represent deviations from the main route).

sectors of several earlier or distinct routes. Some of the sites along it may be identified with confidence, others have been the subject of immense speculation. The first sector corresponds with the main *Tacapae* to *Capsa* (Gafsa) highway, first laid out by Nonius Asprenas in AD 14. At el-Hamma (*Aquae Tacapitanae*) the *limes* road branched southwest towards the Nefzaoua oases following the north side of the Djebel Tebaga. The earliest evidence on this stretch is of a Domitianic milestone. South of the Nefzaoua, the road entered the pre-desert zone and, apart from one or two fixed points such as *Bezereos*, its course is almost entirely hypothetical. Most modern commentators believe that it followed the Wadi ben Hallouf in the Dahar south of *Bezereos* (Bir Rhezene) before cutting back through the Gebel somewhere in the Benia Ceder/Ras el Ain sector.

Rushworth has recently revived an interesting alternative argument that would take the would-be traveller back towards *Tacapae* from *Bezereos*, joining a direct road from *Tacapae* towards Remada and Ghadames only a short distance from where the *limes Tripolitanus iter* had started. The apparently absurd deviation should remind us that the purpose of the Antonine Itinerary was primarily concerned with official peregrinations and not necessarily with providing travellers with shortest routes, as is also apparent from a detailed study of the British section. The sites of *Agma* and *Auzemmi* on the *limes* road would then be equated with *Agma sive Fulgurita villa* on the coast road (Table 3:2) and with *Augarmi* on the western Gefara route (see below, Table 3:5). The suggestion that this western Gefara road was of considerable military importance is supported by the fact that some milestones are known from it. This alternative reconstruction is not without its problems (notably the awkward fact that *Agma* is on the wrong road out of *Tacapae*), but the possibility that the *limes* route

Ant Itin Ref.	Roman names and distances	Modern locations
73.4	*Iter quod limitem Tripolitanum per Turrem Tamalleni a Tacapis Lepti Magna ducit m.p. DCV*	
74.1	*A Tacapis*	Gabes
	18 m.p.	
	Ad Aquas	el-Hamma
	30 m.p.	
	Agarlabas/Agarlavas	Hr Mgarine (?)
	30 m.p.	
	Turre Tamalleni	Telmine
	12 m.p.	
	Ad Templum	
	30 m.p.	
	Bezereos	Bir Rhezene
	32 m.p.	
	Ausilimdi	
	30 m.p.	
75.1	*Agma*	
	30 m.p.	
	Auzemmi	
	30 m.p.	
	Tabalati	Ras el Ain?/Foum Tatahouine area?
	25 m.p.	
	Thebelami/Themalami	Hr Medeina?
	20 m.p.	
	Tillibari	Remada
	30 m.p.	
	Ad Amadum/Aumaudum	Dehibat?
	25 m.p.	
76.1	*Tabuinati/Thrabunacti*	
	25 m.p.	
	Thramusdusin/Tharama	
	30 m.p.	
	Thamascaltin	
	30 m.p.	
	Thenteos	near Zintan (Edref?)
	30 m.p.	
	Auru	Ain el Auenia?
	35 m.p.	
	Vinaza	
	16 m.p.	
	Thalatati/Talalati	
	26 m.p.	
77.1	*Thenadassal/Tenadassa*	Ain Wif
	30 m.p.	
	Mesphe	Medina Doga
	40 m.p.	
	Lepti Magna	Lebda
	[Total] *DCV*	

Table 3:3. The *limes Tripolitanus* road from the Antonine Itinerary (after Cuntz 1929).

rejoined the western Gefara road some way north of its normally accepted junction in the Foum Tatahouine area is certainly worth further consideration. South of Foum Tatahouine the route ran on the margins of Gebel and Gefara towards *Tillibari* (Remada) and Dehibat. From there it will have turned east-northeast climbing on to the Gebel crest and continuing towards Zintan and Gharian. *Thenteos* (Zintan), *Auru* (Ain el-Auenia) and *Thenadassa* (Ain Wif) provide more or less fixed points, even though the next milestones are not encountered until the approaches to Tarhuna. The final sector from *Mesphe*

Tabula Peutingeriana 5.5–6.5	Ravenna Cos. 3.5	Modern Location
Thusuros		Tozeur
30 m.p.		
Aggarsel Nepte	*Nepte*	Nefta(?)
115 m.p. [!?]		
Agarsel	*Agasel*	
14 m.p.		
Puteo	*Putam*	
	[mileage omitted]	
7 m.p.	*Tinzimendo*	*Tingimie*
Mazantanzur		
6 m.p.		
Timezegeri Turris		
10 m.p.		
Avibus [road junction]		Part of el-Hamma oasis?
18 m.p.		
Tacape col		Gabes
[Total length of route *200 m.p.*]		

Table 3:4. The Djerid-Nefzaoua-Gabes route. The course and mileages are for the most part very uncertain.

(Medina Doga) to *Lepcis* is reasonably well known from milestone evidence, the earliest being one of AD 15/16. This Tiberian road ran 70 km into the Gebel Tarhuna to a point which evidently marked the south-western limits of the territory of *Lepcis*.[35]

Three other routes shown on the Peutinger map (Figs 3:2–3:3; Tables 3:2, 3:4–3:5) are even more problematical to trace as there is limited milestone evidence to supplement place-name identifications. The first of these routes (Fig. 3:2, no. 3; Table 3:4) apparently linked the oases of the Djerid with those of the Nefzaoua by a route which ran round the southern edge of the Chott Djerid and then continued to *Tacapae* (presumably on the south side of the Djebel Tebaga). This can never have been much more than a desert/pre-desert track for much of its course. It is possible that *Avibus*, where there was a road junction, is the name for one part of the twin oasis of el-Hamma (the other being *Aquae Tacapitanae*).[36]

Another road ran out from *Tacapae*, evidently in a south or southeasterly direction into the interior portion of the western Gefara (Fig. 3:2, no. 4; Table 3:5). *Martae* is generally agreed to be Mareth, but *Augarmi* has been variously identified as Medenine, the site of Ksar Koutine or Kedama. Ksar Koutine is a fairly major Roman period village or estate centre and therefore perhaps marginally the better candidate. The mileage figures are incomplete and possibly corrupt in any case, so speculation beyond that is hazardous. In any event, the road seems to have been following the southwestern edge of the Gefara plain alongside the Djebel Matmata. The fact that this road

Tabula Peutingeriana 6.5–7.2	Ravenna Cos. 3.5	Modern Location
Tacape col	[*Taccapas*]	Gabes
10 m.p.		
Martae	*Marthae*	Mareth
26 m.p.		
Afas Lupeici	*Afas Lucernae*	
5 m.p.		
Augarmi	*Agarmi*	Ksar Koutine? Hr Kredama
25 m.p.		
Ausere fl.	*Aucertim*	
[mileage omitted]		
Putea	*Ad Putam*	
[mileage omitted]		
Laminie	*Lamie*	
[mileage omitted]		
Veri	*Afas Verim*	
Total length of route 66 m.p.++		

Table 3:5. The inland western Gefara route. Beyond *Veri* the road probably ran south towards *Tillibari* (Remada), cf. Table 3:4.

was marked by milestones emphasizes its military importance and lends some support to Rushworth's view that the *limes* route, after its detour to and from the Nefzaoua, is to be identified with a substantial segment of this road.[37]

The inland route between *Oea* and *Lepcis* via *Flacci Taberna*, *Cercar* and *Subututtu* (Fig. 3:2, no. 5; Table 3:2) is subject to a major error in the mileages given, which produce a lower total than the direct coastal route. Oates and Goodchild proposed that the route in fact ran up into the heart of the Gebel Tarhuna, identifying *Cercar* with the spring of Ain Scersciara (where there was a major Roman villa) and *Subututtu* with the small town of Gasr ed-Daun. This still seems the best explanation, particularly when it is appreciated that the Gebel Tarhuna was one of the main olive oil producing zones and the roads from *Cercar* to *Oea* and from *Subututtu* to *Lepcis* will have carried a substantial amount of the surplus production to market. The *Lepcis* road is in fact to be identified with the final stretch of the *limes* road from *Mesphe* (Medina Doga).[38]

Several other roads are known only from milestones. The Gebel el Asker route linked the towns of *Capsa* and *Turris Tamalleni* (Fig. 3:2, no. 6). Its course across the Chott Fedjedj and the Cherb range is well established by the topographic constraints and by a series of four Trajanic and one Caracallan milestones. The main route across the Gefara and Gebel south of Tripoli, the so-called 'central route', was also important enough to be marked as far south as Mizda (Fig. 3:2, no. 7). No less than 21 milestones are known, the majority of Caracalla, but including examples of Maximinus, Gordian and Gallienus (AD 262). At Mizda this route was joined by another from the northwest (Fig. 3:2, no. 8). The 'upper Sofeggin road' branched from the *limes* road at *Thenteos* (Zintan) and seems to have terminated at Mizda. This route was undoubtedly of military importance and it is likely that both the major road junctions, Zintan and Mizda, were the sites of Roman forts. The 'central route' continued south of Mizda as an unmarked piste to the fort at Gheriat and beyond towards the land of the *Garamantes*.[39]

The official roads were thus of different types. On the one hand there were the military roads linking forts and fortifications, on the other the civil routes linking towns with each other and with their territories. In some cases roads started as military highways but developed into essential civilian lines of communication. The first improvements to the coastal road in the reign of Augustus had a military context but that was doubtless quickly superseded by increased civil usage. Finally, the total number of official roads in Tripolitania was very small in comparison to the geographical area covered. But it would be wrong to think of land communication as being limited to this skeleton. Beyond the routes described above there was an extensive network of minor routes and trackways, structurally little different to the 'Roman roads', criss-crossing the rural landscape and linking it to the urban centres, to the Roman frontier and to the major trans-Saharan desert trackways.[40]

4

THE ARMY AND FRONTIER DEVELOPMENT

1
TERRITORIAL OR HEGEMONIC CONTROL?

Discussion of the frontier situations in Roman Tripolitania is constrained by the unequal and inadequate amounts of information available. With a few exceptions the surviving military epigraphy of the region is concentrated within the third century AD. This seems to have been the period of maximum frontier development, though, as we shall see, the earlier and later phases of activity may be grossly underrepresented in the extant material. The incompleteness of the evidence necessitates some reliance being placed on attested Roman practices elsewhere in Africa, or more generally on the frontiers of the empire, in order to reconstruct a picture of Tripolitanian development. It would be inappropriate to dwell on wider issues of frontier strategy in a book of this type, but it must be made clear at the outset that I believe that a useful basis for comparison does exist between frontier practices and deployments in different parts of the Roman world.

There is a basic distinction, however, between the frontier region in Tripolitania and those of much of the rest of North Africa (Fig. 4:1). Numidia was partly bordered by pre-desert land but many of the garrison posts were located in better watered areas. In the Mauretanian provinces the frontier lines were drawn well to the north of the true desert and were more concerned with control of mountains and high plains. Only in Tripolitania was there an unbroken desert frontier zone. The primacy of desert frontiers over other types of natural demarcation line helps to explain the remarkable economy of force achieved in defending the region (the mountains of the Moroccan Atlas demanded the heaviest concentration of forts, Fig. 4:1).[1]

The expansion of Rome into the Maghreb was not achieved solely by warfare and of the wars which were fought not all were for territorial control. At all stages of the conquest and subsequent occupation, Rome sought to impose her hegemonic control on people dwelling beyond the formal (or informal) limits of the provinces. Before the creation of true frontiers, from the late first century AD onwards, the peace of the region was protected by the effectiveness of a comparatively mobile army and its ability to impose authority (preferably through mechanisms of power other than force) on potential resistance both in territory which Rome perceived as occupied and in the far wider zone of hegemonic control. Overall, the numbers of troops based on the African frontiers were very low (approx. 30,000–40,000 according to most estimates) and the history of the region under Rome was comparatively peaceful. In the core economic territories the *pax Romana* heralded booming prosperity for some. This achievement is rendered more comprehensible when we identify the diplomatic weapons of suasion, coercion and conciliation used by Rome to back up her military organizational superiority. Even when formal frontiers were created, delineating and separating more rigidly lands inside from those outside the empire, the security of the provinces continued to rest to a large extent on hegemonic relationships with peoples living outside. This control took various forms including treaties, in some cases

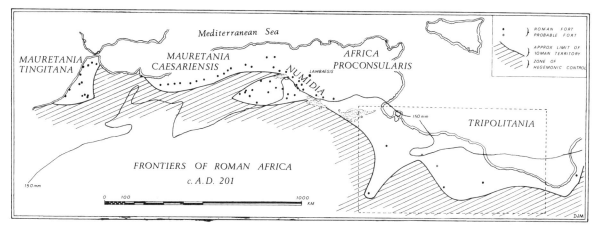

Fig. 4:1 The frontiers of Roman Africa at their maximum extent *c.* AD 201. Note the postulated hegemonic zone in advance of the territorial frontier and the line of the 150 mm rainfall isohyet in relation to the military posts.

tribute levy, in others direct subsidy of tribal groups or leaders, interference in tribal affairs, support for pro-Roman factions, economic regulation and so forth.

The Roman frontier did not separate pacified and sedentarized people from implacably hostile nomadic tribes. Rather, Rome's aim was to achieve territorial security through long-range hegemony. This 'strategy' was by and large intuitive, but it explains many of the similarities between Roman frontiers even in areas where divergent physical conditions necessitated rather different tactical deployments.[2]

The form of the frontier deployment in Tripolitania, then, was conditioned not simply by strategic considerations but by the tactical situations created by regional geography and tribal society. Rome was confronted in Tripolitania by several large confederations or regional groupings of tribes: *Garamantes, Nasamones, Macae* and *Gaetuli.* The *Garamantes* were probably the strongest of these super-tribes and were ruled by a king with centralized authority. In the early principate it is likely that they also maintained a hegemony over some of their northern neighbours, including some of the *Gaetuli* and *Macae.* Confederation seems to have been much weaker or more localized amongst these two groups as one can discern from the relative independence of some of their tribal sub-groups (*Phazanii, Nybgenii, Cinithi* and *Cinyphi).*

These tribes utilized two distinct types of tribal centre, hillforts and oases. An analysis of potential population densities suggests that the oasis centres posed the greater threat to Roman security, though hillforts were perhaps a source of policing problems. The existence of major population centres in the Nefzaoua, at Ghadames, in the Giofra and Fezzan oases and further east at *Augila* required the implementation of control measures both military and diplomatic. The nature of these societies and their close associations with the more settled and sedentary areas required that no matter where a frontier line was established, political and military control had to extend well beyond it. The early history of wars and revolts indicates the establishment and maintenance of a Roman hegemony in the region. Incidents involving the *Garamantes*, the various *Gaetuli* groupings, the *Nasamones* and *Macae* attest the high level of military activity in the region. But comparatively little new territory was actually annexed under Augustus; the more important aim would seem to have been the dismantling of the Garamantian alliance and the creation of tribal allies (*pacati* and *foederati*) from Syrtica, to Fezzan, to Nefzaoua.[3]

The social, political and economic development of those tribes and lands which were eventually annexed by Rome depended on this initial act of pacification. Agricultural expansion was carried out by Libyans and Libyphoenicians but it seems to coincide remarkably well with Rome's final achievement of hegemonic dominance over the desert tribes (see below, chapter 7).

2
WARFARE AND REVOLTS

The evidence relating to Roman campaigning in Tripolitania varies in quality and quantity. There are some battles or wars about which we are entirely ignorant. The style of warfare involved, as far as one can tell, mainly desert campaigning or combating guerrilla tactics. There were few pitched battles, but perhaps more frequently cavalry skirmishes and sieges. In the early centuries AD Rome lost occasional battles, but never a war. Later this seems to have been not quite so certain.[4]

Probably the first and certainly the most famous of Rome's hegemonic campaigns in Tripolitania was that of L. Cornelius Balbus in 20 BC. Balbus celebrated a triumph in Rome on 27 March 19 BC so it is probable that his military activity took place during the preceding year. The detail of his exploits provided by Pliny has fuelled many hypotheses but there is still little scholarly agreement. It is certain, however, that Balbus himself led a campaign against the *Phazanii* and the *Garamantes*. He captured the Phazanian centres of *Cidamus* (Ghadames), *Alele* and *Cilliba* before crossing a stretch of desert (the edge of the Hamada el Hamra?) into Garamantian lands. There he took the *oppida* of *Debris* (Edri?) – notable for its hot springs – *Thelgae* and the capital *Garama* (Germa/Zinchecra).

So much is clear from the first part of Pliny's account. But, using another source, he then listed in detail the places and tribes which Balbus claimed (on plaques carried in his triumphal procession) to have captured. Some further sites can be credibly located in Tripolitania and Fezzan but others almost certainly relate to the Wadi Djedi area of Algeria. Desanges was the first to elaborate the hypothesis of a further campaign or campaigns further west. The campaign in Tripolitania alone (probably starting at *Sabratha* and ending at *Lepcis*) is estimated by Daniels to have lasted at least three months. This makes no allowance for a period of preparation or for mopping-up operations and therefore it seems likely that the subsidiary action to the Wadi Djedi area was delegated by Balbus to his lieutenants. In any case it is implausible that Balbus would have attempted to take all the forces at his disposal on campaign. The logistics of desert campaigning require a small and fairly mobile force so it is unlikely that he took more than a few thousand men to Fezzan. This would have left ample in reserve in case of disaster or for use in other sectors. It is doubtful that the *Garamantes* had much stomach for pitched battles and the mere fact that Balbus had successfully penetrated their desert shield may well have demoralized them and fragmented resistance.

From the start Balbus' mission cannot have been aiming at territorial conquest but, by enforcing Rome's authority, imposing treaties and demonstrating Rome's offensive capabilities, Balbus established hegemonic dominance. The *Garamantes* were clearly considered as part of Rome's *imperium* thereafter. The subsidiary action(s) further west implies a concerted effort by Rome to extend or exert her hegemonic control over other tribes of the desert fringes. It is inappropriate, however, to credit Balbus with a desire to open up the supposed trans-Saharan trade routes. Nor is there any reason to follow Lhote and extend the scope of the campaign south of Fezzan.[5]

During the so-called Gaetulian war (*c*. 3 BC – AD 6), Tripolitania was again the scene of serious fighting. The causes of this revolt were perhaps largely linked to the exercise of hegemonic control. The tribes involved probably included *Gaetuli*, *Nasamones* and *Garamantes*. Dio mentioned some Roman defeats and the situation was serious enough for Augustus to intervene in the appointment of a general for the normally senate-controlled province. Two governors earned the *ornamenta triumphalia* in the fighting. Moreover, Desanges has suggested that a proconsul, L. Cornelius Lentulus, was actually murdered by the *Nasamones* at the height of the crisis. If the *Nasamones* were indeed involved, then the disruption of Roman hegemony spanned the entire zone between *Mauretania* and the borders of *Cyrenaica*. Two factors offer independent support for Desanges' theory. First, there is the inscription erected to Cossus Lentulus by the *civitas Lepcitana* recording that he had liberated the province from the war (*bello gaetulico liberata*). The presence of this unique inscription at *Lepcis* suggests that the region had been the scene of serious fighting and had something to be grateful for. The lands of *Lepcis* are much more vulnerable to attack by tribes from the south or east than from the west towards the Lesser Syrtes. The second point concerns the campaign of Quirinius against *Marmaridae* and *Garamantes* which is mentioned by Florus in connection with the Gaetulian war but which is not securely dated. If we see this incident as a Roman reprisal campaign against the desert tribes at some point between 3 BC–AD 5, we may suspect that the term *Marmaridae* was here used in reference to the *Nasamones* of *Augila*. There was a well established route from *Augila* to Fezzan which Quirinius presumably followed.[6]

In the aftermath of this revolt, the territory of some of the tribes closest to Rome was, at least in part, annexed. This seems to have been the punishment of *Musulames* and *Cinithi*. Some troops probably remained in the region to act as a deterrent and to see through the pacification. The road link between *Ammaedara* and the *Emporia* which was marked out in AD 14 implies that the region remained one of the major 'fronts' and it is possible that a vexillation of the Third Legion was based at or near one of the coastal towns in an as yet undiscovered camp. Resistance was by no means quelled as the Tacfarinan revolt was to show. For the *Cinithi* this was a territorial revolt but for most of the other Tripolitanian tribes it was another opportunity to reject Roman hegemonic authority. The *Garamantes*, for instance, were certainly involved. When the *Legio IX Hispana* was sent to Africa as reinforcements it was posted to Tripolitania in order to prevent raiding by *Garamantes* and others against *Lepcis* (and her territory).

Little else is recorded about the fighting in Tripolitania; it seems to have devolved into raiding and guerrilla warfare and the most significant victories were eventually won elsewhere. Nevertheless, having ended the war in AD 24, Dolabella was honoured by two inscriptions from Tripolitania. Furthermore, after the death of Tacfarinas the *Garamantes* sent peace envoys to Tiberius and this presumably marks the resumption of Roman hegemony in the region. The seriousness of the fighting in Tripolitania is shown by the inscriptions set up in *Lepcis* 11 years later recording the paving of the streets of the town with revenue from the lands 'restored to *Lepcis*'. This suggests that in the early stages of the war parts of the town's *territorium* had been overrun.[7]

The causes of the revolts were plainly more complex than a simple question of resistance to Roman expansionism or a rejection of her hegemonic rule. The *Cinithi,* like the *Musulames,* had rebelled some years after part of their lands had been annexed. They were evidently joined by many of the other Tripolitanian tribes from the zone of hegemonic control in following the leadership of Tacfarinas. There must have been other contributory factors to account for the more widespread disaffection. One possibility is a change in the relationship between pastoral and sedentary groups caused by the expansion of the *territoria* of the Libyphoenician *Emporia* well into the Gebel, which must have been encouraged, or at least condoned, by Rome and which would have affected the traditional land and pasture rights of many tribes. The recent discovery of Flavian boundary stones has solved the enigma of the road built by Aelius Lamia (AD 15–17) *in mediterraneum m.p. XLIV.* The forty-fourth mile from *Lepcis* is coincident with the southwestern limit of the *territorium* of *Lepcis* where it met that of *Oea* (see above, Fig. 3:2). By this date at the latest, then, the *Emporia* were exploiting enormous areas of the Gebel for agriculture and arboriculture and these lands were recognized by Rome. Some of the Libyan elite participated in the new opportunities and wealth. The *Ammonium* of Ras el-Haddagia (near Tarhuna) was dedicated during Lamia's proconsulship by 'NKSF (or TKSF) son of Shasidwasan (or Shasidwasat) son of Namrar (or Tamrar) of the sons of Masinkaw'. Although the inscription was in neo-Punic the names are those of a man of thoroughly Libyan descent. But not all the Libyans could expect to share in the advantages of development. The Arab historian Abd el-Hakam stated that the Libyan peas-

antry were exploited by the Roman (that is Romano-Libyan) seigneurial class and other evidence suggests that slave-run estates were not uncommon in the region. It is possible, therefore, that the lands overrun during the Tacfarinan war and later restored to *Lepcis* may have been an important underlying cause of tribal discontent in Tripolitania. In AD 17 the emergence of a suitable and charismatic leader in Tacfarinas was the catalyst which triggered the latent tribal resistance in a confederation of enormous size.[8]

A critical aspect of the Augustan wars was clearly the exercise of Roman hegemony, which at this stage was probably concentrated on the problem of dismantling the traditional alliances and dominance exercised by the major oasis-based tribes, such as the *Garamantes.* In spite of the campaigns of Balbus and Quirinius, the *Garamantes* had evidently continued to flout Roman authority when it suited them, as Tacitus and Pliny made clear. A longer term solution to the problems of hegemonic control was not achieved until Flavian times.

In AD 69, when *Lepcis* and *Oea* quarrelled over land ownership in the Gebel and then turned to war, *Oea,* as the weaker side, called in the *Garamantes.* Because of the uncertainties of the disputed succession to the imperial throne at this time, the Roman response was slow and *Lepcis* was besieged for several days before the arrival of *alae* and *cohortes* (in advance of Valerius Festus and the Third Legion) put the enemy to flight. Festus subsequently set out on a raid against the Garamantian heartlands using a faster route than previously known (probably the so-called central road via Mizda and Gheriat). This was clearly a reprisal attack, designed to prove once again the Roman ability to pierce the desert shield of the *Garamantes* and to inflict 'unacceptable levels of damage' as punishment.[9] However, Festus may also have been motivated by a desire to impress his new master, Vespasian.

The power of the *Garamantes* seems to have been largely destroyed as a result of this campaign. Their northern influence, which had put them in a position to interfere in the affairs of the coastal cities, was broken for ever. At least one further military campaign to Fezzan is known about but the ultimate objectives lay further south towards Sudan, which implies that the *Garamantes* were no longer the threat they had once been. The date of this campaign is uncertain depending on whether or not one identifies the Roman general involved with the known legate Suellius Flaccus (see further below). Ptolemy, quoting Marinus of Tyre, stated that one Septimius Flaccus took 30 days to reach *Garama* with his army and then marched south to the land of the Ethiopians. A few years later he was followed on this route by a certain Julius Maternus who set out from *Lepcis* and reached *Garama* in only 20 days. He then proceeded south in the company of the Garamantian king on a journey of four months to the land of *Agisymba* 'where the rhinoceros is to be found'. The circumstances of this second expedition have led some commentators to conclude the Maternus was not on a military campaign. There is no mention of an army with him, nor is his name known in the provincial *fasti*. In all probability Maternus was a *negotiator* and the mention of the rhinoceros may give a clue as to his mission. Desanges has suggested a connection between Maternus' expedition and the first appearance of a *rhinoceros bicornis* in the arena at Rome and on Domitian's coinage *c*. AD 92.

At all events the expeditions of Festus, Flaccus and Maternus mark a definite turning point in Roman relations with the *Garamantes*. There are no further outbreaks of war attested in Tripolitania until the early third century, though the subsequent Severan troop deployments suggest that the *Garamantes* may have been involved in that disturbance. The military activity of Festus and Flaccus heralded a period of peaceful collaboration and cooperation and made possible the mission of the civilian Maternus to the deep south.

The exact date of Flaccus' campaign is a complicated issue, bound up with the scant evidence concerning the Nasamonian revolt of AD 85–6. The *Nasamones* were in the unique and possibly unfortunate position of having territory not only in *Africa* but also in *Cyrenaica* and well to the south in the desert oases of the zone of hegemonic control (notably *Augila*). Normal levels of tribal resistance were thus compounded by the fact that the tribe was divided between three Roman administrative categories. The revolt was sparked off by the activities of Roman tax collectors, who were presumably operating along the Syrtic coast which had probably already been 'provincialized' to create the road link to *Cyrenaica*. The *Nasamones* of the coastal region were notorious pirates and the activity of the tax collectors may have been simply part of a policy aimed at tightening controls over them. Delimitation of lands to provide a basis for the tax assessment was another potentially provocative issue which may have been at stake. For whatever reason, the tax collectors were murdered and the revolt spread throughout the Nasamonian confederation, possibly involving other tribes as well. When the legate Suellius Flaccus arrived to quell the rebellion, probably in AD 86, he was surprisingly defeated in a pitched battle. The *Nasamones* failed to follow up their victory, instead looting the Roman camp. There they found a quantity of food and wine and celebrated their success until Flaccus returned with his

regrouped army and massacred the inebriated tribesmen. He clearly went on to exact further gruesome reprisals as Domitian was to claim that he had annihilated the tribe (though that was an exaggeration). In the aftermath of the revolt Flaccus was active in neighbouring *Macae* territory delimiting sub-tribal lands and this strengthens the suspicion that the revolt had not been simply over the question of tax or tribute payments but concerned a more far-reaching process of incorporation and provincialization.

As we have noted above, a campaign was made against the *Garamantes* at about this time by a man referred to by Ptolemy as Septimius Flaccus and it has been speculated that the two Flacci were in fact one and same man. Had there been any Garamantian support for the Nasamonian revolt this would obviously have demanded a firm response. Alternatively Flaccus may simply have wished to reaffirm Roman hegemonic control over the *Garamantes* and to round up any Nasamonian fugitives who would have been potential trouble-makers. Flaccus had to make some deviations on his journey south from *Lepcis* but there is no reference to fighting in Fezzan itself. Since he proceeded south of *Garama* for a considerable distance it is clear that the *Garamantes* had been eager to confirm their treaty and were not considered likely to turn hostile when he extended his lines of communication and retreat. In the sequel to this a few years later, Maternus actually joined the Garamantian king who was going on an expedition against his Ethiopian subjects and thus enjoyed Garamantian protection. If Suellius and Septimius are accepted as the same person then the following outline chronology can be proposed:

AD 69	*Garamantes* join *Oea* against *Lepcis*. Defeated by Roman advance guard.
AD 70	Campaign of Valerius Festus to Fezzan. Major defeat inflicted on *Garamantes* and new treaty terms imposed.
c. AD 85–6	Revolt of the *Nasamones*. Suellius Flaccus active in *Syrtica* and Tripolitania.
AD 87	Delimitation of lands of Syrtic tribes and campaign of Suellius Flaccus to Fezzan and beyond.
AD 88–92	Expedition of Maternus.

The alternative interpretation that Suellius and Septimius were separate legates of the Third Legion still merits close attention. The campaign of Septimius

Flaccus would then have to be fitted in to the chronology either before the Nasamonian revolt or into the same short date bracket as that of Maternus (AD 88–92). One minor detail which perhaps favours the separate identification is the origin of the name of the Lepcitanian Septimii who acquired citizenship in the late first century AD. The presence in *Lepcis* at about the right time of a military governor with this name is an attractive possibility. The question remains open, though, in the absence of independent evidence, it is perhaps slightly more logical to assume that Ptolemy or a later copyist confused the name and that the Nasamonian and Garamantian campaigns of Flaccus followed on from each other and were conducted by the same man.[10]

During these wars of the first century AD Rome had eventually succeeded in smashing the power of two of the most powerful tribal confederations. Garamantian hegemony which had once extended well to the north of Fezzan was henceforth limited to her heartlands alone and tribes like the *Phazanii* were now separately bound to Rome as hegemonic allies.

Although our knowledge of warfare and revolts in the first century is limited to these few incidents, there is some evidence that troops were also active in the Djerid and Nefzaoua during the Flavian period. These oases are in a key strategic position and Roman control of them seems to have extended to military occupation. If there was armed resistance, as is likely, we know nothing of it.[11]

There are no records of revolts or wars in Tripolitania in the second century AD, but it would be unwise to assume that no troops were needed or deployed there. Evidence is presented below to demonstrate the existence of a diplomatic policy, the presence of a military garrison and deterrent measures in the pre-Severan period. Manoeuvres and patrolling-in-force to tribal centres well beyond provincial territory can be postulated even though detailed evidence is lacking.

There was certainly renewed trouble in the early part of Septimius Severus' reign. Late Roman sources reveal that warlike people threatened the security of the region; unfortunately the precise identity of the aggressors is nowhere attested. The breakdown of Roman diplomatic control of the tribes can perhaps be attributed to the uncertainties aroused by the civil wars in the AD 190s. The date span of the campaigns is unknown but they seem to have been in progress when the fort at Bu Njem was established in AD 201 and may have continued to 205. It has been suggested that Severus himself took part in campaigns early in 203, when an inscription records both his imminent return to *Lepcis* (from active campaigning?) and his

victory. These protracted military operations saw a necessary overhaul of Roman diplomatic control but also the strengthening and forward movement of the garrison (see below).

Information for the rest of the third century is equally imprecise and problematic. Damage done to the fort at Gheriat during a war (*bellum*) was repaired under Gordian III, but there are no other clues as to the nature or severity of the trouble. The construction of Gasr Duib in AD 244–6 was specifically to watch one of the routes used by barbarian raiders (... *viam incursib(us) barba[ro]rum constituto novo centenario ... prae[cl]useru[nt]*). The *centenarium* at Gasr Duib is obviously too small an outpost to have dealt with any major incursions and its function should be seen as essentially one of policing rather than to act as a blockhouse.

An archive of day records, reports and letters discovered at Bu Njem demonstrates that this fort was a relatively quiet garrison post in the mid-third century. Typical incidents recorded were the appearance of small groups of *Garamantes* with donkey and mule trains, in one case accompanying a runaway slave, and the arrival or recruitment of tribal spies and informers, and they provide a vivid picture of the generally humdrum life and work of the garrison. The surviving information seems to detail only peaceful policing work and there are no clearcut indications of heightened tensions nor that the garrison felt threatened by hostile tribes. The abandonment of the fort took place c. AD 259–63 (the latter year being when a new fort was established at Ras el-Ain) and was evidently a peaceful withdrawal. The *vicus* continued to be occupied into the fourth century.[12]

3

DIPLOMACY, TRIBAL CONTROL AND TRIBAL DEVELOPMENT IN TRIPOLITANIA

In the preceding section we have seen that the evidence from Tripolitania suggests that it was one of the key battlegrounds during the establishment of Roman hegemonic and territorial control in Africa during the first century AD. In later chapters we shall see that it was also one of the first areas where those controls started to break down in the fourth century AD. The history of Roman diplomacy, suasion and tribal relations is complementary to this picture. The policy behind the long-range desert campaigns of Balbus, Festus and others was not simply to inflict maximum damage and then withdraw. Military action was always followed by the imposition of treaties and diplomatic controls. These were maintained by the exchange of envoys, by military deterrence and on occasion by direct interference. The evidence is sparse, but it is consistent in showing the importance of the hegemonic control or direct supervision of peoples overcome in battle.

The *Garamantes* provide a good case study. As a consequence of the tribe's success in establishing its own political dominance over its northern neighbours it became necessary for Rome to extend her political control to their remote heartlands in Fezzan. One purpose of Balbus' campaign of 20 BC seems to have been to detach the *Phazanii* from Garamantian control. Pliny treated them as distinct tribal groups and this is typical of Rome's policy of divide and rule. The *Garamantes* continued to resist Roman suzerainty and were prominent in several revolts against it under Augustus and Tiberius. But when the Tacfarinan war ended in AD 24 they anticipated Roman action against them by sending envoys to Tiberius. The lessons of the campaigns of Balbus and Quirinius had clearly been learnt. At this stage treaty relations were probably of a simple nature, involving only the recognition of Roman supremacy and a promise not to attack her territory or that of her other allied tribes. There is precious little evidence for the existence of trans-Saharan trade on a large scale in the early Principate and Rome's motivation is best interpreted as hegemonic.

The campaign of Festus in AD 70 marked a turning point in relations between Rome and the tribe. From this period can be dated the start of the mass importation of fine wares from the Mediterranean to Fezzan. Later Roman expeditions proceeded south of *Garama*, indicating that the *Garamantes* themselves were considered pacified and friendly. It is tempting to speculate about how this transformation of a tribe previously described as warlike and ungovernable was achieved. The installation of a pro-Roman king and the encouragement of the elite by gifts and aid are reasonable possibilities. Excavations by Caputo, Ayoub and Daniels in Fezzan have recovered vast quantities of luxury goods (fine wares and glass) and *amphorae* from late first- and second-century burials. Buildings with ashlar footings on the southern side of Zinchecra and under Germa also date from this period and attest the presence of skilled masons at the Garamantian capital (see above, Fig. 2:13). The 'Punico-Roman' mausoleum at Gasr Uatuat near Germa is now paralleled by at least four other exam-

Fig. 4:2 Gasr Uatuat, a Roman-influenced mausoleum from the Garamantian heartlands near Germa, Fezzan (from Barth 1857).

ples providing further evidence for Roman influence and artisans in the region (Fig. 4:2).

However, there is no evidence that a Roman garrison was ever installed in Fezzan, so it seems likely that the presence of skilled stonemasons at this early date is accountable as part of a package of technical aid provided by Rome. The quantity of pottery and fine glassware reaching Fezzan is difficult to explain in terms of trade alone and some of these prestige goods may have been sent as part of a policy of lavishing gifts on pro-Roman elements of the tribal elite.

The expedition of Flaccus may have been made to reaffirm these far-reaching arrangements, perhaps even to support the king against an anti-Roman faction which had grown up because of the Nasamonian revolt. The southward campaign of Flaccus suggests that he was primarily concerned with extending Rome's hegemonic influence in that direction. A few years later Maternus accompanied the Garamantian king on this route, which was under his authority, and this implies that the tribe may have been entitled to act as middlemen for Rome in this particular sector of her Saharan hegemony.

It is not entirely certain whether the *Garamantes* were involved in the early third-century disturbances, though the positioning of the forts at Bu Njem, Gheriat and Ghadames suggests that they were. But apart from this occasion the relationship between Rome and the tribe appears to have been generally peaceful and cooperative (if mutually suspicious) from the late first century onwards. Roman diplomacy and supervision still continued to operate in Fezzan in the later third century. Ostraca from Bu

Njem refer to the dispatch of a soldier *cum Garamantibus* (perhaps to *Garama* itself or accompanying a group northwards?). Other *Garamantes* passed along the desert tracks, presenting 'letters of passage' at Roman outposts; one group was carrying a consignment of barley on a small caravan of donkeys and mules, another group was accompanied by two Egyptians and a runaway slave. The possibility that individual soldiers were posted to Fezzan in some sort of supervisory role receives some support from a graffito cut on a rock on top of the hillfort of Zinchecra by a man called Aurelius. The point to note is that there are indications of detailed surveillance and even supervision well in advance of the Roman frontier. Roman luxury goods were still present in graves of fourth- and fifth-century date, though in general these later graves are poorer than those of the earlier periods. Nonetheless, even as late as the sixth century AD the *Garamantes* made a treaty with the Byzantine rulers of coastal *Tripolitana*.[13]

Unlike the *Garamantes*, the *Phazanii* did not remain forever outside the frontier, with their main population centre at Ghadames (*Cidamus*) receiving a Roman garrison in the third century AD. However, prior to that their treatment by Rome strongly resembles that of the *Garamantes*. There are a number of indications that there were close links with Rome in the first and second centuries; large quantities of second-century Roman fine wares have been noted in the Ghadames oasis (across an area of about 1.5 sq. km) and the ancient necropolis west of the oasis (over 2 km in length) contains the famous 'asnam' (idols), which have been identified as tombs of Romano-Libyan type. Continuous and continuing occupation of the oasis has obscured most of the evidence but, as at Germa, fine pottery and ashlar masonry in a native context outside the territorial limits of the empire suggest the existence of treaty relationships. Rebuffat supports the idea that Ghadames was a Roman protectorate by reference to additional finds of second-century fine wares associated with native style fortifications at minor oases between Ghadames and Nalut.

In the second century Rome supervised her hegemony over the *Phazanii* from the Gebel and Dahar. The establishment of one fort at Remada (*Tillibari*) and the possible construction of another at Zintan (*Thenteos*) at the probable northern extent of their territory suggests that a visible and close deterrent was considered necessary. The later establishment of a Roman garrison at Ghadames itself implies that some sub-tribal groups may have been involved in the disturbances of the early third century. In AD 244–6 the construction of the *centenarium* at Gasr Duib was specifically to watch over one of the approaches

from *Phazania* towards the Gebel because of raiding parties. Almost certainly by this date the Ghadames garrison had been withdrawn and the *Phazanii* had returned to the status of hegemonic allies whose loyalty was sometimes doubtful. On balance, though, the *Phazanii* like the *Garamantes* seem to have been relatively stable and long-term allies. Procopius recorded that the people of *Cidamus* had been allies of Rome from ancient times and their treaty was renewed under Justinian.[14]

The division of the *Nasamones* tribes between three territorial units (two provinces and the zone of hegemonic control) has already been mentioned. The different treatment of the various sub-tribes that this demanded may in part explain the Nasamonian revolt. The regions closest to the Syrtic shore in both *Cyrenaica* and *Africa* were probably incorporated within the provinces at an early date and it is likely that by the Flavian period the tribes were being increasingly regularized and perhaps their territory delimited for tax purposes. But movement between the coast and the interior oases was common and any attempt to control tribal movements or land and grazing rights was liable to be resisted. Roman diplomatic control was exerted over the oases as Quirinius' campaign and Mela's account of the *Augilae* show. The failure of territorial control and diplomatic coercion in AD 85 has already been described. Defeat for the tribe must have been followed by reprisal campaigns against the oases and the imposition of harsh terms on the survivors. But, in spite of the catastrophe, the *Nasamones* did survive and gradually recovered. *Augila* was recorded in Byzantine times as a populous and important centre. These desert-dwelling *Nasamones* were no doubt bound to Rome as allies (*pacati*) but a lapse in Roman authority in the third century may have allowed the infiltration of the tribes from further east. Justinian imposed a treaty on the oasis once more in the sixth century.[15]

To the south and west of the Greater Syrtes were the *Macae* tribe. Their proximity to the Libyphoenician *Emporia* accounts for the early absorption and social development of some of the sub-tribes; the *Cinyphi* for instance, were assimilated by *Lepcis*. Some of the Libyans in the Gebel and the Sofeggin and Zem-Zem basins also adopted elements of a Punico-Roman culture. Other elements of the *Macae* remained truer to their traditional lifestyle as the study of hillforts reveals and as do the Libyan graffiti at Bu Njem. Rome reacted to these different groups in various ways. The presence of *terra sigillata* and early ARS on the hillfort sites demonstrates friendly contact between those groups and the Roman authorities. In at least one case, though, there is reason to suspect direct military supervision of a hillfort by a Roman military post (see below, chapter 5, Gasr Isawi).

The rapid agricultural development of Gebel and pre-desert must have received Roman approval and perhaps supervision. The delimitation of the lands of the main towns was an essential first step and this seems to have been done as early as AD 17 in the case of *Lepcis* at least (Fig. 4:3). The lands of *Lepcis* and *Oea* were resurveyed by Rutilius Gallicus after the war of 69–70. On the Syrtic coast the association between the *Seli* tribe and the towns of *Marcomades* and *Digdiga* suggests that these may have been designated *civitas* centres. The *Seli* were evidently sub-groups of both the *Macae* and the *Nasamones* tribes so the existence of two *civitates* need not surprise us. There is further evidence for the delimitation of tribal lands near *Marcomades* (Sirte). A boundary stone was erected in AD 87 between the *Mudicivvi* and *Zamuci* sub-tribes after a conference and it is unlikely to have been an isolated act. One can infer that there was a more widespread policy of tribal delimitation and political

development in the late first and early second century (see further below). Most of *Macae* territory seems to have come within the province between the late first and late second centuries, well before the establishment of forts at Bu Njem and Gheriat in AD 201.

Another aspect of Roman diplomacy is illustrated by one of the *Macae* sub-tribes. The *Cissipades* were recruited to form a cohort which served in *Moesia* in the late first century. Although this is a unique Tripolitanian example, the levying of recruits from some of the other pacified tribes is a possibility.[16]

The Gaetulian tribes of the western Gebel, the Gefara and the Nefzaoua who were also absorbed into the territorial empire show a similar pattern of development to the *Macae*. Assimilation by the *Libyphoenices* continued though now to the established Roman formula. The *Cinithi* were placed under the supervision of a *praefectus gentis* and *Gigthis* was almost certainly made their *civitas* capital. Their territory was defined from that of *Tacapae* and, though the earliest evidence for the delimitation is two milestones of

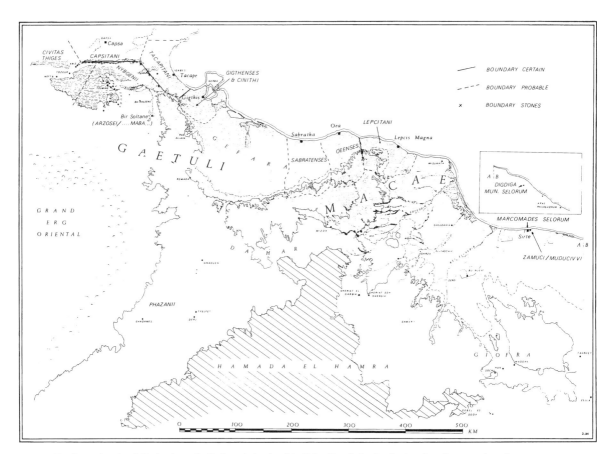

Fig. 4:3 Evidence for the delimitation of tribal and city land in Tripolitania in the first and early second century AD.

Caracalla, it probably took place along with that of the *Nybgenii* under Trajan. The early history of the *Cinithi* had been one of resistance and revolt but in the long term Rome's policy of closely supervised development transformed them into a peaceful and prosperous community based on an urban centre.[17]

An even clearer example of the metamorphosis from 'unruly' tribe to self-governing *civitas* is provided by the *Nybgenii*. The strategic position of the Nefzaoua oases between Numidia and Tripolitania makes their neutrality in the Gaetulian and Tacfarinan revolts improbable and Roman campaigns to the area are likely to have started early. In AD 29–30 Vibius Marsus surveyed part of *Nybgenii* territory, presumably as a basis for tribute assessment in the aftermath of the Tacfarinan revolt. The establishment of first hegemony and then territorial control over the oases of Nefzaoua and Djerid were vital (and underestimated) stages in Roman pacification of Numidia and Tripolitania. Garrisons were probably established on both sides of the Chott Djerid under the Flavians. By AD 83–4 a native *civitas* was organized at *Thiges* (Gourbata?). The first reference to the *civitas Nybgeniorum* is under Trajan in AD 105, and its lands were delimited from those of *Tacapae* and *Capsa* at about the same time (Fig 4:3). Trousset's excellent study of the Trajanic delimitation has shown that it utilized the framework provided by the survey of Vibius Marsus from 75 years earlier.

In another way the timing of the Trajanic delimitation was important since it may have marked the demilitarization of the area and the forward movement of the garrison. A boundary stone was erected between two tribes at Bir Soltane at this same time, suggesting that the territorial frontier then lay well to the south of the Nefzaoua in the Dahar (Fig 4:3). The pacification and social development of the *Nybgenii* continued behind this evolving frontier. Although we lack precise evidence about their passage from conquered tribe to urban-based *civitas*, it is clear that the *Nybgenii* fit into a general framework for successful development. The seal of success in this case was the elevation of the *civitas* capital to the rank of *municipium* under Hadrian.[18]

In these few brief examples I have tried to show how Rome pursued a relatively consistent policy, on the one hand towards tribes outside the territories she annexed and, on the other, towards tribes which fell within her territorial empire. In both cases an initial display of force and brutality was often followed up with policies effecting conciliation and development, and whose main advantages were aimed at the existing tribal elites.

4
THE FRONTIER AND ITS GARRISON

The Tripolitanian frontier developed to meet the needs of hegemonic and territorial control. Its form was further affected by the geography and by the nature of tribal society in the region. But its development can be best understood in relation to an overall Roman frontier strategy. Septimius Severus has sometimes been credited as the creator of the first frontier in the region. However, this interpretation is based on an argument from silence because of the dearth of hard evidence and it contradicts what is understood of Roman frontier strategy elsewhere in the second century. Furthermore, the existence of an open frontier without any garrison until the third century seems inconceivable in the light of what we have established in the previous sections. In short, although one must accept that the archaeological evidence is not good enough to allow definite conclusions to be drawn about the frontier development, nevertheless there are abundant hints about a pre-Severan garrison even in the available evidence (Fig. 4:4).

Early studies of the *limes Tripolitanus* placed a great deal of emphasis on the linear aspect of the *limes* road from *Tacape* to *Lepcis*. However, the early frontiers in Roman Africa were not horizontally linear but based on lines of advance into tribal territory. These '*limites de pénétration*' were well suited to the geographical and political situation in Tripolitania, where the most important consideration was control of the access routes to the major tribal centres in the oases. Roman desert frontiers rarely achieved a true linear deployment because of the comparative facility of control based on the supervision of key routes and water resources. The development of such controls was achieved by the progressive advance of garrison positions in what can be termed a 'rolling frontier'. In western Tripolitania, for instance, the pacification of the *Nybgenii* almost certainly involved the placement of a garrison in one of the oases of the Nefzaoua. When the native *civitas* was organized under Trajan it is likely that the garrison was reduced in size or more likely advanced down the Dahar. Euzennat and Trousset have convincingly argued that the original fort at Remada (*Tillibari*) was a Hadrianic foundation. It is possible that there is another early second century fort, as yet unrecognized, marking an intermediate advance between Nefzaoua and Gebel Demmer. The boundary stone from Bir Soltane, for instance,

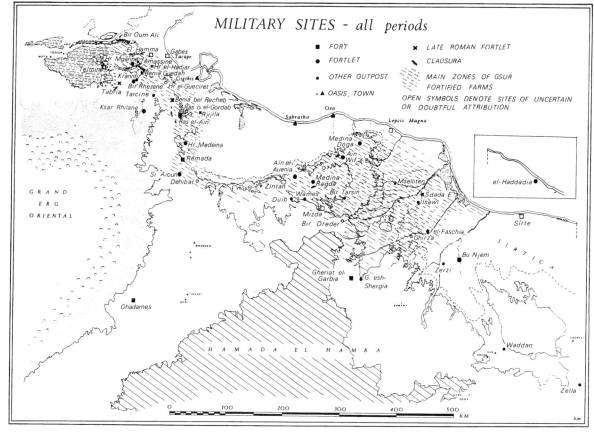

Fig. 4:4 Military sites of all periods in Tripolitania.

shows that the Dahar was 'provincialized' as far south as the Wadi Hallouf under Trajan. The fortlets established by Commodus at *Bezereos* and *Tisavar* in the late second century can be seen not as remote outposts but as part of a policy for policing in greater detail an area already controlled. Under Severus further fortlets and road stations were established down the Dahar corridor and a new fort established in Phazanian territory at Ghadames.

The significance of the road from Tripoli–Mizda–Gheriat in Central Tripolitania has long been recognized. This was probably the route to Garamantian lands explored by Festus in AD 70 and a hypothetical developmental sequence can be proposed. Some pre-Severan military posts on the Gebel Garian are likely and recent observations of Ain Wif suggest that there was a fortlet there at some point during the second century (see below). The position of Mizda, at the junction of two Roman roads (marked by Caracallan milestones) and two caravan routes, implies the existence there of a major site. Barth recognized extensive ruins extending into the plain, but the site of the pre-

sumed fort probably lies under the western oasis. Northwest of Mizda, Medina Ragda, a possible fortlet near the Hadd Hajar *clausura*, has produced abundant late first- and second-century pottery. South of Mizda along the main route towards Fezzan lies a series of small buildings, one in ashlar masonry, associated with first- and second-century pottery. If these are military outposts (and they are certainly too small to be farms) then there is every reason to suspect that Mizda may have been their base fort and was pre-Severan in origin.

A similar case can also be made for the unexplored site of *Thenteos* at Edref near Zintan, undoubtedly the site of a major fort in the third century AD, but on strategic grounds perhaps likely to have originated during an earlier phase of the frontier development.

Finally, recent work at Gheriat el-Garbia has identified some possible pre-Severan activity at the oasis. Prior to the construction of the main fort *c.* AD 201 an L-shaped enclosure of military appearance was tacked on to one side of a native style promontory fort and is probably evidence of a temporary camp (below,

Fig. 6:10). It is also conceivable that the fortlet at Gheriat esh-Shergia was pre-Severan in origin.

Further east in the hinterland of *Lepcis* and the Greater Syrtes the frontier development is harder to trace. Some troops must have remained tied down in the area following the wars of AD 69–70 and 85–7. There is a known fortlet at *Tugulus* (Gasr el-Haddadia) near *Arae Philaenorum* but pottery from the site spans the period from the first century BC to the fourth century AD. The military phase could well be pre-Severan for want of any clearer historical context. In the Sofeggin and Zem-Zem basins several possible fortlets at important locations or wells have normally been assumed to be Severan for no better reason than that they are on the routes leading north from Bu Njem. On the basis of pottery scatters at several of these sites, however, their origins may lie in the second rather than the third century. In addition the *Tabula Peutingeriana* features several sites near the Greater Syrtes whose names may indicate pre-Severan military activity: *Praesidium*, *Praetorium* and *Praesidio*.

Whilst hard epigraphic proof is lacking, then, there are strong hints concerning pre-Severan antecedents for the frontier in Tripolitania. Septimius Severus must be credited with a major reorganization and strengthening of the defences of the region but it is clear that the basis for the deployment was already established on the major routes of penetration to *Phazania* and the Garamantian lands.[19]

A second element crucial to understanding the Tripolitanian frontier is the role played by the series of linear barriers (*clausurae*). A full discussion is reserved for the next chapter but some suggestions can be made here about what these short sections of linear barrier were and what they were not. They did not demarcate provincial lands from those of 'barbarians' nor could they function effectively as defences against raiders. But the location of these obstacles in major passes and across important routes shows that they were connected with the movement of people. Although they lie behind the theoretical line of the frontiers they can be related in part to tribal territories and it is a reasonable supposition that they were erected to regulate transhumance, seasonal labour and trading movements between the predominantly pastoral and predominantly sedentary zones. Policing of such movements was part of Roman strategy from the later first century to the early fifth and this brings us to the problem of dating the *clausurae*. In Algeria to the west, elements of the so-called *Fossatum Africae* (a similar, though more considerable, series of walls and earthworks) were started under Hadrian and it is reasonable to suppose that an early second-century date might be extendable to some of the *clausurae* also. But the construction, use and reconstruction may well have been spread over the next 300 years and it would be a mistake to assume that they were all part of a unitary scheme. Since I shall argue that some at least were constructed in the second century they provide an additional reason for identifying the origins of the frontier then.[20]

Frontier development and dated construction

The earliest deployments of troops were on an *ad hoc* basis, such as the four cohorts sent to *Lepcis* by Metellus in 109 BC or the army with Balbus in 20 BC. The evolution of the deterrent strategy under Augustus required a tactical rethink and in *Africa* (with a single legion only) this involved dividing the army up into mobile battle groups. The record of wars and revolts in Tripolitania demanded the presence of a regional force in the early years of the first century AD. The main base of the *legio III Augusta* in AD 14 was at *Ammaedara* (Haidra, on the Tuniso-Algerian border) but contrary to the normal assumption this fortress cannot have been a full-sized legionary base. As in other areas of territorial expansionism, the Julio-Claudian deployment probably involved splitting the army between a number of mobile battle groups in so-called vexillation fortresses of about half the normal legionary size. The practice of using such intermediate fortresses is particularly well illustrated in Claudian Britain. Topographical examination of the site of *Ammaedara* suggests that the fortress there cannot have been much above 10–12 ha (25–30 acres) in size, prompting the question of where the rest of the legion was stationed at this period.

One important clue is given by the fact that a road was marked out from there to Tripolitania in AD 14, perhaps indicating the existence for a few years at least of a 'vexillation' fortress somewhere in the region. Tacitus informs us that troops were certainly based near *Lepcis* during the Tacfarinan war. At this stage the empire was still expanding and we should not expect any frontier lines or frontier roads as such. Military occupation was probably limited to *Lepcis* and to one or two other key sites. Gabes (*Tacapae*) and el Hamma (*Aquae Tacapitanae*), for instance, control the Arad corridor between them and are in good positions for the intimidation of the Nefzaoua tribes. In AD 69–70 auxiliary units (*alae et cohortes*) arrived at *Lepcis Magna* ahead of the legion. They could perhaps have been based somewhere within western Tripolitania.

Under the Flavians, the legion was reunited in a single fortress at *Theveste* (Tebessa, Algeria) and the entire army became increasingly involved in policing duties, with frontiers being better defined than hitherto.

Some troops must have been left on station, even if only temporarily, after the Garamantian war of 69–70 and the Nasamonian revolt of 85–6. It is logical that the Nefzaoua and Djerid were garrisoned at the same time. They occupy a pivotal position between the tribes of southern Numidia and Tripolitania and earlier revolts had often spread across this entire zone. The construction of a *castellus Thiges* (*sic*) under Nerva was not the first act of the military garrison in this area as is sometimes supposed; in fact, it may well have been one of the last stages of the initial phase of pacification here.

The early years of the second century saw the completion of the pacification of the northern Dahar and the Nefzaoua and perhaps the construction of the first *clausurae* in the Cherb range. The fort at Remada (*Tillibari*) was established close to or on the northern boundary of Phazanian territory. It is certainly a pre-Severan foundation, as an epigraphic reference to repairs in AD 197 makes clear, and the style of its original gates suggests that it is also pre-Commodan. Tumuli on the fringe of the *vicus* have yielded coins of Antoninus and Faustina the Younger and others possibly earlier. Obviously such evidence cannot be pressed but a Hadrianic origin is attractive, particularly in view of structural similarities with the fort of *Gemellae* in Numidia founded in the 130s. The recognition of Remada as a pre-Severan cohort fort has the important effect of showing up the defective reasoning behind the assumption that Severus alone created the frontier (Table 4:1).[21]

I have already speculated on the grounds of strategic necessity that there may have been further early forts at Mizda and Zintan. Apart from the convergence of at least four major routes at Mizda the double oasis is situated at the probable boundaries of both *Macae* and *Phazanii* territory. Most commentators have agreed that Mizda was a garrison post. In view of the early date now applicable to the development of wadi agriculture in the Sofeggin system, Mizda would have been militarily significant in the second century. Zintan also lies at a strategic crossroads and at the probable northern transhuming limits of the *Phazanii*.

The recently discovered *clausura* known as Hadd Hajar, northwest of Mizda has not been accurately dated so far, but from the limited pottery evidence it is possible that it was constructed during (and perhaps late in) the second century AD. A few kilometres to the north of this wall lies the site of Medina Ragda which Brogan cautiously interpreted as a farm. The defensive features of this site might conceivably be found on a civilian site of the third or fourth century. However the *floruit* of Medina Ragda is indisputably in the late first and second century AD. At this early date, these features suggest a military interpretation.

Another site where pre-third-century occupation is likely is Ain Wif (*Thenadassa*). Two visits to the site in 1981 coincided with the construction of a road builders' camp on the southern margin of this site. In this area traces of two phases of military occupation were identified. Pottery recovered from the site, notably in stratified contexts in drain trenches, supported this interpretation and placed the initial phase within the second century. This discovery allows the reinterpretation of an inscription from the site which mentions repairs to the bath-house. The style of lettering on this inscription is not characteristic of the period *c.* 220–30 to which it is normally assigned. But if there was a second century military post with a bath-house here then these repairs can be dated earlier, perhaps to the earliest year of the Severan reoccupation of the post, in the same way that such work was undertaken at Remada in AD 197.

The earliest military sites attested epigraphically are two in western Tripolitania linked with the name of Commodus, Ksar Rhilane (*Tisavar*) and Bir Rhezene (*Bezereos*) (see Table 4:1). Although *Tisavar* was most probably constructed during his reign, this is not absolutely certain in the case of *Bezereos* since the inscription in question was a Severan restitution of a Commodan text and the initial occupation at the site could have been older still. The limitations of the epigraphic evidence are compounded by the lack of modern excavations and pottery analysis at these and most other sites. However, I would suggest that their construction was not a forward move into a hostile and unknown land but rather the infilling of an established framework because of a gradual increase in policing duties.[22]

A major phase of reorganization of the Tripolitanian *limes* began in AD 197 when Anicius Faustus became legate of the *III Augusta*. Repairs to a temple at Remada were followed in 198 by the construction of a new fortlet (*praesidium*) at Si Aioun, south of Remada. This work was carried out by the *Cohors II Flavia Afrorum* and the *numerus collatus*. Trouble brewing in the area for some time had perhaps turned into warfare by AD 201 when a vexillation of the Third Legion founded a new fort at Bu Njem. The larger fort at Gheriat el-Garbia was probably established at the same time. Severan occupation and/or repairs are also attested at *Bezereos* in AD 201 and at Ghadames (*Cidamus*), Ain Wif, Ain el-Auenia, Gasr Zerzi and Bir Tarsin between AD 201 and 211 (Fig. 4:5; Table 4:1). Between AD 201 and 205 the constructional programme was accompanied by some active campaigning.[23]

This epigraphic evidence for the input of troops

Modern name	Ancient name	Date and context	References
Remada	*Tillibari*	Early/mid 2nd C construction of fort? AD 197 repairs to *aedem annorum vetustate dilapsam* 4th C occupation	Euzennat 1973; Euzennat and Trousset 1975; Trousset 1974, 117–18. Notitia Dig., *Occ* 25. 33, 31.21
Ksar Rhilane	*Tisavar*	184–91, construction of fortlet Last coin: Maximin Daia	*CIL* 8.11048 Gombeaud 1901
Bir Rhezene/Sidi Mohammed ben Aissa	*Bezereos/Vezerei*	Commodan establishment AD 201, repairs 4th C occupation	*ILAf* 26 = *ILT* 56, 58 *ILAf* 27, 28 Notitia Dig., *Occ* 31.20
Ain Wif	*Thenadassa*	2nd C (?), fortlet AD 201–211 construction of new outpost/fortlet Early 3rd C (?), reconstruction of baths	Mattingly 1982 *IRT* 868 *IRT* 869
Si Aioun	*(praesidium)*	AD 198, fortlet constructed	*ILAf* 8–9; Trousset 1974, 120
Gheriat el-Garbia	?	AD 198–201 (probably 201) fort constructed Repairs in 240s	*LA* Supp 2, 1966, 107–11; cf. *IRT* 913 Loriot 1971; Mattingly 1985b
Bu Njem	*Gholaia*	24 Jan 201, start of fort construction AD 202 baths AD 205 Return of part of vexillation, construction of temple of Jupiter Hammon AD 222 Repairs to S gate by Porcius Iasucthan > AD 225 Temple of Mars Canapphar AD 222–35 *principia* inscription AD 236–38 *Ara cerei* dedication ad 244–49 Inscription of *praepositus limitis* in *principia* post-AD 238 Repairs to baths AD 253–59 Dated *ostraca* from last phase of occupation, graffito of *miles* in *vicus* AD 259 last dated *ostracon*	Rebuffat 1973b, no. 72–94; 72–26; 1973a *IRT* 913, 918–19 *IRT* 920; Rebuffat 1973b, no. 74–94 Rebuffat 1970b, no. 70–37/45; 1972a, 71–200; 1975b 214–15. Rebuffat 1975b, no. 71–206 Rebuffat 1970b, no. 70–49 Rebuffat 1982b, 912–14 Rebuffat 1985b Rebuffat 1970b, no. 70–46; 1985. Rebuffat 1970b, no. 68–6 Marichal 1992
Bir Tarsin	?	AD 198–211 military construction (outpost?)	*IRT* 887
Gasr Zerzi	?	AD 201–211, outpost built. Erasure of *Leg III Aug* titles after AD 238.	Brogan and Reynolds 1964, 43–44, nos 1–2.
Ghadames	*Cidamus Cydamae*	AD 198–211 Fort (?) built. Caracalla, occupation continues Severus Alexander, repairs Erasure of Alexander's name and possibly Leg III Aug shows military occupation until AD 235 and possibly 238+	*IRT* 909 *IRT* 907; Reynolds 1958, no 1 *IRT* 908 *IRT* 908
Ain el-Auenia	*Auru*	AD 198–211, military buildings (fortlet?) and a temple	Reynolds and Brogan 1960, nos 1–2; Reynolds and Simpson 1967, 45–47.
Gheriat el-Garbia (North)	*(burgus)*	AD 222–35, circular tower constructed *c.* 1 km north of fort	*IRT* 895; Mattingly 1985b.
Gasr Duib	*(novum centenarium)*	AD 244–46 outpost constructed *in regionem limitis Tenthetani*	*IRT* 880; Mattingly 1991

Table 4:1. Dated military construction and repair work in Tripolitania.

Table 4:1. *cont.*

Modern name	Ancient name	Date and context	References
Ras el Ain	*Talalati/Tabalati*	AD 263, fort constructed *opportuno loco a solo for C oh VIII Fida* AD 355–60, major repairs to defences (*propugnacula*) under Flavius Archontius Nilus Late 4th C	*CIL* 8.22765; *ILT* 3; Trousset 1974, 101 *CIL* 8.22766–22767 = *ILAf* 11; 8.22768; Rebuffat 1980, 113–14. *Notitia Dig. Occ.*, 25.31, 31.18
Ksar Tarcine	(*centenarium*) *Tibubuci*	*c.* AD 303, construction of outpost by early *praesides* of province of *Tripolitana*. Coin sequence to end 4th C	*CIL* 8.22763 = *ILS* 9352 Trousset 1974, 91

and constructional activity in the early third century is supplemented by archaeological data. For instance, the sites of Hr Mgarine and Hr Medeina in Tunisia can be proposed fairly confidently as fortlets marking the road stations of *Agarlabas* and *Thebelami* though there is no epigraphic evidence from either site. At any event Severus' frontier deployment must have at least doubled the troops in the region and it involved the permanent outstationing of a considerable number of legionaries (see further below). What Severus seems to have been doing was extending the existing deployment to the south along the major routes of penetration, in order to supervise more closely the desert tribes, whilst also strengthening the lateral lines of communication. The creation of this latter linear aspect in the form of the *limes Tripolitanus* road is

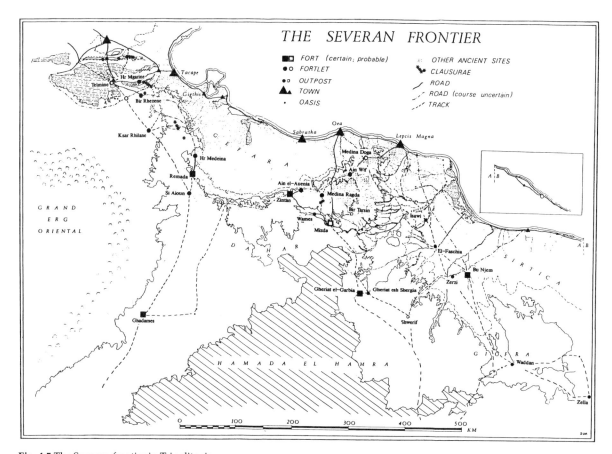

Fig. 4:5 The Severan frontier in Tripolitania.

sometimes credited to Severus, sometimes to his predecessors. The evidence is too uncertain for firm conclusions though Severus certainly established some new fortlets along the *limes* road. However, parts of this route were in military use before this, serving sites such as *Turris Tamalleni, Bezereos, Tillibari, Thenteos* (?) and *Thenadassa*. We should note, though, that at no date did the *limes Tripolitanus* road mark the actual frontier line.[24]

A *burgus* was built at Gheriat in the reign of Severus Alexander. Although the inscription referring to this was for a long time associated with the construction of the fort itself (until the discovery of an early third-century inscription in 1965), Barth stated that he found it built into the circular tower about a kilometre north of the fort (Plate 13). It was still in place over the doorway but he concluded from the style of masonry that the tower was post-Roman and, therefore, that the inscription had been brought there and reused. Goodchild made the same error of interpretation though he admitted that the term *burgus* could be applicable to such a tower. In fact there is no reason to think that the inscription was out of context. The masonry of the tower is paralleled by the recently identified southwest gate of the fort which was rebuilt with semi-circular projecting towers some time after the initial construction. The *burgus* thus refers to the circular tower which served as an important look-out post for the fort and signalling link to the fortlet at Gheriat esh-Shergia (which is visible from the tower but not from the fort).

In AD 238 the *Legio III Augusta* was disbanded with *damnatio memoriae* and the effects must have been profoundly felt in Tripolitania where so many legionary vexillations were outstationed. The archaeological evidence is simply not refined enough for us to assess the full effects but some important sites clearly continued in occupation. This is certain at Gheriat, Bu Njem and *Thenteos* and almost certain at others such as Bir Rhezene, Remada and Ksar Rhilane. At Bu Njem the garrison was a *numerus*, perhaps the same one that had been on station there with a legionary vexillation in AD 236–8. An auxiliary unit (or a detachment from it) took over the garrison duties at Gheriat and is perhaps identifiable as the *Cohors (I) Syrorum Sagittariorum* (see below). Because of their distance from their main legionary base and from the scene of the AD 238 revolt at Thysdrus (El Djem), the Tripolitanian vexillations may not have been actually present at the battle in which the elder Gordians perished and thus have been held less culpable when judgment was passed on the legion. In these circumstances, it is not inconceivable that some of the disbanded legionaries were absorbed on to the rosters of

existing auxiliary units, and this suggests a possible context for the known (but undated) promotion of the Syrian cohort to milliary size. Rebuffat has suggested a similar move at Bu Njem may have rechristened the legionary vexillation as the *vexillatio Golensis*.[25]

In AD 244–6 a *novum centenarium* was built at Gasr Duib in *regionem limi[tis Ten]theitani partitam* under the auspices of the legate of Numidia and a man described as *praep(ositus) limitis (Tripolitanae)*. This small fortlet or outpost was placed in advance of the known Roman road system in order to watch for raiders moving out of the Phazanian pre-desert zone into the Gebel. It was an outstation for the presumed fort of *Thenteos* (Edref, near Zintan)

Bu Njem (*Gholaia*) continued to remain an important command base into the 250s and the *praepositus limitis Tripolitanae* is attested there also, though the fort was under the day-to-day control of a decurion. The outpost positions of *Boinag, Esuba, Hyeruzerian* and the possibly more major site of *Secedi* are mentioned on ostraca and a great deal of communication passed between them and *Gholaia*.

Rebuffat has suggested that the abandonment of Bu Njem more or less coincided with the foundation of an entirely new fort at Ras el-Ain Tlalet in AD 263. The reasons for the withdrawal are unclear but native pressure seems unlikely in the light of the contents of the ostraca. A strategic retrenchment for political reasons or to economize on deployed forces are possible alternatives. Not all the outlying positions were abandoned at a stroke though. Either Gheriat or, perhaps more likely, Mizda was still occupied in AD 275 (the year of the last dated milestone on the central road south of Garian). Excavations of *Tisavar* produced a coin of Maximin Daia below the burning level left when the departing garrison fired the post as part of their orderly withdrawal.

The frontier system recorded in the *Notitia Dignitatum* shows the division of the *limes* into regional sectors each under the control of a *praepositus provinciae/zae* and the whole commanded by a *dux Tripolitan* (in place of the third-century *praepositus limitis*). As we shall see shortly, the origins of this system date back to Severan times and the fully-fledged system was probably in operation before the end of the third century. The surviving list, however, includes corrections and updatings down to the end of the fourth century. So although some of the *limites* named in the list are identifiable with earlier frontier positions many are entirely unknown. The problems with the *Notitia* are discussed further below. The last securely dated new structure on the *limes Tripolitanus* is the *centenarium Tibubuci* built *c.* AD 303 and occupied for about a century thereafter.[26]

Command structure

The first period where there is adequate evidence for the nature of the command structure is the Severan reorganization (Table 4:2). The military zone of Tripolitania fell under the jurisdiction of the legate of the *Legio III Augusta*, who was governor of *Numidia* as well from the early third century. Some of the earliest known subordinate commands were clearly of an extraordinary nature. Aemilius Emeritus, a decurion of the *Ala I Pannoniorum*, was appointed as *praepositus* of an 'expeditionary' force comprising the *Cohors II Flavia Afrorum* and a *numerus collatus* (a type of unit specially created from detachments of existing auxiliary units) which built the *praesidium* at Si Aioun. M. Caninius Adiutor Faustinianus, prefect of the *Coh. II Hamiorum* and *praepositus vex Leg III Aug*, may have been entrusted with a similar mission to establish a series of garrison positions in the Gebel. In both cases the unit to which their command normally related was not necessarily present and the slight available evidence suggests that they remained in *Numidia*. This type of appointment for serving auxiliary officers is paralleled at this period by examples of special expeditionary columns on and beyond the Numidian frontier.

More significant for the future development of the command structures in Tripolitania was the practice of appointing *praepositi* to some of the permanent legionary garrison positions established in the early third century. Tullius Romulus, *(centurio) ex maiorario praepositus vexillationis Leg III Aug*, at Bu Njem in AD 205 is the earliest known. A *praepositus vexillationis* was at one level simply in command of a vexillation of legionaries but the title was limited in Tripolitania to major bases only. More is known of legionary centurions holding this post under Severus Alexander whilst commanding vexillations of the *III Augusta* at the same fort and at Gheriat el-Garbia (see Table 4:2). These were two of the major forts of the zone whose combined garrison was initially intended to be between 1,000 and 1,500 men. From the Bu Njem ostraca of the 250s it is clear that these were not established as remote outpost forts but were centres for observation and patrolling of a wide area, across which outposts were established and manned. Archaeological evidence for sites such as Gasr Zerzi and Gheriat esh-Shergia shows that fortlets dependent on the major command centres also existed from the outset. The *praepositi* at Bu Njem and Gheriat were not simply in command of a single remote fort, therefore, but coordinated a regional network of policing and observation points. At an early date the Severan system contained many of the ingredients of the *limites* command sectors of the *Notitia*. It is logical to assume that other parts of the *limes Tripolitanus* also functioned in this way under the Severans.[27]

The site of *Bezereos* (Bir Rhezene) is an enigmatic one. As described by Trousset, it is at best a 'small fort' and fortlet would be a truer description since it is only approx. 0.33 ha (0.81 acres) in area. Yet calculations from a military roster found there suggest a garrison size of around 300 men. This seems impossibly high unless either a larger site remains unrecognized among the sand dunes or *Bezereos* was the regional centre for a *praepositus* with responsibility for a number of small posts in the Dahar. Recent studies of the text of the inscription have shown that the last surviving line on the principal face contains the start of a man's name who was almost certainly a centurion of the Third Legion and possibly also *praepositus*. There is space on the stone for considerably more detail concerning the circumstances in which it was erected, presumably on a special day in the military religious calendar when all the outpost garrisons were temporarily reunited at the command centre. This interpretation is supported by a consideration of the military lists on the sides of the stone. The list is headed by an *optio*, who I believe was second in command of the detachment at *Bezereos* itself. In smaller letters followed about 300 names of which about 112 can be reconstructed with some certainty. At least eight centurions are mentioned amongst the men and some of these must have been the commanders of other outposts, such as *Tisavar*. It is perhaps significant that *Bezereos* was later the headquarters of a *praepositus* in the *Notitia*.

Remada (*Tillibari*) as a cohort fort was certainly a major garrison post and a number of fortlets can credibly be associated with it. Si Aioun was constructed by men from the *Cohors II Flavia Afrorum* in AD 198 and probably manned by troops outstationed from Remada. One can speculate in a similar way about the fortlet at Hr Medeina (*Thebelami*?), the now destroyed site at Dehibat and another possible outpost at el Magen. Although Aemilius Emeritus commanded the garrison in extraordinary circumstances in 198, as we have seen, it is likely that the prefect of the cohort was the normal commanding officer of the sector. It is not certain at what date he was acknowledged as *praepositus* but one is known for the *limes Tillibarensis* in the *Notitia*.

In summary, then, there is some evidence for the existence of regional command centres with associated outposts commanded by *praepositi* from the years following the Severan reorganization. Their command sectors were not immediately called *limites*, but the system recorded in the *Notitia* was a logical development. The following elements can be suggested for a tentative reconstruction of some of these sectors.

Site	Type	Unit/Detachment	Size	Title of CO(s)	References
Remada *(Tillibari)*	F	*Cohors II Flavia Afrorum*	488/ 608	*Praefectus cohortis*	Euzennat 1973, 14
Si Aioun	O	*Cohors II Flavia Afrorum?*	<50?	Erected by detachment of *Coh II Flavia and numerus collatus* under command of Aemilius Emeritus, *praepositus* (seconded from duties as *decurio ala. I Pannoniorum* It is presumed that troops were outposted from Remada, rank of CO of outpost unknown.	*ILAf* 9
Ksar Rhilane *(Tisavar)*	FL	*vexillatio Leg. III Aug*	c. 80?	a) Ulpius Paulinus > *leg* b) with Vibianus and Myro *optiones*	CIL 8.22759
Bir Rhezene *(Bezereos)*	FL	*vexillatio Leg. III Aug*	c. 160	a) C. Iulius Saturninus > *leg* b) Ianuarius *optio* as deputy c) Other > in roster list of AD 209–11 may be in charge at other outposts	*ILAf* 26 *ILAf* 27 *ILAf* 27; Lassère 1980
Ain Wif *(Thenadassa)*	FL/O	*vexillatio Leg. III Aug* unknown auxiliary detachment	20– 100?	a) building carried out by force commanded by M. Caninius Adiutor Faustinianus, *praep. vex leg III* and on secondment from duties as *praefectus* of *Coh II Hamiorum* (his unit based outside Tripolitania). b) M. Coelius … ninus (rank unknown) c) Iunio Sucesso > *principe leg* was CO of detachment	*IRT* 868 *IRT* 869 *IRT* 869; Speidel 1981
Gasr Zerzi	O	detachment from *vex. Leg. III Aug* based at Bu Njem	<20?	No evidence from epigraphy, hints from *ostraca* received from outposts at Bu Njem that might be *beneficiarii* commanding *stationarii*	Marichal 1992, 108–09.
Ghadames *(Cidamus)*	F? FL??	*vexillatio Leg. III Aug*	c. 500	a) M. Aurelius Ianuarius > *leg* b) … > *leg*	Reynolds 1958, no.1 *IRT* 908
Gheriat el-Garbia	F	*vexillatio Leg. III Aug* Detachment of *Coh I Syrorum*	c. 800 c. 400?	a) > *et praepositus vex leg …* b) unnamed auxiliary officer	*IRT* 895 *AE* 1973, 573
Bu Njem *(Gholaia)*	F	*vexillatio Leg. III Aug* *vex. Leg. III & numerus collatus* *Vexillatio golensis*	c. 480 120? c. 480 c. 480 c. 480	a) C. Iulius Dignus > *leg* b) Q. Avidius Quintianus > *leg* c) Tullius Romulus > *ex maiorario praepositus vex* d) M. Porcius Iasuchan > *leg* e) T. Flavius Apronianus/Vicrius Verus > *leg praepositus vex* f) M. Caecilius Felix > *leg praepositus vex et numerus conlatus* g) Ti Iulius Vitalis *decurio* h) *decurio* of an *ala* i) Octavius Festus *dec p.p.* j) junior officer *librarius*, for example Iunius Amicus *sesquiplicarius qui et librarius*	Reb. 1973b, no. 72–26 *IRT* 918–19 *IRT* 920; Reb. 1973b, no. 74–94. Reb. 1985 Reb. 1975b, no. 71–206; 1967, 67–89 Reb. 1967, no. 67–15; 1982, 912–14. Reb. 1973b, 72–28 ibid, no. 70–64. Marichal 1992, nos 76–79, 82–85. Marichal 1992, p.68, 75.
Gasr Duib	O	Detachment of *Coh I Syrorum?*	<20?	a) post constructed by *tribunus* (? *Coh I Syrorum*) b) officer in charge of outposted troops of unknown rank	*IRT* 880; Mattingly 1991

Table 4:2. Evidence of the command structure of units based in Tripolitania in the third century ad, as revealed by epigraphic evidence from forts (F), fortlets (FL) and outposts (O). Reb = Rebuffat; > = centurion.

Table 4:2. *cont.*

Ksar Tarcine (*Tibubuci*)	O	Unknown	<20?	Unknown	*CIL* 8.22763
Secedi (?)	F	*Cohors VIII Fida*	480?	a) Decurion mentioned on Bu Njem *ostracon*	Marichal 1992, no. 95
Ras el-Ain (*Talalati*)	F	*Cohors VIII Fida*	480?	a) no evidence from Ras el-Ain, presumably a decurion as at *Secedi*	Marichal 1992, nos 94–95

1) Bu Njem; troops: around 480; outposts: Zerzi, Zella, Waddan, el Fascia.
2) Gheriat; 800–1000; Gheriat esh-Shergia, watchtower at el-Garbia, plus other outposts?
3) Ghadames; plus outposts in neighbouring oases?
4) Remada; around 500–600; Si Aioun, el Majen, Dehibat, Hr Medeina.
5) Bir Rhezene; around 300; *Tisavar*, Hr Kranfir? plus other outposts?
6) Nefzaoua; unknown size; Hr Mgarine; *Ad Templum*?
7) Zintan (*Thenteos*); 800; *Auru*, Gasr Duib, plus other outposts?
8) Mizda? 100s (?); Bir Tarsin, Medina Ragda, Saquifah, Wames, perhaps also Ain Wif.

I would suggest, therefore, that the origin of some of the *limites* sectors listed in the *Notitia* can be traced back to the increasingly regionalized command structure initiated under Severus and based on the major garrison posts. For this reason I am inclined to identify *Thenteos* (near Zintan?) as the base fort of the milliary *Cohors I Syrorum Sagittariorum* known on an inscription from one of its probable outstations at Ain el-Auenia (*Auru*). *Thenteos*, of course, was later the centre of the *praepositus limitis Tentheitani*. It is all the more regrettable in view of this that this key site is totally unexcavated and unexamined.[28]

The chain of command in the Severan period was probably from the legate of Numidia direct to the principal fort commanders and from them to the junior officers in command of outposts.

The origins of the system of regional *limites* has normally been dated to AD 244–6 on the basis of the Gasr Duib inscription mentioning a *praepositus limitis* and the *regionem limi[tis Ten]theitani partitam*. This is not evidence for the existence of the *praepositi limitis Tenthetani* of the *Notitia*, as has normally been assumed. An inscription from Bu Njem refers to a *praepositus limitis Tripolitanae* in the year 248 and it is now certain that the *praepositus* mentioned at Duib held the same post. Whilst it is clear that the regional

framework did exist by then (and I have tried to show that it was a logical development from the command structure established by Severus) the existence of an overall *praepositus* for the *limes* is a new and exciting discovery. It imposed an additional link in the chain of command between the Numidian governor and the major garrison points. One possible interpretation is that this office was created post-AD 238 following the disbandment of the legion when, with fewer troops available, greater cooperation between sectors became necessary. It is unclear how long this command survived; some of the Bu Njem ostraca refer to a *praepositus* without making it clear whether he was a regional or zonal commander. The next highest officer at Bu Njem appears to have been a *librarius*. On balance it is likely that after 238 both regional *praepositi* (or their equivalents) and a *praepositus limitis Tripolitanae* existed in the command hierarchy.

The Gasr Duib inscription mentions three individuals in descending order of importance:

Gasr Duib AD 244–6 (*IRT* 880)
(M. Aurelius) Cominius Cassianus leg. augg. pr. pr.
Governor of *Numidia*
|
(?) *Gallicanus [proc. agg.] v.e, praep. limitis (Tripolitanae)*
Zonal commander of *limes Tripolitanus*
|
Numisius Maximus domo [...]sia trib(unus)
Commander of unit based in *limes Tentheitanus* sector

Bu Njem AD 248 (Rebuffat 1985b)
(M. Aurelius) Cominius Cassianus leg. augg. pr. pr.
Governor of *Numidia*
|
Lucretius Marcellus v.e. proc augg nn praeposito limitis Tripolitanae
Zonal commander of *limes Tripolitanus*
|
C. Iulius Donatus dec alae flaviae, praefectus... vexillationi golensi et ...
Commander of unit based at Bu Njem

Numisius Maximus has normally been identified as the soldier left in command of the *centenarium* but this must be highly dubious in view of the tiny size of the post and the exalted status of his superiors named with him on the inscription. Rather we would expect to find reference here to the officer in charge of the larger garrison post from which Gasr Duib was controlled. The inscription makes it clear that this was the presumed fort at Zintan *(Tentheos, Thenteos)*, thus adding considerable weight to the supposition about the status of that site. I have already suggested that the *cohors I Syrorum sagittariorum* may have had a long-term base at *Thenteos* and it is surely significant that that milliary cohort was commanded by a tribune. The final line of the Duib inscription can now be expanded to conclude: *Numisius Maximus ... trib. (coh. I. Syrorum)*. In this it would match in every detail the Bu Njem inscription of the *praepositus limitis Tripolitanae*, where the zonal commander is likewise interposed between provincial governor and fort commander in the dedication.[29]

Units attested in Tripolitania

It is a difficult if not impossible task to suggest reliable figures for the size of the Roman garrison in Tripolitania at various periods (Tables 4:2–4:3). It can be estimated, however, that the sites known to have been occupied under Septimius Severus would have required around 3,000 troops to have been fully manned. Of these perhaps 1,500 to 2,000 were outstationed legionaries of the *Legio III Augusta* (equivalent to about one third of its total strength). This suggests that when Severus wished to strengthen the frontier in Tripolitania there were few auxiliary troops available for redeployment. La Bohec has suggested that the *numerus collatus* (or *conlatus*) known at Si Aioun and Bu Njem is not the title of a single unit but rather the name for a special type of unit which he suggests was recruited from the existing auxiliary units in the province for use in particular circumstances. The use of legionary vexillations and this sort of *numerus* in Tripolitania both attest the special circumstances and scanty manpower reserves of the Severan reorganization.

Two units are known, however, which could well have been in the region earlier. *The Cohors II Flavia Afrorum (equitata)* was the garrison unit at Remada and may have been redeployed there from the Nefzaoua under Hadrian. It was most likely assigned to the Tripolitanian region throughout much of its career and appears to be recorded in the *Notitia*. The unit was also involved in building work at *Tisavar* (Ksar Rhilane) and Si Aioun.

The second unit which I suggest was in the region in pre-Severan times is the *Cohors (I) Syrorum Sagittariorum* known on an inscription from Ain el-Auenia *(Auru)*. This unit probably arrived in Africa in the mid-first century but little is known of it thereafter until it is mentioned at the probable fortlet at *Auru* (AD 198–211). The fact that the garrison left at *Auru* was legionary and the proximity of el-Auenia to the suspected fort of *Thenteos* near Zintan suggests that the latter site may have been the cohort's base under Severus and probably earlier. Another possibility of course would be the supposed fort at Mizda. The cohort was initially of *quinquenaria* size (about 480 strong) but was increased at some point to *milliaria* strength (about 800 strong) since it was commanded by tribunes in third-century inscriptions. Le Bohec attributes the unit with a Tripolitanian posting and its long-term presence at the uninvestigated site of *Thenteos* (Zintan) would help explain the epigraphic *lacunae* in its history. It is likely that the unit retained its associations with Tripolitania beyond AD 238. A fragmentary inscription from Gheriat records the name of an auxiliary unit in garrison in AD 239 whose titles end with the letter G. The expansion *[Coh I Syrorum Sa]g.* is an attractive possibility in view of the unit's known association with the area earlier. As noted already, the tribune mentioned in the Gasr Duib inscription of AD 244–6 is more likely to have been the commander of this cohort than a soldier in charge of such a small outpost. It is conceivable that the Syrian cohort was divided between the forts of Zintan and Gheriat in this phase following the disbandment of the Third Legion.

These two units, it can be argued, formed the core component of the garrison prior to the influx of legionaries under Severus.[30] The recorded presence of a prefect of the *Cohors II H(a)m(iorum)* on an inscription from Ain Wif is not proof that any soldiers of this unit were posted to the region, as already explained. But the uncertainty about the location and movements of most of the garrison units of the Numidian army make estimates of the upper and lower limits of the troops in Tripolitania difficult. It is apparent though that there was a dramatic increase in numbers between AD 198 and 211 and an equally dramatic decrease (by implication) post AD 238. It is uncertain whether elements of the Third Legion were returned to the region after it was re-formed in AD 253.

One additional unit is known in the AD 250s, the *Cohors VIII Fida.* It is thought to have been a late foundation, perhaps following the dissolution of the Third Legion. A decurion of this unit may have been based at the unlocated site of *Secedi* in the mid-third century and cavalry from the cohort are recorded in the Bu Njem *ostraca* as present at the latter fort. Messages

Unit	Date	Location	References
Vexillationes Legionis III Augustae	Late 2C Late 2C/ 201–11+ 201–38 201?–238 Early 3C Early 3C Early 3C	1. *Tisavar* (Ksar Rhilane), fortlet 2. *Bezereos* (Bir Rhezene), fortlet 3. *Gholaia* (Bu Njem), fort 4. Gheriat el Garbia, fort 5. *Cidamus* (Ghadames), fort? 6. *Thenadassa* (Ain Wif), fortlet 7. *Auru* (Ain el-Auenia), fortlet	Unit type: Cagnat 1913; Goodchild 1954a; Lassère 1980; Le Bohec 1989a; Merlin 1921; Saxer 1967. Epigraphy: Le Bohec 1989a; *CIL* 8.11048, 8.22759, *ILAf* 26–29; Suppl *LA* 2, 1967, 107–11, nos 1,4, 8; *IRT* 868–69, 895; 908, 913–16, 918–20; Rebuffat 1967a, inscriptions 67–15, 67–89; 1973a/b; 1982b; Reynolds and Brogan 1960, 51–52, nos 1 and 2; Reynolds and Simpson 1967, 45–47; Reynolds 1958, 134 no. 1.
Cohors II Flavia Afrorum (*equitata*)	2–4C 2C+ 3C+	1. *Tillibari* (Remada), fort 2. *Tisavar* (Ksar Rhilane), fortlet 3. Si Aioun, outpost	Unit: Cagnat 1913, 200; Euzennat 1973, 143; 1977c, 231–35; Le Bohec 1989b, 67–70; Trousset 1974, 114–20. Epigraphy: *CIL* 8.22631; *BCTH* 1919, clviii (stamped tiles); *ILAf* 9; Trousset 1974, 117–18 (inscriptions).
Cohors I Syrorum sagittariorum (*quinquenaria*, then *miliaria*, probably *equitata*)	3C post-238 ?2–3C+ post-246	1. *Auru* (Ain el-Auenia), fortlet? 2. Gheriat el-Garbia(?), fort 3. *Thenteos* (Zintan), fort 4. Gsar Duib, outpost	Unit: Le Bohec 1987; 1989b, Mattingly 1985b; 1991. Epigraphy: Le Bohec 1989b, 84, 89–90; Reynolds and Brogan 1960, 51, no. 1; Mattingly 1991.
Cohors VIII Fida (*equitata*)	pre-263 post-263 pre-263	1. *Secedi* (unlocated, c. 2-3 days march from Bu Njem), fort? 2. *Talalati* (Ras el Ain), fort 3. *Gholaia* (Bu Njem), few cavalry outposted	Le Bohec 1989b, 76–79; Marichal 1992, 66, 200–03. Epigraphy: *ILS* 8923; Trousset 1974, 98; Marichal 1992, no. 95
Numerus collatus (or *conlatus*), *numerus*	198 236–38 238–263	1. Si Aioun, outpost 2. *Gholaia* Bu Njem, fort	Le Bohec 1980; 1985. Marichal 1979, 439, 447; 1992; Rebuffat 1967, inscription 67–15; Rebuffat 1970b, inscription 70–46; Rebuffat 1982b, 912–14

Table 4:3. Units attested in Tripolitana in the second–third centuries AD.

passing between *Secedi* and Bu Njem evidently took about three days to arrive, giving some indication of their relative positions (Mizda or Gheriat el-Garbia are probably at the limits of possible locations for *Secedi*). In AD 263 a new fort was built for the unit at Ras el-Ain Tlalat. This fort was still garrisoned by regular troops, perhaps the remnants of the cohort, when repairs were carried out in AD 355–60.

The most detailed evidence for the later third-century garrison is from the Bu Njem *ostraca*, but the *numerus* they deal with is of very peculiar size, composition and organization. It is likely that the day lists which give a strength of only 42–96 men relate not to the entire garrison but to some sub-division of it, perhaps a squad assigned to the *librarius*. The chain of command has been established as *decurio* (*et praeposi-*

tus), *librarius*, *optio*, *proculcator* (perhaps a sort of spy-master/surveillance officer).[31]

5
CONCLUSIONS : THE WORK OF THE GARRISON

I have argued that Tripolitania was 'garrisoned' throughout the period of the Principate in accordance with changing threats and changing strategy. Much of the hard evidence of documentary or epigraphic sources is lacking and some of my conclusions are based on circumstantial evidence or on hypothesis. However, when set against the background of Roman frontier policy generally it should be clear that there is cause for disquiet about some conventional views. Whilst it is true that Tripolitania was a remarkably peaceful region in the second century, it was also a very disturbed one in the first and early third. It would be contradictory to all we know of Roman frontier development in the second century if a zone like this was left without troops to back up the evident diplomatic pressure on neighbouring tribes and to supervise the development of annexed territories. It would be naïve to imagine that the *Phazanii, Garamantes* and *Nasamones* were so suddenly and so completely pacified.[32] In any case the Roman army had become far more that a mere strike force during the first century and garrisons were not maintained only on high risk sectors.

The policing of the frontier zone and the need for customs control of population and merchandise became of equal importance in areas where physical frontiers were vague and transhumance commonplace. The development of linear earthworks (*fossata* and *clausurae*) reflects the necessity of policing control and regulation of the movement of people, goods and services. They were not in the first instance defensive. Other important duties of the garrison involved information gathering, the regulation or supervision of tribal affairs inside and outside the frontiers and the maintenance of formal links with *foederati* and *pacati*. The Bu Njem *ostraca* refer to spies (tribal informers) who played an important but shadowy role in overseeing affairs in the hegemonic zone beyond the frontier. The army also had to arrange for its own provisioning, normally done at local unit level.[33]

The detailed evidence now available from Bu Njem helps to fill out many gaps in our appreciation of the work of Roman garrisons. For instance, provisions for the fort were clearly obtained in the vicinity of Bu Njem from Libyan producers. The economic interrelationship between fort and farmers was no doubt reinforced by the growth of a large *vicus* (15 ha/37.5 acres) alongside the fort which must have been a major consumer of agricultural surplus. This economic impact of the garrison on the pre-desert society should not be underestimated.

The army also patrolled and policed the area, receiving runaway slaves and tribal 'deserters' or 'refugees', checking out suspicious tribesmen, issuing letters of passage to others. Outposts were occupied on the main routes through the region and at the major wells and cisterns. The caravan trade was carefully monitored at a *statio camellariorum* at Bu Njem. Representatives from the fort were sent *cum Garamantibus* (whatever that meant precisely) and there are other clues concerning diplomatic activity with neighbouring tribes.

The evidence relates to the mid-third century – a period of crisis and disintegration elsewhere in the empire – and shows that Tripolitania was a comparatively orderly and peaceful garrison sector at this stage. The policing functions described above are relatively typical of those that the garrisons would have performed over a century earlier or indeed a century later. St. Augustine's letters provide evidence that the same concern was felt in his day for the regulation of trans-border movement of seasonal labourers. A system like this could work in favour of those both inside and outside the frontier. In normal conditions the transhuming and migrating populations had their rights protected as much as did the sedentary populations and symbiotic coexistence was possible. The more sedentarized zones probably depended on a seasonal influx of labour at harvest time and this often came from tribes which were partly or wholly extra-provincial. Even when Rome's ability to provide a credible deterrent was visibly weakening there were strong socio-economic ties across the frontiers which delayed the breakdown of the frontier system.[34]

The defensive and policing strategies in Tripolitania were aspects common to most Roman provinces; the potential problems of the interaction between transhuming and sedentary communities were peculiarly African. The solution combined Roman strategic aims and local knowledge of the land and people in a flexible deployment. The increasing proportion of Africans in the army (see below, chapter 8) emphasized the regional character of the frontier at the tactical level. However, I hope that it is also clear that the underlying strategy of the Tripolitanian frontier is recognizable in the evidence for other *limites* of the Roman empire.

5

THE ARCHAEOLOGY
OF THE FRONTIER

(First–Third Centuries AD)

1
TYPOLOGY

Typology and chronology were of little concern to the earliest investigators of the *limes Tripolitanus*. In attempting to trace the course of the *limes* road they made identifications between the stations of the early third-century Antonine Itinerary and any conveniently located ruin, without regard for the fact that some were built long after the compilation of the itinerary. Thus the two most prominent *quadriburgi*, Benia Guedah Ceder and Benia bel Recheb, or the fourth-century *centenarium Tibubuci* were cited as 'forts' on the *limes* road. The problem is even more acute for the large numbers of fortified farms commonly described as 'postes militaires' but whose dates and military significance are harder to assess.

In this chapter I have not tried in most cases to class sites by their Latin names, *castra, castellum, praesidium, burgus* and so on. Practice was not consistent enough in ancient times for this to be satisfactory. Rather I have discussed sites under broad headings (fort, fortlet, outpost, tower) with size being the main typological factor, though making allowances for sites which were contemporary or have shared characteristics (Tables 5:1–5:3). I do not believe that sites can be assigned to type-groups solely on the basis of their physical appearance and many of the older descriptions of sites, if taken at face value, suggest inappropriate parallels. Ultimately this analysis is rudimentary in the extreme because too many sites are unsurveyed, unexcavated and undated. The apparent absence of dated forts of first century AD date and the

shortage of epigraphic evidence prior to the Severan period also reflect the poverty of our data-base far more than the ancient reality (see above, chapter 4.4).[1]

2
FORTS OF SECOND- TO EARLY THIRD-CENTURY DATE

Remada (*Tillibari*)

DIMENSIONS: 157 × 124 m   AREA: 1.95 ha (4.87 acres)
FIGURES: 5:1–5:2   EPIGRAPHY: Trousset 1974, 116–18

The presence of a fort at Remada was first reported by Lecoy de la Marche in 1894. Excavations were undertaken early this century by Commander Donau but this work was interrupted by the First World War and during the course of the war the visible remains were obliterated by the construction of a French barracks. The results of Donau's excavation remained unpublished until the 1970s when they were reassessed by Euzennat and Trousset. In modern times little trace of the Roman fort remains but one significant epigraphic find has been made.

Donau's excavations were concentrated on the gates, defences and *principia* of the fort (Fig 5:1). The site, of standard 'playing-card' shape with four gates, faced east. The defensive wall was 2.47 m thick comprising two faces of small, mortared masonry with a sand and rubble fill. In places it survived to 2–3 m height but there was evidence of considerable patching and repair work along it. The gates also provided

Area (across ramparts)	Name	Unit	Garrison size (max.)	Occupation
2.48 ha/6.20 acres	Gheriat el-Garbia	1) *vex. leg. III Aug.* 2) *Detachment of coh I Syrorum (?)*	800–1000?	201–238 post-238
Unknown	Zintan (*Thenteos*)	1) *Coh I Syrorum*	480/800?	3rd C (possibly earlier also)
1.95 ha/4.87 acres	Remada (*Tillibari*)	1) *Coh II Flavia Afrorum*	600?	2nd–5th (?)
1.28 ha/3.21 acres	Bu Njem (*Gholaia*)	1) *vex leg. III Aug* 2) *vex leg III + numerus conlatus* 3) *vexillatio Golensis/numerus*	c. 480 c. 500? c. 500?	201–? 236–238 (perhaps earlier) 238–263
0.86 ha/2.16 acres	Ras el-Ain (*Talalati*)	Cohors VIII Fida	300–400?	post-263
Unknown	*Secedi* (modern location unknown)	Cohors VIII Fida	300–400?	pre-263
Unknown	Mizda	*Unknown*	?	?
Unknown (possibly not a full size fort?)	Ghadames (*Cidamus*)	*vex leg. III Aug*	?	201–238?

Table 5:1. Principal forts of Tripolitania (sites over 0.8 ha/2 acres in area). Some sites that are believed to have been forts, but whose remains have not been traced on the ground are included.

evidence of several phases of occupation. In their original form they were all flanked by internal rectangular towers. The east and west gates were later altered by the addition of a projecting rectangular bastion, the north and south gates by the addition of a semi-circular front. At a later date, further repairs and alterations took place at several of the gates and the north gate, for instance, was narrowed and finally blocked. The parallels for the original internal gate towers are second century, for the second-phase projecting towers late second and third (Fig 5:2).

Donau also ran slit-trenches up the *viae principalis* and *decumana* and opened a number of sondages in the area of the headquarters building (*principia*). The *principia* trenches revealed a series of rooms and corridors whose plan cannot be easily related to that of

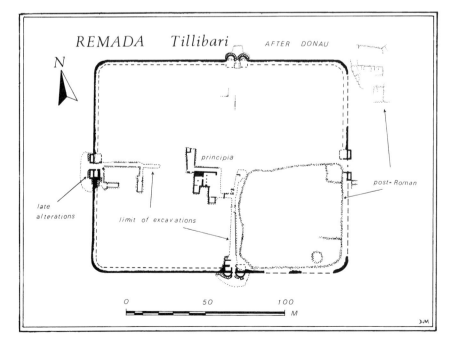

Fig. 5:1 Remada (*Tillibari*), plan of fort showing Donau's excavations. Note the possible late antique enclave in the southeast corner (after Euzennat and Trousset 1975).

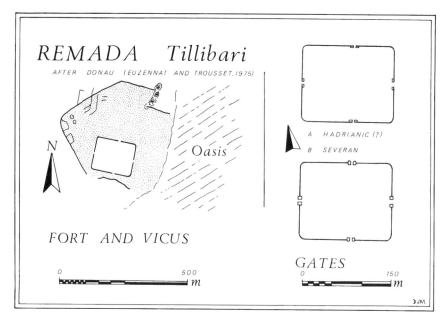

Fig. 5:2 Remada, fort and *vicus* (stippled). The original form of the gates (a) suggests an Hadrianic date, while the modified D-shaped gate towers (b) look Severan in date (after Euzennat and Trousset 1975).

other African examples (Fig. 5:1). Two interconnecting rooms with columns and a raised earth platform supporting a basin and small columns might be interpreted as a chapel but it is in the wrong position to be the *sacellum*. Another room contained plaster fragments covered in graffiti (which Donau could make nothing of) and may have been a *scriptorium*. It is clear though that Donau conflated several phases of building on his plan and his excavations were far from complete. Trousset suggests that as many as five phases were involved.

In the *retentura* Donau examined at least one room of a building he described as a *quaestorium*. This building was evidently over 23 m long, flanking and partly impinging on the *via decumana*. It is therefore not an original structure and the evidence for metal working from the excavated room suggests that it was in fact a *fabrica*.

The earliest epigraphic evidence from the site is an inscription of Anicius Faustus of AD 197, referring to repairs to an *aedes* which had collapsed through age. The original form of the gates suggests that the site originated early rather than later in the second century and there are close similarities with the Hadrianic fort at *Gemellae* (AD 132). The addition of the projecting fronts to the gate towers was probably done as part of the Severan refurbishment of AD 197. Occupation of the fort apparently continued into the fifth century.

In the southeast corner of the fort, Donau noted an enclosure of about 60 x 70 m built in rough style with its foundations about 1 m above Roman ground level.

This is normally referred to as a 'camp Arabe', but a sub-Roman date is possible. The people of *Tillibari* were mentioned by Corippus in his account of the *Laguatan* revolt of AD 546.[2]

Gheriat el-Garbia (Roman name unknown)

DIMENSIONS: 183 × 132 m (Goodchild), 181 x 137 m (ULVS)   AREA: 2.48 ha (6.20 acres)   FIGURES: 5:3–5:4, 6:10   PLATES: 6–9   EPIGRAPHY: *IRT* 895–7; Supp *LA* II (1966)

In 1850, whilst on his way to Fezzan, Barth recognized the northeast gate as the 'well fortified entrance into the Roman station; but of the station itself I was unable to find any traces'. He was misled by the presence of a Berber village on the site and by the contrast between the ashlar masonry used for the lower part of the gate and the much rougher masonry used for the rest of the fort's defences. When Goodchild flew over and visited the site in the 1950s he made out far more of the layout and his plan has remained standard until the site was resurveyed as part of the ULVS work in the area (Fig 5:3).

Goodchild located three of the four gates but failed to find any trace of the southwest gate or southern corner of the fort defences. His conclusion that the wall was never built here because of the natural cliff defences must be doubtful following the identification of one side of the largely robbed-out southwest gate. The rest of the gate and the missing section of wall were presumably used as a quarry for the Berber vil-

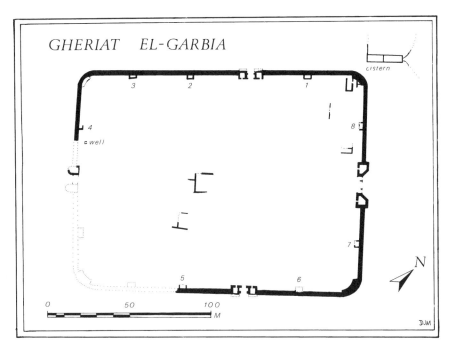

Fig. 5:3 The fort at Gheriat el-Garbia (after ULVS survey).

lage inside the fort (Plates 6 and 7). Where it survives, the fort wall is about 2.4 m thick and 3.5 m high to the bottom of the parapet. In many places the facing stone has been robbed and the rubble core is exposed.

The northeast gate is rightly famous for its triple archway (intact until 1984) and its southeast tower which stands almost to full height (Plate 8). The gate towers have obliquely angled fronts, a feature paralleled at Bu Njem and *Lambaesis*, and were constructed in ashlar blocks up to the bottom of the parapet. The first floor rooms were lit by two large windows in the front walls and were probably constructed on a vault. Goodchild also planned the southeast gate and those to the northeast and southwest were recorded by the ULVS in 1981 (Fig 5:4). The *portae principales* had rectangular, slightly projecting towers and these were faced with ashlars (robbed from their projecting face). Analogy with Bu Njem would suggest that the fourth gate should have been of this type, but Gheriat is highly unusual in having a third distinct type. The southwest gate was flanked by D-shaped projecting towers and whilst there are good Severan parallels several factors suggest that this gate may not have been original. Unlike the other gates it was not faced with ashlars but was constructed entirely in small masonry. As we have noted, the mixture of three distinct gate types is unparalleled in North Africa and this suggests non-contemporaneity. Finally, the circular watchtower 1 km north of the fort, which is securely dated to the reign of Severus Alexander (AD 222–35), was constructed in a similar style and would seem to confirm that the southwest gate was entirely rebuilt 20–30 years after the fort was first occupied.

The major discovery of the 1981 survey was the recognition of eight of the fort's original ten interval towers and three of its four angle towers (Fig. 5:4; Plate 9). Two of the interval towers stood almost to their full height of 9 m. The lower storey was filled with rubble in at least one case and the towers were entered from the parapet at first-floor level. There were no windows on the sides or inside walls of the towers so they were presumably on the outer face at first-floor level. These towers were generally around 4.8 m square.

The angle towers were of an unusually large type, filling the entire corners of the fort. They were built on a specially widened platform in the fort wall, a feature most readily paralleled at *Rapidum* in *Mauretania Caesariensis* – but probably also present at Bu Njem. Welsby has calculated from the evidence of the north tower that they were fronted by as many as five windows.

The interior buildings of the fort have been almost entirely robbed out or obscured by the Berber village which was built within the fort and occupied until recent times. Columns reused in the mosque may have come from the *principia* and some traces of earlier wall alignments are visible amongst the ruins of the village. In 1981 a small bath-house of military type was discovered by a spring on the opposite (western) side of the oasis. Three isolated buildings east of the

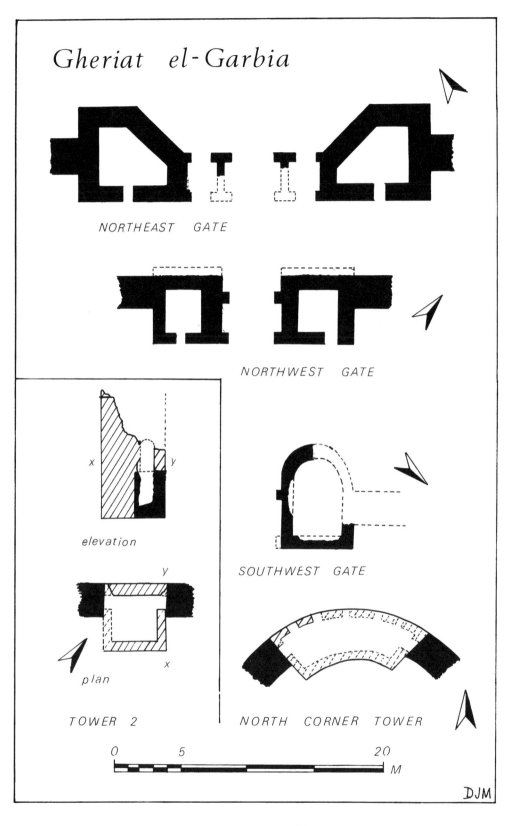

Fig. 5:4 Gates and towers at Gheriat el-Garbia (after ULVS survey).

Gheriat el-Garbia

NORTHEAST GATE

NORTHWEST GATE

elevation

SOUTHWEST GATE

plan

TOWER 2

NORTH CORNER TOWER

0   5   20
                          M

DJM

Fig. 5:5 Bu Njem, the north gate (from Lyon 1821).

fort were possibly temples – a column base being noted here in 1984. Closer to the fort are traces of a *vicus* and necropolis (see Fig. 6:10, below).

The epigraphic evidence from Gheriat shows that the fort was probably built at the same time as Bu Njem in AD 201 and was occupied at least down to the reign of Gordian, when an auxiliary unit had replaced the legionaries disbanded in AD 238. A milestone of Aurelian (AD 275) from south of Garian shows that either Mizda or Gheriat was still in commission at that late date. Pottery data are not refined without excavation, but seem to confirm that occupation was confined to the third century. The size of the fort implies that it was more important than Bu Njem and, as such, it is a possible location for the headquarters of the *praepositus limitis Tripolitanae*.[3]

Bu Njem (*Gholaia*)

DIMENSIONS: 138 × 93 m   AREA: 1.28 ha (3.21 acres)
FIGURES: 5:5–5:6, 6:10   PLATES: 10–11   EPIGRAPHY: *IRT* 913 – 22, *LA* 3 – 4 f.

The site was discovered by the British explorer Lyon in 1819 and his drawing of the north gate, then standing to full height, remains of great value (Fig. 5:5). Other early travellers have left useful observations. The construction of the Turkish and Italian forts nearby might have despoiled the site but led to the discovery of the bath building in 1928. However, the first detailed plan of the site was made by Goodchild on the basis of both field visits and air-photographs. Since 1967 a French team directed by Professor

Rebuffat has conducted extensive excavations at the site and a good deal is now published in full detail.[4]

The fort was provided with four gates and faced east (Fig. 5:6; Plate 10). The rampart wall was 2.40–2.50 m thick and according to Rebuffat it would have stood 5 m high including the parapet. As at Gheriat it was constructed in small masonry, the use of ashlar blocks being reserved for the lower portions of the gates. Most of the ashlars were given a rusticated finish, a distinctive feature of the site. The *porta praetoria* (east gate) was flanked by obliquely angled projecting towers, but was only a single carriageway wide. After the withdrawal of the garrison the gate chambers were converted to a different use, possibly as grain silos. The other three gates were all flanked by square projecting towers and the north and south examples have been excavated. Lyon's drawing (Fig. 5.5) indicates that like the Gheriat examples these were not constructed in ashlar to their full height, with smaller masonry being used in the upper structure. Each of the gate towers had two large windows at first-floor and one or two at second-floor level. These towers must have stood over 8 m high and this point is illustrated by a graffito found in the baths which depicts a fort whose eight gate towers are very high in relation to the walls. Ideas on the reconstruction of Roman fort gates and towers in other parts of the Roman empire may need to be reconsidered. Rebuffat has also uncovered traces of one interval tower and one can infer the presence of another and four angle towers of the same type as at Gheriat (on the basis of a kite air-photograph of the southeast corner of the fort; Plate 10).

Inaccurate Roman surveying of the outer defences

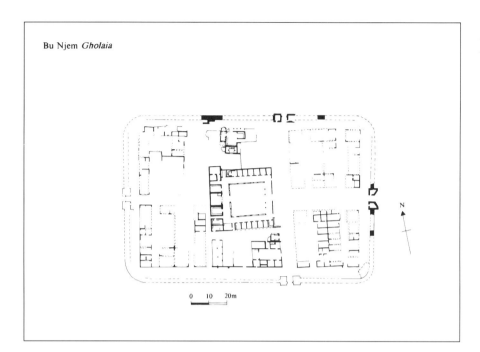

Bu Njem *Gholaia*

0 10 20m

Fig. 5:6 Bu Njem (*Gholaia*) plan (after Rebuffat 1989, with additions).

led to the positioning of the north and south gates at different distances from the eastern defences. This had the effect of putting askew the buildings flanking the *via principalis* as is all too evident on Figure 5:6. The *principia* and four of the six strip buildings in the *praetentura* were laid out in relation to this incorrect alignment. Another peculiarity of the layout of the fort is that it was apparently laid out using cardinal measurements in Punic cubits not Roman feet. The overall dimensions translate as 270 × 180 cubits of 51.55 cm, the 36 m front of the *principia* is equivalent to 70 cubits. Calculations in Roman feet and paces do not produce such satisfactory whole numbers for the common dividers.[5]

The *principia* has been completely excavated (Plate 11), along with the *praetorium*, the baths and a double granary (all in the *latera praetorii*). The *principia* is of fairly standard type. Offices, armouries and other rooms flank a courtyard, to the west of which a cross-hall with tribunal dais separates the court from the rear range. The *sacellum* is centrally placed in this rear range, raised up a few steps over the military strong-room. An important discovery was the identification of the *scriptorium* in the southern range with its writing desk and benches still *in situ*. At least four phases of construction/alterations were identified in the *principia* as a whole and a large quantity of military records written on pot sherds (*ostraca* – giving details of the last phase of military occupation) was found in and around the building. The majority of the 146

ostraca lay in a dump against the outside south wall of the building, close to the *scriptorium*, others came from several locations within the *principia*. These represent the residue of the last batch of temporary records held at the headquarters of the unit; after a few months the information recorded in the day rosters, day by day military reports on activity around Bu Njem and correspondence will have been superseded by events. The final destination for the thousands of such documents that the fort must have generated each year of its existence will have been the huge midden lying to the southwest of the fort (where a few further *ostraca* were indeed found).

The excavations of the baths have produced a wealth of detail about this complex which is preserved up to roof level. Repairs and alterations continued long after AD 238 as, for instance, in the Room of Fortuna. There was at least one well inside the fort, but fetching water and wood for the baths featured prominently among the tasks assigned in the Bu Njem day rosters. The commanding officer's house (*praetorium*) and the double granary lay on the south side of the *principia*, the chapel in the *praetorium* yielding an important text to the *genius Gholaiae*. Although mainly surface clearing was carried out over the barracks, their disposition is clear. Allowing two rooms per *contubernium* and assuming that some of the smaller strip buildings were stores or *fabricae* there is adequate accommodation for six centuries or one cohort (about 480 men). Rebuffat suggests 480–640 as the most likely range, but the question is complicated by the undoubted presence of a cavalry component in the 250s and by changes over time.[6]

Investigation of the cemeteries, of buildings within the *vicus* and of five satellite temples (three of which were dedicated to Jupiter Hammon, Mars Cannaphar and Vanammon) have been other important aspects of Rebuffat's work (Fig. 6:10). The epigraphic archive from the site is particularly rich and dated examples cover the period AD 201–59. It is thought that the fort was probably abandoned *c*. 263. Structural and ceramic evidence, however, shows that some civilian 'squatter' occupation continued into the fourth or early fifth century. By this stage the site was already partly engulfed by sands.[7]

Ghadames (*Cidamus, Cydamae*)

EPIGRAPHY: *IRT* 907–9; Reynolds 1958, no 1

Little survives at Ghadames which can be linked with the probable Roman fort constructed by the Roman vexillation under the command of a centurion. Duveyrier described a square tower in the northwest angle of the town wall, built of small masonry with some brick courses. There was another collapsed tower adjacent. Roman columns and capitals have been found in the el-Aouina square and reused in the main mosque. Recently, Rebuffat has reported finding Roman fine wares over a large part of the oasis adjacent to the necropolis. He has surveyed the tombs (Asnam) and an enigmatic circular tower nearby. Since the exact position and size of the military installation at Ghadames has not been established, we cannot exclude the possibility that it was not a full-size fort, as centurions could command fortlets (cf. *Tisavar* below).

Occupation can be presumed for the period *c*. AD 201–38. There is also evidence for considerable contact between Rome and the oasis in the second century before the garrison was installed.[8]

El-Hamma (*Aquae Tacapitanae*)

EPIGRAPHY: *CIL* 8. 22784

El-Hamma is notable for the Roman baths found there near the French colonial garrison fort, though the question of whether these were of military or civil origin is uncertain. The strategic importance of this oasis, which controls the Arad and the Tebaga gap and lies at an important Roman crossroads, suggests that it may have been garrisoned in the Flavian period. Unfortunately, apart from the baths, little is known of the other ancient ruins.[9]

Telmine (*Turris Tamalleni*)

EPIGRAPHY: *CIL* 8. 83, 84, 23157

The identification of Telmine as a Flavian fort is also circumstantial. The construction of a road between el-Hamma and Telmine under Domitian is highly suggestive. So is the rapidity of the pacification and the development of the tribal *civitas* there under Trajan and Hadrian. If not at Telmine itself a fort must have been placed at one of the neighbouring oases. Some troops may have remained in the area until the late empire.[10]

Mizda (Roman name unknown)

There was undoubtedly a major ancient site at Mizda. Barth described extensive ruins extending into the plain. When the Italian fort was built there it incorporated ancient stone and inscriptions from the region and from Mizda itself into its walls. The site lies at the centre of a network of roads, tracks and routes and was probably close to the boundary of the *Macae* and *Phazanii* tribes. There are no surviving structural remains today, but the most likely location for the fort is underneath the western village in the oasis.[11]

Edref near Zintan? (*Thenteos*)

The discovery of the Gasr Duib inscription confirmed the general location of *Thenteos* in the vicinity of Zintan. De Mathuisieulx had suggested this but the ruins he associated with the Roman 'road station' are those of the fortified olive farm and mausoleum called Gasr Romani. An expedition from Cambridge in 1964 suggested a different site a few kilometres west of Zintan at the Edref crossroads. Though covered by later troglodyte dwellings, Roman foundations extended along the ridge for about 400 m. The site is exactly 30 m.p. from Ain el Auenia (*Auru*).

The existence of a major fort here is admittedly speculation, in part based on the question of the whereabouts of the *cohors I Syrorum Sagittariorum*. This unit was involved in construction work at *Auru* in the early third century, but the permanent garrison left there was a legionary vexillation. The later importance of *Thenteos*, as attested by the Gasr Duib, inscription of AD 244–6 and in the *Notitia*, suggests that it was a fort rather than a road station. My interpretation of the status of the tribune mentioned in the Duib inscription (see above) supports the view that there was a major cohort fort at *Thenteos*. If it had an entire *cohors milliaria* in garrison (around 800 men) it would have been one of the most important forts in the region.[12]

3
FORTS OF MID-THIRD-CENTURY DATE

Ras el-Ain (*Talalati*)

DIMENSIONS: 93 × 93 m.   AREA: 0.86 ha (2.16 acres)
EPIGRAPHY: *CIL* 8 22765–22768   FIGURES: 5:7, 6:11

First identified by Lecoy de la Marche in 1894, Ras el-Ain was subjected to several attempts at excavation which produced two gate inscriptions of AD 263, but little detail of the fort's interior. Some buildings of the *vicus* were excavated including a bath-house. The site is still little changed and would repay modern examination.

The fort is roughly square, with rounded corners, and faces east. Like Bu Njem, its cardinal measurements may be based on the Punic cubit, giving overall

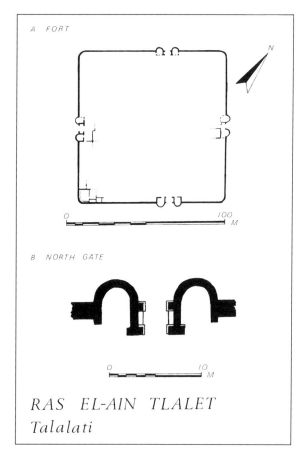

Fig. 5:7 Ras el-Ain Tlalet (*Talalati*), fort built in AD 263:
a) general plan; b) detail of north gate.

dimensions of 180 × 180 cubits. The main wall is only about 1.50 m thick and survives to approx. 2 m height. The four gates were all apparently flanked by D-shaped projecting towers with the piers and voussoirs of the arches being in ashlar. Figure 5:7 corrects the impression given by a recently published plan that these gate towers were simply semi-circular additions to the outside of the rampart. Detailed plans show that the gates were of normal type with the towers serving as guard chambers.

Excavation of the southwest angle produced no trace of an angle tower, but instead a series of storerooms and corridors backing on to the rampart. In general the early excavators found the interior too full of rubble for their speedy operations and so turned to the *vicus* outside (Fig. 6:11).

The fort was built in AD 263 in *opportuno loco a solo* and regular military occupation continued into the later fourth century AD following repairs in AD 355–60. Late Roman, and possibly Christian, burials were made in the corridor of the west gate, so the fort may have been abandoned at some point between AD 360 and the Vandal conquest. In contradiction of the claim that the fort was built on a virgin site, ceramic evidence suggests that the earliest activity here may have been early in the third century. This is to be expected if Ras el-Ain is to be identified with the *Talalati* of the Antonine Itinerary, which may therefore have originated as a civilian settlement or a fortlet of Severan date. The question can only be finally resolved by new excavation.[13]

4
ROAD STATIONS/FORTLETS

It is clear that not all the sites mentioned on the *limes* road in the Antonine Itinerary were military posts. It is not necessary, therefore, to link any suitably located defensive structure to a particular name from the Itinerary. But, conversely, it appears that when troops were posted to a road station or to watch a cistern or well they were provided with some form of defensive enceinte, be it a tower or a fortlet. The earliest certainly dated fortlets are those of *Bezereos* and *Tisavar* (Commodan) and the network was expanded under the Severans. Some outposts might be expected to date from the early to mid-second century whilst the construction of such posts continued into the fourth century (Table 5:2; Fig. 5:8).[14]

Area (across ramparts)	Name	Unit	Garrison size (max.)	Occupation
0.5 ha/1.25 acres	Ain Wif I (*Thenadassa*)	*vex./*part of a unit	100–200?	2nd C?
0.45 ha/1.12 acres	Hr Mgarine (*Agarlabas*)	*vex./*part of a unit	100?	3rd C
0.40 ha/0.99 acres	Hr Medeina (*Thebelami*)	part of *Coh II Flavia Afrorum?*	100?	3rd C
0.36 ha/0.90 acres	Gasr el Haddadia (*Tugulus*)	part of a unit?	100?	1st C? 3rd C?
0.36 ha/0.90 acres	Ksar Tabria	*vex/*part of a unit	100?	3rd C??
0.33 ha/0.81 acres	Bir Rhezene (*Bezereos*)	*vex leg III Aug*	c. 300*	later 2nd–3rd C
0.16 ha/0.40 acres	Ain Wif II (*Thenadassa*)	*vex leg III Aug*	?	3rd C
0.16 ha/0.40 acres	Medina Doga (*Mesphe*)	?	?	3rd C??
?	Ain el-Auenia (*Auru*)	*vex leg III Aug/* part of *Coh I Syrorum?*	?	3rd C
0.14 ha/0.36 acres	El Medina Ragda	?	?	1st–3rd C??
0.12 ha/0.30 acres	Ksar Rhilane (*Tisavar*)	*vex leg III Aug*	c. 80?	Later 2nd–3rd C
0.12 ha/0.30 acres	Si Aioun	*numerus collatus/*part of *Coh II Flavia Af.*	?	3rd C

Table 5:2. Roman fortlets in Tripolitania (sites between 0.11–0.5 ha area). * Some part of the *Bezereos* garrison may well have been distributed among other fortlets, unless a larger site than that known remains unidentified here.

Ain Wif I (*Thenadassa*)

DIMENSIONS: approx. 100 × 50 m (?)   AREA: 0.5 ha (1.25 acres)   EPIGRAPHY: *IRT 868–870*   FIGURE: 5:9

The site at Ain Wif I was for long considered an undefended road station garrisoned by a few soldiers. This theory does not seem to take account of the fact that there is a large military bath-house here nor explain why a 'few soldiers merely' were commanded by a *centurio princeps*. Re-examination of the site revealed the presence of certainly one and probably two phases of military compound. The larger of these has been tentatively ascribed to the second century AD on the

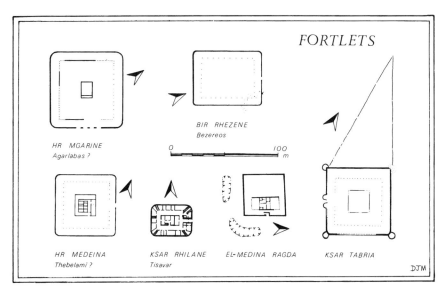

Fig. 5:8 Comparative plans of fortlets (including possible sites) from the *limes Tripolitanus*.

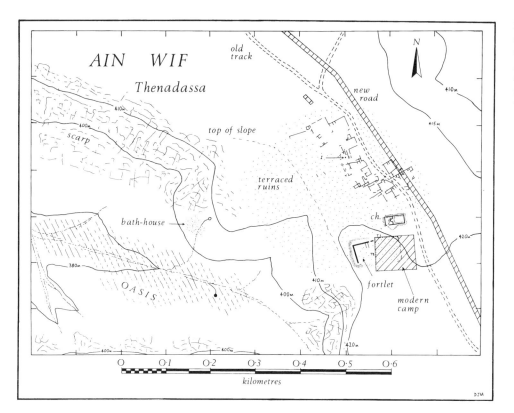

Fig. 5:9 Military structures and civil settlement at Ain Wif (*Thenadassa*) (from Mattingly 1982).

basis of pottery found in modern drain trenches cut through it, whilst the second, smaller fortlet probably relates to the attested occupation during the Severan period (Fig. 5:9).[15]

Bir Rhezene (*Bezereos*)

DIMENSIONS: 50 × 65 m   AREA: 0.33 ha (0.81 acres)
EPIGRAPHY: *ILAf* 26–27   FIGURE: 5:8

The recorded dimensions of the site of *Bezereos* (or *Vezerei*) do not correlate with the importance of the site as suggested by epigraphic discoveries. A fortlet of this small size could not have accommodated the force of 300 men revealed by a military list from the site. In chapter 4 it was suggested, therefore, that either there is a larger site still awaiting discovery under the sand dunes or else *Bezereos* was the command centre for a number of other small outposts in the northern Dahar.

The outer wall of the fortlet was constructed in small masonry with a single gate 'à chicane' in the north side. No detail of the internal buildings has been recorded but an arrangement similar to that at sites like *Tisavar* or Henchir Mgarine is likely.[16]

Hr Mgarine (*Agarlabas?*)

DIMENSIONS: 67 × 67 m   AREA: 0.45 ha (1.12 acres)
FIGURE: 5:8

The fortlet is defined by a masonry enceinte approx. 1.4 m wide. The angles are rounded with no trace of external bastions. The single entrance was probably in the southeast side. A central building constructed in *opus africanum* is relatively well preserved but the site has been heavily robbed of its smaller stonework. Trousset noted an internal wall running parallel to the northwest rampart at a distance of approx. 7 m from it. In 1982 I observed traces of similar walls in the same relationship to the southwest and southeast walls. The site would appear, therefore, to be a larger version of the *Tisavar*-type fortlet with barracks and stores built around the inside of the rampart and with a single freestanding central building (Fig. 5:8). Pottery from the site and its quite extensive *vicus* was predominantly third century in date but some indisputably second- and fifth-century forms were noted, so civilian occupation of some sort may have been over a longer period.[17]

Hr Medeina (*Thebelami?*)

DIMENSIONS: 63 × 63 m   AREA: 0.40 ha (0.99 acres)
FIGURES: 5:8, 5:10

Discovered by Lecoy de la Marche in 1894, this site bears many similarities to that just described. The style of enceinte, the presence of an *opus africanum* building in the centre and the overall size suggest that the sites were broadly contemporary and constructed for a particular size of detachment. The barrack arrangements at Medeina are unrecorded but were probably similar to those at Mgarine. Trousset's recent plan of the site disagrees in important details with de la Marche's on the arrangement of the central building (Figs 5:8, 5:10) and further survey or excavation would be necessary to resolve this problem entirely.[18]

Ksar Tabria (Roman name unknown)

DIMENSIONS: 60 × 60 m   AREA: 0.36 ha (0.9 acres)
FIGURE: 5:8

Although at first sight this fortlet appears to be of late Roman date, on account of its projecting corner towers, on the other hand the small masonry, larger overall size and circular, as opposed to square, bastions distinguish this site from the Benia Guedah Ceder type of *quadriburgus* (see chapter 10). The size and square shape of the site, the presence of a centrally placed free-standing building and barracks around the enceinte are features which could apply to a fortlet of third-century date were it not for the external corner bastions (Fig. 5:8). On Trousset's plan, at least one of these bastions looks as if it may have been added rather than being an original feature. If that were the case then this could be another third-century fortlet which was later modified. A visit to the site will be necessary before this possible third-century phase can be more than a tentative hypothesis.[19]

Ksar Rhilane (*Tisavar*)

DIMENSIONS: 40 × 30 m   AREA: 0.12 ha (0.3 acres)
EPIGRAPHY: *CIL* 8. 11048, 22631, 22579–22761
FIGURES: 5:8, 5:10

Tisavar is the most extensively excavated fortlet in Tripolitania. Although this site was only a quarter the size of Hr Mgarine it was clearly the same basic type of construction, though presumably designed for a smaller garrison (Fig. 5:8). The outer wall was 1.40 m thick with rounded corners. It was constructed up to a

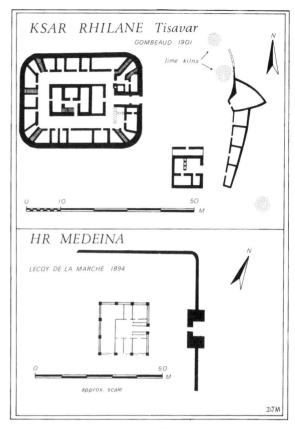

Fig. 5:10 a) The Roman fortlet of Ksar Rhilane (*Tisavar*) (after Gombeaud 1901); b) detail of the fortlet at Henschir Medeina (after Lecoy de la Marche 1894, but cf. 5:8).

height of roughly 1.5 m in ashlar and above that in smaller masonry to a height of about 4 m. The single entrance was in the east side and there were 20 rooms of varying size constructed round the inside face of the enceinte wall, some presumably barracks, others for stores (Fig. 5:10). The parapet walkway was built on the roofs of these rooms and stairways in the corners of the fortlet gave access up to it. The well-built central range of rooms included a chapel to Jupiter and was presumably the administrative centre of the post. Extramural ancilliary buildings included stables and temples (one of which had a trefoil plan and was dedicated to the *Genius Tisavar*).

The Severan garrison may have been equivalent to a century of about 80 men as it was commanded by a centurion and two *optiones*. Military occupation of the site seems to have run from the later second century to the early years of the fourth century. The fortlet seems to have been deliberately burnt after being cleared out by the departing garrison.[20]

Si Aioun (*praesidium...*)

DIMENSIONS: approx. 30 × 40 m   AREA: approx. 0.12 ha (0.3 acres)   EPIGRAPHY: *ILAF* 8–9

I know of no published plan of this site, but the most recent description appears to describe a fortlet of similar type to those above. At 300 m from the fortlet were at least two mausolea and a large group of cisterns lay between these tombs and the fortlet. The central building of the fortlet has completely collapsed but may have been constructed in part in *opus africanum*. Trousset noted that the ruinous main building was surrounded by a masonry enceinte about 30–40 m square, which would make the site overall the same size as *Tisavar*, with a cistern in the southern sector and the main entrance to the east.[21]

Gasr el-Haddadia (*Tugulus*)

DIMENSIONS: approx. 60 × 60 m   AREA: 0.36 ha (0.9 acres)

Goodchild published an air-photograph of this site with an all-too-brief description. The site is approximately square with rounded corners and perhaps had more than one gate. Details of internal buildings do not show on the photograph. The form of the site and the surface pottery combine to suggest a date for its construction between the late first century and early third century AD. The aftermath of the Nasamonian revolt is perhaps the best context, but its small size might suggest a later date.[22]

Ain Wif II (*Thenadassa*), Medina Doga (*Mesphe*), Ain el-Auenia (*Auru*)

DIMENSIONS: Ain Wif II and Medina Doga, approx. 40 × 40 m   AREA: 0.16 ha (0.4 acres)
EPIGRAPHY: Ain Wif: *IRT* 868–70; el-Auenia : *IRT* 857; Reynolds 1955, 5.14; Reynolds and Brogan 1960, Nos 1–2, Reynolds and Simpson 1967, 45–7
FIGURE: 5:9

These sites can be conveniently discussed together, since all three have been claimed to be undefended road stations. The recent identification of a two phase fortlet at Ain Wif reopens the question of the form of military presence postulated for the other two sites. No military inscriptions have been found at Medina Doga, but there is a roughly 40 m square defensive enceinte there, built in ashlar masonry. The second phase fortlet at Ain Wif is approximately the same size though built in smaller masonry (and therefore

almost entirely robbed out). Conversely at Ain el-Auenia inscriptions and tile stamps show that a legionary vexillation was certainly present in garrison and, although so far their barracks have not been located, a fortified post is likely. All three of these road stations possessed bath-houses and later were fairly considerable civilian settlements (chapter 6).[23]

El Medina Ragda

DIMENSIONS: approx. 38 × 38 m   AREA : 0.14 ha (0.36 acres)   FIGURES: 5:8, 5:21

First identified as a military post by de Mathuisieulx in 1904, the site was virtually forgotten until visited by Brogan when she discovered the Hadd Hajar *clausura* a few kilometres to the south of it. She cautiously suggested that the site might be a fortified farm but the subsequent visit by the ULVS favoured the earlier military interpretation.

The site is surrounded by a defensive wall of large ashlars with a single entrance in the east side. The corners are square but there is no trace of external bastions. On the south and east sides there are hints of a possible ditch. The only visible interior building is a rectangular range in *opus africanum* near the entrance (Fig. 5:8). About 50 m northeast of the fortlet is a huge double cistern with impressively constructed vaults (Fig. 5:21).

The surface pottery scatter at the site included large quantities of late first- and second-century fine wares and at this early date the defensive features of the site would be more consistent with a military interpretation. Medina Ragda lies on a major transhuming corridor between the Dahar and the Gebel, and the *clausura* just to the south shows that Roman policing of this corridor was considered important. The fortlet at Medina Ragda was probably occupied from an earlier date than the *clausura*, but a connection between the two is not improbable.[24]

5
OUTPOSTS (*GSUR*, 'FORTIFIED FARMS', *CENTENARIA*)

Unlike most of the sites described above, fortified sites of 0.1 ha area and under are much harder to classify as military or civilian. The criteria applied in the past have proved unsatisfactory, particularly because of the tendency to identify *any* square or rectangular building with reasonably neat masonry and some defensive features as military. Recent work in the

Libyan pre-desert and Gebel has underlined time and again the indigenous origins of most of the settlement and of many of the impressive fortified farms (*gsur*). The previous attempts to date the *gsur* in terms of alleged differences in their masonry construction have been discredited and without some supplementary evidence the style of construction alone cannot be taken to indicate that a building was built by the military. Nor are features like ditches solely restricted to military sites. In some cases the proximity of civilian mausolea can help decide whether a particular *gsur* is of 'native type', but this cannot be infallible either.

Terminology is a complicating factor of course. Indeed the whole question of the *centenaria* in the later Roman empire has often been misconceived. It has been argued that the *centenarium* was a particular class of site and that the name related to the officer in charge (*centenarius*). Alternatively it may derive from the unit intended to serve as the detachment (*centuria*). But the archaeological evidence cannot be reconciled to either view. Compare, for example, the size of *centenarium Aqua Viva* (86 × 86 m = 0.74 ha) built in AD 303 with *centenarium Tibubuci* (15 × 15 m = 0.02 ha) also probably built in AD 303. Neither the commanding officer's rank nor the size of units installed are likely to have been equivalent in these two sites. It is inadvisable, therefore, to read too much into the significance of the name in a late Roman context.

Further confusion has arisen, as we have already observed, through erroneous links established between *centenaria* and *gsur* and between *limitanei* and the *gasr*-dwellers. Goodchild correctly observed that in a few cases, *gsur* built by native Libyans were also called *centenaria*, but his error was to argue that this had military significance and that the same was probably true of the status of most of the other *gsur* as well. We have no way of assessing exactly how many of the *gasr*-dwellers had a designated status as border militia nor do we know what duties this entailed. The use of military terminology by civilians for structures built on their estates, however, is well attested. Indeed, it is interesting that almost all of the epigraphic evidence suggests that the first concern of the *gasr*-builders was protection for their own families and estates; there is no mention of a wider purpose. The military organization behind the known civilian *centenaria* was in all probability extremely loose or non-existent (see chapter 10, below).

Because of these uncertainties it is now necessary to treat each site on its merits and with a good deal of scepticism. Of course some genuine small outposts and towers can be confidently identified by epigraphic means. There must have been some others which were military or para-military in origin, but it would be a futile exercise to list *all* the known *gsur* since a high proportion were indigenous civilian creations, built for reasons of prestige and/or defence. The earliest of the Libyan *gsur* seem to be late second and early third century in date and it is possible that the form followed a military model. But fortified towers had served as granaries in the oases earlier so an indigenous development is not inconceivable. In view of these problems of identification I have limited my examples of 'military' outposts largely to the certain and probable categories (Table 5:3; Fig. 5:11).[25]

Some of the larger outposts were constructed in ashlar masonry and despite the lack of epigraphic proof, their strategic sitings favour a military interpretation.

Area (across ramparts)	Name	Attached to fort/fortlet	Garrison size (max.)	Occupation
0.10 ha/0.25 acres	Gheriat esh Shergia	Gheriat el-Garbia	<50?	later 2nd?–3rd C
0.08 ha/0.20 acres	Hr Krannfir (Khanefi)	Bir Rhezene (*Bezereos*)	<50??	3rd C?
0.06 ha/0.16 acres	Zella I	Bu Njem (*Gholaia*)	?	3rd C?
0.06 ha/0.16 acres	Gasr Isawi (Banat)	?	<50?	later 2nd?–3rd C
0.03 ha/0.08 acres	el-Fascia	Bu Njem?	?	later 2nd?–3rd C
0.03 ha/0.08 acres	Zella II	Bu Njem	?	3rd C?
0.02 ha/0.06 acres	Ksar Tarcine (*Tibubuci*)	Ras el Ain (*Talalati*)	22 maximum	4th C
0.02 ha/0.06 acres	Gasr Duib	Zintan (*Thenteos*)	?	mid 3rd C +
0.02 ha/0.04 acres	Gasr Wames	Zintan (*Thenteos*) or Mizda?	?	mid 3rd C +?
0.01 ha/0.03 acres	Gasr Zerzi	Bu Njem	?	3rd C

Table 5:3. Roman outposts in Tripolitania (sites under 0.10 ha in size, excluding watch-towers and minor observation posts).

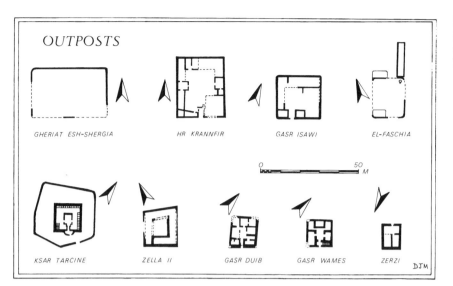

Fig. 5:11 Comparative plans of certain and probable military outposts in Tripolitania.

Hr Krannfir (*Khanefi*)

DIMENSIONS: 31 × 25.4 m   AREA: 0.08 ha (0.2 acres)
FIGURE: 5:11

The site was partially excavated in 1903 and comprises an ashlar enceinte, with a number of rooms inside flanking a central courtyard. The fact that the building lacks bastions favours a second- or third-century date, but no clearer indications were noted in the excavation. One of the internal rooms was a stable with accommodation for at least eight horses, so the detachment was part mounted. The site is also in a good position for observation and signalling towards Bir Rhezene (*Bezereos*) which was presumably its command centre (Fig. 5:17).[26]

Gheriat esh-Shergia

DIMENSIONS: 38.8 × 26 m   AREA: 0.10 ha
(0.25 acres)   FIGURES: 5:11, 5:12   Plate: 12

Three sides of this impressive building survive to a height of about 7 m, built throughout in fine ashlar blocks (Plate 12). The corners were cut round and slightly bevelled, a feature exactly paralleled at Gasr Isawi (see below). Goodchild thought the east wall had fallen away over the cliff escarpment, but examination in 1980 suggested that it may have been demolished when the building was incorporated into an Italian fort and a range of offices or barracks was inserted on this side. The presence in the entrance to one of these now ruined rooms of a pair of massive sill-stones, apparently *in situ*, established the position

of the entrance and east wall of the Roman post (Fig. 5:12). On the much rougher internal face of the enceinte wall there are signs that the rooms were built lean-to against it and that they were two-storeyed.

The outpost was constructed at the top of a scarp overlooking and dominating the esh-Shergia oasis. A signalling link existed between the Roman posts in the Gheriat oases, the tower (*burgus*) at el-Garbia being visible from esh-Shergia. Although normally assumed to post-date the construction of the fort at el-Garbia, it is conceivable that the sequence could be reversed. Of

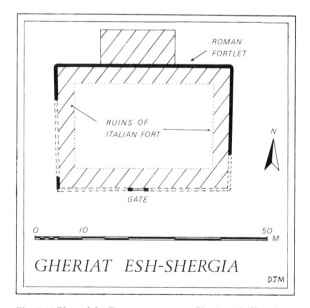

Fig. 5:12 Plan of the Roman outpost at Gheriat esh-Shergia (after ULVS survey).

the two oases esh-Shergia is the larger and perhaps lies on the better route southwards to Fezzan. The possibility of a pre-Severan date is worth bearing in mind in view of the evidence from Gasr Isawi.

Gasr Isawi (*Banat*)

DIMENSIONS: 22 × 25 m   AREA: 0.06 ha (0.14 acres)
FIGURES: 5:11, 5:13

The existence of an almost identical building to the esh-Shergia example called Gasr Isawi, in the Wadi N'f'd, was noted by Goodchild and others and increases the likelihood that both are military. The discovery by the ULVS of a native hillfort about 400 m from the post suggests a probable *raison d'être* for a military presence here.

The main ashlar walls of the building still stand 6 – 7 m high and were backed on the inside by an inner skin of smaller masonry into which the internal rooms were bonded. The layout was apparently based on ranges of rooms around a central courtyard (Fig. 5:11). The well-preserved doorway could be strongly barred and bolted. There was no sign of the provision of a dedicatory inscription (Fig. 5:13). Additional support

for a military interpretation is provided by ancilliary buildings round the main *gasr*. The regular, rectangular ranges are quite unlike the normally somewhat irregular outbuildings around *gsur*.

As well as policing a tribal (and perhaps a market) centre, Isawi is close to several major routes leading north across the Sofeggin. Dating evidence from the site suggests that occupation may have commenced in the later second century, possibly in pre-Severan times.

A number of other sites exhibiting similarly fine masonry may be in this same class, but care is necessary. A strong case can be made out for the site at el-Faschia on the Zem-Zem. This *gasr* with rounded corners and built in massive masonry controls an important Roman cistern on a route towards Bu Njem (Fig. 5:11). One can be less confident about some other possibilities, notably in the Gebel region where the use of ashlar masonry was much more common-place.[27]

The Bu Njem outposts

EPIGRAPHY: Brogan and Reynolds 1960, Nos 1 and 2. Marichal 1979, 448–50; 1992. FIGURE: 5:11

The *ostraca* from Bu Njem occasionally referred to places that may have been military outposts, *Arnum, Boinag, Esuba, Galin...i[...], Hyeruzerian, Secedi*. Although the exact location of these is unknown, and *Secedi* may be a separate cohort fort, there are some good archaeological candidates. There are two *gsur* (28 x 23 m and 18 x 18 m) in the Zella oasis with associated third-century pottery and both may be military in nature. Gasr Zerzi (12.8 x 9.2 m) to the west of Bu Njem is securely dated by inscriptions to the reign of Severus (Fig 5:11). Other sites remain only partially published, but at most of them the pottery is consistent with the Bu Njem type series. Many of the outposts and towers were sited at oases, wells or cisterns on the desert (and pre-desert) tracks. Their function would therefore seem to have been to regulate and oversee all movement through the frontier zone.[28]

Gasr Duib and Gasr Wames

DIMENSIONS: Duib approx. 16.25 × 15 m. Wames 13.20 × 13.20 m   AREA: D 0.02 ha (0.06 acres). W 0.02 ha (0.04 acres)   EPIGRAPHY: *IRT* 880–2 (Duib) FIGURES: 5:11, 5:21

These two sites are sometimes referred to as if both lay on the upper Sofeggin road, but Duib actually lay some kilometres southwest of the known alignment.

Fig. 5:13 The fine ashlar masonry and doorway of the probable Roman outpost of Gasr Isawi in the Wadi N'f'd (after ULVS survey).

Duib was clearly an outpost associated with *Thenteos* (near Zintan) whilst Wames, from its more southeasterly location, probably related to the suspected military post at Mizda. They were not necessarily of contemporary construction, therefore, though their functions may have been similar.

Wames is surrounded by a ditch and has a well preserved tower over the entrance. Post-Roman alterations and refurbishment of Duib make it harder to discern original features there, but the construction is dated to AD 244–6. Another inscription, largely illegible, seems to use the Latino-Punic script. At Wames the space for a large rectangular dedication stone is visible over the entrance but the stone has disappeared. It was probably also constructed during the third century. It is crucially important to note, though, that in many respects these two sites are indistinguishable from the mass of other fortified farms in the region.[29]

Ksar Tarcine (*Centenarium Tibubuci*)

DIMENSIONS: 15 × 15 m   AREA: 0.02 ha (0.06 acres)
EPIGRAPHY: *CIL* 8.22763   FIGURES: 5:11, 5:19

The *gasr* at Tarcine was surrounded by an outer hexagonal enclosure of uncertain function. The ground floor of the *gasr* itself was mainly used for stabling up to 22 horses. The garrison presumably lived on the second floor, reached by a staircase in the southwest corner. The presence of cavalry indicates that the function of the post went beyond the mere act of controlling use of the cistern there and of overseeing movement up the Wadi Hallouf. Some wider patrolling seems to have been envisaged (Fig. 5:11). The post was constructed *c.* AD 303 and was still occupied in the 390s (following the coin evidence). Although it properly related to the fourth-century frontier, in typological terms it was more similar to the smaller outposts of the second/third centuries than the *quadriburgi* of the late Roman frontier (see below, chapter 10).[30]

There are many other *gsur* in Tunisia and Libya which were possibly of military construction. Since in most cases the evidence is unsatisfactory for firm conclusions I have excluded them from this analysis. But I would concede that the following sites recorded by Trousset (1974) are possibilities in view of their location (away from the agricultural settlement) or structural peculiarities: Trousset site nos 96 Ksar Chetaoua; 101 Bir Mahalla; 114 Ksar Chouline; 134 Wadi Ouni; 135 el Majen.

6
TOWERS
(sites under 10 × 10 m)

Similarly, a large number of possibly military watchtowers can be cited but the same difficulties of positive identification exist as for the larger *gsur*. Towers were also built for crop and flock watchers in the agricultural areas. For a few structures, however, greater certainty is possible. There are the towers associated with the *clausurae* (see below), the circular *burgus* at Gheriat el-Garbia, and the towers acting as look-outs for the forts of Benia Guedah Ceder, *Bezereos* and Bu Njem.

Some of the towers were intended simply as observation posts, others for both observation and signalling. Local tradition preserves the memory of signalling between Mergueb ed Diab (the 'eyes' of the fort of *Bezereos)* and Tamezrend in the Gebel Matmata (Fig 5:17). There may have been a network of such signalling stations in the Mizda-Gheriat corridor and near Bu Njem. Nonetheless, the Bu Njem *ostraca* show that the outposts sent frequent messages by hand. In those circumstances horse or mule transport between posts will have been necessary for speedy communication. The manning of the towers was the same as for fortlets, with detachments outposted from the control forts such as Remada, Bu Njem and Gheriat.[31]

7
CLAUSURAE

Since I have attacked the inappropriate usage of Latin terminology, the employment of the terms *fossatum* and *clausura* in this section requires explanation. Both these terms are commonly used in Roman African studies in reference to the linear walls and earthworks of the frontier region, the difference between the two being that a *clausura* is much shorter than a section of *fossatum* and generally blocks a single corridor or defile. Our knowledge of ancient usage is sparse and inconclusive. The word *clausura*, for instance, is only known in a few late Roman and Byzantine sources and in different contexts can be translated as 'the defile', 'the fort in the defile' and 'the fortification in the defile'. It is in the last sense that it is normally employed in modern scholarship. Nor is the ancient use of the term *fossatum* much better known. But the alternatives are equally problematical. Rebuffat has suggested recently that the linear barrier south of *Sala* in *Mauretania Tingitana* was in Latin terminology a *bracchium*, but the evidence is far from convincing.

With more justification he has disposed of the suggestion made by Euzennat and Trousset that one of the Tunisian groups of *clausurae* was referred to as *propugnacula*. One can invoke the case of the *vallum* in Britain and plead that at least the usage of *clausura* and *fossatum* has been consistent (even if some would claim incorrect) and that scholars relate the terms for convenience with a particular group of monuments.[32]

As stated already, the basis for my distinction between the *fossata* of Algeria and the *clausurae* is that the former are significantly longer and were intended to control a multiplicity of routes. In sequence the *clausurae* achieved the same result but each one individually controlled only a single route or defile. The idea that the *fossata* and *clausurae* were part of a complete cordon defence utilizing 'impenetrable' natural obstacles in the gaps between sectors is no longer tenable. But there is a regularity in their pattern of deployment, in that many of the major natural routes and transhumance lines were obliged to cross one of these linear barriers. It is also clear that these earthworks did not mark the official frontier of Rome in

every case. Many of them were erected behind the actual frontier proper, very close to the limits of the agricultural zone at a point where there was a rapid transition from a predominantly agricultural to a predominantly pastoral way of life (Fig. 5:14).

Early French antiquarians initially identified the earthworks as irrigation canals or barrages. Since the recognition that they were elements of a Roman frontier system there has been a great deal of speculation but little agreement about their function and date. In terms of Roman frontier strategy they could be assigned to any period between the late first and early fifth centuries AD. Indeed one of the major errors of some scholars may have been to seek a unitary solution for their development and perhaps in future it will be possible to separate out several different phases of construction.[33]

The Cherb *clausurae*
(Fig. 5:15)

The Cherb range, north of the Chott Fedjedj, formed the boundary between the territory of the *Capsitani*

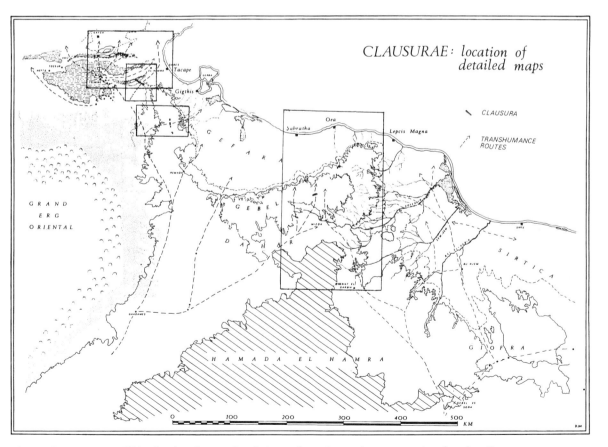

Fig. 5:14 Location map of Tripolitanian *clausurae* in relation to the main transhumance routes of modern times.

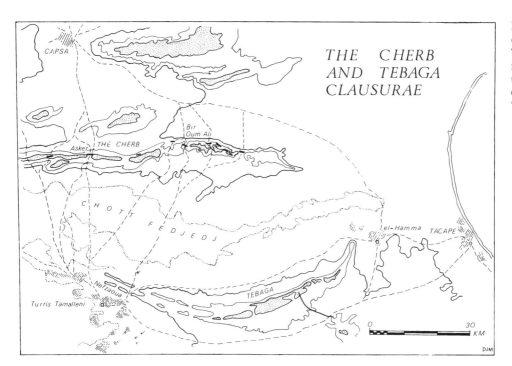

Fig. 5:15 Location of the Cherb and Tebaga *clausurae* in relation to the towns/oases of *Capsa, Tacape* and *Turris Tamalleni.*

and the *Nybgenii*. The range is a difficult one to cross and in the nineteenth century only one or two routes were believed practicable for horses. Goetschy, therefore, poured scorn on the local claim that the Romans had built walls in other passes as well as in these two major corridors across the Gebel Asker and at Bir Oum Ali. Nevertheless a recent French expedition has found evidence for ten or more *clausurae* in the range. As well as those in the Asker and Oum Ali defiles, these are located in the gorges of the Wadi Halfaya Srhira, the Wadi Kerma, the Khanguet Lefaia, on the watershed of the Gebel Batoum and in the Gebel Sif el Laham (Fig. 5:15).

Gebel Asker

Privé, who was one of the first to report the presence of walls in the Cherb, missed the one in the Asker defile, though he certainly passed through. Toutain later reported that Donau had observed a 'barrage' in the wadi in the defile. This wall continued up the valley sides, limiting traffic to a single point. Carton recognized this as a linear barrier. The main Roman road between *Capsa* and the Nefzaoua passed through this control point, showing that in antiquity this route was probably more significant than that via Bir Oum Ali. Traces of the wall are still visible over its length of several hundred metres. The sluice system on which it was carried over the wadi is of particular interest.

Bir Oum Ali

The wall at Khanguet Oum Ali is in an astonishing state of preservation (Plates 14 and 15). In places it still stands to its full height of approx. 6 m and the neat mortared masonry has an extraordinarily fresh look. It was built up and down a series of sharp gradients in order to limit movement down the pass and the wadi bed below to a single crossing point controlled by gate. Like the more ruinous example at Asker, the *clausura* was carried across the wadi over a rock-cut system of sluices. The actual wall was approx. 1.5 m wide with two faces of small neat masonry and a rubble and mortar fill. On the steeper slopes the wall was topped by a triangular cap in the same masonry. In other sections it was open to the air leaving a 'walkway' 0.75 m wide with parapets up to approx. 0.60 m high. The floor and walls of this were partially plastered (Fig. 5:16). Goetschy made an imaginative interpretation of the defensive utility of these features but his vision of men fighting off invaders from the wall's parapet is patently absurd. To use the wall as a shield they would have had to fight on hands and knees and in any case one can question the efficacy of the *clausurae* as defensible lines.

The only evidence for a garrison associated with the wall is provided by the gate (probably flanked by two towers and, to the west, an enigmatic circular structure). Most of this has been obliterated by modern

20 (*Above*) Detail of Imperial family from the Severan quadrifons arch at *Lepcis Magna*, showing (centre from right to left) Septimius Severus, Geta and Caracalla, with the disgraced and defaced praetorian prefect Fulvius Plautianus to the right and Julia Domna to left (the Jamahiriya's Museum, Tripoli).

21 (*Above*) The reconstructed quadrifons arch at *Lepcis Magna* (the scene shown in plate 20 can be seen in the attic of the arch).

22 (*Right*) Detail of figured pilaster from the Severan basilica at *Lepcis Magna*, showing Bacchic scenes in reference to the tutelary deity Liber Pater/Shadrapa.

23 (*Above*) Interior of the Severan basilica, *Lepcis Magna*, looking north.

24 (*Left*) Exterior wall and one of the entrances into the Severan forum at *Lepcis*.

25 (*Below*) General view of *Lepcis Magna* taken from the top of the theatre looking towards the Severan forum complex (right rear) and the harbour (rear left). The building in the centre is the market.

26 (*Above*) The eastern harbour mole at *Lepcis Magna* viewed across the silted harbour mouth. The building on the end of the mole was probably a semaphore tower for guiding ships into the harbour.

27 (*Left*) The office of Sabrathan merchants in the Piazzale delle Corporazioni at Ostia, using the elephant as a commercial or civic emblem.

28 (*Below*) The Hunting baths, *Lepcis Magna*, late second century AD.

29 (*Above*) Interior of frigidarium of the Hunting baths showing scenes of leopard hunting in the arena.

30 (*Below*) *Sabratha*, exterior view of the theatre (source: Barri Jones).

31 (*Above*) The forum at *Gigthis* from the east, looking towards the capitolium.

32 (*Below*) Telmine (*Turris Tamalleni*), architectural elements from the Roman town and view of the oasis adjacent to the modern settlement.

33 (*Top left*) Henchir Sidi Hamdan, *opus africanum* olive oil factory containing a suite of nine olive presses.

34 (*Bottom left*) El-Amud olive farm, press building with single press, detail of lower press room with settling tank and vats.

35 (*Right*) Snemat, an *opus africanum* farm from the Wadi Merdum of first-century AD date, with colossal olive press orthostats (source: ULVS).

36 (*Below*) Wadi walls on the floor of the denuded Wadi Migdal.

37 (*Above*) Surviving Wadi agriculture in the Wadi Beni Ulid showing dense plantations of ancient olive trees, with occasional almonds, dates. The traces of lateral and longitudinal walls can be seen in between the trees. Compare also Plate 2.

38 (*Below left*) Aerial view of an *opus africanum* olive farm, Grarat D'nar Salem (BUN 7) (source: ULVS).

39 (*Below right*) Aerial view of a courtyard farm from the Wadi Ghirza (source: ULVS).

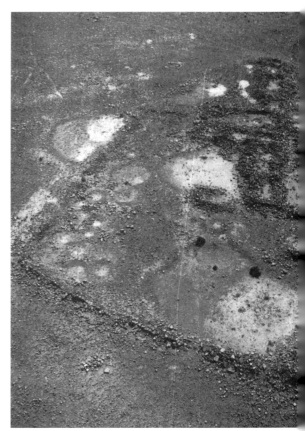

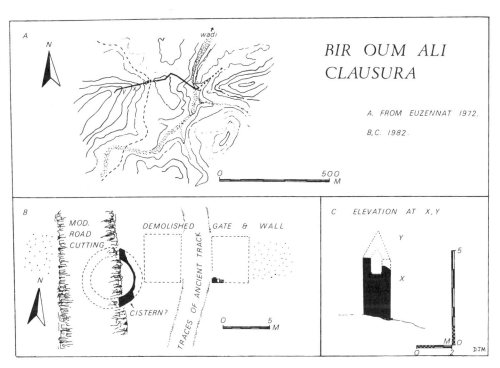

Fig. 5:16 The Bir Oum Ali *clausura*: a) general layout; b) detail of area of gate; c) elevations at points x and y on (a) (after Euzennat 1972).

road improvements which have sliced through the circular feature (4 m internal diameter), but the line of the ancient track and at least one ashlar pier of the gate can still be seen just to the east (Fig. 5:16). Goetschy noted the circular structure in 1894 and interpreted it as either a tower or well-head. But since it is at the lowest point of the wall across the main corridor and adjacent to the gate it is hardly likely to have been an observation tower. An important feature of it is that it is plaster lined and this suggests another possibility, namely that it was a cistern, supplying the needs of the small detachment in the gate-house. This interpretation also provides a possible explanation for the so-called 'parapet walkway' which could obviously function as a catchment system for the cistern during a torrential downpour. Otherwise the nearest source of water is a few kilometres to the north at Bir Oum Ali itself.

Pottery is very sparse in the vicinity of the gate, but one rim sherd identified on site was of second/third century date. Other circumstantial evidence suggests that the *clausura* may have been built in the early second century (see further below).[34]

The Gebel Tebaga *clausura*
(Figs 5:15, 5:17–5:18)
From the late nineteenth century the Tebaga *clausura* has been recognized as a linear earthwork of the Roman frontier. It is over 17 km long, running from the crest of the Gebel Tebaga to the foothills of the Gebel Melab. It thus controls the extremely important corridor linking Dahar and Arad (Figs 5:15, 5:17). There was confusion in early reports of the nature of the obstacle, one described it as a low dry-stone wall 4 m wide, another as an earth bank. In reality both were correct in that it was constructed as a bank and ditch across the alluvial floor of the valley (Plate 16) and as a wall on the Gebel scarps. The combination of bank and ditch produced an obstacle about 15 m wide. The change in constructional technique shows a perfect adaptation to local conditions and is paralleled on the Numidian *fossata* and on the Hadd Hajar *clausura*. In all these cases the changes in construction need not relate to different phases of construction.

A number of towers and a gate have also been noted in association with the *clausura*. Two of the towers are of unusual type and design, being circular in shape (8 m diameter) and surrounded by their own bank and ditch defences (25 m diameter) which join on to those of the *clausura* proper.

The gateway through the *clausura* itself was excavated by Donau in 1904, but Blanchet's account contains valuable supplementary information on the state of the gate prior to this. Donau revealed a double tower of several rooms, separated by a corridor. Some blocks from a demolished mausoleum were reused in the ashlar walls including a funerary inscription (civilian) in the corridor wall. Since his excavation was

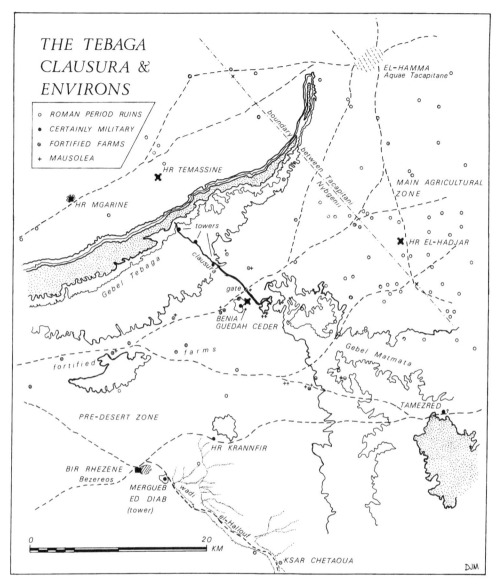

Fig. 5:17 The Tebaga *clausura* in relation to the second-century fortlets at Bir Rhezene and Hr Mgarine and the probable fourth century sites of Benia Guedah Ceder, Hr el-Hadjar and Hr Temassine.

never fully published and the only available plan is that produced by Trousset, Donau's evidence is difficult to assess. However, some modifications to both plan and interpretation can be proposed (Fig. 5:18a). First, there is the question of whether the incorporation of the reused mausoleum blocks was an original feature. The door of the northern tower was blocked in a late alteration (Plate 16) and its southern suite of rooms extends further west than one might expect, raising the possibility that the gate was substantially modified in the late empire. A second peculiarity is that the *clausura* did not run right up to the gate. In fact the gate lies within an outer compound, as was noted by Blanchet (Fig. 5:18b). Clearly more than one

phase of construction and use is involved in this particular case and we must be wary not to read too much into the meagre dating evidence. On the other hand the late second- to early third-century lamp found by Donau below the foundations is not consistent with the mid-fourth-century date assigned to this *clausura* by Trousset. For comparison, the sparse pottery noted on the site in 1982 was third century in date.[35]

The Skiffa group
(Figs 5:19, 5:20)

The presence of a group of *clausurae* in Gebel Demmer has long been suspected, but has only recently

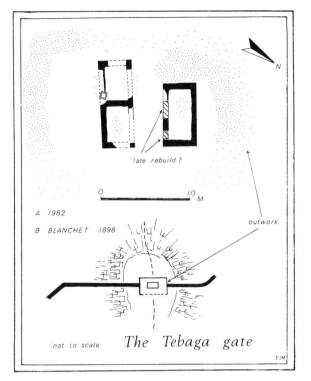

Fig. 5:18 The Tebaga *clausura* gate: a) after Trousset 1974 (with modifications); b) after Blanchet 1898 (NB the clear indication of the outwork).

received the attention which it deserves. Four (perhaps five) are known and more may yet be discovered along some of the other main west to east routes through the range (Fig. 5:19). All these *clausurae* control defiles (or 'passages obligés') which separate the Dahar from the Gefara.

Wadi bel Recheb

The existence of a *clausura* in the Wadi bel Recheb west of the late fortlet at Benia bel Recheb is uncertain because of a double confusion. Lecoy de la Marche was misled by his guide into believing he was in the Wadi bel Recheb when he discovered the Skiffa *clausura* in 1894 (which he believed was a barrage in any case). The account of Hilaire in 1901, however, contained an important double reference relating to this area. First, he correctly pointed out Lecoy's geographical error but then he went on to state that there were two other 'barrages' closer to the fort at Benia. The first was in the Wadi Zraia and is in fact a *clausura*, the second he placed in the Wadi bel Recheb itself. Although it has not been relocated in modern times, Hilaire had differentiated this 'barrage' from the one mistakenly located by Lecoy de la Marche, so it is likely to have been a genuine feature. Given the topographic importance of the bel Recheb corridor, a wall there is likely to have been a *clausura* rather than a barrage.

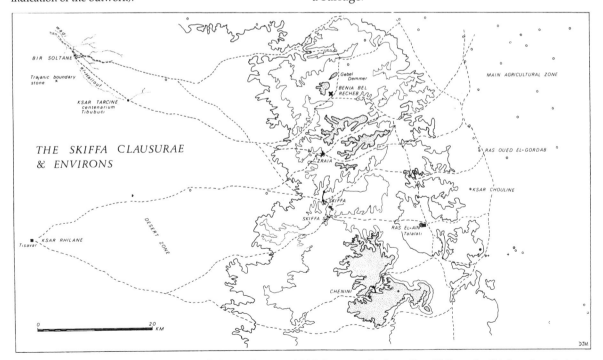

Fig. 5:19 The Skiffa group of *clausurae* in relation to the second/third-century fortlet at Ksar Rhilane, the third-century fort at Ras el-Ain and the fourth-century outpost at Ksar Tarcine and probable fortlet at Benia bel Recheb.

Wadi Zraia

This *clausura* of approx. 400 m length was constructed as a broad bank in the bottom of the defile and as a roughly built, low stone wall on its scarps. The original interpretation of it as a barrage is clearly inappropriate. There is a possible watchtower on a hillock just to the east.

Wadi Skiffa

The *clausura* of Wadi Skiffa is over a kilometre in length (Plate 17) and consists of a wall of 3–4 m width near the sides of the valley and on the scarps which it runs up. In the centre of the valley it has the appearance of either a broad bank or an extremely ruinous wall – perhaps there was originally a slight wall on top of a bank. Where it crossed the main wadi bed it was built over sluices to allow the water to pass below during floods. Two supposed circular towers near to its southern end, in a low lying position, could more likely be interpretable as Libyan tombs. A cemetery of similar, though generally smaller, examples was noted in the vicinity in 1982. On the other hand there is a possible tower on a prominent hillock at the northern end of the *clausura* (Fig. 5:20) and a gate towards the south.

The modern track passes through the *clausura* adjacent to its ruined gate-house. This comprised a two-roomed tower separated by a corridor and was built in small neat masonry with rounded corners. Trousset suggested that it might be a later addition to the *clausura* (presumably on the grounds that it was not built in ashlar masonry) but the gate is now paralleled by the better preserved example at Hadd Hajar and there is no reason to question the contemporaneity of gate and *clausura* in either case (Fig. 5:20b).

Skiffa south

A new *clausura* was discovered in another wadi defile just to the south of Skiffa in 1982. It is surely significant that a modern route is signposted to Ksar Rhilane (*Tisavar*) up this corridor. The central section of the *clausura* had been badly eroded by the wadi and by later agricultural terraces but the 3–3.35 m wide wall was easily visible running up the scarps on both the north and south sides of the defile just to the west of the point at which the plain opens out. It is virtually identical to the Skiffa example in its construction on these steep gradients. Its total length was approx. 200–300 m with no surviving traces of either a tower or gate in association.

Chenini

Another *clausura* of similar type exists in the southerly corridor centred on the wadi Chenini. It is described

as a 3–4 m wide mound of rubble with a total height of 1.5–2 m. There is a possible tower on the scarp at the northern end.[36]

Hadd Hajar
(Figs. 5:20, 5:21)

The discovery of another *clausura* northwest of Mizda is of major significance. It is further valuable evidence that eastern and western Tripolitania were more similar in their frontier development than sometimes assumed. De Mathuisieulx visited the site of the gate (Gasr Saqifah) but did not spot the associated wall and bank and ditch. This omission was remedied through the accurate observation of the compiler of the modern 1:50,000 map sheet and by the intuition of Olwen Brogan, who went to investigate the 6 km long 'ancient wall' so mapped.

The *clausura* crosses a major transhuming corridor between the Dahar and the Gebel Garian (Fig. 5:21, Plate 18). In character it is very similar to the Skiffa and Tebaga examples, being in parts a dry stone wall and in its central sector a bank and ditch. Watchtowers cover the central and western

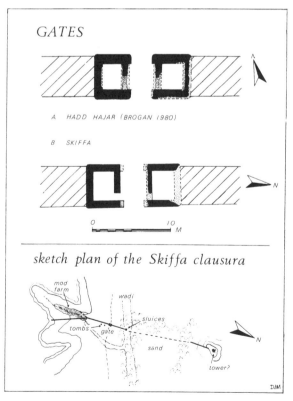

Fig. 5:20 The gate-houses on the Hadd Hajar (a) and Skiffa (b) *clausurae* (after Brogan 1980). Below, sketch plan of the Skiffa *clausura* (after Blanchet 1898, with additions).

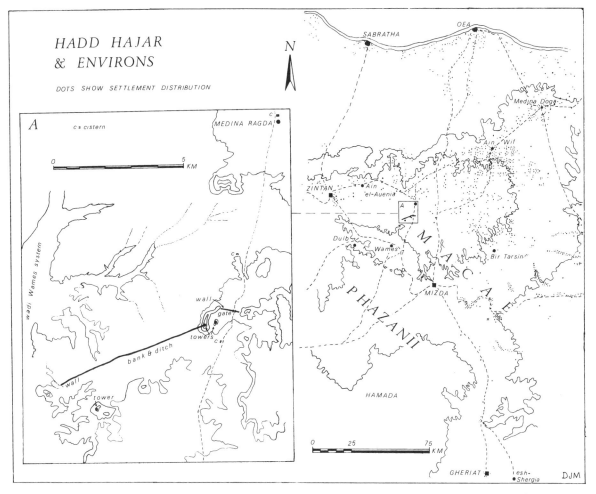

Fig. 5:21 The Hadd Hajar *clausura* in relation to the probable Roman forts at Mizda and Zintan and the outposts of Medina Ragda, Gasr Duib and Gasr Wames.

approaches to the obstacle, whilst the gate is located in a subsidiary corridor to the east (Plate 19). The gate (12 x 5.5 m) was flanked by two towers which are still preserved to 3–4 m height. (Fig. 5:20a).

Very little diagnostic pottery has been recovered from any of these features, but that which has been identified suggests that a later second-century or pre-Severan origin is possible.[37]

The function of the *clausurae*

The defensive value of the *clausurae* has been greatly overestimated on occasion. The original height of most of them was clearly not much over 2–3 m. Bir Oum Ali and perhaps some others in the Cherb were rather higher, mortared walls but they could not serve as fighting platforms. The sort of garrison that could be accommodated in the gate-houses could not be expected to defend the *clausurae* against determined

assailants, whether an invading army or a small raiding band. Nor was this the way Rome defended her frontiers. The small size of the obstacles suggests rather that the aim of the *clausurae* was not to prevent people using the natural corridors, but to oblige them to do so via the controlled crossing points.

The alternative appraisal of the *clausurae* is therefore to see them as control barriers used in the policing and customs duties of the garrison. It is significant that the areas where *clausurae* have been discovered are zones where there is a rapid transition from a predominantly pastoral pre-desert region into a predominantly agricultural one. This is particularly evident on Figures 5:19 and 5:21 where there is a fairly dramatic increase in settlement density from one side of the *clausurae* to the other. There could be no question of a Roman blockade along this line and it was argued above (chapter 2) that transhumance and seasonal labour movements between the zones were considerable in antiquity. The symbiotic relationships between pastoralists, mixed farmers and agriculturalists were undoubtedly affected by the rapid economic development of the better land in the first centuries AD. It can be argued that this was one of the main potential causes of unrest among the pre-desert tribes. On the other hand it was equally important to define their grazing lands and water rights and to regulate their seasonal movements. The *clausurae* were a labour-saving device in the policing of population movements in these sensitive zones. They could serve an economic function as well in terms of customs control of the flocks and goods being moved between 'desert and sown' which were otherwise difficult to assess and tax. This interpretation is supported by the archaeological evidence for controlled gates. In the Tebaga corridor, the 17 km expanse was no doubt difficult to police before all movement up it was focused on a single checkpoint.[38]

It has often been argued that the *clausurae* and *fossata* are entirely distinct from the supposedly defensive frontier barriers of Britain and Germany, but this argument can be stood on its head. One can question whether the great provision of gates through Hadrian's Wall, for instance, has a military rationale in terms of defensive/offensive tactics or whether they were specifically intended to facilitate controlled civilian movement across the frontier. In operation, at any rate, all these barriers were intended to make border policing simpler and less labour-intensive rather than to function as fighting platforms.

There is some documentary evidence which is relevant to the operation of *clausurae* as policing positions where credentials could be checked out or accreditation given to individuals passing through the frontier zone. The seasonal influx of labourers into the agricultural zone for the harvest seems to have been particularly significant. On the other hand, there is little clearcut evidence for customs control or taxation.[39]

The location of the *clausurae* need not have been coincident with the limit of Roman territory. I have suggested that areas where there was a rapid transition from desert to farmland and where different economic modes were traditionally practised in symbiosis required careful policing to maintain the rights and property of all parties. It is noticeable that the areas where no *clausurae* have been found relate either to the rain shadow area of the southern Gebel Demmer and Gefara, where there was little agricultural development, or to the zone of wadi agriculture in eastern Tripolitania. In the latter case the recent ULVS work has revealed that, whilst agricultural

development was on a broad basis, many wadi farmers practised a mixed economy and the importance of pastoralism proportionally increased the further south one went. As a consequence the change from 'desert' to 'sown' was much more gradual in this area. All the same, to the south of this area, in the desert proper, the location of Roman outposts at most major wells and cisterns provided a level of policing commensurate with that which could have been achieved by *clausurae*.

The dating of the *clausurae*

Although Baradez showed that some sections of the *Fossatum Africae*, as he called it, were Hadrianic, many scholars have still preferred to link these earthworks to later periods of history. One school of thought believes that the disbandment of the Third Legion by Gordian III created the need for the 'defensive' earthworks. Another theory has associated them with imagined raids of camel-riding nomads in the late empire (notably from the fourth century onwards). But clearly both of these interpretations assume that the basic function of the obstacle was defensive, whether against armies or raiding bands. However, even a comparatively small *razzia* would have been able to rout the handful of men controlling the gates in the pre-firearms age. As I hope I have demonstrated, we must get away from the blockhouse mentality and look more closely at the possible policing functions of these fortifications. Chronologically these policing activities were an adjunct of Roman strategy from the later first century onwards, so one has a very broad date range for their construction. Although I accept that a unitary solution to the question is unlikely, the best indications are that many of them were constructed prior to the fourth century, though they continued to be maintained and used right up to the end of Roman Africa.[40]

The Cherb *clausurae*, for instance, are generally argued to be early second century because of the known Trajanic delimitation of the lands of the *Nybgenii* and *Capsitani* along that line. The fact that some of these walls were mortared and are of higher quality perhaps favours identifying the Bir Oum Ali wall, for instance, as a prototype. But not all of the Cherb walls are comparable with Oum Ali and they need not all be contemporary.

In contradiction to Donau's evidence for the Tebaga *clausura*, Trousset dated it to the mid-fourth century because of similarities with the Skiffa group. The Skiffa group were assigned by him to this date on the mistaken assumption that a reference to *propugnacula* in an inscription of AD 355–60 at Ras el-Ain referred to the *clausurae* rather than to the fort's òwn defences. This late Roman dating framework is plainly untenable.

The pottery evidence for any of the *clausurae* is frustratingly slight, but for Tebaga there is material of late second- and third-century date. Similarly for Hadd Hajar and perhaps, by analogy, for the Skiffa group. The functional need for these *clausurae* was created by the advance of the frontier in the early second century, so a pre-Severan origin for some of them is possible.

It is clear from a superficial study of the Tebaga gate and its modifications that some of the *clausurae* were in service for a long time. The locations of the fort at Ras el-Ain or of the late fortlets at Benia Guedah Ceder and Benia bel Recheb demonstrate the continuing and perhaps increasing importance of the policing system based on the *clausurae* in the late third and fourth centuries (Figs 5:17, 5:19). On the current state of the evidence there can be no certainty, but a second-century origin for the system seems likely, with additions in the third century and refurbishment and embellishment in the fourth. The existence of a probable fortlet in the Hadd Hajar corridor in the late first century shows that policing tactics were undertaken at an early date. The *clausurae* constituted a logical development from this situation. But without excavation or epigraphic evidence it would be unwise to try and define the chronology of this development in any greater detail. At least some of the *clausurae*, though, seem to be pre-Severan in date and fit in with the theory of earlier development of the Roman frontier in Tripolitania.[41]

6
CITIES, TOWNS AND VILLAGES

This chapter does not present a comprehensive gazetteer of urban sites in Tripolitania, nor does it describe in minute detail the principal monuments of the best-known sites. The former cannot be done in a satisfactory way because of the inequalities of the data available for the various sites and good examples of the latter approach are readily accessible in other publications. Rather, by focusing on questions of urban development, scale and resources, I hope to illustrate the way the cities, towns and villages of Tripolitania fitted into an urban hierarchy and something of the interrelationships between them. The choice of sites described below is largely dictated by the availability of evidence.

There were eventually four cities with the status of *coloniae* in Tripolitania, *Lepcis Magna*, *Oea*, *Sabratha* and *Tacapae* and another six towns ranked as *municipia*. There were in addition nine or ten sites which may have been recognized as *civitates* and a host of 'small towns', villages and military *vici* which never amounted to very much (Fig. 3:2).[1] The discussion that follows will treat these different categories in descending order of importance.

1
LEPCIS MAGNA (LEBDA)

It will be clear from the earlier chapters of this book that *Lepcis Magna* was the major and dominating urban centre in the region. In many Latin sources the name was transliterated as *Leptis Magna*, but the local Latin epigraphy used *Lepcis* to echo more closely the Libyphoenican original *Lpqy*. The epithet *Magna* dis-

tinguished the town from *Leptiminus* on the Lesser Syrtes but might equally have served as a comment on its distinguished history. Even as an independent *civitas* the town was clearly favoured by Rome and the honorary promotions to *municipium* in AD 74–7 and to *colonia* in AD 109 were signs of great distinction at a time when most *coloniae* in Africa were colonies for military veterans who were already Roman citizens. The municipal grant to *Lepcis* enfranchised her nobility through membership of the town council, the appellation *colonia* conferred Roman citizenship on all the townspeople. At the dates at which she achieved them, these were valuable and significant concessions. Subsequently, *c*. AD 203, Septimius Severus granted his home town the highest honour available for a provincial town, the *ius Italicum* status, giving it the same exemption enjoyed by Italian towns from certain forms of taxation. When the province of *Tripolitana* was constituted at the start of the fourth century *Lepcis* was evidently its capital.

The architectural core of the city was extensively cleared of sand and rubble by Italian archaeologists in the early decades of this century, with a great deal of reconstruction work being undertaken. Despite the fact that much remains unpublished in definitive form, the monuments of *Lepcis* are among the most famous in the Mediterranean. At its height, this was an immense city though the frequently reproduced plan of just its central area does not convey this fully. A key factor in the archaeology of *Lepcis* is that early in the reign of Augustus the town opened a quarry at Ras el-Hammam (5 km south of the town) from which it extracted a hard and fine-quality limestone. This stone is largely responsible for the surviving wealth of epigraphic evidence from the site and for the durability of its monuments. In consequence, it is possible to trace the town's development in some detail.[2]

The early Phoenician occupation of the site appears to have depended on the protection afforded to ships by a number of islands at the mouth of the Wadi Lebda (now underlying the north and west moles of the Roman harbour works). Although sea conditions around Lebda are generally good through much of the year, this was far from ideal as a winter harbour and the weakness of the site in this respect poses interesting questions about its further development. However, unlike *Oea* and *Sabratha*, *Lepcis* is located in a dry-farming region (though there were also spring-fed oases nearby). The Gebel Msellata curves north to meet the coast just to the west of Lebda and the Wadi Caam (the famously fertile

Cinyps of Herodotus) lay not far to the east. The agricultural potential of the land around the settlement thus entailed far less initial work than the oases of the Gefara coast. As a roadstead and as a site capable of sustaining itself easily from its immediate hinterland, *Lpqy* had much to recommend it. Nevertheless, the lack of a better year-round harbour was to impede for some time the growth of the site beyond the small initial nucleus on the west bank of the Wadi Lebda.

Traces of the first settlement of the seventh century BC have been detected in very limited work beneath the old forum (Fig. 6:1, no. 13), but because the results were never fully published the evidence remains difficult to assess. Jones has recently noted air-photographic evidence for structures close to the mouth of the Lebda (Fig. 6.1, no. 31), which diverge slightly from the orientation of the earliest gridded

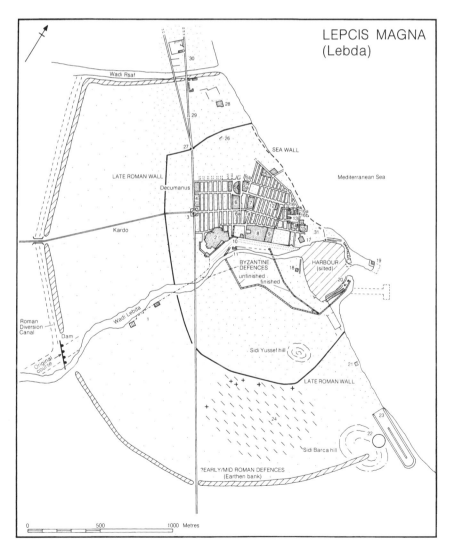

Fig. 6:1 *Lepcis Magna*, overall plan showing the location of the successive defensive circuits and the major monuments referred to in the text. The main built-up area is indicated by stippling, the principal cemetery zone by hatching.

117

streets around the old forum. There is no reason to presume that these structures were themselves pre-Roman in date but they may well have followed a long established orientation. The slanting northeast side of the forum also attests some irregularity of layout, perhaps reflecting the long-term influence of early Libyphoenician structures on subsequent building in this quarter (as may also be observed north of the forum at *Sabratha*, see below). A cemetery of Hellenistic date lies beneath the theatre, with finds including a small amount of sixth/fifth century material, perhaps from earlier graves which had been disturbed or destroyed. It would appear then that the earliest settlement lay on the west bank of the Lebda, close to its mouth and that by the latter centuries BC there was a cemetery in the region of the theatre. But compared to the detailed picture of its Roman period development this is slim evidence indeed.

The discovery of a harbour wharf buried beneath a rich second-century AD villa at Homs, about 3 km west of the mouth of the Lebda, has added an intriguing new twist, in that di Vita wishes to identify this as the main Hellenistic port of *Lepcis* and to associate it with references in a second-century BC source that *Lepcis* (referred to as *Neapolis*) lacked a true harbour and that such a facility existed at Cape *Hermaion* 15 *stades* (2.7 km) west, which is clearly the Homs peninsula. Although it is an attractive possibility that there was a Libyphoenician settlement and harbour at Homs, the wharf described by di Vita employed the Ras el-Hammam limestone and ought not to pre-date the reign of Augustus. It is certainly possible, however, that the early *Lepcitani* sought to ameliorate the disadvantages of the Lebda anchorage by developing harbour facilities on the eastern side of the Homs peninsula. The evident silting up of this quay by the second century AD may indicate why Homs did not develop as a long-term rival to *Lepcis*.[3]

Literary references to *Lepcis* at the end of the second century BC certainly suggest a vigorous urban community, open to Mediterranean shipping and with well-developed urban institutions. Di Vita has argued that the initial laying out of the old forum (Fig. 6:1, no. 13) and its surrounding *insulae* took place in the second or first century BC, certainly prior to the reign of Augustus. There were of course repeated modifications to the forum but he argues that, in its original state, it was dominated by twin temples to the tutelary deities of the town, Milk'ashtart and Shadrapa (later syncretized with the Roman Hercules and Liber Pater). During the reign of Augustus these temples (nos 16, 16a) were rebuilt and it appears that Milk'ashtart's shrine in the centre of the northwest side of the forum was now rededicated to Rome and

Augustus and a smaller temple added (by 5 BC–AD 2 at the latest) on its northern flank to house the displaced god.

If the initial gridded area around the forum was pre-Augustan in date, and I think that di Vita is right in saying it was, there is little doubt about the subsequent extension under Augustus. In 8 BC the market (Fig. 6:1, no. 7; Plate 25) was built on the main street (*kardo*) running southwest and a whole new quarter of rectangular *insulae* must have been laid out. The theatre (no. 5), dedicated in AD 1–2, was just beyond this gridded area and the construction of the *chalcidicum* (no. 6) in AD 12 almost certainly inaugurated the next phase of orthogonal planning, diverging by 17 degrees from the previous one. By the end of the reign of Augustus, then, the southern limits of the town were represented by the intersection of the gridded area with the main coast road (*decumanus*). Just to the north of the spot where the great Severan arch (no. 3) was to be erected, the proconsul Vibius Marsus erected an arch to Augusta Salutaris in AD 29–30, and to its south stood the milestone of AD 15/16 marking the *caput viae* of the road into the Gebel. Quite clearly, these monuments stood at the Tiberian city limits. Other arches of Tiberian date, recording the paving of the streets of the town in AD 35–6, were set up close to the theatre and the market (nos 5b, 7a) at points of intersection between the two zones of Augustan expansion. The known Flavian (no. 32) and Trajanic (no. 6a) arches on the *kardo* were both erected within the Augustan gridded area at important road junctions and no doubt commemorated the promotions in the status of the town.

There is clear evidence, though, for very considerable growth of the town in the later first and second century out to the south and west. An arch of Hadrian or Pius was incorporated in the west gate of the late defences (no. 27) and even further west on the *decumanus* lay an arch of Marcus Aurelius (no. 29). The latter overlay an earlier cemetery, which had in turn been replaced by an industrial quarter involved in glass production. The western suburbs continued some way further towards Homs with a series of multi-roomed structures of vast ground plan (no. 30). These are best interpreted as large-scale warehouses (*horrea*), where agricultural produce (notably oil) could be stored pending export (Fig. 6:2). By the later second century, the street grid extended at least as far as the Hunting Baths (no. 28).[4]

The urban amenities built by the *Lepcitani* were designed and ornamented in a style to fit their high opinion of themselves and their aspirations. The vast majority of building work was paid for by individual members of the local elite, though often formally

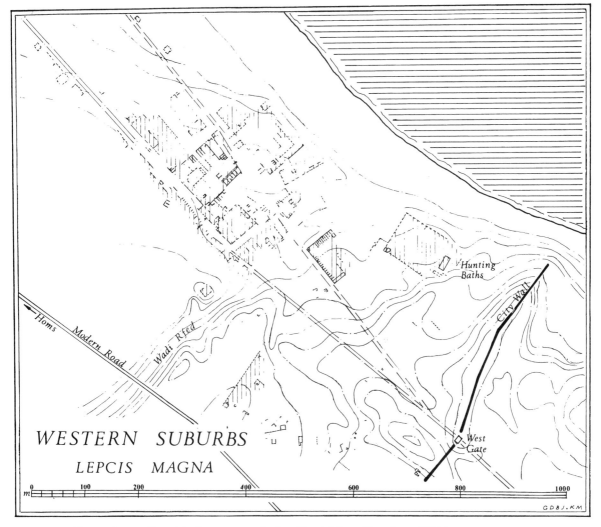

Fig. 6:2 Possible warehouses (*horrea*) in the western suburbs of *Lepcis Magna* (from Jones 1989b).

dedicated in the emperor's name by the proconsul or his legate. Up to the end of the first century dedications were frequently bi-lingual (neo-Punic and Latin) and even when the practice of erecting neo-Punic texts ceased, traditional Punic phrases continued in Latinized form, such as, for example, *amator patriae* or *ornator patriae*. Annobal Tapapius Rufus paid for the original market (8 BC) and theatre (AD 1–2); Iddibal Caphada Aemilius donated the *chalcidicum* (AD 12); Iddibal Tapapius gave a shrine to the Di Augusti in the theatre (AD 43); the forum was fully paved and given colonnades (AD 54) by G'y ben Hanno (Gaius Anno) and the civic basilica (no. 14) probably dates to the same period. In AD 56 the amphitheatre (no. 22) was constructed in an old quarry to the east of the town, and there is evidence of major work at this time

on the western harbour quay, with a portico being completed in AD 62. A temple to Magna Mater (Cybele) was dedicated in the forum in AD 72 by Iddibal son of Balsillec and an imposing temple to the Flavian emperors (no. 17) was added (AD 93/94) to the west side of the harbour. The council house (*curia* = no. 15) was either another late first- or a second-century project. A fourth-century inscription apparently refers to a Trajanic forum and basilica which has yet to be located, always assuming that this was not a disguised reference to the old forum, which certainly received a new temple under Trajan on its west side. Under Hadrian (AD 120) a citizen, Q. Servilius Candidus, paid for the aqueduct bringing water from the Wadi Caam and a series of public fountains. The new water supply enabled the town to build a massive public baths complex (no. 2), one of the largest in the Roman provinces at that date. The town may have possessed a race-course of sorts prior to the construction of its magnificent circus (no. 23), finally completed in AD 162. As Humphrey has argued, parts of the structure may have been built much earlier in the second century. Once again the example at *Lepcis* is one of the largest outside Italy. There were also Antonine improvements to the theatre and baths (with a considerable increase in the amount of marble employed), and several new temples were built, including one on the *decumanus* (no. 4) and a serapeum (no. 12). The well-preserved Hunting baths (no. 28, and Plates 28 and 29) and the Orpheus House (no. 26) in the western suburbs, and the villa of the Nile (no. 21) east of the harbour illustrate smaller-scale civic and rich domestic development in the later second century.[5]

Although the area to the east of the Wadi Lebda is not believed to have been as densely built on as the west bank, it is clear that there was development here also, particularly close to the harbour and along the road leading out to the amphitheatre and circus. Between the amphitheatre and the main coast road lay a major cemetery and several prominent mausolea (no. 24). To the south of the *decumanus* little is known for certain apart from the two major cisterns (no. 1) for water distribution adjacent to the Wadi Lebda. The dam across the Wadi Lebda to the south and the earthen bank flanking the diversion channel which carried the flood waters of the Lebda around the perimeter of the city into the Wadi Rsaf are of enormous interest, but little examined. The function of these features was clearly to limit the possibility of serious damage being done to the centre of the town by flash floods (the potential of which was illustrated as recently as November 1987 by a flood which carried away the bottom end of the colonnaded street). Restricting the volume of water passing down the Lebda stream bed during its rare spates will also have protected shipping in the harbour from damage, and the basin itself from siltation. But as Goodchild and Ward-Perkins realized long ago, the bank may also have served as an early defensive circuit for the town. The bank extended on to the rising ground east of the Wadi Lebda where it can only be seen as a defensive earthwork. Whilst the length of the defences makes it unlikely that this circuit was erected in haste, for instance, to counter the Garamantian threat of AD 69, the first or second centuries AD seem the most likely context for this perimeter. The total area enclosed by the earthworks is in the region of 425 ha (1,000 acres), of which perhaps two thirds was reasonably densely built up (280 ha, 660 acres). This makes it a very substantial town by ancient standards. For comparison,

the late Roman town walls enclosed 130 ha (325 acres) and the Byzantine defences a mere 38 ha (95 acres), soon reduced to 18 ha (45 acres).[6]

Well before the accession of Septimius Severus to the imperial throne, the urban development of *Lepcis* had been impressive, even exceptional, for a provincial town and provides ample testimony to the financial resources of the local elite. Some of the inscriptions recording construction or other gifts by members of the nobility reveal the sums expended. In the lists drawn up for North Africa by Duncan-Jones, *Lepcis* consistently features at the top of the different categories of expenditure. The temple of Magna Mater cost 200,000 sestertii (HS) in AD 72, another unnamed temple HS 80,000 in AD 93/94; the arch of Marcus Aurelius (AD 173/74) cost over HS 120,000; HS 272,500 were spent on a colonnaded enclosure dedicated to Apollo (pre AD 180). A single silver statue of an aunt of Septimius Severus (pre AD 170) was worth over HS 115,000 and a separate donation of no less than 16 statues involved an outlay of HS 1,000,000. Finally, the tomb of P. Lucretius Rogatianus outside the town cost well in excess of HS 80,000. As we have noted already (chapter 3), the resources of the Lepcitanian elite enabled them to enter the ranks of the equestrian and senatorial orders at Rome with increasing frequency during the second century AD and this process culminated with the seizure of power by one of them in the civil war of AD 193–6.[7]

The victory of Septimius Severus was followed by the initiation of a building programme even more extraordinary than the city had previously experienced. The architecture, the scale and the materials used attest that this was an imperial project of the grandest type and one which would have graced Rome as surely as it did the Tripolitanian city. C. Fulvius Plautianus, the Lepcitanian praetorian prefect, seems to have been instrumental in organizing some details of the scheme, with massive quantities of marble and granite columns being ordered up from quarries and imperial stock-yards. The unknown architect was undoubtedly brought in from the eastern Mediterranean, as were many of the best masons and marble workers. The principal monuments in the scheme were:

1 a broad and lavishly ornamented colonnaded street (Figs 6:1, no. 10 and 6:3) running along the west bank of the Lebda and connecting the harbour with the *decumanus*. The presence of the Hadrianic baths (aligned off the normal grid in order to catch the sun on its south-facing hot rooms) necessitated a kink in the road and this junction was marked by a massive nymphaeum (no. 11) facing an exhedra across a small piazza;

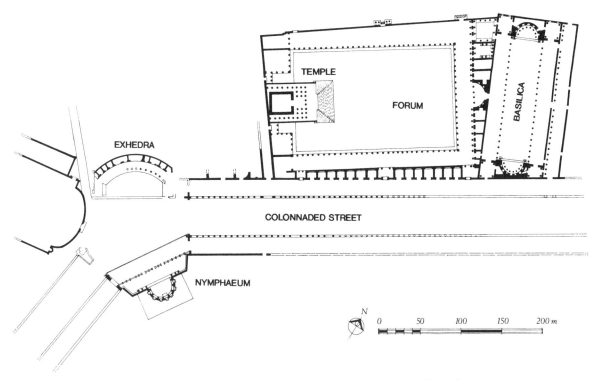

Fig. 6:3 The new civic centre of *Lepcis* in the Severan age (from Ward-Perkins 1993, with additions).

2 an enormous new forum and basilica complex situated on the north side of the colonnaded street, covering no less than seven or eight of the original *insulae* here (Plates 22 to 24). Created in an irregular quadrilateral of 142/123 x 82/92 m, the forum (no. 8) was dominated by a colossal temple at its southwest end, with the basilica (no. 9) placed perpendicularly across the northeast side of the forum;

3 a quadriform arch at the main road junction (no. 3) decorated with reliefs portraying the Severan family (Plates 20 and 21);

4 a major remodelling and extension of the harbour basin, including construction of a new eastern quay (Fig. 6:1, no. 20; Plate 26) and radical extension and improvement to the northern quay and its lighthouse (no. 19). It is likely that the T-shaped addition to the eastern quay that has recently been recognized also belongs to this phase, representing a substantial increase in the harbour facilities at the site.

The work took 20 years to complete, the forum and basilica being dedicated under Caracalla in AD 216. Di Vita has argued that the original plan for the forum basilica complex was to build a double forum, with the basilica separating the two halves of the forum (in a manner reminiscent of Trajan's forum at Rome), but in the event only one half was built. Whilst it is clear

that the Severans intended to make some use of an area of land of uncertain overall dimensions to the northeast of the basilica, the ingenious arguments advanced by di Vita must remain no more than speculation without further research on the ground. As Birley has pointed out, though, there was a very important theme to the monument as built. The elegant pilasters flanking the apses of the basilica were decorated with either Bacchic or Herculean scenes in clear reference to the *dii patrii* or tutelary deities of the town, Liber Pater and Hercules. When Dio complained that Septimius had built an 'excessively large temple to Bacchus and Hercules', it is by no means inconceivable that he was referring to the forum temple at *Lepcis* rather than to an unlocated monument in Rome. Only a few fragments of the dedicatory inscription survives, but an attribution to Liber Pater and Hercules is not excluded and would fit in well with what we know of the singular importance of these two deities at *Lepcis* and of Septimius' civic patriotism.

The scale of use of marble and exotic stone was immense, perhaps best represented by the 112 red Aswan granite columns (each 24 Roman feet high) required for the basilica and temple, or the 400–500 cippolino marble columns for the colonnaded street. Whilst it is clear that imperial finances bore the brunt of the expenditure entailed, local notables may have been encouraged to subscribe to some minor, but still financially significant, elements of the overall scheme. In the end, the ambitious plan almost overstretched the imperial treasury and may well have led to financial embarrassment for some of the nobility. The rest of the third century is notable for the small amount of public works carried out as a result of individual largesse being dispensed in the city.[8]

2
OEA (TRIPOLI)

The relative significance of Roman *Oea* (Liby-phoenician *Wy't*) compared with *Lepcis* and *Sabratha* is difficult to judge on account of the dramatically different preservation of the latter two sites. But there are a number of strands of evidence to suggest that *Oea* was the second city of the region after *Lepcis* for much of its history and that by the Byzantine period it had probably even usurped the primary role of the declining metropolis. The Arabs chose Tripoli as their capital in the region and it has remained so to the present day. The twin secrets of Tripoli's success at all times have been the existence of what is arguably one of the best natural harbours in North Africa and the

adjacent oasis (Fig 6:4, inset). Without the development of the oasis, the harbour would have been of minor use; without the harbour, the oasis might have remained relatively unimportant.

The central Gefara is arid and inhospitable; settlement has relied on two sources of support for its agriculture – the artesian nappes feeding the coastal oases and the flash floods in its wadis. Tripoli and its immediate hinterland have benefited from both, in that the Wadi Megenin is one of the few Gefara wadis whose flood waters regularly reach the coast. The main extent of the Tripoli oasis lay in early modern times to the east and south of the city, with smaller outliers at Gargaresh and Gurgi to the southwest. It is impossible to assess the relative size of the Roman oasis, but in view of what we know of the relative sizes of the built-up area (see below), it is not inconceivable that it was as extensive. *Oea* also exploited a large territory extending many kilometres into the Gebel to south and southeast, but it is clear that it was the quality of the lands closest to the city that allowed it to continue (whilst *Lepcis* and *Sabratha* failed) into the Islamic age as an urban centre of considerable magnitude. Recent archaeological discoveries have shown that the lesser oases of Gargaresh and Gurgi were in effect important suburbs of the town. There were rich villas here, along with tombs of Punic through to late Roman date and much the same was probably true of

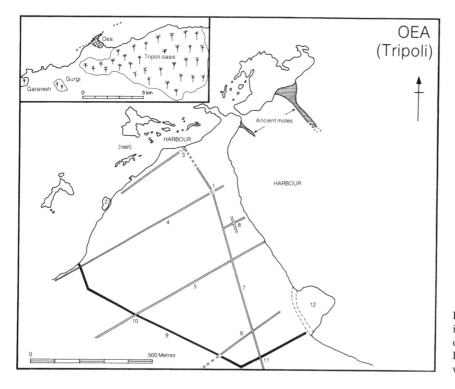

Fig. 6:4 Oea (Tripoli), location in relation to neighbouring oases and detail of the known Roman layout and harbour works.

the larger oasis to the east of Tripoli. There were clearly many villas of extraordinary luxury at points further out along the coast road, such as, for example, those at Tagiura 30 km east of Tripoli (chapter 7) and further important cemeteries or tombs are known also both along the coast and on the routes into the interior (Zanzur, en-Ngila, Ain Zara). The town was the focus, therefore, for a hinterland which was cultivated both intensively and extensively.

The history of *Oea* is briefly told. It was undoubtedly overshadowed by its powerful eastern neighbour, but perhaps to a lesser degree than we might imagine. A small number of neo-Punic texts confirm that the cultural character of the town was essentially similar to that of *Lepcis*. In AD 69 *Oea* attempted to settle a quarrel with *Lepcis* by military means, though needing to call on the *Garamantes* for assistance. As a result of having made this dangerous alliance, it is clear that the *Oeenses* were held responsible for the war with *Lepcis* and quite likely penalized in the settlement which followed. Whilst *Lepcis* was quickly promoted to *municipium* (AD 74–7) and *colonia* status (AD 109), it appears that *Oea* suffered the punishment of retarded promotion. The exact dates of her eventual elevation to municipal and colonial status are unknown, but the latter was certainly attained by the 160s. Even a time-lag of 20–30 years, however, would have done much to wound local pride.

Oea was the home town of Apuleius' friend Sicinius Pontianus and it was at Pontianus' suggestion that Apuleius courted his widowed mother Aemilia Pudentilla. When Pontianus died in AD 158, certain members of the Aemilii and the Sicinii clans closed in and arraigned Apuleius on the serious charge of witchcraft (for how else could a local matron have been persuaded to wed outside the ranks of a local aristocracy which had always been noted for its insularity?). Apuleius used the trial to demonstrate his rhetorical brilliance, rightly castigating some and undoubtedly slandering others of his opponents in a scintillating counter offensive. The trial and the events leading up to it must have been one of the dominant topics of conversation in the town in the late 150s.

The rise of the Severan dynasty undoubtedly brought larger numbers of the town's elite into the higher levels of imperial administration but perhaps with less severe repercussions following the fall of the dynasty than were suffered by *Lepcis*. Although *Lepcis* was the provincial capital in the fourth century it is possible that *Oea* was progressively coming closer to equality in terms of economic importance. Whilst the fourth and early fifth century saw *Lepcis* slide into an early grave, *Oea* seems to have continued to maintain a large urban population. The first Islamic defences are believed to have been built directly on the Roman walls and this suggests that the town captured by Ibn el-Aasi in the 640s was still nearly 50 ha in extent. The defended area at *Lepcis* had shrunk by that date to no more than 18 ha (and *Sabratha* was half that size again). Tripoli was chosen by the Arabs as their capital not simply because of its natural advantages but because it had survived until then as a meaningful centre.[9]

The topography of the ancient city is only comprehensible at a rudimentary level because of the inaccessibility of the Punic and Roman levels below the medieval and modern buildings. A probable Punic settlement and cemetery are known from an area about 1 km east of the presumed line of the Roman town wall and finds of Punic date have also been reported from a site on the coast by the Gargaresh oasis. However, the most intensive settlement of early date might be expected to lie in the area immediately north and northwest of the four-way (*quadrifons*) arch (Fig. 6:4, no. 1) in the heart of Tripoli itself. Here the peninsula on which the town stands narrows in considerably and there are protected anchorages on both sides of it. Another late Punic cemetery has been located on what was probably an offshore island to the southwest of this presumed early core (Fig. 6:4, no. 2). The earliest archaeological evidence so far to have come from *Oea* is of fifth-century BC date but it seems unlikely that development of the site would have lagged so far behind that of *Lepcis* (late seventh century BC).

The harbour facilities of ancient *Oea* are most emphatically represented by two major moles of Roman date on the eastern side of the promontory (Figs 6:4–6:5). It is also apparent, though, that the offshore reef on the west side of the peninsula offered considerable protection from the prevailing winds (most commonly northwesterly) and, although there is less room for manoeuvring here between reef and shore, this would not have been a problem for small craft. It is probable, then, that both sides of the promontory were developed as harbour facilities, and likely that a passage existed between the two sectors close to the southernmost mole on the east side. The depth within the main harbour is well illustrated by a map of 1819 (Fig. 6:5), which shows values from 3–8 m (the soundings are in French feet = 0.324 m). For comparison, the harbour at *Sabratha* allowed considerably less clearance, with depths of 1.5–3.1 m having been recorded. The total sheltered area of the anchorage at *Oea* far exceeds those at *Lepcis* and *Sabratha*, and this is a point of considerable importance to the eventual emergence of Tripoli as one of

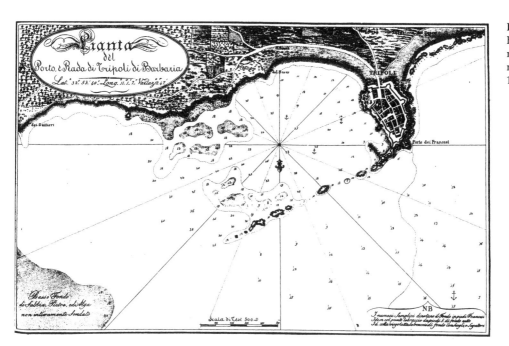

Fig. 6:5 Tripoli harbour in an early nineteenth century map from Lezlne 1972.

the key ports of the southern Mediterranean in medieval and early modern times.

The other traces of Romano-Libyan *Oea* are tantalizingly slight, but nevertheless impressive. As Lezine has observed, the scale of marble use in the *quadrifons* arch at Tripoli (AD 163) is unmatched by any monument of similar date at *Sabratha*. A chance survival of a city whose monuments will have ranked high alongside those of her neighbours, the arch is central to all attempts at studying the urban topography. It marked the intersection of two of the principal streets, the extension into town of the roads leading west to *Sabratha* and east to *Lepcis*. These and other ancient streets have been identified in the pattern of alleys and roads of the medieval medina (Fig. 6:4 presents a minimal view of the evidence). There were at least three major southwest-northeast streets (*decumanes*) (Fig. 6:4, nos 4–6). A further street on a similar alignment (no. 3) may well have originated as a harbour road within the earlier Libyphoenician town. There are hints to the southeast of the arch (e.g. junction no. 8), that the expanded Roman grid may have been based partly on elongated rectangular *insulae* as at *Lepcis* (though this and many other fundamental details still require confirmation through excavation). At any rate it seems clear that the street grid was based on an orthogonal layout, though presumably not of a single phase. As at *Lepcis* and *Sabratha*, we might envisage progressive extensions from an initial core, with slight changes of alignment or of *insula* sizes.

The postulated course of the late Roman wall circuit is equally problematic and possibly unlikely to be resolved due to the almost complete demolition by the Italians of the Islamic defences beneath which which they are thought to have lain. Only at the southwest corner of the city are the Roman defences believed to have encompassed territory excluded by the medieval circuit. The latter turned almost northwards at the Bab el-Zenata (no. 10) in the direction of the Burg Sidi el-Haddar (no. 2). The Islamic walls thus enclosed an area of 44.4 ha, the late Roman ones approx. 49 ha. There is every reason to believe that, at its greatest extent in the second century AD, the Roman town spread some way beyond the late wall circuit, and may have covered as much as double the walled area. This is consistent with a limited amount of archaeological evidence for structures in the zone immediately outside the western defences and with inferences that may be drawn about the population. In the eighteenth century 12,000 people were crammed into the 44.4 ha of the town (as against about 6,000 in the fourteenth). Yet Duncan-Jones has suggested a population of roughly 20,000 plus on the basis of known citizen donations (*sportulae*) in the town. Given the generally less congested conditions in Roman towns, this argues for a considerably greater urban area at its maximum extent in the Roman period.

With the notable exception of the arch erected in honour of Marcus Aurelius by a local notable, C. Calpurnius Celsus, little is known about the buildings and monuments of the Roman town. It is thought that the forum may have lain close to or indeed adjacent to the arch and fragments of a temple dedicated in AD 183–5 to the Genius of the colony were found during clearance around the arch. Another major public building, probably an extensive bath-house, under-lies the castle (Assaray el-Hamra) on what may have been originally an islet (no. 12). Numerous other finds of Roman material have been recorded, but most represent in all probability the fragmentary remains of private housing.[10]

3
SABRATHA (SABRATA)

The location of *Sabratha* (Libyphoenician *Sbrt'n*) is similar in some respects to that of *Oea*. Its immediate Gefara hinterland is quite arid and forbidding but is alleviated by the presence of spring-fed oases close to the coast. The town's economic hinterland may well have extended to the Gebel (over 80 km to the south), but the Gebel Nefusa region itself is not spectacularly well-watered (chapter 1). There is no doubt, then, that the primary agricultural resources of *Sabratha* were far inferior to those available to her eastern neighbours. The existence of an offshore reef as at Tripoli was a factor in the development of the site. The shortage of harbours on this stretch of coast is well attested and *Sabratha* may initially have plugged an awkward gap.

The town made little impact in the pages of the ancient historians and geographers and we are reliant on archaeological and epigraphic discoveries for our reconstruction of its history. The site of the ancient town was abandoned at some point early in the

Islamic period, and there have been extensive excava-tions this century. The recent publication of much of the Italian and British work at the site is of the utmost importance, in that the urban development of *Sabratha* can now be traced in comparatively minute detail. However, the nature of the evidence leaves some important questions unanswered. The local stone is very friable and prior to larger-scale importation of marble or other harder stone for dedication panels in the second century AD, inscriptions seem not to have survived for very long. There is thus a significant chronological gap in the otherwise substantial body of epigraphic evidence from the town, with little known about the town's early institutions, its initial promotions in status, or its leading citizens prior to the adoption of Romanized names. As at *Lepcis*, it is reasonable to presume, though, that local Liby-phoenicians and not settlers dominated the town. The Libyphoenician character of the town is confirmed by the recent discoveries of a *tophet* (to the west of the centre) and a large bowl (*labrum*) dedicated in Latin and neo-Punic to Baal-Saturn. The dates at which the town acquired municipal and then colonial status are unknown, though the latter had certainly been gained by the 180s (and quite possibly by the 140s or 150s). At any rate it was a clear generation or two behind *Lepcis* in achieving the honour and its urban develop-ment also reflects far less spectacular early growth.[11]

The earliest archaeological evidence is from the region to the north of the forum and the east forum temple, where floor levels and post holes have been found in association with late fifth-century BC Greek pottery and Phoenician storage jars (Figs 6:6–6:7). Layers of wind-blown sand separating successive floor levels or hearths perhaps suggest that occupa-tion was only periodic at this stage. This sort of

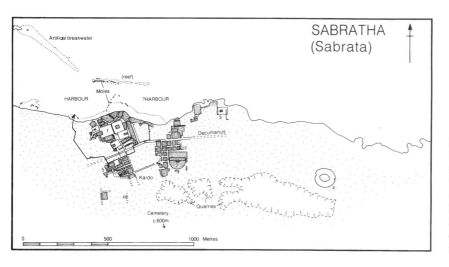

Fig. 6:6 General plan of *Sabratha* showing main excavated sectors., harbour works and outlying monuments and quarries. Key: **1** = forum, **2** = theatre, **3** = Temple of Isis, **4** = amphitheatre, **5** = Regio VI, mausolea A and B.

evidence, obtained in a few restricted sondages, is very difficult to interpret and we must be cautious in drawing conclusions about the early settlement as a whole from such a small sample. Nevertheless, the first stone buildings so far unearthed date to the second half of the fourth century BC and by that time the settlement had expanded southwards to the site of the forum and the east forum temple and into the 'casa Brogan' area (Reg. II, 10). The oblique alignments of the Roman period *insulae* north of the forum (Reg. II, 5–8) clearly reflect something of the original layout below, as limited excavation there and in the forum/temple area has confirmed. At the west end of the later forum there was evidently an open area, perhaps a Libyphoenician market-place and precursor to the forum. The structures below the 'casa Brogan' were not on the same oblique alignment as the rest but for some reason had already established in the fourth century BC the later orientation of this *insula*.

Following the defeat of Carthage by Rome in 202 BC, the *Emporia* were to enjoy greater economic and political freedom and di Vita and Kenrick have both demonstrated the archaeological manifestations of this. There was a major phase of rebuilding and expansion of the town in the first half of the second century BC and di Vita has dated two fine obelisk tombs (mausolea A and B) to this period (Figure 6:6, no. 5). These tombs obviously stood beyond the

southern limits of the town at that date and the eastern boundary may be represented by a possible town wall running north-south up the east side of the 'casa Brogan'. There is evidence to suggest that expansion continued during the first century BC, perhaps in a piecemeal fashion, south of the area later covered by the south forum and Antonine temples. In Regio II, the evidence is a little inconsistent, with *insula* 3 being established by the late first century BC, while the earliest evidence from *insula* 1 indicates a Flavian date for its development. On the other hand, di Vita has evidence for the Punico-Hellenistic mausolea being dismantled and the site developed for housing in the mid-first century BC, with the Regio VI *insulae* firmly established by the end of that century at the latest.

During the first century AD the centre of the town started to take on the monumental character familiar to visitors today (Fig. 6:7). Development in this area, though, was to continue to the later second century. The earliest temples in this area were perhaps the temple of Serapis (the identification with Serapis is not certain) and the capitolium on the west side of the forum. The coins of *Sabratha* of first century BC to early AD feature Serapis and Melqart (Hercules) and early shrines to these deities must have existed and might be expected to have been amongst the first to be given a more monumental appearance. An early temple of Hercules remains to be found. The first east

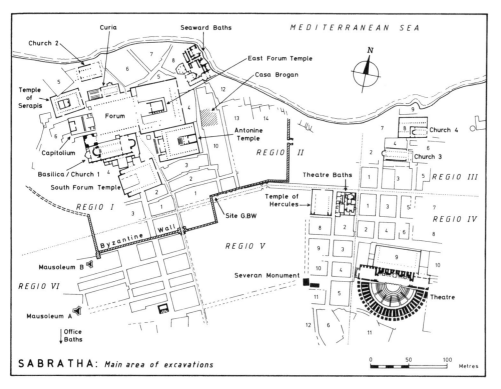

Fig. 6:7 The central area of *Sabratha*, showing principal monuments (from Kenrick 1985c).

forum temple (almost certainly dedicated to Shadrapa/Liber Pater) was constructed in the mid-first century, following clearance of earlier buildings on the site, and the whole forum complex was regularized according to the orthogonal layout dictated by the *insulae* and roads to the south of the old core. The east forum temple had to be rebuilt within a few decades at most and Kenrick accepts di Vita's argument that an earthquake had hit the city in *c.* AD 64–70. There was also rebuilding work in the 'casa Brogan' and the temple of Isis at this time and the first basilica was now added to the south side of a slightly replanned forum.

The second century witnessed major growth of the town towards the east in the direction of the hitherto suburban temple of Isis and the amphitheatre (Fig. 6:6, nos 3 and 4). The exact date of the layout of Regiones III, IV and V is uncertain but the initial delineation of the new quarter may have been quite early in the century, with the actual building work continuing right through the Antonine period. The temple of Hercules was built in the late 180s and it is probable that the theatre (Plate 30) was also a late second-century project (rather than Severan). There was also further southward expansion at this time and major embellishment of the town centre. Up to the second century, most construction utlized a local yellow sandstone which eroded badly when exposed to the elements. Generally, buildings were plastered and whitewashed. During the second century marble started being imported into the town and many of the pre-existing buildings were modified to make use of the more exciting finish it provided. In addition, two major temples were added to the monumental town centre, the so-called Antonine and south forum temples, the former being epigraphically dated to AD 166–9, the latter assignable on architectural criteria to a slightly later date. On various grounds these temples are attributed respectively to Saturn (Phoenician Baal) and Caelestis (Tanit) and presumably replaced earlier, smaller shrines somewhere within the town.

Other urban amenities were evidently also provided for the first time in the later second century. A water supply (aqueduct and 12 public fountains) was provided by a citizen, C. Flavius Pudens, and this will have increased the provision of bath-houses within the town. Furthermore, drains were constructed and most roads paved for the first time. We have already noted the construction of the theatre, and it is likely that the amphitheatre was contemporary. The inscription honouring Flavius Pudens for seeing through the aqueduct scheme mentions that he was the first to put on a gladiatorial display and this must have taken place in the newly completed amphitheatre. There is

little doubt, then, that the late Antonine era marked the peak of local prosperity. At its greatest extent the town and its principal suburbs stretched at least 2 km east-west and 0.7 km north-south (not including the harbour) for a total area in the region of 140 ha (350 acres). Although the periphery may not have been densely built up, this is a considerable area in comparison to the mere 9 ha (22.5 acres) enclosed by the sixth-century Byzantine walls.

A notable feature of the *Sabratha* excavations is the amount of private housing which has been exposed. In the areas uncovered, the peristyle house of the richer citizen is rare and the larger properties may have developed in the wider spaces on the fringes of the town. The character of much of the housing is utilitarian, though with a few notable exceptions, and in some *insulae* there is considerable evidence for industrial activity or olive oil production having taken place. Almost every house had its own subterranean cistern to capitalize on what little rain fell on the roofs of the town.

The harbour at *Sabratha* was perhaps throughout its history the key to its success and is reasonably well understood as a result of underwater archaeology (Fig. 6:6). The initial harbour seems to have developed in the lee of the offshore reef north of the Roman period town centre. There are remains of concrete foundations and of structures built on top of the reef. Further moles were built out towards the centre of the reef, possibly forming a triangular main quay. At some point the harbour was considerably expanded by the construction of an artificial breakwater to the west of the reef, which ran as far as a small natural island. This breakwater protected further moles or quays some 400 m west of the main quay. The gap between breakwater and reef was evidently the principal entrance to the harbour, and a circular foundation on the shore facing it may have supported a light-house or light-tower.[12] The town was an important enough maritime trader to maintain an office at Ostia (Plate 27), where the use of the elephant as the town's symbol has excited considerable comment about the nature of that trade (see p.157, below).

4
TACAPAE (GABES)

The fourth of the *coloniae*, *Tacapae* was situated at the centre of the Lesser Syrtic gulf, in a pivotal position between Tripolitania and *Africa* proper. The town lay alongside one of the most remarkable of the south Tunisian oases and in a geographical sense this can be seen to link it more with the Tripolitanian environment. Little is known archaeologically about ancient *Tacapae*, long dismembered for construction in the oasis villages which continued beyond the life of the Roman town. From historical sources we know that the town originated as a Phoenician *emporium*, that it became a Libyphoenician *civitas* exploiting the abundant springwater of the oasis for its agriculture and that it ranked a *colonia*. But even the date at which the site was granted colonial status is unknown. A limited amount of research has indicated that the town was of large extent and that it lay on the south side of the oasis and the Wadi Gabes. It is possible that the ancient port was further inland than the modern one in a now silted lagoon. On the fringes of the town evidence has been found for pottery production, including lamps and amphorae. In the absence of direct evidence, we might consider that the model of urban development at *Sabratha* could have applied in whole or in part to a site like *Tacapae*.

The oasis of Gabes is of particular interest because it features in an important passage in Pliny's *Natural History*, where he reveals the potential profitability of its irrigated agriculture and the high yields attained. Although the territory of *Tacapae* extended well beyond the oasis into the Arad plain, it is certain that the oasis was the most intensively exploited local resource. Pliny lists dates, olives, figs, pomegranates, grapes, wheat, vegetables and herbs as a series of crops all grown on the same plot, asserting that there was always something ready to be harvested.[13]

5
GIGTHIS (BOU GHARA)

Gigthis is without doubt the best known of the smaller Tripolitanian towns, thanks to extensive French excavations at the turn of the century. However, the nature of those excavations was characteristic of the time, involving wholesale clearance of the central area and detailed study only of the major architectural monuments. Late phases of occupation are referred to in a number of contexts but it is apparent that these were removed with little record in order to reveal the original appearance of the major monuments. Dating evidence at that time was heavily dependent on epigraphy and where no inscription was found only rather vague comments could be advanced. Nonetheless, in spite of these reservations, the remains of *Gigthis* are of the utmost interest for what they tell us about the processes of urbanization at such smaller centres.

The site was rediscovered by Victor Guerin in 1860 in dramatic circumstances. He crossed to the mainland from the island of Gerba in a small boat and almost immediately stumbled across the ruins of the forum. In a few minutes more he had solved the question of the identification of the site by uncovering an inscription recording a dedication by the *Gigthenses publice*. At this point, however, a band of bedouin ('armés jusqu'au dents') appeared on the scene to disrupt the work, but retired when it became clear that

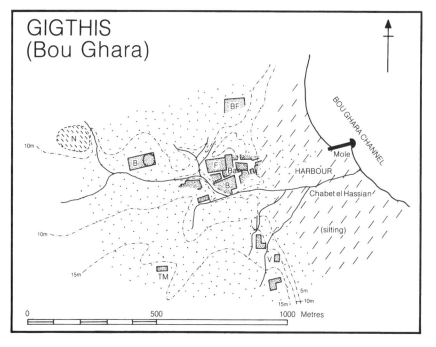

Fig. 6:8 General plan of Gigthis (Bou Ghara). **F** = forum, **Ba** = basilica, **B** = baths, **Bf** = 'Byzantine fort', **V** = villas, **TM** = temple of Mercury, **N** = necropolis.

Guerin's armed party would offer stern resistance. The main work of excavation was carried out in the 1880s and, more importantly, from 1901–06.

Bou Ghara lies at the southwestern extremity of the gulf of Bou Ghara in the lee of the island of Gerba. It is a naturally sheltered location, suitable for a small harbour, and seems to have been in existence by the third century BC at the latest. The site is poorly situated for defence, being very exposed on the landward side, but no sign of ancient defences has been noted (Fig. 6:8). The ancient harbour lay at the mouth of a minor wadi where it cut through a line of cliffs (still very evident to the north and south of the town). The town thus grew up on very uneven ground on the flanks of a minor valley and this is clearly reflected in the irregularity of the discernible street plan. Virtually nothing is known of the early history of the town, though pre-Roman cemeteries have been located to the north, northwest and west of the town. It escaped notice in almost all the Roman sources and we are very dependent on the epigraphic evidence from the excavations for what little we can piece together. The principal structures at the centre of the town were evidently part of a second-century reshaping and monumentalizing of an older core. This growth can in part be related to the town's several attempts to obtain promotion to *municipium* status and subsequently to achieve higher Latin rights (enfranchising all the town council and not just the magistrates). Several embassies were dispatched to Rome whilst the principal local families invested considerable sums in improving the look of the place. Antoninus Pius eventually granted both municipal rank and the more coveted *Latium maius* status. The impetus continued thereafter as the local notables continued to vie with each other to display the greater level of local patriotism and euergetism.

This programme of reconstruction of the forum (Plate 31), its associated temples and minor monuments thus spans the reigns of Hadrian, Antoninus Pius and Marcus Aurelius (Fig. 6:9). That there was an earlier forum we may safely infer from architectural fragments of Julio-Claudian type and several of the temples to traditional Libyphoenician deities, such as Melqart and Shadrapa (albeit in their Romanized guises as Hercules and Liber Pater), must have had antecedents. Neo-Punic inscriptions are known from the town and statues of Augustus and Nerva also reflect first century AD activity. What we see in the town plan as excavated, though, is the partial formalization of a previously more haphazard urban layout. The orthogonal lines of the forum and its temples and shrines, the basilica and the temple of Liber Pater are quite clearly superimposed on a higgledy-piggledy

network of roads and buildings, well represented, for example, by the Rue des Thermes and by the east temple (though the latter was rebuilt at some point in the mid-second century it kept to its traditional orientation). Marble was used in the Antonine reconstruction programme, though always in a limited way. The traditional local stones, normally white-stuccoed for protection, remained the dominant building materials, even for architraves, bases and columns.

Nonetheless, this rebuilding programme reflects considerable vitality and spare cash in the town during the decades when it was seeking and obtaining municipal status. But it is important to keep a sense of perspective and a quick comparison with the plan of the central area of *Sabratha*, for instance, is enough to show that the *Gigthenses* for all their pretension, were not in the same economic league. The architecture is undeniably monumental but the scale of everything is reduced from the more grandiose proportions of the eastern Tripolitanian cities and as we have noted marble was used far more sparingly.

The dating of the forum and its principal temple is generally held to be Hadrianic, with further temples, shrines and monuments being added down to the end of the second century. The evidence for the Hadrianic date is somewhat circumstantial, concerning a group of imperial statues clustered at the west end of the forum and its porticoes, the earliest of the group being dedicated to Hadrian during his reign. It is probably reasonable to ascribe the initial layout and paving of the new forum and construction of its principal temple to his reign. The attribution of the temple is controversial, Constans having argued that it was dedicated to Serapis/Isis, whilst from its position one might expect the capitoline triad or the imperial cult to have been more likely choices. On the other hand, Serapis and Isis were popular cults in Tripolitania and it is likely that one of the unassigned temples or shrines of the forum area was dedicated to them. The temple podium rises over 3 m above the level of the forum paving, protruding approx. 22 m into the 60.6 x 38.5 m forum enclosure. Only two other major structures impinge on this space – to the south of the temple was a sanctuary to the Genius Augusti and to the north a large rectangular room preceded by a vestibule. The central strip of the larger room was paved in marble and against the east and west walls were piers which could have supported raised banks of seating, indicating that this room was almost certainly the *curia*. It is unclear whether this was the *curia* known from an inscription to have been completed in AD 166. It is by no means impossible, though, that a larger and grander council house was added at that date in the unexcavated area to the north of the forum.

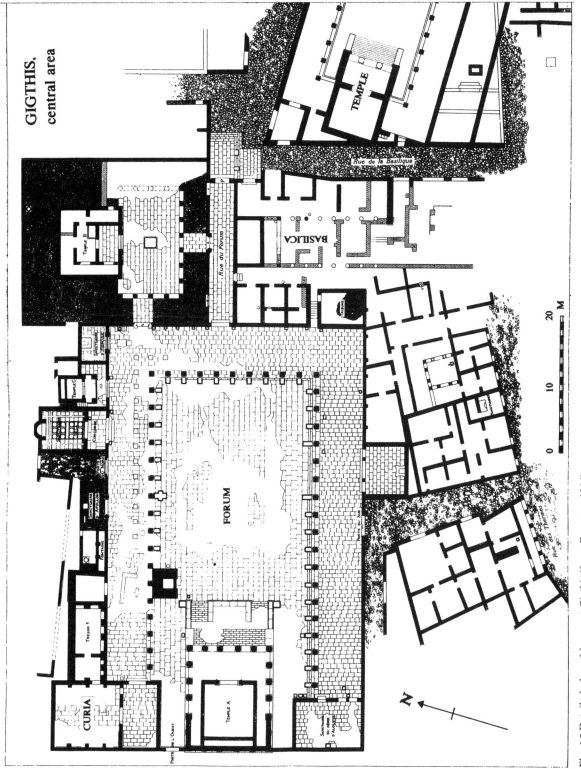

Fig. 6.9 Detailed plan of forum at *Gigthis* (from Constans 1916).

Because of extensive alteration to its fabric little is known of the original plan of the basilica to the east of the forum. But an inscription from the road leading out of that side of the forum would appear to indicate that the large temple to the north of the basilica was dedicated to Liber Pater. After the initial layout of the new forum, the main area available for monumental additions was on its north side between the temple of Liber Pater and the structure just postulated as the *curia*. Next to Liber Pater (Shadrapa), quite naturally, we find a shrine to Hercules (Melqart). Alongside this stood another small temple (perhaps the *aedes picta cum columnis* paid for by Q. Servaeus Macer) which was certainly earlier than the next structure to the west, the temple to Concordia Panthea – erected by M. Ummidius Sedatus in honour of his son's decurionate. On the other side of the north exit from the forum, a small shrine to Apollo was dedicated by the proconsul of AD 162 together with one of his legates (coincidentally called M. Ummidius Annianus Quadratus, but no relation of the local Ummidii). Adjacent to this stood a fountain, probably given in AD 164 by Q. Servaeus Macer, followed by a further room opening on to the forum (perhaps another shrine), then by two rooms with reinforced walls to which access could only be gained through the supposed *curia*. These are normally interpreted as the town's treasury (*aerarium*).

In addition to their extensive funding of the forum building programme, the local elite filled its porticoes with statues and honorific bases to the town's foremost citizens, to patrons of the town and to the emperors. The cruciform base against the north portico was apparently surmounted by a bronze wolf and twins donated by Q. Servaeus Macer probably in the reign of Pius at the time of the town's elevation to municipal status. Servaeus Macer belonged to one of the most prominent families in the town; the *gens* is known from many inscriptions including one honouring Q. Servaeus Fuscus Cornelianus, the governor of Galatia in 230. Other major local families included the Ummidii (three generations were honoured with statues in the forum), the Servilii (best known for their patronage of the late second/third-century temple of Mercury but probably also responsible for the new *curia* of AD 166), the Memmii, Messii and Iulii. Of particular importance is the Cinithian L. Memmius Messius, who demonstrated the Libyan as opposed to Libyphoenican background of some of these leading families (chapter 2, *Cinithi*). Unfortunately the donors of many of the town's public buildings remain unknown (the two baths, the east temple and the market), so on current evidence it would be hazardous to try and rank their importance *vis à vis* each other. The houses of the

richer families were perhaps to be found on the rising ground at the southern edge of town where a number of elegant peristyle villas have been recorded.

Beyond the east temple a gate gave access to the harbour quarter, with the road beyond evidently flanked by warehouses. There is ample evidence for rural exploitation in the vicinity of *Gigthis* (Constans speaks of sites 'presque à chaque pas') and olive oil may have been available for export. A prominent mole (17 m broad by 140 m long) marks the northern flank of the ancient harbour, now completely silted. It was apparently surmounted by a colonnade. Large quantities of murex shell littering the site suggest that there may have been an industrial quarter hereabouts involved in purple dye manufacture and perhaps in processing other marine products, which seem to have been a notable feature of the littoral in this region.[14]

At its maximum extent the town covered perhaps 50 ha (125 acres), though to date no trace has been found of theatre, amphitheatre or circus. In the late Roman period, there appears to have been shrinkage and adaptation of a number of the former public buildings. Nevertheless, the fourth-century governors of the province of *Tripolitana* did visit, with at least one of them becoming a patron of the town, and there was a bishop at *Gigthis* in 411. But the archaeological evidence clearly points to the second and early third centuries as marking the apogee of the town.

6
TURRIS TAMALLENI (TELMINE)

The oasis of Telmine in the Nefzaoua has long been identified as the site of the *civitas* capital of the *Nybgenii* tribe (Plate 32). The oases of the Nefzaoua seem to have had a long history of occupation and the *Turris* element of the name probably refers to a pre-Roman native fortification there. It is almost certain that the oases will have received a Roman garrison for a while in the conquest period. By the late first century AD, though, there are signs that the tribe was considered ready for local self-government and the *civitas* centre was organized as a town on Roman lines. It was certainly in existence when the territory of the tribe was delimited from that of the cities of *Capsa* (Gafsa) to the north and *Tacapae* to the east *c.* AD 105. Under Hadrian the town was granted municipal status and we know of an early third-century proconsul of Africa who served as its patron. There was a bishopric based in the town, although the see was listed as one of those of the fourth-century province of *Byzacena*, rather than *Tripolitana* (perhaps because of the close links between the oases of Djerid and Nefzaoua). Alternatively, there may have been military reasons for linking the Nefzaoua with the late Roman military commands of southern *Byzacena* and *Numidia*, perhaps as a modification to a scheme that would have included this area in the province (where it more logically belonged). The detachment of the Nefzaoua from the old *limes Tripolitanus* frontier zone, whether done at the outset or subsequent to the formation of the province of *Tripolitana* was a geographic anomaly in that the Chotts themselves would have formed a more logical boundary between the provinces.

Archaeology can add little to this picture, because of continuous occupation at the oasis, but the amount of ancient stonework and architectural fragments reused in the houses of Telmine confirm the location and indicate something of the possible sophistication of some of the buildings. Columns and capitals recovered from the mosque belong to a number of distinct structures (Plate 32) and a massive, part ashlar wall surmounts a springhead a short distance from the mosque.[15]

The rapid promotion of an oasis town and its indigenous population (there is no evidence and little likelihood of outside settlers here) is of the greatest interest. It is the clearest example one could wish for of the processes by which hostile peoples were transformed into peaceful and self-governing communities. The appearance of the place can only be guessed at but the worthy, rather than spectacular, architecture and semi-planned layout of *Gigthis* may perhaps be an appropriate comparable image.

7
ZITHA (ZIAN)

Although the site of *Zitha* is poorly understood at present, there are hints that its urban development followed a dramatically different course from that of the other sites considered so far. The site lies a few kilometres inland from Zarzis (*Gergis*), which presumably served as its harbour. It is also close to the south end of the ancient causeway to the island of Gerba and this perhaps explains its early origins. The Zarzis peninsula has long been known for the quality of its olive orchards and the name of the site is very suggestive of a link (Phoenician *zith* = olive). Cultivation of the olive, then, may have been another reason for the establishment and success of the site. The site has yielded Punic and neo-Punic texts which should indicate activity from at least the second century BC, and the pre-Roman *emporium* was important enough to issue its own coins.

The early distinction of *Zitha* ought to have guaranteed it becoming a prominent town under Rome and the signs are that this was starting to happen in the first century AD. The excavation of the forum in the 1880s revealed a series of dedications in which the names of Claudius and at least two Claudian proconsuls can be identified. The forum, with a triple temple arrangement at one end and colonnades around the central space, was constructed between AD 41 and 53. A bust of Claudius found in the central *cella* gives added emphasis to the mid-first-century development. But the size of the forum monuments is very small and, although no scale is given on the published plan, it was plainly much reduced in comparison with that of *Gigthis* (the portico colonnades contained 11 x 9 columns, against 19 x 11). Apart from a temple of Caelestis, situated on a hummock approx. 300 m from the forum, nothing else has been excavated at *Zitha*, and it is clearly hazardous to extrapolate the history of the site. Yet the apparent absence of major additions to the forum after the Julio-Claudian period and its miniature scale is disconcerting, in view of the dramatic evidence of Antonine development from *Sabratha* and *Gigthis*, for instance. Although *Zitha* continued to be occupied well beyond the first century, and at some point was awarded *municipium* status, it does not appear to have fulfilled its early promise. Is this a case perhaps of a successful *emporium* becoming a failed *municipium*?[16]

8
THUBACTIS
(AT OR NEAR MISURATA?)

A fundamental problem presented by a number of the smaller towns of ancient Tripolitania concerns their exact location. In spite of being known to have achieved municipal status, *Thubactis* or *Tubactis* is an archaeological mystery. It was the only substantial town to the east of *Lepcis* before the Syrtic gulf and the mileage distances, though corrupt, suggest that it lay somewhere in the vicinity of the important medieval and modern oasis town of Misurata. No traces of a major settlement have been noted at Misurata itself (though that should not necessarily exclude the oasis from consideration as the Roman town) and three alternative theories have been proposed:

1 Bartoccini identified the town with a small harbour site at Gasr Ahmed on the Syrtic coast a few kilometres east of Misurata. There is a small late-Roman bath here and pottery has been noted at a number of points.

2 Brogan recognized an alternative small harbour on the coast to the northwest of Misurata at Marsa Gezira. There was certainly an important Libyphoenician settlement here, consisting of mud-brick buildings. Tombs of various date have been noted, including some of Roman date.
3 Rebuffat has argued that the town lay on a more inland route which by-passed Misurata and should be located somewhere to the south of Misurata near Taouorga (cf. Fig. 3:2).

In reality none of the solutions proposed seems to have enough solid evidence behind it to be finally acceptable. The Gasr Ahmed baths and anchorage could conceivably have been associated with a villa, rather than a small town, whilst at Marsa Gezira the bulk of the settlement evidence relates to the third—first centuries BC and, although this pre-Roman period settlement was spread over 300 m, there is nothing in the record as yet to confirm the presence of a substantial Roman town. Rebuffat's proposal originated in his desire to equate *Chosol* of the *Tabula Peutingeriana* with *Gholaia* (Bu Njem) and he has no specific site in mind for *Thubactis*; indeed no extensive ruins are known in that area.[17]

The character of the town is thus unknown. But in view of its total obliteration it was perhaps small and unspectacular in the manner of *Zitha*, rather than a rival in any sense to the larger cities. *Lepcis* would certainly have preferred to keep it that way.

9
OTHER TOWNS

The archaeological record for the other towns is very sketchy (Fig. 3:2). *Pisidia* on the Lesser Syrtes and *Digdida* on the Greater Syrtes were apparently *municipia*, the latter associated with the *Seli* tribe, but there has been little investigation at either site. The four towns of the island of Gerba (*Girba, Tipasa, Hare, Meninx*) are little better known, but we might note that *Girba* was the seat of a bishopric in the late empire. Two other settlements along the Syrtic coast were of some consequence, *Marcomades* (Sirte), evidently a *civitas* of the western *Seli*, and *Iscina* (Medina Sultan), which had a noteworthy Jewish community (*loc. iudaeor. Augti.*). A Christian catacomb and some fine pagan tombs are known at Sirte, but at both sites subsequent occupation has obliterated most traces of the Roman period towns.

The hot springs at El Hamma (*Aquae Tacapitanae*) made that oasis a spa centre for nearby *Tacapae*, though occupation by a sedentary indigenous population

could have been early. Apart from the baths, which could be military in origin, little is known.[18]

10
'SMALL TOWNS' AND VILLAGES

All the sites mentioned so far will have aspired to a greater or lesser extent to be recognized both in administrative and in physical terms as 'Roman' towns. Most will eventually have possessed fora, temples, baths and other amenities on a scale commensurate with their resources. There were other sites in the region whose size and complexity identifies them as urban or proto-urban but whose form and organization distinguished them from the chartered towns governed by councils and magistrates. We might include in this category the major oases of the frontier and beyond (*Cidamus* and *Garama* being the prime examples, chapter 2 above). A second category comprises the 'small towns' and villages within the massive *territoria* of the great coastal cities, which due to the factor of distance from the mother city must have served as local regional markets. The case is clearest for the territory of *Lepcis* which is reasonably well defined and which contained at least three minor centres, *Sugolin* (Zliten), *Subututtu* (Gasr ed-Daun) and *Mesphe* (Medina Doga). The first and last of these are sited very close to the edge of the territory, in which location they could have fulfilled an important function as 'gateway' communities or 'ports of trade'. Medina Doga was a large undefended settlement of approx. 15 ha (47 acres), possessing at least two bath buildings and a large colonnaded structure. There was a Christian catacomb and extensive cemeteries nearby. There is evidence in the form of neo-Punic dedications to Ammon and Caelestis (Tanit) for a Libyphoenician presence in this part of the Gebel from the early first century AD. On current evidence, Gasr ed-Daun appears to have been a smaller, more straggling settlement, along the line of the Gebel road. Foundations of buildings, a few columns and capitals, a small bath-house and pottery kilns have been noted here. Ed-Daun lies at the centre of a network of tracks and is thus well placed to have acted as a gathering point for onward transportation of olive oil shipments from the many farms in its vicinity. The relatively low level of development of these small towns strongly suggests that *Lepcis* maintained full administrative authority and economic power over them.

Several further Gebel settlements were of large extent but their interpretation is complicated by the attested presence of a military garrison for some period of their occupation. It is probable, however, that *Thenadassa* (Ain Wif) and *Auru* (Ain el-Auenia) were located just within the boundaries of the *territoria* of *Oea* and *Sabratha* respectively and that occupation pre-dated the Roman road stations established there. Ain Wif covered an area of 10–11 ha (25 acres) running along a ridge and also descending on terraces to the small spring-fed oasis on its west side (Fig. 5:9). The military works on the south side have been described already. On the evidence of the church and of late Roman pottery, occupation continued into the fifth century. Ain el-Auenia is another important spring site and traces of Roman period occupation cover an area in excess of 8 ha (20 acres). Small-scale excavations in 1960 uncovered part of a military bathhouse and architectural fragments from substantial buildings or tombs. The coin list extends from the mid-second to the early fifth century.

Whether we care to see these settlements as small towns or villages, there is a very important distinction to be drawn between the evidence for urbanization here and in most other parts of *Africa Proconsularis*. In comparison to the size of the region, the density of proper towns remained far lower in Tripolitania than was the norm elsewhere in Roman Africa. The failure of the many smaller 'towns' and 'villages' to graduate to full urban status must in large part be attributed to the extraordinary position and power allowed by Rome to the major cities.[19]

11
MILITARY *VICI*

The final category of site to be considered is the military *vicus*, the civilian settlement which grew up around Roman garrison points. In some cases, it is likely that native settlement pre-existed the arrival of the garrison, but even in these cases the construction of the fort will have introduced a whole series of new spatial relationships and may have involved the local population relocating their own dwellings. *Vici* were not simply a response to the recreational and consumer needs of the garrison, though economic motives may have brought some part of their population there. In some instances, political supervision was exercised over tribal groups by fort commanders and it is probable that the tribal leaders will have been required to move to or to spend considerable periods of time in the *vicus*. In certain cases in North Africa, the *vicus* population was eventually recognized as a self-governing town. But in others, and most of the Tripolitanian examples fall in this category, the *vicus* dwindled and

failed after the removal of the garrison's spending power. Nonetheless the size of some of the military *vici* was very large, easily comparable with the 'small towns' just described, and there remain further questions as to why the military-sponsored urbanization should also have been less effective in Tripolitania than elsewhere on the African frontiers.[20]

Bu Njem is by far the best-known site on account of Rebuffat's excavations. Traces of the civil settlement were first noted by Richardson and are clear on Goodchild's air-photograph. It extends over an area of approx. 15 ha (37 acres), of which at least 10 ha (25 acres) were enclosed by a wall showing several stages of development (Fig. 6.10). This wall is rather insubstantial and does not seem to have been primarily defensive in function. Its date is unknown but it clearly post-dated the construction of the fort. There is no evidence for second-century occupation at the site.

Rebuffat has excavated a number of building complexes, notably the 'building of the niches' and the 'building with two windows'. Some of the *vicus* structures were aligned with the fort, but this planned layout is by no means representative of the settlement as a whole, which seems to have grown rapidly and on an irregular basis.

The shifting sands have buried many of these buildings up to their roof level so that they are extraordinarily well-preserved. The vaulted architecture employed is reminiscent of medieval and modern practice in the northern Sahara. In most cases the barrel vaults were formed by bending slender palm trunks and then encasing them with mortar. The excavated rooms seem to have been mainly shops or merchants' offices to judge from their plan and the graffiti found on their walls. The 'building of the niches', for instance, divided up into five two-room units. Libyan graffiti show that the population of the *vicus* was not entirely composed of Latinized traders or campfollowers. On the other hand, pictures of ships and a lighthouse, of wild animals and hunters, suggest that the *vicus* did not exist solely to service the fort. This conclusion is supported by evidence of consumption of imported goods among the civilian population itself. Perfume flasks and make-up pots abound, along with glass, fine pottery and a range of luxury goods. The more basic needs of food, oil and wine had also to be supplied. The *vicus* was thus an important bridge between the Mediterranean economy and the inland pre-desert oasis and farming communities.

The settlement thrived during the third century but after the garrison was withdrawn *c.* 263 it entered a gradual decline. Although there were still some occupants in the early fifth century, large parts of buildings were at that date already abandoned to the sands.[21]

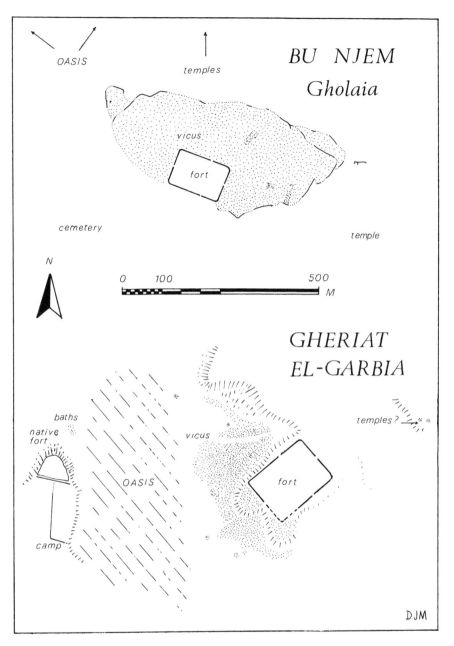

Fig. 6:10 The military *vici* at Bu Njem and Gheriat el-Garbia (after Rebuffat 1975b and ULVS survey).

The existence of a *vicus* at Remada (*Tillibari*) can be surmised from Donau's report which mentioned a walled enclosure around the fort (Fig. 5:2). Donau sectioned the defences in several places and found an earth bank fronted by a dry-stone wall. His interpretation that this 10 ha (25 acres) enclosure was an auxiliary camp or a baggage park was heavily influenced by French military practice at that time. Trousset correctly identified it as a civilian settlement. At least one female civilian is attested on a tombstone from the site.

The *vicus* of Gheriat el-Garbia has been little stud-

ied and most of its traces have been obliterated by subsequent occupants of the oasis. The evidence visible on Goodchild's air-photograph may represent only part of the original settlement. Traces of buildings are visible on the eastern slopes between the fort and the oasis, covering an area of 6–10 ha (15–25 acres) and some clearly relate to the military alignment (Fig. 6:10). As at Bu Njem, however, many structures are far less regularly aligned. The discovery of what appears to be a native fortification, a temporary Roman encampment and a military bath-house on the

135

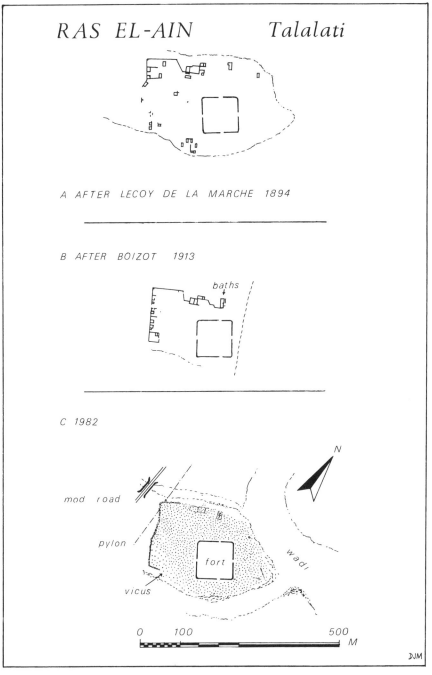

Fig. 6:11 The military *vicus* at Ras el-Ain (after Lecoy de la Marche 1894, Boizot 1913 and pers obs 1982).

west side of the oasis, suggests that the civil settlement may have spread on both sides of the cultivated area. A significant Libyan component may be suspected among the inhabitants. The size of the fort at Gheriat indicates that it contained the largest garrison unit in Tripolitania and its *vicus* may have been similarly populous.

Because of the density of rubble inside the fort of Ras el-Ain (*Talalati*), early investigators turned their attention to the visible *vicus* buildings alongside (Fig. 6:11). The information recorded can be usefully compared with surface traces today. The *vicus* was enclosed and protected to the west by a wall, with the steep embankments of a series of wadis serving as boundaries on the other sides. This well-defined 4 ha (10 acres) promontory was fairly densely built up.

Some of the buildings were attached to the back of the western wall, at least one being a shop or store-house to judge from the quantity of amphora fragments found there. A small bath building was excavated by Boizot on the north side of the site in 1913.

The civil settlement had a long life and may even have pre-dated the fort (founded in AD 263) since some early third-century ARS forms are visible on the surface. Fragments of the inscription detailing rebuilding work of AD 355–60 were reused in later renovation of *vicus* structures and pottery from the site includes ARS and TRS (Tripolitanian Red Slip) of fifth-century date.[22]

Even small military sites could have attendant *vici*. For example, Hilaire noted ruins covering approx. 10 ha between Bir Rhezene (*Bezereos*) and Sidi Mohammed ben Aissa. In 1938, a two-storey house was partially excavated and traces of five other substantial buildings are still visible today, though much of the site is obscured by sand. Civilian burials have also been discovered.

A number of other road stations in both western and eastern Tripolitania have produced evidence of civil settlement associated with military posts. An extreme example is the site of Ksar Rhilane (*Tisavar*) on the edge of the Eastern Erg. The ancillary buildings visible close to the fortlet (Fig. 5:10) seem to be primarily military (stables, a temple of the Genius, other shrines), but Gombeaud mentioned other buildings up to 400 m from the fortlet. These are now mainly obscured by sand dunes, but the possibility of a small *vicus* cannot be ignored.[23]

Judged by the standards of some other African examples, the Tripolitanian *vici* were poor achievers in the long term. In Mauretania and Numidia many *vici* gained self-governing status (9 out of 23 *vici* in

Mauretania Caesariensis) or even became *municipia,* as in the well-documented cases of *Rapidum, Gemellae* and *Ad Maiores*. On current knowledge, the only likely parallel is *Turris Tamalleni*, if it is accepted that a military garrison was installed there in the Flavian period. One may contrast the two types of civil settlement alongside forts, the 'dependent' and 'independent' *vicus*. The dependent *vici* grew up primarily to service the garrison and their economic base was vulnerable once the garrison's spending power was removed. Independent *vici* were better integrated into the broader economic structures of the province and into local administrative arrangements, thereby gaining a better chance of surviving as a market or administrative centre if the troops were redeployed. It is interesting to note, however, that the most successful *vici* in Mauretania and Numidia gained their recognition as self-governing communities whilst the garrisons were still in occupation.[24]

The Tripolitanian *vici* appear either to have declined with the redeployment of the garrison or, in the case of Remada, never to have amounted to much. Sites such as Ain el-Auenia, Ain Wif and Medina Doga perhaps came closest to urban status, but they were in reality never much more than large villages or local markets. The lack of urban growth in the hinterland may in part be ascribed to a lack of will on the part of Rome to promote it. The cultural make-up of the region was polarized between coastal and interior parts (chapter 8), with the Libyphoenician communities of the former much more amenable to Roman-style urban government than the Libyans of the pre-desert hinterland and the oases. It is also the case, though, that the region has struggled in its long history to sustain major urban centres between the coast and the chief oases of the northern Sahara.

7

ECONOMY AND TRADE

1
THE OLIVE OIL PROVINCE

The spectacular wealth of the coastal cities of Tripolitania was generated in a variety of ways, but first place must be accorded to agriculture and, in particular, to the olive. Previous accounts of the economy of Tripolitania have tended to stress the importance of trans-Saharan trade to the sea-borne commerce of the cities, but this supposition is both unverifiable and unquantifiable. Whilst I do not deny the probable existence of some trans-Saharan traffic (see below), the overwhelming impression to be gained from literary and archaeological evidence is that olive oil was the chief currency-earning export of the region. The emphasis in this chapter, therefore, will be on agricultural development and the potential trade in food staples. Other elements of trade and industry may be speculated upon but evidence remains elusive.[1]

During the Roman period there was a massive increase in the extent and scale of agriculture and arboriculture in North Africa as a whole. This revolution did not involve new crops or new methods, but an intensification and expansion of the pre-existing Carthaginian, Libyphoenician and African production. One result of this was a shift from subsistence to market strategies in some regions, a process amplified by the introduction of taxation and by the growth of towns. Official Roman interest in the farming economy initially centred on northern Tunisia, where there were massive imperial estates. A major concern of north Tunisian farming was cereal production, with

the area becoming one of the major suppliers of the city of Rome by the first century AD. Landholding was the subject of several agricultural laws and there is evidence of land survey (centuriation) covering tens of thousands of square kilometres. Such surveying was not simply to provide convenient modules for allocating land, but, of course, also served as a basis for tax assessment.

Under the Flavian emperors a major recensus took place. The legal basis of agricultural tenancy on imperial estates (and possibly private estates also) was formalized by the *lex Manciana* and the delimitation of tribal lands for administrative and fiscal needs was undertaken. As a result of this policy, attributed by some sources to Vespasian's avarice, there was a significant increase in agricultural production and in general prosperity in Africa.[2] We shall see that there are echoes of this in the evidence from late first-century Tripolitania.

The equation between grain for Rome and African wealth is by no means straightforward. A substantial element of the surplus cereal production either came in the form of rents from imperial estates or was levied as tax in kind so its value to the local economy is hard to judge. However, the presence of large numbers of shippers in the North African ports provided opportunities for exporting other commodities. In spite of occasional scholarly doubts as to the viability and extent of a Mediterranean trade in agricultural staples, these were precisely the products which seem to have underpinned the prosperity of Africa. Even on the cereal estates of north Tunisia there was some diversification in the agricultural regime to provide alternative cash crops. Olives and vines were the two

138

most adaptable and remunerative of these and both were established in the region from Punic times. The olive became increasingly important, just as cereal production became less so, as one moved south into the more marginal regions of central and southern Tunisia and Algeria. By the third century AD the extent of olive cultivation in the Maghreb had reached an extraordinary pitch and the total volume of Tunisian olive oil exports was probably the highest in the Roman world. Inevitably, Tripolitania was affected by the trading contacts of *Africa Proconsularis* and by its own olive boom (being a pioneer for marginal zone olive specialization and perhaps a victim of the late Roman supremacy of the Tunisian olive lands).[3]

Reference has been made several times to the fact that Tripolitania was different from much of the rest of Roman Africa. Three factors are particularly significant in economic terms: first, the marginality of the zone (chapter 1); second, the fact that agricultural development had been fostered by a Libyphoenician elite based on the coastal towns who, unlike the

Carthaginian aristocracy, had not been supplanted by Roman landowners; third, the remarkably early date of Tripolitanian prosperity gave its chief city a head start over most other North African towns. There is no reason to assume, therefore, that the spread of agriculture was brought about by Roman 'colonists' or that it involved the wholesale replacement of indigenous socio-economic structures by the Roman market economy.

But nor should we underestimate the essential precariousness of an agricultural economy in what was a marginal environment. Within the area of Roman Tripolitania the potential agricultural land is squeezed severely between sea and desert and the climate is unfavourable for large-scale commercial production of cereals since no part of the zone receives the necessary average annual rainfall of 400 mm plus. Yet the Gebel and coastal area was one of the major olive-oil producing regions of the Roman empire and the pre-desert was also intensively cultivated during the Roman period. Recent work has suggested new

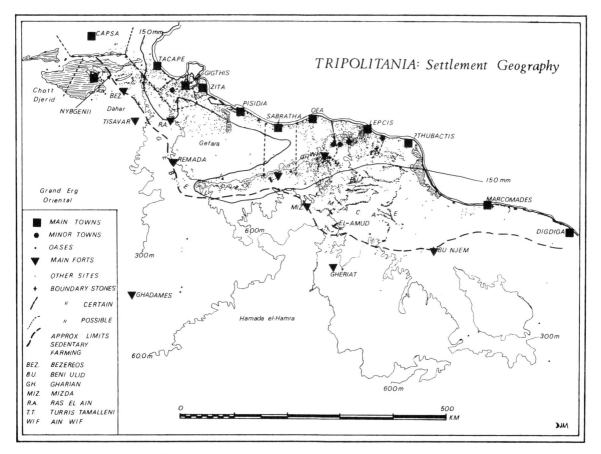

Fig 7:1 Settlement geography in Roman Tripolitania, showing known or postulated *civitas* boundaries and the approximate limit of sedentary cultivation in relation to the 150 mm rainfall isohyet. (from Mattingly 1987a).

possibilities of how and when this agricultural devel-opment was achieved.

When the generalized distribution of ancient sites (as known) is considered (Fig. 7:1), it is apparent that settlement did not obey geographic/climatic 'law'. Sedentary agriculture extended well beyond the sup-posed limits at the 150 mm isohyet and there are still no doubt many sites to seek in the region of Sirte, in the Tunisian Gebel Demmer and the northern Dahar. On the other hand it appears to remain true that the extension of agriculture (excluding oasis cultivation which was much older) to the south of the 150 mm isohyet was a phenomenon of the Roman period. I shall argue below that the development of these mar-ginal zones drew on the manpower, technology, expertise and capital of the indigenous African and Libyphoenician population of the region, who had already brought the coastal and Gebel zones into pro-duction in pre-Roman times. The Roman role was that of a catalyst, providing the necessary conditions of security, land delimitation in favour of elite groups in society, an expanding market economy and overall supervision.[4]

As for the olive, its choice as the mainstay of Tripolitanian agriculture is unsurprising. It is a hardy tree and capable of adaptation to marginal environ-ments. Once established, olive orchards require little work outside the major task of the winter harvest. A large part of the year is free for the production of other crops, which can be intercultivated between the rows of trees. The most important product of the olive tree is the oil which can be extracted by milling and pressing its fruit. Olive oil was a basic food in an-tiquity, as well as being the prime lighting fuel and the essential base for numerous medicaments, soaps, skin oils, perfumes and cosmetics. It is justifiable to suggest that both the scale of reliance on olive oil and its economic importance in antiquity may have been seriously underestimated, particularly when its signif-icance as a food and its uses for lighting and personal hygiene are fully appreciated. Twenty litres per capita may be a useful rule of thumb value for average annual consumption in the Greco-Roman Mediter-ranean heartlands, or at any rate in the oil-rich areas. There was clearly a ready market for surplus olive oil in the ancient world and Tripolitania was one of a number of regions which played a part in supplying that trade.[5]

In this chapter we shall examine the evidence for the agricultural development of two distinct zones: first, the *territoria* of the towns in the coastal plains and in the Gebel; second, the pre-desert lands lying beyond this primary zone. Subsequent sections will turn to the question of trans-Saharan trade and to the

evidence for commerce in a range of commodities, but notably in olive oil, from Tripolitania.

2
COAST AND GEBEL

The exploitation of the Gebel lands is linked to the agricultural development of the coastal plains. By a geographical peculiarity a substantial part of the cen-tral Gefara plain is poorly watered land, with only its east and west extremities being extensively cultivated in ancient times. Much of the best agricultural land in the region is in fact to be found in the foothills and on the plateaux of the Gebel. Particularly in eastern Tripolitania, therefore, the agricultural development of the Gebel was a logical corollary of the territorial expansion of the *Libyphoenices*. Unfortunately, the earl-iest archaeological evidence from the farms of the Gebel Tarhuna, Garian and Nefusa is in the form of a few sherds of first-century AD *terra sigillata*, but in the absence of proper excavation on any of these sites it would be unwise to put much emphasis on this date. For a start, the 3 million pounds of oil fine imposed by Caesar implied large-scale olive oil production from the territory of *Lepcis Magna* by the mid-first cen-tury BC and on any estimate it is apparent that this ter-ritory was not restricted to the coastal plain but was extending up into the Gebel. The road from *Lepcis* into the Gebel Tarhuna built by the Proconsul Aelius Lamia in AD 15/16 was at one time interpreted as a purely military road, designed to facilitate more rapid deployment against the *Garamantes*. No adequate explanation could be given for the significance of the distance of 44 *milia* recorded on the terminal mile-stone at *Lepcis*. However, recent discoveries of Flavian land-boundary stones have shown that the forty-fourth milestone almost certainly would have coin-cided with the southwestern limit of the town's *territorium*, indicating that in Tiberian times the terri-tory was already of vast extent and parts of the fertile eastern Gebel Tarhuna and the Gebel Msellata were probably being exploited by the town-dwellers far earlier. It is unlikely that an early first-century AD temple of Ammon, excavated by Goodchild near Tarhuna, stood in isolation. Inscriptions record the repaving of the town's streets in AD 33–6, with fund-ing coming from the revenues of lands restored to *Lepcis* after the Tacfarinan war. The likely significance is that these lands comprised mature (rather than immature) orchards on the remoter fringes of Lepcitanian territory. In AD 69 *Lepcis* went to war with her neighbour *Oea* over disputed lands along their common boundary (almost certainly located in the Gebel in the area resurveyed in AD 74), perhaps implying that by then there was comparatively little undeveloped land remaining in their *territoria*. The existence of well-developed agricultural lands extending so far into the Gebel certainly helps to explain the wealth of many of the Lepcitanian aristocracy from the Augustan period. The primary cash crop of the Gebel farming was olive oil, as is made clear by the abundant evidence for olive presses, though no doubt a far wider range of produce was grown (Fig. 7:2).[6]

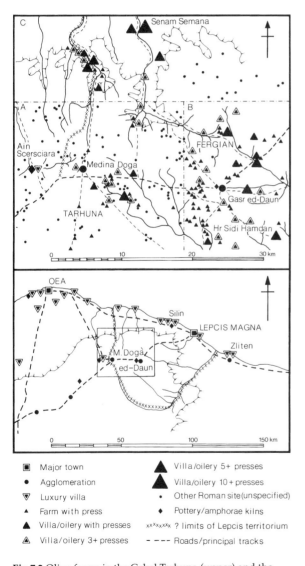

Fig 7:2 Olive farms in the Gebel Tarhuna (upper) and the probable extent of the *territorium* of *Lepcis Magna* (lower). The lower map also indicates the location of luxury villas and amphora kilns in the region (from Mattingly 1988b).

The further development of the Roman Mediterranean economy during the first century AD will have provided an additional incentive to increase production and to expand the area under cultivation. A few observations on the nature and distribution of the olive press sites are appropriate here. There is a sharp contrast between the spartan character of the 'villa' type structures in the Gebel and the luxury villas in the coastal plain, such as Zliten, Taggiura and those near Silin. The latter are quite unlike most North African house-types and their location (Fig. 7:2, lower map), in many cases right on the Mediterranean foreshore, is reminiscent of Italian luxury maritime villas. Most of the known luxury villa sites reached their apogee in the Antonine era, reflecting the increasing historical prominence of Tripolitanians at this period. The lavish mosaic pavements known from a number of these sites, the presence of marble fragments, painted stucco, bath-houses, porticoes, belvederes and other exotic architectural features all indicate the sort of conspicuous consumption we would expect at the out-of-town retreats of an extremely wealthy urban elite. The location of these luxury villas was conditioned by ease of access from the towns, whether by sea or along the main coastal highway; some existed in the very suburbs of the towns. A remarkably similar distribution is to be found in the territory of *Caesarea* in Mauretania, though the sites are far less spectacular, reflecting differences in resources it could be said. Yet this coastal distribution of major luxury retreats overlaps with an area of intense agricultural activity; indeed they were in effect located on estates. For instance the five or six villas at Silin are surrounded by buildings of more mundane functions, including the processing of oil, whose plans are similar to those of the Gebel sites. The names of some of the major estates close to the coastal highway are preserved in the Itineraries (*Fulgurita Villa, Villa Magna, Villa Repentina, Villa Aniciorum, Villa Marci*).[7]

The Gebel 'villas' were utilitarian structures, where evidence for bath-houses, mosaics or wall-paintings is minimal, whilst olive presses abound. The villa at Ain Scerciara, with its mosaics, porticoes and beautiful location close to a springhead and waterfall, is a rare (perhaps unique) exception to this general rule (Fig. 7:2). The evident clustering of oil presses of all types along the line of Roman roads and major trackways of the area implies that a significant portion of the production was intended to be marketed. Some of the smallest farms with single olive presses were less well built and may reflect a second level of economic activity.

The typical press in the Gebel was a massive affair, with stone piers supporting one end of a timber press

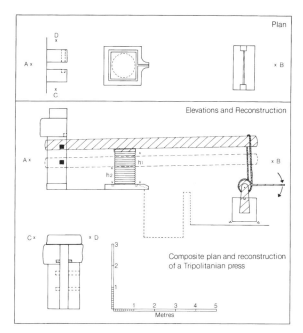

Fig 7:3 Plan and reconstruction of a massive Tripolitanian olive press from the Gebel Tarhuna (from Mattingly 1988a).

beam, the free end being manoeuvred downwards by means of a windlass mounted on a counterweight block (Fig. 7:3). The excellent preservation of the stone uprights at many sites makes the identification and counting of presses relatively easy (Plate 1), though much the best work on these sites was done in the 1890s under the mistaken impression that they were prehistoric megaliths (see above, Fig. 0:1). There are quite a number of sites with multiple banks of presses; three to five are commonly found (Fig. 7:4), a few sites have nine or more (Plate 33) and the uniquely large factory at Senam Semana (Fig. 7:5) had at least 17.

The massive scale of the various elements of these Tripolitanian presses shows that they were amongst the biggest of the ancient world, and I have calculated that individual examples could have had a potential production capacity of about 10,000 litres or kilograms of olive oil in a bumper year (though output would fluctuate wildly year by year). This is compelling evidence for the economic orientation of the majority of the Gebel farms. They were not subsistence small-holdings by and large but centres for substantial estates in which capital had been invested to provide utilitarian living accommodation together with purpose-built and expensive processing facilities. The high quality ashlar masonry used in these structures is not matched by quality of finds and this reinforces the impression that many farms were built

with the capital investment of major landowners but occupied by tenants or slaves.[8]

No doubt many small and less obviously 'Romanized' sites have escaped detection. But the record may be considered relatively complete at least as regards the distribution of *villa rustica* type sites for the Fergian region (Fig. 7:2). The density of such sites and of olive presses in neighbouring Tarhuna or Msellata would undoubtedly be similar if we had fuller records for those areas. The high level of investment demonstrable in the utilitarian villas/farms and press buildings in the Gebel, coupled with the absence of much evidence for conspicuous consumption of profits outside the principal towns and the luxury coastal villas, indicate a pattern of ownership or control of these sites by an urban elite. Nor is there reason to consider that the distribution of olive presses on the Tarhuna plateau was atypically dense in comparison to other parts of the territory of the town, and the limited excavation of domestic quarters or suburbs of *Lepcis* and other towns leaves the question of the scale of oil production there an open one. Nevertheless, particularly in the later empire, olive oil production is well attested in towns in Roman Africa and some presses are known in *Sabratha* and *Lepcis*.

The distance at which this type of villa agriculture was operated from the town is also of considerable

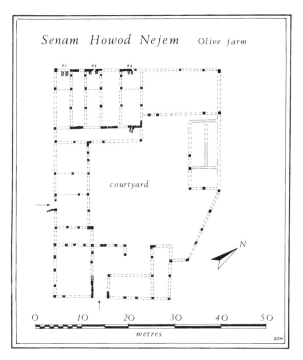

Fig 7:4 Olive farm with three olive presses from the Fergian region (from Mattingly 1985a).

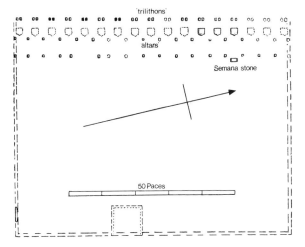

'trilithons'

altars

Semana stone

50 Paces

Fig 7:5 Olive oil factory with 17 presses at Senam Semana (from Cowper 1897, with modifications).

interest. The developed agricultural territory of *Lepcis Magna* can now be estimated at around 3,000–4,000 sq km and this can be compared, for instance, with information on *Caesarea* in Mauretania (Leveau 1984). Leveau has calculated that the villa-dominated agricultural hinterland of *Caesarea* comprised approx. 350 sq km and by most standards it was a well-to-do town. It was capital of the province of *Mauretania Caesariensis*, yet its developed agricultural hinterland was roughly one tenth the size of that of *Lepcis*. In the most densely urbanized parts of *Africa Proconsularis* towns were so close together that in the most extreme cases their territories must have been under 100 sq km. Even allowing for some differences in land quality, this must have implications for any assessment of the relative level of 'success' achieved by each town in the Roman world. The territory of *Lepcis* certainly contained many hundreds of olive presses (perhaps as many as 1,500), and the total potential oil production capacity in good years will have measured millions of litres. Some of the largest press complexes may justifiably be described as oileries. If my estimate of the potential output of the biggest presses is correct, a site such as Henschir Sidi Hamdan (Plate 33) could have had an output of up to 100,000 litres in a bumper year and Senam Semana nearer 200,000 litres. Clearly bumper harvests did not occur every year, but I would argue that the region was geared up to take full advantage of those occasions when they did occur. Although the biggest exporter may have been *Lepcis*, large-scale olive oil production seems likely both in eastern and western Tripolitania. We have earlier noted the derivation of the name of *Zitha* in the Arad plain from the Phoenician word for olive.[9]

The extraordinary size of the agriculturally developed territory of *Lepcis* in conjunction with the comparatively small number of major families in the town (as revealed by the civic inscriptions) will have placed a very considerable resource in the hands of a select group. Not every year need have seen a surplus produced for overseas sale, but the disposal of oil to the internal market will also have been very much in the control of the rich landowners and to their financial benefit. They will have held the largest stockpiles in years of shortage and in any year will have put the greatest quantity on the market. The territories of *Oea*, *Sabratha* and *Tacapae* were also enormous but the quality of the land was overall not as high as that of *Lepcis*.

What is clearly visible for olive oil will have applied to other forms of farming wealth also; it is certainly not my intention to imply that olive oil was the only source of enrichment for the Tripolitanian elite. Mosaics from the coastal villas indicate a wide range of agricultural activities, including olives and cereal cultivation, horse rearing, shepherding and market-gardening. The same picture of mixed farming is evident in the account of the multiple estates of the Oean aristocracy provided by Apuleius. He emphasized wheat, barley, vines and olives along with sheep and goats and horse-breeding. Stock-raising may have had particular significance as a subsidiary production focus for the estates. Aristocratic fortunes, primarily based on farming and the marketing of its products, could be great. Pudentilla, the Oean woman who married Apuleius, had a fortune of 4 million sestertii and this probably did not include the value of the hundreds of slaves who evidently worked on her estates. Nor was Pudentilla the only millionaire at *Oea* and the aristocracy at *Lepcis* were even more wealthy.[10]

There is comparatively little evidence either from the towns or their hinterland of settlers from outside Africa or of retired soldiers. The bulk of the population in both town and country was of Punic or African extraction. Apuleius described the landholding elite of *Oea* as heavily Punicized, with many of them owning multiple estates, scattered throughout *Oea*'s territory and controlled for them by bailiffs or slaves. The question of the extent to which Tripolitania made use of slave labour in Roman times is controversial, though there appear to have been large numbers of rural slaves. Pudentilla, for instance, had at least 400 and the terms used by Apuleius to describe farm workers on her estates (*vilici, equisones, upiliones*) are suggestive of a slave system run by bailiffs, rather than of tenant farmers. Yet knowledge of the labour demands of intensive olive cultivation suggests that a substantial pool of free labour must have existed to cope with the exceptionally high labour requirement at harvest time in November/December, in contrast to the small core of workers needed on a year-round basis. In Tripolitania, the traditional solution has lain in arrangements between the sedentary olive growers and transhuming pastoralists of the area, who provide the additional harvest labour. Even allowing for the fact that olive cultivation was not their sole activity, common sense would suggest that it would not have been financially viable for the olive estates of antiquity to maintain on a year-round basis a slave labour force adequate for the high demands of the harvest. Regardless of whether olive farming was carried out by slaves, free but semi-dependent peasants, tenants, or a combination of all three, it is a reasonable conclusion that in antiquity the harvest involved the influx of additional seasonal labour. The existence of a suitable pool of well-organized and comparatively cheap seasonal labour in Tripolitania (perhaps recruited from the pastoral tribes of the desert fringes) could have helped local producers achieve economies of scale over, for instance, Italian competition.

Several *ostraca* found on Tripolitanian farms apparently give details of farming transactions and organization. Some of them were written in neo-Punic or Latino-Punic. Unfortunately, only one of these is published but as more evidence of this sort becomes available it should clarify many details of both the social and economic organization of agriculture. To the extent that some land was worked through tenants rather than slaves it is likely that rental agreements were in the form of a percentage of the produce rather than specie payments.[11]

Careful management of the available water resources was just as critical in the Gebel and Gefara as in the pre-desert (see below) and this is corroborated by the archaeological evidence. There are many examples of water diversion walls, terraces and dams in the wadi beds. The same technology is still employed on a wide scale in southern Tunisia and in the Libyan Gebel Nefusa. This 'run-off' agriculture relies on the ability of the farmers to take surplus water from as wide a catchment area as possible and entrain it into field systems and cisterns. If uncontrolled, the flash floods (which result from the sudden, torrential downpours of the region) can cause major scouring of the alluvium in the wadi beds. The key to run-off agriculture is in the control of the potential erosive force of the flood and the wide distribution of the water to maximize its effects across the entire valley floor. In the fields, the flow of the water is regulated by the use of sluices, allowing entry into different areas of the system, and by the provision of spillways which control the flow from one terraced field to the next or at the exit of the

system. Similar water control systems are known right across the Maghreb, though only occasionally have they received detailed attention. There is no reason to doubt the pre-Roman origins of this form of agriculture in North Africa.[12]

The old Libyphoenician towns (*Lepcis, Oea, Sabratha, Zitha, Gigthis, Tacape*) continued to act as the major market foci when olive production for export intensified during the Roman period, though a number of small towns and other minor market centres developed in the coastal plains and Gebel (see Fig. 7:1). Periodic rural markets (*nundinae*) were probably the norm here as in other parts of Roman Africa, with these regulated gatherings also serving as prime recruiting sites for casual rural labour and harvesters. A number of the small towns of the Gebel and some of the larger estate centres may have had such market functions granted them by the Roman senate. These *nundinae* probably functioned as a second tier below the coastal entrepôts in a hierarchy of market centres. They may have assumed greater importance as the pre-desert settlement spread to the south of them.[13]

3
THE PRE-DESERT

When Richard Goodchild and John Ward-Perkins first approached the archaeology of the pre-desert, matters seemed fairly clearcut. There was an abundance of fortified farm sites (*gsur*) which they believed on various grounds to post-date the construction of the great Severan forts at Bu Njem and Gheriat el-Garbia in the early third century AD. Although Goodchild and other early investigators were broadly correct to regard the construction of the fortified farms as a third-century and later development, they failed to appreciate that these were not the only (or earliest) substantial settlements in the pre-desert. It was Olwen Brogan who first showed the existence of numbers of undefended farms, often built in the *opus africanum* style, which yielded later first- and second-century pottery when sherded and the work of the UNESCO Libyan Valleys Survey has confirmed her conclusions (Fig. 7:6; Plates 34–35, 38). Trial excavations undertaken at selected sites have suggested that the general picture given by sherd samples from surface collections here are a reasonable indicator of the date span of individual sites and that settlement on a large and organized scale got under way during the second half of the first century AD. There is relatively little material which is unquestionably pre-Flavian and it is likely that the events of the years AD 69–70 may be of relevance, with the

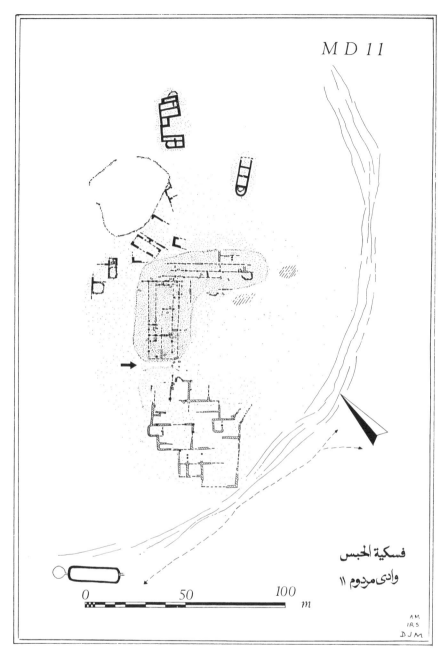

MD 11

فسكية الحبس
وادى مردوم ١١

0   50   100
                m

AM
IRS
DJM

Fig 7:6 *Opus africanum* farm from the Wadi Merdum, close to the Mselliten obelisk tombs. Both tombs and farm are of first/second-century date (from Jones 1985a).

settlement imposed on the *Garamantes* by the Roman legate, Valerius Flaccus, opening up possibilities for increased sedentary farming in the pre-desert margins of the province. As already noted, the Gebel lands were resurveyed at this date and it is possible that the sedentarization of the more marginal pre-desert lands followed. At any rate it is hard to believe that olive plantations in the wadis would have seemed a worthwhile investment until the *Garamantes* were firmly and finally under control. The most likely candidates

for pre-Flavian settlement sites are the hillforts in *Macae* territory (chapter 2 above), which do not appear to have been directly linked with developed wadi agriculture.[14]

Further proof of Roman encouragement of agrarian development can be seen in the evidence from Tripolitania and other parts of Africa of centuriation and of land delimitation programmes. Although there is no evidence for comprehensive centuriation schemes in Tripolitania, land surveys were undoubtedly

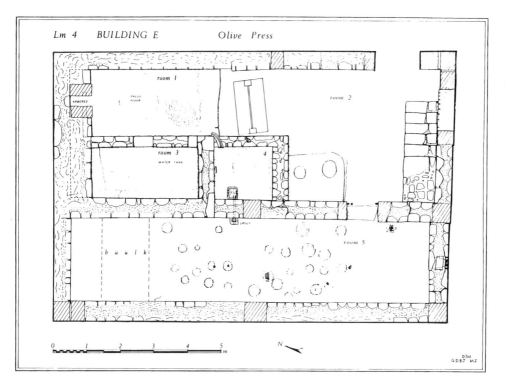

Fig 7:7 Romano-Libyan olive press building from the first–third-century farm Lm 4 in the Wadi el-Amud (from Mattingly and Zenati 1984).

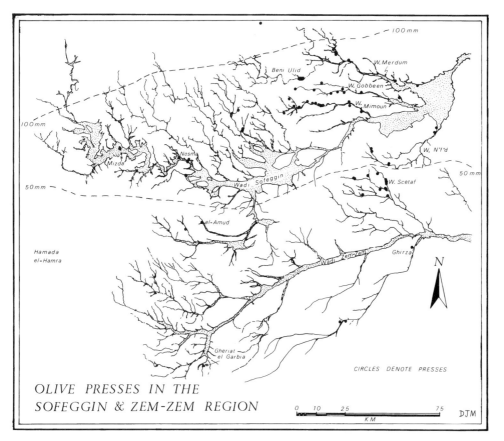

OLIVE PRESSES IN THE
SOFEGGIN & ZEM-ZEM REGION

Fig 7:8 Distribution of olive presses in the Libyan pre-desert (from Mattingly 1985a).

carried out on a grand scale. Apart from the well-known Trajanic demarcation of the lands of the *Nybgenii* from those of the towns of *Capsa* and *Tacapae*, or the Flavian resurvey of the lands of *Lepcis* and *Oea*, there are two boundary stones which relate only to native tribal groups in the Tunisian Dahar and close to the Syrtic town of *Marcomades*. The latter is Flavian, the former Trajanic in date and they hint at a more widespread delimitation of lands across the region in the late first and early second century AD.

In the pre-desert area the evidence recorded by the ULVS suggests that settlement was hierarchical from the point at which it became widespread in the late first century. At the top end of the hierarchy were buildings constructed of ashlar masonry or *opus africanum* and associated cemeteries with fine mausolea. These farms, commonly equipped with olive presses, were undefended, though sometimes they were arranged around an enclosed courtyard. In many respects they are similar to the smaller type of *villa rustica* in the Gebel region, although their olive presses were generally of somewhat smaller scale (Fig. 7.7; Plate 34) and never numbered more than one or two at a site (Fig. 7.8). It is now clear that this class of site was progressively replaced at the top of the hierarchy by fortified farms (the *gsur*) from the third century AD onwards (see below). The mausolea were once thought to be entirely of late Roman date but some (perhaps many) now seem to date to the end of the first or the second century AD (Plates 43–47). Other sites of early date exist and these may be interpreted as farms and farmsteads, with their location often suggesting socio-economic links with the *opus africanum* sites. Once again these sites were undefended, built generally in rougher dry-stone masonry, though often possessing enclosures (Plate 39). In a number of locations larger settlements have been noted, though without any evidence for a large farm or *gasr* at the nucleus. These may be seen as 'hamlets' or 'villages', although quite how they fitted into the social structure is unclear. At a lower level still were small isolated buildings, towers and hutments, some at least of which have proved Roman in date. All these elements can be examined in relation to a well-preserved ancient landscape of field walls, cisterns, catchment systems and boundary markers (Figs 7.9–7.10; Plate 36).[15]

The Punic language and culture of the major landholders who lived in the undefended farms and who were buried in the tombs imply contact with the farmers in the Gebel region (see further, chapter 8, below). However, their Libyan names, together with indications of tribal connections and the fact that these people constituted a rural aristocracy rather than an urban-based one, suggest that the exploitation of the pre-desert was undertaken by members of the main tribal groupings; in eastern Tripolitania this was the *Macae* confederation, in the west it was the *Nybgenii*. Given the basic hostility of the environment, it is a reasonable supposition that these individuals were only able to show such a profit from farming through the systematic exploitation of other people in the region, whether slaves, tenant farmers or dependent peasants. Such ties may already have existed in the pre-Roman tribal society but it is tempting to posit a state-sponsored consolidation of the dominant position of the elite group, notably when tribal lands were delimited in the late first century. So far, then, the Roman contribution to the spread of agriculture was limited to enabling native elites in the towns and of the tribes to take advantage of their traditional position in society through the exploitation of land and labour.

The picture of settlement development in the pre-desert zone of west Tripolitania has been complicated by the insistence of the early researchers on designating almost every site discovered as a military work. But Trousset's work in the area has shown that there was a good deal of agricultural development also. Roman pottery collected from some of these sites includes *terra sigillata* of late first- and second-century date and there are abundant traces hereabouts of agricultural walls and cisterns, as well as a number of explicitly civilian tombstones. A pattern of development similar to that in to eastern Tripolitania is thus emerging for the west, with a late first-century AD extension of agricultural practices from the coastal plain and better watered land into the pre-desert.

At a later date, from the third century onwards, the character of the civilian settlement became more defensive, with the construction of *gsur* and the addition of ditches around some earlier sites. Whether this actually indicates increased insecurity is unclear; it is conceivable that the fortified farms were merely imitative of military-style construction and built in the first instance for motives of prestige. The building type is well suited to pre-desert living conditions, perhaps more so than the earlier farms whose architecture was developed for the conditions of the Mediterranean littoral.

The changeover from undefended farms to fortified farms was gradual, beginning around the end of the second century and continuing into the fourth and fifth centuries and later. Although the *opus africanum* farms were replaced by or incorporated into *gsur*, many of the smaller and less sophisticated farms and farmsteads continued to be occupied alongside the latter. There was, however, a general trend towards greater nucleation of settlement and most *gsur* were surrounded by dependent 'villages'. The typical *gasr* is a tower-like structure of two or more storeys, with a light-well or central court of variable size. The standard of masonry construction varies, but most commonly consists of small, neatly coursed blockwork. The rubble-filled interiors of most ground-floor rooms limits information on their uses, but some of the *gsur* certainly contained olive presses. The building inscriptions ascribing them to notable individuals and the lack of any alternative accommodation for the rural elite indicates that they were habitations and not simply fortified store-houses. There is no reason to argue, from the current evidence, that the first *gasr* dwellers were other than the descendants of those who had built the *opus africanum* farms and created the wadi estates in the first place.[16]

The detailed work of the ULVS has added a wealth of new information on the adaptation of the traditional run-off farming to the pre-desert environment. Even in Roman times there were vast expanses of exposed bedrock on the plateaux above the wadis and there has been some further erosion of the hamada soils since then. Wall systems were concentrated on the alluvium in the valley bottoms or in the few surviving, shallow silt-filled depressions on the hamada.

A number of detailed surveys have been made of field systems in several different topographic locations and have demonstrated the adaptability and success of the technology in wadi cultivation (Plates 36–37). Although the narrow, entrenched wadis seem to have been most densely farmed, similar systems are to be found in broad, shallow wadis also. Two examples of the surveys produced by the Libyan Valleys project will serve to illustrate the richness of the data-base now available.

Major survey and excavation work was carried out in 1984 at the el-Amud farm (Lm4). The farm was established in the second half of the first century AD and continued in occupation until the later third century, by which date its functions may have been taken over by the nearby *gasr* Lm 3. The main buildings at the centre of the estate comprised a rectangular farmhouse in *opus quadratum*, three subsidiary structures in poorer quality masonry and a well-built olive press (Plate 34). Numerous threshing floors are visible on aerial photographs of the site. Field-system walls defined two sides of the farmyard and palaeo-environmental evidence recovered from this area indicated the economic activity of the farm. Barley predominated over wheat in the sample of cereals, and there was also evidence for peas, lentils and other

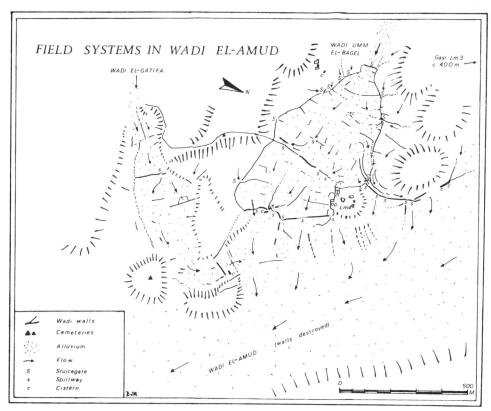

FIELD SYSTEMS IN WADI EL-AMUD

WADI UMM EL-BAGEL

WADI EL-GATIFA

Gasr Lm 3 c. 400 m

N

Lm4

WADI EL-AMUD

(walls destroyed)

0   500 M

Wadi walls
Cemeteries
Alluvium
Flow
S   Sluicegate
s   Spillway
c   Cistern

DJM

Fig 7:9 Field systems associated with the olive farm Lm 4 in the Wadi el-Amud and its tributaries (from Mattingly 1987a).

pulses. Of tree crops, figs, grapes, dates, olives and almonds were present. Sheep and goats dominated the faunal sample, but cattle, pigs, camels, horses, dogs, cats and rabbits were also represented. A large number of gazelle bones presumably indicate that the meat diet was supplemented through hunting.

The el-Amud wadi floor is still regularly ploughed for cereal cultivation (although average rainfall is under 50 mm here), the harvest being in late March/early April. Because of this activity, much of the evidence for wadi walls in the main channel has been destroyed, though some traces were detected on the west side towards the farm (Lm4). The principal surviving wall systems lay in two minor tributary streams of the el-Amud, the Umm el-Bagel and the el-Gatifa, but the main wadi floor was also integral to the estate (Fig. 7:9). Nowadays, flood waters in the Umm el-Bagel run in a scour channel down the centre of the field system and although this has destroyed quite a lot of evidence in its path it has preserved the sides of the system to a remarkable extent, including traces of numerous sluice gates and spillways. In the event of a rain storm, run-off water entered the field system from numerous directions, being entrained by catchment walls down to sluice-gates in the boundary wall. At the west end, where the el-Bagel wadi channel entered, there was a remarkable system of 56 sluice-gates, which could be used to distribute the flood waters across the entire field area and thus to prevent the erosive concentration of water which occurs today. Within the field system, the use of diversion walls and spillways again facilitated the direction of flood water to all parts of the system whilst controlling the force of the flood. Of particular interest are the series of walls on the north side which diverted water back out of the field system in order to prevent the inundation of the farmyard area. This water was not wasted, since it was fed back into fields in the main wadi floor down a series of major spillways. A further series of spillways, mostly in a poor state of preservation, was noted at the east side of the field system, again allowing surplus water to run off into the el-Amud. Traces of a similar, but smaller-scale, wall system were noted in the Wadi el-Gatifa to the southeast. That this was part of the same farm estate was demonstrated by the extension of the boundary wall of the el-Bagel system to include these fields also.

A further indication of the limits of the estate may be given by the location of its two recorded cemeteries. The major cemetery consisted of a series of ashlar tower tombs (Plate 43), surrounded by other graves, on an isolated knoll close to the junction of the el-Gatifa and el-Amud. It may well have been designed as a visible landmark of the southeastern extent of the estate. It was evidently established as a cemetery at an early date since the tombs were dedicated with neo-Punic texts, which described several generations of a Libyan clan (see below). This clearly accords with the argument above, which would identify the first sedentary farmers of the area as members of the *Macae* tribal grouping. The second cemetery lay against the boundary wall connecting the Bagel and el-Gatifa field systems together and was also designed to be visible from a distance, though on a much smaller scale. The use of cemeteries as territorial markers seems to have been relatively common in the region and numerous other examples have been noted during survey work.

The exact limits of the farm estate to the north have not yet been precisely determined. In all probability, however, they lay at least half a kilometre to the northwest, where a *gasr* was built in the third century to replace the earlier farm as the main building of the estate. The estate was on a substantial scale then and presumably relied on the labour of a considerable number of people beyond the owner's immediate family. One subsidiary farmstead is known, at the southwest corner of the Umm-el-Bagel system, and there may well have been others. There were at least seven main cisterns fed by catchment walls within the field systems and these may indicate substantial pastoral interests, with grazing perhaps taking place away from the home farm for part of the year.

One of the most important aspects of the el-Amud work has been to show that the wadi wall technology was integral to the development of sedentary farming in the pre-desert from the beginning. The association between the early farm (latter part of the first century AD forward) and the wall systems can hardly be denied in this case (though the final appearance of the system no doubt took many years to achieve).[17]

The detailed survey of a 3.5 km stretch of the Wadi Mansur offers a useful comparison with the el-Amud example just described (Fig. 7:10). The wadi here is more deeply entrenched and the space for cultivation more constricted. The density of ancient sites and their associated field systems is remarkable. Close to the wadi floor were two first-century open farms (sites Mn 6 (Fig. 7:11) and 82). In the later Roman period a series of *gsur* were constructed on top of the escarpments overlooking both sites (Mn 23/81, 25, 26). As at el-Amud, the pottery evidence suggests direct replacement of the open farm by the fortified farms. Within the zone surveyed there were also numerous farmsteads or smaller buildings (Mn 25A/B, 27–9, 50, 62, 88, 91) and two small 'villages' (Mn 85, 87). *Gsur* Mn 23/81 and 25 also had substantial peripheral settlements. At least ten cisterns were recorded along this

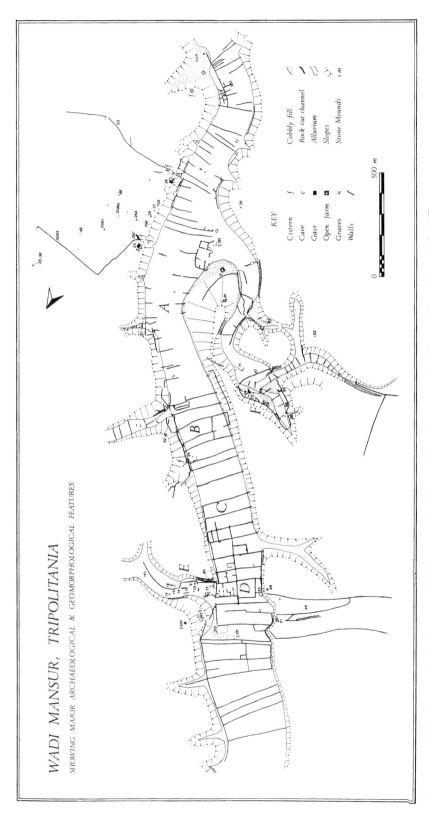

WADI MANSUR, TRIPOLITANIA

SHOWING MAJOR ARCHAEOLOGICAL & GEOMORPHOLOGICAL FEATURES

KEY

Cistern	f		Cobbly fill	
Cave	c		Rock cut channel	
Gasr	■		Alluvium	
Open farm	⊞		Slopes	
Graves	⋇		Stone Mounds	
Walls	∕			

0   500 m

Fig 7:10 The Wadi Mansur, detailed survey of a 3.5 km stretch of the agricultural systems and settlement (from Hunt *et al.* 1987).

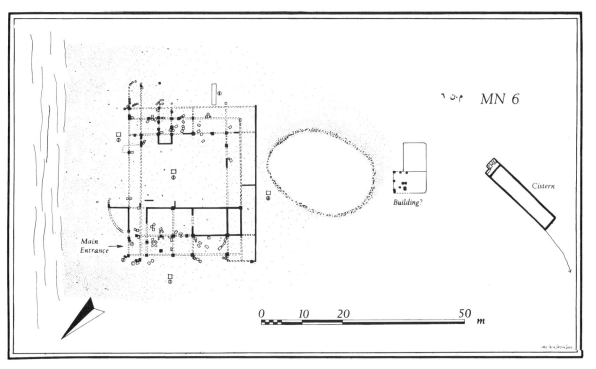

Fig 7:11 The *opus africanum* farm Mn 6 in the Wadi Mansur (from Jones 1985a, cf. 7:10).

section of the wadi and these and the field systems in the wadi bed were serviced by long catchment walls, in some cases extending several kilometres back across the barren hamada, on which most of the cemeteries were also located. The capacity of two of the cisterns was ascertained: approx. 175,000 litres for the large one on the wadi floor adjacent to Mn 6; 136,000 litres for Mn 25C (adjacent to *gasr* Mn 25). Since a single family would require about 10,000 litres per year, these figures indicate that the fully developed system of wadi exploitation almost certainly could support larger numbers of people and/or animals.[18]

Additional information on farming in the pre-desert zone comes in the form of relief carvings, depicting agricultural scenes, on the mausolea of the area. Those from Ghirza illustrating ploughing, sowing, reaping, threshing and winnowing of grain are the best known (Plates 59–60), but there are other scenes representing shepherding, viticulture and arboriculture. Vines are particularly common as a motif in the art of the pre-desert, though wine production is difficult to trace archaeologically. Two of the Ghirza scenes show small camel caravans on the move (Plate 61) and these may well be intended to represent the disposal of surplus produce to market. Several of the Bu Njem *ostraca* of the AD 250s relate to the delivery of small consignments of wheat and oil

by native Libyan camel drivers, and these were presumably from the wadi farming community. (Some *Garamantes* also are referred to transporting barley on mules and donkeys.) If we had a larger sample of such documents they would probably inform us of the local availability of a broader range of crops. The well-developed agriculture of the pre-desert wadis could very well have supplied almost all the subsistence requirements of the military garrison stationed in the region, unlikely though that once seemed.

The recent work on palaeo-environmental samples collected from Ghirza in the 1950s and from the current Libyan Valleys work has revolutionized our outlook on wadi farming. In addition, the growing number of known olive-press sites in the Sofeggin and Zem-Zem wadi systems have confounded earlier expectations of the importance of olive oil production in this marginal zone. The new picture to emerge is of a mixed economy similar to that known in the Gebel area, with a remarkable range of crops being represented (Table 1:1).

Not all species have appeared on every site where samples have been obtained, but some samples were quite small and preservation varied somewhat. In general, though, the results suggest that the agricultural regime was relatively similar in both early and late Roman times. The presence of chaff and other threshing detritus in many samples indicates local production, with hulled six-row barley being by far the most common type. Similarly, olives and grapes are unlikely to have been imports in view of the abundant evidence of presses (it is just possible that some presses were used for both oil production and the vintage, though simple treading basins may have served for wine production in most cases). Water melon is highly unlikely to have been transported very far from where it was grown and, although many of the other products are more transportable (some, like figs, in dried form), there is no reason to doubt that they too could have been cultivated in the pre-desert farms. The weeds in the samples are by and large arid zone species, such as are found in the area today, supporting the view that the climate was similar in antiquity to that of today and that it was the floodwater farming technology which rendered the wadis cultivable in the Roman period.[19]

It is now clear that in spite of the inadequate rainfall and arid climate the pre-desert region of ancient Tripolitania was developed for mixed farming on a considerable scale. The key to success was the simple technology of run-off farming which, by concentrating rainfall from a wide catchment in the wadi bottoms, allowed the alluvium there to receive an artificially high amount of water, equivalent to the average rainfall of better watered zones (Plates 2, 36–37). Experiments aimed at reconstructing similar wadi farms in the Negev desert have shown that the technology does work extremely well in practice and bumper yields have been achieved, rather than mere subsistence returns.

The level of production in the pre-desert presents a delicate problem of interpretation. On the one hand, the existence of extensive settled farming in the marginal zone appears to break all the rules of agricultural feasibility and viability. On the other hand, the results of the Libyan Valleys Survey have shown that it was possible for some individuals to create significant wealth from their farming in this zone. The evidence for this comes in several forms. First, the large quantities of *terra sigillata* and African Red Slip ware pottery reaching even the remoter sites implies involvement in a market economy.

Second, there is the evidence for the 'buying-in' of monumental tombs by members of the rural elite. In some cases we are informed of the sums involved: 25,000 and 3,100 *denarii*, 45,600 and 90,000 *folles*. There are over 60 high-quality tombs scattered across the pre-desert agricultural zone and the total outlay represented must be enormous. The fact that specie payments are mentioned in connection with these tombs demonstrates conclusively the participation of the

rural elite in the Roman market economy. Third, there is the new evidence for the scale of olive oil production in the region. I have argued elsewhere that the numbers of presses now known in the Sofeggin and Zem-Zem region (over 60) represent production well above subsistence level. For instance, production at the el-Amud farm can be estimated to have been in the low thousands, rather than hundreds, of litres per productive year. With a high value per unit volume, oil was the most economic product of the pre-desert for transportation to market. Live animals on the hoof, wine and dates are other possibilities, though they are perhaps less likely to have brought as large a return as oil.

Cereals might be expected to have played no more than a subsistence role were it not for the presence in the region of a special type of market – the Roman military. The supply of Roman forts is a complex issue, but it would appear that wherever possible the military attempted to acquire basic foodstuffs in the immediate vicinity of its garrison posts. We have already noted the significance of the Bu Njem *ostraca* in this respect. The camel drivers, such as Macargus, Iassucthan and Iaremaba, may well have been the producers (or their representatives), disposing of their modest agricultural surplus to the military for profit. The exact nature of the transaction involved is not made clear but a soldier was specially detached from the unit to liaise with the producers/carriers to obtain supplies for the fort. It is quite likely that the military still paid for its supplies at this date. The *pro forma* letter of carriage issued to the camel drivers varies mainly in the terms used to describe the native units of measure employed. Four different terms appear to be used for a unit of 105 litres size, perhaps indicating supplies being bought from several different sub-tribal groups. The following example is typical:

To Octavius Festus, my decurion and praepositus, Aemilius Aemilianus, soldier, sends greetings. I am sending to you, sir, by the driver Macargus, two 'siddipia' of wheat which make 24 (modii) [210 litres]. In the year of the consuls after Thuscus and Bassus [AD 259]
[*Second hand*] Received 21 January [259]

The known third-century forts (with the exception of Ghadames) lay on the margins of the sedentary settlement of the pre-desert. Military contracts could be expected, therefore, to absorb some of the surplus production of this zone. Forts also acted as foci for civilian settlement and in some cases this could be very substantial, as at Bu Njem. But it will also be noted on Figure 7:1 that some parts of the pre-desert were actually closer to the coast than the third-century military markets. In spite of the harshness of the environment, the costs of overland transport of goods to market and the distance of the coastal *Emporia*, the pre-desert was made to bloom and produce a profit in the Roman market economy by the native African elite. True, the profits were limited to a few in the top tiers of society, who lived off the exploitation of the labour of others (whether slave or free) and the impact of the market economy may have been similarly limited to this elite. Much of the population may have been largely oblivious to it, remaining as part of an embedded economy of dues or rents given in labour or in kind to their superiors.[20]

4
THE EVIDENCE OF TRIPOLITANIAN AMPHORAE

A century ago, Heinrich Dressel worked on deposits of Tripolitanian amphorae when he published the amphorae stamps and painted inscriptions (*tituli picti*) from Monte Testaccio in Rome (*CIL* XV). Monte Testaccio is the extraordinary man-made mountain of over 50 million amphorae, mainly olive oil containers, disposed of deliberately after the transfer of their contents into the bulk storage facilities of the vast olive oil warehouses in the main commercial district of the city to the south of the Aventine hill. The hill (50 m high and 1 km in circumference) survives today as the ultimate monument to the importance of olive oil in the Roman economy. The bulk of the stamps and *tituli picti*, however, related not to the Tripolitanian vessels (nor to other African amphorae which were rarely stamped for reasons that are not fully understood), but to the distinctive, globular type from southern Spain (known as Dressel form 20). Dressel and later researchers have tended to concentrate on the epigraphically rewarding Dressel 20 to such an extent that, although Tripolitanian material was abundant on certain parts of Testaccio, it is only 25 years since the first publication of an illustration of a Tripolitanian amphora.[21] Subsequently, some Punic precursors and three main classes of Roman period amphorae of Tripolitanian origin have been identified. It is generally assumed that the principal product carried in Tripolitania types I and III amphorae was olive oil and these have a much wider distribution than type II. In broad terms type I may be dated to the first and second centuries AD, with type III being of second century and later date. Type I occurs at Pompeii in sufficient quantity to confirm a regular

and organized commerce in the first century AD but it is unclear how significant a quantity of oil was involved. The available evidence from Rome and Ostia does not suggest that Tripolitanian oil fulfilled more than a tiny percentage of the needs of the capital at that date. On the other hand, it should be remembered that even a 1–5 per cent market share of the Rome market would have represented a very substantial export. Rodriguez Almeida has recently suggested on the basis of evidence from Monte Testaccio that Rome's total annual oil imports may have been in the order of 10 million litres per year (and this may well be a very conservative estimate). On the evidence from Ostia, the Tripolitanian share in oil imports could have averaged nearer 10 per cent. A potential annual export to Rome in excess of 1 million litres of oil per year is of considerable size (coincidentally the same level as Caesar's fine) and this was clearly not the only external market reached by Tripolitanian oil. To date there have been few discoveries of shipwrecks carrying Tripolitanian cargoes, though it is unclear if this discrepancy is more apparent than real given the imbalance in underwater archaeology research in favour of the European Riviera and the all-too-recent recognition of what Tripolitanian cargoes should look like.[22]

The major evidence for the type III amphorae comes from Ostia and Rome, notably Monte Testaccio where Dressel sampled a major deposit of third-century date on the west flank of the hill of potsherds. It is likely that this deposit relates to the Severan reorientation of oil imports from Tripolitania within the *annona* system (see below). Yet, once again, the type is being recognized increasingly on other sites around the Mediterranean and beyond, and the overall distribution seems to have been quite wide.

A number of kiln sites for the production of the amphorae is known in Tripolitania, some excavated many years ago but with no proper publication of the amphorae found on site. Renewed work on the identification and publication of the kiln sites is needed urgently in order to refine our knowledge of the amphorae typology and chronology (Fig. 7:2). As we shall see, such work could also produce invaluable information about the organization of both oil and amphorae production in the region.

Recent studies have revealed that the very small percentage of Tripolitanian vessels which were stamped contain vital information about the socio-economic organization of oil production and distribution. Only two probable examples of type I stamps are known (probably to be read as *PRO* or *MRO* and *QSCS* or *QSCS*) and only a few examples of type II have been recorded with stamps (including *PBAV* at

Stamp	Identification	Stamp	Identification
1. AVGG	Septimius Severus & Caracalla	32. L.S.PLH/ BVR	L. Silius Plautius Haterianus Blaesilianus (*IRT* 635)
2. AVGGG	Septimius Severus, Caracalla & Geta	33. L.S.PLH/ MYC	L. Silius Plautius Haterianus Blaesilianus (*IRT* 635)
3. IMPANT/ AVG	Caracalla (or Elagabalus?)	34. [L?]SAHCV	L. Silius Amicus Haterianus? (*IRT* 542)
4. [...]DAVG	Severus Alexander	35. CSM/BAICI (?)	C. Servilius Marsus? (*AE* 1959, 271)
5. LAS	L. Avillius [...] or L. Appius [...]?	36. CSMCV	C. Servilius Marsus? (*AE* 1959, 271)
6. S.A.BCV/+++		37. LVTM	L. Volusius [...] or L. Verginius Tiro Marcianus?
7. SAB/ACMV		38. MVC	M. Ulpius Cerialis (*IRT* 388) or family of M. Vibii (*IRT* 578)
8. CBSVR		39. MVM	M. Ulpius [...] or family of M. Vibii?
9. PBAV		40. [...]FCV	
10. LBAI		41. ACVCF	
11. LCS[...]		42. AC[...]	
12. PCAGCV/STID	Family of P. Cornelii (cf *IRT* 263, 592)	43. ADYRMP	
13. PCAG[...] (retro)	Family of P. Cornelii (cf *IRT* 263, 592)	44. ARAP	Asinius Rogatianus APLL or Adelfius (*IRT* 539)
14. PCBSCV	Kinsman of M. Cornelius Bassus Servianus (*IRT* 443)	45. BINOMI[...]	
15. PCRSSV (retro)		46. CEI	
16. PCSSCV/ MARIA[...]		47. CR	
17. OCHO	Family of Calpurnii Honesti? (*IRT* 370–71)	48. CRCA	
18. QCL	Q. Cassius Longinus? (*IRT* 601)	49. FYN	
19. OCLCV	Q. Cassius Longinus? (*IRT* 601)	50. IVI[...]	
20. QCV	Q. Cornelius Valens? (*IRT* 594)	51. KATA*	
21. CPFCV	C. Fulvius Plautianus (cos 293, Praetorian Prefect, father-in-law of Caracalla, executed 205 (*PIR* 2 F554)	52. MD[...]	
22. CFPPP	C. Fulvius Plautianus	53. ONII (?)	
23. CFPPPCV	C. Fulvius Plautianus	54. PC	
24. CAELESTIN	Q. Granius Caelestinus? (*IRT* 532)	55. SA[...]	
25. LMPP++		56. SIAP	
26. QMD (retro)	Q. Marcius Dioga (*IRT* 401)	57. THER	
27. L.PCR	cf. Q. Pompeius Cerealis Felix (*IRT* 444); L. Pompeius Cerialis Salvianus (*IRT* 602)	58. VAR	
28. MPF	Family of Pompeii	59. VIC	
29. POMBAL		60. QPGAT (?)	
30. L.APRI	L. Septimius Aper, cos 207, executed 212 (*IG* 12.7.397.28)	61. [...]FC	
31. L.S.A.CV	L. Septimius Aper or L. Silius Amicus Haterianus (*IRT* 542)	62. SNPS (retro)	

Table 7:1. List of Tripolitania III amphora stamps and suggested identifications with individuals or families known from Lepcitanian epigraphy (after Mattingly 1988b, Table 1, from di Vita-Evrard 1985; Manacorda 1977, 1983).

Bu Njem). On the other hand, first-century AD examples of type I at Pompeii (and presumably elsewhere) seem to have frequently carried painted inscriptions (*tituli picti*) in neo-Punic script and some of these seem to make specific reference to olive oil (*shmn*).

The great majority of the 62 known stamps relates to type III amphorae and most of these seem to be datable to the Severan period, more particularly to the first quarter of the third century. The civic epigraphy of *Lepcis Magna* for this period provides the key to understanding some of the stamps (Table 7:1). A few (nos 1–4) clearly related to imperial lands in the region, initially based on the property of Septimius Severus himself, but added to by confiscations during his and Caracalla's reigns. However, most appear to represent the abbreviated *tria nomina* of individuals. There are further clues as to the identity of some of these. The letters *CV* were a common addition to *tria nomina* initials and the interpretation of this as *clarissimus vir*, an indication of senatorial status, presents no problems. Some of the individuals so dignified can be confidently identified with members of the leading Lepcitanian families, who secured access to the Roman senate in the second and early third centuries. The most notable example is Gaius Fulvius Plautianus, Severus' praetorian prefect, who has long been believed to have been a citizen of *Lepcis* like Septimius Severus himself. In a remarkable series of stamps (nos 21–3) he is identified as praetorian prefect (*PP*), as a senator (*CV* – this a special privilege for the normally equestrian prefect) and as both simultaneously. Since Plautianus was executed in AD 205, these stamps can be reasonably precisely dated to the late second or first years of the third century. Another stamp for which we have a *terminus ante quem* is *L.APRI* (no. 30), which is reasonably assigned to L. Septimius Aper, the cousin of Caracalla who was executed by the latter in AD 212.[23]

It is now clear that the major families of *Lepcis Magna* are attested on these amphorae. Further discoveries of stamps and civic inscriptions will no doubt fill out the picture further but already representatives of the following families are known or suspected: Septimii; Fulvii; Plautii/Silii Plautii; Marcii; Ulpii; Vibii; Cornelii; Servilii; Pompeii; Cassii; Granii; Calpurnii; Verginii. The activities and benefactions of these *gentes* are well known at *Lepcis*.

The second point concerns the association of the names of prominent citizens of *Lepcis Magna* with amphorae (no identifications have yet been made from the stamps with the prosopography of *Oea* or *Sabratha* – though some will surely come in time). Without further investigation of kiln sites and waster deposits in Libya, the mechanics of amphora production will remain unclear. Nevertheless, at Ain Scersiara (within the territory of *Oea*) and near Silin, Goodchild uncovered kilns in close association with major villas, and estate production is a strong possibility in this case. The amphorae stamps reveal that the Lepcitanian elite was concerned in the manufacture of these containers, and by implication also in the production and sale of the contents. They were major oil producers and the stamped amphorae indicate that they had surplus production for export. Here then is a

clear link between olive oil production and the wealthiest section of Lepcitanian society.

The increased incidence of stamps on oil amphorae in the early third century may well have a connection with the granting of the *Ius Italicum* to *Lepcis* by Septimius Severus and the apparently reciprocal gesture of the Lepcitanians in voluntarily making a donation of oil to the city of Rome. The motive behind the generosity of the Lepcitanian city fathers may not have been connected simply with having won an important tax concession from their countryman, Septimius. By the early years of the third century, he was firmly established in power and the position of his sons as heirs apparent well-advanced. As we have seen, there was already a substantial body of Lepcitanians active in different areas of Roman central and provincial administration and their expectation under Septimius may well have been of accelerated careers and improved prospects. Imperial service at the highest level offered prestige, patronage and financial rewards. The donation of oil might then have been seen as a small investment to secure imperial approval and popular standing with the people of Rome.

The possibility that other products were also carried in the Tripolitanian export amphorae cannot be resolved on current evidence. However, analogy with other oil-exporting regions would suggest the probability that some proportion of the trade was in wine and marine products also. Wine production is attested in Tripolitania by literary and iconographic evidence and there is archaeological information from a survey of the coastal region of west Tripolitania indicating a considerable amount of processing of fish and other marine products. The eastern Tripolitanian seaboard has never been researched in comparable detail and the likelihood is that much more evidence of this sort would be revealed by such survey work in future.[24]

5
TRANS-SAHARAN TRADE

In his survey of the Romano-African economy Haywood several times referred to the importance of a trans-Saharan trade in 'exotic wares'. Like others who have been misled by this seductive myth he could offer little hard evidence for what it comprised. Trans-Saharan contact is not in doubt, as the substantial numbers of Roman coins found in and to the south of the Sahara demonstrate (even allowing for some of these having passed along the trade routes long after the Roman period). The experience of the earliest modern travellers to explore the desert routes promoted the belief that trans-Saharan trade had been the foundation of the ancient Tripolitanian economy. As they crossed Tripolitania they were struck by the contrast between the denuded countryside and the magnificent ruined cities of the coast. Since these explorers often travelled in the company of Arab caravans, plying a trade between the Mediterranean world, Niger and Chad, there was a natural tendency for them to rationalize their observation of the apparent wealth of Roman Tripolitania with their own experience of the economic condition of the country.

De Mathuisieulx, for instance, described a caravan that left Tripoli in 1899, only returning three years later from Kano, each of 40 camels carrying a load of about 175 kg. Lyon also listed the goods carried south by a caravan of his day: beads, coral, glass amulets, needles, silks, red cloth, bales of linen, muslin, shawls, Turkish carpets, kaftans, coins, burnooses, copper pots and kettles, brass basins, looking-glasses, swords, guns and pistols, powder, tools, horses. From the Fezzan/Sudan they returned with slaves, gold and ivory (on a small scale), cottons and garments, leather as hides and articles, water skins, ostrich skins and feathers, wooden bowls and mortars, honey, civet, pepper, kola nuts. From such graphic evidence they concluded that a lucrative caravan trade in exotica must have been a staple part of the Roman economy of the region, since the coastal cities lie at the head of several important trans-Saharan routes (Fig. 1:2).

These routes ran from Gabes or Sabrata to Ghadames and on to Ghat, from Tripoli to Mizda to Murzuk and from Lebda to Bu Njem to Socna to Murzuk. The latter two routes to the Fezzan pass close to the old Garamantian capital at Germa whilst the former passes through the territory of the Phazanii. It is self-evident that the participation or acquiescence of these tribes would have been essential for any effective trade to develop. The major objections to the old view of the significance of trans-Saharan trade in the Tripolitanian economy are that it assumes the existence of desirable and important commodities for exchange and second that the chronology of the pacification of the desert tribes occurred after the date at which the major towns were already showing signs of considerable wealth. Whilst I do not wish to deny that some trans-Saharan trade took place in Roman times, I would dispute that its scale and importance in the regional economy were as great as sometimes imagined.[25]

When drawing up a list of possible trade goods it is important to remember that the evidence for commerce in most of them is strongest for the post-Roman period. So, although it is commonly believed that gold, ivory, slaves, precious stones and wild beasts were traded, there is little evidence in the ancient literature (with the possible exception of a type of red carbuncle or cornelian). Some other supposed items of trade, such as emeralds, are entirely modern inventions. Scepticism has grown over the last 20 years about the existence of any trade at all because of this dearth of primary source information.

Nevertheless, like all good myths, there is an element of truth amidst the speculation. Archaeological evidence from Fezzan now provides some primary data, albeit relating only to non-perishable items (Table 2:4). The large quantities of Roman pottery, glass and faience ware which reached *Garama* may in part have been given to the tribal elite as one aspect of treaty relations (Plate 5). But trade is likely to have been a secondary mechanism here. The incidence of Black Glaze wares of pre-Roman date is perhaps best explained as evidence for a far smaller level of trade and exchange. The carriage of fragile pottery and glass on the 30 or so day journey from coast to Fezzan implies the existence of worthwhile products to exchange.[26]

Slaves are the most likely possibility since the *Garamantes* are known to have 'hunted' their negroid Ethiopian neighbours. In the medieval-early modern trade, slaves were one of the most important commodities (interestingly enough, Bu Njem marked the critical point on the route where responsibility for the slaves' well-being shifted from the southern sheiks and traders on to the northern authorities). Two of the Roman *ostraca* from Bu Njem mention slaves, in one instance a runaway slave is brought to the fort (for sale?) by a group of *Garamantes*, while another fragmentary text mentions black slaves (*nigri publici*), though it is unclear whether these were servicing the garrison or being traded towards the coast. On the other hand, references to a *statio camelliarorum* at Bu Njem suggest that its facilities were in regular demand at certain times of the year. The idea of the *Garamantes* preying on their Berber and black neighbours to feed the slave caravans may seem repugnant but has plenty of parallels in more recently documented instances of slave-using states working through the established tribal power structures, a particularly vivid example being that of seventeenth- to nineteenth-century Dahomey. Although we have no indication of the possible scale of the Roman slave trade, the probability that there was a higher occurrence of rural slaves on Tripolitanian estates (compared to the rest of *Africa Proconsularis*) may hint at the plentiful availability of slave labour in this region. The movement of slaves, then, is the most likely explanation for the development of the trans-Saharan trade in Roman times.[27]

Firm conclusions about gold and carbuncles cannot be made either, even though both items have been found at Garamantian sites in Fezzan. There is nothing to suggest that the *Garamantes* were exploited as a source of gold by the Roman authorities, a factor that suggests that the quantities moved along the trans-Saharan routes may have been small. Nor is it easy to imagine the caravan trade being built around the supply of a not very exciting semi-precious stone. These two products were most likely carried as secondary, luxury goods alongside slaves and other commodities.[28]

Similarly, there was a plentiful supply of wild beasts in Tripolitania itself in the first century AD, with even the North African elephant not yet extinct. The Sudan could offer some exotic species, such as the *rhinoceros bicornis*, which may have been taken to Rome for the first time *c.* AD 92 as a result of Julius Maternus' expedition south from Fezzan. But transport of such huge beasts across the Sahara must have been extraordinarily difficult and accordingly rare. It is of course entirely possible that as the elephant became rarer in the Maghreb the trade in ivory from sub-Saharan Africa became more significant. *Lepcis* and *Sabratha* both used the elephant as a form of civic or commercial symbol (Plate 27) and there are inscriptions recording the dedication of elephant tusks to the patron deities of *Lepcis* and *Oea*. This evidence is somewhat circumstantial but both wild beasts and ivory are likely to have been exported from Tripolitanian ports, though neither the scale nor the source of supply from north or south of the Sahara can be determined.[29]

Daniels has referred to evidence for smelting and glassmaking in Fezzan and haematite and natron may have been exportable as raw materials. As with other potential exports, the evidence is very slight.[30]

The new epigraphic evidence from Bu Njem sheds some light on the measures taken by Rome to monitor the caravan trade. In addition to the *statio camellariorum* at Bu Njem itself, many of the minor outposts were provided with very large scale cisterns, such as might have serviced passing caravans. Another of the *ostraca* refers to a consignment of cloth (*syriacas*) though both its origin and destination are unclear. The deployment of the Roman garrison in bases and outposts at the oases and wells along the routes of the northern Sahara demonstrates a concern with observing and controlling movement in the zone (be it for reasons of war, trade, labour relations, pastoralism). Customs dues may well have been levied by the major garrison posts, in the same way that they evidently were at *Zarai* in Numidia before the army post was withdrawn and replaced with a civil *lex portus*.[31]

Perhaps the most important factor to emerge from this discussion is that there was no single, outstandingly important, commodity of trade. As we have seen, Rome's reasons for her initial involvement with the *Garamantes* are unlikely to have been economic ones. Rome needed to establish political and military dominance over the tribe to safeguard the security of the province, not to capture and control already well-developed trade routes. The Roman period trade seems to have developed after the pacification of the tribe in the AD 70s. The chief profits of this trade will have lain on the one hand with the *Garamantes* and on the other with the entrepreneurs who ventured south. Rome will have benefited through customs dues. It is unclear from this analysis to what extent the Tripolitanian cities derived an income from the trade, though individual elite families may conceivably have invested capital in financing caravans. On balance, the evidence at present does not suggest that trans-Saharan trade made a major contribution to the regional economy.

6
OTHER TRADE

As we have already established, the main wealth of Tripolitania lay in her oleoculture and the regional surplus was exported, along with a range of other products. We should not underestimate the contribution to the secondary export list made by stock-raising and its by-products such as leather and wool. The problem with those products, however, is that they are archaeologically elusive and it is impossible to assess the scale of exploitation. All that can be said is that there are some ancient references to stock-raising in the region (see above, chapter 1) and that the environmental conditions of the zone favoured some degree of specialization in animal products. The relative contribution of most other commodities to the regional economy is equally hard to assess, but the likelihood remains that the real foundation of wealth was the farmland and the disposal of its surpluses to domestic and export markets.

Tripolitania was certainly a source of wild beasts for the arenas of the Roman world and we have noted that it could have been a source of slaves. The military pacification of the Libyan tribes of the northern Sahara in the first century AD must have produced significant numbers of Berber slaves for Rome. In the more peaceful era of the *pax Romana*, the slave trade may have increasingly tapped sources of negroid slaves from the deep Saharan oases and beyond. In the same way, the initial expansion of the agricultural zone in North Africa led to the large-scale 'clearance' of abundant wild animals in the frontier zone. As these populations were diminished by hunting, greater reliance may have had to be placed on sources that were further afield or on the traffic in rare or exotic specimens (such as Domitian's rhinoceros).

A number of other commodities were certainly manufactured for export. Some African Red Slip ware (ARS) may have been produced in the coastal region and in late Roman times there was a more distinct local pottery series, Tripolitanian Red Slip (TRS). There were also numerous coarse pottery producers, many specializing in amphorae production for the olive oil industry. Unfortunately only a few of these sites have been located, but comparison with a survey of a similar area on the Tunisian coast would suggest that it was probably on a very considerable scale, particularly close to the coastal cities.

The Lesser Syrtic coast and Gerba in particular are known to have been important producers of purple dye. Thousands of murex shells scattered over the surface of the site of *Gigthis,* for instance, suggest the presence of dye-works and we know of at least one fulling establishment owned by an elite family there. Other fish products were also produced on an important scale along the Lesser Syrtic coast, as work carried out by Trousset and others has demonstrated. No work of this nature has as yet been published for the Libyan sector of the coast but it is highly likely that marine products were likewise a significant export of several parts of the Tripolitanian littoral. Some of the amphora produced in the region could have been used to transport fish sauces and other fish products rather than olive oil. But these are issues demanding far more work in future.[32]

7
TRIPOLITANIA AND MEDITERRANEAN COMMERCE

Who were the trading partners of the Tripolitanian ports? Something has already been said about the unsatisfactory nature of the evidence of Tripolitanian exports, comprising primarily amphorae that have until comparatively recently gone unrecognized on many Mediterranean sites, or 'perishable' goods such as slaves or wild beasts. Distribution maps for Tripolitanian amphorae at present tend to reflect the personal pilgrimages to the museum vaults of the Mediterranean world by the chief scholars involved in their study. Moreover, with the exception of a

very few sites where detailed statistical work has been done on the coarse pottery and amphorae, the quantificative significance of the occurrence of Tripolitanian amphorae can rarely be assessed at even the most basic level. Pompeii, Ostia and Rome offer the best indication to date for a significant level of trade with Tripolitania, but these were not necessarily the only significant markets reached; they are simply those with the clearest evidence. On current evidence, however, it is clear that Tripolitanian amphorae achieved only limited penetration of some regions of the western Mediterranean. The extensive underwater archaeology of the French Riviera has yielded little trace of Tripolitanian cargo and the amphorae are fairly uncommon, though still represented at many sites in *Gallia Narbonensis.* Clearly much more information of this type is needed but the main axis of trade may have been between Tripolitania, Sicily, Italy and the Adriatic.[33]

An alternative approach is to see what can be inferred from the archaeological evidence for imported goods. Luxury goods such as marbles were obviously imported in considerable quantities to the major cities and useful research has been done on the trade links with the east Mediterranean quarries that this reveals. The picture is undoubtedly complicated by the privileged access to state marble supplies that *Lepcis* enjoyed in the early third century, but the scale of marble use in second-century monuments was already somewhat out of the ordinary for Africa.[34]

The bulk of the evidence for imports is ceramic in nature and it is still unclear to what extent pottery goods necessarily reflect the broader pattern of trade. Clearly amphorae used to transport a bulk commodity such as oil, wine or fish products are potentially much more pertinent than fine pottery that may have been shipped (and perhaps trans-shipped) as saleable ballast. In a recent, ground-breaking study Fulford has reviewed and compared the evidence from British excavations at two Libyan cities, *Sabratha* in Tripolitania and *Berenice* in Cyrenaica. Separated by about 750 km across the Greater Syrtic gulf, the two cities display mutually exclusive long-term patterns of ceramic imports and use. Fulford concluded that the two areas belonged to different regional economic systems of Mediterranean trade, an east central axis and a west central axis. Cyrenaica appears to have looked north, particularly towards Crete and the Greek mainland and islands. Tripolitania also had significant trade contact with the countries lying to its north and northwest (*Africa Proconsularis,* Sicily, Italy). The scale of Tripolitanian amphora production was significantly higher than that of Cyrenaica and accounted for a substantial percentage of the amphora from all phases of the *Sabratha* excavations. Coarse pottery from *Sabratha* also supports the orientation of trading contacts towards Carthage and Rome, rather than eastwards towards *Berenice* and Cyrenaica. Broadly speaking, this picture is supported by a range of other evidence suggesting the exclusivity of the two regions, such as coin supply, or the supply of marble and decorative stone.[35]

Yet, undoubted though the disparities between the *Berenice* and *Sabratha* assemblages are, the predominant lines of maritime commerce may mask the true degree of inter-regional trade along the North African littoral between Tripolitania and the eastern Mediterranean. Admittedly, the Greater Syrtes gulf was a notorious hazard to shipping, but coastal cabotage may have carried Tripolitanian products well beyond the nearest harbour at *Berenice*. A scatter of findspots of Tripolitanian amphorae in the Levant requires explanation (not least because as amphora studies in the east Mediterranean improve, the database of Tripolitanian material will undoubtedly grow). These amphorae could have arrived there on grain ships returning from Italy with a mixed cargo of surplus oil picked up in the markets of Rome or Ostia. But the Roman literary sources seem to imply a fairly high degree of navigation, despite the perils, along the African littoral towards Egypt, and this shipping route was of prime importance in the medieval history of Mediterranean trade.[36] The key to a clearer understanding of the question lies in further work on large ceramic assemblages from harbour sites, not just in Tripolitania and Cyrenaica but particularly at the minor anchorages in Syrtica itself.

Finally, it is worth stressing that the export potential of Tripolitania was not limitless. The supply of slaves and wild beasts from Tripolitania was regulated by the natural ecology and the political imperatives of the moment. Neither was a resource that could be dramatically expanded willy-nilly to meet market demand. The olive groves of the region were nowhere near as extensive or as well watered as those of Tunisian *Byzacena* or Spanish *Baetica*. But in both those heavily urbanized regions the profits from the exploitation of the resource were shared by many more competing towns.

Yet it is surely significant that a good share of the profits from the successful marketing of the region's surplus resources through Mediterranean commerce was vested primarily in the hands of the elite of only four or five major cities. The rich of these cities could grow richer on what to us may appear a small percentage of Mediterranean trade (to the extent that that is accurately represented in pottery assemblages). The Tripolitanian elite could have been fabulously wealthy from providing the products (and perhaps also some of the commercial capital) that made up only a few per cent of the overall trade in the Mediterranean region. We can never know what sort of trading figure was actually achieved (and exports probably fluctuated wildly on a year-by-year basis for olive oil, which tends to follow a pronounced biennial production pattern) nor the extent to which the elite may have invested in commerce as well as in agricultural production. But we can judge the results. Compared with the agricultural situation today, Roman Tripolitania was an unlikely economic success story, though the extraordinary prestige and wealth of her leading citizens may give a misleading impression. The economic boom, founded above all on oleoculture, was achieved despite, not because of, the ecological conditions of the region.[37]

8

THE CULTURAL CHARACTER OF TRIPOLITANIA

1
ROMANIZATION AND RESISTANCE

A good deal of attention has been focused recently on the degree of cultural as well as political resistance to Rome in Africa. The discussion has concentrated on the abundant evidence for Libyan, African, Numidian and Libyphoenician cultural continuity beneath a thin veneer of Romanization. Benabou, for instance, has seized on this as proof of passive social resistance to the Roman occupation and colonization of Africa. His position is an extreme reaction to earlier generations of scholars who tended to overlook the considerable native input to 'Roman' Africa. On the other hand, the distinct African cultural base is not surprising when one considers other regional variations in Romanization around the empire.

In reality the Romans were not trying to enforce a complete cultural complex on their subject people. Certainly, the development of towns and an urban-based system of local government followed an approved model. Latin became the official language in the western empire and provincials gradually gained Latin names through enfranchisement. Religious differences were generally resolved by syncretism, linking local gods with the Roman pantheon. Roman tastes in luxuries were encouraged and satisfied through the growth of trade and a cash economy centred on towns. Beyond this the 'specific cultural complex' of the African provinces may be described as Romano-African with some of the strongest influences being Punic and Libyan.[1]

Because there were few Italian settlers and no Roman military colonies in Tripolitania, the indigenous cultural contribution remained paramount. We shall examine some of the evidence for the survival of Punic and Libyan culture in the early principate in both town and country. A brief assessment of the Romanization of the region is also included. It is assumed here that the colonial age dichotomy between African nomads and 'Roman' sedentary farmers is now discredited. Nevertheless, in order to redress the balance, I have concentrated on the evidence of indigenous sedentary farmers rather than on the semi-nomadic pastoralists of the zone.[2]

2
PUNIC AND LIBYAN CULTURE IN THE URBAN CENTRES

Punic nomenclature and culture

Leglay has suggested that one of the main problems facing the Romans in Africa was the need to de-Punicize the population. If that was the objective, however, then they had limited success. One might suggest, alternatively, that the urban civilization of Roman Africa was ultimately based on a Punic foundation. The excavations at *Lepcis Magna* have produced a remarkable epigraphic dossier on her population and detailed studies have shown that the urban aristocracy were mainly of Phoenician or Libyphoenician extraction. Neo-Punic and bilingual inscriptions show their wealth and political

160

dominance in the town in the first century AD.

One of these dominant families was the *Tapapii* whose members are known from the dedicatory inscriptions of a number of monuments. Notable amongst them was Annobal Rufus, son of Himilcho Tapapius, who provided the town with its market (8 BC) and its theatre (AD 1–2, cf Plate 40). Even in the Latin sections of bilingual inscriptions the Punic names are thinly disguised, as in the case of C. Anno and Balitto Annonis Macri (or G'y ben Hanno and Ba'alyaton son of M'qr and grandson of Hanno). Other prominent Libyphoenicians in the first century included Iddibal Himilis, Iddibal Tapapius, Boncarth son of Muthumbal and Iddibal son of Balsillec, grandson of Annobal (see above, chapter 3.3).[3]

Another sign of the Punic character of the town was its political organization. The chief magistrates were called *sufetes* throughout the first century AD, only ceasing when the town became a *colonia* in AD 109. The practice of erecting bilingual or neo-Punic texts also ceased at about this time. Nevertheless, the Punic character of the Lepcitanian elite was still discernible in the Latin names and Latin texts of the second century (see above) and phrases such as *amator civium suorum, amator patriae* and *ornator patriae* were direct translations of neo-Punic titles.

Literary evidence confirms that Punic remained a spoken language in Tripolitania. Apuleius referred to the limited education of his antagonistic stepson, Sicinius Pudens of *Oea,* who had regressed to speaking 'nothing but Punic' (and this in a family with a fortune worth over 4 million *sesterces*). Similarly, the future emperor Septimius Severus was trilingual, having been educated at *Lepcis* in Latin (which he allegedly spoke with an African accent) and Greek and being fluent in Punic. The accusation that his sister Octavilla could scarcely speak Latin (*... vix Latine loquens ...)* is more credible when it is appreciated that Punic probably remained the vernacular language in Tripolitania. Although the use of the neo-Punic script died out, a debased form of written Punic was developed using the Latin alphabet. The origins of Latino-Punic inscriptions can be traced to the second century AD. A stamped tile from the Hadrianic baths reads FELIOTH IADEM SYROGATE YMMANNAI which Levi Della Vida translated as 'made in the workshops of Rogate Ymmannai'. Other Latino-Punic texts from *Lepcis* are funerary in nature and may be of later date, as for instance the stele set up by Barichal Typafi for his son Viystila and his wife Ihi.[4]

In spite of their continuing regional character, the Tripolitanian *Emporia* became in most respects typical towns of the Roman empire, with their constitutions run on Roman lines, education available in both Latin

(now the official language) and in Greek, with Romanized town plans and public buildings and their gods closely identified with Roman ones. There was no inherent contradiction though; beneath this surface gloss Punic culture and language survived.[5]

Libyans in the urban centres

There were many Libyans in the urban centres though the urban aristocracy more often bore Punic names. Amongst the citizen body at large one finds a greater preponderance of Libyan names, though the very fact of commemoration with an inscription shows that these were not amongst the poorest citizens. A series of labelled cinerary urns from *Lepcis* records Ammon, Dicar, Zabdas alongside the Punic names Anno..., Arisu, Balbilla and Imilcho. Other inscriptions refer to Nummius Gaetulicus, M. Pompeius Gaetulicus and Gaetul [...] and Claudius Ladas and Claudius Stiddin. Another Stiddin is known at *Oea.*

Gigthis provides an interesting contrast to *Lepcis* in that some of the *Cinithi* tribe rose to high status in the town and its surrounding *territoria.* L. Memmius Messius was both one of the leading tribesmen of the *Cinithi* and magistrate of *Gigthis.* His kinsfolk are known to have owned a fulling establishment in the town and there was a C. Memmius at nearby *Zitha* (Zian). Inscriptions from prestigious mausolea in the Gefara agricultural zone refer to a Messius Crescens and a Messia Spicula, who may be suspected of belonging to another African family. The culture of these Libyan aristocrats was basically Punic.[6]

Another way of identifying the Libyan element in urban centres might be through the excavation of cemeteries, though those of the Tripolitanian cities are poorly known. Grave types appear to have been predominantly Libyan or Punic, as in rural districts also. There is little evidence in the early period of imported Roman burial habits.[7]

3
ART AND HIGH CULTURE IN TRIPOLITANIA

The architecture, sculpture and painting of the leading Tripolitanian cities often attained the highest standards of Roman provincial art. Whilst the Punic towns of the region had borrowed extensively from Alexandrian art and architecture, under imperial rule they embraced the renascent classicism of Roman art. In the early first century AD *Lepcis* had an array of amenities that would have done credit to most Italian towns. A visitor to the town would undoubtedly have been impressed by the scale and ornamentation of the main temples, the market, the freestanding theatre *cavea*, the amphitheatre and the over-life-size statues of the Julio-Claudian imperial family in the temple of Rome and Augustus. The first century AD also witnessed the first extensive use of marble and mosaics in the town. Mosaic art became a regional speciality, though some of the finest pavements at the Zliten villa are now generally dated to the Severan period rather than to the Flavian era as formerly. The well-known Zliten amphitheatre scenes, showing the whole bloody array of arena games – gladiators, animal hunts/fights and human execution *ad bestias* – ornamented the mosaic border of an ornate *opus sectile* floor. Another coastal villa at Silin, recently excavated, has yielded comparable mosaics, the most notable of which feature a scene showing condemned prisoners being gored and tossed by a huge bull and a detailed representation of the circus at *Lepcis Magna*. The choice of subject matter reflects not only the urban connections of the aristocratic families who owned these two luxury coastal villas, but also the extent to which the stature of public benefactors might be judged in terms of the gruesome opulence of the Roman style games they sponsored.

The ornamentation and building programme of the Severans took the city to new heights of conformity with the artistic culture of Rome. The elite upper class of Tripolitania had the wealth and the cultural awareness to buy into what was perceived to be most refined about architecture, craft and artistic production. But it is easy to be misled by this adhesion to the fashions of high culture into believing that the ordinary people were equally enthusiastic in their responses to classical art. Survivals of Punic and late antique art suggest that there were other traditions in the region and that these can be traced through many of the less Romanized creations of indigenous artisans in the Roman period.[8]

In particular, the craft workshops responsible for the many ornamented tombs of the rural districts used scenes from local life as well as from the repertory of the classical pattern book. This type of art has rarely been treated as though it was in any way distinct from that of the high art of the cities in terms of its cultural reference points. Accordingly it has sometimes been dismissed as second-rate imitation of classical style. But the evidence presented in this chapter for profound cultural differences between town and country in Tripolitania suggests that this is an important area for future re-evaluation. The characteristic products of the tomb builders of the Gebel and pre-desert zones merit detailed study, then, as representative of a distinctive and flourishing rural

culture, as much African as classical in inspiration (Fig. 8.4; Plates 43–45, 47, 59–61).

4
PUNIC AND LIBYAN IN RURAL AREAS

It has sometimes been claimed that the Punic language and culture of the rural areas was quickly extinguished under Rome. This idea is based on the mistaken assumption that it had never been well established there in the first place. However, the monarchies of *Mauretania* and *Numidia* were highly Punicized and the widespread influence of Punic culture and language among some of the other tribal groups is likely. St Augustine's well-known comments on the survival of Punic in rural areas should be taken at face value, particularly in view of the unequivocal evidence from rural Tripolitania presented below.[9]

Several discrete bodies of information lead us to the same conclusion; the first of these is the architectural evidence. The earliest farming settlements in the Gebel and pre-desert regions of Tripolitania were centred on undefended farms constructed in the *opus africanum* style. Relief carvings from these buildings of the Tanit symbol and of phallic symbols, designed to ward off the evil eye, are typically Punic. The *opus africanum* style of building originated in the Phoenician and Punic centres in Africa.

Associated with many of these early farms were elaborate tombs in ashlar masonry the commonest form being the so-called obelisk tomb (see above, Fig. 0.1; Plate 44). Although they were at one time mostly assigned a late Roman date, to go with the *gsur*, it is now clear that many of the tombs, and the obelisk type in particular, are datable to the first two centuries AD. The obelisk tomb had Phoenician antecedents, clearly demonstrated by two fine Punico-Hellenistic examples found at *Sabratha*.[10]

In the ULVS study area, obelisk tombs on the Wadi Merdum at Mselletin and Bir Gebira had fragmentary neo-Punic dedications and are to be associated with open farms whose occupation began in the second half of the first century AD. Similarly, in the Wadi el-Amud the early farm (see above) lay in close proximity to a cemetery containing two elaborate obelisk or tower tombs whose dedications were in neo-Punic (Fig. 7:9; Plate 43). Similar tombs (with a pronaos formed by columns at second-storey height) have been recorded in the Wadis Migdal (Plate 45) and Messeuggi, and once again there are farms yielding first- and second-century pottery close by. In the Wadi N'f'd a pair of obelisk tombs was erected at the mouth of a tributary (known today as the el-Amud; Plate 44), but the ULVS failed to locate an early site close to them. However, de Mathuisieulx recorded the existence of a 'bourgade', built in ashlar masonry, a few metres above the wadi floor below the south obelisk. This seems to be a reference to an *opus africanum* farm rather than a *gasr*, but the area indicated is now covered by shifting sand dunes. Yet another example of the association between early settlement and obelisk tombs is to be found in the Wadi Antar, where an obelisk tomb stood in close proximity to another tomb which has been dated on epigraphic grounds to the late first or very early second century. Further examples exist in the Wadi Umm el-Agerem, though the tombs there probably date from the late second or early third century (Fig. 8:4). In general, therefore, the spread of obelisk mausolea was early in date and reflects the Punic culture or tastes of the wealthy elite in the zone.[11]

The same was also true of western Tripolitania as is illustrated by the el-Amrouni mausoleum, south of Foum Tatahouine. Although for long considered third century AD or later in date, recent commentators have tended to date it to the first or second century AD since the dedication was made in both Latin and neo-Punic. This was also an obelisk tomb. The architectural style of this and other tombs in the region can justifiably be described as Libyco-Punic even if architectural details, such as engaged pilasters with Corinthian capitals, reflect Mediterranean borrowings.[12]

Further neo-Punic inscriptions from the hinterland of Tripolitania include the dedication of a Libyan temple near Tarhuna and an *ostracon* (dealing with farming matters) from near Cussabat. There is also the evidence of Punic names to be considered. From the Gebel region came Balsilech Subath (who allegedly lived to be over 110) and a certain Hanno. Iddibal, Annibal/Annobal, Imilcho, Arisam and Bodastart are attested on sites south of the Wadi Sofeggin. Of course, some of these Punic names may have been assumed by people of Libyan descent, and Punic nomenclature was much less common than Libyan, even among the elite, in the Tripolitanian hinterland. Although the rural population were Punicized to a degree and seem to have spoken Punic, they were not strictly Libyphoenicians and there is no certain evidence for 'colonists' sent out beyond their *territoria* by the Tripolitanian towns. However, a small number of civilian names encountered in the Bu Njem documents appear to be Aramean or Syrian in origin: Aban, Barlas, Malchus.[13]

Scholars of Punic and neo-Punic have demonstrated that the so-called Latino-Libyan inscriptions of Tripolitania were essentially Latino-Punic in character, though the language was clearly a rather debased form of Punic. Translation of some, but by no means all, texts has been possible. A series of hybrid texts using a mixture of Latin and Punic words demonstrates that the vernacular language was still Punic. The use of the Punic phrase *avo sanu* for *vixit annis* ('lived for ... years') is one revealing example of this.[14]

Outside the *territoria* of the coastal cities, the process of agricultural development was carried out primarily by members of the *Gaetuli* and *Macae* regional sub-tribes. Many of these spoke Punic and had some cultural associations with the *Libyphoenices*. They may have gained agricultural experience and capital working land within the *territoria* of the towns (which must have impinged on traditional tribal lands). However, their names show clearly that they were representatives of a Libyan rural elite. In the hinterland of western Tripolitania one finds, *inter alia*, Miha Vasa, Iurathe, Iuzale, Thanubra and Assioda. In the eastern Gebel lands lived M. Ulpius [...] Chinitiu [...], Issicuar, Semp and Eisrelia, Muthunilim, Stiddin, Thlana Marci Cecili son of Mupal, Shasidwasan son of Tamrar of the sons of Masinkaw and many others.[15]

The most important group of names, however, comes from the Sofeggin and Zem-Zem region. Quite detailed information about family relationships can be established in a few cases. Neo-Punic inscriptions from two tombs at the main cemetery in the Wadi el-Amud allow partial family trees to be established (Figs 8:1–8:2). The date range is probably late first to second century AD. From the larger tomb (Plate 43) came the following text:

The tomb in absolute ownership, which Masawkan made for his father Yamrur, son of Gatit of the M.s.li and for his mother Zut, daughter of Gatidan (or Ganidan) the T.g.l.bi (or N.g.l.bi) and for his son and for his wife Asliyat daughter of Yankdassan, son of Siyuk of the T.g.l.bi (or N.g.l.bi). O woe that there are four! The tomb was made at his expense and during his life and the lives of his sons Arisam and Iosdan.

The second and third inscriptions came from the smaller monumental tomb in the cemetery, mentioning another man called Arisam and a man called Nimran. These texts cannot be certainly genealogically linked to the first one, but a close family link may be suspected.

Stele which was set up to Nimran Y[...] by his sons. The builder was Arisam.

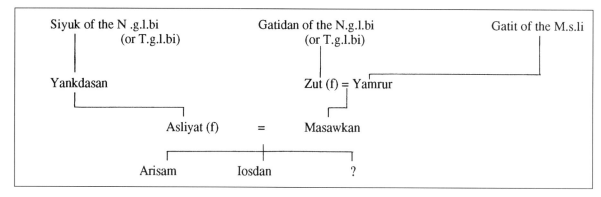

Fig. 8:1 Partial family tree from the el-Amud (tomb 1), second half first to early second century AD (cf. Fig. 7:9; Plate 43).

This stele was set up for Nimran, son of Masukkasan, son of [...]w.n.t (or [...]w.t.t) ... the builders were ...s.p.n.p.l (or .s.p.t.p.l) son of [...] and Arisam son of Bod'astart

Of the 16 people named on these inscriptions only three have Punic names (two of these, the tomb builder and his father, may not be related to the rest). The third case, though, is the son of an undoubted Libyan family and demonstrates the dangers of assuming that Punic names were used exclusively by people of Libyphoenician origin. The grandparents of Asliyat and Masawkan were referred to in relation to their Libyan tribal clans (the N.g.l.bi or T.g.l.bl and the M.s.li). The pattern of intermarriage between the two clans is interesting, with Yamrur of the M.s.li marrying into one of the families of the N.g.l.bi and his son marrying the daughter of another. These inscriptions

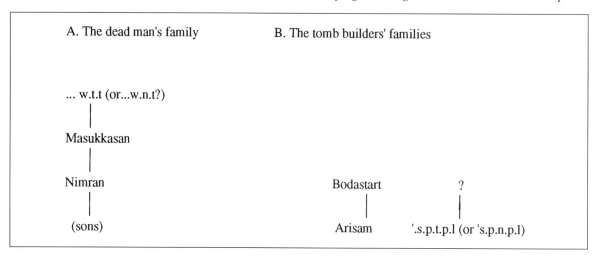

Fig. 8:2 Partial family tree from the el-Amud (tomb 2), late first to early second century AD.

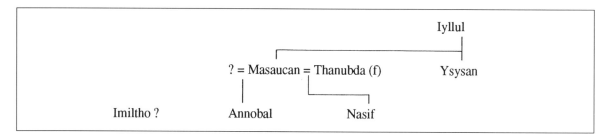

Fig. 8:3 Partial family tree from the Wadi Umm el-Agerem, second or third century AD (cf. Figs 8:4–5; Plates 41, 46, 47).

164

record at least four generations (and probably more) of one of the wealthiest families in the Sofeggin region in the late first and early second centuries AD, but there is little sign of increasing Romanization. Similarly, unpublished *ostraca* from this farm, of probable third-century date, were written in Latino-Punic (Plate 42).[16]

Two Latino-Punic inscriptions from a cemetery in the Wadi Umm el-Agerem allow another partial family tree to be reconstructed (Fig. 8:3). The texts come from two fine obelisk or tower tombs from a prominent cemetery (Fig. 8:4; Plates 41, 46, 47) close to the major farm/*gasr* complex in the wadi.

> Masaucan and Ysysan have made this tomb for their father Iyllul ... the builders were Imiltho and Annobal son of Masauchan Chaross.

> Thanubda and her son have made this monument to Masauchan, son of Iylul, with 2,100 denarii, to which were added by the builder Annobal 1,000 denarii ...

This is again a wealthy Libyan family group who spoke Punic and still used some Punic names alongside their more common Libyan ones. Their farm (Ag 1) had started as an undefended *opus africanum* structure (Fig. 8:5; Plate 48), but probably in the third century it was incorporated into the structure of a conventional *gasr*. The fact that Annobal, the tomb builder in both cases, contributed to the costs of the tomb for Masauchan suggests that the latter was his father, though the phrasing implies that Thanubra was not his natural mother. The relationship (if any) of the other tomb builder is unknown.[17]

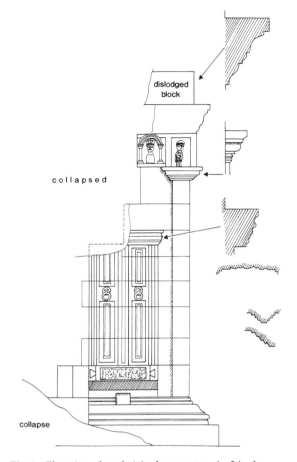

Fig. 8:4 Elevation of tomb A in the cemetery Ag 2 in the Umm el-Agerem, from which came text 2 disscussed above (from ULVS survey).

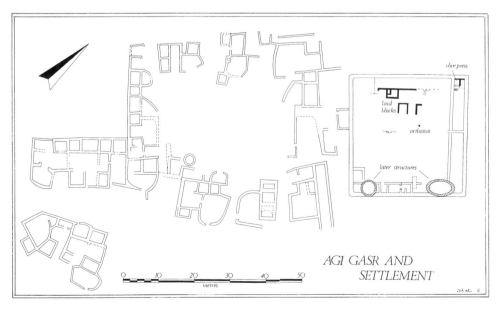

AGI GASR AND SETTLEMENT

Fig. 8:5 The main fortified farm (*gasr*) and settlement Ag 1 from the Wadi Umm el-Agerem (cf. Fig. 11.2; Plate 48). Within the structure of the *gasr* traces of an earlier *opus africanum* farm can be made out (from Jones 1985a).

So far we have dealt exclusively with the elite group who aspired to and attained a higher level of acculturation. There were other Libyans in the zone whose culture was far less Punicized. Chabot recorded a number of inscriptions using a Libyan alphabet in western Tripolitania and, although it was once thought that there were no texts in the Libyan alphabet from the eastern region, over 40 examples are now known besides the more extensive archive from the Bu Njem *vicus*. There are many others from Fezzan also. In spite of the knowledge of Punic among the elite, then, Libyan was also a major spoken language in the rural areas and had a number of dialects (see further, chapter 11).[18]

5
ROMAN LANGUAGE AND CULTURE

It should already be apparent that Romanization came a poor second to the earlier and continuing Punicization of Tripolitania. But it is not necessary to conclude, as did Benabou, that this was a result of cultural resistance to the imperial power. One comes back to the question of what level of social and cultural change Rome actually tried to achieve in the provinces. The aims of Romanization were primarily political – to create stable conditions of local government centred on towns, with Latin as the language of officialdom. At a far lower level it was directed at tribal elites beyond and in the frontier zones and was designed to reconcile them to Roman authority. This sort of Romanization, working through treaties, grants of Roman citizenship, the export of high prestige goods and services, was designed to create cultural links between Roman and native. It was not intended that Libyans be turned into Romans, rather that potential enemies were to be persuaded in the

first instance to identify just a little with Roman civilization. The process is fairly clear, for instance, in Rome's dealings with the *Garamantes* (see above, Chapters 2–3).

Within the Roman province, the towns conformed to the pattern of Romanized centres in spite of their continuing and strong Punic links. How else to explain the success of L. Septimius Severus? Because Roman rule was carried out at local level by pre-existing elites (wherever suitable candidates were found) it was inevitable that their culture should survive beneath a veneer of Romanization. To some extent the same principles extended to Roman control over the deeper hinterland. It seems certain that Rome attached great importance to the existence of a Libyan elite whose high culture was that of the Libyphoenicians but whose tribal connections covered a much wider area through the principle of tribal hierarchy. Some of these people were no doubt established alongside the Libyphoenician farmers of the Gebel and, whether by opportunity or inducements, they were encouraged to extend sedentary agriculture on to their tribal lands in the marginal pre-desert zone.

The culture, language and nomenclature of these people was comparatively little affected as we have seen, though a few did acquire Roman citizenship prior to the third century. One such was T. Flavius Capito who erected a small temple at Tininai, perhaps in the late first century to judge from the pottery collected from this site by the ULVS. He was probably related to a T. Flavius Ninus Achul commemorated on a tomb inscription from the Wadi Antar nearby. The latter text also referred to the dead man's father, Uzale, his grandfather, Masinthan, and to a woman whose name was probably Thanecum and who was almost certainly his mother (Fig. 8:6). On this evidence the Libyan origin of both T. Flavii seems certain, perhaps even from the same family. As first generation citizens they received the grant no later

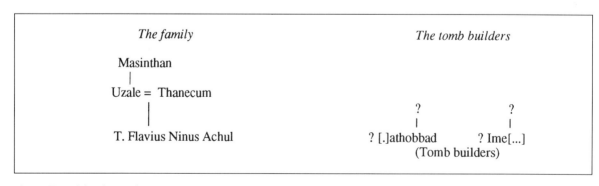

The family

Masinthan
|
Uzale = Thanecum
|
T. Flavius Ninus Achul

The tomb builders

?   ?
| |
? [.]athobbad   ? Ime[...]
(Tomb builders)

Fig. 8:6 Partial family tree from Wadi Antar cemetery, late first to early second century AD.

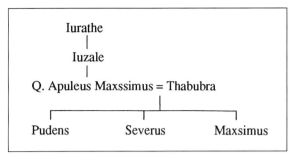

Iurathe
|
Iuzale
|
Q. Apuleus Maxssimus = Thabubra

Pudens   Severus   Maxsimus

Fig. 8:7 Partial family tree from el-Amrouni, late first century to early second century AD.

than AD 96 and, with Flavius Ninus dying at age 39, his tomb should belong in the early years of the second century at latest. There is an interesting contrast to be drawn between this Libyan family, embracing Latin names and erecting Latin inscriptions, and the probably contemporary el-Amud family, still utilizing the neo-Punic script.[19]

There is similar evidence for Romanized Libyans from western Tripolitania, such as the L. Domitii in the western Gefara and Gebel Matmata. L. Domitius Aumura and L. Domitius Tellul were plainly native Libyans and the wife of the former man, Arellia Tommassa, may have been ancestrally related to Arellia Nepotilla, the wife of M. Manlius Ingenus who constructed the *turris Maniliorum Arelliorum* at a later date.[20]

The process of enfranchisement is also illustrated in the well-known Latin funerary dedication of Q. Apuleus Maxssimus (*sic*) from el-Amrouni (Fig. 8:7). The inscription is most likely first or second century AD as there was a parallel neo-Punic text on the obelisk-type tomb. Apuleus was nicknamed *Rideus* ('Smiley') and lived to be 90.

The members of the family of Apuleus were evidently Punicized Libyans who lived in and farmed the marginal agricultural zone. The poor spelling of the Latin text demonstrates that both Apuleus, despite the grant of citizenship, and his stone-cutter were only superficially Romanized.[21]

The art and architecture of many of the funerary monuments, from simple cairns to tombs decorated with relief carvings, follow recognizable Punico-Libyan or Romano-Libyan styles. They are best not judged by stringent standards of classical art but analysed as the invaluable record of an important cultural fusion. Few would now accept Smythe's harsh verdict on the Ghirza tombs as 'debased classical tombs in indifferent taste'. There were undoubtedly many classical motifs selected at random from the constructor's pattern book, but these are accompanied by vigorous representations of those

who commissioned the tombs and of their rural life as they wished themselves and it to be remembered.[22]

6
RELIGION IN ROMAN TRIPOLITANIA

The religion of the people of Tripolitania remained fairly traditional until the rise of Christianity. The most detailed recent study of cults and temples in Tripolitania has also stressed the particularism of the region. In Tripolitania both the Punic and native African religious traditions exhibited significant non-conformity with those of other Libyphoenician/Carthaginian cities or of interior lands such as Numidia. There was also a significant divergence between the cults represented in the coastal cities and those of the rural hinterland.

Roman cults had their main impact in the cities, of course, where both orthodox classical and monumental Semitic style temples were erected. The old tutelary deities of many cities retained their significance under Rome, being syncretized with suitable Roman alternatives and worshipped under the joint names. The most emphatic example of this trend is at *Lepcis*, where the Phoenician gods Milk'ashtart (probably synonymous with Carthaginian Melqart) and Shadrapa were equated respectively with Hercules and Liber Pater (Bacchus). Although the temple of Milk'ashtart appears to have been elbowed off its prime site on the Old Forum by a Temple of Rome and Augustus (a clear sign of the ambitious attitude of the *Lepcitani* towards Rome), it was relocated close by. Septimius Severus seems to have made his new forum and basilica complex a vast monument to the tutelary gods. The massive temple in the forum may well have been jointly dedicated to them (Dio refers to Severus wasting a huge sum on a temple to them!); scenes of Hercules and Bacchus were intricately cut into the pilasters of the basilica. The Saecular Games at Rome in AD 204 also seem to have been conducted under the auspices of Severus' favoured pair of gods.[23]

Milk'ashtart and a third Phoenician god at *Lepcis*, El Qone Aras, are not otherwise attested in North Africa. This is perhaps a reflection of the close links that *Lepcis* maintained with her mother city Tyre and the comparative autonomy she had from Carthaginian dominance. *Sabratha* and some of the smaller centres show greater conformity with the Carthaginian pantheon, dominated by Baal-Hammon and Tanit (both attested at *Sabratha* in neo-Punic dedications, but not at *Lepcis*). Tanit is traceable in the cult of Roman Caelestis and Baal-Hammon was normally conflated with Saturn. While these two cults were enormously popular and widespread in other regions of North Africa, their importance in Tripolitania seems to have been much more limited. Caelestis for instance is only attested at *Sabratha, Lepcis,* Tarhuna and *Zitha,* and Saturn only at *Sabratha.*[24]

The most prominent Roman deities were undoubtedly those that combined Roman and Libyphoenician attributes as with Liber Pater (*Lepcis, Oea, Sabratha, Gigthis*) and Hercules (*Lepcis, Sabratha, Gigthis*). The popularity of Mercury (attested at *Lepcis, Oea, Sabratha, Gigthis*) suggests that he too was syncretized with an important local Punic cult. Venus (celebrated at *Lepcis*) was probably equated with Phoenician Astarte. Of the innovations introduced by Rome, the imperial cult undoubtedly became a major focus of civic ceremonial at several towns. Overall, though, the Tripolitanian cities showed considerable loyalty to their Phoenician/Punic tutelary deities.

The 19 excavated temples and over 40 different deities attested at *Lepcis* is somewhat atypical of the region, with a wide range of imported cults existing alongside the old Phoenician ones. But several of the other harbour cities have yielded evidence for a variety of eastern cults, notably Isis (*Sabratha*) and Serapis (*Lepcis, Sabratha, Gigthis*).

Despite the large archive of religious dedications from several of the coastal cities, it is particularly striking that there is not a single case of a Libyan cult recorded from them. A recent attempt to identify Gurzil in a neo-Punic text at *Oea* has not met with the acceptance of the editors of *IPT* and cannot be pressed. There are some slight signs in the eastern Gebel of Libyphoenician influence, represented by the temple at Gasr el-Gezira to Hercules (Melqart?) and a dedication from Tarhuna to Caelestis (Tanit symbols are also known in this area). By way of contrast, much of the rural hinterland and the smaller coastal settlements showed an overwhelming preference for Libyan cults, with temples of Ammon known at several points along the coast road.

The dominant religion in rural Tripolitania and among the desert tribes was Libyan Ammon, a quite distinct cult from that of Punic Baal-Hammon. There were apparently many rural shrines or *Ammonia* in the region (*Arae Philaenorum,* Breviglieri, Bu Njem, Zaviet et Mahgiub (15 km west of Misurata), Senam Tininai (assuming that Jupiter here indicated Jupiter Ammon as at Bu Njem), and an unlocated site approx. 24 km west of *Sabratha*). *Ammonia* are also mentioned in the sources dealing with the tribes of the desert oases, stretching from the great oracular centres of the Ammon cult at *Siwa* and *Augila* to *Garama* and beyond.

The Roman fort and *vicus* at Bu Njem was surrounded by no less than five outlying temples, and the three surviving dedications provide interesting information about the local cults, as well as about the religious outlook of the garrison. The dedications of two of the deities worshipped by the garrison at Bu Njem conflated, in one case, Jupiter with Hammon (Ammon) and, in the other, Mars with Libyan Canapphar. The third text is to the otherwise unknown Libyan god, Vanammon (presumably progeny of Ammon himself?). This sort of religious partisanship for and *interpretatio* (syncretism) of local cults in the frontier regions is amply paralleled in other provinces, such as Britain.[25]

Yet the underlying message to be derived from this brief analysis is that the religious make-up of Tripolitania was extremely unusual, a sort of cultural dimorphism between on the one hand the old Punic cities and on the other an extremely deep Libyan hinterland. The particular strength of Ammon worship in the desert and pre-desert margins is in marked contrast to the other evidence we have seen for the elites of these regions embracing elements of Punic or Roman culture and architectural fashions.

7
THE ARMY

Recent research shows that the Roman army, far from being a model of Roman *civilitas*, was itself thoroughly Punicized or Libyanized by the third century AD. We have noted already the apparent use of Punic measures in the laying out of the camp at Bu Njem. The garrison in Tripolitania in the third century was predominantly recruited from people born in Africa and although the Bu Njem evidence provides some indications of classical pretensions, such as the two acrostic poems set up by the centurions, Q. Avidius Quintianus and M. Porcius Iasucthan, the general level of classical knowledge seems to have been low. Iasuchtan's name is Libyan, while many Latin cognomina are typical of the theophoric forms favoured by Punic communities, Donatus, Rogatus, Saturninus, etc. Lassère's study of the list of about 300 names from *Bezereos* likewise reveals a high proportion of African combinations of Latin nomenclature. Typically African cognomina there include Auctus, Ammon, Crescens, Donatus (x 4), Faustus, Felix (x 8), Fortunatus (x 4), Honoratus, Ianuarius, Impetratus, Novatianus, Proculus (x 3), Rogatus (x 3), Sallustianus (x 7), Saturninus, Victor (x 5), Victorianus.[26]

This picture is typical of the *legio III Augusta* from

the second century onwards as has been demonstrated on the extensive prosopographical dossier of inscriptions from the legionary headquarters at Lambaesis. The auxiliary units posted in Tripolitania may have become no less dependent on local sources of recruits, though the demographic evidence available does not permit certainty. The *Cohors II Flavia Afrorum* naturally had always had an African base of recruitment, and though a specialist unit such as the archers of the Syrian cohort might be thought more likely to have maintained a link with the home region this is by no means certain.[27]

Marichal despairs of the 'latin créole' used by some of the troops at Bu Njem when sending dispatches and even the scribes at the fort were far from word-perfect. One letter received at the fort was written in Latino-Punic. In a region where the chief spoken languages were Punic and Libyan, it made sense to have a garrison who could communicate in the vernacular but it imposed limitations on the usefulness of the army as agents of Romanization. In this respect the superficiality of the *Romanitas* of the army is not significantly different from most other frontier provinces. Rome had no great scheme for supplanting indigenous cultures, nor did she have the physical means to enforce her will in such matters. Romanization involved the absorption of local religion and culture into the Roman system. The background, language and culture of many of the military 'agents of civilization' favoured a high degree of cultural assimilation. The process was a two-way one also, in which the enemies of Rome participated, with the differences between Roman and 'barbarian' gradually becoming indeterminate. Such cultural inversion on the frontiers could, of course, be a factor in the ultimate failure of an imperial authority to maintain its borders.[28]

8
CONCLUSIONS

In normal circumstances the sequel to the Roman military conquest was not the imposition of an Italian, or wholly alien, culture on subject peoples. The key to Roman success was not the crushing of local resistance to the point of extermination but the voluntary assimilation of local peoples into a system of government based on wealth and oligarchic power. Resistance to Rome was often overcome or minimized by suitable inducements to existing elite groups. The participation in Roman government of the *Libyphoenices* from the towns of Tripolitania produced centurions, procurators, senators, governors, praeto-

rian prefects and even emperors. In the frontier zone, the energy of the elite was directed towards the accumulation of wealth within the Roman economic system. Beyond the frontiers, Roman diplomacy concentrated on maintaining a dominant pro-Roman faction among the tribal elites through gifts, services and support.[29]

In rural areas, the active involvement of the native people was no doubt on a lower level than in the towns. When Synesius spent time in the Cyrenaican country, well away from the towns, he rejoiced in the simple, ageless quality of rural life, for:

> As to the Emperor, as to the favourites of the Emperor .... no one, or hardly any one, speaks of them here. Our ears have rest from such stories. No doubt men know well that there is always an Emperor living, for we are reminded of this every year by those who collect the taxes: but who he is, is not very clear.

These comments might equally be applicable to the interior of Tripolitania under Rome.[30] The region was generally pacified, relatively prosperous and, though not very Romanized, the elite were reconciled to Roman rule for as long as it worked to their advantage. The most visible signs of Roman rule were the garrison posts and the annual visits of the tax-men. But an equally profound, but less obvious, Roman influence was exercised over the social and economic development of the region. Most scholars would now agree that the extent of Roman involvement stopped well short of official colonization of the frontier region, but we cannot entirely divorce the indigenous development of marginal zone farming from Roman stimuli. The timing of the first settlement of sedentary estates in the Sofeggin, for instance, corresponded with the final pacification of the tribes in the area and the official delimitation of their lands in the Flavian period. It is worth speculating that, having identified an elite group amongst the more northerly tribes, Rome fostered economic development as an incidental side effect of rewarding this group with land and incentives such as Roman citizenship. Through land delimitation Rome would have been able to transfer the title of some lands from the whole tribe to individuals. The creation of cash wealth augmented the power of the traditional leaders of the northern clans and the mixed farming regime may have gained further recruits from southerly, transhuming clans. However, these changes, brought about by the establishment of the Roman military control, created a rural aristocracy whose lifestyle and estates were modelled not on a Roman pattern but in equal measure on those of the pre-existing Libyphoenician aristocracy of the *Emporia* and on their own Libyan culture.

In spite of occasionally protracted and bitter wars of conquest, Roman imperialism was in general fairly enlightened when it came to dealing with defeated enemies. In contrast to many more recent imperial and colonial interludes, the Roman empire was not handicapped by the same level of racial and religious bigotry, which has done so much to discredit modern colonialism. In addition to the unprecedented military success of her armies, Rome's great strength was her ability to assimilate the diverse people she conquered into the Roman system. The keys to this were the *limited* aims of Romanization and the conciliation of the ruling classes and dominant social groups. Paradoxically, the growth of the Roman world brought about the dilution of Roman culture rather than its wholesale export.[31]

9

LATE ROMAN HISTORICAL SUMMARY

1
THE PROVINCE OF *TRIPOLITANA*

The creation of the province of *Tripolitana* related to an empire-wide pattern of sub-division of provinces during the first Tetrarchy under Diocletian and Maximian between AD 294–305. Various theories exist concerning the exact date and context of the change. Some scholars have argued that the Diocletianic reforms represented a single and generally applied policy across the empire, linked chronologically with the appointment of the junior Caesars in 293. However, the evidence from some provinces suggests a later sub-division, perhaps signifying that a more piecemeal pattern of provincial fractionalization may have been followed according to distinct regional timetables. For the African provinces, the campaigns of Maximian in 296–7 have frequently been seen as an appropriate watershed from which the division of *Mauretania* and *Africa Proconsularis* can be traced. Recently a very strong case has been made for placing the sub-division of the latter into *Africa Proconsularis* (or *Zeugitana*, northern Tunisia), *Valeria Byzacena* (central and southern Tunisia) and *Tripolitana* in the autumn of 303, coincident with the timing of the sub-division of *Numidia* into *Numidia Militiana* and *Numidia Cirtensis*.[1]

The arguments in favour of the 303 date are compelling and require the least amount of special pleading with the limited available epigraphic data. As di Vita-Evrard has noted, this date may also have relevance for other provinces where the Tetrarchic reform is poorly dated. The crucial points are:

1) the detachment from *Africa* of *Byzacena* and *Tripolitana* must have been a single act, as the separation of only one would have caused administrative anomalies;
2) the existence of a separate province of *Tripolitana*, with its *limes* zone, had implications for the military organization of *Numidia* – restructuring of these provinces at the same moment would have been a logical step;
3) the division of *Numidia* can be accurately dated to the latter part of 303;
4) the earliest inscription of a governor (*praeses*) of *Tripolitana* mentions two successive governors (C. Valerius Vibianus and Aurelius Quintianus) and must date to shortly after 303 as the second man is also known to have been the first governor of *Numidia Cirtensis* in 303. The Tripolitanian position will have been a promotional step, since the early *praesides* had command of the troops based there whereas no army units were based in *Numidia Cirtensis*. It is possible that Quintianus may have gone straight on to *Tripolitana* from the Cirtan position and, if so, it is likely that the Tripolitanian governors on the *centenarium Tibubuci* dedication were the first two holders of the new office;
5) altars and monuments to the Tetrarchs are known to have been set up by *praesides* in both *Tripolitana* and *Byzacena* to mark the provincial boundary. Although not closely datable, this would have been an early duty of the first governors of the new provinces.[2]

171

The rationale behind the creation of the new provinces can be assessed at two levels, global and regional. Tripolitania had for long been recognized as a quasi-separate unity, the *regio Tripolitana,* and the economic growth of *Byzacena* had demarcated it as a fiscal administrative region separate from that of north Tunisia. But the geographical logic was probably secondary to the political imperatives of the day. The Tetrarchs favoured smaller provincial commands, organized within regional dioceses and prefectures. The new administrative arrangements involved considerable expansion in the imperial civil service and set in train a pattern of bureaucracy that was to become progressively more top-heavy during the fourth century. The vicar of Africa (responsible for the provinces of *Byzacena, Tripolitana, Numidia* and *Mauretania*), for instance, had a staff of 300, the proconsul of Africa 400. Other governors will have had about 100 paid staff. The hierarchy of posts and the limits of responsibility within this bureaucracy were complex and, on occasions, contradictory. Both the praetorian prefect for Italy, Africa and Illyricum and the vicar of the African diocese reported direct to the emperor, though the prefect was technically the superior officer of state. The vicar in turn had limited powers of intervention with the provincial governors below him, other than in matters concerning the *annona,* the maintenance of the food supply of the city of Rome being his principal responsibility. The proconsular governor of *Zeugitana* was of higher rank than the Vicar and thus not subject to his authority. The other main function of the vicar and the provincial governors was judicial, operating two tiers of assize courts.

In the early years of the Diocletianic system the army units in the African provinces were controlled by the *praesides* under the supervision of the vicar. But by the mid-fourth century neither the *vicarius* nor most of the governors had military responsibilities, with the possible exception of the Tripolitanian *praesides.* Instead the military units in the African provinces were at some point placed almost exclusively under the control of military specialists, counts and dukes. The date of the earliest *comes Africae* is uncertain, but Gratian (father of the emperors Valentinian I and Valens) is a likely candidate at some stage in the 330s. By the 360s, control of the Tripolitanian border units seems to have passed from the provincial governor to the count. The power of the *comites Africae* frequently eclipsed that of the *vicarii* in the second half of the fourth century and the position of a minor governor in dispute with the count could be perilous (as we shall see in the story of Count Romanus).

The status of the governors of the individual provinces varied also according to well-defined criteria (Table 9:1). The remnants of *Africa Proconsularis* retained the proconsular status for its governors, although the governorship was more frequently held by men from distinguished senatorial families at the start of their careers, rather than as the culmination of a career as had earlier been the case. Nonetheless, many of the known holders of the office in the fourth century went on to glittering careers. Tenure of the office was normally of short duration, rarely more than a year or two. Likewise *Numidia* (reunited as a single province based on *Cirta* in 314 and promoted to consular rank in 320) attracted men of high birth and importance in court circles. *Byzacena* was also raised c. 340 to consular rank, probably on account of its economic importance, but seems to have received men of slightly lesser note than went to *Numidia.* By way of contrast, *Tripolitana* remained a praesidal province, governed by men of equestrian rank with limited social or political consequence in court affairs. Significantly, little is known of the prior or subsequent career

Title	Command	Date from	Rank
Praefectus praetori	*Italia, Africa, Illyricum*	303	*vir illustris*
Proconsularis Africae	*Zeugitana*	303	*vir spectabilis*
Vicarius Africae	*Africa, Numidia, Byzacena, Tripolitana, Mauretania* (civil powers)	303	*vir spectabilis*
Comes Africae	*Numidia, Tripolitana, Mauretania, Byzacena* (military powers)	330s f	*vir spectabilis*
Consularis	*Numidia*	320	*vir clarissimus*
Consularis	*Byzacena*	340s f	*vir clarissimus*
Praeses	*Numidia Militaris*	303–314	*vir perfectissimus*
Praeses	*Byzacena*	303–340s	*vir perfectissimus*
Praeses	*Tripolitana*	303	*vir perfectissimus*
Praeses	*Numidia Cirtenses*	303–314	*vir perfectissimus*

Table 9:1. The hierarchy of civil government in the African provinces in the fourth century AD.

40 (*Above*) Dedication inscription of the theatre at *Lepcis Magna*, AD 1–2, recording the benefaction of Annobal Tapapius Rufus in Latin and neo-Punic.

41 (*Left*) Latino-Punic dedication of the tomb of Masauchan in the Wadi Umm el-Agerem (cf. Plates 46–8) (source: ULVS).

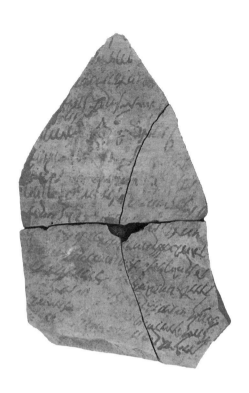

42 (*Left*) Latino-Punic *ostracon* from the el-Amud olive press building. Although not yet deciphered it is probable that this document records some sort of transaction or farm accounts.

43 (*Below*) Tower or obelisk tomb at el-Amud built by Masawkan, probably late first century AD.

44 (*Top left*) Obelisk tomb from the Wadi N'f'd.

45 (*Top right*) Tower or obelisk tomb from the Wadi Migdal.

46 (*Bottom left*) Aerial view of cemetery Ag 2 in the Wadi Umm el-Agerem, showing a line of six ashlar tombs and associated satellite burials. The tomb featured in Plates 41 and 47 is the second from the left end of the line (source: ULVS).

47 (*Bottom right*) Elevation of the tomb of Masauchan in the Wadi Umm el-Agerem. The inscription featured in Plate 41 is visible below the false door (source: ULVS).

48 (*Top left*) Aerial view of the main *gasr* (Agl) in the Wadi Umm el-Agerem, close to cemetery Ag 2, showing traces (left) of the earlier *opus africanum* farm incorporated into the interior of the later fortified farm. The extensive subsidiary settlement to the right is thought to be of late Roman date, cf. Figs 8:5, 11:2 (source: ULVS).

49 (*Top right*) Fortified farms (*gsur*) in the lower Wadi Mansur, here with little more than a few hundred metres separating neighbouring structures.

50 (*Bottom left*) A classic example of the tower-like *gsur* in the Bir Scedua basin (BS 4).

51 (*Bottom middle*) Interior of another of the Bir Scedua *gsur* with characteristic niches and neatly coursed masonry.

52 (*Bottom right*) General view of the Ghirza settlement looking north (source: ULVS).

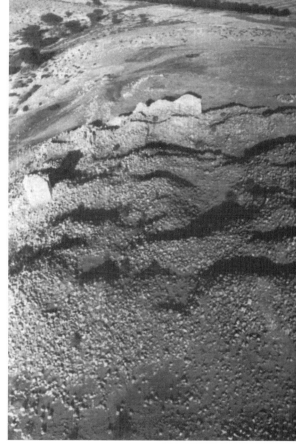

53 (*Above left*) Detail of one of the fortified farms (building 26) of the Ghirza settlement (source: ULVS).

54 (*Above right*) Aerial view of the ruinous remains of building 31, one of the two main complexes at Ghirza. It comprised a central *gasr*-like building, with well-built subsidiary ranges erected on all sides (source: ULVS).

55 (*Bottom left*) Aerial view of one of the smaller *gsur* of the Ghirza settlement (building 1) with its attendant satellite structures (source: ULVS).

56 (*Bottom right*) The northern group of mausolea at Ghirza (from right to left tombs North A, B, C, D, E, F) (source: ULVS).

57 (*Left*) Tomb North C at Ghirza, detail of west side (source: ULVS).

58 (*Below*) The church at Souk el-Oti, Wadi Buzra, looking west. In the foreground is the back of the eastern apse, inserted in a secondary phase into the nave.

59 (*Above*) Ploughing and sowing scene, tomb South C,
Ghirza (the Jamahiriya's Museum, Tripoli).

60 (*Left*) Reaping scene, tomb North
B, Ghirza. Note the ears of grain laid
on the threshing floor to left (the
Jamahiriya's Museum, Tripoli).

61 (*Below*) Camel caravan, tomb South C, Ghirza, perhaps
showing surplus produce of region being taken to market
(the Jamahiriya's Museum, Tripoli).

patterns of the *praesides* of *Tripolitana*. Indeed of the provinces that emerged from the Diocletianic reforms, once *Numidia* was reunited *c.* 314 and promoted to consular rank *c.* 320, *Tripolitana* would appear to have been the least important in terms of the stature of its governors. However, unlike most of the other civil governors of the African provinces, the Tripolitanian *praesides* are attested down to *c.* 360 as having military responsibilities for the border troops stationed on the *limites*. Donaldson has argued that this was the normal situation until the 370s at least, but the traditional view that the *comes Africae* was exercising full military authority at the time of the *Austuriani* raids in the 360s has much to recommend it.

In the later fourth century the meagre military forces were certainly under the control of other officials. The *Notitia Dignitatum* records a *dux provinciae Tripolitanae* (subordinate to the *comes Africae*) alongside the civil *praeses*; in AD 393 there was a *dux et corrector limitis Tripolitani* (presumably combining civil and military responsibilities); and in 406–08 we find a *comes et dux provinciae Tripolitanae* probably operating alongside the *praeses*. These men were of higher rank, the *dux* of the *Notitia* being a *vir spectabilis*, the *dux et corrector* and the *comes et dux* being *viri clarissimi*. The reasons for the higher grade of military personnel in the province in the late fourth and early fifth century will be considered in the next chapter. Overall, however, the impression is that *Tripolitana* became something of a backwater after the division of the old province.[3]

Tripolitana survived as a Roman province for some years after the Vandal conquest of much of the rest of the Maghreb in the years following AD 429. After the fall of Carthage in 439, and the completion of the Vandal takeover of all the provinces to the west in 442, *Tripolitana* was presumably attached to the diocese of *Oriens* for a few years until it was ceded to the Vandals in 455. The Roman province was succeeded by a Byzantine one of the same name after the reconquest by Belisarius in 533, but Byzantine *Tripolitana* was a mere shadow of the former region (see chapter 12)

Some scholars have wished to trace the erosion of territory to a far earlier date. Courtois suggested that from its foundation the province of *Tripolitana* comprised little more than the coastal strip in the east, with the frontier extending into the interior only in the western part of the province, but his extreme position has been countered by most subsequent analyses. On the other hand, it is clear that the late empire was a period of fundamental change in almost every aspect of provincial life. This chapter will focus on the period from the Tetrarchic reforms to the Vandal invasion and seek to examine the possible causes of change and decline in the fortunes of the region.[4]

2
THE TRIBAL SITUATION

The picture presented by late Roman sources of the tribal groupings living within and beyond the fringes of the province shows some degree of continuity with the earlier sources (chapter 2 above). However, there are numerous mentions of new groupings, that represented either the coalescence of existing tribes into larger confederations or the impact of newly arrived desert tribes from further east or a combination of the two factors. The full significance of a revival or revitalization of tribal aggression can only be guessed at but the overall effect is clear from the periodic records of renewed instability on the frontier from the late third century onwards. Two of the names that appear in the late empire seem to have had specifically broad connotations, *Laguatan* and *Arzuges*.

The *Laguatan*

The *Laguatan* confederation provide an element of coherence to the otherwise confused events of the later Roman empire, the Vandal period, the Byzantine reoccupation and the Arab invasions. It is known under several variant names, *Laguatan* and the plural form *Ilaguas* (used by Corippus in the sixth century), *Leuathae* (Procopius, likewise in the sixth century) and *Lawata* (in the early Arab sources). The form *Laguatan* is adopted here as Corippus generally gave transcriptions rather than Latinized versions of Libyan names. Careful study of Corippus' epic poem, *Iohannidos*, reveals that the *Laguatan* were a great confederacy composed of many sub-tribes. There has been unnecessary confusion amongst modern commentators who have often described the sub-tribes as distinct tribal groupings. The confederation seems to have been known by the name *Austuriani* or *Ausuriani* in the fourth and early fifth centuries, since Corippus traced the military confrontation between the *Laguatan* and Rome to the late third century and there is other evidence to suggest that the *Austuriani* corresponded to a sub-tribe of the group known later as *Laguatan*.[5]

Both Corippus and Procopius indicated that the *Laguatan/Leuathae* were the principal tribal group in Tripolitania in the sixth century. By the time of the Arab invasions *Lawata* tribes were to be found over much of the territory between Cyrenaica and eastern Algeria. The confederation clearly absorbed many of the earlier tribes of this vast region, but the nucleus of this super-tribe was probably built around a migration of new people from the eastern Sahara. Their point of origin is thought to have been the northern oases of the western Egyptian desert, an area they

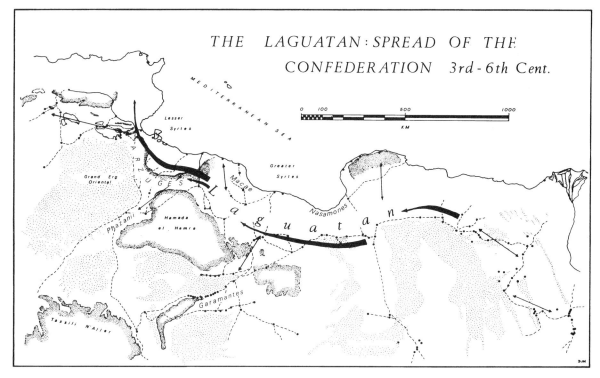

THE LAGUATAN : SPREAD OF THE CONFEDERATION 3rd - 6th Cent.

Fig. 9:1 The spread of the *Laguatan* confederation along the oases of the northern Sahara (from Mattingly 1983).

were traditionally linked with as *Botr* berbers. These *Botr* 'néoberbères' moved westwards along the Siwa–Augila chain of oases from the third century AD onwards, an action which was to destabilize the frontiers of *Cyrenaica* and *Tripolitana* (Fig. 9.1).[6]

The hierarchical structure of this confederation can be easily demonstrated. The 'countless' tribes of the *Laguatan*, under the control of great chieftains such as Antalas, Ierna and Carcasan, defeated the Byzantine army on several occasions. Corippus could not resist calling these chieftains 'tyrants' but it is clear from his account that the major decisions of war and peace were taken by all the assembled sub-chiefs. The selection of an overall chieftain by the *Laguatan* was a wartime measure. In times of peace the individual sub-tribes seem to have conducted their own political relations with *Byzantium*. In AD 544, 80 *Laguatan* chiefs presented themselves to the new Byzantine *dux* for confirmation of their peace-treaties. Some of these sub-tribes may have been of minor importance, but since the tribes represented were presumably only those closest to *Tripolitana*, the scale of the *Laguatan* confederation must have been enormous. In certain cases Corippus established hierarchical links between sub-tribal names and the *Laguatan*. Carcasan, for instance, was the chief of the *Ifuraces* tribe before he

became the overall chieftain of the *Laguatan*.[7] Quite a list can be compiled of *Laguatan* sub-tribes (cf. Table 2:3).

Austuriani, Ausuriani, Austur

The first Roman contact with the *Laguatan* was at the end of the third century AD, when Maximian made two raids to the Syrtic region. The next major problems recorded were caused by the *Austuriani* tribe in the second half of the fourth century and early fifth century. This tribe is assumed to have been the same as the raiders who devastated *Cyrenaica* in the early fifth century and who were described by Synesius as *Ausuriani*. To have attacked both *Cyrenaica* and *Tripolitana* these tribes must have had Syrtic bases, presumably in the southern oases. This is also the region the *Austur* of Corippus came from. The *Austuriani* have generally been viewed by modern commentators as a separate entity from the *Laguatan*, yet in the sixth century the *Austur* were considered a sub-tribe of the *Laguatan*: clearly they represent a historical stage in the rise of the *Laguatan*, with the change of name probably reflecting a shift in the sub-tribal balance of power. The identification of the *Austuriani* with the *Laguatan* establishes a common origin of the raids in the late Roman period.[8]

Ifuraces

Carcasan served under Ierna as chief of a *Laguatan* sub-tribe, the *Ifuraces*, and following the death of Ierna in AD 547 he was elected chief of the confederation. The *Ifuraces* were, thus, unquestionably a sub-tribe of the *Laguatan*.

Mecales

The *Mecales* were mentioned by Corippus, along with the *Ifuraces* in a passage concerning the Tripolitanian tribes. *Imaclas* may be the plural form for this tribal name. They were most likely a *Laguatan* tribe.

Mazices/Mazaces/Mazax *and* Ursiliani/Urceliana

The *Mazices* and *Ursiliani* were described by Vegetius as desert tribes of Syrtica. The names reappear in Corippus as *Mazax* and *Urceliana*, although *Mazax* is generally used as a synonym for *Laguatan* rather than to indicate a sub-tribal ethnic group and the Libyan ethnic name *Mazices* was very common in North Africa. The *Urceliana manus* were encountered by the Byzantine army in the western Gefara and forced into an alliance. This apparent westward movement of the *Ursiliani/Urceliana* is additional reason for identifying them as a migratory *Laguatan* tribe.[9]

Other sub-tribes and allies

The *Anacutas, Silcadenit, Silvacae* and *Silvaizan* are representative of a great number of other minor tribal names mentioned by Corippus which might relate to *Laguatan* tribes or to allied tribes from *Tripolitana* and *Byzacena*. The military confederation extended beyond those *Laguatan* tribes that were allied on ethnic grounds. For instance, the *Nasamones, Seli, Macae* and *Gaetuli* were progressively absorbed into the hegemony. Following Ierna's defeat in 547 a new *Laguatan* confederacy was gathered. Horsemen spread the news to all the barbarians under their domination (*a Syrtibus alae/invitantque feras regni sub imagine gentes*). The army that was gathered included the Nasamonian cultivators of the Syrtic shore and the barbarian neighbours of the *Garamantes*.[10]

Lawata, Hawara, Nefusa

The early Arab historians encountered the *Lawata* people across an enormous geographical zone from the Egyptian deserts to the Aures in Algeria and also in north Tunisia. In Tripolitania the principal sub-divisions in Arab times were the *Hawara* and the *Nefusa*. The segmental structure of these sub-tribes is apparent, down to the level of the family unit.[11]

In sum, the *Laguatan* appear to have started as a new generation of Berber tribes migrating through the deserts from the east. The process may have been slow at first, a gradual movement from oasis to oasis. The tribesmen possessed many things in common with the established tribes, notably *Ammon* worship, and the migration seems to have absorbed elements of the existing tribes. The confederation was swelled by each military victory as further tribes accepted the hegemony. A more crucial phase was entered when the *Laguatan* came within range of the 'ecological niches' of *Tripolitana* and *Cyrenaica*. At first there was plunder and destruction but later some of the *Laguatan* settled. It is inaccurate to describe the *Laguatan* as camel-riding nomads who were simply intent on the destruction of settled farming. It also obscures the significance of their role in the downfall of the Roman *limes*.

The *Laguatan* have generally been described as a nomadic tribe of the most 'aggressive' type. If they are identified with the *Austuriani* of the fourth and fifth centuries AD, as I have argued, then their association with destructive raiding is established for a period of over 300 years. But not all the references to the *Laguatan* depicted them as unsettled nomads. The 80 *Laguatan* (*Leuathae*) sub-chiefs who presented themselves, as representatives of the Tripolitanian tribes, to Sergius, the new Byzantine governor at *Lepcis*, requested the confirmation of their treaties. The hinterland zone of *Tripolitana* included the region of *gasr*-settlement of Gebel and pre-desert, where Arab writers recorded the take-over of lands by the *Laguatan*. Some of the *Laguatan* sub-tribes were therefore established by the sixth century in a seigneurial capacity in agricultural regions of Tripolitania, alongside those of the original settlers who had joined their confederation. Furthermore, the *Laguatan* chiefs complained to Sergius that Byzantine troops had been pillaging their crops. This reversal of roles is a useful corrective to the view that the *Laguatan* were simply migratory nomads. An important faction of the confederation was eager to settle and exploit agricultural land whose owners had been dispossessed and driven off. Arab sources recorded the presence of *Laguatan* in practically every 'ecological niche' between the Nile and the Aures, so the process of sedentarization seems to have consistently followed the process of migration and conquest. The growth of the confederation through association of already sedentarized tribes amplified this trend.[12]

The *Arzuges/regio Arzugum*

From the fourth century AD Roman sources referred to people called *Arzuges* and a *regio Arzugum*, located in the old frontier zone of *Tripolitana*. The *regio* was in some way connected with, but at the same time distinct from, *Tripolitana*. Records of ecclesiastical councils show that the area had separate bishops and that those of *Tripolitana* came only from the coastal towns. In AD 411 the bishop of Tozeur passed through the *regio Arzugum* whilst on his way to Carthage, presumably by boat from *Tacapae*. This suggests that the old territory of the *Nybgenii*, the Nefzaoua, lay within the region. A letter of St Augustine also mentioned the *regio Arzugum* and distinguished it as the most southerly part of the North African provinces and as lying south of *Tripolitana*. In another correspondence further details emerge which confirm that the *regio* was the frontier zone of the old province of *Tripolitana*. The letters described pagan barbarians being allowed into the province to seek work as crop watchers or porters after swearing oaths before the commander of the border troops. Orosius stated that the *regio* was indeed formerly part of *Tripolitana*. However, he also added a rider to the effect that *Arzuges* was a term applicable to the tribes all along the *limites* of Africa. Corippus referred to the 'savage land of the *Arzuges*' in the sixth century, though seemingly by then it was of diminished importance. Such a description is well suited for the pre-desert frontier zone, as Goodchild long ago noted.[13]

On the origin of the term *Arzuges*, opinion is also divided. Bates established a tenuous etymological connection with the name *Austuriani* but has not been followed in this interpretation by other commentators. The Trajanic boundary stone from Bir Soltane which named the *Arzosei* is more often used as evidence for a tribal origin. A recently published inscription of the AD 240s records some sort of dedication by the governor of *Numidia* to the *Arzugi*, surely the earliest mention of either the region or its people. It is worth considering that the name may not be that of a tribal *gens* at all but, as Orosius implied, a general Libyan term of late date applicable to all the *gentiles* of the frontier zone in Roman Africa. At any rate, it developed a special significance for the frontier zone of *Tripolitana* and it is clear that the *Arzuges* comprised elements of the earlier population of that frontier zone, *Gaetuli, Macae* and *Libyphoenices*.[14]

The growth of the *Laguatan* confederation in *Tripolitana* in the fifth and sixth centuries must have been at the expense of the *Arzuges*. In the sixth century the *regio Arzugum* had shrunk both in size and importance. The decline of the *Arzuges* is indicative of the revived tribalism in many areas following the Vandal conquest and the collapse of Roman rule.

Some of the tribal names recorded by Corippus, especially those which bear comparison with earlier ethnic labels or which suggest associations with the wooded Gebel area, may have been those of the descendants of the *Arzuges*: the *Anacutas* and *Astrikes*, the *Muctunia manus*, the *Silcadenit, Silvacae, Silvaizan*. To these may be added the populations of *Talanteis* and *Tillibaris*, surely the old *limes* stations of *Talalati* and *Tillibari*, the Bir ed-Dreder *tribuni* and some of the mixed Libyan and Libyphoenician *gsur*-dwellers of pre-desert and Gebel.[15]

3
MILITARY PROBLEMS

When the fort at Bu Njem was abandoned *c*. 263, it was part of an orderly redeployment, apparently not brought about by unrest along the frontier. By the end of the third century, however, the *Laguatan* had unexpectedly emerged as a new threat to the region. It is likely that at this stage they were operating along the great east to west chain of oases on the line Siwa–Augila–Giofra. During his military expedition to Africa in the 290s, Maximian apparently made two expeditions against these new tribes, perhaps re-establishing a basis for treaty relations. At any rate we have no record of further trouble until the mid-fourth century.[16]

In the 360s the *Austuriani* unleashed a series of great raids against *Tripolitana* from their oasis bases in Syrtica, the immediate *causus belli* being the execution by burning of one of their chiefs. This man, Stachao, had been arrested within the province and accused of spying out the land and inciting trouble. The evidence was clearcut, according to Ammianus, and the punishment was defined by law. Under the terms of normal frontier control he had probably been able to enter provincial territory under the pretext of legitimate business (transportation of goods, flock or crop-watching, or as an harvester). The fact that Stachao was stirring up trouble amongst people within the frontier shows that the breakdown of treaty arrangements had already begun before his execution.[17]

Epigraphic evidence suggests that the build up of tension had been going on for some time and this makes the Roman authorities all the more culpable for their failure to anticipate the invasion or to remedy the situation when it happened. Flavius Archontius Nilus, who was *comes* as well as *praeses provinciae Tripolitanae c.* AD 355–60, had military as well as civil responsibilities. He is known on inscriptions from *Lepcis, Gigthis* and the fort at Ras el-Ain (where major repairs were undertaken). Another governor at about this time was Flavius Nepotianus, though his term of office is imprecisely placed between 355–70. He, too, was *comes et praeses* and the style and wording of the honorific inscription erected to him at *Lepcis* is very close to those erected to Nilus. It is possible therefore that he was governor before the great Austurian invasions began in 363. Indeed the *Lepcis* inscription has a smug and self-confident tone which would have been entirely inappropriate in the aftermath of the disasters of the mid-360s. If, as I believe, he was governor between 355–62, then there was a harsh irony in the claim in this inscription that, having defeated the barbarians, he had made the frontiers secure even against future attacks.[18]

Nilus and Nepotianus may have been the last *praesides* to exercise military powers. It was a period of rising tension and Nepotianus evidently took the field and gained a minor success. They were credited with strengthening both city and provincial defences. But it appears that command of the troops based permanently in *Tripolitana* was passed to the *comes Africae* in the period immediately before the first invasion, perhaps coincident with the appointment in AD 363 of a new *comes*, Romanus, whose infamy was recorded in some detail by Ammianus. It would appear that this was the moment when the Stachao incident occurred and, before the province could be reinforced, it was overrun.

The *Austuriani* raids were swift and fierce and were apparently not opposed by any significant body of troops. In 363 they reached the fertile hinterland of *Lepcis* (presumably the Gebel Tarhuna and Msellata regions) where they remained for three days pillaging and burning. Silva, the leading *curialis* of *Lepcis*, was captured on one of his country estates and carried off (presumably to be offered for ransom). Some time later, following an appeal from the Lepcitanians, Romanus arrived at *Lepcis* with the field army but refused to launch a retaliatory campaign unless the *Lepcitani* provided supplies and 4,000 camels. When these were not forthcoming after about 40 days he simply marched away. Although generally condemned for his apparent extortion it is not implausible that Romanus felt himself genuinely under-equipped and under-provisioned to pursue the tribesmen to their desert bases. Moreover, the African army were owed arrears of pay at this time and their willingness to undertake a desert campaign under their new commander was perhaps open to question. For their part, the *Lepcitani* may well have been unable to meet Romanus' requirements because of the losses they had already suffered to their camel herds and agricultural surpluses.

Although some military units were briefly placed under the control of the *praeses*, when these troops were returned to Romanus in 365 a further raid occurred and this time the death and devastation was shared by the *territorium* of *Oea*. Many leading citizens died, most, like Rusticianus, a former provincial priest, and Nicasius, an *aedile*, caught on their rural estates. The following year, and still unopposed by a Roman army, the *Austuriani* came again and actually besieged *Lepcis* and laid waste and looted numerous estates. Olives and vines are mentioned as having been chopped down on this occasion. Mychon, another important *curialis* from *Lepcis,* was captured on the outskirts of the town. He attempted to escape by jumping into an empty well, sustaining minor injuries. The tribesmen pulled him out and paraded him before the walls of the city until his wife raised a substantial ransom. However, after being hauled up the walls by a rope, he died within a few days from the after-effects of his ordeal. The siege of *Lepcis* had lasted for eight days when, having sustained some casualties, the 'somewhat disappointed' *Austuriani* withdrew.

Romanus and a number of other corrupt imperial agents contrived to cover up this incident for many years and little seems to have been done to repair the damage done to the province and to Roman deterrent diplomacy.[19]

The *Austuriani/Laguatan* repeated their raids against both *Tripolitana* and *Cyrenaica* in the late fourth and early fifth century. Contrary to the arguments advanced by Donaldson, it is very unlikely that the civil *praesides* continued to have military responsibilities at this date. Action was sometimes taken by the *comes Africae* himself, as in the case of Flavius Victorianus who was active in *Tripolitana* between 375–8, though fighting a defensive action rather than launching an offensive campaign against the tribal centres. An alternative strategy was to bolster the low-grade border troops with a few higher calibre units under the command of a subordinate of the *comes*. Changes in the command structure in the later fourth century are probably to be interpreted in this light. In 393 a certain Silvanus was described as *dux et corrector limitis Tripolitani*, from his title evidently with some civil responsibility but still subordinate to the *comes Africae*. This may have been a short-term measure since by 406 a separate command had been created, that of *comes et dux provinciae Tripolitanae*. One of the men of *vir clarissimus* rank to hold this office, Flavius Ortygius (between 408–23) was commemorated for having repelled an Austurian attack. His tenure of the office may well have been closer to 408, since the *Notitia* (probably achieving its final form for this part of Africa towards 423) records simply a *dux* and gives him the higher rank of *vir spectabilis*. The gradual increase in the rank of military commander and the evidence from the *Notitia Dignitatum* for the presence of a few units of good quality troops (*ripenses*) suggests that the threat of warfare on the Tripolitanian frontier had again increased in this period.[20]

4
THE NATURE OF TRIBAL ATTACKS: THE MYTH OF THE CAMEL

What was the nature of the threat posed by African tribal groups in the late empire? The belief has been widespread that the Roman *limites* in Africa were confronted and overrun by an enemy whose potency was revived by the diffusion of the camel. It has even been claimed that the frontier earthworks, *clausurae* and *fossata,* were erected as late as the fourth century AD as barriers against such nomadic raiding. Such theories, especially prevalent in nineteenth- and early twentieth-century scholarship, were coloured by the European colonial experience of 'aggressive nomadism', involving camel-riding Touareg and others operating from oasis bases deep into the Sahara. Although there is now a trend towards modifying some of these ideas, their influence is pervasive and a more thorough reappraisal is necessary.

There are four main defects in these arguments. First, the existence of the camel in the northern Sahara can be demonstrated at a much earlier date than the period when the raiding commenced, with its use being essentially as a beast of burden or a working farm animal. Second, there is no evidence to support the idea of a transformation of the camel into a beast of warfare in the later period. The case cannot be convincingly made because it is based almost entirely on modern colonial experience and the incautious interpretation of a few source references. A third point concerns the implied responsibility of the camel for the unleashing of the desert tribes and the decline of Rome. As well as being entirely unprovable it offers a very limited explanation for the end of the Roman *limites*. Fourth, there is ample literary evidence for the later Roman and Byzantine periods which details the practices of equine cavalry warfare among the supposed 'camel nomads'. This is entirely conclusive evidence to demolish the myth of the camel.

The camel was present in the northern Sahara in late prehistoric times, probably towards the end of the first millennium BC. Archaeological evidence, in particular relief carvings, demonstrates the use of the camel as both a farm animal and beast of burden in

the second and third centuries AD. The introduction of the camel cannot then be placed as late as the fourth century nor, alternatively, explained away as a 'gift' from Septimius Severus to his homeland. The North African camel probably originated in Egypt and its diffusion was along the east-to-west caravan routes.

There is in fact no clearcut evidence for the camel playing other than a passive role in the warfare of the late Roman period. Representations of camels ploughing are common in Tripolitania and there is also evidence for their use on the caravan routes and for local haulage of goods. These are tasks the camel is well suited to. Particularly on desert marches the camel's greater carrying capacity, hardiness and low water consumption give it a distinct advantage over horses, mules and oxen. But it is a mistake to believe that the diffusion of the camel rendered these other animals superfluous in desert transport. Furthermore, although the camel is the superior animal for desert travel, particularly in a stone desert where it is less prone to lameness, one can question the assumption that it is a superior beast for warfare. The greater short-range speed and agility of the horse are compensation enough. Indeed, there is no evidence that the fighting potential of ridden camels was exploited until well after the Arab conquest of the Maghreb.[21]

The historical evidence used to identify the camel with the destructive raids is very thin. Vegetius mentioned 'camel-riding' tribes from the Syrtic region, the *Mazices* and *Ursiliani*. Another possible piece of evidence is the description of the *Laguatan* confederation gathered by Carcasan which included cavalry, infantry and 'those who rode camels following the custom of the Moors'. Also Procopius and Corippus referred to the Libyan custom of forming defences for their encampments by placing rings of tethered camels round the outside. The 'passive' use of camels here had a disruptive effect on attempted enemy cavalry attacks and the tactic was successful on at least one occasion during the *Laguatan* wars with the Vandals and *Byzantium*.[22]

The references to camels, particularly in the latter example, have led to a concentration on this one aspect of late tribal warfare to the exclusion of conflicting, or clarifying, information. Reading the secondary literature, one would imagine that the tactic of counter-attack from behind a wall of camels was the only strategy employed by the *Laguatan* against regular field armies. Camels were certainly present in large numbers in the region – Courtois calculated that thousands of them were needed by the *Laguatan* to form their 'camel-ramparts' and Synesius, for instance, bewailed the fate of *Cyrenaica* when the *Ausuriani* raiders in the early fifth century rustled

5,000 camels to carry off their booty. Similarly, when Romanus demanded that the *Lepcitani* provide 4,000 camels for a retaliatory expedition against the *Austuriani*, the *Lepcitani* were outraged not so much because the number was inconceivably high, but because their camel herds had probably been too depleted by the raids to meet it.[23]

There is no reason to doubt, then, that the *Laguatan* possessed large numbers of camels but the same was also true of the cities of the *Pentapolis* and *Tripolitana*. Some of the camels could have been ridden by the *Laguatan*, though the only example in Corippus did not refer to a battle. The *Ausuriani* used the camels they rustled in *Cyrenaica* to carry away their booty, not for riding. Nor did Ammianus Marcellinus or Synesius, an eye-witness to the raids, mention camels being ridden by the raiders. In two of his letters Synesius described chance meetings with small groups of the barbarians who rode horses and who dismounted to fight.[24]

The *Iohannidos* of Corippus is by far the most important source for the practice of warfare in the Byzantine period and although he had access to eye-witness accounts, he nowhere mentioned camels ridden in battle. On the contrary his accounts of battles were full of references to *Laguatan* cavalry. He described the battles at two levels. On the one hand, they were a string of personal combats between the glorified Roman heroes and individual Libyans in the tradition of epic poems. There is a second level of treatment, which used contemporary information to provide a generally reliable overall picture of the battles. From both categories of description the information on the *Laguatan* is the same, namely, that they fought as light armed cavalry (the elite troops) and infantry. There are over 50 references to Libyans riding horses in battle. Procopius also confirmed that the *Laguatan* warriors of the sixth century still depended on the skill and sheer numbers of their equine cavalry for their success.[25]

It is clear from this evidence that the importance of the horse in warfare had not diminished in the sixth century, let alone by the third or fourth, as has sometimes been argued. The camel remained primarily a beast of burden, carrying goods and the non-combatant camp followers. Along with the other pack-animals the camels were used to form a rudimentary cordon around the camp. The *Laguatan* warriors, then, did not ride camels but Corippus did reveal the identity of those amongst the Libyan people who did. As well as carrying the baggage and tents of the *Laguatan*, the camels bore their women and children.[26]

The defensive walls of camels were a passive rather than an active use of the animal, and depended for their success on the unsettling effect of the camels' smell on attacking cavalry. The *Laguatan* fought on foot when defending these fortifications, standing between the legs of the camels for cover. The ranks of camels were only part of the total defences, however, as the full obstacle course also included tethered rows of cattle and mules as well as sheep and goats. This type of defence was a logical response from people on the move in the semi-desert, in the same way that the cordon of covered wagons was used on the trails of the American west. The defences were constructed from the non-combatant animals in order to protect the goods and families of the *Laguatan* during the battle. The horses were not included in the defences for the obvious reason that they were needed for the serious fighting. The *Laguatan* cavalry was well capable of fighting and winning battles. The defensive strategy was only resorted to when the odds clearly favoured the Byzantine army in a pitched battle or when the cavalry had suffered an initial defeat and staged their last-ditch resistance at their camp. Ibn Khaldun recorded the same practice among the Berber tribes after the Arab conquest, where lines of camels and baggage animals drawn up behind the fighting men steadied their nerve and gave them a position to fall back on. The same tactic is probably to be inferred in the comment of Vegetius that certain tribes drew camels up into lines. Since the camels and flocks of the tribes were an important resource, their employment as vulnerable defensive lines in battle was not undertaken lightly. Fighting from such positions, therefore, was not the battle tactic of choice but a sign of desperation when cornered. The preferred fighting option was in the open field with swift, light-armed equine cavalry.[27]

The tribes in the late Roman period thus posed a rather similar type of threat to the horse-riding Libyans of earlier times. Why, then, was the military response to the tribal unrest so feeble? The principal answer lies in the unwillingness of the central government to commit (even on a temporary basis) field army units to a provincial backwater, such as *Tripolitana* had become. The *Notitia Dignitatum* listing of the troops of the *dux provinciae Tripolitanae*, which probably dates to the early fifth century, shows that he had no field army units at his disposal and only two higher grade units of border troops (*ripenses*) (see chapter 10 and Table 10.2 below). The field army units were primarily brigaded in western *Byzacena*, *Numidia* and *Mauretania*, where serious revolts such as that of Firmus (AD 373–5) were inevitably given a higher priority by the state than the protection of *Tripolitana*. All the available evidence, therefore, suggests that Rome made little attempt to wrest the initiative back from the *Laguatan* by launching campaigns against their centres. The installation of a garrison at *Lepcis* is evidence that the zone of effective military control in east *Tripolitana* had retreated towards the coast. Although locally recruited border troops remained in forts in both east and west *Tripolitana*, their numbers, armament and status had in all probability been downgraded to the point where they were of little use for anything but policing work. The number of cavalry amongst the border troops was probably far lower than in earlier times.

Minor raiding could be dealt with by such troops but anything on the scale of the *Austuriani* attacks, arguably involving hundreds or thousands of tribesmen, will have simply bypassed the garrison points with impunity. When diplomatic arrangements with the desert tribes broke down there would always be a time-lag before adequate troops could be on the spot to cope with major incursions. Against this background, it is likely that frontier deterrence increasingly gave way to attempts to buy off some of the tribes and to persuade them either to defend the province against their compatriots or simply to refrain from further attacks.

The situation in *Cyrenaica* at the same time was recorded in some detail and seems to have been remarkably similar. Synesius frequently castigated the efforts of the border units for their failure to take to the field against the raiders, but his letters also reveal the progressive fall in the rosters of units such as the *Unnigarde*, who comprised a mere 40 men, and were threatened with loss of their mounts and demotion to militia status. The inability and unwillingness of such units to venture out against the larger groups of raiders had severe repercussions in both zones. Agricultural territory was lost to the cities, treaties between Rome and both the enemies and the guardians of the frontiers became increasingly expensive and the *Laguatan* confederation grew by absorbing the populations of the previous frontier zones.[28]

Following the ceding of *Tripolitana* to the Vandals in AD 455, the *Laguatan* grew even more powerful in the Tripolitanian hinterland and the remaining Gebel lands of the cities were probably lost by the early sixth century when the Vandals themselves were defeated in battle and *Lepcis* abandoned and sacked. Similar advances were made by the *Laguatan* in *Cyrenaica* and the Byzantine government was forced to concentrate its military effort on the coastal cities and on maintaining diplomatic relations with the interior tribes. In *Tripolitana* the sixth-century Byzantine reoccupation was virtually limited to the coastal region. Most of John Troglitas' battles with the *Laguatan* took place close to the coast. His one attempt to campaign into the desert (perhaps advancing down the Dahar corridor) ended in an ignominious withdrawal when his supplies became suddenly exhausted.[29]

His problems resembled those of the late Roman period. The reaction to a regional threat was generally slow, by which time considerable damage could have been done, and, although fairly proficient in battle, his troops were not markedly superior to their native opponents. The failure to repeat the audacious long-range campaigning of earlier years was the crucial weakness, however, and eroded the basis of Roman deterrent diplomacy. In *Tripolitana* the late Roman decline of the frontier was aggravated further by two factors, namely, by its isolation from the command centre and bases of the field army and by the unforeseen and unchecked rise of the *Laguatan* confederation.

5
EARTHQUAKES

Tribal incursions were not the only catastrophes confronted by *Tripolitana* in the fourth century. Di Vita has argued from extensive evidence at *Sabratha* that the town was badly damaged in the wave of earthquakes that struck parts of North Africa and the eastern Mediterranean in AD 365. He has also argued, though with less solid evidence, that there was an earlier major earthquake in AD 306–10. The British excavations at *Sabratha* have produced ample evidence in support of the earthquake in the 360s and some more tenuous structural evidence from the east forum temple for the earlier incident. In the light of this, both di Vita and Kenrick have rejected Bartoccini's interpretation of the mid-fourth-century damage to practically all the major public buildings as being due to an (unrecorded) sack of the city by the *Austuriani*. In any case, the ability (or desire) of such raiders to have brought about the collapse of the major architectural structures of the town must be doubted. The scale of destruction is appropriate to a major earthquake and, as Kenrick suggests, this must have been accompanied by significant loss of life as well as property.[30]

Nor was *Sabratha* the only Tripolitanian city affected, since di Vita adduces similar evidence for *Lepcis* as well. *Oea*, of course, is not accessible for archaeological evaluation but its median position between the other two principal centres would suggest that it is unlikely to have escaped unscathed. At *Lepcis* there are indications of two phases of earthquake damage and destruction in the fourth century, the first of which may have affected *inter alia* the

Serapeum, the Flavian temple and the amphitheatre. The proposed date of *c.* 306–10 is derived from di Vita's own excavations in the *Lepcis* Serapeum and in Regio VI at *Sabratha*, though the chronological connection between those dated contexts and the other visible signs of late Roman structural damage and repair to buildings is difficult to establish. On the other hand, there is epigraphic evidence for significant rebuilding work undertaken by the Constantinian *praeses* Laenatius Romulus *c.* 324–6 in the central area of *Lepcis*. Among the monuments known to have undergone restoration at this juncture were the basilica, the old forum portico and the portico by the market. Other structures with archaeologically or epigraphically attested renovation in the first quarter of the fourth century include the Serapaeum, the Flavian temple, the Basilica Ulpia, the *schola* and the amphitheatre.

Evidence for earthquake damage in the 360s is absolutely incontrovertible at *Sabratha* and *Lepcis*. The problem lies in assigning a date (or dates) to it. There is, of course, a catastrophic earthquake recorded in the ancient sources as having taken place on 21 July 365, and scholars have commonly seized on this as a context for archaeologically attested seismic damage. But, as seismologists have pointed out, a single quake with a single epicentre could not possibly have caused all the reported instances of damage to Roman cities at about this date in a zone from Algeria through to the eastern Mediterranean. Di Vita has responded that, although it is impossible that the damage could have been done simultaneously at so many sites, a wave of successive shocks moving from west to east is plausible. Similarly, in a phase of heightened seismic activity, it is also probable that some damage was done (or completed) by minor quakes in the build-up to and the after-shocks following a succession of major earthquakes. So, although it is likely that the Tripolitanian evidence does relate primarily to damage sustained in AD 365, some structures weakened in that quake may not have collapsed until hit by more minor tremors in subsequent years.

In terms of collapsed and weakened buildings the restoration costs must have been extraordinarily high for the Tripolitanian towns to bear. Quite apart from the likely destruction of large areas of domestic and commercial premises, the damage at *Sabratha* appears to have included the civic basilica, curia, parts of the forum colonnades and paving, capitolium, east forum temple, Antonine temple, south forum temple, theatre, marine baths and temple of Isis. At *Lepcis* there is less clearcut evidence for widespread destruction but a number of individual buildings show clear signs of partial collapse: the Flavian temple (already at this date converted into habitations), the Serapaeum, the theatre, amphitheatre, circus, Hadrianic baths and the major diversion dam on the Wadi Lebda (leading to problems with flooding in the city centre).[31]

The scale of earthquake damage to the civic centre of *Sabratha* was particularly severe and the repairs to the civic fabric of the province must have been a terrible drain on resources just at the time that the leading families suffered terrific losses from their agricultural estates. Di Vita has also argued that there is evidence of earthquake destruction at some of the principal luxury villas along the Tripolitanian coast at this time. However, the possibility of human agency must here be given greater consideration. A large number of important town councillors and local officials were evidently surprised on their country estates by the *Austuriani* raiders of the 360s and Ammianus specifically mentions the extensive damage done to rural property. The most luxurious of the coastal villas were obvious targets for the raiders to have attacked, so the dereliction and lack of subsequent reoccupation of these properties was more likely due to human than natural causes.[32]

The conjuncture between this phase of earthquake damage and the major onslaught of the *Austuriani* may not be coincidental. The stricken cities must have seemed a soft target at that moment but we should not exclude the possibility that the Saharan oases centres had also suffered damage and loss, provoking unrest among the tribes. The Giofra oases, for instance, lie at the southern end of the major fault system in eastern Tripolitania, the Hun graben, and more recent quakes appear to have been frequently centred in this area. Earthquake activity on the coast, therefore, should have had its counterpart in some parts of the interior.

6
CIVIL LIFE AND CIVIL GOVERNMENT

Some recent work on late Roman life in the African provinces and *Cyrenaica* has proposed a significant revision to the general view that this was a time of degeneration and decline. The case has more credibility in some areas (*Africa*, *Byzacena*) than others (*Cyrenaica*, *Tripolitana*). *Lepcis Magna* is assumed to have been the capital of the province of *Tripolitana* on account of the numerous dedications there by, for, or on behalf of the *praeses*, the *vicarius* of Africa or the *vice agens* of the praetorian prefect – these being the senior officials with regular dealings with the province. The rank of the governor and the generally low-grade status of the border troops reflect a diminished level of imperial interest in the region from the very start of its existence as a separate province. But although the towns of *Tripolitana* may have passed their peak by the late second or early third century AD, the region was not entirely lacking in signs of vitality in the early fourth century. A variety of disasters, both human and natural, and official injustices were to change that irrevocably in the course of the century.

In the early part of the fourth century there was renewed building work or renovation at a number of cities although, as we have seen, this may have been occasioned by earthquake damage *c.* 306–10. Constantinian building at *Lepcis* is attested epigraphically, notably by the *praeses* Laenatius Romulus in 324–6, and the unfinished major bath complex in Regio V of the city most probably pre-date the AD 365 earthquake. Town walls at *Lepcis* and *Sabratha* are probably to be dated to the first quarter of the fourth century though it is uncertain whether various mid-fourth-century inscriptions at *Lepcis* mentioning *moenia* record repairs to town walls or to other public buildings in the town. Those inscriptions and others from *Sabratha* (for instance, repairs to the temple of Hercules in the 340s by the *praeses* Flavius Victor Calpurnius) provide valuable, if sparse, indications of continuing vitality.

The major evidence for fourth-century activity at *Lepcis* came from a series of dedications to the emperors, provincial governors and other officials set up by the *Lepcitani* in the increasingly congested Severan forum. A few of the leading families in the town were still of equestrian status, holding posts carrying *vir perfectissimus* or *vir clarissimus* rank, but the prominence of Lepcitanians in the imperial government and bureaucracy was less pronounced than before. Local society, however, continued to be dominated by the most important of these clans, Flavii Vibani, Volusii, Aemilii. Some of these families continued to support games in the local amphitheatre.[33]

The vitality of town life at the major centres was undoubtedly further undermined by the problems that beset the province in the 360s. Signally, there are no dated records of building activity at *Lepcis* after 360. The military disasters of the 360s were accompanied by a failure of the imperial government to do justice to the complaint made by the province against the failure of the *comes Africae* Romanus to take military action in their defence. The civil repercussions of the raids are only known to us because after the cover-up was exposed in the 370s Ammianus Marcellinus selected it as a suitable cautionary tale of official corruption and intrigue.

Following the first *Austuriani* raid in 363, the provincial council of *Tripolitana* initiated the process of complaint against Romanus, using the occasion of the accession of Valentinian as a context for sending envoys to make an appeal for assistance and justice. The complaint against an imperial official as powerful and well-connected as Romanus was a very risky manoeuvre and his side of the argument was forcefully presented by his supporters at court. Valentinian initially refused to accept either version of events and ordered a full inquiry, though this was soon stalled by Remigius, the Master of the Offices and a kinsman of Romanus. However, some troops were temporarily placed under the command of Ruricius, the *praeses* of *Tripolitana*, though once again Romanus' supporters quickly reversed this decision.

At the time of the second and third raids, the original envoys sent to Valentinian in 364 had still not returned from the imperial court at Trier. A second embassy was now sent, meeting the first envoys in Carthage where they had been sent to discuss their complaints with the vicar and Count Romanus himself. Perhaps because of this inauspicious development, the second embassy continued to Trier to press its appeal to the emperor, who had in the meantime sent a special envoy, Palladius, to assess the situation on the ground. Palladius brought with him arrears of pay owed to the troops in Africa, and Romanus arranged for the unit commanders to return a substantial part of this as personal gifts to the envoy on account of his importance at court.

Palladius was appalled by the state of the province and the destruction wrought by the raiders. Two Lepcitanians, Erechthius and Aristomenes, made detailed statements to him about the losses of the town. But when Palladius threatened to expose Romanus, the latter sprang his own trap – revealing his knowledge of Palladius' dishonesty over the military pay. Palladius was now obliged to back Romanus and, as a result of the former's report to Valentinian that the Tripolitanians were guilty of false testimony, the full weight of judicial savagery was directed against those involved in the case on behalf of the province. Knowing its cause was lost and under enormous pressure from an agent of Romanus, Caecilius (evidently a native of *Tripolitana*), the city council of *Lepcis* was persuaded to disown its second group of envoys for having over-stepped their brief. Of the four envoys, two had died during their travels but the surviving member of the second embassy, Jovinus, was executed along with three other citizens, Caelestinus, Concordius and Lucius (presumably leading *curiales* who had been at the forefront in urging the policy of appealing to Valentinian). The remaining envoy from the first mission was also put on trial and would probably have been sentenced to death had he not bribed his guards and escaped into hiding. Erechthius and Aristomenes, who stood accused of misleading Palladius, would have had their tongues cut out had they too not fled incognito to a place 'far from *Lepcis*'. The *praeses* of *Tripolitana*, Ruricius ('whose lies were aggravated by his intemperate language'), was sentenced to death and executed at *Sitifis*, perhaps Romanus' headquarters. A notable feature of the entire case is that the emperor, in assessing Romanus' conduct, does not at any stage seem to have paid much attention to the reports that emanated from his own provincial governor on the spot. The word of a mere *vir perfectissimus* was not to be set against that of a *vir spectabilis*.

The state of the province in the 360s was altered dramatically by a combination of factors, starting with serious losses to the rural infrastructure and wealth of the province, compounded by serious earthquake damage to the civic centres and exacerbated by the public clash between the province and the count Romanus and the humiliation and execution of Ruricius. Romanus enjoyed a long tenure of office as *comes*, being still in post at the time of the revolt of Firmus in 373.

The latter incident proved to be the unravelling of the official conspiracy and cover-up concerning the Tripolitanian complaints of the 360s. Theodosius, the *magister equitum* and leader of the expeditionary force sent by Valentinian to counter the rebellion led by Firmus, arrested Romanus on the grounds that his vindictiveness towards Firmus was partly responsible for the outbreak. Amongst his papers was a letter revealing that Palladius had lied to the emperor in support of Romanus. Palladius was arrested, but committed suicide, Romanus' agent Caecilius admitted under torture to having persuaded the Lepcitanians to disown their own envoys and Erechthius and Aristomenes emerged from hiding to tell their story to a new commission comprising the vicar and proconsul of Africa. As for Romanus, he continued to plead his own innocence to Gratian, after the death of Valentinian in 375. It is unclear to what extent the imperial authorities made amends to the Tripolitanians.[34]

The later civic epigraphy of *Tripolitana* is notable for the grandiloquent language with which governors and officials were honoured for their services to the community. Undoubtedly much of this was hyperbole and claims that individuals had restored the frontiers, beaten off the barbarians, revived the fortunes of the town and so forth must be treated with a degree of scepticism. *Sabratha*, however, shows some signs of a concerted effort to overcome the earthquake damage

of 365. Although parts of the town were abandoned permanently, there was a well-organized attempt to rebuild the civic centre. Reusable materials, especially marble, were stockpiled in the shattered theatre and in the vaults of the Capitoline temple, while a number of important structures were fully reconstructed, most notably the civic basilica (converted into a church subsequently), the curia and the north forum portico, and some new churches were built (churches 3 and 4). This work was slow (certainly continuing in the late 370s) and only achieved with official help, whether from individual *praeses* or by more direct appeals to the emperor, as Lucius Aemilius Quintus (honoured at *Sabratha*, *Gigthis* and *Lepcis Magna*) seems to have done on behalf of the impoverished towns. At *Lepcis*, by contrast, there is little evidence of urban renewal after 365, though the churches of the city are poorly dated. However, the cumulative picture from excavations of a number of the earlier major buildings is of widespread change of use for the former public spaces. Some at least of the luxury coastal villas of the elite seem to have been permanently abandoned after the 360s and those rural estates that endured took on an increasingly fortified appearance (chapters 10–11).[35]

7
CONCLUSION: STABILITY OR DECLINE?

It is not being unduly pessimistic to say that the fourth century, and particularly its middle decades, brought catastrophic change to the province as a whole. The combined effects of the *Laguatan/ Austuriani* attacks, earthquakes and discriminatory or indifferent treatment by the high officials of state left the province a much changed place. Early fourth-century building schemes at *Lepcis* had not been sustained and there are comparatively few records of renovation or new construction after the 340s. The breaching of the diversionary dam on the Wadi Lebda (perhaps in the earthquakes of the mid-360s) may have had a double negative effect, first by exposing areas of the town to the threat of inundation during flash floods, and second by accelerating the siltation of the town's harbour basin into which the Lebda flowed. The market was sub-divided into small habitations by the early fifth century, the theatre and amphitheatre became fortified residences (as did the amphitheatre at *Sabratha* in late antiquity), numerous temples were abandoned or similarly converted to domestic or commercial premises. The character of the great civic monuments – especially the pagan

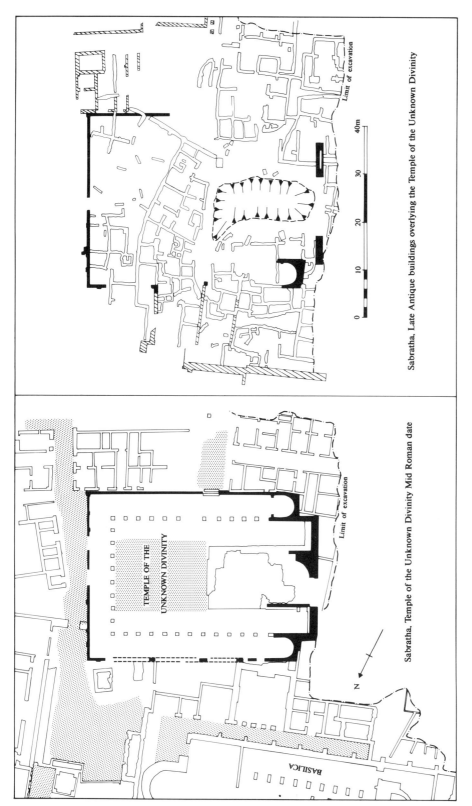

Sabratha, Late Antique buildings overlying the Temple of the Unknown Divinity

Sabratha, Temple of the Unknown Divinity Mid Roman date

Fig. 9:2 Late antique structures on the podium of the Temple of the Unknown Divinity, (= South Forum Temple), *Sabratha* (after Joly and Tomasello 1984).

temples – was altered radically with houses and workshops created out of their fabric. The Flavian temple at *Lepcis* was converted into houses and pottery workshops, built both under and over the vaults of the ruined temple. Similar structures have been traced at *Sabratha* from the final phase of the south forum temple (Fig. 9:2). From the 360s it appears that large areas of *Lepcis* were no longer occupied, with sand and rubble filling the buildings and minor streets. The main roads passing through these quarters were kept open by the device of bricking up the doorways of the abandoned properties on either side. Procopius confirms that even prior to the Vandal take-over, a large part of the city had been abandoned to the sand dunes. By the time of the Byzantine reconquest, the town itself had been temporarily deserted as a result of the complete loss of neighbouring land to the *Laguatan*.

Abandonment of outlying areas and conversion of public buildings to private or commercial use does not imply terminal decadence and 'squatter occupation' has been a much misused concept in assessing the vitality of late antique towns. There is increasing evidence for this sort of change in late antique towns in North Africa. However, the Tripolitanian cities seem to have been undergoing the transformation from an earlier date than many other parts of Africa and there is no doubt that some sort of qualitative change in the standard of life was involved.[36]

There are few mitigating circumstances to be adduced from the surviving records. *Tripolitana* fell from prosperity and influence as fast as the region had earlier risen. The military and socio-economic consequences of such a turn-about were undoubtedly grave.

10
LATE ROMAN FRONTIER ARRANGEMENTS

1
DIPLOMACY IN THE LATE ROMAN PERIOD

Diplomacy retained an important role in the policing of the Tripolitanian frontier in the late Roman period, but there were crucial differences to the frontier situations of earlier times. The quality and number of troops based in *Tripolitana* in the fourth and fifth centuries were generally inadequate to undertake punitive or intimidatory warfare and the lack of an effective deterrent was to undermine frontier diplomacy. Moreover, although Rome resisted renouncing her claim to empire, when the garrisons were withdrawn from Bu Njem, Gheriat and Ghadames in the second half of the third century some territory must have returned to the trust of tribal *foederati* or *pacati*. By withdrawing from these advanced desert 'listening posts', Rome can no longer have been so well informed of events beyond the province nor so much in control of movement on the desert routes. Nonetheless, from the remaining forts, the army sought to maintain the earlier policy of treaty relations and policing. The situation described by St Augustine and Publicola in their exchange of letters gives a valuable insight. Publicola expressed anxiety about the employment of barbarians from beyond the frontiers on his estate where they were used as crop-watchers, shepherds, harvesters or transporters of goods. They were allowed to pass through the frontier in the *regio Arzugum* upon swearing pagan oaths before the decurion or tribune of the border guard, who then provided them with a letter of passage. Publicola was worried about the possibility of committing a sin by employing on his land men who had sworn pagan oaths. But Augustine in his reply concluded that it was a worse sin 'to swear falsely by the true God than to swear truly by the false gods ... for not only on the frontier, but throughout all the provinces, the security of peace rests on the oaths of barbarians'. The transborder movement described in the letters shows that treaty relations continued to exist with the desert tribes, who still migrated to fulfil a symbiotic role with the sedentary farmers. Taken literally, though, Augustine's comments show a growing lack of confidence in the ability of the Roman garrison to cope if the barbarians decided *en masse* to break their oaths.[1]

The works of the Byzantine authors Corippus and Procopius provide ample illustrations for the continuation of a policy of employing Libyan chiefs as subsidized allies, and of 'buying' loyalty from tribal groups with gifts and regalia. The events following Belisarius' arrival in Africa in 533 are particularly illuminating:

> All who ruled over the Moors ... sent envoys to Belisarius saying that they were slaves of the emperor and promised to fight with him. There were some also who sent their children as hostages and requested that the symbols of office be sent to them according to ancient custom. For it was a law among the Moors that no one should be a ruler over them, even if he were hostile to the Romans, until the emperor should give him the tokens of office. ... Now these symbols are a staff of silver covered with gold and a silver cap (not covering the whole head, but like a crown and held in place by bands of silver), a kind of white cloak gathered by a golden brooch on the right shoulder in

the form of a Thessalian cape and a white tunic with embroidery and a gilded boot. And Belisarius sent these things to them and presented each with money. However they did not come to fight for him ... they waited to see what would be the outcome of the war.[2]

These practices are specifically stated to have been a continuation of late Roman policy. Yet in spite of the inherent weaknesses of a system based more on good faith and bribes than on a credible deterrent, at times it could work fairly well. The main problems for the Byzantine government in fact arose because of its own governors breaching agreements, acting duplicitly and breaking oaths.[3]

The scanty historical record is punctuated by the attested raids of the *Austuriani/Laguatan* and it is all too easy to assume that frontier relations between Rome and the neighbouring peoples degenerated once and for all into one of confrontation and antipathy. Yet the testimony of St Augustine and the hints about continued diplomatic activity remind us that there were likely periods of peace and reconciliation, when the frontier continued its earlier function as a filter for more symbiotic contacts between desert and sown.

2
THE *NOTITIA DIGNITATUM*: THE *PRAEPOSITI LIMITES* AND THE MILITARY GARRISON

Epigraphic evidence for the late Roman garrison in *Tripolitana* is almost non-existent and archaeological traces are also disappointingly slight. The main source of information, as for many other areas of the empire, is the *Notitia Dignitatum*, with its listing of official offices and military units in the provinces. The exact date of the sections of the *Notitia* relevant to the western provinces vary, but the African segment appears to be one of the latest in the reign of Honorius. The cumulative nature of the record has often been remarked on, with additions being made over time to a list that was otherwise inconsistently revised. It is improbable, therefore, that the document provides a snapshot view of the deployment of 423 or thereabouts.

The military garrison of the African provinces in the fourth century consisted of two main types of unit. First, there were the established border troops within the Diocletianic frontier provinces, *Tripolitana*, *Mauretania Caesariensis*, *Mauretania Sitifensis* and *Numidia Militaris*. These were the remnants of the auxiliary units of the second- and third-century deployment, in many cases continuing on in the same forts that they had occupied then. The sectors of the frontier covered by these forts, defined as *limites*, were commanded by *praepositi*. In the *Notitia*, the entries for the African provinces normally refer to the officer in charge, for example the *praepositus limitis Tenthettani*, rather than to the unit in garrison. The assumption must be that these *limes* sectors all originated around the fort of a regular unit of the border army. Over time, however, these units, officially classed as *limitanei*, were progressively reduced in status, manpower and efficiency, perhaps in part by extremely localized recruitment. It is possible that some units and *limes* sectors continued to exist only on paper by the early fifth century or that the appointment of *praepositi* for these sectors was no longer on the same basis as earlier. We simply cannot tell from the *Notitia* alone.[4]

The second type of troops were the successors to the legions of the early empire and comprised the elite fighting units of the army, both infantry and cavalry. Because of the political conditions of the late empire, many of these units were maintained in the direct control of the emperors or their principal representatives. From the reign of Constantine, this type of unit seems increasingly to have been differentiated from the border troops by the term *comitatenses*. Initially there were few of these new-style field army units in Africa, probaby formed around elements of Maximian's expeditionary force of 297–8, but their number grew steadily throughout the fourth century, at some point in the 330s requiring the appointment of a supreme military commander with responsibility for all the African provinces, the *comes Africae*. By the early fifth century, there were no less than 19 cavalry vexillations and 12 infantry *numeri*, modern estimates putting the manpower of these 30-plus units at about 22,000. The emphasis on mobile cavalry forces (around 10,500 cavalry to only 11,500 infantry is an extraordinarily high ratio in the late Roman army) is entirely in agreement with the analysis (see above, chapter 9) that the African tribes continued to pose a significant cavalry threat.[5]

Although the garrison bases of these field army units are very poorly attested epigraphically, the troops appear to have been distributed between western *Byzacena*, *Numidia* and *Mauretania*, though not attached to the *limes* sectors. Some of them were probably brigaded in the major towns to the rear of the frontier proper (*Sitifis, Thamugadi, Theveste, Thelepte,* etc.). These were evidently considered the regions facing the highest intensity threat in the early fourth century. *Tripolitana* was initially left with simply its old border units under the command of the *praeses* of the province. After the *Austuriani* raid of 363, the *comes* Romanus brought part of the field army with him to *Tripolitana*, but, having decided against a desert campaign, he returned to his Numidian base with all these troops. The border units in the province also seem to have been under his command, perhaps as a new development following the first signs of trouble in the region in the late 350s. Given the conflict that developed between him and the Tripolitanian cities, it is improbable that he posted any field army units to the region over the subsequent decade of his tenure of office. There is no evidence of *comitatenses* units being posted in *Tripolitana*, though in the late 370s another *comes*, Flavius Victorianus, did campaign there.[6]

The *Notitia* presents the evidence for the early fifth-century African garrison in several separate lists. The field army troops commanded by the *comes* were included separately as infantry and cavalry in the lists of the *magister peditum praesentalis* and the *magister equitum praesentalis*. The regular border troops (*limitanei*) were listed separately for the *comes Africae*, who had charge of all the *limes* sectors of southern *Byzacena* and *Numidia* and a number of other sectors in both *Tripolitana* (Table 10.1) and *Mauretania*, and for the *duces* of *Tripolitana* (see Table 10.2) and *Mauretania*. Only the Tripolitanian sectors need be discussed in detail here.

There was some overlap between the lists of the *comes Africae* and the *dux* which suggests that they are not exactly contemporary. It is unclear whether the list of the *comes* represented the situation in *Tripolitana* prior to the creation of the ducate or to a late reshuffle of forces in which some sectors reverted to his direct control. There may have been a distinction, however, in content between the two lists: that of the *comes* specified that all the frontier sectors mentioned involved *limitanei*, whereas this was not made explicit in the much longer list of the *dux*. The interpretation of the evidence of the *Notitia* is far from straightforward and no consensus view has yet emerged.[7]

The location of the 16 *limes* sectors assigned to the *comes* have been much discussed, but only three or

four seem to be relevant to *Tripolitana* (Table 10.1). Of these, one appears to be a clear reference to the remnant of the old *Cohors II Flavia Afrorum*, still based at *Tillibari* (Remada), and another to the *limes Tablatensis/Talalatensis* is almost certainly to be equated with the garrison based at Ras el-Ain (*Talalati*). The *limes Thamallensis* is to be identified with the Nefzaoua oases, centred on the town of *Turris Tamalleni* (Telmine). The incorporation of the Nefzaoua oases into the province of *Byzacena* is, at first sight, a geographical anomaly. It is possible, though, that this was done some time after the creation of the province specifically in order to facilitate the military supervision of these important oases by the *comes*. The next entry, the *limes Montensis* based *in castris Neptanis* or *Leptitanis*, poses several problems in that neither the oasis of *Nepta* (southern end of the Djerid) nor *Lepcis Magna* are particularly close to mountains. Correlation with Nefta and the Cherb mountain chain to the north of the Chotts Djerid and Fedjedj seems the more likely solution, however, because the names in this part of the count's chapter then fall into a perfect east to west sequence from the *limes Thamallensis* to the *limes Zabensis* in *Mauretania Sitifensis*. The fact that the Tripolitanian *limites* assigned to the count lay in the westernmost part of the province has on occasion prompted speculation about the withdrawal of regular troops from the eastern part of the frontier zone. An alternative, of course, is that it made strategic sense for these sectors to be part of the overall command structure of the count rather than monitored at long range by a governor based at *Lepcis*.[8]

Twelve *praepositi limites* and two separate units of *ripenses* (top grade *limitanei*) were named in the list of the *dux provinciae Tripolitanae* (Table 10:2; Fig. 10:1). Apart from the two specifically mentioned units of *limitanei* (the *milites fortenses* or *hortenses* and the *milites munifices*), a further two can be identified from the recurrence of names (the *limites Tillibarensis* and *Talalatensis*) from the list of the count. The remaining 10 *limites* included two that can be certainly identified with second/third-century garrison posts (*limes*

Notitia refer.	Commander and Sector	2–3 C.	Modern location
Occ 25.21	*praepositus limitis Thamallensis*	F?	Nefzaoua oases
Occ 25.22	*praepositus limitis Montensis in castris Neptanis* (or *Leptitanis*)	F?	Djerid oases or *Lepcis Magna*
Occ 25.31	*praepositus limitis Tablatensis*	F3	Ras el-Ain/ Tatahouine region
Occ 25.33	*praepositus limitis Secundaeforum in castris Tillibarensibus**	F2–3	Remada region

Table 10:1. Tripolitanian *limes* sectors under the direct command of the *Comes Africae* according to the *Notitia*. **Secundaeforum* is normally corrected to read *Secundanorum*, but *Secundae Afrorum* is also possible, providing a reference for the continued presence of the unit attested here in the second/third century. 2–3 C. indicates military presence (F = fort) in 2nd/3rd centuries.

Notitia refer.	Command Structure	2–3 C.	Modern location
Occ 31.17	*sub dispositione viri spectabilis ducis provinciae Tripolitanae:*		Entire frontier zone
Occ 31.18	*praepositus limitis Talalatensis*	F3	Ras el-Ain/Tatahouine region
Occ 31.19	*praepositus limitis Tenthettani*	F2–3	Zintan region
Occ 31.20	*praepositus limitis Bizerentane*	F2–3	Bir Rhezene region
Occ 31.21	*praepositus limitis Tillibarensis*	F2–3	Remada region
Occ 31.22	*praepositus limitis Madensibus*		Dehibat region?
Occ 31.23	*praepositus limitis Maccomadensis*		Sirte region
Occ 31.24	*praepositus limitis Tintiberitani*		unknown, E. Tripolitania?
Occ 31.25	*praepositus limitis Bubensis*		unknown, E. Tripolitania?
Occ 31.26	*praepositus limitis Mamucensis*		Eastern Tripolitania
Occ 31.27	*praepositus limitis Balensis*		unknown, E. Tripolitania?
Occ 31.28	*praepositus limitis Varensis*		unknown, E. Tripolitania?
Occ 31.29	*Milites fortenses in castris Leptitanis*		*Lepcis Magna*
Occ 31.30	*Milites munifices in castris Madensibus*		Near Sebkha Tauorgha?
Occ 31.31	*praepositus limitis Sarcitani*		unknown, E. Tripolitania?

Table 10:2. The list of the *dux provinciae Tripolitanae* from the *Notitia Dignitatum.* 2–3 C. indicates military presence (F = fort) in 2nd/3rd centuries.

Tenthettani = *Tentheos* or *Thenteos* (Zintan) and *limes Bizerentane* = *Bezereos* (Bir Rhezene)). The sector based on *Marcomades* can be associated with the Syrtic town of that name, which could have received a garrison in the fourth century on account of its position in the front line of *Austuriani* attacks. The *limes Madensis* was listed separately from the *milites munifices in castris Madensisibus*. Were there two separate units at the same site or two separate frontier posts with the same or a very similar name? A recent study of the Libyan name *Mada* has suggested either a correlation with the site known in the Antonine Itinerary as *Ad Amadum* on the *limes Tripolitanus* road south of Remada (probably in the vicinity of Dehibat) or alternatively a connection with the Sebkha Taourgha close to the Syrtic shore in eastern Tripolitania.

Attempts to identify the remaining names in the list with toponyms from earlier sources are speculative. One new possibility is suggested by the Bu Njem documentation: could the *limes Sarcitani* have a connection with the unlocated fort of *Secedi*? If so, then this *limes* sector probably lay about two days' travel north or northwest of Bu Njem. Little can be said about the rest of the names but it seems significant that we have a fairly full record of *limes* sectors in western Tripolitania and a very poor representation in the eastern part of the territory. In view of the well-attested evidence for raids on *Tripolitana* emanating from the Syrtic region and from the desert margins to the south of *Lepcis* it is inherently improbable that the eastern part of the province was left without border troops. Most of the unidentified sectors, therefore, will have lain either between *Thenteos* and the western

coast of the Greater Syrtes or along the Syrtic coast road towards the east from Sirte. The former zone would include the oasis of Mizda, a likely base for one of the *limites*, and the area of the Libyan Valleys survey.

Although the order of citation of sector names in the duke's list appears to have no geographical coherence, some degree of rationality may underlie it, with the sectors divisible into a western group and an eastern group. Assuming that the first reference to *Mada* in the list is identifiable with *Ad Amadum* in the western part of the province, the first five sectors listed can all be assigned to locations in that zone, with Zintan being the most easterly site. The remaining group of seven *limites* and the two units of higher grade *limitanei* were certainly or probably based in eastern Tripolitania and Syrtica. As far as we can judge, the *limites* were designed to police the areas of primary contact between sedentary farming and pastoral herding. The two independent and higher calibre units of *ripenses* will have fulfilled a more defensive role, being stationed at *Lepcis* itself and, assuming that the Sebkha Tauorgha was known as *lacus Madensis*, close to the main coastal approach route to the city on the western shore of the Greater Syrtes.

The more mobile and effective fighting units of *ripenses* were probably a late addition to the provincial garrison, certainly not present at the time of the 363–6 raids (nor before the deposition of Romanus as *comes* in the 370s). One possible context for their creation and deployment in the region may have been 375–8, when Victorianus, perhaps Romanus' direct successor as *comes*, is known to have been active in

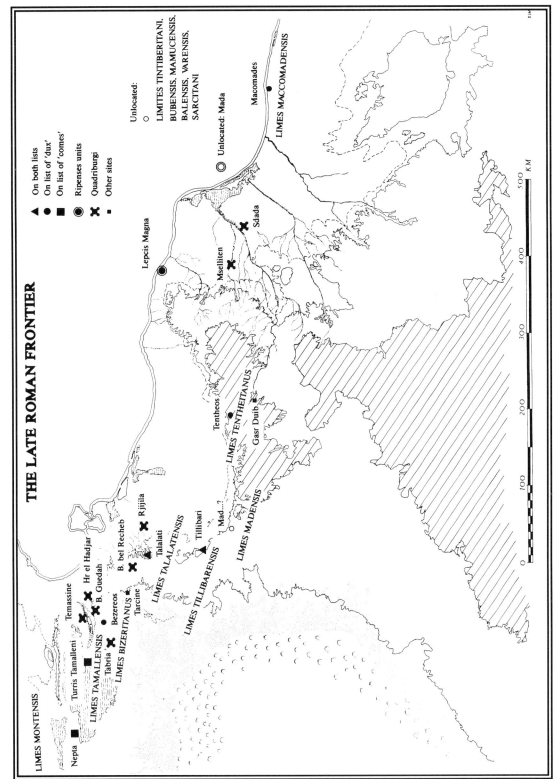

THE LATE ROMAN FRONTIER

On both lists ▲
On list of 'dux' ●
On list of 'comes' ■
Ripenses units ◎
Quadriburgi ✖
Other sites ▪

Unlocated: ○

LIMITES TINTIBERITANI,
BUBENSIS, MAMUCENSIS,
BALENSIS, VARENSIS,
SARCITANI

Unlocated: Mada

LIMES MACCOMADENSIS
Macomades

Lepcis Magna

Sdada

Mselliten

LIMES TENTHEITANUS
Tentheos
Gasr Duib

LIMES MADENSIS
Mad...?

LIMES TILLIBARENSIS
Tillibari

LIMES TALALATENSIS
Talalati
Rijila
B. bel Recheb

LIMES BIZERITANUS
Tarcine
Bezereos
B. Guedah
Tabria
Hr el Hadjar

LIMES TAMALLENSIS
Turris Tamalleni
Temassine
Nepta

LIMES MONTENSIS

500 KM 400 300 200 100 0

Fig. 10:1 The *limes* sectors in fourth-century *Tripolitana* from the *Notitia Dignitatum*.

190

Tripolitana. Following the exposure of Romanus' misdeeds towards the city of *Lepcis* and the province, the imperial government may have made a conciliatory gesture by providing such reinforcements to the garrison. However, a more likely occasion was surely the moment when the post of *dux* was created near the end of the fourth century or when its rank was raised to that of *vir spectabilis* at the beginning of the fifth. In these cases, the decision to provide extra troops would evidently have been a response to renewed raiding by the *Austuriani.*[9]

The *Notitia* provides a model that can be tested against the archaeological evidence, both from *Tripolitana* and from other African provinces. We would expect to see the continuation of occupation at the main forts on which the sectors were based, with some new construction of typically late-style fortlets and outposts. The linear barriers, where they existed earlier, would have been maintained, possibly added to in other locations. In Algeria there is clear evidence for this sort of policy being vigorously pursued on a number of the *limes* sectors, with the maintenance of the *fossatum Africae*, the construction of *quadriburgi* and continuing garrisons at sites such as *Gemellae.*[10]

Evidence is more scanty in *Tripolitana*, not least because almost half the *limites* are not securely located. Late military occupation at both *Talalati* (Ras el-Ain) and *Tillibari* (Remada) is proved archaeologically and in the latter case the unit in garrison in the early fifth appears to be the same as that of the second–third century, the *Cohors II Flavia Afrorum*. The same may well be true of the *Cohors VIII Fida* at *Talalati*, though unfortunately the mid-fourth-century inscription mentioning repairs to the fort battlements does not identify the garrison. *Thenteos* (Zintan) is unexplored but the *Cohors I Syrorum*, assumed in garrison in the third, could well have formed the basis of the fourth-century *limitanei*. Nothing is known in

detail of late Roman occupation at *Bezereos* (Bir Rhezene), and even the nature of its later third-century garrison is uncertain. The brigading of the *milites Fortenses* at *Lepcis* is known only from the *Notitia* but must surely have involved either dispersed billeting or a military compound within the late Roman walled circuit.

As regards new military constructions, a number of the distinctive late Roman *quadriburgi* are known (Table 10.3). These fortlets, described below, have projecting towers at the corner angles (and sometimes at the gates also) and present a significant departure from earlier Roman military architecture. Unfortunately, none of these Tripolitanian examples has yielded a military dedication, and indeed the latest dated new construction from the frontier is the tower-like outpost of *centenarium Tibubuci* (Ksar Tarcine) erected *c.* 303–05. Several of the western Tripolitanian *quadriburgi* were constructed in close proximity to the *clausurae* (notably Henschir Benia Ceder and Henschir Benia bel-Recheb) and presumably the continued manning of these customs barriers was part of their function. They are generally of very small size in comparison with those known in *Numidia* for instance. In eastern Tripolitania there are very few ruins that can with confidence be assigned a late Roman military function. Overall the paucity of archaeological features corresponding to the 12 *limites* and two forts of *milites* is extremely puzzling.

My initial view on this question was that the shortage of evidence for the presence of regular soldiers on the eastern Tripolitanian *limites* was due to the devolution of military affairs at some point to frontier militia (*gentiles*). I am now more inclined to believe, though certainty is impossible, that the state attempted to maintain a semblance of the original system but that the numbers of *limitanei* under each *praepositus* were reduced progressively to a minimal

Name	Area	Unit
Remada (*Tillibari*)	1.95 ha/4.87 acres	remnants of *coh II Flavia Afr.*
Ras el-Ain (*Talalati*)	0.86 ha/2.16 acres	remnants of *coh VIII Fida?*
Ksar Tabria	0.36 ha/0.90 acres	outpost for *Bezereos?*
Bir Rhezene (*Bezereos*)	0.33 ha/0.80 acres	remnants of 3rd C garrison?
Sdada east	0.27 ha/0.66 acres	?
Benia Guedah Ceder	0.24 ha/0.60 acres	outpost for *Bezereos?*
Hr el Hadjar	0.15 ha/0.38 acres	outpost for *Bezereos?*
Benia bel Recheb	0.14 ha/0.36 acres	outpost for *Talalati?*
Hr Temassine	0.08 ha/0.19 acres	outpost for *Bezereos?*
Gasr Bularkan	0.05 ha/0.12 acres	?
Hr Rjijila	0.04 ha/0.09 acres	outpost for Ras el Ain?
Zintan (*Thenteos*)	unknown	remnants of *coh I Syrorum?*
Lepcis Magna	unknown	*milites fortenses*
Mada (near Sebkha Tauorgha?)	unknown	*milites munifices*

Table 10:3. Sizes of certain and probable forts and fortlets occupied in the fourth century.

police presence on many sectors. How big, then, were the *limitanei* units commanded by the fourth-century *praepositi*? In the third-century *limes* structure that was subsumed into the Diocletianic system, quingenary or milliary units seem to have been envisaged (around 480 or 800 men). The use of irregular vexillations of legionaries and of *numeri* may have introduced some lower figures, but 300 men are attested at *Bezereos* in the early third century and several hundred still seem to have been at Bu Njem in the late 250s. It is implausible that the fourth- and fifth-century *limites* were based around such large concentrations, especially as the Diocletianic overhaul of the mid-third-century system of *limes* sectors is unlikely to have involved the deployment of additional troops. Furthermore, evidence from other provinces shows that the rosters of many of the auxiliary units surviving into the fourth century were allowed to drop well below the previous muster levels. Continued occupation of a large cohort fort need not indicate a similarly large number of men occupying each barrack block, as excavations on Hadrian's Wall in Britain have demonstrated. In a military backwater, such as *Tripolitana* was in the early fourth century, the process of slimming down the units based there probably began quite early. I am doubtful if any of the *limes* sectors counted for more than 100–200 troops and some of them may have fallen some way below 100. The small number and size of the known Tripolitanian outposts of late date is very suggestive of a limited availability of troops for detached duty. The total provincial garrison under Diocletian may have numbered between 1,500 and 2,000 men; by the early fifth century –

excluding the two *ripenses* units – it could have declined to well under 1,000.[11]

It is possible that in the early fifth century some of the troops may have faced downgrading to militia status (*gentiles*), as happened in *Cyrenaica* at this time. Given the involvement in both areas of the *Laguatan* tribes (*Austuriani/Ausuriani*) the pattern of events in the *Pentapolis* can add something to our understanding in *Tripolitana*. Synesius several times complains about the behaviour of Cerealis, the military governor of *Cyrenaica*, responsible in his view for the military unpreparedness of the border defences. Cerealis is accused of weakening the defences by taking away 'the possessions of the soldiers', by billeting troops on the towns for financial reasons rather than for strategic ones. For example, the unit of *Balagritae*, 'before Cerealis had taken command of the province ... were mounted bowmen; but, when he entered upon his functions, their horses were sold and they became only archers'. Similarly, the *Unnigardae* unit, celebrated by Synesius for having dared to fight off some of the raiders, though numbering no more than 40 men at the time, were subsequently threatened with demotion to the status of local militia. The realities of such a step would have involved the loss of the emperor's largesse, their remounts, arms and pay. Synesius wrote to their former commander asking him to use his influence not merely to secure a reprieve for the unit but to increase its numbers: 'For who would not admit that 200 *Unnigardae* ... would suffice, when commanded by you, to bring the Ausurian war to an end for the emperor.' The arithmetic is obviously based on flattery and optimism in equal measure but

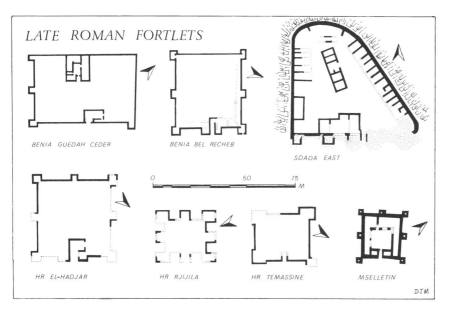

Fig. 10:2 Late Roman fortlets in *Tripolitana*, cf. table 10.3.

the letter reveals much about the low expectations of frontier troops in the fifth century and the extent to which the frontier was succumbing to successive cost-cutting exercises as much as to a superior enemy.[12]

Thinly spread between 12 policing sectors, covering 1,000 km of frontier and increasingly poorly equipped, it is small wonder that such forces were simply swept away or bypassed by the major incursions of the period. Even the two new units brought into *Tripolitana* at the end of the fourth century are unlikely to have totalled more than 1,000 men, perhaps considerably less. Their deployment reveals that the imperial government was attempting to do something about the military condition of the province, though continuing raids in the early fifth century would suggest that the presence of fresh troops was not an effective deterrent. Frontier security within the increasingly poorly garrisoned *limites* sectors was augmented in certain cases by making use in various ways of native *gentiles*, recruited from the broad group of people defined as the *Arzuges*.[13]

3
LATE ROMAN FORTIFICATIONS

All the known late Roman fortlets in *Tripolitana* are very small in size, particularly when compared to those of *Numidia*. They are treated as a group here because they all share the late Roman characteristic of projecting angle towers, though they are by no means all contemporary (Fig. 10:2; Table 10:3). None has yielded any inscriptions.

Benia Guedah Ceder

DIMENSIONS: 60 × 40 m   AREA: 0.24 ha (0.6 acres)
FIGURES: 5:16, 10:2

Frequently mentioned by early French explorers of the Tebaga corridor and excavated by Donau in 1902 and 1904, the site is still in a remarkable state of preservation. The enceinte is built in high-quality ashlar masonry with square bastions projecting at the south, east and west corners. There is another in the middle of the southwest side. The single gate in the southeast side opens on to a Z-bend corridor. Most of these ashlar walls are 0.60–0.80 m thick and have been robbed down to within a metre or two from ground level. The upper walls were apparently originally constructed in smaller masonry though Donau and others interpreted this as a sign of possible Byzantine reuse.

The main building of the fort interior is in ashlar masonry and still stands 3 m high against the northwest wall. Its single entrance was defensible. One of the interior rooms was a stable, with water troughs. Donau's account records that he uncovered traces of barracks and stores built against the inside of the enceinte using smaller masonry. These buildings had been almost entirely robbed, of course, and little trace now remains. There is no reason why these have to be considered as a later addition to the site.

The style of building in an African context is fourth century, but in the absence of epigraphic evidence precision is difficult. Pottery identified on the site and at the nearby *clausura* might push its origins back to the later third century.[14]

Wadi Temassine

DIMENSIONS: 30 × 25 m   AREA: 0.08 ha (0.19 acres)
FIGURE: 10:2

This is a much smaller version of the *quadriburgus* type with four square corner bastions. The entrance is in the east side but no trace of internal buildings survives and no dating evidence has been recovered.[15]

Henchir el-Hadjar

DIMENSIONS: 38.80 × 38.80 m   AREA: 0.15 ha (0.38 acres)   FIGURE: 5:17, 10:2

The site is situated between Benia Buedah Ceder and Gabes (Fig. 5.17) and its plan suggests broad contemporaneity with the former (Fig. 10.2). The ashlar enceinte was reinforced by four corner bastions and five more at the centres of its sides and flanking the gate. It was also surrounded by a ditch and counterscarp. No trace of internal buildings has been noted. Some late Roman pottery including Christian lamps have been collected from the site.[16]

Ksar Tabria

DIMENSIONS: 60 × 60 m   AREA: 0.36 ha (0.9 acres)
FIGURE: 5:8

Trousset's plan of this site, taken from an aerial photograph, puts it in a different category from the other late fortlets. It is much larger and had circular corner bastions and D-shaped gate towers. A central building is visible but the area described as intervallum was almost certainly taken up by barracks. Outside the fortlet to the north is an enigmatic triangular enclosure. Trousset dates the site as Constantinian following Petrikovits' analysis of fortifications in northwest Europe. The bastions certainly suggest fourth century occupation but some features suggest an earlier construction date (see above).[17]

Benia bel Recheb

DIMENSIONS: 40 × 36 m   AREA: 0.14 ha (0.36 acres)
FIGURES: 5:19, 10:2

This site also presents many similarities with Benia Guedah Ceder. Although there were no ashlar buildings inside the enceinte, the fortlet was not empty of structures. Barracks and store-buildings were noted by early researchers (in particular in the northern corner) and these structures in smaller and rougher masonry were still visible in 1964. As on many other sites in the region, this smaller masonry has been the first target for stone-robbers whilst the large ashlars, being less transportable, have tended to survive. The apparent emptiness of Benia bel Recheb and indeed its allegedly unfinished state reflect the post-Roman history of the ruins, not their original construction. As with the other Benia, the bel Recheb fortlet was built in proximity to a sector of several *clausurae* (see above, chapter 5:7 and Fig. 5:19).[18]

Henchir Rjijila

DIMENSIONS: 17 × 21 m   AREA: 0.04 ha (0.09 acres)
FIGURE: 10:2

This was another very small example of the type. Little detail has been recorded but the outline of the site with its bastions is clear from Trousset's plan.[19]

Gasr Bularkan (Mselletin)

DIMENSIONS: 22 × 22 m   AREA: 0.05 ha (0.12 acres)
FIGURE: 10:2

Once again this site reproduced the plan of a fourth century fortlet in miniature. The construction of a site of this nature, with its seven square bastions, is at least indicative of the continued presence of *some* regular troops in eastern Tripolitania at a late date.[20]

Sdada east

DIMENSIONS: *c.* 66 × 55 m   AREA: approx. 0.27 ha (0.66 acres)   FIGURE: 10:2

The Italian fort on Sdada hill overlooks the major inland short-cut from the southwestern edge of the

Greater Syrtes towards *Lepcis* and *Oea*. Opposite Sdada on the east side of the N'f'd a possibly military site was located in 1980 (ULVS site Nf 83). It owes its shape to its position on an irregular spur but the site was surrounded by a well-built wall 2 m thick. On the landward side this was augmented by a series of square bastions also built in small masonry. The regular layout of the internal buildings is also suggestive of a military interpretation.[21]

4
BORDER MILITIA AND *GENTILES*: THE 'SOLDIER-FARMERS' OF *TRIPOLITANA*

Imperial action is likely to have explored other (and cheaper) possibilities for strengthening the frontier zone. A *prime facie* case can be made for the recruitment of native Libyan potentates as allies (*foederati*). The small number of official troops emphasizes the increased reliance on treaty relationships with tribes or chieftains of the zone and helps to explain why, when such agreements broke down, the *Laguatan* were able to raid with impunity.

A few points should be made here about the views of Ward-Perkins, Goodchild and others concerning a class of soldier-farmers whom they incorrectly described as *limitanei*. A.H.M. Jones made the point long ago that *limitanei* were in fact the official troops maintained in proper forts with pay, rations and arms provided by the government and a militia recruited from veterans or the indigenous population would have been in law *gentiles* or *veterani*.

A second point of revision concerns the developmental sequence proposed by Goodchild for his *limitanei* settlements. Recent work has disproved his belief in the Severan origin of the Tripolitanian frontier and of the third-century origin for the farming settlement under its protection. He sought an explanation for the fortified farms by interpreting a passage in the largely spurious life of Severus Alexander as referring to land allocations to border troops in *Tripolitana*. Ignoring the question of the reliability of the source, these supposed land-handouts followed wars in *Mauretania Tingitana, Illyricum* and *Armenia*, and so were without any apparent relevance to *Tripolitana*.[22]

A third unfortunate aspect has been the tendency for British and French archaeologists to identify any defended buildings in the frontier zone as 'postes militaires' or as of 'essentially military character'. There is a plethora of fortified farms (*gsur*) in this zone, yet many of them were demonstrably constructed by the indigenous population (Plates 49–55). Indeed fortified farms are now a recognized phenomenon the length and breadth of the Maghreb provinces. Although Goodchild showed his awareness of many of the pitfalls, he ended up being too much influenced by the few genuine military or paramilitary examples. Without excavation or further detailed study it will not be possible to disentangle military *gsur* from the fortified farms which were erected for reasons of prestige and defence by a civilian population who had, in many cases, been in the zone for a hundred years or more before the Severan frontier was created.[23]

Although there was no officially organized mass settlement of the pre-desert in order to create a class of soldier-farmers, it is equally certain that some of the Libyan elite were recruited by Rome to assist in some way with the defence of their locality when the official garrison was thinned out or withdrawn. In some sectors the official troops could have been superseded by native recruits dignified with Roman names and titles who perhaps received small stipends. Use of military terminology (*centenarium*, *turris*) in the dedicatory inscriptions of fortified farms has sometimes been used as grounds for identifying such individuals, but the evidence is shaky. Nor can the fact that the constructors of fortified farms were sometimes motivated by concerns about raiders (whether barbarians or people of the frontier zone (*gentiles*), as in a text from a *gasr* at Sidi Sames in the Gebel Tarhuna) count as evidence for official military responsibilities.[24]

Considerable caution needs to be exercised, then, in interpreting the possible military or paramilitary aspects of the Tripolitanian *gsur* and it must be stressed that the vast majority can only be considered as civilian farming communities. It has been argued above (chapter 7) that the norm of rural development in the pre-desert region of eastern Tripolitania involved the development of estates based around *opus Africanum* farms in the late first–early second century AD, followed in the third and fourth centuries by the construction of fortified residences on the same estates. A few sites or groups of sites have been selected for more detailed commentary here as they do not at first sight conform to this norm. Ghirza and the Bir Scedua *gsur* are unusual settlements because in both cases the evidence for early Roman occupation is weak and the late Roman occupation is atypical in nature. The late Roman cemetery at Bir ed-Dreder is even more extraordinary in that it is located adjacent to no major settlement. Finally, a number of

sites in western Tripolitania that have commonly been presented as military are reviewed and shown to conform to the pattern of the eastern Tripolitanian farming settlements.

The Bir ed-Dreder/Bir Scedua sites

Goodchild developed many of his key theories about frontier militias and soldier farmers from his study of the Bir Scedua *gsur*. This remarkable group of sites, located on the southern side of the Wadi Sofeggin, shares many architectural characteristics and these may reflect a specific group identity (Figs 10:3–10:4; Plates 50–51). Goodchild believed that the uniformity confirmed the official settlement of soldier farmers, but a more credible case can be made for an ethnic explanation. The revived importance of tribal based structures in the late Roman period is evident at other sites such as Ghirza, which appears to have been a sub-tribal centre. Though far more dispersed than the Ghirza site, the dense *gasr* distribution in the Scedua basin indicates the presence of a large population while the homogeneity of the construction of the *gsur* suggests agnate links between them. Their Libyan character is established by the nomenclature in a Latino-Punic funerary inscription.[25]

The Bir ed-Dreder cemetery (Fig. 10:4), located about 15 km southwest of the Scedua basin, contained at least 80 cremation burials, many marked by ashlar stele of a distinctive type set in socles and capped with rough capitals. The stele showed that some of the dead men bore Roman as well as Libyan names and had been given the title of *tribunus*. The Latin names fall into two distinctive groups: four stele recorded men called Flavius (three being qualified as *tribunus*), and three others were named Iulius (though only one of these was designated tribune). The combination of Flavii and Iulii may suggest a context for the earliest of these inscriptions *c.* 340–50 (when Iulius Constans and Flavius Iulius Constantius were emperors), though the date range for the cemetery could extend well beyond that.

Although there is a total absence of major settlement sites in the Wadi Dreder, Goodchild disassociated this cemetery from the Scedua *gasr*-dwellers because he had already noted some cemeteries in the Scedua basin itself and because he felt that the Dreder wells lay beyond the limits of wadi agriculture. He suggested instead that the Dreder *tribuni* were 'nomadic *foederati*' patrolling the desert ahead of the agricultural zone, while some other commentators have preferred to see them as more regular soldiers. These explanations are unsatisfactory and new evidence suggests a revised interpretation. The Latino-Punic texts are extremely fragmentary and modern

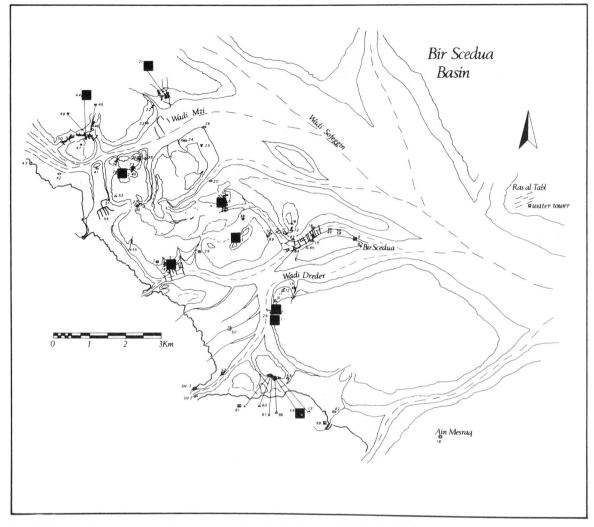

Fig. 10:3 The fortified farms in the Bir Scedua area (from Buck, Burns and Mattingly 1983).

attempts to make complete sense of them must be treated with some caution. Nevertheless, it would appear that, with the exception of the word *tribunus*, the vocabulary used includes terminology suggestive more of tribal than official military organization. It is possible that the Flavii and Iulii represent two distinct clans of a single sub-tribe. Not all the graves of those honoured with inscriptions were for men designated *tribuni* so the rank was not an honour shared among an entire tribal grouping. A number of family relationships are possible and it is probable that several generations of tribal leaders were buried here, assuming that the Roman title of tribune was reserved for only the leading individuals (the title was recorded in seven instances by Goodchild). However, the other graves marked with inscribed stele seem

also to have been for high status individuals within the tribe. The grave type at Bir ed-Dreder is almost unique in the ULVS, but there are in fact many similarities in grave and tomb types between the Dreder and Scedua cemeteries and the latter seem to be located only at the northeastern limits of the Scedua settlement. Though unsuited for agriculture, the wells at Bir ed-Dreder would give it a great importance in a mixed or pastoral economy. Since the Scedua *gsur*-dwellers seem to have practised a mixed economy it seems likely that the Dreder cemetery was a territorial 'marker' at the southwestern limits of their primary grazing lands.[26]

The Dreder *tribuni* can therefore be identified as the Scedua *gasr*-dwellers, forming a cohesive tribal group, perhaps divided between two clans. The

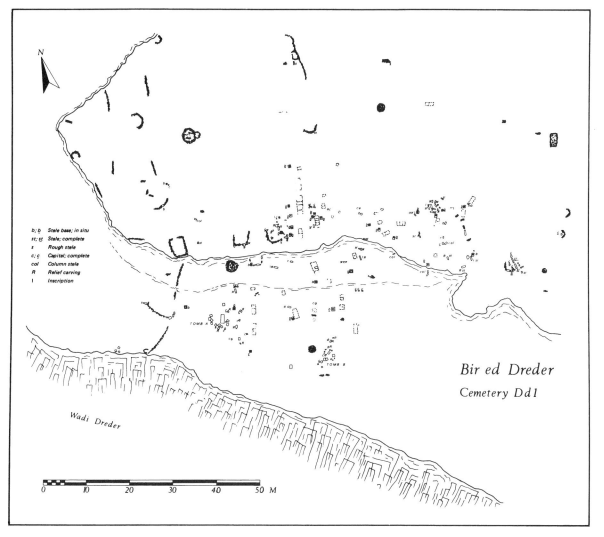

b; b   *Stele base; in situ*
st; st   *Stele; complete*
s   *Rough stele*
c; c   *Capital; complete*
col   *Column stele*
R   *Relief carving*
I   *Inscription*

Bir ed Dreder

Cemetery Dd1

Wadi Dreder

Fig. 10:4 The Bir ed-Dreder cemetery of the *tribuni*. There were two small ashlar tombs (**a** and **b**), numerous small cremation graves marked by stele and a number of other funerary monuments (such as tumuli) (from Buck, Burns and Mattingly 1983).

attested practice of conferring Latin names and titles on allied tribes in the late Roman empire is well illustrated here. Yet the Latinity of the *tribuni* appears to have been minimal and it is hard to visualize them fulfilling an official role as *praepositi* responsible for reporting to the governor in the same manner as commanders with border troops assigned to them. These were not, then, *praepositi* of one of the missing *limes* sectors. The military character and organization of these people was clearly loose and if their 'recruitment' took place in the 340s, this was probably long after their arrival in the area and the construction of the *gsur*. The unique style of their funerary monuments and the comparatively late *floruit* of their settlement in the Scedua are distinctive features, and

generally supportive of the view that they were a tight-knit tribal grouping. They came to have some formal relation with the frontier but I think it was as *gentiles* bound by treaty to assist in its protection.

Ghirza

The concentration of about 40 major buildings (including six castle-like *gsur*) and numerous ancilliary structures at Ghirza constitutes the largest nucleated settlement of *gsur* in the pre-desert. Spread across an area of approx. 500 x 300m and bisected by a tributary stream-bed of the Wadi Ghirza, the settlement has attracted attention since its rediscovery by Smythe in the 1820s and was the focus of Italian interest in the 1930s and of a programme of survey and

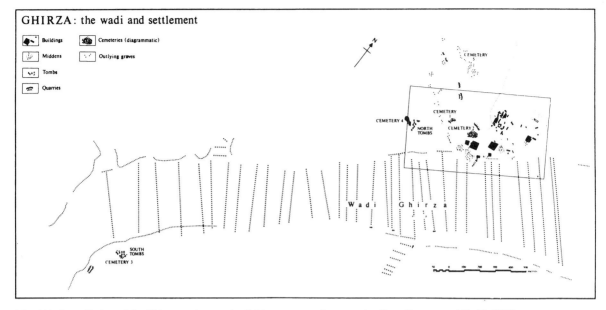

Fig. 10:5 Overall plan of the Ghirza settlement, its field systems and cemeteries (from Brogan and Smith 1985).

excavation by Brogan and Smith in the 1950s (Plate 52). The site is one of the most unusual in the Libyan pre-desert, and also that for which the most detailed archaeological picture has been built up (Figs 10:5–10:6). Traces of cross and side walls on the alluvium of the wadi floor adjoining the settlement, show that it was intensively cultivated for a total distance of 2.9 km (approx. 122 ha/301 acres). Botanical remains from the middens indicate cultivation of barley, wheat, olives, vines, figs, almonds, dates, pulses and possibly water-melon.

There were no less than five major cemeteries (two featuring complexes of ashlar-built mausolea) and numerous outlying graves surrounding the site. Seven of the mausolea were constructed in a cemetery located at the southern limits of the settlement's field system, another seven tombs stood on the opposite side of the wadi immediately south of the settlement itself (Plates 56–57).

At the core of the inhabited area lay two enormous *gsur*, almost completely without parallel in the subsequent extensive work of the ULVS in the region. These structures (buildings 31 and 34) comprised what appeared to have been relatively standard courtyard *gsur* at their core, but with a far larger *gasr*-like structure set around them (Plate 54). Building 31 was approx. 47 m sq, while 34 was an irregular quadrilateral (39.5 x 46 x 46 x 48.5 m). There were other *gsur* with their own satellite structures in the settlement but all are of far smaller scale (Plates 53, 55). The presence of two major cemeteries and two unusually large but comparable structures dominating the settlement

suggests that the population here may have comprised two distinct families or clans.

Six Latin inscriptions, three Latino-Punic texts and no less than 27 Libyan graffiti are known from the site. Of the Libyan texts, 11 were inscribed on cult objects or on the walls of an important pagan temple (building 32), 12 on other buildings of the settlement and three cut into the Romano-Libyan mausolea. The personal nomenclature of the Latin and Latino-Punic inscriptions reveals that the elite residents were Libyans, though some possessed Roman *nomina*. The undoubted Libyan character of the inhabitants strongly favours the interpretation that this was a sub-tribal centre in the late Roman period. A few sherds of first-century AD pottery have been found at the site, but no structures of that date have been isolated and the extensive settlement that can be seen today appears to be uniformly late Roman in date. If there was an early settlement here, then, it does not seem to have amounted to much. Yet for the wealth of its tombs and the material culture contained in its particularly massive middens, Ghirza appears to have been the the most thriving individual pre-desert settlement of the fourth–sixth centuries. Although the period of greatest prosperity appears to have been the early fourth century, when the most splendid of the mausolea were erected, the site does not seem to have suffered unduly from the unrest of the *Austuriani* raids and the latest of the mausolea probably date to the early fifth century. Some of the mausolea are decorated with scenes from everyday life, including hunting, farming and the presentation of produce to a

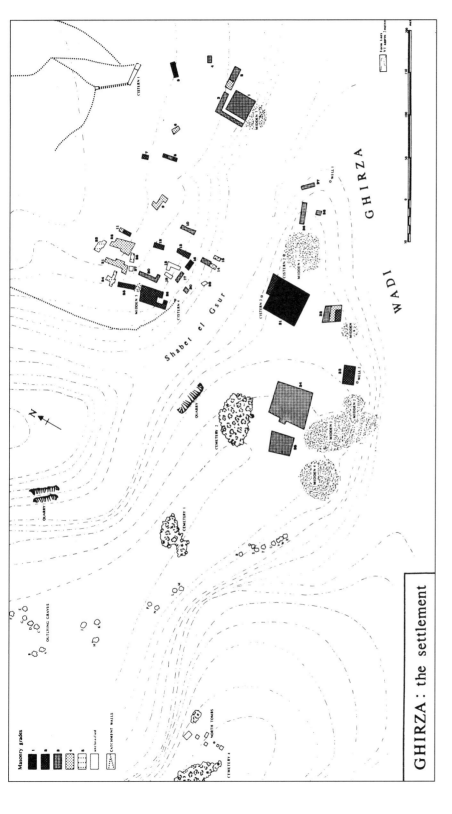

Fig. 10.6 Ghirza, detailed plan of the settlement (cf. Plates 52–55) (from Brogan and Smith 1985).

seated person (presumably the deceased in some sort of chiefly role). Several scenes show human combat, between naked or semi-naked 'barbarian' Libyans and the *gasr*-dwellers. Once again, there are no grounds for trying to fit this evidence into the formal structures of the military command of *limes* sectors. The inhabitants of Ghirza clearly dominated a larger area of the pre-desert than the 3 km strip of wadi that they actually farmed but I suggest that they did this as tribal clans, no doubt possessing favourable status as *gentiles* with the military administration. In a region short of regular troops they may well have become accustomed to see to their own defence against intruders.

The *gentiles* of the pre-desert have sometimes been accused of collusion with the *Laguatan* in the raids against the territories of the coastal towns. In their defence, it should first be noted that many of the raids may have bypassed the difficult terrain of the Sofeggin and Zem-Zem valleys (studded as they were with fortified strong-points) and taken the shorter routes closer to the Syrtic coast. In time, however, as the Roman frontier decayed and, after the Vandal conquest, ceased to exist at all, the *gentiles* will have had to reach an accommodation with the spreading power of the *Laguatan* confederation. Whatever its precise history, Ghirza was clearly not created as an official settlement of soldier/farmers. Its origins were in a Romano-Libyan farming community not a veteran settlement. In the next chapter we shall see that Ghirza and Bir Scedua/Bir Dreder were not the only significant concentrations of *gsur* in the eastern pre-desert.[27]

Some Tunisian misfits

In the absence of a detailed survey for western Tripolitania equivalent to the ULVS, there are considerable discrepancies in our understanding of rural settlement in the two regions. Most previous discussions of the western frontier zone have tended to ignore or down-play the evidence for a substantial civil presence in the frontier zone, for the establishment of some of this settlement at a date comparable to the first settlement in the Libyan pre-desert (that is in the late first century AD) and for the existence of fortified farms here also. The following examples simply illustrate the potential for reinterpretation of many sites in this zone that have hitherto been considered military.

In the Tebaga corridor, there is a series of sites exhibiting shared characteristics but whose interpretation is difficult (Fig. 5:17). Most of these were constructed in part ashlar masonry, *opus africanum* or *saxa quadrata*, and on the visible evidence would have been single-storey. Their appearance would be that of farms, were it not for the presence of large ditches with counterscarp banks around some of them. French antiquarians unswervingly referred to them as military posts but this may be doubted for several reasons. First, they are too large and too close to each other for them to be interpreted as towers in a signalling chain. Nor would so many observation posts have been necessary in this flat corridor. Second, the case rests on the erroneous assumption (partly corrected by Trousset's work) that there was no ancient agricultural development in the area. There is, however, abundant archaeological evidence for this as well as civilian epitaphs from the Tebaga corridor. The ribbon-like siting of these sites show that they related to a route passing through the Tebaga *clausura* towards *Aquae Tacapitanae*, but obviously there are economic as well as military explanations for such a distribution. The fact that several such sites are not ditched suggest that the fortifications may not be an original feature but a later development as happened with civilian farms in Libya. Several of the sites have indeed yielded first- and second-century fine wares on inspection. 'Fortified farms' is, therefore, a more acceptable interpretation of this group of sites.[28]

Similar conclusions can be reached for other well-known sites which have often been presented as military. Henschir el Gueciret (*Turris Maniliorum Arelliorum*) has been interpreted as military on the basis of its ancient name alone. Yet the dedicatory inscription mentions only the extended family, friends and servants of the man on whose estate (*praedium*) the tower-like residence had been erected and no actual Roman officials are referred to at all. The building itself is easily paralleled by other civil fortified farms and the military had no exclusive claim on the use of the word *turris*. In this example and others from Libya, the construction of the fortified farm by the estate-owner was primarily for the benefit of himself and his family. The economic development of the marginal zone lands had advanced rapidly, as we shall see, and the indigenous farmers were wealthy and status conscious enough by the third century to build fortified farms.[29]

An equally dubious 'military' site is that at Ras el Oued Gordab, where a complex of buildings was excavated without turning up any military inscription or paraphernalia. This site lay well to the rear of the *limes* in an area of extensive agricultural settlement (Fig. 5:17). In the context of the Libyan pre-desert it would now be viewed as a civilian fortified farm on the available evidence, but it still features regularly in the literature as a supposedly definite military site.[30]

One final point needs stressing with relation to the

vitality of the frontier zone in the late Roman period. The progressive withdrawal of regular troops did not lead to total anarchy and economic collapse in the frontier region. In fact it was the urban centres of the coast and their *territoria* whose economy crashed first. The inland region declined more slowly, in part because local self-defence was well-organized around the fortified farms of the region and in part perhaps because the frontier people were gradually assimilated into the *Laguatan* confederation. The fusion between Romanized pre-desert farmers and the *Laguatan* may be indicated by the evidence for Ghirza becoming progressively more Libyan in culture and outlook through the fifth and sixth centuries.

11
ECONOMY AND CULTURE IN LATE ROMAN TRIPOLITANIA

1
RURAL LIFE IN GEBEL AND PRE-DESERT

Rural settlement morphology in the late Roman period became more and more defensive in character. The traditional dating of the fortified farms (*gsur*) to the third century AD and later is largely confirmed by the most recent work, though the very earliest examples seem to have been built at the end of the second century. The heyday of *gasr* construction, to judge from the groups of sites that have been most systematically examined (Ghirza, Bir Scedua, Wadi Buzra, Wadi Umm el-Kharab) was the fourth century. It is possible that military outposts served as a model for some of the early civilian *gsur*. The attested insecurity of the zone at the beginning of the third century, and at intervals through the fourth and fifth, was another reason in favour of a shift to a more defensive style of construction. Equally, the evident prosperity of many of the major landholders suggests that prestige and social status may also have played a part in the widespread adoption of the building style.

No single scheme for the classification of *gsur*, whether based on morphology of ground plan, architectural features or quality of masonry, has gained widespread acceptance. There are endless minor variations in plan and constructional technique presented by the hundreds of examples now known (Fig. 11:1). Some features such as vaulted chambers and battered outer walls and distinctive plasterwork appear to be generally, though not exclusively, a late feature, extending into the Islamic era. Equally, ashlar or near ashlar

construction is normally indicative of very late second- or third-century work. The vast majority of all the *gsur* were small (10–20 m sq) tower-like buildings with a single entrance and one, two or three storeys of rooms normally arranged around a court or central light-well (Plates 50–51). A small number of examples (such as the early third-century site of Mm 10 in the Wadi Mimoun) were much bigger, as were the remarkable and atypical main buildings of fourth-century Ghirza (Plate 54). But such exceptions are rare.

The standards of construction were generally fairly high, with neatly coursed mortared masonry frequently enlivened by decorative door surrounds and internal arches. Some of the architectural features noted imply the presence of skilled masons who had connections with the Gebel and coastal regions. The construction and ornamentation of *gsur* probably absorbed a lot of the surplus capital of the region in this period. With the notable exception of Ghirza, there appear to have been far fewer ashlar mausolea erected in the region in the fourth and fifth centuries than had been commissioned by the second- and third-century inhabitants. Although different socio-economic factors could have lain behind these two very different forms of prestige buildings, there is no reason to doubt that both *gsur* and tombs served to emphasize the personal and communal power of the rural leaders.[1]

In the Gebel regions, there is indisputable evidence from several fortified farms that they were erected on the estates of powerful families, with defence against attacks by 'barbarians or *gentiles*' the motivation in at least one case. Here, then, it would appear that the *gsur* represent the addition of fortifications to existing

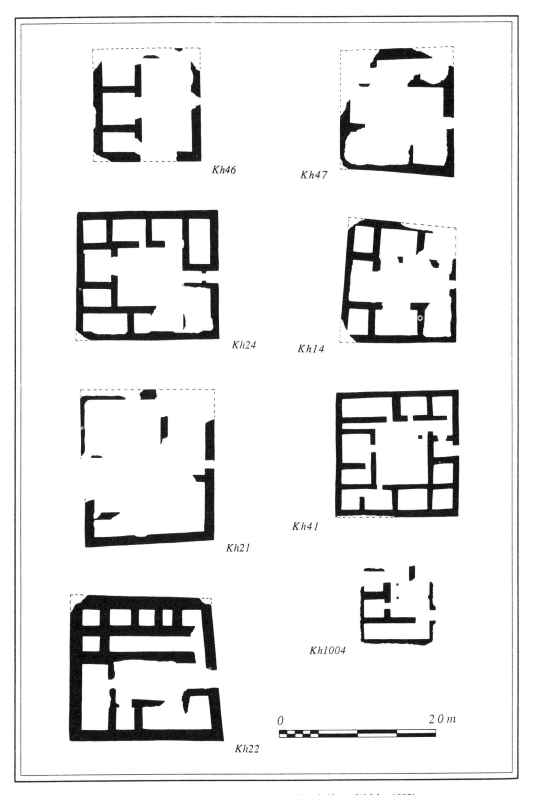

Kh46

Kh47

Kh24

Kh14

Kh21

Kh41

Kh1004

Kh22

0   2 0 m

Fig. 11:1 Comparative plans of *gsur* from the Wadi Umm el-Kharab (from Welsby 1992).

rural estates. The *Austuriani* attacks, especially of the mid-fourth century and later, provide sufficient explanation.

On the other hand, although a number of clear cases of continuity from open farm to *gasr* have been established, some aspects of the late Roman settlement pattern in the pre-desert suggest that a different mode of land organization may have partially replaced the early Roman one. Many *gsur* marked a continuation of existing settlements, possibly organized as large estates centred on *opus africanum* style farms owned by a Libyan group of landholders. However, certain wadis, such as the Ghirza or the Umm el-Kharab, have very high concentrations of *gsur* in such close proximity to each other that the carrying capacity of the adjacent wadi floor agriculture seems to be exceeded (Fig. 10:3). In the latter example,

there appears also to be a case for a phase of discontinuity between the earlier farms being abandoned in the third century and the *gsur* being constructed in the fourth.

Whereas the earlier pattern had been one of dispersed farms and farmsteads, there is a clear tendency towards greater settlement nucleation later. Many *gsur* also have quite large settlements of ancillary buildings around them, reflecting a relocation of rural population (Fig. 11:2; Plates 48, 55). There is some evidence to link distinct concentrations of *gsur* to a revival of tribal links in the area and the hypothesis can be advanced that these served as regional tribal centres (see further below). The evidence from the pre-desert would seem to suggest that initially the estate pattern of the open farms did continue but that this gave way increasingly during the fourth and fifth

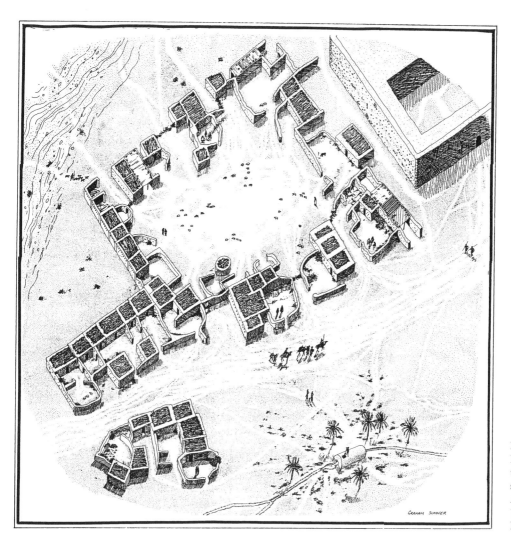

Fig. 11:2
Reconstruction of the subsidiary settlement by *gasr* Ag 1 (from Jones 1985a, cf. Fig. 8:5, Plate 48).

centuries to a pattern of territorial control based on localized clusters of *gsur*.[2]

The documentary sources and the evident decline in the prosperity of the towns indicate that their *territoria* must have become less productive in the course of the fourth and fifth centuries. The *Austuriani* apparently cut down trees and vines in their raid of 365 and the attacks on individual estates involved the plunder or destruction not only of crops but also of buildings and equipment. Unfortunately, no archaeological excavations have yet been carried out on farms in the Gebel Tarhuna to assess their fate in this period. However, the distribution of fortified farms recorded by Oates in the Fergian region of the Tarhuna plateau was significantly thinner than that of the earlier Roman farms and oileries. Some parts of the territory, for instance the area southeast of Gasr ed-Daun, seem to have been comprehensively abandoned, although previously densely covered by olive farms. It seems reasonable to infer from this that there was a decline both in the number of people engaged in farming and in the area under cultivation. Oates associated some of the fortified residences with attempts by the Romano-Libyan elite to defend their estates, but argued convincingly that the majority of the late settlements and the reoccupation of a small number of the earlier olive farms dated to the *Laguatan* takeover of the Gebel lands. Many of the earlier olive presses were no longer maintained, and where presses were adapted in the new buildings, the beam length and overall scale of production was clearly much reduced.[3]

In the pre-desert zone the picture is more confusing. The farming settlements in the wadis south of Syrtica that had thrived in the second and third centuries were for the most part abandoned. Subsequent settlement congregated around the coastal plain, where a few fortified farms were constructed. Similarly, in the Zem-Zem and Sofeggin areas, there are signs that some wadis had passed their peak in the third century or went through a phase of decline then. In other cases, however, there is little doubt that the wadi floor farming systems were greatly extended and made more complex in the late Roman period. This has been demonstrated with particular clarity in the Wadi Umm-Kharab and the Wadi Buzra, where early Roman settlement was limited to certain parts only of the wadi. Although the economy of the province as a whole was in decline, it is interesting that some parts of the frontier zone seem to buck this trend. However, it is possible that the economic relationships were once again becoming embedded in social relations rather than responding to new marketing possibilities.[4]

2
GASR SOCIETY

It has been suggested rather optimistically that, although the people of the frontier zone were predominantly of Libyan or Punic descent, they 'n'en étaient moins loyaliste et romain d'ésprit'. An alternative view of the Roman/native interaction expresses it in terms of Rome building 'a network of families, groups and communities with vested interests in the prolongation of Roman rule'. This relationship may have been threatened when the material prosperity of the province of *Tripolitana* declined in the fourth century. At the same time taxation was rising and the security of the zone breaking down. Once the material advantages of Roman rule were under threat, we cannot assume that blind loyalty and 'Roman spirit' alone will have maintained the long-standing relationship between the authorities and the rural elite. It would be surprising for such a relationship not to undergo changes in the new circumstances.

As we have seen, Courtois was wrong to imagine that the interior part of eastern Tripolitania was abandoned by Rome early in the fourth century simply because it was not very Romanized.[5] Throughout the African provinces Romanization was strongest in the towns and many rural areas retained a strong Punic and Libyan character into the fifth century and beyond. The low level of Romanization in the interior of Tripolitania only became significant at the point when the rural elite became disaffected with Roman rule and opted out of the system. Secession from Rome was not the culmination of long resistance in most cases but marked the relatively abrupt end of centuries of participation.

There is little evidence for increasing Romanization of the pre-desert *gasr* dwellers in the third and fourth centuries. Latin inscriptions continued to be comparatively rare and, in the known examples, the Latin was generally ungrammatical and mis-spelt. The majority of the texts from eastern Tripolitania (from tombs and *gasr* dedications) were cut in Latin letters but used a debased form of the Punic language. Indeed inscriptions which started in Latin show a tendency to lapse into this vernacular language.[6] Although some of the men and women recorded bore Roman *nomina* their *cognomina* remained staunchly Libyan. An inscription from the Bir Scedua area, probably of late third-century date, refers to M[asa]uchan, son of Iylul. These are the same names already encountered on a tomb in the Wadi Umm el-Agerem (see above, chapter 8) and, though the same man cannot be buried in two places, it is possible that there was a family connection between the two areas. Similarly we find a man called Marcius Metusan, whose father was called Fydel or Fidel, both at Ghirza and at a *gasr* in the Wadi Migdal (about 100 km away). The coincidence suggests that they may belong to different generations of the same extended family group or clan. Hierarchical tribal links between extended family groups or clans and marriage alliances will have strengthened the bonds between clans, even where they were exploiting lands some distance apart.[7]

As the official garrison of the region was thinned out in the fourth century, the existence of what was essentially a clan-based society, centred on individual fortified farms, became increasingly important. Many of the names recorded at Bir ed-Dreder are paralleled elsewhere in the ULVS study region. For example, at Bir Dreder one finds Iulius Nasif (*tribunus*), Flabius Isiguar (*tribunus*) and Yriraban, son of Isicuar, [...]imnus Nimira and Flabius Masin[th]an (*tribunus*), whilst for comparison one can cite M. Nasif, Issicuar, Isicua[r], Marcius Nimira and Nimmire and Iulius Severus Masinthan from other sites in eastern Tripolitania. Another name, Macarcum, recurs in Corippus as Magargum.[8]

Ghirza is another site with a very obvious importance in the late Roman period as a sub-tribal centre (Figs 10:5–10:6; Plates 52–61). The settlement is thought to have been dominated by two extended family groups and three inscriptions from one of the cemeteries allow some partial family trees to be reconstructed (Fig. 11:3):

(The tomb) of Marcius Nasif and Marcia Mathlich (their) mother. Marchius Nimira and Fydel, their sons, made this for their beloved parents. (Tomb North A, *IRT* 899)

Marchius Fydel and Flavia Thesylgum, father and mother of Marchius Metusan who made for them this memorial. I have calculated the expenditure exactly. There was disbursed in wages in coin n(inety) thousand folles of denarii simplices, besides food for

the workmen. May my sons and grandsons read and visit the monument in good fortune and may they make monuments like it. (Tomb North B, *IRT* 900)

Marchius Chullam and Varnychsin, father and mother of Marchius Nimmire and Maccurasan, who made for them this memorial. We have calculated the expenditure exactly. There was paid out in wages in coin 45,600 folles of denarii simplices, besides food for the workmen. May our sons and grandsons visit the tomb in fortune. (Tomb North C, *IRT* 898)

All the known funerary inscriptions at Ghirza came from the northern group of mausolea (Plate 56), where *IRT* 899 appears to be from the earliest tomb (A), *IRT* 900 the next (B), then *IRT* 898 (C). All probably date to the first half of the fourth century, with the later tombs of this cemetery, D to F, being added in the period through to the early fifth century (perhaps by the sons and grandsons who were exhorted to do so). At that stage there was evidently a good deal of disposable wealth available, and the construction costs make clear that food and wages were supplied to the artisans employed. Tombs B and C were probably very close in date to judge from the similarity in the wording of the inscriptions and of their architecture and ornamentation (Plate 57). They seem to relate to different branches of the clan assumed to have monopolized this cemetery. A Latino-Punic text thought to come from Ghirza (and thus probably also from the North Tombs) mentions another man called Nasif and seems to concern a monument erected to him by his daughter Thualath. Presumably this was a later generation of one of the families discussed above. The existence of several related families making up two clans of a sub-tribe based at Ghirza might be surmised by the existence of six *gsur* but only two elite cemetery areas.[9]

Another interesting aspect to note is the importance attached to the continuation of respect for dead ancestors, not simply in the present generation, but in the future ones as well. This receives added support from another inscription, poorly preserved and found

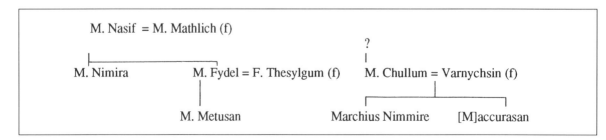

Fig. 11:3 Partial family tree from the North cemetery at Ghirza, fourth century AD (cf. Plates 56–57).

out of context close to the three tombs already referred to. It mentioned a celebration of the *parentalia* and recorded the sacrifice of 51 bulls and 38 goats for the occasion. This does not appear to have been a small family gathering and the use of the Latin term probably relates not to the normal Roman festival of the *parentalia* but to a Libyan ancestor cult identified with what appeared to be its nearest Roman equivalent. The scale of the sacrifice, and of the presumed accompanying feast, looks to be more appropriate for a sub-tribal group than a single family. The importance of ancestry and lineage are, of course, fundamental to the functioning of the hierarchical structures of Libyan tribes (see chapter 2, above).

The status of the leading men buried with their wives in these tombs is further reinforced by some of the lively relief carvings that decorate their friezes. Two scenes from tombs North B and C are of particular importance, in that they show chieftains seated on cross-legged chairs holding scrolls and attended by individuals bearing specific symbols of office or gifts (a sceptre, a wine jug, bows and arrows). Another scene that is common to both tombs appears to show a prisoner suffering corporal or capital punishment. Whatever gloss we may put on the nature of authority being exerted in the first scene, the second would seem to imply that the Ghirza chieftains enjoyed a considerable degree of judicial autonomy from the state (or perhaps exercised such power on the state's behalf). Several scenes from other tombs show fighting between well-dressed and well-armed men (presumably the *gasr*-dwellers) and semi-naked or naked Libyans and, once again, these images raise questions about the freedom of the pre-desert communities from normal civil rules. Although at one level the tombs celebrate individual families there are many features about Ghirza that seem to fit more easily into a tribal or chiefly framework than into a pattern of elite-run rural estates. Scenes of agricultural activities and camel caravans on the tombs suggest two possible sources of income (Plates 59–61), though the wealth of the settlement seems out of proportion to the extremely marginal environment of the southern Zem-Zem.

Not all the elite individuals at Ghirza were as Romanized as the Marcii. Two other men commemorated on inscriptions at Ghirza were known simply by their Libyan names – Nasif and Isiguar – three inscriptions were written in Latino-Punic and there are many Libyan texts from the site also. Significantly, there was no church at Ghirza but a major pagan temple (see below).[10]

It is a reasonable hypothesis that at neither Bir ed-Dreder/Bir Scedua nor Ghirza were the *gsur*-dwellers recruited *stricto sensu* as 'soldier-farmers' or militia but that the Roman government recognized and exploited the relative autonomy and local political dominance of sub-tribal groups. There are a number of other major concentrations of late Roman settlement in the pre-desert that seem to be of a similar character to those at Ghirza and in the Scedua basin. The *gsur,* church and associated settlements at Souk el Oti (Souk el Awty) in the Wadi Buzra and the dense concentration of *gsur* in the Wadi Umm-el-Kharab have recently been examined in some detail. As at Ghirza and Scedua, neither of these areas seems to have been of outstanding importance in the initial phase of wadi settlement, but came into their own in the fourth and fifth centuries. Sites in both the Umm el-Kharab and the Buzra continued in occupation into the seventh century (and possibly beyond, though diagnostic pottery unfortunately does not exist to prove this). The architecture of the Kharab *gsur* has been studied in detail (Fig. 11:1), with three main types of layout being defined (though with many minor divergencies being noted). Although one unique *gasr* has been interpreted as a fortified storage building, the others are seen as dwellings. Some sophisticated aspects of ornamentation and standard techniques and materials of construction were interpreted as evidence for the work of specialist constructors. The diversity in building plan and the limited dating evidence available suggest that the eight *gsur* were built over a considerable period of time.[11]

The church at Souk el Oti is of particular significance in that it is one of only two known in the pre-desert region (see below). The tribal group who occupied the Wadi Buzra region were evidently Christianized and the size of the settlement adjacent to the church suggests that the site probably functioned also as a regional market centre (Fig. 11:4; Plate 58).

There are other instances of particularly large fortified farms and associated villages, or of significant groupings of *gsur* in the ULVS area. It is a reasonable assumption that these sites demonstrate something of the local balance of power in the late Roman period. Tribal leaders and regional clans will have maintained relations between the hundreds of fortified farms but with the major sites perhaps fulfilling primary functions such as market centres and as points of socio-political control.

Close parallels can be drawn from late fourth-century *Mauretania Sitifensis* and *Caesariensis,* where the great landowners in the frontier zone (who were also tribal leaders) were delegated frontier roles by Rome as in the documented case of Sammac and Firmus. The murder of the pro-Roman Sammac in 373

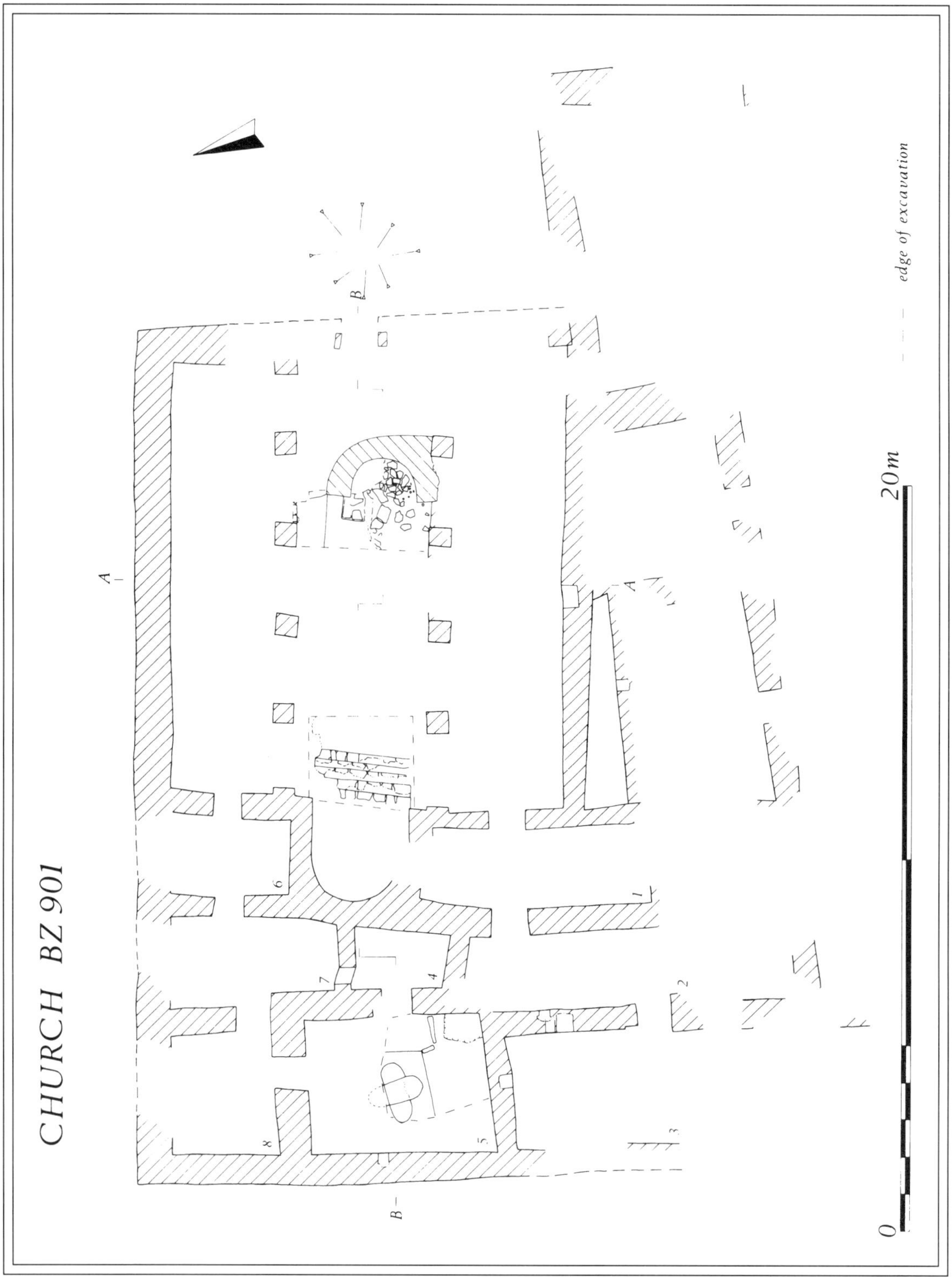

Fig. 11:4 Plan of the church at Souk el-Oti (after Welsby 1991).

seems to have been an intra-tribal affair rather than an overtly rebellious act, since his half-brother and killer, Firmus, seems to have hoped that his action would have no political repercussions. Ammianus tells us that Romanus, still *comes Africae,* suppressed Firmus' explanation of his conduct in order to seek personal revenge for the death of Sammac (who had been a favourite of his) and this provoked the actual revolt. Matthews has shown convincingly that the events of the revolt related to the old frontier zone, where Sammac, Firmus and other Moorish chiefs fulfilled certain duties of frontier control on Rome's behalf. They also exercised their power from fortified farmhouses not dissimilar to the Tripolitanian ones, and the location of Sammac's strong point, the *fundus Petrensis,* is known from its impressive dedicatory inscription. This well-known Latin inscription spells out in flowery language the important roles that Sammac considered himself to be playing in the maintenance of peace on behalf of Rome. There were few regular troops left in the region and the Moorish chiefs evidently arranged treaties and provided a certain amount of local policing centred on their impressive fortified farmhouses. Some of these chieftains, including Nubel, the father of Sammac and Firmus, also held official army posts in the field army and Gildo, a third brother, was later *comes Africae.*[12]

Just as in *Tripolitana,* the Mauretanian frontier zone came to be dominated by an elite group whose power was based on traditional tribal ties, on their position as the major landholders in the region and on Roman support for them. A distinguishing feature in the Mauretanian case was the greater level of participation in imperial administration and military career structures. The distinction reflects the relative importance of the two theatres, with the Mauretanian leaders much more in contact with high-status Roman military personnel.

The decline of the inland cash economy in *Tripolitana* in the fourth century – caused by shrinking Mediterranean trade and a reduced market – ought to have created a certain amount of disaffection amongst the pro-Roman Libyan nobility. But the ties that bound the frontier people to Rome seem to have changed, with the importance of military and political strength rising above wealth from surplus-oriented farming as indicators of social prestige. Given these changing conditions some of the leading frontier farmers may have been very receptive to the possibility of obtaining treaties, honorary titles, gifts and even stipends from Rome. References to this sort of treaty relationship in Byzantine times declared it to be a continuation of late Roman practice in the area.

Although Libyco-Punic culture continued to be important in the frontier zone there was also something of a resurgence of a more purely Libyan culture. At Ghirza, for instance, four of the main buildings had Libyan dedications on their doorways. Another building in the settlement proved on excavation to have been a pagan temple and yielded 20 votive altars, 3 of which were inscribed with undeciphered Libyan slogans. None of the temple dedications was in Latin or Punic, perhaps a sign that the region was becoming decreasingly literate in those languages in the transition to the post-Roman period.[13]

The role played by the *Laguatan* confederation in the revived tribalism and de-Romanization of the region was significant. New tribes migrated westwards in the late Roman period, assimilating existing populations of the oases of the northern Sahara into their confederation. The *Nasamones, Garamantes* and *Phazanii* tribes, who had remained generally reliable hegemonic allies of Rome, were destabilized at a time when the military and diplomatic effectiveness of the frontier had been weakened by establishment cut-backs.

The farmers of the frontier zone were faced with a dilemma. They needed to defend their lands, but for their farming and shepherding to be feasible they also had to maintain symbiotic relationships with the transhuming people from the oases and these people were now *Laguatan* or allies of the latter. In the event it was the *territoria* of the coastal cities that suffered the worst onslaught of the *Laguatan* raids and one may surmise that the people of the frontier zone were gradually assimilated by the confederation. The continued occupation of some of the pre-desert *gsur* into the fifth and sixth centuries attests to the stability of the symbiotic relationship between pastoralist and sedentarist despite the collapse of Roman authority. The Vandals and Byzantine officials continued to make treaties with the tribal groups of *Tripolitana,* but these were more like insecure non-aggression pacts than the earlier pattern of hegemonic alliances backed by force. The Libyan revival was strongest in eastern Tripolitania initially, but by the early fifth century, western Tripolitania and even the coastal regions were coming under the influence of the renewed tribalism.

3
CHRISTIANITY AND PAGANISM IN *TRIPOLITANA*

Roman Africa was one of the earliest of the western Mediterranean provinces to have a substantial Christian community and in consequence produced a notable crop of martyrs in the persecutions of the third and initial years of the fourth centuries. The lifting of the threat of further persecution by Constantine, with some measure of positive discrimination running in their favour, saw the rapid advance of the now legitimate Christian Church in communal life in the early fourth century. Nowhere is this more clearly documented than in North Africa, where a wealth of archaeological evidence for the churches established by the flourishing Christian communities is supplemented by an extraordinarily detailed archive of contemporary documentation on Church history.

The prime reason for the abundance of textual material, however, is that from the very beginning of Constantine's reign the Church in Africa had started on a schismatic course that was to split it into two camps, the Catholics and the Donatists. The origins of the schism lay in the events of the Great Persecution of 303, because, alongside the many martyrs, there were clearly many officers of the Church who had survived the events by compromising their faith (primarily by handing over Church scriptures to the authorities – hence the Latin term for them, *traditores*). The Bishop of Carthage died just as the persecution ended and a successor, Caecilianus, was hastily appointed, without respect for either tradition or for the views of the Numidian bishops. The appointment was challenged by the Numidian primate and a rival bishop, Maiorinus, was elected. Constantine, however, recognized Caecilianus as the legitimate bishop and chose to channel his financial aid for the African Church through the latter's office. It is easy to understand why Rome preferred to deal with the 'Church of compromise' rather than with a group of hard-line bishops who did not intend to let either the Church or the state draw a veil over the events of the persecution.

In 313 Maiorinus died and a man called Donatus was elected by the opponents of Caecilianus as their rival bishop, soon giving his name to the schismatists, the Donatists. There were now two rival Churches in Africa, both claiming to be the true faith and with radically different policies on crucial matters such as the redemption of the *traditores*. Despite the fact that several Church councils and official investigations into the circumstances surrounding the election of Caecilianus found in favour of the Catholics, the Donatists refused to give up their cause. After riots in Carthage, the repression of the Donatists began (317), giving the rival Church its first martyrs. The popularity of Donatism continued to grow, however, particularly in the inland regions of *Africa, Byzacena* and *Numidia*, where the cult of the martyrs appears to have been a feature of the Early Church that struck a

cord with the Romano-Africans. In many of the larger towns of the provinces, sees of both the official and Donatist Churches were set up, and periodically there was sectarian violence between the rival factions within the towns. For the most part the state continued its firm support for the Catholics and indulged in periodic purges against the Donatists, especially when the latter developed a paramilitary (or terrorist) wing (depending on the viewpoint of the commentator). The *circumcelliones*, as they were known, were again particularly active in *Numidia*. In the late fourth century Augustine lent his considerable weight to the Catholic cause and in response to Catholic agitation the emperor Honorius sent a special tribune to Africa in an attempt to solve the issue once and for all. A council was held before the tribune, Marcellinus, in Carthage in June 411 which all Donatist and Catholic bishops were invited to attend. The decision of Marcellinus was once again in favour of the Catholics, and he ordered all Donatist property confiscated and banned them from meeting together. Despite this final decision, the controversy dragged on and in many districts, particularly rural ones, the Donatists were still a force to be reckoned with in the later sixth century.[14]

It is against this background that the evidence for the spread of Christianity in *Tripolitana* must be considered. In this respect, the region stands out once again from the other African provinces, in that it is clear that Christianity was by no means as successful here as it was elsewhere. The first bishop recorded, with his see at *Lepcis,* was Archaeus, an immigrant to judge from the name, in the late second century. At the time of the mid-third-century persecution there were others at *Girba, Oea* and *Sabratha*. Against the hundreds of bishoprics established in *Africa, Byzacena, Numidia* and in the Mauretanian provinces, *Tripolitana* for much of the fourth century at least seems to have had just five, with the addition of *Tacapae* to those previously mentioned. This was certainly the case as late as 397, when a proposal to increase the number of bishops required at the ordination of a new bishop was rebutted on the grounds that any change to the rules would create exceptional difficulties for the five Tripolitanian sees. There were some bishoprics in the ecclesiastical *regio Arzugitana*, probably located in the oases of the Nefzaoua and Djerid and thus attached to the province of *Byzacena*. The Church sources talk of the Tripolitanian sees as being frequently separated from those of *Arzugitana* by barbarian peoples. Special dispensation seems to have been made for *Tripolitana* to send a single bishop to represent the other sees at councils in Carthage or Hippo, as is attested in AD 393, 403 and 418. The reasoning behind this policy may have taken account of limited Church resources in the province, as well as the factors of distance and the small number of bishoprics.

However, at the Carthage conference in 411, there were eight Tripolitanian sees represented, possibly due to the deliberate tactic on both sides of the argument of swelling their numbers by creating some rather peripheral bishoprics. *Girba* and *Tacapae* were represented by both a Catholic and Donatist in Carthage for the council (though in the event Felix the Donatist bishop of *Tacapae* was too ill to attend proceedings). *Gigthis*, *Sabratha* and the see for the *plebs Sinnipsensis* (*Cinyps*) were solely Catholic, while *Lepcis*, *Oea* and *Villa Magna* were represented by Donatist bishops only. The uncontested nature of some of the sees is made certain by the detailed verbal record of the 411 conference but the evidence is inconclusive for *Lepcis* and *Oea* while at *Sabratha* the absence of a Donatist rival was presented as a recent occurrence. Major cities like *Lepcis* would more commonly have been expected to have representatives of both Churches. From other testimony it is clear that by no means all bishops on both sides had been able to attend.

Amongst the hundreds of bishops present in 411, only Salvianus (*Lepcis*, Donatist) appears to have played a significant role, perhaps as one of a team of seven advisers to their seven spokesmen. In the 390s, the Donatist bishop of Sabratha had given influential support to a sub-schism within his own movement (once again caused by a disputed election to the see at Carthage) and had been excommunicated from the Donatist Church along with 12 other 'Maximianists'. For the most part, though, the Tripolitanian Church was on the fringe of things and the major incidents and violence of the Donatist controversy took place elsewhere in Africa. It is likely that Donatism was generally stronger than Catholicism in *Tripolitana*, though the archaeological evidence for Donatists is meagre. The Donatist bishops at the 411 conference seem to have been somewhat better organized.[15]

The spread of Christianity in *Tripolitana* had its greatest success in the coastal cities and in the eastern Gebel region. At *Girba* one church has been excavated, at *Sabratha* four are known, and at *Lepcis* six (though some of those in the latter two cases were only founded in the Byzantine period). The major study of Tripolitanian churches adds a further six in the eastern Gebel, but only two churches in the Sofeggin wadi basin and none at all in the Zem-Zem. Christian catacombs are known from *Sabratha*, *Marcomades* and Tarhuna; two open Christian cemeteries have been excavated on the fringes of the Tripoli oasis at Ain

Zara and en Ngila. Partial excavation of a fortified building at Henschir Taglissi (12 km south of Garian) has yielded a remarkable series of finely decorated lintels and architectural pieces, proclaiming the strong Donatist sympathies of its owner, Aemilianus, but with no certain structural evidence for a chapel or church there. Finds of other Christian buildings, inscriptions, burials or cemeteries and Christian symbols strengthen the evidence for highly Christianized communities in the Gebel Tarhuna, Garian and Nefusa, but for minimal penetration of Christianity amongst the pre-desert *gasr*-dwellers. There is little evidence for the impact of Christianity in the hinterland of western Tripolitania where, signally, Trousset did not record the existence of a single church along the *limes*.[16]

Three of the churches excavated at *Sabratha* were characteristic of pre-Byzantine basilicas in *Tripolitana*. This type of church was a three-aisled basilica, with a raised apse at the western end and the chancel and altar prominently positioned in the central section of the nave. With variations in scale and decoration, this was the most common model adopted in the late fourth- and fifth-century churches throughout the province and is well-attested in the other African provinces too. Only one of the six churches located at *Lepcis*, constructed over a demolished pagan temple in the old forum, can be shown to conform to a pre-Byzantine type, this being an early fifth-century three-aisled type with an eastern apse and twinned columns.[17]

Various fragments of Christian architectural fragments and inscriptions have been found in Tripoli but no *in situ* remains of a church. The cemeteries of Ain Zara (14 km southwest of Tripoli) and of en Ngila (18 km southeast of the city) are of late antique or Islamic date demonstrating the long-term survival of Chritianity in the Tripoli oasis. The earliest tombs at Ain Zara are believed to post-date 451 and five dated graves at en Ngila fall between 945 and 1003.[18]

In the *territoria* of the coastal cities, the earliest churches again seem to conform to the late fourth-century three-aisled type with raised western apse. Examples have been excavated at el-Asabaa, Tebedut (with large altar platform visible in the centre of the nave); Ain Wif (*Thenadassa*) and Breviglieri (Hr el-Aftah). Breviglieri was a particularly ornate example and shows evidence for a subsequent Byzantine enlargement, including the addition of a cruciform baptistery. The decorative carving for brackets, imposts and lintels has a distinctive regional style and quality and has been interpreted as the work of a master craftsman or school. The construction of these churches may be dated broadly to the late fourth or early fifth century. An early sixth-century coin hoard, whose latest issues pre-date the Byzantine reconquest, was buried below secondary paving in the church at el-Asabaa.

A probable church at Gasr Maamùra had a trichoncos form, so far unique in *Tripolitana*. Its massive apsidal vaults seem to have been covered originally with glass mosaic. The site was part of a *gasr*-like complex, situated on a precipitous ridge. The small church at Wadi Crema was possibly entirely Byzantine in date, possessing an eastern apse level with the nave floor. The insertion of cruciform baptisteries and other structural modifications of the church complexes at el-Asabaa and Breviglieri, indicate continuing use of these churches well into the sixth century or later.

Ain Wif was a 'small town', developed around a small military post of second/third-century date. The churches at Breviglieri, Gasr Maamùra, Tebedut, on the other hand, were associated with substantial fortified buildings. It is unclear what sort of community was served by the other churches, but a close link with neighbouring *gsur* is possible. The Donatist inscriptions in the fortified building of Aemilianus at Hr Taglissi also show a close connection between the church and the *gasr*-dwellers.[19]

Only two churches are known in the Libyan predesert, Chafagi Aamer in the upper Wadi Sofeggin, near Mizda, and Souk el Oti (el Awty) in the Wadi Buzra, south of Beni Ulid in the middle Sofeggin. As a result of excavations in 1989 at the latter site, both can now be viewed as examples of the standard Tripolitanian pre-Byzantine type. However, cruciform baptisteries were added to both buildings and at Souk el Oti an eastern apse was inserted into the nave, to conform with Byzantine custom (Fig. 11:4; Plate 58). In order to allow continued entry into the church through its east door, this new apse was built nearly 2 m down the length of the nave and slightly offset from the main axis (its odd position leading previous investigators to speculate that this was a Mihrab, representing conversion of the church to mosque). Although Islamic religious use of the church must now be dismissed, the dating of the Souk el Oti settlement spans the period fourth–seventh century and continuity beyond that date is a possibility (given the non-recognition of diagnostic pottery for the sub-Roman period). The church itself is likely to have been built no earlier than *c*. 400. When abandoned as a religious building, the church appears to have been converted into a stable. Chafagi Aamer and Suk el Oti are part of large *gasr* settlements that could have served as important regional *foci*.[20]

The size of all the churches in the Tripolitanian hinterland was fairly small, their external measurements (including apses but excluding additional suites of rooms) ranging from 34 x 19 m (Ain Wif) to 13.1 x 10 m (Wadi Crema). The communities that they served on a regular basis were perhaps based around the occupants of individual *gsur* and dependent settlements. A relationship between some of the *gasr*-dwellers and Christian worship is supported by the evidence for the distribution of Christian symbols (chi-rho monogram, alpha and omega, monogram cross, Latin cross, Greek cross, etc.). These have been found on at least five fortified farms in the Gebel region (another seven fragments are unprovenanced or out of context, but may well have come from domestic buildings rather than churches), on another *gasr* lying between Gebel and Sofeggin and on a single *gasr* in the Sofeggin basin (near Chafagi Aamer). The type and style of imagery employed also supports the view that the interior spread of Christianity was a comparatively late phenomenon, roughly of 375–425. Despite the superb quality of preservation of the *gsur* in the pre-desert wadis, in comparison to those of the Gebel, the lack of additional identified churches or Christian symbols would suggest that this region was generally resistant to the spread of Christianity. The Christian communities at Souk el Oti and Chafagi Aamer must have been fairly isolated in what seems to have remained a staunchly pagan region. Once again, this recalls the correspondence between Augustine and Publicola, concerning the latter's qualms about using labourers who had sworn pagan oaths on his estate in the *regio Arzugum*. In penning his practical reply (that Publicola should not worry too much and must make the best of it), Augustine was no doubt all too well aware of the limited penetration of the Church in the old frontier zone.[21]

In summary, then, the province was largely spared the worst traumas of the Donatist controversy but may have shown some Donatist tendencies. Christianity was well established in the cities and in the Gebel lands in the eastern part of the province (where it survived down to the eleventh century among the Nefusa communities). In contrast, the limited acceptance of Christianity in the frontier region indicates the continuing strength of Punic and Libyan traditions there.

Most of the known late pagan temples were small shrines, in fact much harder to differentiate archaeologically than churches, and many of the elaborate mausolea served as *foci* for the Libyan ancestor cult. Two important Libyan deities attested in late antiquity were Ammon and his bull-headed progeny Gurzil. They played a prominent role in the *Laguatan* wars with *Byzantium* in the sixth century. Ierna, who was the *Laguatan* commander-in-chief in 546, was also high priest of Gurzil. A connection has sometimes been suggested between the names Gurzil and Ghirza, not least because El Bekri wrote in the eleventh century of an inland site called Gurza where paganism was still practised. There is now some additional evidence to suggest that this etymological connection may be correct. An inscription, found by Ghirza tomb North A, refers to a sacrifice involving no less than 51 bulls and a relief panel on another tomb shows a bull being sacrificed. Moreover, one of the major buildings at Ghirza has proved on excavation to be a major temple of Semitic type. It is far larger than the normal cult shrines (such as Tininai) and 20 votive altars were recovered, along with stone bowls and other cult objects. The significant number of Libyan inscriptions in this building has already been remarked on above. If Ghirza was indeed the centre of the Gurzil cult in the late Roman period then it provides an additional reason as to why the settlement became so large and remained comparatively wealthy. As a tribal and religious centre, probably with attendant market functions, the site was undoubtedly one of the most important in the entire pre-desert zone. The close religious affinities between the Romano-Libyan people of Ghirza and the Ammon worshipping *Laguatan* could ultimately have cut across whatever loyalty they had to Rome and facilitated their absorption into the confederation.[22]

12

DE-ROMANIZATION AND SECESSION

1
ENDING UP OR OPTING OUT?

Both the Romanization and de-Romanization of *Tripolitana* involved above all the 'estate of management' (the Libyan elite) and not the 'estate of production' (the peasantry). There is no evidence of a 'peasants' revolt' against Roman rule, as one scholar has argued. The social status of the rural poor was if anything rather worse at the end of the Roman period than it had been earlier, with tribal ties and obligations taking on a more feudal aspect. Under the *pax Romana* tribal society and tribal hierarchy had come to be exploited by a seigneurial class enjoying Rome's favour and support. It was the same once pro-Roman elite who led the secession from Rome, when their best interests were no longer served by remaining a part of the empire. We have noted how this also applied in *Mauretania*. The *Laguatan* provided a complicating factor in *Tripolitana* but even the migratory elements of these tribes were transformed from raiders to settlers during the fifth and sixth centuries, with their leaders seeking to establish themselves in a seigneurial role on lands in the old *territoria* of the cities.[1]

Second, it is apparent that resistance and secession were not the inevitable outcomes of the cultural make-up of the Tripolitanian frontier zone. The people were not very Romanized and their language, culture and religion remained predominantly Punic or Libyan in nature. Yet the Roman system endured for as long as it had the active support of the Libyan

elite in the countryside and it was only during the fourth and fifth centuries that the basis of that support was effectively eroded.

The reasons for this change are several and complex. The farming of the marginal frontier environment did not come to a sudden end, as one might expect it to have done had there been major climatic change. But one can suggest that its initial development was something of an anomaly in such an arid zone. Over time the productivity of heavily cultivated marginal soils can start to decline alarmingly.[2] The shrinkage of the artificial cash economy of the Mediterranean region in the fourth century AD perhaps precipitated a return to an economy based more closely on subsistence production and tribal dues and obligations. The economic advantages of remaining part of a Roman province were among the first things to be lost with the decline of the province's Mediterranean trade.

At the same time the Roman military establishment was reduced to the bare essentials. The isolation of the province from the nearest field army units under the command of the *comes Africae* effectively left the frontier out on a limb and invited attack by tribes no longer inhibited and controlled by the earlier Roman policy of deterrence. *Laguatan* did not possess any secret weapon, they fought as light-armed horsemen – just as the the *Garamantes* or *Nasamones* had previously done. There is no reason to believe that they posed a significantly bigger threat. The failure to punish the *Laguatan,* by punitive raids against their oases centres, destroyed the credibility of the frontier in eastern Tripolitania and severed the last links of self-interest of many of the Libyan elite with the provincial structure. As a result the *Laguatan* consolidated their position and their confederation spread to engulf the people of *Tripolitana*. The petty warlords and tribal chiefs continued to make non-aggression pacts with Rome but in the final phase, even before the Vandals occupied the coastal towns, interior *Tripolitana* was in all probability already being transformed into a largely autonomous Libyan and tribal-dominated territory.

2
VANDAL AND BYZANTINE
TRIPOLITANA

When Boniface, *comes Africae* from 423 to 430, was suspected of disloyalty by the empress Placidia and refused to respond to her summons, she sent two expeditions, including a Gothic army, to recover the African provinces. In desperation, Boniface sought assistance, but his choice of allies proved an unfortunate one for, having already invited the Vandals across from Spain into Africa, he was then reconciled with the imperial house but found that his invited guests refused to leave. The defeat of Boniface in 430 by Gaiseric and his Vandals marked the beginning of the end of Roman Africa. For the next two decades the Vandals gradually consolidated their position, the sieges of major cities culminating in the fall of Carthage in 439. By a treaty of 442, the emperor ceded all the African provinces to the west of *Tripolitana* and for a further 13 years the latter continued its tenuous existence. Even when it was ceded to them in 455, it is not apparent that the Vandals paid a great deal of attention to *Tripolitana*.[3]

For this reason the region was selected as the base of several attempts by the eastern emperors to recapture Africa. Early efforts failed, as in 470, when Leo dispatched a force under Heracleius to *Tripolis*. After initial success against the meagre Vandal garrison based there, Heracleius embarked on a disastrous land march on Carthage itself. In the early sixth century a defeat was also suffered by the Vandals in *Tripolitana* (or alternatively in southern *Byzacena*) at the hands of a *Laguatan* chieftain, Caboan. When the successful Byzantine reconquest of Africa was launched by Justinian in 532 it was in response to yet another revolt against Vandal authority in the Tripolitanian region, this time led by a leading citizen of one of the towns, Pudentius. Justinian sent him a small force under the general Tattimuth and, with no significant Vandal force based in the region at that time, they proclaimed Byzantine rule there in 532. The full-scale invasion force under Belisarius was sent the following year.[4]

For much of Roman Africa the Vandal conquest did not result in cataclysmic change. The conquerors seized some of the best lands of *Proconsularis* and *Byzacena* for themselves without displacing the dependent peasantry. Elsewhere, the Romano-Africans continued to farm the land as before, as is clear from the Albertini Tablets, a cache of late fifth-century documents from a pre-desert estate on the Algerian/Tunisian border. The cultivation of this estate was carried out by many tenant farmers working small plots of land in the wadi beds, and provides a vivid illustration of the sort of farming documented by the ULVS in the Tripolitanian pre-desert also. The Vandals also concluded treaties with the various Berber tribes and kingdoms beyond their territory. Even in some of the areas of *Mauretania* which had passed out of Roman control prior to the Vandal conquest Latin inscriptions show that a vague semblance of *Romanitas* continued for many years. However, little is known of the precise dealings between Vandals and *Laguatan*.[5]

The Byzantine reconquest a century later in AD 533 once again brought about a seigneurial change on the best agricultural land, notably that in northern Tunisia. Once the Vandals were disposed of, the Byzantine army came into conflict with some of the Berber tribes and new frontiers were created in several sectors. The reconquered territory of *Tripolitana*, however, did not extend much beyond the coastal plain and peace depended on treaty relationships with individual *Laguatan* sub-tribes.

The peace was destroyed in 544 by the massacre of 79 *Laguatan* sub-chiefs after Sergius, the Byzantine *dux*, had sworn safe-conduct for them on the Holy Scriptures. It took four years of savage fighting to quell the revolt. One of the *Laguatan* commanders in this revolt may have had a connection with Ghirza, since Ierna was high priest of the god Gurzil. At any rate the temple at Ghirza was destroyed at about this date (and perhaps other parts of the settlement), possibly as the result of a Byzantine reprisal in the aftermath of the revolt.[6]

During the period of Byzantine rule there was a further decline in Latinity, Romanization and urban life. Many of the Byzantine officials of course were Greek-speaking foreigners and it is uncertain to what extent they built a close *rapprochement* with the town-dwellers. Town life of sorts continued at the main cities, *Tacapae*, *Gigthis*, *Lepcis*, *Sabratha* and *Oea* (now the most important city of the region). However, at both *Lepcis* and *Sabratha*, the Byzantine 'cities' were little more than fortified harbours, with the new defences enclosing only a tiny percentage of the ground covered when the towns were at their peak (at *Lepcis* just 44 ha/110 acres, later reduced to 28 ha/64 acres, compared to 130 ha/325 acres within the late Roman circuit; at *Sabratha* only 9 ha/22.5 acres). A number of new churches were built under the auspices of the Byzantine officials, primarily one suspects to serve the needs of the garrisons rather than from concern to embellish the towns. As noted above (chapter 9), the late antique townscapes were very different from those of the principate, with many irregular private dwellings invading the interior space of ex-public buildings or encroaching on street frontages, and theatres and amphitheatres becoming fortified residences. There are no indications that Byzantine rule in the region did anything to check this decivilizing of the towns. Life in towns, if not exactly akin to Roman town life, continued into the Arab period.

In rural areas the Byzantine reconquest was not entirely popular since these new *Romanoi* proved to be more efficient tax-collectors than the Vandals had been. Christianity was to prove the most resilient aspect of Roman culture and in some areas it lingered on well into the Middle Ages. But even before the Arab invasions the general social pattern was changing back towards a rural-based, fragmented tribal society.[7]

3
SUB-ROMAN AND ARAB TRIPOLITANIA

This trend was amplified following the Arab conquest of the Maghreb, though life of some sort continued in many urban centres beyond the mid-seventh century. In the long term, though, the Maghreb declined from being one of the most densely urbanized areas of the western Mediterranean to being one of the least urbanized by the later Middle Ages. During this same period, sedentary agriculture was increasingly supplanted by semi-nomadic pastoralism and political and military power was frequently in the hands of vast tribal confederations. The cultures which emerged dominant from centuries of political and religious turmoil were Libyan (Berber) and Arabic. The long-term legacy of both Punic and Roman civilization to the Maghreb has been small.[8]

The Vandals and Byzantines had never occupied much more than the coastal strip in *Tripolitana*, the rest of the country being occupied by *Laguatan* sub-tribes. Although Roman rule continued without interruption in *Cyrenaica* into the seventh century direct control was increasingly confined to no more than the coastal cities and their immediate hinterland. When the first Arab invasion took place in 642 the interior tribes, who were described by Arab sources as *Lawata* (= *Laguatan*), controlled the plateau and had treaties with the Byzantine government. Amr Ibn el-Aasi, the Arab commander, ignored the Byzantine forces that were preparing to make a last stand at coastal *Tauchira* (Tocra). Instead he made for *Barca*, on the plateau, there concluding a treaty with the *Lawata* of the region. The relatively insignificant Byzantine forces were dealt with at a later date. The implication of this is surely that political dominance over the more numerous *Laguatan* was the key to controlling the region.[9]

Resistance in *Tripolitana* to the first Arab raid in AD 643 was entirely ineffectual. *Oea* was captured by an unexpected attack through an unprotected gap at the seaward end of her western defences. The successful Arabs immediately rode on through the night to surprise *Sabratha* early the next day with her 'gates wide open'. The first attack was primarily one seeking booty and the Arabs duly departed eastwards heavily laden. The Byzantine officials seem to have fled by sea during the siege and it is not clear if they had returned when the Tripolitanian cities were again taken by the Arab armies moving west in a more concerted fashion in 645.[10]

There is some evidence for continued occupation and mixed farming in the former frontier zone long after the Arab conquest, though interpretation of the archaeological record is at present hampered by a lack of diagnostic pottery series for this period. The Arab government based in Tripoli frequently encountered trouble in its dealings with the interior tribes. As happened in *Cyrenaica*, the tribes retained their local autonomy in return for acknowledging Arab hegemony and paying tribute. In the ULVS study area it is apparent that *gsur* were still being built in the ninth century AD and there are hints of continued occupation at a number of earlier sites. In the eleventh century el-Bekri referred to the fertility of the Sofeggin valley, to a *gasr* in the Wadi Mimoun, and to the continued importance of *Gurza* (Ghirza) as a pagan religious centre. The old temple at Ghirza was reoccupied by a merchant in the tenth and eleventh centuries, so the religious ritual by this date may have become centred on the tombs. In the Wadi Mimoun and in its tributary, the Wadi Buzra, there is evidence for settlement continuing at least until the seventh century, notably at Souk el Oti and Souk el Fogi (the 'upper' and 'lower' markets) on the Buzra. The existence of these local markets may imply the more widespread continuation of wadi farming and pastoralism in the region.[11]

Gradually, some of the remoter and more marginal wadis were abandoned for sedentary farming and from about the eleventh century there appears to have been an increasing concentration of population in the northern wadis, notably in a series of major villages such as Ben Telis on the Wadi Beni Ulid. This area became the political and military centre of the Orfella tribe. The Orfella confederation incorporated both Arab and Libyan groups from the region, as is demonstrated by the continuity of wadi agriculture in the Wadi Beni Ulid to the present day.

Continuity is also to be found in the Berber communities of southern Tunisia and northwest Libya. Relic Berber populations survived the invasions in remote, fortifed villages in the Gebel Matmata, Gebel Demmer and Gebel Nefusa, and, once again, these are regions where the technology of flood-water farming in the wadis has survived almost unchanged. Christianity endured amongst some of the Nefusa tribes until the eleventh century and Christian inscriptions of tenth- and eleventh-century date have also been found near the Tripoli oasis. In the aftermath of the Beni Hillal invasions and the ending of religious toleration Islam triumphed and the culture of the Berbers today is essentially Libyan and Arab in equal measure. The important factor to appreciate, though, is that social and cultural changes were relatively slow and superficial up until the eleventh and twelfth centuries AD. In the interim period, *Tripolitana* remained what it had become in the late Roman period, namely a region of revived Libyan tribal societies.[12]

4
DECLINE AND FALL

The collapse of a great superpower has many repercussions for its constituent territories. However, the fall of Rome was not solely responsible for the decline of *Tripolitana*. Other factors can be advanced at the regional level – above all concerned with its marginality. Time and again in this book, we have observed points of geographic, climatic, environmental, economic and cultural disjunction between Tripolitania and the rest of Roman Africa. In addition, the accidents of imperial succession, first bringing Septimius Severus to power then wiping out his dynastic successors, had their part to play in the making and breaking of the region's good fortune. So, too, did the attested 'invasions' of *Laguatan*, though I have questioned whether the threat was really as great as the inadequacy of the response has made it appear. Earthquakes have also been blamed for hastening decline, though it must be borne in mind that the region had suffered earlier seismic shocks and rebuilt in style.

The really significant 'tremors' were the military, political and economic ones of the later fourth and early fifth century that brought about the total collapse of the western empire. The after-shocks of the sixth and seventh centuries completed the levelling of the ground on which medieval Tripolitania was to be built.

NOTES

Preface (pp?–?)

1 The term *Tripolitana* is employed in the book only in reference to specific Roman usage: the third-century *regio* (region) and the fourth-century province. Tripolitania, on the other hand, is used freely with reference to the geographical region later covered by the province: di Vita-Evrard 1985b; Romanelli 1933. Up to the end of the third century AD, this zone was administered as part of *Africa Proconsularis*, though it is clear that it was always somewhat distinct in geography, culture and history from the rest of the African province. The Romans knew the region first as the *Emporia*, or the 'land between the two Syrtes' and in the third century there was a *regio Tripolitana*. General histories of the region or of Africa: Benabou 1976; Merighi 1940; Romanelli 1959; also Barton 1972a; Decret and Fantar 1981; Law 1978; MacKendrick 1980; Mahjoubi and Salama 1981; Rachet 1970; Raven 1993. Mapping of ancient Tripolitania: Cagnat and Merlin 1914/1932; Goodchild 1954b/c; Hafemann 1975.

2 Pre-eminence of *Lepcis*: Duncan-Jones 1962, 57; Gascou 1972a; 1982; *IRT* pp. 76–8; Lepelley 1981a, 337.

3 Explorers in Tripolitania and northern Fezzan: Lyon 1821, 18–66, 323–37; Denham and Clapperton 1826, xv–xvi, 305–11; Richardson 1848, I, 26–384, II, 442–82; Barth 1857, I, 57–147, III, 448–511; Duveyrier 1864; Tissot 1888, 708–10; Nachtigal 1974, 38–66. Fatalities included Oudney of the Denham and Clapperton expedition and Major Laing (Bovill 1964).

4 Smythe's account was published by Beechey and Beechey 1828, 72–8 (*Lepcis*), 504–12 (interior). Ibid, 12–208 deals with the Beecheys' Tripolitanian journey.

5 Tunisia: Tissot 1888; Goetschy 1894; Lecoy de la Marche 1894; Toutain 1895; 1896; 1903a/b; 1905; 1906; Gaukler 1897/1904; 1900; 1902; Blanchet 1898; 1899; Donau 1904a/b; 1906; 1909a/b; Pericaud 1905; Toussaint 1905; 1906; 1907; 1908; Gueneau 1907; Boizot 1913; Cagnat 1913; 1914b. Libya: Cowper 1896; 1897; 1899; Myres 1899; de Mathuisieulx 1901; 1902; 1904; 1905; 1912. Olive presses: Mattingly 1988a.

6 Towns: Aurigemma 1916; 1929; 1933; 1940c; 1960; 1967; Bartoccini 1927a; 1928a; 1929a/b; 1931; Caputo and Levi della Vida 1935; Guidi 1929; 1930; 1933; 1935a/b; Romanelli 1916; 1925. Interior: Bartoccini 1928b; Bauer 1935; Cerrata 1933; Coro 1928; 1935; Gentilucci 1933; Petragnani 1928. Fezzan: Pace, Serge and Caputo 1951.

7 Interior: Brogan and Smith 1957; 1985; Goodchild 1948; 1949a/b; 1950a/b/c; 1951b; 1952a; 1954a/b/c/d; Haynes 1959; Ward-Perkins 1950; Ward-Perkins and Goodchild 1949; Towns: Bartoccini

1958b; Bianchi-Bandinelli *et al.* 1966; Caputo 1959; 1987; Degrassi 1951; Goodchild 1949b; 1950d; Kenrick 1986; Squarciapino 1966; Ward-Perkins 1993; Ward-Perkins and Goodchild 1953; Ward-Perkins and Toynbee 1949. Work of 1960s-1980s: Brogan 1964; 1971a/b; 1977; 1980; Brogan and Reynolds 1964; 1985; Daniels 1970a/b; 1971a; 1975; 1989; di Vita 1964a/b; 1966; 1967; Rebuffat 1989; Reynolds and Brogan 1960.

8 Tunisia: Euzennat 1972; Trousset 1974; 1976; 1978; 1984a/b; 1987. Libya: Barker 1985; Barker and Jones 1981; 1982; 1984; 1985; Barker *et al.* 1991; forthcoming; Jones 1985; Jones and Barker 1980; 1983; Mattingly 1987a; 1989a/b; Rebuffat 1982c; 1988c; Reddé 1985; 1988.

9 Desert vs sown: Benabou 1976; Gautier 1952; Gsell 1933; Guey 1939; Leschi 1942; Rachet 1970; Van Berchem 1952; Wheeler 1954; Winkler 1910. Land delimitation and sedentarization of pastoralists: Berthier 1968; Lancel 1955; Leschi 1948. Modern colonial activity creating image of past: Moore 1940. Cf also Oliver 1979.

10 *Limitanei*: HA, *Severus Alex* 58.4–5; *Cod.Theod* 7.15.1; Carcopino 1925, 1933; Goodchild 1949a/c; 1950a/c; 1951b; 1952b/c; 1954d; Ward-Perkins and Goodchild 1949. Incorrect term: Jones 1971. Earlier settlement: Brogan 1964; 1971a; di Vita 1964a; *supra* n. 8.

11 The minimalist view and anti-colonialist history are often combined, as in Benabou 1976. Note also, Benabou 1978; Garnsey 1978; Leveau 1978; Thébert 1978 on cultural aspects. Minimal Roman involvement in native frontier groups: Shaw 1980; 1984; Whittaker 1978a; 1989a; 1994.

Chapter 1 (pp1–16)

1 Distinctiveness of Tripolitania from rest of Maghreb: Despois 1964, x, 68–72; 97–111; Despois and Raynal 249–54; cf. Sherwin-White 1944.

2 Ancient settlement noted: Barth 1857, 51–103; Cowper 1897, 224–95; Nachtigal 1974; 38–41.

3 Ancient sources, North Africa general: Gsell 1918/1929, I, 1–158 (geography, flora and fauna), 159–76 (agriculture/pastoralism). Tripolitania: Fantoli 1933. Tripartite division: Strabo 17.3.19; Pliny *NH* 5.26; Corippus *Ioh* 2.51–62, 2.78–80, 6.104–05, 6.270–95, 6.581.

4 Gebel: Livy 29.33.8–9; Orosius 1.2.90; Pliny *NH* 5.26–38; Strabo 17.3.17–20. Desert: Corippus *Ioh* 6.294–5; Horace *Odes* 1.22; Plutarch *Cato Y* 56; Strabo 17.3.20; Lucan, *Pharsalia* Book 9; Squarciapino 1980; cf. Capot-Rey 1953, 94–7; Holmboe 1936, 95–176. Oases: Herodotus 4.181–5; Lucan 9.522–27; cf. also Diodorus Siculus 3.49.2–3; Procopius *de aed.* 6.2.14–20; Strabo 2.130, 17.1.5.

5 Coastal features: Strabo 17.3.17–18, 17.3.20; cf. Brogan 1975a, 52;

218

Gsell 1928b; Paskoff *et al.* 1991; Smythe 1854; Trousset 1992. Shifting sand: Procopius *de aed* 6.4.1; Haynes 1959, 72. Navigational perils: Lucan 9.338–44. Pliny *NH* 5.26; Silius Italicus 1.408–10, 3.320 (Nasamonian wreckers); Strabo 17.3.20; Synesius *Letters* 4. Trade: Fulford 1989.

6 Drought: Sallust 17.5–6; HA *Hadrian* 22.10; Corippus 6.247; cf Garnsey 1988 on the periodicity of Mediterranean crop failure. Dams: Strabo 17.3.18; Frontinus *de controv. agrorum* 2 (trans. Dilke 1971, 65, from Blume *et al.* 1848/1852, I, 36). Lamasba: *CIL* 8.4440, 18587; Shaw 1982. Archaeology of hydrology: Baradez 1949a; 1957; Barker and Jones 1982; Birebent 1962; Carton 1896/1897; Crova 1967; 1912; Gauckler 1900/1912; Gilbertson *et al.* 1984; Gsell *et al.* 1902; Shaw 1984; Trousset 1986; Vita-Finzi 1969.

7 Water resources: Strabo 17.3.1, 2.130; Sallust *BJ* 89.4, 91.2–3. Bu Njem baths: *IRT* 918; Haynes 1946, 75–6; Rebuffat 1987b. Ghibli: Corippus *Ioh* 8.370–73 (10 days' duration); Herodotus 4.173, on the extermination of the *Psylli* tribe doing battle with the south wind; Lucan 9.447–500.

8 Tree cover or lack, Maghreb: Sallust *BJ* 17.5–6; Pliny *NH* 5.6, 5.9. Tripolitania: Pliny *NH* 5.26; Strabo 17.3.18. Olive orchards: Pliny 15.3.8 (negative view); cf. Silius Italicus 3.324 (Athena gave the gift of the olive to Africa before anywhere else); Caesar *BAf* 97.3 (annual fine of 3 million pounds of oil exacted from *Lepcis*); cf Camps-Fabrer 1953; 1985; Gsell 1925; Mattingly 1988a/b/c. Lotus: Pliny *NH* 13.104. Tripoli's forest: el-Tidjani = Rousseau 1853, 150–51; Brett 1978a, 56–7. Reliefs, mosaics: Aurigemma 1926a; 1960; Barker and Jones 1981, 37; Brogan and Smith 1985; Romanelli 1930. Bu Njem: Marichal 1992.

9 Sofeggin and Zem-Zem: van der Veen 1981; 1985a/b; Barker and Jones 1982, 17–19. Negev: Evenari *et al.* 1971, 122; Mayerson 1962, 211–69. Fezzan: Herodotus 4.181–5; Pliny *NH* 13.33; Lucan 9.522–7; Daniels 1989; van der Veen 1992. Bu Njem construction: Rebuffat 1969, 210; 1982c.

10 Faunal record, decline: Bovill 1968, 6–9, 15. Late prehistoric times and rock art: Barker 1989. *Venationes*: Pliny *NH* 8.62. Wild beast zone: Herodotus 4.181; Pliny *NH* 5.26, 8.32. Elephant as civic emblem: Aurigemma 1940a; Romanelli 1920. Agriculture vs predators: Diodorus Siculus 4.17.4–5; Strabo 17.3.15.

11 Faunal evidence, pre-desert: Barker 1985; Barker and Jones 1982, 17–19; Clarke 1986. Modern stock: Franchetti *et al.* 1914, figs 272–3, 275–8 (horses), 280–86 (donkeys), 287–98 (camels), 318–35 (sheep), 336–45 (goats).

12 Southern Tunisia: Despois 1964, 68–72; Despois and Raynal 1967, 249–54, 428–31; Trousset 1974, 13–28. Libya: Ghisleri 1912; Goodchild 1950c; Haynes 1959, 13–17; Kanter 1967, 76–102; Nyop *et al.* 1973; Ward 1967; 1968a/b. The calculation of area excludes the main desert masses (Erg, Hamada, Syrtica).

13 Desert character and geology: Anketell 1989; Coque 1962; Despois and Raynal 1967, 252–4, 428–30; Hey 1962; Kanter 1967, 76; Salem and Busrewil 1980. 3% agriculture: Allan 1969, 1. Cf. Penrose *et al.* 1970 (Libya); Poncet 1963, 278–91 (Tunisia).

14 Three zones: de Mathuisieulx 1904, 48–59; Haynes 1959, 13–15; Louis 1975, 18–22. Local variation: Brehony 1960, 60 (five sub-zones of the Gebel Tarhuna).

15 Jurassic dome: Kanter 1967, 79–81. Gebel cliffs: Despois 1964, 68–80; Trousset 1974, 13–19. Matmata/Demmer: Despois and Raynal 1967, 252–4; Louis 1975. Nefusa/Gharian: Despois 1935, 9–45; Franchetti *et al.* 1914, 81–126; de Mathuisieulx 1904, 48–64. Tarhuna/Msellata: Brehony 1960, 60; Cowper 1897; Goodchild 1951b, 72–5; Oates 1953, 81–2; Taylor 1960, 96.

16 Kanter 1967, 79; Louis 1975, 19–20; Vita-Finzi 1969, 7.

17 'Passages obligés': Trousset 1974, 26; Brogan 1980, 45–52. Soils: Herodotus 2.10–12; Franchetti *et al.* 1914, 155–88; Kanter 1967, 80–81; Vita-Finzi 1969, 7–12.

18 Gefara: Anketell 1989; Vita-Finzi 1969, 7–12; Willimot 1960. Alluviation: Vita-Finzi 1969, 39 (cisterns in Wadi Lebda excavated by Italians and now reburied under 3 m of silt); Vita-Finzi and Brogan 1965, 65–71 (Wadi Megenin floods carrying silt 60 km across Gefara to Tripoli). Gefara as desert: Richardson 1848, 26 (cf Brett 1976); as steppe: *IRT* p. 203. Ancient settlement: Brogan 1965a,

47; Louis 1975, 18–22; Vita-Finzi and Brogan 1965; AMS 1:50,000 series and Tunisian 1:200,000 series maps. Oases: Beechey and Beechey 1828, 33–112; Franchi 1912; Kanter 1967, 77–8; de Mathuisieulx 1912, 196–200.

19 Dahar: Barker *et al.* 1983; Despois 1964, 68–72, Louis 1975, 17–21; Martel 1968; Vita-Finzi 1969, 41–4.

20 Chotts: Despois 1964, 37–40. Limiting movement: Trousset 1978, 164–73; 1982a, 45–59. Nefzaoua oases: Carton 1914/1915; Despois 1964, 428–31; Moreau 1947, 13–21; Poncet 1963, 273–91; Sarel-Sternberg 1963, 123–33. Djerid oases: Gendre 1908; Guides Bleus 1967, 289–96; Trousset 1976, 21–33; 1986a.

21 Hamada el-Hamra: Kanter 1967, 81–2.

22 Hun graben: Brogan 1965b, 57; Kanter 1967, 82–3; Rebuffat 1967a, 56–61. Syrtica: Reddé 1988, 12–14. Sebkha Tauorgha: Strabo 17.3.20; *Tab. Peut* 7.4; Brogan 1975a.

23 Sahara: Bagnold 1941; Bovill 1968, 1–16; Briggs 1960; Capot-Rey 1953, 7–35. Sinawen: Richardson 1848, 78. Eastern oases: Herodotus 4.181–5; Bates 1914, 1–38; Fakry 1973, 1–25; cf 1974; Luni 1980; Mills 1980; Rebuffat 1970c/d; Wendorf and Marks 1975. Fezzan: Barth 1857, 134–49; Kanter 1967, 84–5; Klitsch and Baird 1969; Lyon 1821, 67–84; RSGI 1937, 39–138; Ward 1968b; cf Rouvillois-Brigol *et al.* 1973 (Algerian oases). *Garamantes*: *infra*, chapter 2.

24 Rainfall: Capot-Rey 1953; Despois 1964, 3–30, map A; Fantoli 1952.

25 Cereals limit: Despois 1964, 99. Olives: Despois 1964, 104 (180 mm); Taylor 1960, 88–90 (150–200 mm).

26 Table 1:2 figures calculated from: BMA 1947, 68–75; Despois and Raynal, 1967, 22; Energoproject 1980, 7–10; Fantoli 1952; Kanter 1967, 97–100; Moreau 1947, 22–49; Polservice 1980, A88; Poncet 1963, 278–9.

27 Inequality of rainfall: Despois 1964, 15–19; Penrose *et al.* 1970, 108. Tarhuna: Brehony 1960, 61. Garian: BMA 1947, 69–75; Taylor 1960, 90 (one good olive crop in five years). Beni Ulid droughts: Nachtigal 1974, 41–4 (1866–9); *Tripolitania* 2 (1932), 10 (1926–32); Ward 1967, 55 (1959–64).

28 Importance of hydraulic technology in exploitation of Tripolitania: Baduel and Baduel 1980; Carton 1912; Gilbertson 1986; Gilbertson *et al.* 1984; Ginestous 1913; Laboulle 1933; Romanelli 1926; Trousset 1986a/b; 1987. Flash floods: Barker and Jones 1981, 34 (2 m flood in Wadi Beni Ulid); cf. Kassam 1973; Moreau 1947, 31–4 (in April 1939, 72 mm rain fell in a few hours at Kebili. Cf. 20 mm for entire year 1944–5); Nachtigal 1974, 44; *Tripolitania* 2 (1932), 10; Vita-Finzi 1969, 38–42. Flood-water farming technology: Barker and Jones 1982; 1984; Despois 1935, 97–120; Louis 1975, 183–9. Cf. Evenari *et al.* 1971, 95–119; Mayerson 1962; Kennedy 1982.

29 Temperature: Despois and Raynal 1967, 422; Kanter 1967, 97; Polservice 1980, A89; RSGI 1937, 105; Trousset 1974, 14–15. Humidity: Trousset 1974, 15. Dew/frost: Denham and Clapperton 1826, 502; Richardson 1848, II, 443; Taylor 1960, 88–9 (olives). Evaporation: Capot-Rey 1953, 36–68. An extreme temperature of 52°C in the shade was recorded in the Tunisian Dahar by Blanchet 1899, 149–50.

30 Ghibli/sandstorms: BMA 1947, 9; de Mathuisieulx 1912, 69; Franchetti *et al.* 1914, 66–7; Johnson 1973, 14. El Golea: Briggs 1960, 7.

31 Capot-Rey 1953, 91; Trousset 1974, 15–16, attribute continuing and damaging changes in Saharan flora and fauna to the action of man.

32 Vegetation, Gefara: Clarke 1960, 52; Despois 1964, 93–5; Kanter 1967, 77–9. Gebel: Brehony 1960, 60; Despois 1935, 77–91; Franchetti *et al.* 1914, 203–47. Syrtica, Chotts: Kanter 1967, 80–83; Trousset 1974, 15–16. Charcoal burning: Franchetti *et al.* 1914, 371, figs 210, 212; Johnson 1973, 24–8 (Cyrenaican parallels). Sofeggin and Zem-Zem: Beechey and Beechey 1828, 508; Denham and Clapperton 1826, xvi. Hamada: Barth 1857, 125–30.

33 Gefara cultivation: Penrose *et al.* 1970; Polservice 1980, B1. Wells: Allan 1969, 6. Coastal oases: de Mathuisieulx 1912, 196–200; Franchi 1912. Olives: Poncet 1963, 284. Gebel cultivation: Barth 1857, 63–4; Despois 1935, 97–120; Franchetti *et al.* 1914, 433–55; Louis 1969; 1975, 158–75; Lyon 1821, 30–31; Taylor 1960, 88–99. Cereals: Despois 1935, 121–5 (variability of yield); Polservice 1980, quotes yields of 327–44 kg/ha for 1974 and 1978, well below

normal Mediterranean yields (for which see International Yearbook of Agricultural Statistics 1922–38, top Egypt (1,710 kg/ha), bottom Algeria (540 kg/ha), Tunisia (400 kg/ha) and Libya. Pre-desert: Beechey and Beechey 1828, 507; Lyon 1821, 35; Nachtigal 1974, 42–3. Oases: Bates 1914, 9–12 (Augila – 116,000 date palms, Siwa – 163,000, Dakhla – 200,000); Moreau 1947, 125 (Nefzaoua 700,000 trees); RSGI 1931, 579 (Fezzan – 900,000 trees). Varied oases crops: Barth 1857, 90; Lyon 1821, 72–3, 270–73; RSGI 1931, 579 (the list includes turnips, beans, peas, carrots, onions, peppers, garlic, melons, olives, figs, apples, peaches, apricots, grapes, mint and herbs).

34 Wild animals: *BMA* 1947, 36; Capot-Rey 1953, 9, 91 (ostriches extinct in Tunisia 1790, Algeria 1845); cf. Daumas 1950/1971, 50–62 on ostrich hunting in the 1840s; Holmboe 1933, 27–9 (leopard, jackals and hyenas close to Syrtic coast); Kádár 1972.

35 Domesticated animals, Libya: Kanter 1967, 104; cf. Polservice 1980, B27. Tunisia: Moreau 1947, 166. Adaptation: Behnke 1980; Briggs 1960, 17–33; Johnson 1969, 7–10; 1973, 40–47; Evenari *et al.* 1971, 301–23. Sheep: Franchetti *et al.* 1914, 519–97; Camels: Johnson 1973, 44, 59–66. Ancient pastoral practices: Barker 1981; 1983.

36 Climatic change: Allan 1981; Barker 1989; Goudie 1977; Shaw 1976; 1981b. Current arid phase: Churcher 1980, 286–93; Ritchie 1980, 414–17. Libyan Valleys: Barker and Jones 1982, 7; Barker *et al.* 1983; Gilbertson and Hunt 1988; Gilbertson *et al.* 1987; Hunt *et al.* 1985; 1986; 1987. But cf. Burns and Denness 1985 (who argue for significant oscillation).

37 Vita-Finzi 1969, 7–44 (Tripolitania), 92–120 (general theory); cf. 1960; 1978, 40–42. Note also Rebuffat 1969, 196; Rouvillois-Brigol 1985; Trousset 1974, 19–20; 1986b. ULVS work: Barker *et al.* 1983; Gilbertson and Hunt 1988; 1990; Gilbertson *et al.* 1987; Hunt *et al.* 1985; 1986; 1987

38 Erosion and its causes: Barker and Jones 1982, 26; Despois 1964, 83–6; Franchetti *et al.* 1914, 371; Johnson 1973, 24–8, 58; Vita-Finzi 1969, 26–34; 1978, 34–5. Neglected Gebel: Barth 1857, 63–4; Oates 1953, 96, 115–17. Modern redevelopment in Gebel and Gefara: BMA 1947, 39–42; Brehony 1960; Poncet 1963, 284–90; Taylor 1960

39 Forts and transhumance: Demougeot 1960; Lassère 1977; Trousset 1974; Whittaker 1978a. Transhumance: Scylax 109, refers to an annual migration made by *Macae* from the coast to the interior; cf. Garnsey 1978, 132; Lawless 1972, 128–34. Modern textbook: Whittaker 1978a, 232.

40 Gefara: Brogan 1965a; Clarke 1960; Louis 1975, 20, 38–42; Vita-Finzi and Brogan 1965. Western Gebel: Despois 1935; Louis 1975; Prost 1954a/b. Gebel arboriculture: Despois 1935, 109 (200,000 olives, 340,000 figs, 65,000 palms, 6,000 almonds and vines, 2,000 pomegranates or others in the Nefusa). Farming systems: Despois 1935, 97–120; Prost 1954a.

41 Eastern Gebel: Brehony 1960, 62–4. Ancient ruins: Mattingly 1985a; 1988a/b. Breviglieri: Brehony 1960, 63–4. Nefzaoua: Sarel-Sternberg 1963, 123–7, 130. Bled Segui: Trousset 1978, 157.

42 Ghadames and Derj: Cauneille 1963, 102; Euzennat and Trousset 1975; Richardson 1848, I. Sofeggin and Zem-Zem: Barker and Jones 1982. Beni Ulid orchard: Barth 1857, 450; Lyon 1821, 35–7, 61; Nachtigal 1974, 42. Fezzan: Cauneille 1963; Klitsch and Baird 1969. Syrtica: Cauneille 1963, 101, 105; Cerrata 1933; Goodchild 1952d; Laronde 1987; Reddé 1985.

Chapter 2 (pp17–49)

1 Nature of opposition: Dyson 1974; Warmington 1974. Primary sources: Bates 1914; Brogan 1975b; Camps 1960; 1980; Desanges 1962; Fentress 1979, 18–60; Gsell 1918/1929, V; 1928b.

2 Anthropological comparison: Berque 1953; Fentress 1979, 4–6; Gsell 1918/1929, vol. I, 275–326; Louis 1975.

3 Conflict theory: Benabou 1976; Gsell 1933; Guey 1939; Leschi 1942; MacKendrick 1980; Rachet 1970. Cf the nuanced and geographically slanted account of the native African peoples by Fevrier 1989, II, 113–57.

4 Bates 1914, esp. 51–71 (analysis of primary sources with maps); Desanges 1962. Cf. also Brogan 1975b; Daniels 1970a; 1971a.

5 Anachronisms: Bates 1914, 67–9; Desanges 1980b; Fentress 1979,

18–42; Pliny *NH* 5.43–6, echoes Mela (1.8.41–8) which in turn draws on Herodotus (4.174, 4.183, 4.186). Locational errors: Pliny 5.34 and Strabo 1.5.33 misplaced the *Asbytae* (known in Cyrenaica from other sources, Desanges 1962, 147–9; cf. Rebuffat 1967b). Ptolemy 4.6.3 likewise located the *Cinyphii* well to the west of their known position in the Wadi Caam (*Cinyps*). Official bias: Tacitus *Ann* 2.52, 3.20–21, 3.73–4, for a wholly unsympathetic account of tribal resistance in Africa (brigands, vagrants, renegades). Attitude towards nomads: Fentress 1979, 18–21; Shaw 1981c; 1983; Trousset 1982b. Balbus: *infra*, chapter 4; Desanges 1980b.

6 Ptolemy: Bates 1914, map VIII (basic plot out), map IX (substantially revised version) illustrate the immediate problems. Maps of tribal pattern: Bates 1914, map VII; Desanges 1962, map 5 and Rachet 1970, map IV, all deal with Pliny as a source, producing radically different distributions. Even greater problems occur in reconciling the positions of a single tribal group as given in several sources, cf. Desanges 1962, maps 4–8, 10.

7 The 516 *populi*: Pliny *NH* 5.29–30; Desanges 1962, 75–143. Berber origins: Bates 1914, 39–51; Camps 1980; Chamoux 1953, 35–68. Libyan language, dialects: Brogan 1975b; Brogan and Smith 1985; Chabot 1940, i–vii; Daniels 1975; Galand 1988; Gsell 1918/1929, I, 409–10; Marichal 1979, 436–7; Rebuffat 1975a; Reynolds, Brogan and Smith 1958. Hercules and Libyans: Sallust *BJ* 18.1–12. Numidian kingdom: Buck 1984; Camps 1960; Gsell 1918/1929, V–VII. Massinissa: Sallust *BJ* 5.4. Numidian confederation: Lucan 4.669–90. *Gaetuli*: Caesar *BAf* 32.3, 35.4, 46.4, 55; Dio 55.28.3–4; Florus 2.31; cf. Fentress 1982, 325–34; Trousset 1982b, 98.

8 *Musulames*: Camps 1960, 72–5; Desanges 1962, 117–21; Fentress 1979, 66, 74–7 and map 5 (p. 63). *tribus Gubul, tribus...*: AE 1917–18, 39; *ILAlg* I.2836. *Regio Beguensi*: CIL 8. 270 = 11451; Desanges 1962, 83. *Tribus Misiciri*: *ILAlg* I. 138, 174, 156 = CIL 8.5217–5218; Desanges 1962, 115–16. *MSKRH*: Camps 1960, 248–50, fig. 26; Desanges 1962, 271; Fentress 1979, 45–6.

9 Euzennat 1974; Seston and Euzennat 1971, 468–90 (esp. 478–9); Sherwin–White 1973.

10 Segmented societies: Dunn, 1973, 85–107; 1977; Gellner 1969, 35–68; Johnson 1973, 33–9; Vinogradov 1973, 67–84. Berber structures: Bates 1914, 113–17; Gellner 1969; Gellner and Micaud 1973; Gsell 1918/1929, V, 27–81; Rachet 1970, 22–3. Leadership: Gellner 1969, 81–93. Azgar: Bates 1914, 114–15. Strength and weakness of segmentary structure: Fentress 1979, 45; Gellner 1969, 40–46, 69; Hart 1973, 25–58; much of the detailed argument on tribal hierarchy can be found in Mattingly 1992.

11 *Quinquegentiani*: Courtois 1955, 120; Desanges 1962, 67; Euzennat 1984; Galand 1971; 277–9 (noting that five has been a significant number in many more recent Berber alliances). Other confederations: Fentress 1982, 330–34 on the *Gaetuli*. Britain and Germany: Birley 1974a, 13–25; Mann 1974b, 34–42; Mann 1979b, 144–51; Todd 1975.

12 Latin terminology: Fentress 1979, 43–4, 'it is not certain that the limits of the application of *gens* and *natio* were any more apparent to the Romans than they are to us'; cf. also Berque 1953; Fentress 1982. Tribal hierarchy: Tacitus *Ann* 2.52 refers to Tacfarinas as *natione Numida and dux (gentium) Musulamiorum*; ILS 2721 refers to a *praefectus ... nationum Gaetulicarum sex quae sunt*. Pliny's view: *NH* 5.1, 5.29–30.

13 Chieftains: Sallust *BJ* 5.4, *rex Numidarum*; Pliny *NH* 8.40, *rex Garamanticae*; Tacitus *Ann* 2.52, *dux Musulamiorum, dux Maurorum*; Corippus *Ioh* 4.597, *princeps ... Ierna*; *Ioh* 1.463, 1.465, *Antalas ... tyrannus*; Lepelley 1974, *praefectus*; CIL 8.17327, *universi seniores Mas[...]rensium ... anno Fortunatiani mag(istratus)*. Elders: CIL 8.15667, *seniores Ucubitani*, cf 8.15721–2; 8.17327; Seston and Euzennat 1971, 478–9 (*populares*). Leaders described: Tacitus *Ann* 2.52, 3.20–21, 3.73–4; Amm.Marcellinus 29.5.1–56; CIL 8.9047, *Faraxen rebellis cum satellitibus suis*; Corippus *Ioh* 2.109, 4.597, 4.631, 4.639, 6.104, 6.143, 6.170.

14 *Zegrenses*: supra, n. 9. *Baquates*: Carcopino 1943, 258–75; Desanges 1962, 28–31; Frezouls 1957; 1980; Shaw 1987; Sigman 1977. *Bavares*: Camps 1955; Courtois 1955, 96–7; Desanges 1962, 46–8. *Macennites*: Desanges 1962, 33–4. Altars of peace: Christol 1988; Frezouls 1957

(full texts); 1980; Romanelli 1962; Shaw 1987. The altars, republished as *IAM* 2.348, 384, 349, 350, 356, 402, 357, 358, 359, 360, 361, are dated as follows, AD 169–75, 173–5, 180, 200, 223–4 (or 233–4), 239–41, 241 (?x2), 245, 277, 280. Note also *IAM* 2.376 (a Baquatian chief of AD 140); *CIL* 6.1800 (son of Aurelius Canartha, chief in AD 180). Significance of altars: Romanelli 1962, 212; Shaw 1987; *contra*, Frezouls 1957; 1980; Rachet 1970 and Sigman 1977, who view relations as frequently disrupted by war, with the altars marking the re-establishment of peace. Cf. Mattingly 1992, 53–5.

15 Ptolemy's coordinates: Bates 1914, 60–65; Rivet and Smith 1979, 103–47 (for Ptolemy's British geography). Pliny's confusions: *NH* 5.26–8, 33–4. *Psylli*: Herodotus 4.173; Bates 1914, 58. Conceptual framework: Mela 1.8.41–8; Pliny *NH* 5.43–6; Fentress 1979, 21–2. Mela's comments: 1.8.41–8, *quamquam in familias passim et sine lege dispersi nihil in commune consultant, tamen quia singulis aliquot simul coniuges et plures ob id liberi adgnatique sunt nusquam.*

16 Diodorus Siculus 3.49.1–3 (Loeb trans.). Protection alliances: Louis 1975, 91–4; Sarel-Sternberg 1963, 126.

17 *Macae*: Desanges 1962, maps 4–8, 10. Previous studies of Tripolitanian tribes: Bates 1914; Brogan 1975b; Desanges 1962.

18 *Lotophages*, location: Dionysius 206; Herodotus 4.177; Mela 1.37; Pliny 9.60; Polybius 1.39.2; 34.3.12; Ptolemy 4.3.6; Scylax 110; Strabo 3.4.3 (cf.17.3.7). Absorbed by *emporia*: Brogan 1975b, 278. Sub-tribes: Stephanus Byzantinus 33.

19 *Libyphoenices*, location: Diodorus Siculus 20.55.4; Livy 21.22; 25.40; Pliny 5.24; Ptolemy 4.3.6; Strabo 17.3.19. Phoenician *emporia*: *infra*, chapter 3. Agricultural development of hinterland: Mattingly 1987a. *Cinithi*: Florus 2.31; Tacitus *Ann* 2.52; *IRT* 859 (*Chinitiu*). Libyphoenician character of people: Mattingly 1987b. El-Hakam: (trans Gateau 1947), 35–7; cf. Oates 1953, 113. Rivalry *Lepcis/Oea*: Tacitus *Hist* 4.50.

20 *Gaetuli*, location: Pliny 5.9–13; 5.43. In Tell region: Apuleius *Apol.* 24.1; Sallust *BJ* 19.7; 80.1–2; 88.3; Caesar *BAf* 32.3; 35.4; 55; 56.4; Desanges 1964b, 33–47; Fentress, 1979, 47, 56–7; 1982; Trousset, 1982b, 98. Southern limits: Desanges 1957, 34–40; Fentress, 1979, 111; Gsell 1918/1929, V, 111 (identifying the Wadi Djedi as the *Nigris* of the sources). In Syrtic region: Virgil *Aen.*5.192, in *Gaetulibus Syrtibus*; Florus 2.31, *Gaetulos accolas Syrtium*; Strabo 17.3.19; 17.3.23. Other southern locations: Orosius 1.2.90. Scale of confederation: Strabo 17.3.2; Mela 1.23; *CIL* 5.5267 (six tribes in Numidia).

21 Pastoral lifestyle: Sallust *BJ* 19.6; 103.4; Mela 3.104; Pliny 10.201; Orosius 1.21.18. *Phazanii*: Pliny 5.35–6; Ptolemy 4.7.10.'Fezzan' near Mizda: AMS 1:250,000 Ed. 1, Mizda *NH* 33.1, grid ref. TQ 3048. *Alele, Cilliba*: Euzennat and Trousset 1975, 57–8, 66; cf. Bates 1914, 73–90; Gsell 1918/1929, I, 309–26, the initial 't' and final 'i' indicate the feminine tense in Berber. Route to Ghadames: Rebuffat 1972a, 322–4. *Phazanii, Nybgenii* transhumants: Euzennat and Trousset 1975, 57, fig. 15; Sarel-Sternberg 1963, 123–33, nineteenth-century transhumance from the Nefzaoua extended south of Remada and Tuareg raiding well to the north. Sub-tribes: Ptolemy 4.3.6 (*Tidamensi*); Desanges 1962, 91–2 (*Cidamensi*), 91–2, 138; cf. Brogan 1975b, 279–80. Archaeology of *Cidamus* (Ghadames): Rebuffat 1969, 194–5; 1972a, 322–3; 1975c, 498–9; cf. Coro 1956, 3–26 and Mercier 1953, 17–47 (tombs). Ethnographic evidence from Ghadames: Duveyrier 1864, 249–54; Richardson 1848, 92–384. Fortifications at other oases: Rebuffat 1972a, 323–4 (Sinaouen, Tfelfel, Materes and Chawan).

22 Twinned tribes: Ptolemy 4.3.6./4.6.6; cf. ibid, 4.3.6./4.7.10; cf. Corippus *Ioh* 2.75 (*Astrikes*); Desanges 1962, 80–81. *Nybgenii*: Cagnat 1909; Carton 1914/1915; Trousset in *Encyclopédie berbère*. Other Nefzaoua oases with ruins: Trousset 1974, sites 1, 3, 4, 5, 6, 7, 8, 9, 10, 11, 12, 13, 14, 15, 16, 17. Population: Sarel-Sternberg 1963, 124. Djerid oases: Trousset 1976; 1980b. Neighbours of *Phazanii*: Ptolemy 4.7.10. Delimitation of lands: Trousset 1978; *ILAf* 30 (Bir Soltane).

23 Gefara and Gebel *Gaetuli*: Ptolemy 4.3.6; Pliny 5.34–5; cf. Florus 2.31; Tacitus *Ann* 2.52.*Cinithi*: Desanges 1962, 86, 135 (*Sintae*). *Gigthis* and *Cinithi*: *CIL* 8. 22729, *L. Memmio Messio/ L.f. Quir. Pacata. Flam. Perpetuo divi Traia/ni Chinithio in quin/que decurias a divo Hadriano adlecto Chinithi ob merita/ eius et singularem pietatem. Qua*

nationi suae prae/stat sua pecuni/a posuerunt. Prefect: *CIL* 8.10500, *L. Egnatuleio P.f. Gal. Sabino. Pontific/ Palatuali proc Aug XXXX Galliarum/ proc Aug ad Epistateian Thebaidos/ proc Aug ad census accipendos/ Macedoniae praef gentis Cinithiorum/ trib leg IIII Scythicae l[...].*

24 *Macae*, location: Herodotus 4.175; 4.42; Scylax 109; Silius Italicus 2.60; 3.275; 5.194; 9.11; 9.89; 9.222; 15.670; Diodorus Siculus 3.49, Pliny 5.34, St Hippolytus *Chron*.145, *Excerpta Barbari*, p.202, *Liber.Gen.*, p.20. Ptolemy's two locations: 4.3.6; 4:6.3; 4.6.6. Orfella region and *Macae*: Rebuffat 1982c, 196–9; 1988c; cf. Cauneille 1963, 105.

25 *Macae* sub-tribes: Diodorus Siculus 3.46, 1–3. *Cinyphii*: Silius Italicus 2.60; 3.275; cf. Pliny 4.6.3; Herodotus 4.42. *Cissipades*: Pliny 5.28; cohort of *Cissipades CIL* 3.14429. *Elaeonoes*: Ptolemy 4.3.6. *Machyles*: Pliny 7.15. *Samamukii, Mamucii, Zamuci, Muducivvi: Not. Dig. Occ.* 31.26; Ptolemy 4.3.6; 4.6.6; *IRT* 854 (boundary stone). *Seli*: Tabula Peutingeriana *Seg* VII; Pliny 7.14 (*Psylli*)

26 *Nasamones*, location: Herodotus 4.172–5; Lucan 9.438–44; Silius Italicus 1.408–10; 3.320. *Augila*: Mela 1.8.41–8 (*Augilae*); Procopius, *de aed.* 6.2.15–20; cf. Corippus *Ioh* 6.145–87, 6.55. Nasamonian kings: A misreading of Dio 67.5.3 has been used as evidence, despite this being shown to be spurious by Gsell 1894, 234, n.6.

27 *Garama*: Pliny 5.36; Ptolemy 4.6.12. *Garamantes*, primary sources: Daniels 1969, 1970a; Desanges 1962, 93–6; Pace, Sergi and Caputo 1951, 151–200. Archaeological work: Ayoub 1962; 1967a/b; Daniels 1968; 1969; 1970a/b; 1971a/b; 1973; 1975; 1977; 1989; Pace, Sergi and Caputo 1951, 201–442; Ruprechtsberger 1989. Anthropology: Pace, Sergi and Caputo 1951, 443–542. Confederation: Daniels 1970a, 36–7. Three bands of oases: Daniels 1971a, 269–70; 1973, 36–7. Palaeolithic/neolithic in Libya and Fezzan: Barker 1989; Graziosi 1933; 1935; Hivernel 1985; Mori 1969; Souville 1970.

28 Burials and demography: Daniels 1969, 34; 1989, 49. Foggaras: Briggs 1960, 10–11; Daniels 1975, 251; Fentress 1979, 169–71 (for Roman or earlier date); Klitsch and Baird 1969, 73–80. Poncet 1963, 280–82; Trousset 1986a, discuss the agriculture and *foggaras* of the Nefzaoua and Djerid (17 km length utilizing 28 springs).

29 Lifestyle of *Garamantes* described in sources: Herodotus 4.183; Mela 1.23, 1.45; Pliny 5.26, 5.35–8, 6.209, 8.142; Lucian *de Dip* 2; Tacitus *Hist* 4.49: *gentem indomitam et inter accolas latrociniis fecundam*. Garamantian agriculture: Daniels 1973, 35; 1971a, 283 reveals that carbonized wheat, date stones and grape pips were found in excavation in Fezzan (cf also Van der Veen 1992). Date of first wheat cultivation: Daniels 1989; Van der Veen 1992.

30 Limits of Garamantian lands: Herodotus 4.183; Pliny 5.26; Ptolemy 4.6.3–5 (*fauces*); Ptolemy 4.6.3; Tacitus *Hist* 4.50. Kings: Pliny 8.142; Ptolemy 1.8.4; cf. El-Bekri, p. 32–5; Ayoub 1962, 20; 1967a, 21–2; Daniels 1970a, 27–35. 'Royal graves': Ayoub 1967a, 1–11, 27–48; 1967b, 213–19. Ammon cult: Lucan 9.511f; Silius Italicus 1.414–17, 2.56–67, 3.6–11, 3.647–714. Egyptian depictions of Libyans: Bates 1914; Daniels 1970a. Racial stock: Daniels 1970a, 27–35; Pace, Sergi and Caputo 1951, 443–542.

31 Richness of grave goods in Fezzan: Daniels 1973, 39 records the following from a single tomb – a saddle quern and rubber, an incense cup, 11 amphorae, five glass bowls, nine small Egyptian faience bowls, 31 imported fineware bowls and dishes. This is not atypical, cf. Ayoub 1967b, 213–19. Sudan in nineteenth century: Moorehead 1960, 58, records Speke's gifts for Mukesa, king of Buganda as including rifles and guns, a gold watch, a telescope, an iron chair, beads, silk, knives forks and spoons. Ashlar buildings and tombs: Daniels 1971a.

32 Contemporary semi-nomadism in North Africa : Bataillon 1963; Cauneille 1963; Clarke 1953; 1959; Johnson 1969 (esp. 15–19); Lawless 1972; 1976; Sarel-Sternberg 1963. Ancient pastoralists: Barker 1981; 1989; Fentress 1979, 18–60, 191–200; Lassère 1977, 344–50; Rebuffat 1990a; Shaw 1978; 1981c; 1983; Trousset 1980a/c; 1982b; Whittaker 1978a, 332–37.

33 Conflict: *supra*, n.3. Symbiosis: Johnson 1969, 11–12; 1973, 29–91; Lawless 1972; Trousset 1980a, 935; Whittaker 1978a, 232–7, 244–50. Eviction theory: Trousset 1980a, 931–4 (discusses and discounts).

34 Mixed economy: Diodorus Siculus 3.49.1–3; cf. Berthier 1981, pls

8–9; Camps 1960, 72–7; Fentress 1979, 66–7 (*Musulames*); Daniels 1989 (*Garamantes*). 'Nomadism' in sources: Fentress 1979, 18–60, 191–200; Shaw 1981c; 1983. Origins of agriculture: Diodorus Siculus 4.17.4–5; Polybius 37.3; Strabo 17.3.15; cf. Camps 1960, 58–91, 209–13. Massinissa and grain exports: Camps 1960, 200 (the totals were large, in 200 BC 200,000 bushels (36,016 hectolitres)). Fortified granaries: Caesar *BAf* 20; Sallust *BJ* 90.1.

35 Eastern Libyans: Bates 1914, 118–41 (dress and ornamentation), 142–71 (material culture); 172–209 (religion). Berber culture: Camps 1980, 145–92; *Encyclopédie berbère*, numerous entries. Resistance or assimilation?: Benabou 1976; 1978; Garnsey 1978; Janon 1977, 474–7; Leveau 1978; Mattingly 1987b; Thébert 1978; Whittaker 1978b.

36 Ammon: Bates 1914, 189–200; Camps 1980, 215–20; cf. Leglay 1966. Zeus Ammon: Herodotus 1.46, 2.18, 2.32, 3.25. Jupiter Hammon: *IRT* 920. Ammon and travellers: Bates 1914, 200; Rebuffat 1970c, 182. Ammon, the oasis cult: Lucan 9.522–7, *Esse locis superos testatur silva per omnem/ Sola virens Libyen. Nam quidquid pulvere sicco/ Separat ardentem tepida Berenicida Lepti/ Ignorat frondes; solus nemus abstulit Hammon/ Silvarum fons causa loco, qui putria terrae/ Alligat et domitas unda conectit harenas.* Cult of dead: Bates 1914, 191–95 (Egyptian evidence); Herodotus 4.190 and Mela 1.8.46 hint at such practices amongst the *Nasamones*. Oracles: Bates 1914, 190–95, the importance of *Siwa* seems to have declined whilst *Augila* became a more important source for Roman Africa (Silius Italicus 3.6–11, 3.647–714; Lucan 9.522–7; Procopius *de aed.* 6.2.15–20). *Ammonia* in Tripolitania: *Tab.Peut.* 7 (*Ad Ammonem*, 16 m.p. west of *Sabratha)*; Ptolemy 4.3.42; Goodchild 1951b; 1952d, 159, 167; Rebuffat 1970b/c; 1977a; Reddé 1992. Revival: Corippus *Ioh* 3.77–155, 6.145–87, 6.556, 7.515–20, 8.252.

37 Veneration of dead: Frend 1971. And living: Gellner 1969, 8–9, 31–4. Numidian/Mauretanian kings: *RIL* 2 (Dougga); Camps 1960, 279–95; 1980, 220–4. 'Baraka' of Antalas: *Ioh* 3.77–155, 3.158–70. Ierna: 2.109–12, 5.22–31, 5.495–502. Carcasan: 6.145–87; 6.556, 7.515–20, 8.252. Rushworth 1992, accepts my conclusions about the importance of *baraka*.

38 Camps 1980, 309–10; Duclos 1973, 217–29; Gellner 1969, 4, 26–8.

39 Saharan chariots: Herodotus 4.183; Camps and Gast 1982; Graziozi 1969, 3–20; Law 1967, 181–3; Lhote 1982. Elite vehicle: Camps 1989. Numidian cavalry: Silius Italicus 1.215–19 (skill without bridle); Livy 24.48.3–8 (Syphax and lack of infantry); 29.34.47 (Carthaginian recruitment of Numidian cavalry), 35.11.4–13 (in action in Spain), 44.13.13–14 (in Macedonia with Rome); Lucan 4.715–87 (Curio ambushed by Juba's cavalry).

40 Libyan cavalry: Lucan 4.677–83 (*Nasamones, Garamantes, Mazax* with Numidians); Silius Italicus 2.56–7, 2.82–3 (Libyan contingents allegedly led by Asbyte, a Garamantian princess); 3.287–93, 5.185, 9.220, 15.672 (Hannibal's Libyan allies in Italy). Libyan horse breeding: Strabo 17.3.19; cf. Daumas 1850/1968.

41 Infantry: Caesar *BAf* 14 (engagement with Juba). Use of spears: Herodotus: 7.71; Diodorus Siculus 3.49.5; Caesar *BAf* 14; Silius Italicus 3.275–7 (*cateia* or barbed spear of *Macae*), 4.445 (*telis Garamantica pubes*); Strabo 17.3.7. Bows and slings: Diodorus Siculus 3.49.5; Bates 1914, 1914. High status of cavalry: Daumas 1850/1971, 10–62, 80–97. Arms and armour general: Bates 1914, 142–51; Pringle 1981. Shortage of metals: Diodorus Siculus 3.49.4–5; cf. Daniels 1971a, 265 (*Garama*).

42 Small shields and lack of body armour: Diodorus 3.49.4–5; Bates 1914, 148; Goodchild 1952c, 152 (cf. Corippus *Ioh* 2.130–37). Tacfarinas, pitched battle: Tacitus *Ann* 2.52. Skirmishing tactics: *Ann* 3.20–21, 3.32, 3.72–4, 4.23–5; cf. Juba's success, Caesar *BAf* 14, *BCiv* 2.38–42 and Lucan 4.715–87; cf. Jugurtha, Sallust *BJ* 55, 97–101.

43 Covering wells: Pliny *NH* 5.38. Roman desert campaigns: Pliny *NH* 5.35–8; Daniels 1970a, 13–17 (3 month, 3,000 km round trip); Dio 60.9.1–6; cf. de la Chapelle 1934 (Roman desert campaigning in Morocco).

44 Numidian heartlands: Berthier 1981, 112–17, 144–53; cf. Camps 1960. *Thugga*: *RIL* 1–2 (and cf. 3–7); Camps 1960, 176–9, 255–7, 265–71. *Zama*: Sallust *BJ* 56–57. *Oppidum Suthul*: *BJ* 37. *Mons saxeo*: *BJ* 92–95; Florus 1.36.14. Hillforts in Byzantine period: Procopius

Wars 4.4.26–7, 4.6.4–14, 4.13.33–4, 4.19.21–4.20.29 (described as *pyrgoi*).

45 Oasis *oppida, Capsa*: Sallust *BJ* 89–91 (N.B. 89.6–7, *Capsenses una modo atque ea intra oppidum iugi aqua cetera pluvia utebantur*); Berthier 1981, 71–3. Later town: *CIL* 8.22796; Camps 1960, 276. Neighbouring *oppida*: *BJ* 92.1–4. British *oppida*: Suetonius *Vesp* 4; Cunliffe 1973, 16–18.

46 North Africa hillforts: Fentress 1979, 30–39; Ferchiou 1990; Gsell 1918/1929, V, 232–45, 250–57. Morocco: Marion 1957; 1959; cf. Fentress 1979, 35–6; Lawless 1970, I, 55–87, II, 1–20. El Krozbet: Baradez 1949a, 251, 253; Fentress 1979, 39. Kalaat Senane: Berthier 1981, 73–9, figs 8–9.

47 *Pyrgoi* in oases: Diodorus Siculus 3.49.1–3. Balbus: Pliny *NH* 5.35–7. Algerian locations: Desanges 1957. Other desert sites: Pliny 5.35–7; Ptolemy 4.6.

48 Magrusa/Mdhaweb: Allan 1980, 26; Barker and Jones 1982; Brogan 1971a, 127; Jones 1985, 265–8; Jones and Barker 1980, 29–34.

49 The Banat village: Burns and Mattingly 1981, 27–9.

50 Dating of hillforts: Dore 1985, 121–2; 1988, 70. Other examples: Rebuffat 1982c (Bir Zayden). Western Gebel: Despois 1935, 171–277; Louis 1975, 37–125 (N.B. 46–53, Roman material from Chenini).

51 Zinchecra: Daniels 1968; 1970b; 1973, 37. Move to Garama: Daniels 1970b, 66; 1971a, 262–5. Other Garamantian hillforts and oases: Daniels 1970b; 1971a, 267–78; 1973, 35–40; 1989. Ocba's campaign: el Bekri (1913 trans.), 32–5. *Garama*: Ayoub 1962, 12–20; 1967a, 12–26; Daniels 1970a; 1971a, 264–5; 1973, 36–7; 1989, 51–6. Saniat Gebril: Daniels 1971a, 264–5; 1971b, 6–7.

Chapter 3 (pp50–67)

1 Phoenician *Lepcis*: Carter 1965, 130–32; di Vita 1969, 196–202; 1982a, 516; cf. Sallust *BJ* 9.1, 80.1. *Lepcis* preferred to *Leptis* form: cf. Pflaum 1959; Reynolds and Ward-Perkins 1952; Romanelli 1924. Greeks on *Cinyps*: Herodotus 5.43. Carthaginian dominance: Lancel 1992; Warmington 1969, 17–82; Whittaker 1974; 1978c. *Sabratha*: di Vita 1969, 196–202; Kenrick 1985c, 2–4; 1986, 312–13. *Emporia*: Rebuffat 1990c.

2 One Talent tribute: Livy 34.32.3–5; di Vita 1982a, 593–4.

3 Massinissa: Livy 29.33.8–9; 34.62.1–18; Appian *Af Wars* 69; Polybius 31.21; Sallust *BJ* 78. Jugurthan war: Sallust *BJ* 77.1–3; Romanelli 1959, 72–88. Herennius: Cicero *II Verr* 1.14, 5.155; Rebuffat 1986, 179–87.

4 Curio's defeat: Caesar *BCiv* 2.23.44. Juba vs *Lepcis*: Caesar *BCiv* 2.38. Cato: Caesar *BAf* 97.3; Plutarch *Cato Y* 56; Lucan 9.375–949. *Thapsus*: *BAf* 79.1–88; Dio 43.9.4–5; Romanelli 1959, 111–28. *Lepcis* fined: *BAf* 97.3; Mattingly 1985a, 32; 1988b, 37. Status of *Emporia*: di Vita 1982a, 520–9.

5 Triumphs: *CIL* 2, p. 50. Balbus: Pliny *NH* 5.35–7. Formation of *Proconsularis*: Dio 53.12; Strabo 17.3.25; Suetonius *Aug* 47. Governor murdered: Desanges 1969. Quirinius: Florus 2.31; Birley 1988a, 231 n.5. Gaetulian war: *ILS* 120; *IRT* 301 (*Lepcis*); Velleius Paterculus 2.16; Florus 2.31; Dio 55.28.1–4; Orosius 6.21.18; Benabou 1976, 63–6; Romanelli 1959, 182–6. Tacfarinas: Tacitus *Ann* 2.52, 2.74, 3.20–21, 3.32, 3.73–4, 4.23–5; Benabou 1976, 75–84; Romanelli 1959, 229–44; *AE* 1961, 107–08 (*Lepcis* and *Oea*). Paving of streets: *IRT* 330–31.

6 Coinage: Jenkins 1969; 1974. Status: n. 4 above, Birley 1988a, 8.

7 Imperial cult: Birley 1988a, 9–15; di Vita 1982a, 550–53. Patrons: Birley 1988a, 14.

8 Reform of AD 39: Tacitus *Hist* 4.48.3–6; Dio 59.20.7; Benabou 1976, 85–9; Romanelli 1959, 246–51. War between *Lepcis* and *Oea*: Tacitus *Hist* 4.50; Pliny *NH* 5.38; Romanelli 1959, 288–91. Rutilius Gallicus: Statius *Silvae* 1.4; *CIL* 5.6690; di Vita-Evrard 1979. Promotion to *municipium*: di Vita-Evrard 1979, 1984 (*Lepcis*); Gascou 1972a, 82–3; 1982, 171, 307–10 (*Oea* and *Sabratha*).

9 *Lepcis* exceptional: Birley 1988a, 1; di Vita 1982a, 526–9. Trial of Priscus: Birley 1988a, 21–2. Trial of Apuleius: Birley 1988a, 25–33; Pavis d'Escurac 1974; Ward 1968a.

10 Events of AD 192–6: Birley 1988a, 81–128.

11 Severus in Tripolitania AD 203: Birley 1988a, 146–54. *Regio Tripolitana*: di Vita-Evrard 1985b. *Procurator ratio privata*: *CIL*

8.11105, 16542–16543. *Procurator ad olea*: *AE* 1973, 76; Manacorda 1977a. *Curatores r.p.*: *CIL* 14.3593; *AE* 1957, 161; 1959, 271. *Limes Tripolitanu*s: Ant.Itin. 73.4; di Vita-Evrard 1985b; Rebuffat 1985b; 1988b.

12 Oil dole: HA *Severus* 18.3. Plautianus: Birley 1988a, *passim*.

13 Revolt of Gordians and frontier restructuring: Herodian 7.4; HA *Gordian* 7; Le Bohec 1986b; 1989a, 451–88; Loriot 1975; Rebuffat 1982a; 1985b; 1988b; Romanelli 1959, 448–63. War: Mattingly 1985b.

14 Lepelley 1967; 1979/1981a; 1981b.

15 Proconsul and legates: Barton 1972b; Thomasson 1960; 1984; di Vita-Evrard 1985c, 155–9; 1990. At *Lepcis*: indexes *IRT*. Proconsuls and roads/land delimitation: di Vita-Evrard 1979; 1988; Trousset 1978. Etrilius Lupercus: *IRT* 330–31.

16 *Curatores*: Jacques 1984, esp. 221–47. Large territories: Mattingly 1988b. Density of towns: Picard 1959, 22, 45–50; di Vita 1983, 356.

17 Punic style government: di Vita 1982a, 537–50. Names at *Lepcis*: Benabou 1976, 511–50; Birley 1988b; Amadasi Guzzo 1983. '*Municipium* sufetal': Benabou 1976, 518–20; di Vita-Evrard 1984.

18 *Nybgenii*: Trousset 1978. *Cinithi*: *CIL* 8.22729. *Seli*: *Tab.Peut.* seg VIII.

19 Activities of elites: Garnsey and Saller 1987, 112–25. *Lepcis*: Benabou 1976, 520–35; Birley 1988a, 23–46; di Vita-Evrard 1982; 1985a; Torelli 1971; 1973. *Oea* and *Sabratha*: Thompson 1971. Tripolitanian equestrians and senators: Pflaum 1950; 1960/1961; 1978; Romanelli 1927; Thompson 1971.

20 Punic epigraphy: *IPT*; Levi della Vida 1927; 1935; 1949; 1951. Latin epigraphy: *IRT*; Reynolds 1955. Tapapii: Amadasi Guzzo 1983. Annobal Rufus: *IPT* 21, 24; *IRT* 319, 321–323. Bodmelqart (*flamen*): *IPT* 21. Bodmelqart (*sufes*): *IPT* 22. Iddibal: *IRT* 273. Ithymbal: *IRT* 341. *Sufes* in 60s: *IPT* 18. Latin name?: Torelli 1973, 401–02.

21 Replacement of Punic names: Birley 1988b, 1–19; cf. 1988a, 14–24. Sestius: *IRT* 318, 347; *IPT* 27.

22 Macer and Septimii: Birley 1988a, 212–13; 1988b, 9, 16–17. Gaius Anno: *IRT* 338; *IPT* 26. Gaius Phelyssam: *IRT* 615.

23 Annaeus Cornutus: Birley 1988b, 5–6. Capella: Suetonius Vesp. 3.1. L. Septimius Severus: Statius *Silvae* 4.5; Birley 1988a, 220; *IRT* 412. P. Septimius Aper and C. Septimius Severus: Birley 1988a, 214, 219. Arch: *AE* 1967, 536.

24 Fulvii Lepcitani: Romanelli 1958; Benabou 1976, 514–15. Plautianus: Birley 1988a, 221. Fulvius Pius: *PIR*2 F 533. Silii Plautii: di Vita-Evrard 1982. Silius Amicus: *IRT* 542; *AE* 1974, 618. Other senators: di Vita-Evrard 1985a; Mattingly 1988b, Table 1. Marcius Dioga: Benabou 1976, 524–31. Ulpius Cerealis: *IRT* 388, 440.

25 *Colonia*: *supra*, n. 8. Aemilius Frontinus: *IRT* 230. Sicinius Clarus: *IGR* 1.685, 766,828. Messius Rufinus: *IRT* 29. General discussion: Thompson 1971.

26 Municipal development, general: Broughton 1929; Fevrier 1982; 1989; Gascou 1972a; 1982, 136–320; Kotula 1974a, 111–31; 1974b; Lepelley 1979/1981a; Romanelli 1975. *Tacapae*: Ant. Itin. 59.6; *Tab.Peut.* VI.5; Procopius *de aed.* 6.4.14; Gascou 1982, 307–08. *Sabratha*: Ant. Itin. 61.3; *IRT* 6, 104, 111; Gascou 1972a, 82; 1982, 171, 307–10; Lepelley 1981a, 372–80. *Oea*: Ant. Itin. 62.2; *Tab. Peut.* VII.3; *IRT* 230, 232; Gascou 1972a, 82–3; 1982, 171; Lepelley 1981a, 371–2. *Lepcis*: Ant. Itin. 63.2; *Tab.Peut.* VII.4; *IRT* 282–4, 353, 467, 563; *AE* 1950, 206, 208. Gascou 1972a, 75–80, 197 (*ius Italicum*); 1982, 165–71; Lepelley 1981a, 335–67. *Turris Tamalleni*: Ant. Itin. 74.3; *CIL* 8.83–4; Cagnat 1909; Gascou 1972a, 134–5; 1982, 189. *Gigthis*: Ant. Itin 60.1; *CIL* 8.11031, 33707, 22737 = *ILT* 41; Gascou 1982, 192–3; Lepelley 1981a, 368–71. Zita: Ant. Itin. 60.2; *Tab. Peut.* VI.5/VII.1; *Ravenna Cos.* V.5; *CIL* 8. 11008, 11002; Gascou 1982, 308. *Pisidia*: *Tab. Peut.* VII.1 (cf. Ant.Itin. 64.3, *Fisidia vicus*); Gascou 1982, 308–10. *Tubactis*: *Tab. Peut.* VII.4–5 (?cf. Ant.Itin. 64.3, *Thebunte*); Ravenna Cos. V.6 (*Thubacis, Thubactis*); Gascou 1982, 307–10; Brogan 1975a and Rebuffat 1973c on the problems of location. *Digdida/Vigdida*: *Tab.Peut.* VIII.1–2; Ant.Itin. 65.4; Gascou 1982, 309–10.

27 Tripolitanian harbours and anchorages: Bartoccini 1958b; Brogan 1975a; Carter 1965, 123–32; di Vita 1974; Laronde 1988; Miro and Fiorenti 1977, 5, 75; Trousset 1992; Yorke 1967, 18–24; 1986, 243–5; Yorke *et al.* 1966.

28 *Gergis*: Toussaint 1908, 405–06. *Marcomades*: *Tab. Peut.* VIII.1

(*Marcomades Selorum*); Ant. Itin. 64.8 (*Marcomadibus Sirtis*); *Not.Dig. Occ.* XXXI.23. *Iscina*: *Tab. Peut.* VII.1–2 (*loc. Iudaeor. Augti.*); Ant. Itin. 65.1; Goodchild 1964. *Aquae Tacapitanae*: *Tab. Peut.* V.3–4; Ant.Itin. 74.1. *Martae* and *Augarmi*: *Tab. Peut.* VI.5–VII.1; Tissot 1888, 694 and Carton 1897, 373–8 5 (Ksar Koutine); Feuille 1940 (Hr Kedama). Island of Gerba: *Tab. Peut.* VII.1; Pliny *NH* 5.41 (*Meninx* and *Thora*); Strabo 17.3.17. Ponte Zita: Ant.Itin. 60.2.

29 *Sugolin*: *Tab. Peut.* VII.4; Stillwell 1976, 1000–01 (Dar Buk-Ammarah villa). *Subututtu*: *Tab. Peut.* VII.3–4; Oates 1953; 1954. *Mesphe*: Ant. Itin. 77.2; Goodchild 1950a. *Thenteos, Auru, Thenadassa*: Ant. Itin. 76.4–77.1; Mattingly 1982; Ward-Perkins and Goodchild 1949. *Vici*: see chapter 6.

30 Cf. *supra*, n. 16. Also Garnsey and Saller 1987, 28–32.

31 Roman roads of Tripolitania: Cuntz 1929; Miller 1887; 1916; Goodchild 1948, 1–28; 1971, 155–62, 164–9; cf. Salama 1951a; Tissot 1888.

32 Milestones as propaganda: Goodchild 1948, 7; 1971, 160–61; Salama 1951b. Milestones from Tripolitania: *CIL* 8.10016–19, 21916–19; *ILAf* 652–7; *ILT* 1719–20, 1722; *IRT* 923–72; di Vita-Evrard 1979; 1988; Goodchild 1948; 1971; 1976c; Rebuffat 1982c, 196; Reynolds 1955, S.3.

33 The coast road: *Tab. Peut.* VI.5–VIII.2; Ant.Itin. 59.6–65.6; Aurigemma 1926b; Bartoccini 1948, 150–57; Goodchild 1948, 9–10; 1952d; 1954b/c; Tissot 1888, 196–243. Milestones: di Vita-Evrard 1988 (Caecina, *c.* AD 12); cf. *CIL* 8.10016 (Nervan); 10017; *ILAf* 652–3; *ILT* 1719; *IRT* 923–9, 972; Salama 1965, 39 (Diocletian). Sebkha Taourgha and Syrtica: Brogan 1975a, 58; Goodchild 1954b; Rebuffat 1973c, 134–45; 1982a, 196 (milestone); Tissot 1888, 223–33.

34 Passage round the Syrtic gulf: Beechey and Beechey 1828; Holmboe 1936; Reddé 1988. *Thubactis*: Bartoccini 1927b (Gasr Ahmed, east of Misurata); Brogan 1975a (Marsa Gezirah, northwest); Rebuffat 1973c (inland and southwest); Tissot 1888 (Misurata).

35 The *limes Tripolitanus* road: Goodchild 1948, 11–13; 1971, 158–9; Hammond 1965; 1967; Hammond *et al.* 1964; Rushworth 1992, 141–5; Tissot 1888, 697–709; Trousset 1974, 29–38. Gabes to el-Hamma: *CIL* 8.10018 (Nonius Asprenas AD 14), 21916–19; *ILAf* 654; Le Boeuf 1905, 346–50; Toutain 1903c. El-Hamma to Telmine: Donau 1907, 52–67, 173–90; *ILAf* 656. Telmine to Libyan border: Blanchet 1898; 1899; Cagnat 1913; 1914b; Euzennat and Trousset 1975; Hilaire 1901; Rushworth 1992; Toutain 1903a; Toussaint 1905/1907. Libyan Gebel: *IRT* 931–9a/b, 954; di Vita-Evrard 1979; Goodchild 1951b, 75–88; 1976c; Hammond 1967; Oates 1953; Reynolds 1955, S. 3; Ward-Perkins and Goodchild 1949, 17–20.

36 Djerid to Gabes route: Tissot 1888, 691–7.

37 The inland west Gefara route: *ILAf* 657 = *BCTH* 1914, 614 for a milestone of Constantius Chlorus from the 17th or 27th mile. Cf. Rushworth 1992, 143–4.

38 Inland route (Tripoli to Lebda): Goodchild 1948, 25; 1951b, 75–88; Oates 1953, 89–92. Milestones: *IRT* 930–39; di Vita-Evrard 1979, 67–77; Romanelli 1939, 92–8.

39 Gebel Asker: Donau 1904b, 354–9; 1909b, 277–81; Toutain 1906, 242–50; Trousset 1978, 165–8; *ILAf* 655; *ILT* 1722. The 'central road': Goodchild 1948, 14–20; 1971, 159, 168–9; *ILAf* 651; *IRT* 940–62. 'Upper Sofeggin road': Goodchild 1948, 21–3; 1971, 160; *IRT* 963–9.

40 Goodchild 1948, 7; 1971, 157; Salama 1951a, 57–97; Trousset 1982a, 45–59.

Chapter 4 (pp68–89)

1 African and Tripolitanian frontier studies: Daniels 1987; di Vita 1964a; 1982a; Euzennat 1977a/b; 1986; Fentress 1979; 1985; Goodchild 1950c; 1954a; Haynes 1959; Mattingly 1989b; 1992; Rebuffat 1979; Trousset 1974; 1984a; 1986b; Ward-Perkins and Goodchild 1949. Grand strategy: Luttwak 1976; cf. *contra*, Isaac 1990; Mann 1974; 1979a. Current approaches: Breeze and Dobson 1987; Birley 1974a; Isaac 1990; Jones 1978; *Limes* 1–*Limes* 14 (numerous papers); Webster 1979; Whittaker 1989a; 1994. Primacy of desert frontier: Correspondence de Napoleon 1.30, 1870, 10, 'De tous les obstacles qui peuvent couvrir les empires, un désert ... est incontestablement le plus grand. Les chaines de montagnes ... tiennent le second rang, les fleuves le troisième'; cf. Isaac 1990; Luttwak 1976, esp. 74–80.

2 Economy of force: Luttwak 1976; expanded discussion in Mattingly 1984; 1992. Nomads and sedentarists: *supra*, chapter 2, ns 3 and 19.

3 Relations with *Garamantes*: Bovill 1968; Daniels 1971a; Law 1967. With *Gaetuli*: Fentress 1982. With *Nasamones, Macae*: Desanges 1969.

4 Record of wars: *supra*, n. 1. Style of warfare: Rebuffat 1982a, 490–92. Roman defeats: Dio (Epitome) 67.3.5 (turned to victory).

5 Balbus: Pliny *NH* 5.35–7; Strabo 3.5.3; Velleius Paterculus 2.51.3; *Ins.Ital* 13 (*Fasti Triumphalis*), 569 – *L. Cornelius P.f. Balbus procos ex Africa Vi K April A. DCCXXXIV*; Thomasson 1960, II, 11. Campaign: Daniels 1970a, 13–21; 1989; Desanges 1957; 1978, 189–95; Lefranc 1986; Lhote 1954 (argued that Balbus penetrated Tassili n'ajjer mountains to reach river Niger); Romanelli 1950; 1977. Size of force: cf. Ocba in AD 666–7 who conquered the Giofra, Fezzan and Ghadames with a force of only 400 cavalry (El-Bekri, trans. de Slane 1913, 32–5). *Garamantes* under Rome's *imperium*: Virgil *Aen* 6.791–7.

6 Gaetulian war: Dio 55.28.1–4; Florus 2.31; Orosius 6.21.18 (extraordinary nature of appointment of Cossus Lentulus); Velleius Paterculus 2.6. (Passienus and Cossus Lentulus won triumphal honours). Involvement of western Numidian *Gaetuli*: Desanges 1964b. Murder of proconsul (L. Cornelius Lentulus): Eustathius *Comm* 5.209–10; Justinian *Inst* 2.25; Desanges 1969. Cossus Lentulus: *IRT* 301. Quirinius: Florus 2.31; Benabou 1976, 69–73 (assumed to have been governor of Crete and Cyrenaica, but Syme (quoted by Birley 1988a, 231, n.5) has suggested he could have been proconsul of Africa in either 3 BC or AD 2).

7 Road of AD 14: *CIL* 8.10018; the interpretation is *contra* Lassère 1982b; cf. Syme 1951. Tacfarinan revolt AD 17–24: Tacitus *Ann* 2.52, 2.73–4, 3.20–21, 3.32, 3.73–4, 4.23–5; Aurelius Victor *de Caes* 2.3; Velleius Paterculus 2.130.5. IX legion at *Lepcis*: Tacitus *Ann* 3.74. Dolabella: Bartoccini 1958a; *AE* 1961, 107–08. Garamantian envoys: *Ann* 4.25. Lands of *Lepcis*: *IRT* 330–331, *... ex reditibus agrorum quos Lepcitanos restituit*.

8 Aelius Lamia, road: *IRT* 930; di Vita-Evrard 1979; cf. Romanelli 1939, 104–10. *Ammonium*: Goodchild 1951b; Levi della Vida 1951. Exploitation of peasants: Abd el-Hakam (trans. Gateau 1947), 35–7. Rural slaves: *ILS* 2927 (*Gigthis*); Apuleius *Apol* 93.4; Garnsey 1978, 235–7; Gsell 1932; Pavis d'Escurac, 1974, 92.

9 War between *Lepcis, Oea*: Tacitus *Hist* 4.50. Campaign of Festus to Fezzan: Pliny *NH* 5.38; Daniels 1969, 37–8.

10 Campaign of Flaccus to Fezzan: Ptolemy 1.8, 1.10; Desanges 1964a; 1978, 197–213. Maternus: Ptolemy 1.8; Desanges 1964a; 1978, 197–213; Daniels 1969, 37–8; cf. Kirkwan 1971. Nasamonian revolt: Zonaras 11.19 = Dio (Epitome) 77.3.5; Eusebius *Chronic* 1.10 (for the date); Benabou 1976, 106–08; Romanelli 1959, 301–03. Delimitation of *Macae* lands: *IRT* 854 = Romanelli 1939, 110–18. Septimius and/or Suellius Flaccus: one man, Desanges 1964a; Romanelli 1959; Thomasson 1960; 1984; two men, Birley 1971, 255; 1988a, 17–18; Desanges 1978, 210–13.

11 Activity in Nefzaoua and Djerid: *CIL* 8.23165 and *ILAf* 656; Donau 1907, 66–67, for Javolenus Priscus legate *c*. AD 83–4 on access roads to both oases groups.

12 Warfare under Severus: HA *Severus* 18.3, *Tripolim ... contusis bellicosissimis gentibus securissimam reddidit ...* ; Aurelius Victor *de Caes* 20.19, *Tripoli cuius Lepti oppido oriebatur, bellicosae gentes submotae procul ...* Bu Njem: Rebuffat 1973b. Campaign of Severus in AD 203: Birley 1988a, 146–54; Guey 1950, 55–67. *Bellum* at Gheriat: Loriot 1971. Gasr Duib: *IRT* 880; Ward-Perkins and Goodchild 1949, 26–8. Bu Njem letters: Marichal 1979, esp. 448–51; Rebuffat 1977c, 407–08 (possible reference to fray); 1989.

13 Garamantian envoys to Rome: Tacitus *Ann* 4.23. Roman goods in Fezzan graves: Ayoub 1967a, 1–11, 27–48; 1967b, 213–19; 1968a, 58–81; Daniels 1971a, 266–7; 1977, 5–7; 1989; Pace, Sergi and Caputo 1951, 201f. Ashlar in buildings at Zinchecra and Germa: Ayoub, 1967a, 12–26; Daniels 1970b, 55–7, 66; 1971a, 262–5; 1973, 36. Mausolea: Barth 1857, 144–7; Daniels 1971a, 267–8; 1975, 24–5; Duveyrier 1864, 275. Roman technical aid and subsidy: Daniels 1970a, 24–5; 1971a, 262–5; Mattingly 1992, 54–7; Rebuffat 1971a;

Romanelli 1962, 229–26 (drawing parallels with the *Baquates* of Morocco (*supra* chapter 2, n. 14)). Letters of passage: Marichal 1979, 451; cf. the practice attested by St Augustine *Letters* 46–7 of allowing tribesmen from outside the province to cross the border to be employed as seasonal labour. Late Roman graves: Daniels 1977. Byzantine treaty: John of Biclar 569.1 (*c*. AD 568).

14 Roman finds at Ghadames: Rebuffat 1969, 194–5; 1972a, 322–4. 'Asnam': Rebuffat 1972a, 333; 1975c, 498–9; Mercier 1953. Other evidence for ancient Ghadames: Coro 1956; Mercier 1953. Roman finds in neighbouring oases: Rebuffat 1972a, 323–4. Severan garrison: *IRT* 907–09. Byzantine treaty: Procopius *de aed* 6.3.9–11, the *Cidamensi* 'had been at peace with Romans from ancient times', though Justinian had had to 'win them over', implying some gap in relations; cf. Rebuffat 1982a, 492–9; Trousset 1984a, 11–12.

15 *Augila*: Mela 1.8.46. AD 85 revolt: *supra*, n. 10. Sixth-century *Augila*: Procopius *de aed* 6.2.18–20.

16 *Macae*: Mattingly 1987a/b (assimilation and culture); Rebuffat 1975a (graffiti at Bu Njem); 1982c (Bei el Kebir area). Land survey, Rutilius Gallicus: di Vita-Evrard 1979, 77–98. *Seli*: *Tab. Peut.* 8.1–8.2 (*Marcomades Selorum, Digdida municipium Selorum*). *Muducivvi, Zamuci*: *IRT* 854. *Cissipades*: *CIL* 16.39, 16.46 (Upper Moesia), 3.14429 (Lower Moesia).

17 Prefect of *Cinithi*: *CIL* 8.10500. Association with *Gigthis*: *CIL* 8. 22729. Territory of *Gigthis*: *CIL* 8.11022 establishes that the western limits of the territory lay 22 *milia* from the town, probably at or near the Wadi Zeuss (implying an area in excess of 1,500 sq km).

18 Conquest of Nefzaoua: Trousset 1982a. Vibius Marsus: Trousset 1978. Flavian garrison: *supra*, n. 11. *Thiges*: *CIL* 8.23165 (on the approach to the Djerid); Trousset 1982a. *Civitas Nybgeniorum*: *CIL* 22796; *ILAf* 655; Cagnat 1909; Carton 1914/1915; *Encyclopédie berbère* cah prov 36. Trajanic delimitation: Trousset 1978, 165–73. Bir Soltane: *ILAf* 30. Municipal status: *CIL* 8.83.

19 Severus 'creator': Cagnat 1914b; Gsell 1933; Haynes 1959, 36–41; Mann 1974a, 526; 1979a, 179–80; Ward-Perkins and Goodchild 1949, 18. 'Limes' de pénétration': Euzennat 1977b, 536–9; Trousset 1984a. Desert frontiers: *supra*, n. 1. Early garrison at Telmine and in Dahar: Euzennat 1977c, 134; Euzennat and Trousset 1975; Gascou 1982, 189. Other pre-Severan development: Mattingly 1989b, 137–9; Rebuffat 1980a, 108–09. *Tab. Peut.*: 7.1, 7.5, 8.1.

20 *Fossata, clausurae*: Baradez 1949a; 1967; Trousset 1980a; 1984b.

21 *Lepcis* garrison: Sallust *BJ* 77.1. *Ammaedara*: pers. obs. of small size. IX legion at/near *Lepcis* AD 22: Tacitus *Ann* 3.74. Garrison of Nefzaoua: Trousset 1982a; cf. *CIL* 8.23166 (*Thiges*). Cherb *clausurae*: Trousset 1978, 166–73. Remada: Bechert 1971, 241–5, 261, 285 (style of gates); Euzennat and Trousset 1975, 45 (date). *Gemellae*: Baradez 1948; 1949a/b; Trousset 1977a.

22 Mizda: Barth 1857, 99–103 (location); Ward-Perkins and Goodchild 1949, 29 (fort). Medina Ragda and Hadd Hajar: Brogan 1980; de Mathuisieulx 1904, 18; Mattingly 1989b. Ain Wif: *IRT* 868, 869; Mattingly 1989b. Tisavar: *CIL* 8.11048; Trousset 1974, 92–4. Bezereos: *ILAf* 26; Trousset 1974, 75–8. Commodan policing posts in Africa: *CIL* 8.2494–2495, 20816, 22629.

23 Remada temple: Euzennat 1973, 143. Si Aioun: *ILAf* 8–9. Bu Njem: Rebuffat 1973b. Gheriat: di Vita 1966b, 107–11. Bezereos: *ILAf* 26–8. Ghadames: *IRT* 909. Ain Wif: *IRT* 868–9. Ain el-Auenia: Reynolds and Brogan 1960, 51–4, nos 1–2. Gasr Zerzi: Brogan and Reynolds 1964, 43–4, nos 1–2. Bir Tarsin: *IRT* 887; cf. Ward-Perkins and Goodchild 1949, 24 and n. 28 (no site located at Tarsin). Campaigns of AD 201–05: Rebuffat 1973b; 1989; *contra*, Speidel 1988.

24 Hr Mgarine, Hr Medeina: Trousset 1974. *Limes Tripolitanus* road: *supra*, chapter 3, n. 34. Severan garrisons on *limes* road: certain or probable, *Agarlabas, Bezereos, Thebelami, Tillibari, Thenteos, Auru, Thenadassa*; cf. di Vita 1964a, 287–90; Hammond 1967, 16–18.

25 Gheriat *burgus*: *IRT* 895; Barth 1857, 123–4; Goodchild 1954a (=1976, 54–55 and n. 26); Mattingly 1985b. Sites occupied post-AD 238: *IRT* 896; Mattingly 1985b (Gheriat); Rebuffat 1985b; 1988b (Bu Njem); *IRT* 880 (*Thenteos*). *ILAf* 26 (Bir Rhezene, titles of *Leg. III* reingraved post-253); *Not. Dig.* Occ. 25.33, 31.21; Euzennat and Trousset 1975, 23–6 (Remada); Gombeaud 1901, 91–2 (Ksar Rhilane, the two thirds of the identifiable coin sequence was

mid-third-century date). Bu Njem garrison: Rebuffat 1982b, 912–14; 1985b. Gheriat garrison: Mattingly 1985b.

26 *Praepositus limitis (Tripolitanae)*, Gasr Duib: *IRT* 880; Mattingly 1991; Rebuffat 1985b, 129. At Bu Njem: Rebuffat 1985b; 1988b. Garrison life: Marichal 1979; 1992. Abandonment: Rebuffat 1982a, 508–09. Ras el-Ain: *CIL* 8.22765 = *ILT* 3; Rebuffat 1979; Trousset 1974. Last milestones on central road: *IRT* 953 (AD 271) and 943 (AD 275). Last coin, Tisavar: Gombeaud 1901, 91–2; Trousset 1974, 92–4. *Notitia*: *infra*, chapter 9.

27 Expeditionary units commanded by auxiliary officers: *CIL* 8.2466, 21567; Picard 1944, 45–6. Aemilius Emeritus also known in Numidia: *CIL* 8.2465, 17953. Legionary centurions in charge of vexillations: Saxer 1967 (vexillations); Smith 1979 (*praepositi*); Speidel 1981 (*centurio principe*). Bu Njem centurions: Rebuffat 1985c. Bu Njem outposts: Marichal 1979, 449–50; Rebuffat 1982a.

28 *Bezereos*: Trousset 1974, 75–8, 132. Military list: *ILAf* 27; Lassère 1980. Religious calendar and lists: Rebuffat 1982b; 1988a. Remada: *ILAf* 9 (Si Aioun); Merlin 1909, 91–101 (tile stamps at *Tisavar*); Euzennat and Trousset 1975, 67; Trousset 1974, 121–2. *Praepositus Tillibarensis*: *Not.Dig.* Occ. 25.33, 31.21. Zintan/*Thenteos*: the date of development of this fort could well have been early, there is no evidence incompatible with it having been already based in the region by the second century, Mattingly 1985b; 1991.

29 *Praepositus limitis*: *IRT* 880; *Not.Dig.*Occ. 31.19 (*Tenthettani*); Ward-Perkins and Goodchild 1949, 26–8; van Berchem 1952, 39–42; cf. Rebuffat 1985b; 1988b (Bu Njem). *Ostraca*: Marichal 1979; 1992. Gasr Duib/Bu Njem texts compared: Mattingly 1991; Rebuffat 1985b; 1988b.

30 Garrison of Tripolitania: Cagnat 1913 (now superseded); Le Bohec 1978; 1989a/b; Picard 1944; Saxer 1967; Smith 1979. *Numerus collatus*: Le Bohec 1980; 1986a; 1989b. *Cohors II Flavia Afrorum*: Cagnat 1913; Euzennat 1973; 1977c; Euzennat and Trousset 1975, 60–61; Le Bohec 1989b, 67–70; Trousset 1974, 94, 114–20. *Cohors I Syrorum sagittariorum*: Reynolds and Brogan 1960, 51, no. 1 (*Auru*); *CIL* 8.21038 (a tribune of the cohort in retirement at *Lambaesis*). At Gheriat: Le Bohec 1987; 1989b, 88–90; Mattingly 1985b. Fort postulated at Zintan: Mattingly 1985b; 1989b; 1991.

31 *Cohors VIII Fida*: *CIL* 8.22765 (Ras el-Ain); *CIL* 8.22766, 22767, 22768 (repairs); Le Bohec 1978; 1989b; Marichal 1979, 450; 1992, 65–6, 72–4 (small detachment at Bu Njem pre-AD 263); Rebuffat 1989. Bu Njem *numerus*: Marichal 1979, 436–52; 1992, 63–6; Rebuffat 1982a, 492–6.

32 Cf. Mann 1974a, 526, who saw the changes under Severus as transforming a frontier situation which was otherwise 'typical of the Republican period' for its low level of development.

33 Policing work: Marichal 1992, 106–14; Rebuffat 1982a 490–92. Customs control: Cagnat 1914a; Darmon 1964; Fentress 1979, 208–09 (for *Zarai* and *Lambaesis* tariffs); Marichal 1992, 112–13; Rebuffat 1979, 232–5. *Clausurae* for policing not defence: Mattingly and Jones 1986; Trousset 1980a; 1984b. Diplomacy and tribal supervision: *supra*, this chapter. Provisioning: Marichal 1979, 448; 1992, 99–106 show camel drivers bringing supplies to the fort of Bu Njem; cf. Davies 1987; Manning 1975; Bowman and Thomas 1983; Bowman *et al.* 1990 (for supporting data from Britain to show garrisons seeking food in their immediate localities); Whittaker 1989a, 51–77; 1989b, 64–80.

34 Bu Njem food supplies: Marichal 1979, 448; 1992, 101–02 shows the quantities brought by individuals to have been small, those of grain varying from 24–108 *modii* (210–945 litres). Patrols and outposts: Marichal 1979, 450; 1992, 106–11; Rebuffat 1970b (Zerzi); 1970d (Zella); Rebuffat and Marichal 1973, 181–6. *Statio camellariorum*: Marichal 1979, 451; 1992, 112–13; Rebuffat 1982c, 196. Relations with *Garamantes*: Marichal 1979, 451; 1992, 110–14. St Augustine *Letters* 46–7.

Chapter 5 (pp90–115)

1 Early investigators of *limes* road: for example, Cagnat 1913, 531–2; de Mathuisieulx 1904, 11–16; Hilaire 1901, 95–105; Toutain 1903a, 391–409; cf. Hammond 1967, 5–15; Le Bohec 1989a, 437–50. Problems of site classification: cf. Rebuffat 1980a, 112–18, 122–3;

Trousset 1974, 131–42. Size categories employed: over 0.8 ha (2 acres) = fort; 0.1–0.8 ha (0.25–2 acres) = fortlet; 0.01–0.1 ha (0.03–0.25 acres) = outpost; under 0.01 ha (0.25 acres) = tower. Excavated forts in Africa: Baradez 1948; 1949b; 1966a/b; Cagnat 1913; Callu *et al.* 1965; Rebuffat 1972b; 1975e; 1982; Rebuffat and Hallier 1970. General studies of Roman forts: Hassall 1983; Johnson 1983; Lander 1984.

2 Remada. Early research: *BCTH* 1919, clviii; Cagnat 1913, 530; Donau 1909a, 39; Euzennat and Trousset 1975 (Donau's excavation); Hilaire 1901, 104; Lecoy de la Marche 1894, 405–06. Recent discoveries/observation: Brogan 1965a, 53; Euzennat 1973; Euzennat and Trousset 1975 (=1978); Hammond 1967, 11. Gates: Bechert 1971, 241–3 (square projecting); 261, 276 (D-shaped); Euzennat and Trousset 1975, 55–9, fig. 14; Daniels 1987 and pers.obs. show the same combination of towers at Sadouri in Algeria, suggesting a Severan date for that fort. *Principia*: Euzennat and Trousset 1975, 28–30; cf. Rebuffat 1975b/d; Trousset 1977a, 572. *Fabrica*: Euzennat and Trousset 1975, 28. Parallels and date: Euzennat 1973 (Severan inscription); Euzennat and Trousset 1975, 55 (Hadrianic); Trousset 1977a (*Gemellae*). Corippus: *Ioh* 2.78–80.

3 Gheriat. Early accounts: Barth 1857, 123–5; Cagnat 1913, 553–5; Petragnarni 1928, 96–7. Goodchild's work: 1952b, 77 (best version of air–photo); 1954a (=1976a, 50–56). Recent research: di Vita 1966b, 94–111; Jones 1989a, 34–5; Jones and Barker 1983, 57–67; Rebuffat 1967a, 51; Welsby 1983, 57–64. Robbed defences: Goodchild 1954a, 54; Welsby 1983, 60. Northeast gate: Goodchild 1954a, 53; cf. Cagnat 1913, 456–63 (*Lambaesis*); Rebuffat 1967a, 71–84. Southwest gate: Welsby 1983, 61; cf. Mattingly 1985b (cf. tower). Interval towers: Welsby 1983, 61–2. Parallels for angle towers: Christofle 1938, 120–21 and Seston 1928, 155, 162 (*Rapidum*); Cagnat 1913, 458 and Trousset 1977a, 571, 573 (?similar at *Lambaesis* and *Gemellae*); Welsby 1988 (with superb reconstruction drawings of towers and gates); 1990; see also this volume, Bu Njem. West side of oasis: Jones and Barker 1983, 58, 64–7. Size of fort: double area of Bu Njem – could have accommodated equivalent of a *cohors milliaria* (about 800 men).

4 Bu Njem. Early travellers: Cagnat 1913, 555–8 (from Duveyrier's notes); Lyon 1821, 65–6; Nachtigal 1974, 47; Richardson 1848, II, 443–53; Vivien de Saint-Martin 1863, 119–21. Italian and British work: Bartoccini 1928b; Goodchild 1954a (=1976, 47–50); Haynes 1959, 140–41; Lavagnini 1928; Petragnarni 1928, 96–97; Merighi 1940, 17–18. French work: 1969; 1971b; 1972a; 1975c; 1977b; 1982c; full bibliographies in Rebuffat 1985a; 1989. Chronology of occupation: Rebuffat 1989; cf. Speidel 1988.

5 Defences: Barker and Jones 1981, 12 (air-photo); Rebuffat 1967a, 54–5; 1970a, 10–11, 87; Welsby 1988. Gates: Lyon 1821, 65–6 (north); Rebuffat 1967a, 71–84; 1969, 199–203 (east and north); 1973a, 99–120; 1975b, 214–15; 1977a, 47–50 (south). Graffito of fort: Rebuffat 1970b, pl. xxviid; 1989, fig. 2. Towers: Birley 1988a, pl. 21 (air-photo); Rebuffat 1970a, 10–11. Layout and cubit base of measurements: Rebuffat 1989, 161–2 (cf. Joppolo 1967 for continuity of Punic measures at the market in *Lepcis Magna*).

6 *Principia*: Rebuffat 1967a, 85–92; 1969, 204–06; 1970a, 14–17; 1970b, 107–21; 1972a, 336–7; 1975b, 189–209; 1989. *Ostraca*: Marichal 1992; Baths: 1970a, 13–14; 1970b, 121–33; 1972a, 331–35; 1975c, 503; 1977a, 44–7; 1989. Well: Cagnat 1913, 556 (close to north gate). *Praetorium*: Rebuffat 1975c, 502–04; 1977a, 42–3; 1989. Granaries: 1977a, 44, fig. 5; 1989. Barracks: Rebuffat 1970a, 11–13; 1977a, 38–42; 1989. Garrison size: Marichal 1992, 63–75; Rebuffat 1977a, 38–42; 1989; cf. Hassall 1983.

7 Temples: 1970b, 135–6; 1972a, 327–9 (Jupiter Hammon and an unknown deity); 1975b, 215–18 (Mars Canapphar); 1977a, 39 (map), 51–6; 1990b (general overview of all temples). Epigraphy: di Vita-Evrard and Rebuffat 1987; Marichal 1979; 1992; Rebuffat 1967a, 97–103; 1970a, 34–5; 1970b, 138–43; 1973a; 1973b; 1973c; 1975b, 218–20; 1977a, 56–9; 1982b; 1985b; 1987; 1988a/b; Rebuffat and Marichal 1973. Abandonment and squatters: Rebuffat 1967a, 71–84; 1970a, 23–30; 1989.

8 Ghadames: Coro 1956, 3–26; Duveyrier 1864, 249–66; Goodchild 1954a (=1976, 56); Mercier 1953, 17–47; Rebuffat 1969, 194–5; 1972a,

322–3; Reynolds 1958, 135–6; Richardson 1848, I, 211, 355–7. Towers: Duveyrier 1864, 251. Fort or fortlet: Mattingly 1989b.

9 El-Hamma: Blanchet 1899, 145–6; Privé 1895, 84–95; Toussaint 1905, 63. Military origins: *CIL* 8.22784 (fragmentary text from el-Hamma) mentions a soldier *Ianuariius sesqui[plicarius]*. *Aquae Flaviae*: *CIL* 8.17725.

10 Telmine, fort: Euzennat 1977c, 134; Gascou 1982, 189. Oasis and town: Cagnat 1909; Carton 1914/1915; Tissot 1888, 46, 701–03; Toussaint 1905, 71–2;Toutain 1903a, 289–303; Trousset 1974, 43–6. Late empire garrison?: *Not.Dig.* Occ. 25.21, *limes Thamallensis* garrisoned by *limitanei*.

11 Mizda: Barth 1857, 99–103; Petragnarni 1928, 112–13; Ward-Perkins and Goodchild 1949, 29. Italian fort: *IRT* p. 215 and nos 883–4. Roads: Goodchild 1948, 5–6; 14–23.

12 *Thenteos*: de Mathuisieulx 1904, 11–16; 1905, 82–7; 1912, 53–4; Euzennat and Trousset 1975, 53; Hammond 1964, 10; 1967, 13. *Cohors Syrorum* in Tripolitania: Le Bohec 1987; Mattingly 1985b; 1991.

13 Ras el-Ain, early investigation: Boizot 1913; Cagnat 1913, 202, 531; Donau 1909a, 38–9; Hilaire 1901. 101–03; Lecoy de la Marche 1894, 395, 399–402; Rebuffat 1980a, 111–12; Toutain 1903a, 351–4; Trousset 1974, 98–102. Epigraphy: Heron de Villefosse 1894a, 472, 475–6; Renault 1901; Trousset 1974, 101–02. D-shaped gate towers: Lecoy de la Marche 1894, 401; Trousset 1974, 99. Burials: Trousset 1974, 100. Southwest corner: Trousset 1974, 99–100; Dating: pottery noted on site in 1982 included Hayes ARS forms 23B, 27/31, 31, 181 (late second–third century), 68 and 70 (late fourth–fifth), TRS form 9 (fifth).

14 Outstationing of troops: Marichal 1979; Rebuffat 1982a (Bu Njem); cf. Breeze 1977, 1–6; Reynolds 1971b; Welles *et al.* 1959, 22–46, 191–404 (*Dura Europus*). Road stations: Haynes 1959, 138 and Ward-Perkins and Goodchild 1949, 21–4 (undefended); Mattingly 1982 (defended).

15 Ain Wif: Mattingly 1982, 73–80; Ward-Perkins and Goodchild 1949, 21–4; 1953, 44 (church). Date: Mattingly 1982, 78–9.

16 Bir Rhezene: Donau 1909a, 35–8; Hilaire 1901, 97, 99; Lassère 1980; Merlin 1921; Poinssot 1937; Tissot 1888, 687, 705; Toussaint 1905, 72; 1906, 231; Toutain 1903a, 324–5; Trousset 1974, 75–8, 132 (plan).

17 Hr Mgarine: Hammond 1964, 14; Toussaint 1905, 70; Trousset 1974, 52 132 (plan). Dating: Hayes ARS forms 27, 27/31, 181 (Severan) common, one rim ARS 6c (second) and examples of 50, 91, 92 (fifth).

18 Hr Medeina: Hammond 1967, 11; Lecoy de la Marche 1894, 407–08; Toussaint 1906, 236; Toutain 1903a, 401; Trousset 1974, 109–10, 132.

19 Ksar Tabria: Toussaint 1905, 70–73; Toutain 1903a, 324; Trousset 1974, 73–5.

20 Ksar Rhilane: Cagnat 1913, 558–61; Gombeaud 1901; Lecoy de la Marche 1894, 396–7; Gaukler 1900; Hilaire 1901, 100; Toussaint 1907, 312–14; Toutain 1903a, 373; Trousset 1974, 92–4. Excavations: Gombeaud 1901, 81–94. Ancillary buildings: Trousset 1974, 92–4; Rebuffat 1980a, 110–11. Abandonment: Gombeaud 1901, 93.

21 Si Aioun: Cagnat 1913, 205, 558; Donau 1909a, 40–43; Hilaire 1901, 104; Merlin 1909, 98; Toutain 1903, 396; Trousset 1974, 118–20.

22 El-Haddadia: Goodchild 1952d (=1976a, 157–8, pl.53). Occupation span of site (civil and military): Bakir 1967, 251.

23 Road stations: Hammond 1964; 1967. Ain Wif II: Mattingly 1982. Medina Doga: Goodchild 1951b, 74–9 (plan); Ain el-Auenia: Cambridge 1960 (plans); Reynolds and Brogan 1960, 51–2; Reynolds and Simpson 1967, 45–7.

24 Medina Ragda: Brogan 1980, 51; Cagnat 1913, 557–8; de Mathuisieulx 1904, 16; 1912, 60–61. J.N. Dore, pers.comm. notes the presence of abundant *terra sigillata* and early ARS, but comparatively little late ARS or TRS.

25 Military interpretation: Toussaint 1906, 230–36. Civilian use of fortified farms: Barker and Jones 1981; 1982; Buck, Burns and Mattingly 1983, 52–4; Jones 1985a; Mattingly 1989a/b. Date by masonry: Brogan and Smith 1985; di Vita 1964a, 71–3; Goodchild 1950a, 41–4. Derivations of *centenarium*: Gauckler 1902; Goodchild 1949a, 32–4; Leschi 1943; Smith 1971 (*centuria*); Toutain 1903a, 372–4; Ward-Perkins and Goodchild 1949, 28. Civil *gsur* with

military names: Courtois *et al.* 1952, Act VIII (*centenarium*); *CIL* 8.22774 (*turris*).

26 Hr Krannfir: Cagnat 1913, 539–42; Toussaint 1906, 231; Toutain 1903a, 325–30 (plan); Trousset 1974, 79.

27 Gheriat esh-Shergia: Barth 1857, 125; di Vita 1964a, 71–3; Goodchild 1954a, 50; Ward-Perkins and Goodchild 1949, 30. ULVS 1980: unpublished survey. Signalling link: Mattingly 1985b; Trousset 1990. Shergia, Gasr Isawi parallels: di Vita 1964a, pl.xxxv b/c/d; Goodchild 1976a, pl. 31. Isawi: Brogan and Smith 1985 (for Gasr Banat, the adjacent tomb); Burns and Mattingly 1981, 24–33; de Mathuisieulx 1904, 27–9; 1912, 71–7; Goodchild 1950a, 41–3; Ward-Perkins and Goodchild, 1949, 30. Date: J.N.Dore, pers.comm., notes two sherds of first-century *terra sigillata Italica* along with Hayes ARS forms 5, 23, 27, 27/31 (second–third century) and 50, 58, 32/58, 59, 69 and TRS 2, 3.

28 Bu Njem outposts: Marichal 1979; 1992; cf. Pliny NH 5.37 (*Boin = Boinag*). Zella: Rebuffat 1970c; 1970d, 17–18. Zerzi: Brogan and Reynolds 1964, 43–6; Rebuffat 1970b, 136–7; 1982a, pls. Other: Rebuffat 1972a, 324–6; 1975c, 499; 1982c, 197–9 (Shwerif, Oum el-Gueloub). Wells and cisterns: Brogan 1965b (Wadis Neina and Bei el Kebir); Brogan and Reynolds 1964; Rebuffat 1982a (Zerzi).

29 Duib: *IRT* 880, 881 (Latino-Punic); di Vita-Evrard 1991; Goodchild 1971, 160 (location); Mattingly 1991; Ward-Perkins and Goodchild 1949, 24–5. Wames: de Mathuisieulx 1905, 88–9 (plan); Goodchild 1976a, pl. 19 (air-photo); Smith 1971, 302–03 (plan).

30 Tarcine: Blanchet 1898, 93; Cagnat 1913, 535–6; Hilaire 1901, 99–100; Gauckler 1902; Toutain 1903a, 360–75; Trousset 1974, 90–92. Excavation: Gauckler 1902, 321–41. Last coin: Eugenius AD 392–4.

31 Towers: Baatz 1970; di Vita 1964a, 87–8 (Mizda-Gheriat); Gichon 1974; Mattingly 1985b (Gheriat); Rebuffat 1978, 845–6; Trousset 1990 (with full list). Messages by hand: Rebuffat 1982a, 483–5.

32 Terminology, *clausurae*: Napoli and Rebuffat 1983; Pringle 1981, 96 (Byzantine use); Rebuffat 1980a, 113–14; Trousset 1984b. *Fossatum*: *Dizionario epigrafico di antichita Romane* 4 (1958), 15–16. *Bracchium*: Rebuffat 1980c; 1981; cf. *RIB* 722 (an annex or *vicus* defence at Brough by Bainbridge). *Propugnacula*: Trousset 1974, 139–41; rebutted by Rebuffat 1980a, 113–14; 1984, 3–26. *Vallum*: Bruce 1979, 30–33.

33 Archaeology, *fossata*: Baradez 1949a; 1967; Fentress 1979, 111–12; Gsell *et al.* 1902; Guey 1939; Jacquot 1911; 1915; Jones and Mattingly 1980; Van Berchem 1952, 42–9. *Clausurae*: Mattingly and Jones 1986; Trousset 1980; 1984b. Links with transhumance routes: Lassère 1977; Whittaker 1978 (maps).

34 Cherb: Goetschy 1894, 593–4; Privé 1895, 87–104; Toussaint 1905, 63–4; cf. Euzennat 1972, 21–3; Trousset 1976, 25–7; 1978, 165–73. Gebel Asker: Carton 1914, 256–9; Privé 1895, 102–04; Toutain 1906, 245; Trousset 1978, 168–73. Asker road: *supra*, chapter 3. Bir Oum Ali: Carton 1914, 359; Euzennat 1972, 21–3; Goetschy 1894, 593–6; Privé 1895, 101–02; Trousset 1976, 25–7; 1978, 66–79; 1980a, 936–40; 1984b. Cistern: Goetschy 1894, 595 (plan). Date: Single rim sherd of Hayes ARS form 23B noted.

35 Tebaga: Blanchet 1898, 71–4; 1899, 147–8; Cagnat 1913, 546–8; Donau 1904a, 472–5; Fentress 1979, 98–100; Tissot 1888, 690, 820; Toutain 1903a, 322; Trousset 1974, 62–7; 1984b, 385–7. Strategic importance of Tebaga corridor: Moreau 1947, 8; Trousset 1974, 63–4. Varied construction: Baradez 1949a; Blanchet 1898, 71–4; Donau 1904a, 472–3; Trousset 1974, 62–7, pls 23–4. Towers: Trousset 1974, 64–5, fig. 8. Gate: Blanchet 1898, 72–3; 1899, 145–6 (plan) Donau 1904a, 472–3; 1909a, 32 (reused tomb dedication); Trousset 1974, 65–7, fig. 9. Outer enclosure: Blanchet 1898, 73; 1899, 147–8 (central structure 6 x 10 m, outer enceinte 15 x 24 m); still partly discernible in 1982. Date: Donau 1904a, 475; Trousset 1974, 62–7; 139–41; pottery observed on site in 1982 included Hayes ARS forms 27/33, 181 (third century).

36 Skiffa group: Blanchet 1899, 139–45; Euzennat 1972, 11–12; Hilaire 1901, 100–01; Lecoy de la Marche 1894, 396, 402; Mattingly and Jones 1986; Trousset 1974, 97–102; 1984b. ?Benia bel-Recheb: Hilaire 1901; Lecoy de la Marche 1894, 396; Trousset 1974, 96–7. Wadi Zraia: Hilaire 1901, 100–01; Toutain 1903a, 360; Trousset 1974, 97, fig. 29; 1984b, 384, fig.1. Wadi Skiffa: Blanchet 1898, 76; 1899, 140; Cagnat 1913, 534–5; Hilaire 1901, 100–01; Lecoy de la Marche 1894,

396; Toussaint 1906, 234; Trousset 1974, 97, 139–41. Towers: Trousset 1974, 97. Gate: Blanchet 1898, 75–7; 1899, 140–41; Cagnat 1913, 534–5; Trousset 1974, 97. Skiffa south: Mattingly and Jones 1986, 89–93. Chenini: 1974, 102, 139–41; 1984b, 387.

37 Hadd Hajar: Brogan 1971b; 1980; Cagnat 1913, 557; de Mathuisieulx 1904, 16; 1912, 60–61; Holmes 1972, 6–7.

38 Function of *clausurae*: Mattingly and Jones 1986; Trousset 1980a; 1984a/b. Transhumance control: see also Garnsey 1978, 232; Whittaker 1978a, 342–48; *contra*, Gsell 1933; Guey 1939, 226–45.

39 Seasonal labour movement: St Augustine *Letters* 46–7; *Cod Theod* 7.15.1; Marichal 1979, 448–51. Customs control: Rebuffat 1977c, 405–07; 1979, 230–32; cf. Darmon 1964.

40 Hadrianic dating of *fossata*: Baradez 1949a, 153–5; 1967, 200–10; Birley 1956, 29. Gordian: Van Berchem 1952, 42–9 (now much discredited). Camel nomads: Gsell 1933; Guey 1939; Euzennat 1977a, 437–8. Late use: *Cod.Theod*. 7.15.1; Jones and Mattingly 1980.

41 Date of Cherb sector: Euzennat 1972, 21–33; Trousset 1976, 31; 1978, 168–73; 1980a, 936–40; 1984b, 394. Tebaga and Skiffa: Mattingly and Jones 1986, 92–5; Rebuffat 1980a, 113–14; Trousset 1974, 139–41; 1984b, 394–7.

Chapter 6 (pp116–37)

1 Cf. chapter 3, nos 25–9.

2 History of *Lepcis*: Birley 1988a, 1–36; Di Vita 1982a; Gascou 1972a, 75–80; 1982, 165–71; Haynes 1959, 31–67; *IRT* pp. 73–86; Lepelley 1981a, 335–67; Romanelli 1925. Archaeology: Bakir 1981; Bianchi-Bandinelli *et al.* 1966; Haynes 1959, 71–106; Manton 1988, 62–71; Romanelli 1925, folded map, for an overall survey of 1915, which pre-dated the excavations; Squarciapino 1966.

3 Phoenician settlement: Carter 1965; Di Vita 1969; Jones 1989b; Whittaker 1974; 1978c. Theatre cemetery: Miro and Fiorentini 1977. Homs harbour: di Vita 1974; Jones 1989b.

4 Old forum: di Vita 1968b; 1982a, 550–58; cf. Ward-Perkins 1982, 30–31, 44–9 (for a contrary view). Roman development of street grid: Romanelli 1940; Ward-Perkins 1982, 30–36. Market: Degrassi 1951. Theatre: Caputo 1987. *Chalcidicum*: Bianchi Bandinelli *et al.* 1966, 71–4. Augusta Salutaris arch and Tiberian milestone: *IRT* 308 and 930. Street paving: *IRT* 330–31. Flavian and Trajanic arches: *IRT* 342, 284/353; Bianchi Bandinelli *et al.* 1966, 72–4. Antonine and Aurelian arches: *AE* 1967, 536; Bianchi Bandinelli *et al.* 1966, 101–04; Ioppolo 1970, 231. *Horrea*: Jones 1989a/b.

5 Market and theatre: *IRT* 319, 321–3. *Chalcidicum*: *IRT* 324. Di Augusti: *IRT* 273. Forum paving: *IPT* 26; *IRT* 338. Amphitheatre: di Vita-Evrard 1965. Harbour portico: *IRT* 341. Magna Mater and Flavian temple: *IRT* 300, 348. Trajanic forum: *IRT* 543. Aqueduct: *IRT* 275, 357–9; Vita-Finzi 1978, 34–6. Hadrianic baths: *IRT* 361; Bartoccini 1929b. Circus: di Vita-Evrard 1965; Humphrey 1986. Antonine temples: Bianchi Bandinelli *et al.* 1966, 84–6, 89–90, 103–04; 108–10. Hunting baths: Ward-Perkins and Toynbee 1949. House of Orpheus: Guidi 1935b. Villa of Nile: Guidi 1933.

6 East cemetery: Bianchi Bandinelli *et al.* 1966, fig. 224; Romanelli 1925. Cisterns and Lebda dam: Bianchi Bandinelli *et al.*. 1966, 117–19, figs 220–23; Goodchild and Ward-Perkins 1953, 45–7 and pl.xv. Urban defences: Goodchild and Ward-Perkins 1953.

7 Expenditure: Duncan-Jones 1962; 1963; 1982, 90–119.

8 Severan buildings: Bartoccini 1927a; 1928a; Bianchi Bandinelli *et al.* 1966, 91–8; di Vita 1982b; Jones and Kronenburg 1988; Squarciapino 1966, 95–110; 1974; Ward-Perkins 1948; 1993. Severan arch: Bartoccini 1931; Bianchi Bandinelli *et al.* 1966, 67–70. Harbour: Bartoccini 1958b; Laronde 1988. Liber Pater and Hercules: Dio 76.16.3; Birley 1988a, 150–51. Marble imports: Walda and Walker 1984; 1988; Ward-Perkins 1951; 1993.

9 Tripoli, second city: Lezine 1972, 58. Oasis: Franchi 1912. Wadi Megenin: Vita-Finzi and Brogan 1965. Gargaresh and Gurgi: Bakir 1967, 241–4, 250. Villas: Bakir 1967, 246–8 and pl. xci; di Vita 1966a. Cemeteries: Aurigemma 1932. Neo-Punic texts: *IPT* 5–8. History of Tripoli: Gascou 1972a, 82–3; 1982, 171; Haynes 1959, 101–06; Lepelley 1981a, 371–2; Ward 1969a. Apuleius: Birley 1988a.

10 Archaeology of Tripoli: Aurigemma 1916; 1967; Haynes 1959, 101–04; Jones 1989b; Lezine 1972, 55–60; Romanelli 1916.

Population: Duncan-Jones 1982, 265–6; Lezine 1972, 60–62. Arch: Aurigemma 1970.

11 *Sabratha*, location: *IRT* p. 21–3. History: Gascou 1972a, 82; 1982, 171, 307–10; Haynes 1959; Lepelley 1981a, 372–80; Ward 1970. Urban development: Bartoccini 1950; di Vita 1976; 1978; Kenrick 1985c; 1986, esp.312–18; Manton 1988, 71–9; Ward-Perkins 1982, 36–43.

12 Libyphoenician settlement: Kenrick 1986, 8, 10–12, 124–8, 142–5, 312–13. *Tophet* and neo-Punic inscriptions: *IPT* 1–4; Rossi and Garbini 1977; Mabruk *et al* 1988. Late Hellenistic *Sabratha*: di Vita 1968a; 1971; 1976; 1978; 1983; Kenrick 1986, 313–14. Temple of ?Serapis: Kenrick 1986, 115–17. *Capitolium*: ibid, 95–114. Forum and east forum temple: ibid, 13–37, 55–67. Casa Brogan: ibid, 141–66. Temple of Isis: Pesce 1953. Basilica: Kenrick 1986 68–95. Temple of Hercules: Caputo and Ghedini 1984. Theatre and east quarter: Caputo 1959; Kenrick 1986, 213–26. Antonine temple: ibid, 169–213; cf. Bartoccini 1964. South forum temple: Joly and Tomasello 1984. Water supply and Flavius Pudens: *IRT* 117 (also honoured in nos 118–25). Domestic housing: Kenrick 1986, 141–67, 236–41. Harbour: ibid, 242–5.

13 *Tacapae*: Gascou 1982, 307–08; Hilaire 1900; Monlezun 1885; Toussaint 1908, 401–02; Toutain 1903a, 274–6. Oasis: Pliny *NH* 18.188; Trousset 1986a, 167–70, 173–6.

14 *Gigthis*, discovery and early work: Constans 1916, 1–11. History: ibid, 12–23; Gascou 1982, 192–3; Lepelley 1981a, 368–71. Archaeology: Constans 1916, 23–110; Ferchiou 1984; Stillwell 1976, 353–4; Tlatli 1971, 61–71. Epigraphy: Ben Abdullah 1986, Tripolitaine nos 1–18; Constans 1914; 1915. Forum: Constans 1916, 23–58. Servaei, Servilii and Ummidii: Ben Abdullah 1986, 5–6, for the *stemmae*. Temple of Mercury: Constans 1916, 104–10. Baths: ibid, 73–86. East temple: ibid, 59–63. Market: ibid, 87–91. Rich houses: 100–04. Harbour quarter and mole: ibid, 68–70. Marine products: Trousset 1992.

15 Telmine: *supra*, chapter 5, n. 10. Archaeological evidence: Trousset 1974, 43–6.

16 *Zitha*: Gascou 1982, 308; Tissot 1888, 204–07. Epigraphy: *CIL* 8.11002–16. Archaeology: Reinach and Babelon 1886, 54–65 (forum); *BCTH* 1905, ccix–ccx (temple of Caelestis). Coinage: Kenrick 1986, 256.

17 *Thubactis*: Bartoccini 1927b (Gasr Ahmed); Blake 1968; Brogan 1975a, 52–5 (Misurata, Marsa Gezira and Gasr Ahmed); Rebuffat 1973c, 139–43 (south of Misurata); Tissot 1888, 204–07 (Misurata).

18 Other *municipia*: Gascou 1982, 307–10. Syrtic towns: Bartoccini 1929b; Cerrata 1933, 205, 212–13, 220–23; Goodchild 1964; Reddé 1988. El Hamma: Privé 1895, 87–8.

19 Small towns: Jones 1989b; Mattingly 1988b; cf. Rodwell and Rowley 1975; Burnham and Wacher 1990. Medina Doga: Goodchild 1951b, 76–9; Levi dell Vida 1951, 93–6 (Ammon); Rossi and Garbini 1977 (Caelestis). Gasr ed-Daun: Oates 1953, 89–92. Ain Wif: Mattingly 1982. Ain el-Auenia: Cambridge 1960.

20 *Vici*: Jones 1984; Jones and Walker 1983; Mattingly 1986; Salway 1965.

21 Bu Njem: Goodchild 1976a, pl. 22 (air-photo); Rebuffat 1967a, 63–8; 1969, 207–11; 1970a, 21–30, 90–92; 1970b, 133–5, 161; 1975a, 165–87; 1977a, 39–40 (plans), 50–56; 1977c, 408–10; Richardson 1848, 445.

22 Remada: Euzennat and Trousset 1975, 19–20; Trousset 1974, 116–17. Gheriat: Goodchild 1954a = 1976a, 54 and pl. 23; Jones and Barker 1983, 64–7. Ras el-Ain: Boizot 1913 (baths); Heron de Villefosse 1894a; Lecoy de la Marche 1894, 395, 399–402; Trousset 1974, 98–102. Dating: pers.obs. of Hayes ARS forms 27, 27/31, 31, 181, 23b (over 20 rim sherds), 68, 70, 84 (or TRS 9).

23 Bir Rhezene: Hilaire 1901, 47; Poinssot 1937; 1940; Trousset 1974. Ksar Rhilane: Gombeaud 1901, 89–92; Rebuffat 1980a, 111–12; Trousset 1974, 93–4.

24 Successful *vici* (*Rapidum, Gemellae, Ad Maiores*): *CIL* 8.2482, 9195–92226a, 20833–42; Lawless 1970, 183–7 (Mauretanian evidence); Mattingly 1986.

Chapter 7 (pp138–59)

1 Trans-Saharan trade: Di Vita 1982a, 588–94; Haywood 1938, 62–9,

111. Importance of olive oil: Gsell 1925; Haywood 1941; Mattingly 1985a; 1987b; 1988a/b/c; 1993; Mattingly and Hitchner 1993.

2 African farming boom: Picard 1956; Raven 1993; Shaw 1984. Agricultural laws: Van Nostrand 1925, 9–11. Centuriation: Chevallier 1958; Dilke 1971, 151–8; Saumagne 1929; Soyer 1973; 1976; Trousset 1977b. *Lex Manciana*: Courtois *et al.* 1952, 81–187; Kehoe 1988; Kolendo 1976; Romanelli 1974, 319–63. Flavian policy and recensus: Leglay 1968; di Vita-Evrard 1979; 1986 (*fossa regia*).

3 Tunisian olive cultivation: Camps-Fabrer 1953; 1985; Carandini 1983; Hitchner 1988; 1989; Hitchner *et al.* 1990; Hitchner and Mattingly 1991; Mattingly 1988c; Peyras 1975.

4 The arguments are laid out in detail in Mattingly 1987a; 1988b; 1989b.

5 Importance of olive oil: Amouretti 1986; Brun 1987; Forbes and Foxhall 1978; Mattingly 1988d. Modern oleoculture in Tripolitania: Despois 1935; Franchetti *et al.* 1914; Taylor 1960.

6 Caesar's fine: *BAf* 97.3; Mattingly 1988b, 37; Rebuffat 1990c, 124–6. *Territoria*: di Vita-Evrard 1979. Olive presses: Mattingly 1985a (map); 1988b (map); Oates 1953; Percival 1976, 61–6.

7 Coastal luxury villas: Aurigemma 1926a (Zliten); Bartoccini 1927b; di Vita 1966b (Taggiura); Mahjub 1984; Picard 1985; 1986; Salza Prina Ricotti 1971 (Silin). *Caesarea* villas: Leveau 1984, esp. 399–410. Estates on coast road: Kolendo 1986; Picard 1986.

8 Press production capacity: Mattingly 1988a; 1993; cf Hitchner *et al.* 1990, 248–55; Hitchner and Mattingly 1991; NB also Forbes 1992, for some doubts on the figures. Prehistoric megaliths: Cowper 1897; cf. Myres 1899; Mattingly 1988a.

9 Overall olive oil production: Mattingly 1988b, 36–8; 1993. *Caesarea*: Leveau 1984. Oileries in western Tripolitania: Trousset 1974, 56–7, 157.

10 Apuleius: *Apol.* 44.6; 71.6; 87.7; Birley 1988a, 26–33; Pavis d'Escurac 1974.

11 Slaves in African farming: Apuleius *Apol.* 87.7; 93.4; *CIL* 8.22721; Gsell 1932, Garnsey 1978, 235–7 (*contra*, Pavis d'Escurac 1974). Tenancy vs slavery in ancient farming: Foxhall 1990; Kehoe 1988 (who emphasizes the potential benefits of share-cropping to both landlord and tenant); Rathbone 1981; Spurr 1986. Tripolitanian harvest arrangements: Taylor 1960. *Ostraca*: Levi della Vida 1964b.

12 Run-off agriculture in the Gebel: Despois 1935; Louis 1975; Prost 1954a; Trousset 1987

13 Rural markets: Shaw 1981a; cf Jones 1989b for a possible marketing model.

14 Pre-desert agriculture: Barker and Jones 1982; 1984; 1985; Barker *et al.* forthcoming; Mattingly 1985a; 1987a, 50–56; 1989b, 141–7. Landmark early studies: Brogan 1971; Goodchild 1952b/c; 1976 (various papers). Chronology of settlement: Dore 1983; 1984; 1985; 1988; Dore and van der Veen 1986; Mattingly 1987a, 50–51.

15 Settlement hierarchy: Barker and Jones 1982, 2–7; Jones 1985a, 263–88; Rebuffat 1988c. Mausolea: Brogan 1971; Brogan and Smith 1985, 119–224; Ferchiou 1989; Mattingly 1987b, 76. Preserved landscapes: Barker 1985; Hunt *et al.* 1986; Trousset 1987.

16 Western Tripolitanian farming settlement: Guery 1986; Mattingly 1987b, 85; Trousset 1974; 1987. Open farm to *gasr* transformation: Barker and Jones 1984; Jones 1985a, 280–82; Mattingly 1987a, 50–51; Mattingly *et al.* forthcoming; Welsby 1992. Function of *gsur*: Reddé 1988. Fortified granaries in Berber societies: Despois 1935; Louis 1975; Mattingly and Hayes 1992, 414–18; Prost 1954b.

17 El-Amud: Barker and Jones 1982, 16–18; 1984; Brogan 1964; Clarke 1986; Gilbertson and Hunt 1990; Mattingly 1987a; van der Veen 1985b.

18 Wadi Mansur: Gilbertson *et al.* 1984; Hunt *et al.* 1986; Jones 1985a, 273–4.

19 Relief carvings showing agricultural activity: Barker and Jones 1980; Brogan 1965a (Tigi); Brogan and Smith 1985 (Ghirza); Romanelli 1930. Bu Njem *ostraca*: Marichal 1992, 99–106. Minimal view of oleoculture in pre-desert: Euzennat 1985. Palaeobotanical evidence: van der Veen 1981; 1985a/b (cf. 1992 for Fezzan). Faunal data: Clarke 1986.

20 Profits of farming: Mattingly 1987a, 59–60; 1989b, 146. Olive presses in pre-desert: Mattingly 1985a, 38–43; 1993; Mattingly and

Hitchner 1993 (smaller scale than those of the Gebel); Mattingly and Zenati 1984. Military supply: Marichal 1992 (the quoted *ostracon* is no. 79, the translation is my own); cf. Bowman and Thomas 1983, 83–96; Bowman *et al.* 1990; Davies 1987; Whittaker 1989a/b.

21 Monte Testaccio: *CIL* 15 (Dressel's work on the inscriptions/stamps); Mattingly 1988c, 54–5; Rodriguez Almeida 1975; 1978; 1984. First recognition of Tripolitanian amphorae: Panella 1968, 104; Zevi and Tchernia 1969. This section of the chapter is closely based on part of my article 1988b.

22 Tripolitania I, II, III: Manacorda 1977a/b; Panella 1972, 78–88; 1973, 562–9; 1977; Peacock and Williams 1986, 166–70; Riley 1979. Tripolitania I at Pompeii: Bisi 1977; Panella 1977. Mediterranean distribution: Carandini and Panella 1981; Manacorda 1977a; 1983, 491; Panella 1983; 1986; Riley 1979, fig.22. Shipwrecks: Parker 1992.

23 Amphora kilns: Bartoccini 1929a, 93–5; Goodchild 1951b, 85–8, 96–9; cf. Arthur 1982. Tunisian olive oil amphora kiln sites: Ben Lazreg and Mattingly 1992; Peacock *et al.* 1989; 1990. Stamped amphorae: di Vita-Evrard 1985a; Manacorda 1977a; 1983; Mattingly 1988b, 32–5.

24 Wine from Africa: Lequement 1980; Leschi 1947. Fish products and wine with olive oil exports: Parker 1992; Ponsich 1988. Marine products from western Tripolitania: Paskoff et al. 1991; Trousset 1992.

25 Trade in 'exotic' wares: Bovill 1968; di Vita 1982a, 588–94; Haywood 1938, 66–8, 111; Law 1967; Lhote 1954. Coinage south of Sahara: Mauny 1956. Early modern travellers with caravans: Barth 1857, 99 (met a caravan near Mizda with 25 camels and 60 slaves); De Mathuisieulx 1904, 75–8; Lyon 1821, 152–7. Caravan routes and rate of travel: Bates 1914; Luni 1979; Rebuffat 1970c/d; Richardson 1848, 480 gave the following jouney times – Tripoli to Ghadames 15 days; Ghadames to Ghat 20 days; Ghat to Murzuk 15 days; Murzuk to Tripoli 30 days; Nachtigal 1974, 42, also gave 30 days for the Fezzan to Tripoli route; Barth 1857, 451, made the journey in the fast time of 18 days.

26 Myth of Garamantian emeralds: Monod 1974. *Garamantes* and trade: Daniels 1970a, 42–4.

27 Slaves: Bovill 1968, 6–40; Law 1967, 181–200. *Ostraca*: Marichal 1992, 109. Negro slaves in Roman empire: Desanges 1976; Law 1967, 195. Dahomey compared: Law 1992. Roman slavery: Hopkins 1978.

28 Cornelian: Pliny *NH* 5.37; 37.92–3, 104, 175. Finds of gold, silver, bronze, coins, ivory and cornelians in Garamantian excavations: Ayoub 1967a, 16–20; 1968a, 41–53; 77–81; Daniels 1971a, 261–85; 1973, 39–40, 1977, 5–7.

29 Elephants on north side of Sahara: Pliny *NH* 5.26. Rhinoceros: Desanges 1964a. Elephant as civic symbol: Meiggs 1973, 283, 287, pl. 23a; Romanelli 1960. Dedications of tusks: *IRT* 231, 295; Aurigemma 1940a; Romanelli 1920. Other wild animals for arenas: Bovill 1968, 6–12

30 Daniels 1969, 48–51 (natron is an important raw material in glassmaking).

31 Marichal 1992, 112–13; Rebuffat 1982a, 502–06. Customs' tariffs: Cagnat 1914a, 142–6; Darmon 1964, 7–23; Fentress 1979, 183–4.

32 Pottery: Hayes 1972; 1980. Purple dye: Pliny *NH* 9.60; Bartoccini 1959b, 187; Reese 1980, 79–93 (esp. 79–86). *Gigthis*: Constans 1914, 178–82; *AE* 1915, 44. Coastal fish product manufactories in Tunisia: Oueslati *et al.* 1987; Paskoff *et al.* 1991, 535–45 (map p. 537); Trousset 1992, 321–8 (map p.320).

33 Roman trade: Hopkins 1980; 1983; Woolf 1992. Mediterranean trade and amphora studies: *Amphores* 1989; Keay 1992; Fulford and Peacock 1984; Peacock and Williams 1986, 2–66; Tomber 1993. Southern Gaul: Hitchner, pers. comm.

34 Marble trade and Tripolitania: Ballance and Brogan 1971; Walda and Walker 1984; 1988; Ward-Perkins 1951; 1993.

35 Trade patterns compared: Fulford 1989. *Berenice* excavations: Bailey 1985; Kenrick 1985a/b; Lloyd 1977; Riley 1979. *Sabratha* excavations: Dore 1988; Dore and Keay 1989; Kenrick 1985c; 1986.

36 Medieval trade along African littoral: Goitein 1967/1983; cf Smythe 1854 (for a description of the navigational characteristics of Syrtica)

37 Tripolitanian olive boom: Mattingly 1988b/c.

Chapter 8 (pp160–70)

1 Romanization in Africa: Benabou 1976, 261–380 (religion), 385–469 (urbanization), 470–570 (language and nomenclature); Benabou 1978/Leveau/Thébert 1978, 64–92; Desanges 1980a/Garnsey 1978; Ilevbare 1973; Whittaker 1978a/b. On the processes: Gascou 1972, 45–54; Leglay 1968, 220–22; Romanelli 1975; Seston and Euzennat 1971; Sherwin-White 1973. Demography: Benabou 1976, 470–570; Lassère 1977; 1982. Romanization in other provinces: Alcock 1993; Bartel 1980; Burnham and Johnson 1979; Blagg and King 1984; Blagg and Millett 1990; Jones 1984; Millett 1990. Roman sources on Romanization: Dio 56.18; Tacitus *Agricola* 21.30–32. This chapter is an abridged and revised version of my article, Mattingly 1987b.

2 Antipathetic towards 'African' nomads: Gautier 1952, 208–09; Gsell 1933, 125–44; Guey 1939. More positive evaluations of nomad/sedentarist interaction: Trousset 1980; 1982; Whittaker 1978, 332–50.

3 De-punicization: Leglay 1968, 202–03. Persistence of Punic culture in Africa: *L'Africa romana* 7, 1990, took the survival of Punic culture as a key theme, see in particular Fantar 1990; also Millar 1968. Persistence at *Lepcis*: Benabou 1976, 511–50; Birley 1988a, 8–22; Levi della Vida and Amadasi Guzzo 1987; Reynolds and Ward-Perkins 1952; Thompson 1971. Latin and Punic inscriptions: *IRT* 273; 294; 300; 319; 321–3; 324; 338; 341; 745; *IPT* 21–6 (neo-Punic numbers 19, 28–31, 33 in *IRT*). Procopius *de aed.* 6.3.9–12, still described the Tripolitanian population as a Phoenician race.

4 *Sufetes*: *IRT* 347; 348; 349a; 412; 418 (latest is of AD 93–4). Neo-Punic phrases in Latin texts: *IRT* 567; 603; 95; 275; 347; 318; 321–3. Spoken Punic: Apuleius *Apol.* 98.8 (*... loquitor nunquam nisi punice ...*); Birley 1988a, 35. Septimius Severus and his sister: HA *Severus* 1.4; 15.7; 28.9; Aurelius Victor, *de Caes.* 20.8; Birley 1988a, 23–36. Latino-Punic/'Latino Libyan' texts: Levi della Vida 1927; 1963; 1965, 60 (for the Hadrianic text); cf Beguinot 1949; Goodchild 1950b; 1954d. A useful summary and full bibliography of subsequent work is Amadasi Guzzo 1990. Stele of Barichal Typafi: *IRT* 828; cf. also 826–7.

5 Amadasi Guzzo 1984, 189–96; Benabou 1976, 511–50; Lepelley 1981a, 355–67; Reynolds and Ward-Perkins 1952, 73–86.

6 *Lepcis* cinerary urns: *IRT* 754. Other Libyans at *Lepcis* and *Oea*: *IRT* 236; 539; 649; 707; Reynolds 1955, 128 no. S8. *Gigthis* and west Gefara: *ILAf* 15; 22; 25; *ILT* 50; *CIL* 8.11007; 11014; 22729 (L. Memmius Messius); Constans 1914; Thompson 1971, 241.

7 African funerary traditions: Abou-hamed 1975; 1977; Bates 1914, 178–84; Ben Lazreg and Mattingly 1992, 301–24; Buck, Burns and Mattingly 1983, 45–51; Merighi 1940; Reygasse 1950; Roffo 1938; Rowe 1956; 1959; Sjöström 1993, 88–90.

8 Art in Roman Tripolitania: Aurigemma 1962; di Vita 1968a; 1971 (Alexandrian influences); Squarciapino 1974; Walda 1985; Walda and Walker 1989. Mosaics: Aurigemma 1962; Dunbabin 1978; Foucher 1964; Johnston 1982; Mahjub 1984; 1988; Picard 1985; Precheur Canonge 1962; Romanelli 1965. Punic and Libyan influences: Di Vita 1990c; Walda 1985; Ward-Perkins 1971. Severan pinnacle: Squarciapino 1974; Strong 1973; Ward-Perkins 1993.

9 Survival of Punic language: St Augustine *Letters* 108.5.14; 209; *Iohannis Ep.* 11.3; Courtois 1950 was doubtful, but his views were correctly rebutted by Millar 1968. Punic influence on Numidian kingdom: Camps 1960, 159–84; 1979, 43–53; Galand 1980.

10 *Opus africanum* construction: Barker and Jones 1981, 38; 1982, 6–7; Di Vita 1964a, 67–71; Oates 1953, 81–117. Tanit symbols: Brogan and Smith 1967, 139–41; Cowper 1897, 153, 156. Obelisk tomb type: Barth 1857, 113–14; 118–19; Brogan 1971, 122–7; Brogan and Smith 1985, 182–9; 207–09; di Vita 1971, 171–80; Haynes 1959, 156–8; cf. Horn and Ruger 1980, 145–71. *Sabratha* tombs: di Vita 1968a; 1971; 1976; 1978; 1983. Other mausolea of interior Tripolitania: Aurigemma 1954; Brogan 1965a; 1978; Brogan and Smith 1985.

11 Tombs. Wadi Merdum: Brogan 1971, 124–5. The Bir Gebira inscription translates, *Tamrar, daughter of [...]*; Brogan and Smith 1967, 141–2. Wadi el-Amud: Brogan 1964, 48–50; Levi della Vida 1964a, 48–50; for work on the associated farm, Barker and Jones

1984, 1–44. Wadis Migdal/Messeuggi: Brogan 1971a, 126; di Vita 1964a, 70–75. Wadi N'f'd: Burns and Mattingly 1981, 26; de Mathuisieulx 1904, 27–8; Haynes 1959, 156–7. Wadi Antar: Brogan and Reynolds 1985, 13–22. Wadi Umm el-Agerem: Barker and Jones 1982, 6–7; Brogan 1971a, 126; Mattingly *et al.* forthcoming.

12 Tomb at el-Amrouni: *CIL* 8.22758; Berger 1895, 71–83; Brogan 1965a, 54–6; Ferchiou 1989,47–76; Trousset 1974, 110–13; Vattioni 1981, 293–9.

13 Punic inscription/*ostraca*: Levi della Vida 1951; 1964a; *IPT* 76, 86. Balsilech: Brogan 1962; Hanno: Levi della Vida 1964a; Annibal, Iddibal: Marichal 1992, 261–2. Annobal, Imiltho: *IRT* 906; Reynolds 1955, 141–2. Arisam and Bodastart: Levi della Vida 1964a.

14 Latino-Punic inscriptions from the Gebel/pre-desert: Amadasi Guzzo 1990 (summary and full bibliography); Levi della Vida 1927; 1963; 1965. *Avo sanu*: *IRT* 894; Bartoccini 1929a, 187–200 (same formula still in use in Christian catacomb in Sirte).

15 Libyan names in western Tripolitania, Miha Vasa: *ILT* 51 (Matmata). Iurathe, Iuzale, Thanubra: *CIL* 8.22758 (el-Amrouni). Assioda: Donau 1909a, 32–3. Eastern Tripolitania, Chinitiu: *IRT* 859 (Jefren). Issicuar, Semp, Eisrelia: *IRT* 867 (Bir el-Uaar). Muthunilim: *IRT* 873; Levi della Vida 1963, 79–80 (near Gasr Doga). Stiddin: *IRT* 875 (Breviglieri). Thlana Marci Cecili: *IRT* 877; Levi della Vida 1963, 87. Shasidwasan: Levi della Vida 1951, 65–8.

16 El-Amud: Brogan 1964a, 48–50; 1971a, 124 (translation); Levi della Vida 1964a, 57–63. Cf Barker and Jones 1984 for the site.

17 Umm el-Agerem: *IRT* 906; Levi della Vida 1963, 71–7; 1965, 60 (preferred version of the texts); Reynolds 1955, 141–2, S. 24. See also Barker and Jones 1982, 6–7; Brogan 1971a, 126; Elmayer 1984; Jones 1985a, 180–82 (with plan of farm/*gasr*); Mattingly *et al.* forthcoming.

18 Libyan inscriptions, dialects: Chabot 1940; Fevrier 1956; Galand 1988; Rebuffat 1975a. Western Tripolitania: *RIL* 60–63; cf. Trousset 1974, 42, 71, 73, 79. Eastern Tripolitania: Goodchild 1950b, 141, knew of no Libyan texts; cf. now Brogan 1975b, 268–78; Brogan and Smith 1985, 250–57; Reynolds *et al.* 1958, 112–15 (Ghirza); Daniels 1975, 249–65 (Fezzan); Rebuffat 1975a (Bu Njem); Sattin 1976, 161–77 (Wadi Mimun). The alphabets are all slightly different and suggest a multiplicity of different dialects, a point supported by the apparent occurrence of four different Libyan words for the same sized unit of wheat mentioned in the Bu Njem *ostraca*, Marichal 1992, 101.

19 Acquisition of Roman citizenship pre-216: Dondin-Payre 1981; Oliver 1972; Seston and Euzennat 1971; Sherwin-White 1973. Tininai temple: *IRT* 888. Wadi Antar inscription: Brogan and Reynolds 1985, 13–22.

20 Domitius Tellus: *ILT* 51 (Matmata); Domitius Aumura/Domitius Maculus: *ILT* 52, 54 (Hr Oum el-Abbes). Arellia Nepotilla: *CIL* 8.22774; Trousset 1974, 85–6.

21 El-Amrouni and Smiley's people: *CIL* 8.22758; Berger 1895, 71–83; Ferchiou 1989; Trousset 110–13; Vattioni 1981.

22 Ghirza tombs: Brogan and Smith 1985, 119–227. Smythe's report featured in Beechey and Beechey 1828, 509–12.

23 Religion in Tripolitania: Brouquier-Reddé 1992a, 117–23; 1992b; Merighi 1940, 85–102. Temple architecture: Brouquier-Reddé 1992b; Joly and Tomasello; Kenrick 1986; Pensabene 1990; Romanelli 1970. Syncretization: Amadasi Guzzo 1984; Pisanu 1990 (*Gigthis*). Hercules/Liber Pater at *Lepcis* and Rome under Severus: Birley 1988a, 151, 159.

24 Saturn/Baal-Hammon: Benabou 1976, 261–80; Leglay 1966, esp. 107–52; 1968, 234–46. Punic cults in Tripolitania: Brouquier-Reddé 1992a, 117–20; 1992b (with full citations of all the relevant epigraphic data).

25 Rural temples: Brogan and Oates 1953, 74–80 (Gasr el-Gezira); Brogan and Smith 1985, 80–92 (Ghirza); Brouquier-Reddé 1992a, 121–3; 1992b Goodchild 1951b, 79–84 (Ras el Haddagia); 1952d, 156–63 (*Arae Philaernorum*) ; Haynes 1959, 161–3. Bu Njem: Rebuffat 1990b, 119–59 (with plans of temples and texts of all relevant inscriptions). Britain: Jones and Mattingly 1990, 264–86.

26 Centurions at Bu Njem: *IRT* 920; Rebuffat 1975b, 214–15; 1977c, 406–07; 1985c; 1987. Names at Bu Njem: Marichal 1992, 63–70.

Names at *Bezereos*: Lassère 1980, 955–75.

27 Recruitment and origin of troops: Cagnat 1913, 287–308; Lassère 1980; Le Bohec 1980; 1989a, 491–530; 1989b, 88–91, 172; Marichal 1992, 63–6; Rebuffat 1972a, 334–5; 1975b, 214–15; 1985c (*Iasucthan*); 1989.

28 Latin créole: Marichal 1979, 436–7, 448; 1992, 46–8. Army and Romanization: Le Bohec 1989a, 531–72; 1989b, 170–81. Cultural inversion on the frontier: Bohannon and Plog 1967; Buck 1985; Kirk 1979; Whittaker 1994.

29 Limited aims: Garnsey 1978; Mattingly 1992; Whittaker 1978, 331–2. Tripolitanian senators and equestrians: Thompson 1971, 245–8 (list).

30 Cyrenaican countryside: Synesius, *Letters*, 148.

31 Excesses and failings of modern imperialism/colonialism: Brown 1972 (US frontier and native Americans); Abun-Nasr 1975, 232–392; Horne 1977; Woolman 1969 (Maghreb).

Chapter 9 (pp171–85)

1 AD 293 date: Jones 1964, 42–7. African reform of 297–8?: Chastagnol 1967, 119–22; Lepelley 1981a, 106, 262; Romanelli 1959, 511–19. *Tripolitana* created 303: di Vita-Evrard 1985c, 162–77 (an excellent review of all evidence and earlier theories).

2 Detailed arguments/references: Di Vita-Evrard 1985c, 168–71. *Numidia* divided in 303: *AE* 1942–3, 81; cf. *CIL* 8.18698. First Tripolitanian governors: *CIL* 8.22763 = *ILS* 9352. Boundary markers: *CIL* 8.23179 = *ILAlg* I, 3832 (altar to Genius of Tetrarchs on the provincial boundary between *Thelepte* and *Theveste*); Goodchild 1952d, 168–70 (statues of Tetrarchs set on inscribed columns at *Arae Philaenorum* – the governor's name is missing but Valerius Vibianus would be a likely candidate). Applicability of 303 reform to other provinces: di Vita-Evrard 1985c, 171–5.

3 Provincial administration in African provinces: Warmington 1954, 1–7; cf. Jones 1964, 321–606; Matthews 1989, 253–78 for overviews of late imperial administration. Gratian first *comes Africae*?: Amm. Marcellinus 30.7.2–3; Pallu de Lessert 1892, 61–4. On relative status of provincial governors: Chastagnol 1967, 121–34; Pallu de Lessert 1892; Warmington 1954, 2–3. Military powers: Donaldson 1985, 165–77.

4 Interior lands of eastern Tripolitania abandoned by Tetrarchs?: Courtois 1955, 70–79, 94–5; rebutted by *inter alia*, di Vita 1964a; Salama 1965.

5 Poem of Corippus: Diggle and Goodyear 1970. Confusion over *Laguatan*: Bates 1914, 67–8, 71; Brogan 1975b, 282–4; Courtois 1955, 102–04, 344–50; Desanges 1962, 82, 101–02; Jerary 1976. Cf Mattingly 1983. *Austuriani/Laguatan*: Corippus *Ioh* 1.480–83; 5.178–80; 7.530–33; Mattingly 1983, 97

6 Camel nomads thesis: Gsell 1933, 149–66. Arab sources: Abd el-Hakam 35–7; Ibn Khaldun 168, 226, 273. Botr and Beranes: Camps 1980, 127–8 distinguishes between the Botr 'néoberbères' and the Beranes of earlier migrations (paleoberbères); cf. the less satisfactory solution proposed by Bulliet 1981.

7 Byzantine sources on sixth-century *Laguatan*: Corippus *Ioh passim*; Procopius *BV* 4.21.2–22; 4.22.13–20; 4.28.47; *de aed* 6.4. Jerary 1976, 26–129 translates and comments on much of the source evidence. Byzantine campaigns: Pringle 1981, 13–16, 29–40; cf Jerary 1976, 130–78. Tyrants: Corippus *Ioh* 1.463–65; 2.343. Election of war leaders: *Ioh* 6.142–4. Decisions of war: *Ioh* 4.316–37; 6.143–4. Eighty sub-chiefs: Procopius, *BV* 4.21, 1–11. Scale of confederation: Corippus *Ioh* 2.7, '*gentibus innumeris*'. Carcasan: *Ioh* 4.639–41.

8 Maximian's campaigns: Corippus *Ioh* 1.480–82; 5.178–80; 7.530–33. *Austuriani* raids in Tripolitania: Amm. Marcellinus, 26.4.5; 28.6.1–5; 10–14; *IRT* 480, Reynolds, 1977, 13. *Ausuriani* raids in Cyrenaica: Synesius *Letters* 57, 58, 104, 108, 125, 130; *Catastasis*, I col. 1568–9; 1572. On Synesius, Goodchild 1976b, 239–54; Tomlin 1979, 259–70 (a sharp analysis). *Austur*: Corippus *Ioh* 2.89; 91–6; 209; 345; 5.192; 7.283.

9 *Ifuraces*: Corippus *Ioh*, 2.113; 3.412; 4.639–41; 8.490, 648. *Mecales/Imaclas*: Corippus *Ioh* 2.75; 3.410–12. *Mazax*: Vegetius *ep. re. milit.* 3.23; Corippus *Ioh* 1.549; 5.80; 376; 6.44; 167; 450. *Urceliana*: *Ioh* 2.75; 6.390. African *Mazices*: Desanges 1962, 34, 63, 112–13, 271 lists

four separate groups. Late Roman sources located *Mazices* in the Great Kharga oasis of the western Egyptian desert (Nestorius, *Hist. Eccl.* 1.7); near the *Garamantes* (*Liber Gen.* p. 167); near the *Austuriani* (Philostorgius, *Hist Eccl.* 11.8).

10 *Nasamones*: *Ioh* 6.198; 552; 589; 692; 7.465; 510; 8.95 (often used as synonym for *Laguatan*). Seli: *Ioh* 2.117–18 (warriors from *Digdiga Selorum*). *Gaetuli* and *Macae*?: *Ioh* 2.74–75 (*Astrikes = Astakoures* of Ptolemy?) and 2.62 (*Macares = Macae*?). Confederation of 547: *Ioh* 6.188–201.

11 Arab sources: Ibn Khaldun, 168; 226; 273; Ibn Abd el-Hakam, 35–7; El Bekri, 25–6; 31. Modern analyses: Brogan 1975b, 282–4; Camps 1980, 124–8; Jerary 1976, 91–129; Oates 1953, 113; 1954, 110–11. Ethnic origins of modern tribal groupings in Tripolitania: Bulugma 1960, 111–19; Despois 1935.

12 Sergius and the 80 chiefs: Procopius *BV* 4.21.2–11; 22.12–20. Take-over of agricultural lands: Ibn Abd el-Hakam, 35–7. Growth of confederation through assimilation and sedentarization: Mattingly 1983, 100–06.

13 *Regio Arzugum*: Courtois 1955, 94, notes 1–5 give full references; see also Denys le Petit, *Codex canonum ecclesiae africanae* 49; 52. Bishop of Tozeur: *Gesta col. Carth.* 1.208; Courtois 1955, 34; Trousset 1982a (he presumably crossed the Chott Djerid en route to *Tacapae*). St Augustine: *Letters* (ed. Schaff 1892) 93.8.24; 93.8.46–7 (Publicola). Orosius: *adv. pag.* 1.2,90 (*quamvis Arzuges per longum Africae limitem generalitor vocentur*). Corippus: *Ioh* 2.148 (*horrida tellus Arrzugis*); Goodchild 1950a, 30–31; cf also Courtois 1955, 93–5.

14 Origins: Bates 1914, 68, n. 7. Arzosei: *ILAf* 30; Brogan 1975b, 280–81; Desanges 1962, 77–80. Third-century inscription: Le Bohec 1989c, 202–03.

15 *Arzuges* assimilated by *Laguatan*?: Corippus *Ioh* 2.52–5; 62; 75; 79–80 (*Talanteis* and *Tillibaris*); 116; 120.

16 East–west spread: Ibn Khaldun (De Slane 1925/1956), 168–82, 231–6, 280–81; Mattingly 1983. Campaigns of Maximian: Corippus *Ioh* 1.480–83; 5.178–80; 7.530–33.

17 Execution of Stachao: Amm. Marcellinus 28.6.2–4; *Cod. Theod.* 7.1.1. Barbarians working inside frontiers: St Augustine *Letters* 46–7.

18 Archontius Nilus: Aurigemma 1940b, 132–40; Chastagnol 1967, 126, 129; Guey 1951, 248–52; Pallu de Lessert 1901, II, 302–03. At *Lepcis*: *IRT* 562–3. At *Gigthis*: *CIL* 8.11031. At Ras el-Ain: *CIL* 8.22768; *ILAf* 11. Nepotianus: Caputo 1951, 243–7; Chastagnol 1967, 126, 129; Guey 1951, 248–52. At *Lepcis*: *IRT* 565, lines 13–20 (... *quod limitis defensionem tuitonemq(ue) perpetuam futuris etiam temporibus munitam securamq.ab omni hostili incursione praestiterit* ...).

19 On Romanus: Warmington 1956, 55–64. Events of 363 raid: Amm. Marcellinus 28.6.4–6. Second raid: 28.6.7–19. Ruricius: Chastagnol 1967, 129; cf. Amm. Marcellinus 28.6.11; *Cod. Iust.* 11.48.5.

20 Raids on Cyrenaica: Synesius *Letters* 13, 57, 62, 67, 69, 78, 94, 95, 104, 107, 108, 113, 122, 125, 130, 132, 134; *Catastasis* I, col. 1568–9, 1572; Mattingly 1983; Tomlin 1979. Victorianus: *IRT* 570 = Reynolds 1955, 130, lines 6–9: *quod defessa territoria nimia incursatione ba[r]barorum*. cf. *CIL* 8.10937 for date of governorship. Silvanus: *Cod.Theod.* 12.1.133. *Comes et dux*: *Cod. Theod.* 11.36.33 (Nestorius in AD 406); *IRT* 529 (Flavius Macedonius Patricius, date unknown). Ortygius: *IRT* 480 = Reynolds 1977, 13: ... *Austurianam furore repraessa*. Civil/military powers split: cf Donaldson 1985.

21 Camel nomadism: Camps 1980, 124–8; Gautier 1937, 208–09; 1950, 129–41; Gsell 1933, 149–66; Leschi 1942, 47–62; Pringle 1981, 16. Linear barriers as defences: Guey 1939, 178–248; Trousset 1974, 141. Symbiosis between pastoral/sedentary communities: Fentress 1979, 98–102, 112; Trousset 1980a, 931–43; 1981. Origins of camel in Maghreb: Bulliet 1975; Demougeot 1960, 209–47. Camel in *Cyrenaica*: Robinson 1927, PL. XLII, 1–5 (camels on coins of 46 BC). Camel in Tripolitanian reliefs: Brogan 1954, 126–31; 1965a, 47–56; Brogan and Smith 1985, 220–21; Bulliet 1981, 108–11; Goodchild 1952c, 152; Romanelli 1930, 53–75. Camels in Africa: Caesar *BAf* 68.4; *Cat. Musée Alaoui , Tunis* I, 1897, 139, 144 (terracotta camels from Sousse). Camels as pack-animals: Brogan 1954, 129, pl. xviia; Brogan and Smith 1985, pl. 67b, 110b; Marichal 1979, 448; 1992, 100–06. Superiority of camel for desert travel: Bates 1914, 16–17; Bovill 1968, 15–16; Briggs 1960, 17–23; Evenari *et al.* 1971, 308–11.

Arab invaders on horseback: Demougeot 1960, 247; El Bekri (De Slane 1913), 32–5 (for Ocba's conquest of Fezzan in AD 666–7 with a force of 400 cavalry supported by camel baggage train).

22 *Ursiliani* and *Mazices*: Vegetius 3.23. Moorish camel riders: Corippus *Ioh* 6.194–5. Rings of camels as makeshift defences: Corippus *Ioh* 2.91–6; 474; 4.597–618; 5.351; 377; 421–33; 8.40; Procopius *BV* 3.8.25–8; 4.11.17–56.

23 *Laguatan* counter-attacks from behind camel defences: Camps 1980, 124–27; Courtois 1955, 100, n. 7 (5,000 camels in the 'rampart'); Gautier 1952, 182–5; Pringle 1981, 15–16, 248. Cyrenaican camels rustled: Synesius *Catastasis* I, col. 1569; *Letters* 130; Tomlin 1979, 266. Romanus' demand: Amm. Marcellinus 28.6.5.

24 *Ausuriani* and horses: Synesius *Letters* 104, 108 (ridden); 104, 108, 130 (large numbers of horses rustled by the raiders); 104, 125, 130, 132, 133 (importance of cavalry forces and horses in combating the raiders).

25 Epic style of Corippus: Alix 1899, 31–7; Pringle 1981, 2, 35. References to horses in Corippus: Mattingly 1984, 400, n. 31. References to cavalry warfare in Procopius: *BV* 4.12.3–28; 4.11.20 (cf. 4.11.17–56, Solomon's attack on a camp surrounded by a camel cordon).

26 Women/children riding camels: Corippus *Ioh* 5.421–33; 6.82–6. Procopius *BV* 4.11.18–19, described the Moorish women and children on campaign, tending the camels and other animals at the camp

27 Camel mixed with flocks/herds in defences: Corippus *Ioh* 2.91–9; 4.597–619; 5.489–92. Pitched battles: Corippus *Ioh* book 5 (unnamed site in *Byzacena*); book 6 (*Marta*); book 8 (*Latara*). Only in the first of these battles was the initial defeat of the *Laguatan* cavalry followed by a desperate and unsuccessful attempt to defend the encampment with its animal defences. Other possible references to Berber tribes using tethered animal lines: Ibn Khaldun *Muqaddima* 2.78 (trans. Rosenthal) describes a similar tactic (called *al-Majbudah*) among the Berbers in medieval times. Vegetius 3.23 (the camels were apparently drawn into lines, perhaps for defence).

28 Garrison at *Lepcis*: *Not. Dig.* Occ. 25.22; 31.29. Failure of Cyrenaican troops: Synesius *Letters* 69, 107, 122, 125, 130. The *Unnigarde*: Synesius *Letters* 68; *Catastasis* I, col. 1568.

29 Vandal problems with *Laguatan*: Procopius *BV* 3.8.15–29; *de aed.* 6.4.6–10. Decline of Cyrenaican cities: Reynolds 1971a, 53–8. Late Roman/Byzantine military problems with Libyan tribes: Jones 1971, 290–92; Pringle 1981, 9–50. Campaign of John Troglitas: Corippus *Ioh* 6.261–378.

30 Sabratha earthquakes: di Vita 1978, 18–22; 1990a, 441–65; Kenrick 1986, 5–6, 315–16. *Austuriani* 'sack': Bartoccini 1950, esp. 33–4; *IRT* p. 23. On the seismicity of Tripolitania: Ambraseys 1984.

31 AD 306–10 quake: di Vita 1990a, 441–52; Kenrick 1986, 5–6, 315. AD 365 earthquake: di Vita 1980; 1990a, 452–65 and 464–94 (general review of evidence and theories on extent and scale 365 quake); 1990b, 136–7 (theatre); Goodchild 1967b; Jacques and Bousquet 1984; Kenrick 1986, 5–6, 315–16; Lepelley 1984; Rebuffat 1980b; *Tremblements* 1984.

32 Di Vita 1990a, 455–7; cf. Amm. Marcellinus 28.6.2–13.

33 Urban/rural vitality in late empire: Lepelley 1967 (land); 1979, 1981a (African towns); Roques 1985 (*Cyrenaica*). Tripolitanian cities in fourth century: Lepelley 1981a, 335–80 presents all the evidence for *Lepcis, Gigthis, Oea, Sabratha*. Constantinian building: *IRT* 467–8; 543 (?). Unfinished baths: Goodchild 1965 (cf. the fanciful interpretation of Bianchi Bandinelli *et al.* 1966, 107–10). Laenatius Romulus: *IRT* 467–8; 464; di Vita 1990a, 446–7. Walls: di Vita 1990a, 451 (Sabratha); Goodchild and Ward-Perkins 1953, 42–3, 47–53, 69–71 (*Lepcis* – though they suggest that the walls may be as early as Gallienus). General building work at *Lepcis*: Lepelley 1981a, 337–41 (nine inscriptions). Temple of Hercules: *IRT* 55. Dedications to emperors: e.g. *IRT* 462–3; 477–8; Lepelley 1981a, 341–3. To *praesides* or *vice agens praefectorum praetorio*: *IRT* 475; 480; 519; 561–3; 565–6; 574–6; Lepelley 1981a, 434–47. Local families of note: e.g. *IRT* 564; 567–8; 578; 595; Lepelley 1981a, 347–54. Games: *IRT* 564; 567.

34 Romanus and *Tripolitana*: Amm. Marcellinus 28.6.1–30; Lepelley

1981a, 354–62; Matthews 1989, 383–7; Warmington 1954, 55–64.

35 *Sabratha* revival: *IRT* 103 (AD 378 records work of governor Flavius Vivius Benedictus *post-ruinam*); Kenrick 1986, 315–16. Aemilius Quintus: *IRT* 111; 588; *CIL* 8.27.

36 *Lepcis* change in building use: di Vita 1990a, 461–5; 1990b, 134–6; Fiandra 1975 (Flavian temple); Goodchild 1976a, 114–17 (coin hoards from late structures in market). Change in nature and appearance in late antique towns: Ward-Perkins *et al.* 1986 (Ptolemais); *contra*, the generally more optimistic view of Lepelley 1981a; Roques 1985.

Chapter 10 (pp186–201)

1 Publicola correspondence: St Augustine *Letters* (ed. Schaff 1892), 93.8.46–7; Goodchild 1950a, 36. Verbal oaths: Procopius *BV* 4.21.17–22 shows the continued importance of such measures under Byzantine rule; Denti di Pirajno 1957, 37–9, records similar oaths sworn by the Tripolitanian tribes who submitted to the Italians in the 1920s.

2 Procopius *BV* 3.25.3–7 (Loeb translation).

3 Continuation of pre-Vandal policy: Procopius *BV* 3.21.2–11. Byzantine breaches of agreements: *BV* 4.21.2–11; 4.21.16–22; *Anecdota* 5.28–38 (on the massacre of 79 *Laguatan* chiefs who had been promised safe conduct).

4 The late Roman army and the *Notitia Dignitatum*: Clemente 1968; Jones 1964, 607–86; 1429–50; Seeck 1896. Africa and the *Notitia*: Cagnat 1913, 728–39; Rushworth 1992, 60–117; Van Berchem 1952; 1977. Status of border troops: Jones 1971; Rushworth 1992, 100–117.

5 Field army units: Rushworth 1992, 60–99 (an outstanding analysis of the composition, evolution and deployment of the African field army). Size of late field army units: Rushworth 1992, 93.

6 Brigading of field army units: Rushworth 1992, 93–9 (with map). Campaign of 375–8: *IRT* 570 = Reynolds 1955, 130.

7 Field army lists: *Not. Dig.* Occ. 7.140–52; 7.179–98. List of *comes*: Occ. 25.1–46; Rushworth 1992, 100–03. List of *dux et praeses Mauritaniae*: Occ. 30.1–29; Matthews 1976; Rushworth 1992, 104–09. List of *dux provinciae Tripolitanae*: Occ. 31.1–41; Mattingly 1984, 248–51 (for my earlier view, now much modified); Rushworth 1992, 110–14; Trousset 1974, 149–55.

8 *Secundae afrorum* at Remada: Rushworth 1992, 12, n. 13; cf. Euzennat and Trousset 1975, 61. Military abandonment of eastern Tripolitania: Courtois 1955, 70–79.

9 *Mada* and the *limes Madensis*: Peyras and Trousset 1988, 197–8. *Secedi*: Marichal 1992, docs 94/95, p. 75, 106–07. Geographical logic of order of citation of *Notitia* lists: cf. Jones and Mattingly 1990, 33–7 (for the British evidence). Assignment of *ripenses* units to *Tripolitana*: Rushworth 1992, 75 (375/378 date). First mention of *dux et corrector*: *Cod. Theod* 12.1.133 (AD 393). First mention of *dux et comes*: *Cod. Theod* 11.36.33 (AD 406).

10 Numidian frontier in late Roman period, *quadriburgi*: Baradez 1949a; Daniels 1987, 260, 262–3; Fentress 1979, 105–08; Leschi 1943; Rushworth 1992, 117–21. *Fossatum*: Baradez 1949a; 1967 (Hadrianic foundation); Birley 1956; Jones and Mattingly 1980 (continued use in fourth century). *Gemellae*: Baradez 1949b; Trousset 1977a.

11 Demotion to *gentiles*: Mattingly 1984, 250–51 (modified here); cf. Rushworth 1992, *passim* (for a cogent argument about the continuing distinction between the roles of *limitanei* and *gentiles* on the African frontier). Falling rosters in fourth century: Duncan-Jones 1990, 105–17, 214–21; James 1984; cf. the inflated figures of Jones 1964, 1450, table xv. Barracks on Hadrian's Wall: Daniels 1980.

12 Synesius on Cerealis: *Letters* 130. On the *Balagritae*: *Letters* 132. On the *Unnigardae*: Letter 78; cf. *Catastasis* I, 1568. All translations from Fitzgerald 1926. See also Tomlin 1979.

13 *Ripenses* establishment: Jones 1964, 1450 suggests the impossibly high total of 3,500 for the two contingents. The exact establishment of these atypical units is unknown.

14 Benia Guedah Ceder: Blanchet 1898, 74; Cagnat 1913, 542–7; Donau 1904a, 467–77; Tissot 1888, 689–90; Toussaint 1905, 69; Toutain 1903a, 315–22, 339–41; Trousset 1974, 67–8. Pottery observed on site included Hayes form 27/33, though this would

probably be residual from some earlier activity.

15 Wadi Temassine: Toussaint 1905, 69; Toutain 1903a, 239; Trousset 1974, 53. A fourth-century site was found on a possibly associated site close by, Trousset 1974, 53.

16 Henchir el-Hadjar: Tissot 1888, 690; Toussaint 1905, 70; Toutain 1903a, 304, 334; Trousset 1974, 59–60 (with plan).

17 Ksar Tabria: Petrikovits 1971, 178–218; Toussaint 1905, 70–3; Toutain 1903, 324; Trousset 1974, 73–5.

18 Benia bel Recheb: Blanchet 1898, 78; 1899, 142–3; Cagnat 1913, 532–4; Hammond et al 1964, 16; Hilaire 1901, 100–01; Toussaint 1906, 233; Toutain 1903a, 348, 354–60; Trousset 1974, 95–6, 133–5. Internal buildings: Cagnat 1913, 533; Hammond et al. 1964, 16. Supposedly unfinished: Blanchet 1898, 78.

19 Henchir Rjijila: Donau 1909a, 50; Lecoy de la Marche 1894, 409–10; Toutain 1903a, 396; Trousset 1974, 105–06.

20 Gasr Bularkan (Mselletin = ULVS site Md 2): Goodchild 1950a = 1976a, 38–41.

21 Sdada east (= ULVS site Nf 83): Burns and Mattingly 1981, 30–31.

22 Concept of soldier farmers in Tripolitana and incorrect use of term limitanei: Brogan 1955; Goodchild 1949a/b/c; 1950a; 1952c; Ward-Perkins and Goodchild 1949. Correct meaning of limitanei: Jones 1964, 646–9; 1971, 293–4, 298; Isaac 1988. Review of the question: Mattingly 1989b, 135, 141–3. Spurious reference to land-allocation: HA Severus Alexander 3–5; see di Vita 1964a, 71–3, 80–86 for early doubts.

23 French 'postes militaires': Toussaint 1906, 230–36 (almost any square or defended building is classified as military); Trousset 1974, 110 (for an example of occasional lapses in the same way: Bir Fatnassia 'établissement assez important ... sans doute poste militaire' despite its proximity to the unquestionably civilian mausoleum at el-Amrouni). On the gsur: Barker and Jones 1982, 3–7; Brogan and Smith 1985, 45–80, 228–32; Buck, Burns and Mattingly 1983, 42–54; Goodchild 1949a, 32–4; 1949b, 39–41; 1950a, 41–3; Jones 1985a, 278–84; Mattingly 1989a; 277–8; 1989b, 141–3; Sjöström 1993, 81–5 and gazetteer with many plans; Rebuffat 1980a, 114–17; Reddé 1988, 71, 81–82; Rushworth 1992, 197–217; Trousset 1974, 136–39 and gazetteer; Ward-Perkins 1950, 25–30; Ward-Perkins and Goodchild 1949, 29–32; Welsby 1992, 73–99. Pan-Maghreb phenomenon: Anselmino et al. 1989; Goodchild 1951a; 1953; Mattingly and Hayes 1992, 414–18.

24 Gsur decribed as centenaria: IRT 877 (Breviglieri), 889 (Gasr Shemek); cf. IRT 875 (the expansion of CTN must be considered doubtful). Gsur as turris: IRT 876; CIL 8.22774. Discussion: Brogan and Smith 1985, 79–80; Elmayer 1983; 1984; 1985; Goodchild 1949a, 32–4; Ward-Perkins and Goodchild 1949, 94. Sidi Sames inscription: Goodchild 1976a, 111–12.

25 Bir Scedua: Buck, Burns and Mattingly 1983, 42–54 (recent work); cf. Goodchild 1950a = 1976a, 41–4; 1950c = 1976a, 14–15; Ward-Perkins and Goodchild 1949 = 1976a, 26–29. Latino-Punic inscription: Reynolds 1955, 138, S20.

26 Bir ed-Dreder: Buck, Burns and Mattingly 1983, 45–51; Goodchild 1954d, 91–107 = 1976a, 59–71. Nomadic federates: Goodchild 1954 d= 1976a, 70–71. Regular soldiers: Rebuffat 1977c, 413–14; cf also Courtois 1955, 92–5; di Vita 1964a, 97–8. Rushworth 1992, 197–208, hedges his bets: the tribuni were officially appointed as praepositi but in charge of gentiles not limitanei. Tribal interpretation: Elmayer 1984, 93–100; 1985, 78–9.

27 Ghirza: Early modern visitors: Beechey and Beechey 1828, 504–12; Denham and Clapperton 1826, 305–09; de Mathuisieulx 1904, 22–6; 1912, 71–7. Italian work: Bauer 1935, 61–78. Summary accounts: Brogan and Smith 1957; 1985, 45–6; 227–32; Smith 1986; Vergera-Caffarelli 1960. Wadi farming: Brogan and Smith 1985, 40–46. Botanical remains: van der Veen 1981; 1985b. Cemeteries: Brogan and Smith 1985, 100–14. Ashlar mausolea: ibid, 119–224. Buildings 31 and 34: ibid, 62–8, 76. Epigraphy: Brogan and Smith 1985, 181 (Latino-Punic), 250–7 (Latin), 260–63 (Libyan); IRT 898–903; Reynolds 1955, 139–40, S 21–2. Building 32 (temple): Brogan and Smith 1985, 80–92.

28 Tebaga corridor sites: Rebuffat 1980a, 122–3; Trousset 1974, sites 50–51, 60–68. Farming sites: Trousset 1974, sites 35 (olive press), 29,

32, 33, 38, 42, 63, 65 (wadi walls, etc.). Mausolea and civil epitaphs: ibid, sites 50, 51, 57, 59 (x3), 62, 65. Chronology: Guery 1986.

29 Hr el-Gueciret: CIL 8.22774; Cagnat 1913, 565–8; Pericaud 1905, 259–69; Toutain 1903a, 384–5; Trousset 1974, 85–6.

30 Ras el-Oued Gordab: Cagnat 1913, 363–5; Moreau 1904, 369–76; Rebuffat 1980a, 122–3; Trousset 1974, 103.

Chapter 11 (pp202–13)

1 Fortified farms: Barker and Jones 1981, 33–42; 1982, 5–8; Brogan and Smith 1985, 45–80, 228–32; Buck, Burns and Mattingly 1983, 52–4; Elmayer 1985; Goodchild 1950a, 41–4; Jones 1985a, 278–84; Mattingly 1989a, 277; 1989b, 141–3; Mattingly and Hayes 1992, 414–18; Oates 1954; Reddé 1988, 71, 81–2; Sjöström 1993, 81–5; Trousset 1974, 136–39; Welsby 1992, 73–99. Dating: Dore 1984, 54–7; 1985, 112–13, 116–23; 1988, 65–70; 1990, 9–17. Attempts to classify gsur: Goodchild 1950a, 41–3; Brogan and Smith 1985, 47, 76–80; Welsby 1992, 73–5; Sjöström 1993, 81–5.

2 Fortified farms in Gebel: Goodchild 1951b, 88–93; 1976a, 111–12 (tower erected in anticipation of attacks by barbarians or gentiles); Oates 1954, 93–110. Continuity on pre-desert estates: Dore 1984; 1985; Jones 1985a, 280–81; Mattingly et al. forthcoming. Discontinuity and unusual settlement concentrations: Barker et al 1991; Brogan and Smith 1985; Dore 1990; Jones 1985a, 280–83, for the 'villages' dependent on the gsur.

3 Late Roman settlement in Gebel Tarhuna: Oates 1954, 91–116 (92 for the distribution map, cf. Oates 1953, 94 for the Roman distribution). Olive presses: ibid. 96–101.

4 Abandonment of Syrtic farms: Rebbufat 1988c, 60–65; Reddé 1985; 1988, 78–80. Differential patterns in ULVS wadis: Dore 1985. Buzra/Kharab: Barker et al. 1991; Dore 1990; Welsby 1991; 1992.

5 Loyalty of frontier dwellers: Rebuffat 1969, 193; cf. Garnsey 1978, 235. Abandonment of east Tripolitania: Courtois 1955, 70–79, 93–5.

6 Non-official Latin texts from the Sofeggin/Zem-Zem region: IRT 883, 888, 891, 894a, 898, 899, 900, 905; Brogan 1964a, 53 = Reynolds 1985; Brogan and Smith 1985, 260–63, nos 1–2, 4,6; Reynolds 1955, S16, S22; B. The most important of many Latino–Punic texts are: IRT 886 (20+ texts), 889, 890, 893, 902, 903, 906;Brogan 1977, 108–09; Brogan and Smith 1985, 260–63, nos 5, 7, 9; Reynolds 1955, S20, S21, S24; Reynolds and Brogan 1960, nos 6 and 7. Hybrid texts: IRT 884, 885, 894, 900, 910; Reynolds and Brogan 1960, 53, no. 5.

7 Masauchan and Iylul: Reynolds 1955, 138 S20 (Bir Schedua); IRT 906 = Reynolds 1955, 141–2, S 24; Levi della Vida 1963, 71–7; 1965, 60 (Agerem). Metusan and Fydel: IRT 900 (Ghirza); Reynolds and Brogan 1960, 53, no 3 (Migdal).

8 Iulius Nasif: IRT 886f = Goodchild 1954d, no. 6. Flabius Isiguar and Yriraban: IRT 886k and h = Goodchild 1954d, 14 and 9; Nimira: IRT 886g =Goodchild 1954d, no 7; Flabius Masinthan: IRT 886j = Goodchild 1954d, 13; Macarcum, IRT 886a and c = Goodchild 1954d, nos 1 and 3. Parallels: M. Nasif, IRT 899, 901 (Ghirza); Issicuar, IRT 867 (Bir el-Uaar); Isiguar: IRT 902 (Ghirza); Marcius Nimira, IRT 898, 899 (Ghirza); Masinthan, IRT 884 (upper Sofeggin, near Mizda); Magargum: Corippus Ioh 5.283; cf. Marichal 1992, docs 68, 79, 88 for a third century 'chamelier' called Macargus.

9 Ghirza inscriptions: reviewed by Brogan and Smith 260–63, nos 1–9; cf. IRT 898–903; Reynolds 1955, 139–40, S21–3. The translations are taken from Brogan and Smith 1985. North tombs: Brogan and Smith 1985, 121–77. Latino-Punic text: IRT 901; Elmayer 1984, 101–02. Two clans: Brogan and Smith 1985, 46, 78.

10 Parentalia inscription: Reynolds 1955, S22 = Brogan and Smith 1985, 182, 262. Discussion of parentalia: ibid, 230 (the assertion that the inscription shows a 'high degree of assimilation of Roman funerary custom' may be questioned). Chieftain scenes: ibid, 137, 153, 223–4 (pl. 63a/c, 78) Execution scenes: ibid, 224 (pl. 63b, 79a). Fighting scenes: ibid, 223 (pl. 61b, 123a, 124a).

11 Wadi Buzra: Barker et al. 1991, 50–58;Ward-Perkins 1950; Ward-Perkins and Goodchild 1949 = 1976a, 61–80. Wadi Umm el Kharab: Barker et al. 1991, 34–51; Burns and Mattingly 1981, 24–33; Welsby 1992, 73–99. Dating: Dore 1990, 9–17; Barker et al. 1991, 46–9; 52–7; Welsby 1991, 76–8; 1992, 97. Specialist constructors: Welsby 1992, 97.

12 Sammac and Firmus: Amm. Marcellinus 29.5.1–13. *Fundus Petrensis*: *ILS* 9351. Nubel's army command: *CIL* 8.9255. Analysis of Mauretanian situation: Lawless 1970, 105–12; Matthews 1976; Rushworth 1992, 208–29.

13 Ghirza temple: Brogan and Smith 1985, 80–92. Libyan texts: ibid, 250–57 (cf. Brogan 1975b, 269–76).

14 Christian Africa and religious conflict: Fevrier 1989, 161–83; Frend 1952; 1978, 410–90; Raven 1993, 144–94; Warmington 1954, 76–113. Events of Great Persecution and origins of the schism: Birley 1987 (a very good introduction to the debate as a whole); Frend 1952, *passim*; Warmington 1954, 76–102. Chronology of Donatism: Birley 1987, 37–40 gives a detailed listing.

15 Tripolitanian bishoprics: Birley 1987, 34–7; Ward-Perkins and Goodchild 1953, 2–5. References to the Church councils etc. are given by Birley.

16 Archaeological traces of Christianity: di Vita 1967; Ward-Perkins and Goodchild 1953 are the fundamental surveys; note also Sjöström 1993, 90–91 (a gazetteer). Coastal cities: Ward-Perkins and Goodchild 1953, 7–35. Gebel region: ibid, 35–50. Sofeggin: ibid, 50–56. Aemilianus, Donatist: ibid, 39–43; *IRT* 863. Christian symbols: ibid, 72–8 (with map p. 73). Western Tripolitania: Trousset 1974.

17 *Sabratha* churches: Kenrick 1986, 83–95; Ward-Perkins and Goodchild 1953, 5–19. Standard Tripolitanian church type: ibid, 57–60. *Lepcis* church 2: ibid, 24–9.

18 Christian remains at *Oea*: ibid, 19–22; *IRT* 254–5. Cemeteries of Ain Zara/en-Ngila: Aurigemma 1932; Paribeni 1927; *IRT* 261 and 262; also di Vita 1967, 136; Ward-Perkins and Goodchild 1953, 21–2.

19 Gebel churches: ibid, 35–7 (Asabaa); 42–3 (Tebedut); 44 (Ain Wif); 44–7 (Breviglieri); 47–8 (Gasr Maamùra, cf. Oates 1954, 107–10); 37–8 (Wadi Crema); 38–43 (Hr Taglissi). Breviglieri stone-carving: de Angelis d'Ossat and Farioli 1975; see also di Vita 1967.

20 Pre-desert churches, Chafagi Aamer: Barth 1857, 107–10; de Mathuisieulx 1906, 90–92; Ward-Perkins and Goodchild 1953, 50–4. Souk el-Oti: Barker *et al.* 1991;Ward-Perkins and Goodchild 1953, 54–6; Ward-Perkins 1950; Welsby 1991. Excavation in 1989: Welsby 1991, 61–80 (62 (plan), 70–2 (raised west apse, nave, east apse), 73 (baptistery), 76–8 (chronology), 78–9 (post-Christian use)).

21 Size: Welsby 1991, 76–7 (after Ward-Perkins and Goodchild 1953). Christian symbols: Ward-Perkins and Goodchild 1953, 41–3, 48–50, 54, 56, 72–8. Date of spread of Christianity: ibid, 76–7. Augustine/Publicola: *Letters* 46–7.

22 Ancestor cult: Bates 1914, 181–2; Reynolds 1955, S22 = Brogan and Smith 1985, 182, 262 (51 bulls sacrificed). Ammon worship, small shrines, Goodchild 1951b, 81–4; 1952d, 158–9. Ammon and Gurzil in late antiquity: Corippus *Ioh* 2.109–12, 405; 3.77–170; 5.25, 39, 498; 6.116, 145–87, 556; 7.512–20; 8.300–17 619. El Bekri: De Slane 1913, 31–2; Brogan and Smith 1985, 36, 231–2 reserve judgement on the identification. Ghirza temple: Brogan and Smith 1985, 80–92. Altars, cult objects and inscriptions: ibid, 243–57.

Chapter 12 (pp214–17)

1 Peasants' revolt: Bulliet 1981. Secession in *Mauretania*: Matthews 1976. Transformation of *Laguatan* from raiders to farmers: Mattingly 1983, 105–06.

2 Decline of yields on marginal land: Chatterton and Chatterton 1985.

3 Events of Vandal invasion: Courtois 1955, 155–214; Raven 1993, 194–6; Sjöström 1993, 35–9; Warmington 1954, 13–14.

4 Rebellion of Heracleius: Procopius *BV* 3.6.9–27. Vandal defeat by Caboan: *BV* 3.8.15–29. Pudentius and Byzantine reconquest: *BV* 3.10.22–4. See also Courtois 1955; Diehl 1896; Pringle 1981; Sjöström 1993, 38–41.

5 Vandal Africa: Bourgeois 1980; Courtois 1955, 311–23 (political and economic structures); 325–50 (Vandal/Berber relations); Raven 1993, 196–208. Late antique Latin inscriptions in Mauretania: Warmington, 1954, 69–75. Tablettes Albertini: Courtois *et al.* 1952; Hitchner 1989.

6 History of Byzantine Africa and Tripolitania: Diehl 1896; Pringle 1981, 1–44; Raven 1993, 209–30; Sjöström 1993, 39–42; Trousset 1985. Relations with *Laguatan*: Pringle 1981, 208–86. Revolt of 544–7: Corippus *Ioh passim*; Procopius *BV* 4.21.1–4.28.52; Pringle 1981, 29–39. Ierna and Gurzil: Corippus *Ioh* 2.109–12; Brogan 1975b, 276; Brogan and Smith 1985, 232.

7 Characteristics of Byzantine rule in reconquered west Mediterranean lands: Christie 1989 (synthesis of recent research). Archaeological evidence for occupation of cities: Goodchild and Ward-Perkins 1953, 54–69, 71–3 (*Lepcis*); Kenrick 1986, 227–33, 316 (*Sabratha*); Pringle 1981, 208–86; Ward-Perkins and Goodchild 1953, 5–34 (churches). Changing townscapes: Cyrenaican comparanda: Jones 1985b, 36–40; Ward-Perkins *et al.* 1986. Efficient tax collection unpopular: Procopius *BV* 3.3.25–7; 4.8.25.

8 History of the Maghreb in Arab times: Abun Nasr 1975; Brett 1978a/b; Elfasi 1988; Oliver 1978; Sjöström 1993, 42–55; Vonderheyden 1927.

9 Arab invasion of *Cyrenaica*: Ibn Abd el-Hakam (Gateau1947), 35–7; Goodchild 1967; Jones 1985b, 36–40; Mattingly 1983, 99.

10 Arab invasion of *Tripolitana*: Ibn Abd el-Hakam (Gateau1947), 35–7; Pringle 1981, 44–50; Raven 1993, 224–30; Sjöström 1993, 42–3; Ward 1970, 24.

11 Arab sources for *Tripolitana*: El Bekri (de Slane 1913), 25–35; el-Edrisi (Dozy and Goedje 1866), 154; Ibn Ghalbun (quoted by Ward 1970, 24). Archaeological evidence: Barker and Jones 1981, 42 (uncalibrated radio-carbon date of AD 860+80 from a structural timber in a *gasr* on the Wadi Mansur). Islamic architectural features of *gsur*: Goodchild 1950a, 42; Sjöström 1993, 82–3. Medieval Ghirza: Brogan and Smith 1985, 80–92, 274–308 (finds included Fatimid coins and Beni Hammad pottery). Souk el Oti and Souk el Fogi: Barker and Jones 1982, 32; Barker *et al.* 1991, 50–58; Ward-Perkins 1950; Ward-Perkins and Goodchild 1953, 6, 54–6; Welsby 1991.

12 Beni Ulid and Orfella: Barker and Jones 1981, 38–42; Cauneille 1963 (modern Orfella); Jones 1989c, 46–7 (for the medieval village of Ben Telis); Sjöström 1993, gazetteer. Relic Berber communities in Gebel: Despois 1935, 279–91; Louis 1969; 1973; 1975, 23–125; Prost 1954b, 239–53; Sjöström 1993, gazetteer, for archaeological evidence. Christian communities: El-Bekri (de Slane 1913), 26 revealed that some of the Nefusa tribesmen were still Christian in his day; Allan 1973, 147–9 (little evidence for subsequent conversion of churches to mosques). Christian cemeteries: *IRT* 261–2; Aurigemma 1932; di Vita 1967; Paribeni 1927.

BIBLIOGRAPHY AND ABBREVIATIONS

Explanations of the most commonly used abbreviations are included in this bibliography. Other abbreviations follow the system of *L'Année Philologique*. Works are arranged by author in alphabetical order and for each author they are listed in chronological sequence.

ABOU-HAMED, M.S. 1975. 'Archaeological News : Tripolitania.' *LA* 11–12: 297–302.

ABOU-HAMED, M.S. 1977. 'Neo-Punic tombs near Lepcis Magna.' *Lib Studs* 8: 27–34.

ABUN-NASR, J. M. 1975. *A History of the Maghreb* (2nd edn) Cambridge.

AE = L'Année Epigraphique. Revue des publications épigraphiques relatives à l'antiquité romaine. Paris.

Af Ital = Africa Italiana. Rome.

ALCOCK, S. 1993. *Graecia Capta. The landscapes of Roman Greece.* Cambridge.

ALIX, J. 1899–1902. Corippe, 'La Johannide'. *RT* 6, 1899: 31–9; 148–60; 314–24; 453–62; *RT* 7, 1900: 106–20; 184–95; 372–7; 477–88; *RT* 8, 1901: 210–13; 327–35; *RT* 9, 1902: 83–96.

ALLAN, J. A. 1969. 'Some recent developments in Libyan agriculture.' *Middle East Economic Papers 1969,* American University of Beirut: 1–17.

ALLAN, J. A. (ed.) 1981. *The Sahara. Ecological change and early economic history.* Wisbech, Camb.

ALLAN, J.A. (ed.) 1982. *Libya since Independence.* London.

ALLAN, J. H. 1980. 'Lift off.' *Popular Archaeology,* September 1980: 25–7.

ALLAN, J. W. 1973. 'Some mosques of the Jebel Nefusa.' *LA* 9–10:147–69.

AMADASI GUZZO, M.G. 1983. 'Una grande famiglia di Lepcis in rapporto con la ristrutturazione urbanistica della citta (I sec AC – I sec DC).' *Architecture et societé de l'archaisme grec à la fin de la republique romaine* (Coll EFR 66): 377–85.

AMADASI GUZZO, M.G. 1984. 'Les divinités dans les inscriptions de Tripolitaine: essai de mise au point.' *BCTH* n.s.17B: 189–96.

AMADASI GUZZO, M.G. 1990. 'Stato degli studi sulle iscrizioni latino-puniche della Tripolitania.' *L'Africa romana* 7: 101–08.

AMBRASEYS, N.N. 1984. 'Material for the investigation of the seismicity of Tripolitania (Libya).' In A. Brambati and D. Slejko (eds) *The O.G.S. Silver Anniversary Volume.* Trieste: 143–53.

AMOURETTI, M–C. 1986. *Le Pain et l'Huile dans la Grèce Antique.* Université de Besançon, Paris.

AMPHORES 1989 = *Amphores romaines et histoire économique. Dix ans de recherches.* CEFR 114, Rome.

ANKETELL, M. 1989. 'Quaternary deposits of Northern Libya – lithostratigraphy and correlation.' *Lib Studs* 20: 1–29.

ANRW = Aufstieg und Niedergang der Römischen Welt. Geschichte und Kultur Roms in Spiegel der neueren Forschung. Temporini, Hildegard et al. (eds) Berlin and New York.

ANSELMINO, L. *et al.* 1989. *Il castellum di Nador. Storia di una fattoria tra Tipasa e Caesarea (I–VI sec d.C).* Rome.

Ant af = Antiquités africaines. CNRS, Paris.

ARTHUR, P. 1982. 'Amphora production in the Tripolitanian Gebel.' *Lib Studs* 13: 61–72.

AURIGEMMA, S. 1916. 'Le fortificazioni della città di Tripoli.' *Notiz. Arch. del Ministero delle Colonie* 2 : 217–300.

AURIGEMMA, S. 1926a. *I Mosaici di Zliten.* (*Africa Italiana* monograph), Rome/Milan.

AURIGEMMA, S. 1926b. 'Pietre miliari Tripolitane.' *Riv. della Trip.* 2, 1924:3–15

AURIGEMMA, S. 1929. 'Mosaici di Leptis Magna tra l'uadi Lebda e il circo.' *Af Ital* 2: 246–61.

AURIGEMMA, S. 1932. *L' 'Area' cemetriale cristiana d'Ain Zara presso Tripoli di Barberia.* Rome.

AURIGEMMA, S. 1940a. 'L'éléphante di Leptis Magna e il commercio dell'avorio e delle "ferae *Libyca*e" negli Emporia Tripolitani.' *Af Ital* 7: 67–86.

AURIGEMMA, S. 1940b. 'Due iscrizione tripolitane.' *Af Ital* 7: 132–40.

AURIGEMMA, S. 1940c. 'Sculpture del Foro vecchio di Leptis Magna raffiguranti la dea Roma e Principi della casa di Guilio Claudio.' *Af Ital* 8: 1–94.

AURIGEMMA, S. 1954. 'Il mausoleo di Gasr Doga in territorio di Tarhuna.' *QAL* 3: 13–31.

AURIGEMMA, S. 1960. *L'Italia in Africa, vol. I, Mosaici.* Rome.

AURIGEMMA, S. 1962. *L'Italia in Africa, vol. II, Le Pitture.* Rome.

AURIGEMMA, S. 1967. 'L'ubicazione e la funzione urbanistica dell'arco quadrifronte di Marco Aurelio in Tripoli.' *QAL* 5 : 65–78.

AURIGEMMA, S. 1970. *L'arco quadrifronte di M. Aurelio e di L.Vero in Tripoli* (*LA* Supp 3), Tripoli.

AYOUB, M. S. 1962. *Excavation at Germa, the capital of the Garamantes. Preliminary Report.* Tripoli.

AYOUB, M. S. 1967a. *Excavations in Germa.* Tripoli.

AYOUB, M. S. 1967b. 'The Royal Cemetery at Germa.' A preliminary report. *LA* 3–4: 213–19.

AYOUB, M. S. 1968a. *Fezzan, a short history.* Tripoli.

AYOUB, M. S. 1968b. *The Rise of Germa.* Tripoli.

234

BAA = Bulletin d'Archéologie Algérienne. Algiers.

BAATZ, D. 1970. *Die Wachttürme am Limes*. Aarlen.

BADUEL, A. and Baduel, P. 1980. 'Le pouvoir de l'eau dans le sud Tunisien.' *R.O.M.M*. 30.2: 101–34.

BAGNOLD, R. A. 1941. *Libyan Sands. Travel in a dead world*. London.

BAILEY, D. 1985. *Excavations at Sidi Khrebish, Benghazi (Berenice) III.2. The Lamps* (LA Supp 5.3), Tripoli.

BAKIR, T. 1967. 'Archaeological News 1965–1967: Tripolitania.' *LA* 3–4: 241–51.

BAKIR, T. 1981. *Historical and archaeological guide to Leptis Magna*. Dept of Antiquities, Tripoli.

BALLANCE, M. H. and Brogan, O. 1971. 'Roman marble, a link between Asia Minor and Libya.' In A.S. Campbell (ed.) *Geology and history of Turkey:* 00–00

BAR = British Archaeological Reports, British Series. Oxford.

BAR S = British Archaeological Reports, International Series. Oxford.

BARADEZ, J. 1948. 'Gemellae, un camp d'Hadrien et une ville des confins sahariens aujourd'hui enséevis sous les sables.' *CRAI* 1948 : 390–95.

BARADEZ, J. 1949a. *Vue aérienne de l'organisation romaine dans le sud Algérienne. Fossatum Africae*. Paris.

BARADEZ, J. 1949b. 'Gemellae, un camp d'Hadrien et une ville des confins sahariens aujourd'hui enséevis sous les sables.' *RAf* 93 : 5–24 (cf. 1948 above).

BARADEZ, J. 1957. 'Travaux hydrauliques romaines révélés par photographies aériennes dans un région aujourd'hui steppienne.' *Actes du 79ème Congrès National des Sociétés Savants, Alger 1954*. Paris : 273–5.

BARADEZ, J. 1966a. 'Deux amphithéatres inédits du "limes" de Numidie: Gemellae et Mesarfelta.' In *Mélanges d'archéologie, d'épigraphie et d'histoire, offerts à Jerome Carcopino*. Paris: 55–63.

BARADEZ, J. 1966b. 'Les thermes légionnaires de Gemellae.' In *Corolla Memoriae Erich Swoboda Dedicata*: 14–22.

BARADEZ, J. 1967. 'Compléments inédits au "Fossatum Africae".' *Limes* 6: 200–10.

BARKER, G. W. W. 1981. 'Early agriculture and economic change in North Africa.' In Allan 1981: 131–45.

BARKER, G. W. W. 1982. 'Natural resource use, lessons from the past.' In Allan 1982: 2–8.

BARKER, G. W. W. 1983. 'Economic life at Berenice: the animal and fish bones, marine molluscs and plant remains.' In Lloyd 1979: 1–49.

BARKER, G.W.W. 1985. 'The UNESCO Libyan Valleys Survey: developing methodologies for investigating ancient floodwater farming.' In Buck and Mattingly 1985: 291–307.

BARKER, G.W.W. 1986. 'Prehistoric rock art in Tripolitania'. *Lib Studs* 17: 69–86.

BARKER, G.W.W. 1989. 'From classification to interpretation: Libyan prehistory 1969–1989.' *Lib Studs* 20: 31–43.

BARKER, G.W.W., Gilbertson, D.D., Griffin, C.M., Hayes, P. and Jones, D.A. 1983. 'The Unesco Libyan Valleys Survey V: Sedimentological properties of Holocene wadi floor and plateau deposits in Tripolitania, Northwest Libya.' *Lib Studs* 14: 69–85.

BARKER, G.W., Gilbertson, D.D., Jones, G.D.B. and Welsby, D.A. 1991. 'ULVS XXIII: the 1989 season.' *Lib Studs* 22: 31–60.

BARKER, G.W.W., Gilbertson, D.D., Jones, G.D.B. and Mattingly, D.J. Forthcoming. *Farming the Libyan Desert. The UNESCO Archaeological Survey in Tripolitania 1979–1989*. 2 vols, UNESCO, Paris.

BARKER, G. W. W. and Jones, G. D. B. 1981. 'The Unesco Libyan Valleys Survey 1980.' *Lib Studs* 12: 9–48.

BARKER, G. W. W. and Jones, G. D. B. 1982. 'The Unesco Libyan Valleys Survey 1979–1981: Palaeoeconomy and environmental archaeology in the predesert.' *Lib Studs* 13: 1–34.

BARKER, G.W.W. and Jones, G.D.B. (eds). 1984. 'The UNESCO Libyan Valleys Survey VI: Investigations of a Romano-Libyan farm, part 1.' *Lib Studs* 15: 1–45.

BARKER, G.W.W. and Jones, G.D.B. 1985. 'Investigating ancient agriculture on the Saharan fringe: the UNESCO Libyan Valleys Survey'. In S. Macready and F.H. Thompson (eds) *Archaeological Field Survey in Britain and Abroad*. London: 225–41.

BARKER, G.W.W., Lloyd, J.A. and Reynolds, J. 1985. *Cyrenaica in Antiquity*. BAR S236, Oxford.

BARTEL, B. 1980. 'Colonialism and cultural responses: problems related to Roman provincial analyses.' *World Archaeology* 12.1:11–26.

BARTH, H. 1857. *Travels and Discoveries in North and Central Africa*. London (reprint 1965).

BARTOCCINI, R. 1927a. 'Il Foro imperiale di Leptis.' *Af Ital* 1 : 53–74.

BARTOCCINI, R. 1927b. 'Rinvenimenti vari di interesse archeologico in Tripolitania (1920–1925).' *Af Ital* 1: 213–48.

BARTOCCINI, R. 1928a. 'Il Foro imperiale di Leptis.' *Af Ital* 2: 30–49.

BARTOCCINI, R. 1928b. 'La fortezza Romana di Bu Ngem.' *Af Ital* 2: 50–58.

BARTOCCINI, R. 1929a. 'Scavi e rinvenimenti di Tripolitania negli anni 1926–27.' *Af Ital* 2: 77–110, 187–200.

BARTOCCINI, R. 1929b. *Le terme di Leptis*. Bergamo.

BARTOCCINI, R. 1931. 'L'Arco quadrifonte dei Severi a Lepcis (Leptis Magna).' *Af Ital* 4: 35–152.

BARTOCCINI, R. 1948. Review of Goodchild 1948. *Epigraphica* 10: 150–57.

BARTOCCINI, R. 1950. 'La curia di Sabratha.' *QAL* 1: 29–58.

BARTOCCINI, R. 1958a. 'Dolabella e Tacfarinas in un'iscrizione di Leptis Magna.' *Epigraphica* 20: 3–13.

BARTOCCINI, R. 1958b. *Il porto romano di Leptis Magna*. Rome.

BARTOCCINI, R. 1964. 'Il tempio Antoniniano di Sabratha.' *LA* 1: 21–42.

BARTON, I. M. 1972a. *Africa in the Roman Empire*. Accra.

BARTON, I. M. 1972b. 'The Proconsuls of Roman Africa.' *Museum Africum* 1: 51–64.

BATAILLON, C. 1963. 'Les Rebaia, semi-nomades du Souf.' In *UNESCO 1963*: 113–21.

BATES, O. 1914. *The Eastern Libyans*. London (reprint 1970).

BAUER, G. 1935. 'Le due necropoli di Ghirza.' *Af Ital* 6: 61–78.

BCTH = *Bullétin archéologique du comité des travaux historiques et scientifiques*. Paris.

BECHERT, T. 1971. 'Römische lagertore und ihre Bauinschriften.' *BJ* Band 171: 201–87.

BEECHEY, F. W. and Beechey, H. W. 1828. *Proceedings of the Expedition to explore the north coast of Africa from Tripoly eastward*. London.

BEGUINOT, F. 1949. 'Di alcune iscrizioni in carattari Latini e in lingua sconosciuta trovante in Tripolitania.' *Rivista degli Studi Orientalia* 24 : 14–19.

BEHNKE, R.H. 1980. *Herders of Eastern Cyrenaica*. Chicago.

BEN ABDULLAH, Z.B. 1986. *Catalogue des inscription païennes du musée du Bardo*. CEFR 92, Rome.

BENABOU, M. 1976. *La résistance africaine à la romanisation*. Paris.

BENABOU, M. 1978. 'Les Romains ont-ils conquis l'Afrique?' *Annales E.S.C.* 33: 83–8.

BEN LAZREG, N. and Mattingly, D.J. 1992. *Leptiminus (Lamta) a Roman port city in Tunisia. Report no. 1. JRA* Supp.4, Ann Arbor.

BERQUE, J. 1953. 'Qu'est ce que qu'une tribu Africaine?' In *Hommages à L. Febvre*. Paris: 261–80.

BERGER, P. 1895. 'Le mausolée d'El-Amrouni.' *Rev. Arch.* 3rd series. 26: 71–5.

BERTHIER, A. 1968. 'Nicibes et Suburbures. Nomades ou sédentaires?' *BAA* 3: 293–300.

BERTHIER, A. 1981. *La Numidie. Rome et le Maghreb*. Paris.

BIANCHI-BANDINELLI, R., Caffarelli, F. V. and Caputo, G. 1966. *The Buried City: Leptis Magna*. New York.

BIREBENT, J. 1962. *Aquae Romanae. Recherches d'hydraulique romaine dans l'est Algérien*. Algiers.

BIRLEY, A. R. 1971. *Septimius Severus, the African Emperor*. London.

BIRLEY, A. R. 1974a. 'Roman frontiers and Roman frontier policy, some reflections on Roman Imperialism.' *Transactions of the Architectural and Archaeological Society of Durham and Northumberland* 3: 13–25.

BIRLEY, A.R. 1987. 'Some notes on the Donatist schism.' *Lib Studs* 18: 29–41.

BIRLEY, A.R. 1988a. *The African Emperor. Septimius Severus*. London.

BIRLEY, A.R. 1988b. 'Names at Lepcis Magna.' *Lib Studs* 19: 1–19.

BIRLEY, E. 1956. 'Hadrianic frontier policy.' *Limes* 2: 25–33.

BISI, A.M. 1977. 'A proposito di alcune iscrizioni puniche su anfore di Pompei.' In Carandini 1977: 151–3.

BLAGG, T.F.C. and King, A.C. (eds) 1984. *Military and Civilian in Roman Britain*. BAR 136, Oxford.

BLAGG, T.F.C. and Millett, M. 1990. *The Early Roman Empire in the West*. Oxford.

BLAKE, G. H. 1968. *Misurata: a market town in Tripolitania* (Dept of Geography, University of Durham, research paper 9).

BLANCHARD, M. 1978. 'Fragments de mosaïques de Djerba conservées au musée de Blois.' *Ant af* 12: 217–39.

BLANCHET, P. 1898. 'Sur quelques points fortifiés de la frontière saharienne de l'empire romain.' *RSAC* 32: 71–96.

BLANCHET, P. 1899. 'Mission archéologique dans le centre et le sud de la Tunisie (avril-août 1895).' *Nouvelles arch. des Missions* 9: 103–56.

BLUME, B. *et al.* 1848/1852. *Die Schriften der römischen Feldmesser*. Berlin.

BMA 1947. See British Military Administration 1947.

BOHANNAN, P. and Plog, F. (eds) 1967. *Beyond the frontier. Social process and culture change*. New York.

BOIZOT, Capt. 1913. 'Fouilles exécutées en 1912 dans le camp romain de Ras el-Ain-Tlalett (Tunisie).' *BCTH* 1913: 260–66.

BOURGEOIS, C. 1980. 'Les vandales, le vandalisme et l'Afrique.' *Ant af* 16: 213–28.

BOVILL, E. W. (ed.) 1964. *The Letters of Major Alexander Gordon Laing 1824–26*. Missions to the Niger I, Hakluyt Society, 2nd series CXXIII.

BOVILL, E. W. 1968. *The Golden Trade of the Moors* (2nd edn). Oxford.

BOVEY, D. 1979. 'The Sahara Gallery.' *Popular Archaeology*, Oct. 1979: 10–12.

BOWMAN, A. K. and Thomas, J. D. 1983. *Vindolanda: the writing tablets*. (*Britannia* monograph series 4), London.

BOWMAN, A., Thomas, J.D. and Adams, J.N. 1990. 'Two letters from Vindolanda.' *Britannia* 21: 33–52

BREEZE, D. J. 1977. 'The garrisoning of Roman fortlets.' *Limes* 10: 1–6.

BREEZE, D. J. and Dobson, B. 1987. *Hadrian's Wall* (3rd edn). London.

BREHONY, J. A. N. 1960. 'Semi-nomadism in the Jebel Tarhuna.' In Willimot and Clarke 1960: 60–69.

BRETT, M. 1976. 'The journey of al-Tijani to Tripoli at the beginning of the fourteenth century AD/eighth century AH.' *Lib Studs* 7 : 41–51.

BRETT, M. 1978a. 'Tripoli at the beginning of the fourteenth century AD/eighth century AH.' *Lib Studs* 9: 55–9.

BRETT, M. 1978b. 'The Arab conquest and the rise of Islam in North Africa.' In Fage 1978, 490–556.

BRETT, M. 1978c. 'The Fatimid revolution and its aftermath in North Africa.' In Fage 1978: 589–637.

BRIGGS, L. C. 1960. *Tribes of the Sahara*. Harvard U. P.

British Military Administration 1947. *Handbook on Tripolitania*, Compiled from official sources. Tripoli.

BROGAN, O. 1954. 'The camel in Roman Tripolitania.' *PBSR* 22: 126–31.

BROGAN, O. 1955. 'When the home guard of Libya created security and fertility on the desert frontier: Ghirza in the third century A.D.' and 'Obelisk and temple tombs of Imperial Roman date near Ghirza.' In *The Illustrated London News* 22 January 1955: 138–42 and 29 January 1955: 182–5.

BROGAN, O. 1962. 'A Tripolitanian centenarian.' In *Hommages à Albert Grennier* (Collection Latomus 58): 368–73.

BROGAN, O. 1964. 'The Roman remains in the wadi el-Amud.' *LA* 1:47–56.

BROGAN, O. 1965a. 'Henschir el-Ausaf by Tigi (Tripolitania) and some related tombs in the Tunisian Gefara.' *LA* 2: 47–56.

BROGAN, O. 1965b. 'Notes on the wadis Neina and Bei el-Kebir and some predesert tracks.' *LA* 2: 57–64.

BROGAN, O. 1971a. 'First and second century settlement in the Tripolitanian pre-desert.' In Gadallah 1971 : 121–30.

BROGAN, O. 1971b. 'Expedition to Tripolitania 1971.' *Lib Studs* 2: 10–11.

BROGAN, O. 1975a. 'Round and about Misurata.' *Lib Studs* 6 : 49–58.

BROGAN, O. 1975b. 'Inscriptions in the Libyan alphabet from Tripolitania and some notes on the tribes of the region.' In Bynon and Bynon 1975: 267–89.

BROGAN, O. 1977. 'Some ancient sites in eastern Tripolitania.' *LA* 13–14 [1984]: 93–129.

BROGAN, O. 1978. 'Es-Sernama Bir el-Uaar: a Roman tomb in Libya.'

In R. Moorey and P. Parr (eds) *Archaeology in the Levant. Essays for Kathleen Kenyon*: 233–7. Warminster.

BROGAN, O. 1980. 'Hadd Hajar, a "clausura" in the Tripolitanian Gebel Garian south of Asabaa.' *Lib Studs* 11 : 45–52.

BROGAN, O. and Oates, D. 1953. 'Gasr el-Gezira, a shrine in the Gebel Nefusa of Tripolitania.' *PBSR* 21: 74–80.

BROGAN, O. and Reynolds, J. M. 1964. 'Inscriptions from the Tripolitanian hinterland.' *LA* 1: 43–6.

BROGAN, O. and Reynolds, J.M. 1985. 'An inscription from the Wadi Antar.' In Buck and Mattingly 1985: 13–23.

BROGAN, O. and Smith, D. E. 1957. 'The Roman frontier at Ghirza, an interim report.' *JRS* 47: 173–84.

BROGAN, O. and Smith, D. E. 1967. 'Notes from the Tripolitanian pre-desert 1967.' *LA* 3–4: 139–44.

BROGAN, O. and Smith, D.J. 1985. *Ghirza: a Romano-Libyan Settlement in Tripolitania*. Libyan Antiquities Series 1, Tripoli, 1984 [1985].

BROUGHTON, T. R. S. 1929. *The Romanization of Africa Proconsularis*. Baltimore.

BROUQUIER-REDDÉ, V. 1992a. 'La place de la Tripolitaine dans la géographie religieuse de l'Afrique du nord.' In *Histoire et archéologie de l'Afrique du Nord. Spectacles, vie portuaire, religion. Actes du Ve Colloque international*. Paris: 117–23.

BROUQUIER-REDDÉ, V. 1992b. *Temples et cultes de Tripolitaine*. CNRS, Paris.

BROWN, D. 1972. *Bury my Heart at Wounded Knee. An Indian history of the American West*. London.

BRUCE, J. C. 1979. *Handbook to the Roman Wall*. (13th edn revised by C. M. Daniels) Newcastle.

BRUN, J-P. 1987. *L'oléiculture antique en Provence*. CNRS, Paris.

BUCK, D.J. 1984. 'The role of states in the Eastern Maghreb, 500 BC–AD 500.' *The Maghreb Review* 9 (1–2): 1–11.

BUCK, D.J. 1985. 'Frontier processes in Roman Tripolitania.' In Buck and Mattingly 1985: 179–90.

BUCK, D.J. and Mattingly, D.J. (eds) 1985. *Town and Country in Roman Tripolitania. Papers in honour of Olwen Hackett*. BAR S 274, Oxford.

BUCK, D. J., Burns, J. R. and Mattingly, D. J. 1983. 'Archaeological sites of the Bir Scedua basin: settlements and cemeteries.' In Jones and Barker 1983: 42–54.

BULLIET, R. W. 1975. *The Camel and the Wheel*. Harvard.

BULLIET, R. W. 1981. 'Botr et Beranès: hypothèses sur l'histoire des Berbères.' *Annales E.S.C.* 36: 104–16.

BURNHAM, B. C. and Johnson, H. B. (eds) 1979. *Invasion and Response. The case of Roman Britain* BAR 73. Oxford.

BURNHAM, B. C. and Wacher, J. 1990. *The Small Towns of Roman Britain*. London.

BURNS, J.R. and Denness, B. 1985. 'Climate and social dynamics: the Tripolitanian example, 300 BC–AD 300.' In Buck and Mattingly 1985: 201–25.

BURNS, J. R. and Mattingly D. J. 1981. 'The wadi N'f'd survey'. In Barker and Jones 1981: 24–33.

BYNON, J. and Bynon, T. (eds). 1975. *Hamito-Semitica*. Mouston.

CAGNAT, R. 1909. 'Les Nugbenoi de Ptolémée.' *CRAI* 1909: 568–79.

CAGNAT, R. 1913. *L'armée romaine d'Afrique et l'occupation de l'Afrique sous les Empereurs* (2nd edn) Paris.

CAGNAT, R. 1914a. 'A new customs list.' *JRS* 4: 142–6.

CAGNAT, R. 1914b. 'La frontière militaire de la Tripolitaine à l'époque romaine.' *MAI* 39: 77–109.

CAGNAT, R. and Merlin, A. 1914/1932. *Atlas archéologique de la Tunisie* (2nd series). Paris.

CAGNAT, Merlin and Chatelain 1923. See *ILAf*.

CALLU, J-P., Morel, J-P., Rebuffat, R. and Hallier, G. 1965. *Thamusida* I. Paris. For Vol II see Rebuffat and Hallier 1970.

Cambridge 1960. *Cambridge Tripolitania Expedition 1960. General Report* (privately circulated report). Cambridge.

CAMPS, G. 1955. 'Les Bavares, peuple de Maurétanie Césarienne.' *RAf* 99: 241–88.

CAMPS, G. 1960. 'Massinissa ou les débuts de l'histoire.' *Libyca* 8.1:1–320.

CAMPS, G. 1980. *Berbères. Aux marges de l'histoire*. Toulouse.

CAMPS, G. 1989. 'Les chars sahariens. Images d'une societé aristocratique.' *Ant af* 25: 11–40.

CAMPS, G. and GAST, M. (eds) 1982. *Les chars préhistoriques du Sahara.* Aix-en-Provence.

CAMPS -FABRER, H. 1953. *L'olivier et l'huile dans l'Afrique romaine.* Algiers.

CAMPS-FABRER, H. 1985. 'L'olivier et son importance économique dans l'Afrique romaine.' In *L'huile d'olive en Méditerranée.* Maison de la Méditerranée, Aix-en-Provence.

CAPOT-REY, R. 1953. *Le Sahara Français (L'Afrique Blanche Française II).* Paris.

CAPUTO, G. 1951. 'Flavius Nepotianus "comes et praeses provinciae Tripolitanae".' *REA* 53: 234–47.

CAPUTO, G. 1959. *Il Teatro di Sabratha e l'architettura teatrale africana.* (MAL VI), Rome.

CAPUTO, G. 1987. *Il Teatro Augusteo di Leptis Magna.* (MAL III), Rome.

CAPUTO, G. and GHEDINI, F. 1984. *Pitture del tempio d'Ercole di Sabratha.* (MAL XIX), Rome.

CAPUTO, G. and LEVI DELLA VIDA, G. 1935. 'Il teatro Augusteo di Leptis Magna secondo le ultime scoperte e un'iscrizione bilingue in latino e neo-punico.' *Af Ital* 6: 91–109.

CARANDINI, A. (ed.) 1977. *Instrumentum Domesticum di Ercolano e Pompei nella Prima Età Imperiale.* Rome.

CARANDINI, A. 1983. 'Pottery and the African economy.' In Garnsey *et al.* 1983: 145–62.

CARANDINI, A. and PANELLA, C. 1981. 'The trading connections of Rome and central Italy in the late second and third centuries: the evidence of the Terme del Nuotatore excavations, Ostia.' In A. King and M. Henig (eds) *The Roman West in the Third Century.* BAR S 109: 487–503.

CARCOPINO, J. 1925. 'Le 'limes" de Numidie et sa garde syrienne d'après inscriptions recemment découvertes.' *Syria* 6: 30–57 and 118–49.

CARCOPINO, J. 1933. 'Note complémentaire sur les Numeri syriens.' *Syria* 14: 20–55.

CARCOPINO, J. 1943. *Le Maroc Antique.* Paris.

CARTER, T. H. 1965. 'Western Phoenicians and Lepcis Magna.' *AJA* 69: 123–32.

CARTON, L. 1896/1897. 'Etudes sur les travaux hydrauliques des romains en Tunisie.' *RT* 3: 373–85, 530–64. *RT* 4: 27–85.

CARTON, L. 1912. 'L'hydraulique dans l'antiquité en Barbarie.' *RT* 19: 221–30.

CARTON, L. 1914/l915. 'Nybgenii et Nefzaoua.' *RT* 21: 207–16; 354–68. *RT* 22: 35–7.

CASEY, P. J. (ed.) 1979. *The End of Roman Britain.* BAR 71, Oxford.

CAUNEILLE, A. 1963. 'Le semi-nomadisme dans l'ouest Libyen (Fezzan, Tripolitaine).' In *UNESCO* 1963: 101–12.

CERRATA, L. 1933. *Sirtis.* Avellino.

CHABOT 1940. See *RIL.*

CHAMOUX, F. 1953. *Cyrène sous la monarchie des Battiades.* Bibliothèque des écoles françaises d'Athènes et de Rome, fasc. 177. Paris.

CHASTAGNOL, A. 1967. 'Les gouverneurs de Byzacène et de Tripolitaine.' *Ant af* I : 119–34.

CHATTERTON, B.A. and L. 1985. 'A hypothetical answer to the decline of the granary of Rome.' *Lib Studs* 16: 95–9.

CHEVALLIER, R. 1958. 'Essai de chronologie des centuriations romaines en Tunisie.' *MEFR* 70: 61–128.

CHRISTIE, N.J. 1989. 'The archaeology of Byzantine Italy: synthesis of recent research.' *JMA* 2.2: 249–93.

CHRISTOFLE, M. 1938. *Rapport sur les travaux de fouilles et consolidation effectuées en 1933–1934–1935–1936 par le service des monuments historique de l'Algérie.* Algiers.

CHRISTOL, M. 1981. 'L'armée des provinces Pannoniennes et la pacification des révoltes maures sous Antonin le Pieux.' *Ant af* 17: 133–41.

CHURCHER, C. S. 1980. 'Preliminary observations on the geology and vertebrate Palaeontology in the northwestern Dakhleh oasis: a report of the 1979 fieldwork.' *The SSEA Journal* X. 4: 379–95.

CIL 8 = *Corpus Inscriptionem Latinarum* Vol VIII, ed. G. Wilmanns *et al.* Berlin, 1881–1942.

CLARKE, G. 1986. 'ULVS XIV: Archaeozoological evidence for stock-raising and stock-management in the pre-desert.' *Lib Studs* 17: 49–64.

CLARKE, J. I. 1953. 'Summer nomadism in Tunisia.' *Econ Geog* 31: 157–67.

CLARKE, J. I. 1959. 'Studies in semi-nomadism in North Africa.' *Econ Geog* 35: 95–108.

CLARKE, J. I. 1960. 'The Siaan: pastoralists of the Jefara.' In Willimot and Clarke 1960: 52–9.

CLEMENTE, G. 1968. *La Notitia Dignitatum.* Cagliari.

CONSTANS, L. A. 1914. 'Inscriptions de Gigthis (Tunisie).' *MEFR* 34: 267–86.

CONSTANS, L. A. 1915. 'Inscriptions de Gigthis (Tunisie),' suite. *MEFR* 35: 327–44.

CONSTANS, L. A. 1916. 'Gigthis.' *Nouvelles arch. des Missions* n.s.14: 1–113.

COQUE, R. 1962. *La Tunisie Présaharienne. Etude géomorphologique.* Paris.

CORO, F. 1928. *Vestigia di colonie agricole Romane. Gebel Nefusa.* Rome.

CORO, F. 1935. 'I milliari Romani della carovaniera Zintan–Mizda.' *Atti del II Congresso di studi Colonici* 2 : 69–75.

CORO, F. 1956. 'Gadames Archeologica. Storia degli studi delle esplorazioni e dei risultati su alcuni fra i piu tipici antichi monumenti dell' oasi famosa. Libia.' *Rivista Trimestriale di Studi Libici.* 4.34: 3–26.

COURTOIS, C. 1950. 'Saint Augustin et la problème de la survivance du Punique.' *RAf* 94: 259–82.

COURTOIS, C. 1955. *Les Vandales et l'Afrique.* Paris.

COURTOIS, C., LESCHI, L., PERRAT, C. and SAUMAGNE, C. 1952. *Les Tablettes Albertini : actes privées de l'époque Vandale.* Paris.

COWPER, H.S. 1896. 'The senams or megalithic temples of Tripoli.' *The Antiquary* 32: 37–45, 68–74.

COWPER, H. S. 1897. *The Hill of the Graces.* Glasgow.

COWPER, H.S. 1899. 'Tripoli Senams: idols or olive presses?' *Proceedings of the Society of Antiquaries* 1899: 297–300.

CRAI = Comptes Rendus à l'Académie des Inscriptions et Belles Lettres. Paris.

CROVA, B. 1967. 'Opere idrauliche romane all'uadi Caam, il Cinyps della Tripolitania romana.' *QAL* 5: 99–120.

CT = Les Cahiers de Tunisie, Tunis, Faculté des Lettres.

CUNLIFFE, B. 1973. *The Regni.* London.

CUNLIFFE, B. 1978. *Iron Age Communities in Britain* (2nd edn). London.

CUNTZ, O. (ed.) 1929. *Itineraria Romana I : Itineraria Antonini.* Lipsiae.

DANIELS, C. M. 1968. 'Garamantian excavations: Zinchecra 1965–1967.' *LA* 5:113–94.

DANIELS, C. M. 1969. 'The Garamantes.' In Kanes 1969 : 31–52.

DANIELS, C. M. 1970a. *The Garamantes of southern Libya.* London.

DANIELS, C. M. 1970b. 'The Garamantes of Fezzan, excavations on Zinchecra 1965–1967.' *AJ* 50 : 37–66.

DANIELS, C. M. 1971a. 'The Garamantes of Fezzan.' In Gadallah 1971: 261–85.

DANIELS, C. M. 1971b. 'Excavations at Saniat Gebril, wadi el-Agial, Fezzan.' *Lib Studs* 2: 6–7.

DANIELS, C. M. 1973. 'The Garamantes of Fezzan, an interim report of research.' *Lib Studs* 4: 35–40.

DANIELS, C. M. 1975. 'An ancient people of the Libyan Sahara.' In Bynon and Bynon 1975: 249–65.

DANIELS, C. M. 1977. 'Garamantian excavations (Germa) 1977.' *Lib Studs* 8 : 5–7.

DANIELS, C. M. 1980. 'Excavations at Wallsend and the fourth-century barracks on Hadrian's Wall.' *Limes* 12 : 173–93.

DANIELS, C.M. 1987. 'Africa.' In J. Wacher (ed.) *The Roman World*, vol 1: 223–65.

DANIELS, C.M. 1989. 'Excavation and fieldwork amongst the Garamantes.' *Lib Studs* 20: 45–61.

Interim reports on Daniels' work in Fezzan in the years 1965, 1967, 1968, 1969 and 1971 are housed in the Libyan Society Library, SOAS, London.

DARMON, J-P. 1964. 'Note sur le tarif de Zarai.' *CT* 12 : 7–23.

DAUMAS, 1850/1968. *The horses of the Sahara* (trans. S. M. Ohlendorf). Austin and London.

DAUMAS, 1850/1971. *The ways of the desert* (trans. S.M. Ohlendorf). Austin and London. (The original French edition incorporated both these titles in a single volume.)

DAVIES, R. W. 1971. 'The Roman military diet.' *Britannia* 2 : 122–48.

DAVIES, R. W. 1987. *Service in the Roman Army*. Edinburgh.

DE ANGELIS D'OSSAT, G. and Farioli, R. 1975. 'Il complesso palaeocristiano di Breviglieri (el Khadra).' *QAL* 7: 28–156.

DECRET, F. and Fantar, M. 1981. *L'Afrique du Nord dans l'Antiquité, histoire et civilisation*. Paris.

DEGRASSI, N. 1951. 'Il mercato Romano di Leptis Magna.' *QAL* 2: 27–70.

DE LA CHAPELLE, F. 1934. 'L'expédition de Suétonius Paulinus dans le sud-est du Maroc.' *Hesperis* 19: 107–24.

DE MATHUISIEULX, H. M. 1901. *A travers le Tripolitaine*. Paris.

DE MATHUISIEULX, H. M. 1902. 'Rapport sur une mission scientifique en Tripolitaine.' *Nouvelles arch. des Missions* 10: 245–77.

DE MATHUISIEULX, H. M. 1904. 'Rapport sur une mission scientifique en Tripolitaine.' *Nouvelles arch. des Missions* 12: 1–80.

DE MATHUISIEULX, H. M. 1905. 'Rapport sur une mission scientifique en Tripolitaine.' *Nouvelles arch. des Missions* 13: 73–102.

DE MATHUISIEULX, H. M. 1912. *La Tripolitaine d'hier et de demain*. Paris.

DEMOUGEOT, E. 1960. 'Le chameau et l'Afrique du Nord romaine.' *Annales E.S.C.* l: 209–47.

DENHAM, D. and Clapperton, H. 1826. *Narration of travels and discoveries in Northern and Central Africa in the years 1822–1824*. London (reprinted 1965 as Missions to the Niger III, Hakluyt Society. 2nd series CXIX, ed. E. W. Bovill).

DENTI DI PIRAJNO, A. 1957. *A cure for serpents* (Eng. trans.), London.

DESANGES, J. 1957. 'Le triomphe de Cornelius Balbus (19 B.C.).' *RAf* 101:5–43.

DESANGES, J. 1962. *Catalogue des tribus africaines de l'Antiquité classique à l'ouest du Nil*. Dakar.

DESANGES, J. 1964a. 'Note sur la datation de l'expédition de Julius Maternus au pays d'Agisymba.' *Latomus* 23: 713–25.

DESANGES, J. 1964b. 'Les territoires gétules de Juba II.' *REA* 66: 33–47.

DESANGES, J. 1969. 'Un drame africain sous Auguste: le meutre du Proconsul L. Cornelius Lentulus par les Nasamons.' *Hommages à M. Renard*: 197–213.

DESANGES, J. 1976. 'The iconography of the Black in ancient North Africa.' In *The Image of the Black in western art I, from the Pharaohs to the fall of the Roman Empire*. Menil Foundation.

DESANGES, J. 1978. *Recherches sur l'activité des Méditerranéens aux confins de l'Afrique*. CEFR no 38. Rome.

DESANGES, J. 1980a. Permanence d'une structure indigène en marge de l'administration romaine: la Numidie traditionelle. *Ant af* 15: 77–89.

DESANGES, J. 1980b. *(Pliné l'Ancien), Histoire Naturelle, Livre V, 1–46 (L'Afrique du Nord)*. Paris.

DE SLANE, M. 1913. *Description de l'Afrique septentrionale. El Bekri* (reprint 1965). Paris.

DE SLANE, M. 1925/1956 *Ibn Khaldun. Histoire des Berbères et des dynasties Musulmanes de l'Afrique septentrionale* (revised edn in 4 vols) Paris.

DESPOIS, J. 1935. *Le Djebel Nefousa (Tripolitaine) Etude géographique*. Paris.

DESPOIS, J. 1964. *L'Afrique du Nord. Vol I of L'Afrique Blanche (française)* (3rd edn). Paris.

DESPOIS, J. 1973. *Maghreb et Sahara, Etudes géographiques offerts à Jean Despois*. Paris.

DESPOIS, J. and Raynal, R. 1967. *Géographie de l'Afrique du nord-ouest*. Paris.

DIEHL, C. 1896. *L'Afrique byzantine: histoire de la domination byzantine en Afrique (533–709)*. Paris.

DIGGLE, J. and GOODYEAR, F. R. D. 1970. *Flavii Cresconii Corippi Iohannidos seu de bellis Libycis Lib. VIII*. Cambridge.

DILKE, O. A. W. 1971. *The Roman land surveyors: an introduction to the Agrimensores*. Newton Abbot.

DI VITA, A. 1964a. 'Il "limes" Romano di Tripolitania nella sua concretezza archeologica e nella sua realtà storica.' *LA* 1: 65–98.

DI VITA, A. 1964b. 'Archaeological news : Tripolitania.' *LA* 1: 133–42.

DI VITA, A. 1966a. 'La villa della Gara delle Nereidi.' *LA Supp* 2: 11–64.

DI VITA, A. 1966b. 'Recenti scavi e scoperte in Tripolitania.' *LA Supp* 2 : 65–111.

DI VITA, A. 1967. 'La diffusione del Cristianismo nell' interno della Tripolitania attraverso i monumenti e sue sopravivenze nelle Tripolitania araba.' *QAL* 5: 121–42.

DI VITA, A. 1968a 'Influence grecque et tradition orientale dans l'art punique de Tripolitaine.' *MEFR* 80 : 7–85.

DI VITA, A. 1968b. 'Shadrapa et Milk'ashtart dei patri di Leptis ed i templi del Lato nord-ouest del foro veccio leptitano.' *Orientalia* 37: 201–11.

DI VITA, A. 1969. 'Le date di fondazione di Leptis e di Sabratha sulla base dell'indagine archeologica e l'eparchia carthaginese d'Africa.' *Hommages à M. Renard* III (Coll. Latomus 103): 196–202.

DI VITA, A. 1971. 'Les Emporia de Tripolitaine dans le rayonnement de Carthage et d'Alexandrie: les mausolées punico-Hellenistiques de Sabratha.' In Gadallah 1971: 173–80.

DI VITA, A. 1974. 'Un passo dello "Stadiasmos tes megales thalasses" ed il porto ellenistico di Leptis Magna.' *Mélanges P. Boyance*. Rome: 229–49.

DI VITA, A. 1976. 'Il mausoleo punico-ellenistico B di Sabratha.' *Rom.Mitt.* 83: 273–83.

DI VITA, A. 1978. 'Lo scavo a nord del mausoleo punico-ellenistico A di Sabratha.' *LA* 11–12 (1974–5) [1978]: 7–111.

DI VITA, A. 1980. 'Evidenza dei terremoti del 306–310 e del 365 B.C. in Tunisia.' *Ant af* 15: 303–07.

DI VITA, A. 1982a. 'Gli Emporia di Tripolitania dall'età di Massinissa a Diocleziano: un profile storico-istituzionale.' *ANRW* II, Principat 10.2: 515–95.

DI VITA, A. 1982b. 'Il progetto originario del forum novum Severianum a Leptis Magna.' *150 Jahr-Feier Deutsches Archaologisches Institut Rom* (Rom. Mitt. Erganzungsheft 25): 84–106.

DI VITA, A. 1983. 'Architettura e societa nelle citta di Tripolitania fra Massinissa e Augusteo: qualche nota.' *Architecture et societé de l'archaisme grec à la fin de la république romaine* (Coll EFR 66):355–76.

DI VITA, A. 1990a. 'Sismi, urbanistica e chronologia assoluta.' In *L'Afrique dans l'Occident romain*. CEFR 134, Rome: 425–94.

DI VITA, A. 1990b. 'Il teatro di Leptis Magna: una rilettura.' *JRA* 3: 133–46.

DI VITA, A. 1990c. 'Antico e tardo-antico in Tripolitania: sopravivenze e metologia.' *L'Africa romana* 7: 347–56.

DI VITA-EVRARD, G. 1965. 'Les dédicaces de l'amphithéatre et du cirque de Lepcis.' *LA* 2: 29–37.

DI VITA-EVRARD, G. 1979. 'Quatre inscriptions du Djebel Tarhuna: le térritoire de Lepcis Magna.' *QAL* 10: 67–98.

DI VITA-EVRARD, G. 1982. 'Note sur trois sénateurs de Lepcis Magna. Le clarissimat des Plautii.' *Epigrafia e ordine senatorio I* (Tituli 4): 453–65.

DI VITA-EVRARD, G. 1984. 'Municipium Flavium Lepcis Magna.' *BCTH* n.s. 17, fasc. B: 197–210.

DI VITA-EVRARD, G. 1985a. 'Note sur quelques timbres d'amphores de Tripolitaine.' *BCTH* n.s. 19 (1983) [1985]: 147–59.

DI VITA-EVRARD, G. 1985b. '"Regio Tripolitana" – a reappraisal.' In Buck and Mattingly 1985: 143–63.

DI VITA-EVRARD, G. 1985c. 'L. Volusius Bassus Cerealis, légat du Proconsul d'Afrique T. Claudius Aurelius Aristobulus, et la création de la province de Tripolitaine.' *L'Africa romana* 2: 149–77.

DI VITA-EVRARD, G. 1986. 'La "Fossa Regia" et les diocèses d'Afrique proconsulaire.' *L'Africa romana* 3: 31–58.

DI VITA-EVRARD, G. 1988. 'Le plus ancien milliare de Tripolitaine: A. Caecina Severus, proconsul d'Afrique.' *LA* 15–16 (1978–9) [1988]: 9–44.

DI VITA-EVRARD, G. 1990. 'IRT 520, le proconsulat de Cn Calpurnius Piso et l'insertion de Lepcis Magna dans la provincia Africa.' In *L'Afrique dans l'Occident romain*. CEFR 134, Rome: 315–31.

DI VITA-EVRARD, G. 1991. 'Gasr Duib: construit ou reconstruit sous les Phillipes.' In *L'armée et les affaires militaires. Actes du IVe Colloque International sur l'histoire et archéologie de l'Afrique du nord*. CTHS, Paris: 427–44.

DI VITA-EVRARD, G. and Rebuffat, R. 1987. 'La dédicace des thermes.' *Karthago* 21: 107–11.

DONALDSON, G. 'The "praesides provinciae Tripolitaniae" – civil administrators or military commanders.' In Buck and Mattingly 1985: 165–77.

DONAU, R. 1904a. 'Le castellum de Benia-Guedah-Ceder.' *BCTH* 1904: 467–77.

DONAU, R. 1904b. 'Note sur la voie de Turris Tamalleni à Capsa et sur quelques ruines romaines situées dans le Bled Segui.' *BCTH* 1904: 354–9.

DONAU, R. 1906. 'Notes sur des ruines du sud Tunisien.' *BCTH* 1906: 113–22.

DONAU, R. 1907. 'Etude sur la voie romaine de Tacapae à Turris Tamalleni.' *Bulletin de la Societé archéologique de Sousse* 1907: 52–67; 173–90.

DONAU, R. l909a. 'Recherches archéologiques.' *BCTH* 1909: 30–50.

DONAU, R. l909b. 'Note relative à deux nouveaux documents découverts sur la voie de Capsa à Turris Tamalleni.' *BCTH* 1909: 277–81.

DONDIN-PAYRE, M. 1981. 'Recherches sur un aspect de la romanisation de l'Afrique du nord: l'expansion de la citoyennette romaine jusqu'à Hadrien.' *Ant af* 17: 93–132.

DORE, J. N. 1983. 'The Pottery from the Unesco Libyan Valleys Survey.' In Jones and Barker 1983: 54–7.

DORE, J.N. 1984. 'The pottery from the LM4 complex (el-Amud).' In Barker and Jones 1984: 22–31.

DORE, J.N. 1985. 'Settlement chronology in the pre-desert zone: the evidence of the fine ware.' In Buck and Mattingly 1985: 107–25.

DORE, J.N. 1988. 'Pottery and the history of Roman Tripolitania: evidence from Sabratha and the Unesco Libyan Valleys Survey.' *Lib Studs* 19: 61–85.

DORE, J.N. 1990. 'ULVS XX: First report on the pottery.' *Lib Studs* 21: 9–17.

DORE, J.N. and Keay, N. 1989. *Excavations at Sabratha 1948–1951. II, The Finds. Part 1, the amphorae, coarse pottery and building materials* (M. Fulford and M. Hall, eds). London.

DORE, J.N. and Veen, M. van der. 1986. 'ULVS XV: radio-carbon dates from the Libyan Valleys Survey.' *Lib Studs* 17: 65–8.

DOZY, R. and Goeje, M. J. 1866. *Edrisi: description de l'Afrique et de l'Espagne*. Leiden (reprint 1969, Amsterdam).

DUNBABIN, K.M.D. 1978. *The Mosaics of Roman North Africa*. Oxford.

DUNCAN-JONES, R. P. 1962. 'Costs, outlays and "summae honorariae" from Roman Africa.' *PBSR* 30: 47–115.

DUNCAN-JONES, R. P. 1963. 'Wealth and munificence in Roman Africa.' *PBSR* 31: 159–78.

DUNCAN-JONES, R. 1982. *The Economy of the Roman Empire. Quantitative Studies* (2nd edn). Cambridge.

DUNCAN-JONES, R. 1990. *Structure and Scale in the Roman Economy.* Cambridge.

DUNN, R. E. 1973. 'Berber imperialism: The Ait Atta expansion in southeast Morocco.' In Gellner and Micaud 1973: 85–107.

DUNN, R. E. 1977. *Resistance in the Desert*. London.

DUVEYRIER, H. 1864. *Les Touareg du nord. Exploration du Sahara*. Paris (reprint 1973, Nendeln).

DYSON, S. L. 1971. 'Native revolts in the Roman Empire.' *Historia* 20: 267–74.

DYSON, S. L. 1974. 'The role of comparative frontier studies in understanding the Roman frontier.' *Limes* 9: 277–83.

DYSON, S. L. 1975. 'Native revolt patterns in the Roman Empire.' *ANRW* II, 3: 138–75.

ELFASI, M. 1988. *Africa from the Seventh to the Eleventh Century.* UNESCO general history of Africa III, London.

ELMAYER, A. F. 1983. 'The reinterpretation of Latino-Punic inscriptions from Roman Tripolitania.' *Lib Studs* 14: 86–95.

ELMAYER, A. F. 1984. 'The reinterpretation of Latino-Punic inscriptions from Roman Tripolitania.' *Lib Studs* 15: 93–105.

ELMAYER, A.F. 1985. 'The "centenaria" of Roman Tripolitania.' *Lib Studs* 16: 77–84.

Energoproject 1980. *Bani Walid project. Hydro-Climatology Study.*

Tripoli SPLAJ, Secretariat for agrarian reform and land development (soil and water department).

EUZENNAT, M. 1972. 'Quatre années de recherches sur la frontière romaine en tunisie méridionale.' *CRAI* 1972: 7–27.

EUZENNAT, M. 1973. 'Tillibari, forteresse du "limes Tripolitanus".' *BCTH* 1973: 143–4.

EUZENNAT, M. 1974. 'Les Zegrenses.' *Mélanges W. Seston*: 175–86.

EUZENNAT, M. 1977a. 'Recherches récentes sur la frontière d'Afrique (1964–74).' *Limes* 10: 429–44.

EUZENNAT, M. 1977b. 'Les recherches sur la frontière romaine d'Afrique.' *Limes* 11: 533–43.

EUZENNAT, M. 1977c. '"Equites secundae Flaviae".' *Ant af* 11: 131–5.

EUZENNAT, M. 1984. 'Les troubles de Maurétanie.' *CRAI* 1984: 372–93.

EUZENNAT, M. 1985. 'L'olivier et le "limes", considerations sur la frontière romaine de Tripolitaine.' *BCTH* n.s. 19, fasc. B: 161–71.

EUZENNAT, M. 1986. 'La frontière d'Afrique 1976–83.' *Limes* 13: 573–83.

EUZENNAT, M. and Trousset, P. 1975. *Le camp de Remada, fouilles inédites du commandant R. Donau*. Aix-en-Provence (privately circulated) = *Africa* 5–6, 1978: 111–89.

EVENARI, M., Shanon, L. and Tadmor, N. 1971. *The Negev. The challenge of a desert*. Harvard.

FAGE, J. D. (ed.) 1978. *The Cambridge History of Africa II, c. 500 B.C.–A.D.1050.* Cambridge.

FAKRY, A. 1973. *The Oases of Egypt. I, Siwa.* Cairo.

FAKRY, A. 1974. *The Oases of Egypt. II, Bahariyah and Farfara oases.* Cairo.

FANTAR, M. 1990. 'Survivances de la civilisation punique en Afrique du nord.' *L'Africa romana* 7: 53–71.

FANTOLI, A. 1933. *La Libia negli scritti degli antichi*. Rome.

FANTOLI, A. 1952. *La piogge della Libia*. Rome.

FENTRESS, E. W. B. 1978. *The economic effects of the Roman army on southern Numidia*. (D.Phil. thesis Oxford) published as:

FENTRESS, E. W. B. 1979. *Numidia and the Roman army. Social, military and economic aspects of the frontier zone*. BAR S.53, Oxford.

FENTRESS, E. W. B. 1982. 'Tribe and faction: the case of the Gaetuli.' *MEFR* 94–1982–1: 325–34.

FENTRESS, E.W.B. 1985. '"Limes" – Africa.' *Dizionario Epigrafico di Antichita Romana* IV, fasc 43.2–3 (1376): 21–47.

FENTRESS, E.W.B. and Perkins, P. 1988. 'Counting African Red Slip ware.' *L'Africa romana* 5: 205–14.

FERCHIOU, N. 1984. 'Gigthis à une époque mal connue, la phase julio-claudienne.' *BCTH* n.s. 17B: 65–74.

FERCHIOU, N. 1989. 'Le mausolée de Q. Apuleus Maxsimus à El Amrouni.' *PBSR* 57: 47–76

FERCHIOU, N. 1990. 'Habitats fortifiés pré-impériaux en Tunisie antique.' *Ant af* 26: 43–86.

FEUILLE, G. 1940. 'Note sur les ruines de l'Henchir Kedama.' *BCTH* 1938–40: 260–65.

FÉVRIER, J. G. 1956. 'Que savons nous du Libyque?' *RAf* 100: 263–73.

FÉVRIER, P. A. 1982. 'Urbanisation et urbanisme de l'Afrique romaine.' *ANRW* II, Principat 10.2 : 321–96.

FÉVRIER, P.A. 1989. *Approches du Maghreb romain*. 2 vols. Aix-en-Provence.

FIANDRA, E. 1975. 'I ruderi del tempio flavio di Leptis Magna.' *LA* 11–12: 147–63.

FITZGERALD, A. 1926. *Letters of Synesius*. London.

FITZGERALD, A. 1930. *The Essays and Hymns of Synesius of Cyrene.* 2 vols. London.

FORBES, H. 1992. 'The ethnoagricultural approach to ancient Greek agriculture. Olive cultivation as a case study.' In B. Wells (ed.) *Agriculture in Ancient Greece*, Acta Instituti Atheniensis Regni Sueciae, series 4, 42: 87–101.

FORBES, H. and Foxhall, L. 1978. '"The Queen of all trees". Preliminary notes on the archaeology of the olive.' *Expedition* 21.1: 37–47.

FOUCHER, L. 1964. 'Sur les mosaïques de Zliten.' *LA* 1: 9–20.

FOXHALL, L. 1990. 'The dependent tenant: land leasing and labour in Italy and Greece.' *JRS* 80: 97–114.

FRANCHETTI, L. *et al*. 1914. *La missione Franchetti in Tripolitania (il Gebel)*. Florence/ Milan.

FRANCHI, S. 1912. *Richerche e studi agrologici sulla Libia. I, La zona di Tripoli*. Bergamo.

FREND, W. H. C. 1971. *The Donatist Church* (2nd edn). Oxford.

FREND, W. H. C. 1978. 'The Christian period in Mediterranean Africa, *c*. A.D. 200–700.' In Fage 1978: 410–90.

FRERE, S. S. 1978. *Britannia. A history of Roman Britain* (revised edn). London.

FREZOULS, E. 1957. 'Les Baquates et la province romaine de Tingitaine.' *BAM* 2:65–116.

FREZOULS, E. 1980. 'Rome et la Maurétanie Tingitane: un constat d'échec?' *Ant af* 16: 65–93.

FULFORD, M. 1989. 'To east and west: the Mediterranean trade of Cyrenaica and Tripolitania.' *Lib Studs* 20: 169–91.

FULFORD, M. and Peacock, D.P.S. 1984. *The Avenue du President Bourgiba, Salambo: the pottery and other ceramic objects. Excavations at Carthage: the British Mission* 1.2. Sheffield.

GADALLAH, F. F. (ed.) *Libya in History. Proceedings of a conference held at the faculty of Arts, University of Libya, 1968*. Benghazi.

GALAND, L. 1971. 'Les Quinquegentanei.' *BAA* 4: 277–9.

GALAND, L. 1989. 'Les alphabets libyques.' *Ant af* 25: 69–81.

GARNSEY, P. D. A. 1978. 'Rome's African Empire under the Principate.' In Garnsey and Whittaker (eds) *Imperialism in the Ancient World*: 223–54. Cambridge.

GARNSEY, P.D.A. 1988. *Famine and Food Supply in the Graeco-Roman World*. Cambridge.

GARNSEY, P., Hopkins, K. and Whittaker, C.R. 1983. *Trade in the Ancient Economy*. London.

GARNSEY, P. and Saller, R. 1987. *The Roman Empire. Economy, Society and Culture*. London.

GASCOU, J. 1972a. *La politique municipale de l'Empire romain en Afrique Proconsulaire de Trajan et Septime Sévère*. (E.F.R.) Paris.

GASCOU, J. 1972b. 'Lepti Minus, colonie de Trajan?' *Ant af* 6: 137–43.

GASCOU, J. 1982. 'La politique municipale de Rome en Afrique du Nord' (Parts 1 and 2). *ANRW* II, Principat 10.2: 136–320.

GATEAU, A. 1947. *Conquête de l'Afrique du Nord et de l'Espagne. Ibn Abd-el Hakam* (2nd edn). Algiers.

GAUCKLER, P. 1897/1904. *Enquête sur les installations hydrauliques romaines en Tunisie*, fasc. I.l and II.3., Paris. The full edition was in 2 vols, 1900/1912, and comprised eight fascicules.

GAUCKLER, P. 1900. 'Notes sur les fouilles executées dans le Sahara tunisien.' *CRAI* 1900: 541–7.

GAUCKLER, P. 1902. 'Le "centenarium" de Tibubuci (Ksar Tarcine, sud Tunisien).' *CRAI* 1902: 321–40.

GAUTIER, E. F. 1937/1952. *Le passé de l'Afrique du Nord* (1st/2nd edn). Paris.

GELLNER, E. 1969. *Saints of the Atlas*. London.

GELLNER, E. and MICAUD, C. (eds) 1973. *Arabs and Berbers. From tribe to nation in North Africa*. London.

GENDRE, F. 1908. 'De Gabes à Nefta (Le Nefzaoua et le Djerid).' *RT* 15: 383–411: 499–520.

GENTILUCCI, I. 1933. 'Resti di antichi edifici lungo l'uadi Sofeggin.' *Af Ital* V:172–87.

GHISLERI, A. 1912. *Tripolitania e Cirenaica dal Mediterraneo al Sahara*. Milan/Bergamo.

GIARDINA, A. (ed.) 1986. *Società romana e impero tardoantico III: le merci gli insediamenti*. Laterza, Rome.

GICHON, M. 1974. 'Towers on the "limes Palestinae" (forms, purpose, terminology and comparisons).' *Limes* 9: 513–30.

GILBERTSON, D.D. 1986. 'Runoff (floodwater) farming and rural water supply in arid lands.' *Applied Geography* 6(1): 5–11.

GILBERTSON, D.D., Hayes, P.P., Barker, G.W.W. and Hunt, C.O. 1984. 'The UNESCO Libyan Valleys Survey VII: an interim classification and functional analysis of ancient wall technology and land use.' *Lib Studs* 15: 45–70.

GILBERTSON, D.D. and HUNT, C.O. 1988. 'ULVS XIX: A reconnaissance survey of the Cenozoic geomorphology of the Wadi Merdum, Beni Ulid, in the Libyan pre-desert.' *Lib Studs* 19: 95–121.

GILBERTSON, D.D. and Hunt, C.O. 1990. 'ULVS XXI: Geomorphological studies of the Romano-Libyan farm.' *Lib Studs* 21: 25–42.

GILBERTSON, D.D., HUNT, C.O., BRIGGS, D.J., COLES, G.M. and THEW, N.M. 1987. 'ULVS XVI: The quaternary geomorphology and calcretes of the area around Gasr Banat in the pre-desert of Tripolitania.' *Lib Studs* 18: 15–27.

GINESTOUS, M. 1913. 'L'hydrauliche agricole dans la Tunisie méridionale.' *RT* 20: 557–63.

GOETSCHY, F. 1894. 'Note sur un passage du Cherb barré par une muraille romaine.' *RSAC* 29: 593–8.

GOITEIN, S.D. 1917/1983. *A Mediterranean Society*. 4 vols. Berkeley.

GOMBEAUD, Lt. 1901. 'Fouilles du castellum d'el-Hagueuff (Tunisie)' *BCTH* 1901: 81–94.

GOODCHILD, R. G. 1948. *The Roman roads and milestones of Tripolitania. (Discoveries and researches 1947). Reports and Monographs 1*. Tripoli.

GOODCHILD, R. G. 1949a. 'Some inscriptions from Roman Tripolitania.' *Reports and Monographs* 2: 29–35.

GOODCHILD, R. G. 1949b. 'Recent explorations and discoveries.' *Reports and Monographs* 2: 37–41.

GOODCHILD, R. G. 1949c. 'Where archaeology and military training go hand in hand: Roman "home guard" outposts in Tripolitania.' *Illustrated London News* 15 October 1949: 594–5.

GOODCHILD, R. G. 1950a. 'The "limes Tripolitanus" II.' *JRS* 40: 30–38 = 1976a: 35–45.

GOODCHILD, R. G. 1950b. 'The Latino-Libyan inscriptions of Tripolitania.' *AJ* 30: 135–44.

GOODCHILD, R. G. 1950c. 'Roman Tripolitania: reconnaissance in the desert frontier zone.' *Geog. J.* 115: 161–78 = 1976a: 3–16.

GOODCHILD, R. G. 1950d. 'Two monumental inscriptions of Lepcis Magna.' *PBSR* 18 : 72–82.

GOODCHILD, R. G. 1951a. 'Libyan forts in south-west Cyrenaica.' *Antiquity* 25: 131–44 = 1976a : 173–86.

GOODCHILD, R. G. 1951b. 'Roman sites on the Tarhuna plateau of Tripolitania.' *PBSR* 19: 43–65 = 1976a : 72–106.

GOODCHILD, R. G. 1952a. 'Mapping Roman Libya.' *Geog. J.* 118: 142–52 = 1976a, 145–54.

GOODCHILD, R. G. 1952b. 'Farming in Roman Libya.' *Geog. Mag.* 25: 70–80.

GOODCHILD, R. G. 1952c. 'The decline of Libyan agriculture.' *Geog. Mag.* 25: 147–56.

GOODCHILD, R. G. 1952d. 'Arae Philaenorum and Automalax.' *PBSR* 20: 94–110 = 1976a: 155–72.

GOODCHILD, R. G. 1953. 'The Roman and Byzantine "limes" in Cyrenaica.' *JRS* 43: 65–76 = 1976a: 195–209.

GOODCHILD, R. G. 1954a. 'Oasis forts of "Legio III Augusta" on the routes to the Fezzan.' *PBSR* 22: 56–68 = 1976a : 46–58.

GOODCHILD, R. G. 1954b. *Tabula Imperii Romani : Lepcis Magna (sheets H.33 1.33)*. Oxford.

GOODCHILD, R. G. 1954c. *Tabula Imperii Romani : Cyrene (sheets H.34 I.34)* Oxford.

GOODCHILD, R. G. 1954d. 'La necropoli Romano-Libica di Bir ed-Dreder.' *QAL* 3 : 91–107 = 1976a, 59–71 (Eng. trans. 'The Romano-Libyan cemetery at Bir ed Dreder').

GOODCHILD, R. G. 1964. 'Medina Sultan (Charax-Iscina-Sort).' *LA* 1: 99–106 = 1976a : 133–42.

GOODCHILD, R. G. 1965. 'The unfinished imperial baths of Lepcis Magna.' *LA* 2: 15–28 = 1976a : 118–32.

GOODCHILD, R. G. 1967a. 'Byzantines, Berbers and Arabs in seventh century Libya.' *Antiquity* 41: 114–24 = 1976a: 255–67.

GOODCHILD, R. G. 1967b. 'A coin hoard from Balagrae (el-Beida) and the earthquake of A.D.365.' *LA* 3–4: 203–12 = 1976a: 229–38.

GOODCHILD, R. G. 1971. 'Roman roads in Libya and their milestones.' In Gadallah 1971 : 155–72.

GOODCHILD, R. G. 1976a. *Libyan Studies : Selected papers of the late R. G. Goodchild* (ed. J. M. Reynolds). London. (Page references in the footnotes to articles reprinted here normally relate to the reprint and not to the original publication.)

GOODCHILD, R. G. 1976b. 'Synesius of Cyrene, Bishop of Ptolemais.' In Goodchild 1976a: 239–54.

GOODCHILD, R. G. 1976c. 'Inscriptions from western Tarhuna.' In Goodchild 1976a : 107–13.

GOODCHILD, R. G. and WARD-PERKINS, J.B. 1953. 'The Roman and Byzantine defences of Lepcis Magna.' *PBSR* 21: 42–73.

GOUDIE, A. S. 1977. *Climatic change*. Oxford.

Governo della Cirenaica. Undated. *Elenco di termini topographici e di voci che entrano comunemente in uso nella toponomastica della Cirenaica.* Official publication, Benghazi.

Governo della Cirenaica 1930. *Principali comunicazioni della Cirenaica* Official publication, Benghazi.

Governo della Libia 1936. *Elenco dei nomi di località contenuti nei fogli di cui al segeunte prospetto, fasc. 1. Tripoli.* Official publication, Tripoli.

Governo della Tripolitania 1916. *Elenco dei nomi di località della Tripolitania settentrionale.* Official publication, Tripoli.

GRAZIOSI, P. 1933. 'Graffiti rupestri del Gebel Bu Ghneba nel Fezzan.' *Af Ital* V: 188–97.

GRAZIOSI, P. 1935. 'Incisioni rupestri di carri dell'uadi nel Fezzan.' *Af Ital* VI: 54–60.

GRAZIOSI, P. 1969. 'Prehistory of southern Libya.' In Kanes 1969: 3–20.

GREENE, K. 1986. *The Archaeology of the Roman Economy*. London.

GSELL, S. 1894. *Essai sur le règne de l'empereur Domitien*. Paris.

GSELL, S. 1918/1929. *Histoire ancienne de l'Afrique du nord.* 8 vols. Paris.

GSELL, S. 1925. 'L'huile de Leptis.' *Riv. della Tripolitania* 1, 1924–5; 41–6 = Gsell 1981: 151–6.

GSELL, S. 1928b. 'Connaissances géographiques des Grecs sur les côtes africaines de l'océan.' *Mémorial Henri Basset* I: 293–312 = Gsell 1981: 175–94.

GSELL, S. 1932. 'Esclaves ruraux dans l'Afrique romaine.' *Mélanges Gustave Glotz* : 397–415 = Gsell 1981: 253–71.

GSELL, S. 1933. 'La Tripolitaine et le Sahara au III siècle de notre ère.' *MAI* 43, 1: 149–66 = Gsell 1981: 157–74.

GSELL, S. 1981. *Etudes sur l'Afrique Antique, scripta varia*. Lille.

GSELL, S. *et al.* 1902. 'Enquête administrative sur les travaux hydrauliques anciens en Algérie.' *Nouvelles arch. des Missions* 10: 1–143.

GUENEAU, Capt. 1907. 'Ruines de la région de Negrine.' *BCTH* 1907: 314–35.

GUERY, R. 1986. 'Chronologie de quelques établissements de la frontière romaine du sud tunisien, à partir de la céramique collectée sur les sites.' *Limes* 13: 600–04.

GUEY, J. 1939. 'Note sur le "limes" romain de Numidie et le Sahara au IVe siècle.' *MEFR* 56: 178–248.

GUEY, J. 1950. '"Lepcitana Septimiana"' VI. *RAf* 94 : 52–83.

GUEY, J. 1951. 'Note sur Flavius Archontius Nilus et Flavius Nepotianus.' *REA* 53: 248–52.

GUIDI, G. 1929. 'La date di costruzione della basilica di Leptis Magna.' *Af Ital* 2: 231–45.

GUIDI, G. 1930. 'Il teatro romano di Sabratha.' *Af Ital* 3: 1–52.

GUIDI, G. 1933. 'La villa del Nilo.' *Af Ital* 5: 1–56.

GUIDI, G. 1935a. 'Criteri e methodi sequiti per il restauro di teatro romano a Sabratha.' *Af Ital* 6: 30–53.

GUIDI, G. 1935b. 'Orfeo, Liber Pater e Oceano in mosaici della Tripolitania.' *Af Ital* 6: 110–55.

HAFEMANN, D. 1975. 'Roman cultural landscape at about A.D.300.' *Afrika-Kartenwerk – series N, N15. Historical Geography.*

HAMMOND, N. 1965. 'The lost Roman road of Tunis and Libya.' *Illustrated London News* 10 July 1965: 27–9.

HAMMOND, N. 1967. 'The "limes Tripolitanus": a Roman road in North Africa.' *Journal of the British Archaeological Association* 3.30: 1–18.

HAMMOND, N. *et al.* 1964. *Cambridge limes Tripolitanus Expedition* (privately circulated report).

HART, D. M. 1973. 'The tribe in modern Morocco: two case studies.' In Gellner and Micaud 1973: 25–58.

HASSALL, M. W. C. 1983. 'The internal planning of Roman auxiliary forts.' In B. Hartley and J. Wacher (eds) *Rome and her northern provinces (Papers presented to Sheppard Frere)*. Sutton: 96–131.

HAYES, J. W. 1972. *Late Roman Pottery*. London.

HAYES, J. W. 1980. *A supplement to Late Roman Pottery*. London.

HAYNES, D. E. L. 1946. *A short historical and archaeological introduction to Ancient Tripolitania*. Tripoli.

HAYNES, D. E. L. 1959. *The Antiquities of Tripolitania*. Tripoli.

HAYWOOD, R. M. 1938. 'Roman Africa.' In T. Frank (ed.) *An economic survey of the Roman Empire* vol. 4: 3–119. Baltimore.

HAYWOOD, R.M. 1941. 'The oil of Leptis.' *Classical Philology* 1941: 246–56.

HERON DE VILLEFOSSE, 1894a. 'Rapport sur la mission du Lieutenant d'artillerie, H. Lecoy de la Marche, dans le sud Tunisien.' *CRAI* 1894: 469–81.

HERON DE VILLEFOSSE, 1894b. 'Inscription latine trouvée à Gourbata (Tunisie).' *CRAI* 1894: 228–32.

HEY, R. W. 1962. 'The Quaternary and Palaeolithic of northern Libya.' *Quaternaria* 6: 435–49.

HILAIRE, Capt. 1900. 'L'emplacement de Tacape.' *BCTH* 1900: 115–25.

HILAIRE, Capt. 1901. 'Note sur la voie stratégique romaine qui longeait la frontière militaire de la Tripolitaine. Essai d'identification des gîtes d'étapes de la portion de cette voie comprise entre ad Templum et Tabuinati.' *BCTH* 1901: 95–105.

HITCHNER, R.B. 1988. 'The University of Virginia-INAA Kasserine Archaeological Survey 1982–1986.' *Ant af* 24: 7–41.

HITCHNER, R.B. 1989: 'The organization of rural settlement in the Cillium-Thelepte region (Kasserine, central Tunisia).' *L'Africa romana* 6, 387–402.

HITCHNER, R.B. *et al.* 1990. 'The Kasserine Archaeological Survey 1987.' *Ant af* 26: 231–60.

HITCHNER, R.B. and Mattingly, D.J. 1991. 'Fruits of Empire. The production of olive oil in Roman Africa.' *National Geographic Research and Exploration* 7.1: 36–55.

HIVERNEL, F. 1985. 'The UNESCO Libyan Valleys Survey XI: Preliminary lithic report.' *Lib Studs* 16: 29–50.

HOLMBOE, K. 1936. *Desert Encounter. An adventurous journey through Italian Africa* (Eng. edn). London.

HOLMES, P. 1972. 'Tripolitania, Hadd Hajar.' *Lib Studs* 3: 6–7.

HOPKINS, K. 1978. *Conquerers and Slaves*. Cambridge.

HOPKINS, K. 1980. 'Taxes and trade in the Roman empire (200 BC–AD 400).' *JRS* 70: 101–25.

HOPKINS, K. 1983. 'Models, ships and staples. In P. Garnsey and C.R. Whittaker (eds) *Trade and Famine in Classical Antiquity*. Cambridge: 84–109.

HORN, H. G. and Ruger, C. B. 1980. *Die Numider*. Bonn.

HORNE, A. 1977. *A savage war of peace: Algeria 1954–1962*. London.

HUMPHREY, J.H. 1986. *Roman Circuses. Arenas for Chariot Racing*. London.

HUNT, C.O., Gale, S.J. and Gilbertson, D.D. 1985. 'The UNESCO Libyan Valleys Survey IX: Anhydrite and limestone karst in the Tripolitanian pre-desert.' *Lib Studs* 16: 1–13.

HUNT, C.O., Mattingly, D.J., Gilbertson, D.D. *et al.* 1986. 'ULVS XIII: interdisciplinary approaches to ancient farming in the Wadi Mansur, Tripolitania.' *Lib Studs* 17: 7–47.

HUNT, C.O., Gilbertson, D.D. *et al.* 1987. 'ULVS XVII: palaeoecology and agriculture of an abandonment phase at gasr Mm10, Wadi Mimoun, Tripolitania.' *Lib Studs* 18: 1–13.

IAM = Inscriptions Antiques du Maroc 2. Inscriptions Latines. (eds. M. Euzennat, J. Marion, J. Gascou, and Y. de Kisch) CNRS, Paris, 1982.

ILAf = Inscriptions Latines d'Afrique (Tripolitaine, Tunisie, Maroc) (eds R. Cagnat, A. Merlin and L. Chatelain). Paris, 1923.

ILAlg = Inscriptions Latine d'Algérie (eds S. Gsell, H. C. Pflaum *et al.*). Paris, 1922f.

ILEVBARE, J. A. 1973. 'Some aspects of social change in North Africa in Punic and Roman times.' *Museum Africum* 2: 24–40.

ILS = Inscriptiones Latinae Selectae (ed. H. Dessau). Berlin, 1892–1916.

ILT = Inscriptions Latines de la Tunisie (ed. A. Merlin). Paris, 1944.

IOPPOLO, G. 1970. 'Introduzione all'indagine stratigrafia presso l'arco di Marco Aurelio a Leptis Magna.' *LA* 6-7: 231–6.

IPT = Iscrizioni puniche della Tripolitania (1927–1967) (eds G. Levi della Vida and M. Amadasi Guzzo). Rome, 1987.

IRT = Inscriptions of Roman Tripolitania (eds J. M. Reynolds and J. B. Ward-Perkins). Rome, 1952.

ISAAC, B. 1988. 'The meaning of "limes" and "limitanei" in ancient literary sources.' *JRS* 78: 125–47.

ISAAC, B. 1990. *The Limits of Empire. The Roman Army in the East.* Oxford.

JACQUES, F. 1984. *Le privilège de liberté. Politique impériale et autonomie municiple dans les cités de l'occident romain (161–244).* Rome.

JACQUES, F. and Bousquet, B. 1984. 'Le raz du marée du 21 juillet 365.' *MEFR* 1984: 423–61.

JACQUOT, L. 1911. 'Autour de Bou Taleb.' *RSAC* 45: 273–87.

JACQUOT, L. 1915. 'Le Krett'Faraoun.' *RSAC* 49: 115–20.

JAMES, S. 1984. 'Britain and the late Roman army.' In T.F.C. Blagg and A.C. King, *Military and Civilian in Roman Britain*. BAR 136, Oxford: 161–86.

JANON, M. 1977. 'Lambèse et l'occupation militaire de la Numidie méridionale.' *Limes* 10: 473–86.

JENKINS, G. 1969. *Sylloge Nummorum Graecorum. North Africa, Syrtica, Mauretania.* Copenhagen.

JENKINS, G. K. 1974. 'Some ancient coins of Libya.' *Lib Studs* 5: 29–35.

JERARY, M. T. 1976. *The Luwata: Prolegomena, source book and preliminary study.* (Unpublished Ph.D. thesis, University of Madison, Wisconsin.)

JOHNSON, A. 1983. *Roman forts.* London.

JOHNSON, D. L. 1969. *The Nature of Nomadism.* (University of Chicago, Dept of Geography research paper no. 118.)

JOHNSON, D. L. 1973. *Jabal al-Akhdar, Cyrenaica: an historical Geography of settlement and livelihood.* (University of Chicago, Dept of Geography research paper no. 148.)

JOHNSTON, D. E. 1982. 'Some mosaics and murals in Roman Tripolitania.' In J. Liversidge (ed) *Roman Provincial wall painting of the western Empire.* BAR S. 140, Oxford: 193–208.

JOLY, E. and Tomasello, F. 1984. *Il tempio a divinita ignota di Sabratha.* (MAL XVIII), Rome.

JONES, A. H. M. 1964. *The Later Roman Empire, 284–602.* 3 vols. Oxford.

JONES, A. H. M. 1971. 'Frontier defence in Byzantine Libya.' In Gadallah 1971: 289–98.

JONES, G. D. B. 1978. 'Concept and development in Roman frontiers.' *Bull. of John Rylands Library* 1978: 115–44.

JONES, G. D. B. 1979. 'Invasion and response in Roman Britain.' In Burnham and Johnson 1979: 57–79.

JONES, G.D.B. 1984. '"Becoming different without knowing it". The role and development of "vici".' In Blagg and King 1984: 75–91.

JONES, G.D.B. 1985a. 'The Libyan Valleys Survey: the development of settlement survey.' In Buck and Mattingly 1985: 263–89.

JONES, G.D.B. 1985b. 'Beginnings and endings in Cyrenaican cities.' In Barker *et al.* 1985: 27–41.

JONES, G.D.B. 1989a. 'The development of air photography in North Africa.' In D. Kennedy (ed) *Into the Sun. Essays on Air Photography in Archaeology presented to D. Riley.* Sheffield: 25–43.

JONES, G.D.B. 1989b. 'Town and city in Tripolitania: studies in origins and development 1969–89.' *Lib Studs* 20: 91–106.

JONES, G. D. B. and Barker, G. W. W. 1980. 'Libyan Valleys Survey.' *Lib Studs* 11: 11–36.

JONES, G. D. B. and Barker, G.W.W. 1983. 'The Unesco Libyan Valleys Survey IV: the 1981 season.' *Lib Studs* 14: 39–68.

JONES, G.D.B. and Kronenburg, R. 1988. 'The Severan buildings at Lepcis Magna.' *Lib Studs* 19: 43–53.

JONES, G. D. B. and Mattingly, D. J. 1980. 'Fourth-century manning of the "Fossatum Africae".' *Britannia* 11: 323–6.

JONES, G.D.B. and Mattingly, D.J. 1990. *An Atlas of Roman Britain.* Oxford.

JONES, G. D. B. and Walker, J. 1983. 'Either side of Solway. Towards a minimalist view of Romano-British agricultural settlement in the north-west.' In J. C. Chapman and H. C. Mytum (eds) *Settlement in North Britain 1000 BC–AD 1000.* BAR 118, Oxford: 185–204.

JOPPOLO, G. 1967. 'La tavola delle unita di misura nel mercato Augusteo di Leptis Magna.' *QAL* 5: 89–98.

KÁDÁR, Z. 1972. 'Some problems concerning the scientific authenticity of classical authors on Libyan fauna.' *Acta Classica Université scient. Debrecen* 8: 11–16.

KANES, W. H. (ed) 1969. *Geology, Archaeology and Prehistory of the southwestern Fezzan, Libya* (Petroleum Exploration Society of Libya, Eleventh annual field conference 1969). Castelfranco-Veneto.

KANTER, H. 1967. *Libyen-Libya.* Berlin/New York.

KASSAM, A. 1973. 'Les pluies exceptionelles de septembre et octobre 1969 en Tunisie.' In Despois 1973: 193–218.

KEAY, S. 1992. 'Amphorae and the Roman economy.' *JRA* 5: 353–60

KEHOE, D.P. 1988. *The Economics of Agriculture on the Roman Imperial estates in North Africa.* Hypomnemata 89, Gottingen.

KENNEDY, D. L. 1982. *Archaeological explorations on the Roman frontier in north-east Jordan. The Roman and Byzantine military installations and road network on the ground and from the air.* BAR S 134, Oxford.

KENRICK, P.M. 1985a. 'Patterns of trade in fine pottery at Berenice.' In Barker *et al.* 1985: 249–57.

KENRICK, P.M. 1985b. *Excavations at Sidi Khrebish, Benghazi (Berenice) III.1. The Fine Pottery (LA Supp 5.3).* Tripoli.

KENRICK, P.M. 1985c. 'The historical development of Sabratha.' In Buck and Mattingly 1985: 1–12.

KENRICK, P.M. 1986. *Excavations at Sabratha 1948–1951. A report on the excavations conducted by Dame Kathleen Kenyon and J. Ward-Perkins.* London.

KIRK, W. 1979. 'The making and impact of the British Imperial North-west frontier in India.' In Burnham and Johnson 1979: 39–55.

KIRKWAN, L. P. 1971. 'Roman expeditions to the Upper Nile and the Chad-Darfur region.' In Gadallah 1971: 253–61.

KLITZSCH, E. and Baird, D. W. 1969. 'Stratigraphy and Palaeohydrology of the Germa (Jarma) area of southwest Libya.' In Kanes 1969: 67–80.

KOLENDO, J. 1976. *Le colonat en Afrique sur le haut empire* (reprinted 1992). Paris.

KOLENDO, J. 1986. 'Les grands domains en Tripolitaine d'après l'Itinéraire antonin.' In *Histoire et archéologie de l'Afrique du Nord III, Montpellier 1985:* 149–62. Paris.

KOTULA, T. 1974a. 'Snobisme municipal ou prosperité relative. Recherches sur le statut des villes nord-Africaines sous le Bas-Empire romain.' *Ant af* 8: 191–208.

KOTULA, T. 1974b. 'L'affaire des Emporia: problème d'histoire et de chronologie.' *Africana Bulletin* 20: 47–61.

KOTULA, T. 1976. 'Les Africains et la domination de Rome.' *DHA* 2: 337–58.

LA = Libya Antiqua, Annual of the Department of Antiquities of Libya, Tripoli.

LA Supp = Supplements to Libya Antiqua, Tripoli.

LABOLLE, M. 1933. 'L'hydraulique romaine (Bassin de l'oued Hallouf à Augarmi).' *Bull. mensuel de la Soc. Arch. Hist. et Geog. de Constantine.* 8.62, May 1933: 134–41.

LANCEL, S. 1955. 'Suburbures et Nicibes : une inscription de Tigisis.' *Libyca* 3: 289–94.

LANCEL, S. 1992. *Carthage.* Paris.

LANDER, J. 1984. *Roman Stone Fortifications. Variations and change from the first to fourth century AD.* BAR S 206, Oxford.

LARONDE, A. 1987. *Cyrène et la Libye héllenistique.* Paris.

LARONDE, A. 1988. 'Le port de Lepcis Magna.' *CRAI* 1988: 337–53.

LASSÈRE, J.-M. 1977. *Ubique Populus.*

LASSÈRE, J.-M. 1980. 'Remarques onomastiques sur la liste militaire de Vezereos (ILAf 27).' *Limes* 12: 955–75.

LASSÈRE, J.-M. 1982a. 'L'organisation des contacts de population dans l'Afrique romaine sous la Republique et au Haut-Empire.' *ANRW* II, Principat 10.2: 397–426.

LASSÈRE, J.-M. 1982b. 'Un conflit "routier": observations sur les causes de la guerre de Tacfarinas.' *Ant af* 18: 11–25.

LAVAGNANI, B. 1928. 'Epimetron, il centurione di Bu Njem.' *Rivista di Filologia* 6: 416–22.

LAW, R. C. C. 1967. 'The Garamantes and Trans-Saharan enterprise in classical times.' *Journal of African History* 8.2: 181–200.

LAW, R. C. C. 1978. 'North Africa in the Hellenistic and Roman periods, 323 BC–AD 305.' In Fage 1978: 148–210.

LAW, R.C. 1992. 'Warfare on the West African slave coast, 1650–1850.' In B. Ferguson and N. Whitehead (eds) *War in the Tribal Zone.*

Expanding States and Indigenous Warfare, School of American Research Advanced Seminar Series, Santa Fe: 103–26.

LAWLESS, R. I. 1970. *Mauretania Caesariensis: an archaeological and geographical survey.* 2 vols. (Unpublished Ph.D. thesis, Durham 1970.)

LAWLESS, R. I. 1972. 'The concept of "Tell" and "Sahara" in the Maghreb: a reappraisal.' *Trans. Inst. Br. Geog.* 57: 125–37.

LE BOEUF, Capt. 1905. 'La voie romaine de Tacapes à Aquae Tacapitanae.' *BCTH* 1905: 346–50.

LE BOHEC, Y. 1978. 'Les auxiliaires de la troisième légion Auguste.' *BCTH* n.s.12–14, 1976–1978: 109–22.

LE BOHEC, Y. 1980. 'Un nouveau type d'unité connu par l'épigraphie africaine.' *Limes* 12: 945–54.

LE BOHEC, Y. 1986a. 'Encore les "numeri collati".' *L'Africa romana* 3: 233–41.

LE BOHEC, Y. 1986b. 'La stratégie de Rome en Afrique de 238–284.' In *Histoire et archéologie de l'Afrique du Nord, 3e Colloque International Montpellier.* Paris: 377–90.

LE BOHEC, Y. 1987. 'Les syriens dans l'Afrique romaine, civils ou militaires?' *Karthago* 21: 81–92.

LE BOHEC, Y. 1989a. *La IIIe Légion Auguste.* Paris.

LE BOHEC, Y. 1989b. *Les unites auxiliaires de l'armée romaine dans les provinces d'Afrique Proconsulaire et de Numidie.* Paris.

LE BOHEC, Y. 1989c. 'Inscriptions inédites ou corrigées concernant l'armée romaine d'Afrique.' *Ant af* 25: 191–226.

LECOY DE LA MARCHE, H. 1894. 'Recherche d'une voie romaine du Golfe de Gabes vers Rhadames.' *BCTH* 1894: 389–413.

LEFRANC, J.–P. 1986. 'La géologie, Pliné l'Ancien et l'histoire de Cornelius Balbus (20 avant J.C.). Nouvelles identifications.' *Histoire et archéologie de l'Afrique du Nord* 3: 303–16.

LEGLAY, M. 1966. *Saturne Africain histoire.* Bibliothèque des écoles françaises d'Athènes et de Rome, fasc. 205). Paris.

LEGLAY, M. 1968. 'Les Flaviens et l'Afrique.' *MEFR* 80: 201–46.

LEPELLEY, C. 1967. 'Déclin ou stabilité de l'agriculture africaine au Bas Empire.' *Ant af* 1: 135–44.

LEPELLEY, C. 1974. 'La préfecture de tribu dans l'Afrique du Bas-Empire.' *Mélanges W. Seston*: 285–95.

LEPELLEY, C. 1979. *Les cités de l'Afrique romaine au Bas-Empire. I, La permanence municipal.* Paris.

LEPELLEY, C. 1981a. *Les cités de l'Afrique romaine au Bas-Empire. II, Notices d'histoire municipal.* Paris.

LEPELLEY, C. 1981b. 'Le crise de l'Afrique romaine au début du Ve siècle d'après les lettres nouvellement découverts de Saint Augustin.' *CRAI* 1981: 445–46.

LEPELLEY, C. 1984. 'L'Afrique du nord et le prétendu séisme universel du 21 juillet 365.' *MEFR* 1984: 463–91.

LEQUEMENT, R. 1980. 'Le vin africain à l'époque imperiale.' *Ant af* 16: 185–93.

LESCHI, L. 1942. 'Rome et les nomades du Sahara central.' *Travaux de l'Institut de Recherches Sahariennes* 1 : 47–62 = 1957 : 65–74.

LESCHI, L. 1943. 'Le centenarium de Aqua Viva.' *RAf* 87: 5–22 = 1957: 47–57.

LESCHI, L. 1947. 'La vigne et le vin dans l'Afrique ancienne.' *Bulletin économique et juridique de l'O.F.A.L.A.C.*: 101–04 = 1957: 80–84.

LESCHI, L. 1948. 'Une assignation des terres sous Septime Sévère.' *RSAC* 66: 103–16 = 1957 : 75–9.

LESCHI, L. 1949. 'Découvertes épigraphiques dans le camp de Gemellae (El Kasbat, Algérie).' *CRAI* 1959: 220–26 = 1957: 318–24.

LESCHI, L. 1953. 'Inscriptions Latine de Lambèse et de Zana.' *Libyca* 1: 189–205.

LESCHI, L. 1957. *Etudes d'épigraphie d'archéologie et d'histoire africaines.* Paris.

LEVEAU, P. 1978. 'La situation coloniale de l'Afrique romaine.' *Annales E.S.C.* 33: 89–92.

LEVEAU, P. 1984. *Caesarea de Maurétanie: une ville romaine et ses campagnes.* (Collection de l'Ecole Française de Rome 70) Paris/Rome.

LEVI DELLA VIDA, G. 1927. 'Le iscrizioni neopuniche della Tripolitania.' *Rivista della Tripolitania* 3: 91–116.

LEVI DELLA VIDA, G. 1935. 'Due iscrizioni imperiali neopuniche di Leptis Magna.' *Af Ital* 6: 1–29.

LEVI DELLA VIDA, G. 1949. 'Iscrizioni neopuniche di Tripolitania.' *Rendiconti della classe di scienze morali, storiche e filologiche.* Series 8.4: 399–412.

LEVI DELLA VIDA, G. 1951. 'The neo-Punic dedication of the Ammonium at Ras el-Haddagia.' *PBSR* 19: 65–8 = Goodchild 1976a: 93–6.

LEVI DELLA VIDA, G. 1963. 'Sulle iscrizioni "Latino-Libiche" della Tripolitania.' *Oriens Antiquus* 2: 65–94.

LEVI DELLA VIDA, G. 1964a. 'Le iscrizioni neopuniche di wadi el-Amud,' *LA* 1, 57–63

LEVI DELLA VIDA, G. 1964b. 'Ostracon neopunico della Tripolitania.' *Orientalia* 33: 1–14.

LEVI DELLA VIDA, G. 1965. 'Parerga neopunica.' *Oriens Antiquus* 4: 59–72.

LEVI DELLA VIDA and Guzzo 1987. See *IPT*.

LEZINE, A. 1972. 'Tripoli. Notes archéologiques.' *LA* 5 (1968) [1972]: 55–67.

LHOTE, H. 1954. 'L'expédition de Cornelius Balbus au Sahara.' *RAf* 98: 41–81.

LHOTE, H. 1982. *Les chars rupestres Sahariennes, des Syrte au Niger par le pays du Garamantes et des Atlantes.* Toulouse.

Lib Studs. = *Libyan Studies. Annual Report of the Society for Libyan Studies*, London.

Limes 1 = E. Birley (ed.) *Congress of Roman Frontier Studies, 1949.* Durham, 1952.

Limes 2 = E. Swoboda (ed.) *Carnuntina. Ergebnisse der Forschung über die Grenzprovinzen des römischen Reiches:Vortrage bein internationalen Kongress der Altertumsforscher Carnuntum 1955.* Cologne, 1956.

Limes 3 = *Limes Studien: vortrage des III intern. Limes-Kongress in Rheinfelden, Basel 1957.* 1959.

Limes 5 = *Quintus Congressus Internationalis Limitis Romani Studiosorum.* Zagreb, 1963.

Limes 6 = *Studien zu den Militargrenzen Roms: Vortrage des 6. Internationalen Limes Kongress in Sud-deutschland.* Cologne, 1967.

Limes 7 = *Roman Frontier Studies, 7th Congress.* Tel Aviv, 1971.

Limes 8 = E. Birley, B. Dobson and M. Jarrett (eds) *Roman Frontier Studies 1969, 8th International Congress of Limesforschung.* Cardiff, 1974.

Limes 9 = D. M. Pippidi (ed.) *Actes du IX congrès international d'études sur les frontières romaines, Mamia 6–13th septembre 1972.* Bucharest/Cologne, 1974.

Limes 10 = *Studien zu den Militärgrenzen Roms II: Vortrage des 10 Internationalen Limeskongress in der Germania inferior.* Cologne, 1977.

Limes 11 = Fitz (ed.) *Acten des Internationalen Limeskongress, 1976.* Budapest, 1977.

Limes 12 = W.S. Hanson and L. J. F. Keppie (eds) *Roman Frontier Studies 1979. Papers presented to the 12th International Congress of Roman frontier studies.* 3 vols. BAR S.71, Oxford, 1980.

Limes 13 = *Acten des 13 Internationalen Limeskongresses Aalen, Sept. 1983.* Stuttgart, 1986.

Limes 14 = *Der römischen limes in Osterreich. Akten des 14 Internationalen Limeskongress 1986 in Carnuntum.* Vienna, 1990.

LLOYD, J. A. (ed.) 1977. *Excavations at Sidi Khrebish, Benghazi (Berenice) I.* (*LA* Supp 5.1). Tripoli.

LLOYD, J. A. (ed.) 1979. *Excavations at Sidi Khrebish, Benghazi (Berenice) II.* (*LA* Supp 5.2). Tripoli.

LORIOT, X. 1971. 'Une dédicace à Gordian III provvenant de Gheria el-Garbia.' *BSAF* 1971: 342–6.

LORIOT, X. 1975. 'Les premières années de la grand crise du IIIe siècle.' *ANRW* 2.2: 745–53.

LOUIS, A. 1969. 'Aux Matmata et dans les ksars du sud. L'olivier et les hommes.' *Cahiers des Arts et Traditions Populaires* 3: 41–66.

LOUIS, A. 1973. 'Kalaa, ksour de montagne et ksour de plaine dans le sud-est Tunisien.' In Despois 1973: 257–70.

LOUIS, A. 1975. *Tunisie du sud. Ksars et villages de crêtes.* CNRS, Paris.

LUNI, M. 1979. 'Il caravanserraglio di Cirene ed indagine preliminare sui percorsi interni della Cirenaica.' *QAL* 10: 49–65.

LUNI, M. 1980. 'Apporti nuovi nel quadro della viabilità antica della Cirenaica interna.' *QAL* 11: 119–37.

LUTTWAK, E. N. 1976. *The Grand Strategy of the Roman Empire.* Baltimore/London.

LYON, G. F. 1821. *A narrative of travels in North Africa in the years 1818, 1819 and 1820.* London.

MABRUK, G., Di Vita, A and Garbini, G. 1988. 'La tomba del "defunto eroizzato" a Sabratha.' *LA* 15–16 (1978–9) [1988]: 45–67.

MACKENDRICK, P. 1980. *The North African stones speak.* London.

MAHJOUBI, A. and Salama, P. 1981. 'The Roman and post-Roman period in North Africa.' In G. Mokhtar (ed.) *General History of Africa II. Ancient civilisations of Africa.* UNESCO/Heinemann, London: 465–512.

MAHJUB, O. 1984. 'I mosaici della villa Romana di Silin.' *III Colloquio Internazionale sul mosaico antico, Ravenna 1980.* Girasole, Ravenna: 299–306.

MAHJUB, O. 1988. 'I mosaici della villa Romana di Silin.' *LA* 15–16 (1978–9)[1988]: 69–74.

MAI = Mémoires de l'Institut National de France, Académie des Inscriptions et Belles Lettres. Paris.

MANACORDA, D. 1977a. 'Testimoniaze sulla produzione e il consumo dell'olio tripolitano nell III secolo.' *Dialoghi di Archeologia* 9–10.1–2: 542–601.

MANACORDA, D. 1977b. 'Anfore.' *Ostia* 4 (= *Studi Miscellani* 23): 117–254.

MANACORDA, D. 1983. 'Prosopografia e anfore Tripolitane: nuove osservazioni.' In *Produccion 1983:* 483–500.

MANN, J. C. 1974a. 'The frontiers of the Principate.' *ANRW* II.l: 508–33.

MANN, J. C. 1974b. 'The Northern frontier after AD 369.' *Glasgow Archaeological Journal* 3: 34–42.

MANN, J. C. 1979a. 'Power, force and the frontiers of the Empire' (review article of Luttwak 1976). *JRS* 69: 175–83.

MANN, J. C. 1979b. 'Hadrian's Wall: the last phases.' In Casey 1979: 144–51.

MANNING, W. H. 1975. 'Economic influences on land use in the military areas of the Highland zone during the Roman period.' In J. G. Evans, S. Limbrey and H. Cleere (eds.) *The Effect of Man on the Landscape: the Highland Zone* (CBA Research Report 11). London: 112–116.

MANTON, E.L. 1988. *Roman North Africa.* London.

MARICHAL, R. 1979. 'Les ostraca de Bu Njem.' *CRAI* 1979: 436–52.

MARICHAL, R. 1992. *Les Ostraca du Bu Njem. LA* Supp 7, Tripoli.

MARION, J. 1957. 'Les ruines anciennes de la région d'Oujda (dit du Ras Asfour).' *BAM* 2: 117–73.

MARION, J. 1959. 'L'éperon fortifié de sidi-Medjahed (Oranie).' *Libyca* 7: 27–41.

MARTEL, A. 1968. *Les confins Saharo-tripolitains de la Tunisie (1881–1911).* 2 vols. Paris.

MATTHEWS, J. 1976. 'Mauretania in Ammianus and the Notitia.' In P. Bartholemew and R. Goodburn (eds) *Aspects of the Notitia Dignitatum.* BAR S15, Oxford: 157–86.

MATTHEWS, J. 1989. *The Roman Empire of Ammianus.* London.

MATTINGLY, D. J. 1982. 'The Roman road-station at Thenadassa (Ain Wif).' *Lib Studs* 13: 73–80.

MATTINGLY, D. J. 1983. 'The Laguatan: a Libyan tribal confederation in the late Roman Empire.' *Lib Studs* 14: 96–108.

MATTINGLY, D.J. 1984. *Tripolitania: a comparative study of a Roman frontier province.* (Unpublished Ph.D. thesis, University of Manchester.)

MATTINGLY, D.J. 1985a. 'Olive oil production in Roman Tripolitania.' In Buck and Mattingly 1985: 27–46.

MATTINGLY, D.J. 1985b. 'IRT 895 and 896: two inscriptions from Gheriat el-Garbia.' *Lib Studs* 16: 67–75.

MATTINGLY, D.J. 1986. 'Soldier or civilian? Urbanisation on the frontiers of Roman Africa.' *Popular Archaeology* Dec. 1985/Jan. 1986: 61–6.

MATTINGLY, D.J. 1987a. 'New perspectives on the agricultural development of Gebel and pre-desert in Roman Tripolitania.' *Revue de l'Occident Musulman et de la Mediterranée* 41–2: 45–65.

MATTINGLY, D.J. 1987b. 'Libyans and the "limes": culture and society in Roman Tripolitania.' *Ant af* 23: 71–94.

MATTINGLY, D.J. 1988a. 'Megalithic madness and measurement. Or how many olives could an olive press press?' *Oxford Journal of Archaeology* 7.2: 177–95.

MATTINGLY, D.J. 1988b. 'The olive boom. Oil surpluses, wealth and power in Roman Tripolitania.' *Lib Studs* 19: 21–41.

MATTINGLY, D.J. 1988c. 'Oil for export: a comparative study of Roman olive oil production in Libya, Spain and Tunisia.' *JRA* 1: 33–56.

MATTINGLY, D.J. 1988d. 'Olea Mediterranea?' *JRA* 1: 153–61.

MATTINGLY, D.J. 1989a. 'Field survey in the Libyan Valleys.' *JRA* 2: 275–80.

MATTINGLY, D.J. 1989b. 'Farmers and frontiers. Exploiting and defending the countryside of Roman Tripolitania.' *Lib Studs:* 135–53

MATTINGLY, D.J. 1989c. 'Ancient olive cultivation and the Albertini Tablets.' *L'Africa romana* 6: 403–15

MATTINGLY, D.J. 1991. 'The constructor of Gasr Duib, Numisius Maximus, trib(unus Cohortis I Syrorum sagittariorum).' *Ant af* 27: 75–82.

MATTINGLY, D.J. 1992. 'War and peace in Roman Africa. Some observations and models of State/Tribe interaction.' In B. Ferguson and N. Whitehead (eds) *War in the Tribal Zone. Expanding States and Indigenous Warfare,* School of American Research Advanced Seminar Series, Santa Fe: 31–60.

MATTINGLY, D.J. 1993. 'Maximum figures and maximizing strategies of oil production? Further thoughts on the processing capacity of Roman olive presses.' In M.–C. Amouretti and J.–P. Brun (eds) *La production du vin et de l'huile en Méditerranée .* Paris: 483–97.

MATTINGLY, D.J., Barker, G.W.W and Jones, G.D.B. Forthcoming. 'Architecture, technology and society: Romano-Libyan settlement in the Wadi Umm-el Agerem.' In Sandro Stucchi papers.

MATTINGLY, D.J. and Hayes, J.W. 1992. 'Nador: a fortified farm in Algeria.' *JRA* 5: 408–18.

MATTINGLY, D.J. and Hitchner, R.B. 1993. 'Technical specifications of some North African olive presses of Roman date.' In M.–C. Amouretti and J.–P. Brun (eds) *La production du vin et de l'huile en Méditerranée:.* Paris: 439–62.

MATTINGLY, D.J. and Jones, G.D.B. 1986. 'A new "clausura" in western Tripolitania: Wadi Skiffa south.' *Lib Studs* 17: 87–96.

MATTINGLY, D.J. and Zenati, M. 1984. 'The excavation of building Lm 4E: the olive press.' In Barker and Jones 1984: 13–18, 21–2.

MAUNY, R. 1956. 'Monnaies antiques trouvées en Afrique au sud du "limes" romain.' *Libyca* 4: 249–60.

MAYERSON, P. 1962. 'The ancient agricultural regime of Nessana and the central Negeb.' In H.D. Colt (ed.), *Excavations at Nessana (Anjia Hafir, Palestine)* I, 211–69. London.

MEIGGS, R. 1973. *Roman Ostia.* Oxford.

MEFR = Mélanges de l'école française de Rome, Antiquités (1971f). Formerly *Mélanges d'archéologie et d'histoire de l'école française de Rome.*

Mélanges Piganiol = Mélanges d'archéologie et d'histoire offerts à Andre Piganiol (ed. R. Chevalier). Paris, 1966.

Mélanges W. Seston = Mélanges d'histoire ancienne offerts à W. Seston. Paris, 1974.

MERCIER, M. 1953. 'Les idoles de Ghadames.' *RAf* 97: 17–47.

MERIGHI, A. 1940. *La Tripolitania antica.* 2 vols. Verbania.

MERLIN, A. 1909. 'Inscriptions Latines nouvellement découvertes en Tunisie.' *CRAI* 1909: 91–101.

MERLIN, A. 1921. 'Le fortin de Bezereos sur le "limes" Tripolitain.' *CRAI* 1921: 236–49.

MERLIN, A. 1944. See *ILT.*

MILLAR, F. 1968. 'Local cultures in the Roman Empire: Libyan, Punic and Latin in Roman Africa.' *JRS* 58: 126–34.

MILLER, K. 1887. *Die Weltkarte des Castorius gennant die Peutingersche Tafel.* 2 vols. Ravensburg.

MILLER, K. 1916. *Itineraria Romana. Römische Reisewege an der hand der Tabula Peutingeriana* (reprint, 1962). Stuttgart.

MILLETT, M. 1990. *The Romanization of Britain. An essay in archaeological interpretation.* Cambridge.

MILLS, A. J. 1980a. 'The Dakhleh oasis project. Report on the second season of survey'. *The SSEA Journal* 10.4: 251–82.

MILLS, A. J. 1980b. 'Lively paintings. Roman frescoes in the Dakhleh oasis.' *Rotunda* 13, 2. Toronto.

MIRO, E. de and Fiorentini, G. 1977. 'Leptis Magna. La necropoli Greco-Punica sotto il teatro.' *QAL* 9: 5–75.

MONLEZUN, Capt. 'Les ruines de Tacape (Gabes).' *BCTH* 1885: 126–31.

MONOD, T. 1974. 'Le mythe de "l'émeraude des Garamantes".' *Ant af* 8: 51–66.

MOORE, M. 1940. *Fourth shore. Italy's mass colonisation of Libya*. London.

MOOREHEAD, A. 1960. *The White Nile*. London.

MOREAU, P. 1904. 'Le castellum de Ras-oued-el-Gordab, près de Ghoumrassen.' *BCTH* 1904: 369–76.

MOREAU, P. 1947. *Les lacs de sel aux chaos de sable. Le Pays des Nefzaouas*. Tunis.

MORI, F. 1969. 'Prehistoric cultures in Tadrart Acacus, Libyan Sahara.' In Kanes 1969: 21–30.

MSAF = Mémoires de la Societé Nationale des Antiquaires de France.

MYRES, J. L. 1899. 'On the age and purpose of the megalithic structures of Tripoli and Barbary.' *Proceedings Society Antiq*, Jan 1899: 280–93.

NACHTIGAL, G. 1879. *Sahara und Sudan* (reprint, 1967). Graz.

NACHTIGAL, G. 1974. *Sahara and Sudan* Vol I (= Nachtigal 1879, translated from the German by A.G.B. and H. J. Fisher). London.

NAPOLI, J. and Rebuffat, R. 1983. 'Clausurae.' *Cah. Armée Romaine et les Provinces* (ed. prov., tirage limité).

Not.Dig. = Notitia Dignitatum accedunt Notitia urbis Constantinopolitanae et Laterculoa Provinciarum, ed. O. Seeck. Frankfurt, 1876 (reprint, 1962).

Nouvelles arch. des Missions = Nouvelles archives des missions scientifiques et littéraires. Paris.

NYOP, R. F. *et al.* 1973. *Area Handbook for Libya*. Foreign Area Studies, Washington.

OATES, D. 1953. 'The Tripolitanian Gebel: settlement of the Roman period around Gasr ed-Daun.' *PBSR* 21: 81–117.

OATES, D. 1954. 'Ancient settlement in the Tripolitanian Gebel, II: the Berber period.' *PBSR* 22: 91–117.

OLIVER, J. H. 1972. 'Text of the "Tabula Banasitana", A.D.177.' *AJPh* 93: 336–40.

OLIVER, R. (ed.) 1978. *The Cambridge History of Africa, III: c. A.D.1050–1600*. Cambridge .

OLIVER, R. 1979. 'Colonization and Decolonization in tropical Africa 1885–1965.' In Burnham and Johnson 1979: 13–23.

OLIVER, R. and Fagan, B. M. 1975. *Africa in the Iron Age, c. 500 B.C.–A.D.1400*. Cambridge.

PACE, P., Sergi, S. and Caputo, G. 1951. 'Scavi Sahariani.' *Monumenti Antichi* 41: 150–549.

PALLU DE LESSERT, A. C. 1896/1901. *Fastes des provinces africaines (Proconsulaire, Numidie, Maurétanies) sous la domination romaine, I: République et Haut Empire. II Bas-Empire*. Paris.

PANELLA, C. 1968. 'Anfore.' In *Ostia* 1 (= *Studi Miscellani* 13): 97–134.

PANELLA, C. 1972. 'Annotazioni in margine alle stratigrafie delle Terme Ostiensi del Nuotatore.' In *Recherches sur les amphores romaines*. (Collection Ecole Française de Rome 10): 69–106.

PANELLA, C. 1973. 'Anfore.' In *Ostia* 3 (= *Studi Miscellani* 21): 460–696.

PANELLA, C. 1977. 'Anfore Tripolitaine a Pompei.' In Carandini 1977: 135–49.

PANELLA, C. 1983. 'I contenitori oleari presenti ad Ostia in età antonina: analisi tipologica, epigrafica, quantitativa.' In *Produccion* 1983: 226–61.

PANELLA, C. 1986. 'Le anfore tardoantiche: centri di produzione e mercati preferenziali.' In Giardina 1986: 251–84.

PARIBENI, R. 1927. 'Sepolcreto cristiano di Engila presso Suanni Beni Adem.' *Af Ital* 1: 75–82.

PARKER, A.J. 1992. *Ancient Shipwrecks of the Mediterranean and Roman Provinces*. BAR S 580, Oxford.

PASKOFF, R., Slim, H. and Trousset, P. 1991. 'Le littoral de la Tunisie dans l'antiquité: cinq ans de recherches géoarchéologiques.' *CRAI* 1991: 515–46.

Pauly-Wissowa = Paulys Real-Encyclopädie der classischen Altertumswissenschaft. Neue Bearbeitung begonnen von Georg Wissowa. Stuttgart and Munich, 1893f.

PAVIS D'ESCURAC, H. 1974. 'Pour une étude sociale de l'Apologie d'Apulée.' *Ant af* 8: 89–101.

PBSR = Papers of the British School at Rome.

PEACOCK, D.P.S. and Williams, D.F. 1986. *Amphorae and the Roman Economy. An introductory guide*. Harlow.

PEACOCK, D.P.S., Bejaoui, F. and Belazreg, N. 1989. 'Roman amphora production in the Sahel region of Tunisia.' *Amphores* 1989: 179–222.

PEACOCK, D.P.S., Bejaoui, F. and Ben Lazreg, N. 1990. 'Roman pottery production in central Tunisia.' *JRA* 3: 59–84.

PENROSE, E., Allan, J. A. and McLachlan, K. S. (eds) 1970. *Agriculture and the Economic development of Libya*. 4 vols. (Libyan–London Universities Joint Research Project.) London.

PENSABENE, P. 1990. 'Il tempio di Saturno a Dougga e tradizioni architettoniche d'origine punica.' *L'Africa romana* 7: 251–93.

PERCIVAL, J. 1976. *The Roman Villa*. London.

PERICAUD, Lt. 1905. 'La "turris Maniliorum Arelliorum" dans le massif des Matmata (Tunisie).' *BCTH* 1905: 259–69.

PESCE, E. 1969. 'Exploration of the Fezzan.' In Kanes 1969: 53–65.

PETRAGNARNI, E. 1928. *Il Sahara Tripolitano*. Rome.

PETRIKOVITS, H. von. 1971. 'Fortifications in the North-western Roman Empire from the third to the fifth centuries A.D.' *JRS* 61: 178–218.

PEYRAS, J. 1975. 'Le "fundus aufidianus": étude d'un grand domaine romain de la région de Mactar (Tunisie du nord).' *Ant af* 9: 181–22.

PEYRAS, J. and Trousset, P. 1988. 'Le "lac Tritonis" et les noms antiques du Chott el Jerid.' *Ant af* 24: 149–204.

PFLAUM, H. G. 1950. *Les procurateurs équestres sous l' Haut-Empire romain*. Paris.

PFLAUM, H. G. 1959. 'Nomenclature de Leptis Magna et de Lepti Minus.' *BSAF* 1959: 85–92 = 1978: 199–206.

PFLAUM, H. G. 1960/1961. *Les carrières procuratoriennes équestres sous l'Haut Empire romain*. 3 vols. Paris.

PFLAUM, H. G. 1978. *Afrique Romain. Scripta Varia* I. Paris.

PICARD, G. C. 1944. *Castellum Dimmidi*. Algiers.

PICARD, G. C. 1956. 'Néron et le blé d'Afrique.' *CT* 4: 163–73.

PICARD, G. C. 1959. *La civilisation de l'Afrique romaine*. Paris.

PICARD, G.C. 1985. 'La villa du Taureau à Silin (Tripolitaine).' *CRAI* 1985: 227–41.

PICARD, G.C. 1986. 'Banlieues de villes dans l'Afrique romaine.' In *Histoire et archéologie de l'Afrique du Nord III, Montpellier 1985*: 143–8.

PINDER, M. and Parthey, G. 1860. *Ravennatis Anonymi Cosmographia et Guidonis Geographia*. Berlin.

PISANU, M. 1990. 'La vita religiosa a Gigthis: testimonianze epigrafiche e monumentali.' *L'Africa romana* 7: 223–31.

POINSSOT, L. 1937. 'Communication.' *BCTH* 1936–7: 321–5.

POINSSOT, L. 1940. 'Sur une maison romaine de Bezereos.' *BCTH* 1939–40: 259.

Polservice 1980. *Tripoli Region. Existing conditions and evaluation of development potentials* Vol l, report 2. Warsaw.

PONCET, J. 1963. *Paysages et problèmes ruraux en Tunisie*. Paris.

PONSICH, M. 1988. *Aceite de oliva y salazónes de pescado. Factores geo-económicos de Bética y Tingitania*. Madrid.

PRÉCHEUR-CANONGE, T. 1962. *La vie rurale en Afrique du nord d'après les mosaiques*. Tunis.

PRINGLE, D. 1981. *The Defence of Byzantine Africa from Justinian to the Arab Conquest*. 2 vols. BAR S.99, Oxford.

PRIVÉ, Capt. 1895. 'Notes archéologiques sur l'Aarad, le Madjourah et le Cherb.' *BCTH* 1895: 78–132.

Produccion 1980 = Produccion y Comercio del aceite en la Antigüedad. Primer Congreso Internacional. Univ. Complutense, Madrid.

Produccion 1983 = Produccion y Comercio del aceite en la Antigüedad. Segundo Congreso Internacional. Univ. Complutense, Madrid.

PROST, G. 1954a. 'Utilisation de la terre et production dans le sud Tunisien: Matmata et Ouderna.' *CT* 2: 28–66.

PROST, G. 1954b. 'Habitat et habitation chez les Ouderna et les Matmata.' *CT* 2: 239–531.

QAL = Quaderni di Archeologia della Libia. Rome.

RACHET, M. 1970. *Rome et les Berbères. Un problème militaire d'Auguste à Diocletian*. Brussels.

RAf = Revue Africaine. Journal des travaux de la societé historique Algérienne.

RAL = Rendiconti della classe di Scienze morali, storiche e filologiche dell' Accademia dei Lincei, Rome.

RATHBONE, D.W. 1981. 'The development of agriculture in the "ager Cosanus" during the Roman Republic: problems of evidence and interpretation.' *JRS* 71: 10–23.

RAVEN, S. 1993. *Rome in Africa*. (3rd edn.) London.

REBUFFAT, R. 1967a = Rebuffat, R., Deneauve, J. and Hallier, G. 1967. 'Bu Njem 1967.' *LA* 3–4:49–137.

REBUFFAT, R. 1967b. 'Les erreurs de Pliné et la position de "Babba Iulia campestris".' *Ant af* 1: 31–57.

REBUFFAT, R. 1969. 'Deux ans de recherches dans le sud de la Tripolitaine.' *CRAI* 1969: 189–212.

REBUFFAT, R. 1970a = Rebuffat, R., Gassend, J. M., Guery, R. and Hallier, G. 1970. 'Bu Njem 1968.' *LA* 6–7: 9–105.

REBUFFAT, R. 1970b. 'Bu Njem 1970.' *LA* 6–7: 107–65.

REBUFFAT, R. 1970c. 'Zella et les routes d'Egypte.' *LA* 6–7: 181–7.

REBUFFAT, R. 1970d. 'Routes d'Egypte de la Libya interieure.' *Studi Magrebini* 3: 1–20.

REBUFFAT, R. 1971a. 'Notes sur les confins de la Maurétanie Tingitane et de la Maurétanie Césarienne.' *Studi Magrebini* 4: 33–64.

REBUFFAT, R. 1971b. 'Recherches en Tripolitaine du sud.' *Rev. Arch.* 1971 n.s.2: 177–84.

REBUFFAT, R. 1972a. 'Nouvelles recherches dans le sud de la Tripolitaine.' *CRAI* 1972: 319–39.

REBUFFAT, R. 1972b. 'Les fouilles de Thamusida et leur contribution à l'histoire du Maroc.' *BAM* 8 : 51–65.

REBUFFAT, R. 1973a. 'Les inscriptions des portes de Bu Njem.' *LA* 9–10: 99–120.

REBUFFAT, R. 1973b. 'L'arrivée des romains à Bu Njem.' *LA* 9–10: 121–34.

REBUFFAT, R. 1973c. 'Gholaia.' *LA* 9–10: 135–45.

REBUFFAT, R. 1975a. 'Graffiti en Libyque de Bu Njem.' *LA* 11–12: 165–87.

REBUFFAT, R. 1975b. 'Bu Njem 1971.' *LA* 11–12: 189–242.

REBUFFAT, R. 1975c. 'Trois nouvelles campagnes dans le sud de la Tripolitaine.' *CRAI* 19 75: 495–505.

REBUFFAT, R. 1975d. 'Les principia du camp romain de Lalla Djilaliya (Tabernae).' *BAM* 9: 359–76.

REBUFFAT, R. 1975e. 'Au delà des camps romains.' *BAM* 9 : 377–408.

REBUFFAT, R. 1977a. 'Bu Njem 1972.' *LA* 13–14: 37–77.

REBUFFAT, R. 1977b. 'Dix ans de recherches dans le prédesert de Tripolitaine.' *LA* 13–14: 79–91.

REBUFFAT, R. 1977c. 'Une zone militaire et sa vie économique: le "limes" de Tripolitaine.' *Colloques Nationaux du CNRS 936: Armées et Fiscalité dans le monde antique*. Paris: 395–419.

REBUFFAT, R. 1978. 'Végèce et la télégraphe Chappe.' *MEFR* 90–1978–2: 829–861.

REBUFFAT, R. 1979. 'La frontière romaine en Afrique, Tripolitaine et Tingitaine.' *Ktema. Civilisations de l'Orient, de la Grèce et de Rome Antique* 4:225–47.

REBUFFAT, R. 1980a. 'A propos du "limes Tripolitanus".' *Rev Arch* 1980, 1: 105–24.

REBUFFAT, R. 1980b. 'Cuicul le 21 juillet 365.' *Ant af* 15: 309–28.

REBUFFAT, R. 1980c. 'Le fossé romain de Sala.' *BAM* 12: 237–58.

REBUFFAT, R. 1981. 'L'ouvrage linéaire romain de Rabat (Maroc).' *Caesarodunum. Bull. de l'Institut Latines et du centre de recherches A. Piganiol XVI, Actes du colloque: frontières en Gaule*: 210–22.

REBUFFAT, R. 1982a. 'Au-delà des camps romains d'Afrique mineure, renseignement, contrôle, pénétration.' *ANRW*, II. Principat. 10.2: 474–513.

REBUFFAT, R. 1982b. '"Ara Cerei".' *MEFR* 94–1982–2: 911–19.

REBUFFAT, R. 1982c. 'Recherches dans le désert de Libye.' *CRAI* 1982: 188–99.

REBUFFAT, R. 1984. 'Propunacula.' *Latomus* 43.1: 3–26.

REBUFFAT, R. 1985a. 'L'arrivée des romains en Tripolitaine intérieure.' *BCTH* n.s. 19, fasc. B [1985]: 249–56.

REBUFFAT, R. 1985b. 'Le "limes" de Tripolitaine.' In Buck and Mattingly 1985: 127–41.

REBUFFAT, R. 1985c. 'Les centurions de Gholaia.' *L'Africa romana* 2: 225–38.

REBUFFAT, R. 1986. 'Un banquier à Lepcis Magna.' *L'Africa romana*. 3: 179–87.

REBUFFAT, R. 1987. 'Le poème de Q. Avidius Quintianus à la déesse Salus.' *Karthago* 21: 93–105.

REBUFFAT, R. 1988a. 'L'inscription de l'ara cerei.' *LA* 15–16 (1978–9) [1988]: 113–24.

REBUFFAT, R. 1988b. 'L'inscription du limes de Tripolitaine.' *LA* 15–16 (1978–9) [1988]

REBUFFAT, R. 1988c. 'Les fermiers du desert.' *L'Africa romana* 5: 33–68.

REBUFFAT, R. 1989. 'Le camp romain de Gholaia (Bu Njem).' *Lib Studs* 20: 155–67.

REBUFFAT, R. 1990a. 'Nomadisme et archéologie.' In *L'Afrique dans l'Occident romain*. CEFR 134, Rome: 231–47.

REBUFFAT, R. 1990b. 'Divinités de l'oued Kebir.' *L'Africa romana* 7: 119–59.

REBUFFAT, R. 1990c. 'Où étaient les Emporia?' In *Mélanges Sznycer* II: 111–26.

REBUFFAT, R. and Hallier, G. 1970. *Thamusida* II. Paris.

REBUFFAT, R. and Marichal, R. 1973. 'Les ostraca de Bu Njem.' *REI* 51: 281–6.

REDDÉ, M. 1985. 'Occupation humaine et mise en valeur économique dans les vallées de la Libye: l'exemple de la wadi Tlal.' *BCTH* n.s. 19B: 173–82.

REDDÉ, R. 1988. *Prospections des vallées du nord de la libye (1979–1980). La région de Syrte à l'époque romaine*. (Armée romaine et les provinces IV.) Paris.

REESE, D. S. 1980. 'Industrial exploitation of murex shells: purple dye and lime production at Sidi-Krebish, Benghazi (Berenice).' *Lib Studs* 11:79–93.

REINACH, S. and Babelon, E. 1886. 'Recherches archéologiques en Tunisie.' *BCTH* 1886: 4–78.

RENAULT, H. 1901. 'Note sur l'inscription de Ras el Ain et le limes tripolitain à la fin du 3e siècle.' *BCTH* 1901: 429–37.

Reports and Monographs = Reports and Monographs of the Department of Antiquities in Tripolitania. British Military Administration, Tripoli.

REYGASSE, M. 1950. *Monuments funéraires préislamiques de l'Afrique du Nord*. Paris.

REYNOLDS, J. M. 1955. 'Inscriptions of Roman Tripolitania (*IRT*): a supplement.' *PBSR* 23: 124–47.

REYNOLDS, J. M. 1958. 'Three inscriptions from Ghadames in Tripolitania.' *PBSR* 26: 135–6.

REYNOLDS, J. M. 1971a. 'The cities of Cyrenaica in decline.' In *Thèmes de recherches sur les villes antiques d'occident*. Strasbourg: 53–8.

REYNOLDS, J. M. 1971b. 'Zawiet Msus.' *LA* 8: 39–42.

REYNOLDS, J. M. (ed.) 1976. See Goodchild 1976a.

REYNOLDS, J. M. 1977. 'The Austuriani and Tripolitania in the early fifth century.' *Lib Studs* 8: 13.

REYNOLDS, J. M. and Brogan, O. 1960. 'Seven new inscriptions from Tripolitania.' *PBSR* 28: 51–4.

REYNOLDS, J. M., Brogan, O. and Smith, D. 1958. 'Inscriptions in the Libyan alphabet from Ghirza in Tripolitania.' *Antiquity* 32: 112–15.

REYNOLDS, J. M. and Simpson, W. G. 1967. 'Some inscriptions from el-Auenia, near Yefren in Tripolitania.' *LA* 3–4: 45–47.

REYNOLDS, J. M. and Ward-Perkins, J. B. (eds) 1952. *Inscriptions of Roman Tripolitania*. See IRT.

RICHARDSON, J. 1848. *Travels in the Great Desert of the Sahara in the years of 1845 and 1846*. 2 vols. London.

RIL = Recueil des Inscriptions Libyques. ed. J. B. Chabot. Paris, 1940.

RILEY, J. 1979. 'Coarse pottery.' In J.Lloyd (ed) *Excavations at Sidi Khrebish Benghazi (Berenice)*. Supplements to *Libya Antiqua* V.2: 91–467.

RITCHIE, J. C. 1980. 'Preliminary observations on the botany of the Dakhleh oasis, Egypt.' *The SSEA Journal* X.4: 397–422.

Riv della Trip = Rivista della Tripolitania, Rome.

RIVET, A. L. F. and Smith, C. 1979. *The Place-names of Roman Britain*. London.

ROBINSON, E. S. G. 1927. *British Museum Catalogue of Greek coins : Cyrenaica*. London.

RODRIGUEZ ALMEIDA, E. 1975/1978. 'Bolli anforari di Monte Testaccio, parts I and II.' *Bulletino della Commissione Archeologia Communale di Roma* 84: 199–248 and 86: 107–37.

RODRIGUEZ ALMEIDA, E. 1984. *Il Monte Testaccio. Ambiente, storia, materiali*. Quasar, Rome.

RODWELL, W. and Rowley, T. 1975. *Small Towns of Roman Britain*. BAR 15, Oxford.

ROFFO, P. 1938. 'Sépultures antéislamiques en pierres sèches.' *RAf* 79: 197–243.

ROMANELLI, P. 1916. 'Scavi e scoperte nella citta di Tripoli.' *Notiz. Arch. del Ministero delle Colonie* 2: 300–64.

ROMANELLI, P. 1920. 'Iscrizione Tripolitana che ricorda un'offerta di denti di avorio.' *RAL* 5.29: 376–83 = 1981: 31–8.

ROMANELLI, P. 1924a, 'Del nome delle due Leptis Afrique.' *RAL* 5.33: 253–62 = 1981: 39–48

ROMANELLI, P. 1925. *Leptis Magna*. Rome.

ROMANELLI, P. 1926. 'La politica Romana delle acque in Tripolitania.' *La Rinascilta della Tripolitania*. Milan: 568–76 = 1981: 49–56.

ROMANELLI, P. 1927. 'Ricordi di Tripolitani a Roma e in Italia.' *Bull. Comm. Arch. Communale di Roma* 51: 69–84 = 1981: 57–72.

ROMANELLI, P. 1930. 'La vita agricola attraverso le reppresentazioni figurante.' *Af Ital* 3: 53–70.

ROMANELLI, P. 1933. 'L'origine del nome "Tripolitania".' *Rend Pont. Accad. Rom. Archaeologica* 9: 25–31 = 1981: 73–9.

ROMANELLI, P. 1939. 'Tre iscrizioni tripolitane di interesse storico.' *Epigraphica* 1: 99–118 = 1981: 87–106.

ROMANELLI, P. 1940. 'Gli archi di Tiberio e di Traiano in Leptis Magna.' *Af Ital* 7: 87–105 = 1981: 449–67.

ROMANELLI, P. 1950. 'Note storico-geografiche relative all'Africa al tempo di Augusto.' *RAL* 8.5: 472–92 = 1981: 125–45.

ROMANELLI, P. 1958. '"Fulvi Lepcitani".' *Archaeologia Classica* 10: 258–61 = 1981: 157–60.

ROMANELLI, P. 1959. *Storia delle province romane dell'Africa*. Rome.

ROMANELLI, P. 1960. 'Di alcune testimonianze epigrafiche sui rapporti tra l' Africa e Roma.' *CT* 31: 63–72 = 1981: 185–202.

ROMANELLI, P. 1962. 'Le iscrizioni volubitane dei Baquati e i rapporti di Roma con le tribu indigene dell'Africa.' *Hommages à Albert Grenier*, Brussels: 1347–66 = 1981: 207–26.

ROMANELLI, P. 1965. 'Riflessi di vita locale nei mosaici Africani.' *La mosaique Greco-Romaine. Colloq. intern. CNRS Paris 1963*. Paris: 275–85 = 1981: 241–57.

ROMANELLI, P. 1970. *Topografia e archeologia dell'Africa Romana*. Enciclopedia Classica III.x.7. Rome.

ROMANELLI, P. 1974. 'Le condizioni giuridiche del suolo in Africa.' *Atti Convegno Intern. I diritti locali nelle province romane con particolare riguardo alle condizioni giuridiche del suolo*. Rome: 171–215 = 1981: 319–63.

ROMANELLI, P. 1975. 'La politica municipale romana nell'Africa Proconsulaire.' *Athenaeum* 53: 144–71 = 1981: 365–92.

ROMANELLI, P. 1977. 'La campagna di Cornelio Balbo nel sud Africano.' *Mélanges offerts à Leopold Sedar Senghor*. Dakar: 429–38 = 1981: 393–402.

ROMANELLI, P. 1981. *In Africa e a Roma*. Rome.

ROQUES, D. 1985. *Synésios de Cyrène et la Cyrénaïque du bas-Empire*. Paris.

ROSENTHAL, F. 1958. *Ibn Khaldun – The Muqaddimah, an introduction to history*. 3 vols. (2nd edn 1980). London.

ROSSI, M. and Garbini, G. 1977. 'Nuovi documenti epigrafici dalla Tripolitania romana.' *LA* 13–14: 7–20.

ROUVILLOIS-BRIGOL, M. 1985. 'La steppisation en Tunisie depuis l'époque punique: determinisme humain ou climatique?' *BCTH* n.s. 19B: 215–24.

ROUVILLOIS-BRIGOL, M., Nesson, C. and Vallet, J. 1973. *Oasis du sahara algérien*. Paris.

ROUSSEAU, A. 1853. 'Voyage de Scheik el-Tidjani dans le régence de Tunis pendant les années 706, 707 et 708 de l'héjire (1306–1307).' *Journal Asiatique* 5.1: 102–69.

ROWE, A. (ed.) 1956. *Cyrenaican expedition of the University of Manchester 1952*. Manchester.

ROWE, A. (ed.) 1959. *Cyrenaican expedition of the University of Manchester in 1955, 1956, 1957*. Manchester.

RSAC = Recueil des notices et mémoires de la Societé archéologique de Constantine.

RSGI 1937 = Real Societa Geographica Italiana. 1937. *Il Sahara Italiano. Fezzan e oasi di Gat*. Rome.

RUPRECHTSBERGER, E.M. 1989. 'Die Garamantien.' *Antike Welt* 20 Jahrgang 1989 (special theme issue).

RT = Revue Tunisienne.

RUSHWORTH, A. 1992. *Soldiers and tribesmen: the Roman army and tribal society in late Roman Africa*. Unpublished Ph.D. thesis, University of Newcastle upon Tyne.

SALADIN, H. 1902. 'Fouilles à Henchir Bou-Guerba, Tunisie.' *BCTH* 1902: 405–11.

SALAMA, P. 1951a. *Les voies Romaines de l'Afrique du nord*. Algiers.

SALAMA, P. 1951b. 'Les bornes milliaires de Djemila (Cuicul).' *RAf* 45: 213–72.

SALAMA, P. 1965. 'Déchiffrement d'un milliaire de Lepcis Magna.' *LA* 2: 39–45.

SALEM, M.I. and Busrewil, M. T. (eds) 1980. *The Geology of Libya. 2nd Symposium on the Geology of Libya, held at Tripoli Sept. 16–21, 1978*. 3 vols. London.

SALWAY, P. 1965. *The Frontier people of Roman Britain*. Cambridge.

SALWAY, P. 1981. *Roman Britain*. Oxford.

SALZA PRINA RICOTTI, E. 1971. 'Le ville marittime di Silin (Leptis Magna).' *Rendiconti/Atti della Pontificia Accademia Romana di Archeologia*, series 3.43 (1970–71): 135–63.

SAREL-STERNBERG, B. 1963. 'Semi-Nomades du Nefzaoua.' In UNESCO 1963: 123–36.

SASEL, J. 1963. '"Clausurae Alpium Iuliarium".' *Limes* 5: 155–61.

SATTIN, F. 1967. 'Le incisioni rupestri di Gasr Mimun.' *LA* 3–4: 161–77.

SAUMAGNE, C. 1929. 'Les vestiges d'une centuriation romaine à l'est d'El-Djem.' *CRAI* 1929: 307–13.

SAXER, R. 1967. 'Untersuchungen zu den Vexillationem des Römischen Kaiserheeres (Augustus bis Diocletian).' *Epig Stud* 9: 30–31, 100–10.

SCHAFF, P. (ed.) 1892. *A select library of the Nicene and Post-Nicene fathers of the Christian Church I, The confessions and letters of St. Augustine*. New York.

SEECK, O. 1876. See *Not.Dig*.

SESTON, W. 1928. 'Le secteur de Rapidum sur le "limes" de Maurétanie Césarienne après les fouilles de 1927.' *MEFR* 45: 150–83.

SESTON, W. 1974. See *Mélanges W. Seston*.

SESTON, W. and Euzennat, M. 1971. 'Un dossier de la chancellerie romaine: la "Tabula Banasitana". Etude de diplomatique.' *CRAI* 1971: 468–90.

SHAW, B. D. 1976. 'Climate, environment and prehistory in the Sahara.' *World Archaeology* 8.2: 133–49.

SHAW, B. D. 1978. *Pastoralists, peasants and politics in Roman North Africa*. (Unpublished Ph.D., University of Cambridge.)

SHAW, B. D. 1980. 'Archaeology and knowledge: the history of the North African provinces of the Roman empire.' *Florilegium* 2: 28–60.

SHAW, B. D. 1981a. 'Rural markets in North Africa and the political economy of the Roman Empire.' *Ant af* 17: 37–83.

SHAW, B. D. 1981b. 'Climate, environment and history: the case of Roman North Africa. In T. M. L. Wigley *et al.* (eds) *Climate and History*. Cambridge.

SHAW, B. D. 1981c. 'Fear and loathing: the nomad menace in Roman Africa.' In C.M.Wells (ed.) *Roman Africa/L'Afrique Romaine. The 1980 Vanier lectures*. Ottawa: 29–50.

SHAW, B. D. 1982. 'Lamasba: an ancient irrigation community.' *Ant af* 18: 61–103.

SHAW, B. D. 1983. '"Eaters of flesh, drinkers of milk": the ancient ideology of the pastoral nomad.' *Ancient Society* 13–14 (1982–83): 5–31.

SHAW, B.D. 1984. 'Water and society in the ancient Maghrib: technology, property and development.' *Ant af* 20: 121–73.

SHAW, B.D. 1987. 'Autonomy and tribute: mountain and plain in Mauretania Tingitana.' *R.O.M.M.* 41–42: 66–89.

SHERWIN-WHITE, A. N. 1944. 'Geographical factors in Roman Algeria.' *JRS* 34:1–10.

SHERWIN-WHITE, A. N. 1973. 'The Tabula of Banasa and the "Constitutio Antoniniana".' *JRS* 63: 86–98.

SIGMAN, M. C. 1977. 'The Romans and the indigenous tribes of Mauretania Tingitana.' *Historia* 26: 415–39.

SJÖSTROM, I. 1993. *Tripolitania in Transition: late Roman to early Islamic Settlement.* Aldershot.

SMITH, D. J. 1971. 'The "centenaria" of Tripolitania and their antecedents.' In Gadallah 1971: 299–321.

SMITH, D.J. 1985. 'Ghirza.' In Buck and Mattingly 1985: 227–39.

SMITH, R. E. 1979. '"Dux, praepositus".' *ZPE* 36: 263–78.

SMYTHE, W.H. 1854. *The Mediterranean. A memoir.* London.

SOUVILLE, G. 1970. 'L'industrie préhistorique recueillie à Bu Njem (1967–1968).' *LA* 6–7: 169–73.

SOYER, J. 1973. 'Les cadastres anciens de la région de Saint-Donat (Algérie).' *Ant af* 7: 275–92,

SOYER, J. 1976. 'Les centuriations romaines en Algérie orientale.' *Ant af* 10: 107–80.

SPEIDEL, M. P. 1981. '"Princeps" as a title for "ad hoc" commanders.' *Britannia* 12: 7–13.

SPEIDEL, M. 1988. 'Outpost duty in the desert. Building the fort at Gholaia, Bu Njem, Libya.' *Ant af* 24: 99–102.

SPURR, S. 1986. *Arable Cultivation in Roman Italy.* London.

SQUARCIAPINO, M.F. 1966. *Leptis Magna.* Basle.

SQUARCIAPINO, M.F. 1974. *Sculture del foro Severiano di Leptis Magna.* (MAL X), Rome.

SQUARCIAPINO, M. F. 1980. 'Sulle antiche fonti riguardanti le relazioni dei Romani con le region trans-Saharane in età imperiale.' *QAL* 11: 113–18.

SSEA Journal = The Journal of the Society for the Study of Egyptian Antiquities. Toronto.

STEVENSON, E. L. (ed.) 1932. *Geography of Claudius Ptolemy.* New York.

STILLWELL, R. (ed.) 1976. *The Princeton Encyclopaedia of Classical Sites.* Princeton.

STRONG, D. 1973. 'Septimius Severus at Leptis Magna and Cyrene.' *Lib Studs* 4: 27–34.

SYME, R. 1951. 'Tacfarinas, the Musulamii and Thuburscu.' In P. R. Coleman-Norton (ed.), *Studies in Roman economic history in honour of A. C. Johnson.* Princeton: 113–31.

TAGART, C. 1982. 'A glass fish beaker from Fezzan.' *Lib Studs* 13: 81–4.

TAGART, C. 1983. 'Roman faience from the vicinity of Germa, wadi el-Agial, Fezzan.' *Lib Studs* 14: 143–54.

TAYLOR, A. R. 1960. 'Regional variations in olive cultivation in north Tripolitania.' In Willimot and Clarke 1960: 88–99.

THÉBERT, Y. 1978. 'Romanisation et déromanisation. Histoire décolonisée ou histoire inversée.' *Annales E.S.C.* 33: 64–82.

THOMASSON, B. E. 1960. *Die Statthalter der Römischen Provinzen Nordafrikas von Augustus bis Diocletian.* 2 vols. Lund.

THOMASSON, B.E. 1984. *Laterculi Praesidium* I. Gothenburg.

THOMPSON, L. A. 1971. 'Roman and native in the Tripolitanian cities in the early Empire.' In Gadallah 1971: 235–50.

TISSOT, C. 1888. *Géographie comparée de la province romaine d'Afrique* II. Paris.

TLATLI, S. 1971. *Antique Cities in Tunisia.* Guides Ceres, Tunis.

TODD, M. 1975. *The Northern Barbarians.* London.

TOMBER, R. 1993. 'Quantitative approaches to the investigation of long-distance exchange.' *JRA* 6: 142–66.

TOMLIN, R. S. O. 1979. 'Meanwhile in North Italy and Cyrenaica.' In Casey 1979: 253–70.

TORELLI, M. 1971. 'Le curie di Leptis Magna.' *QAL* 6: 105–11.

TORELLI, M. 1973. 'Per una storia della classe dirigente di Lepcis Magna.' *Rendiconti dell'Accademia Lincei,* series 8.28: 377–410.

TOUSSAINT, P-M. 1905–1908. 'Résumé des reconnaisances archéologiques exécutées par les officiers des Brigade Topographiques d'Algérie et de Tunisie pendant le campagne de 1903–1904.' *BCTH* 1905: 56–74. 'Campagne de 19041905.' *BCTH* 1906: 223–41. 'Campagne de 1905–1906.' *BCTH* 1907: 302–14. 'Campagne de 1906–1907.' *BCTH* 1908: 393–409.

TOUTAIN, J. 1895. 'Notes sur quelques voies romaines de l'Afrique Proconsulaire (Tunisie méridionale et Tripolitaine).' *MEFR* 15: 201–29.

TOUTAIN, J. 1896. 'Les Romains dans le Sahara.' *MEFR* 16:63–77.

TOUTAIN, J. 1903a. 'Notes et documents sur les voies stratégiques et sur l'occupation militaire du sud Tunisien à l'époque romaine.' *BCTH* 1903: 272–409.

TOUTAIN, J. 1903b. 'Note sur une inscription trouvée dans le Djebel Asker.' *BCTH* 1903: 202–07.

TOUTAIN, J. 1903c. 'Les nouveaux milliaires de la route de Capsa à Tacape découverts par M. le capitaine Donau.' *MSAF* 114: 153–230.

TOUTAIN, J. 1905. 'La "limes Tripolitanus" en Tripolitaine d'après les récentes découvertes de M. de Mathuisieulx (1901–04).' *BCTH* 1905: 351–65.

TOUTAIN, J. 1906. 'Nouvelles découvertes sur la voie de Capsa à Turris Tamalleni (sur deux communications de Comm. Donau).' *BCTH* 1906: 242–50.

Tremblements 1984. *Tremblements de terre: histoire et archéologie. IVème rencontres intern. d'archéologie et d'histoire d'Antibes.* Valbonne.

TROUSSET, P. 1974. *Recherches sur le 'limes Tripolitanus' du chott el-Djerid à la frontière tuniso-libyenne.* Editions CNRS, Paris.

TROUSSET, P. 1976. 'Reconnaisances archéologiques sur la frontière saharienne de l'Empire romain dans le sud-ouest de la Tunisie.' *Actes 101e Congrès National des Societés Savantes, Lille. Archéologie:* 21–33.

TROUSSET, P. 1977a. 'Le camp de Gemellae sur le "limes" de Numidie d'après les fouilles de Colonel Baradez (1947–50).' *Limes* 11: 559–76.

TROUSSET, P. 1977b. 'Nouvelles observations sur la centuriation romaine à l'est d'El Jem.' *Ant af* 11: 175–207.

TROUSSET, P. 1978. 'Les bornes du Bled Segui. Nouveaux aperçus sur la centuriation romaine du sud Tunisie.' *Ant af* 12: 125–78.

TROUSSET, P. 1980a. 'Signification d'une frontière: nomades et sédentaires dans la zone du "limes" d'Afrique.' *Limes* 12: 931–43.

TROUSSET, P. 1980b. 'Les milliaires de Chebika (sud Tunisien).' *Ant af* 15: 135–54.

TROUSSET, P. 1980c. 'Villes, campagnes et nomadisme dans l'Afrique du nord antique: representations et réalités.' *Actes de la Table Ronde.* Aix-en-Provence: 195–203.

TROUSSET, P. 1982a. 'Le franchissement des chotts du sud Tunisien dans l'antiquité.' *Ant af* 18: 45–59.

TROUSSET, P. 1982b. 'L'image du nomade saharien dans l'historiographie antique.' *Production pastorale et sociéte 1982,* no. 10 (Maison des sciences de l'hommes): 97–105.

TROUSSET, P. 1984a. 'L'idée de frontière au Sahara d'après les données archéologiques.' In P. Baduel (ed.), *Enjeux Sahariens:* 47–78.

TROUSSET, P. 1984b. 'Note sur un type d'ouvrage linéaire du "limes" d'Afrique.' *BCTH* ns 17B: 383–98.

TROUSSET, P. 1985. 'Les "fines Antiquae" et la reconquête Byzantine en Afrique.' *BCTH* ns 19B: 361–76.

TROUSSET, P. 1986a. 'Les oasis présahariennes dans l'Antiquite: partage de l'eau et division du temps.' *Ant af* 22: 161–91.

TROUSSET, P. 1986b. 'Limes et "frontière climatique".' *Histoire et archéologie de l'Afrique du Nord, 3e Colloque International, Montpellier,* 1985: 55–84.

TROUSSET, P. 1987. 'De la montagne au désert: limes et maîtrise de l'eau.' *R.O.M.M.* 41–42: 90–115.

TROUSSET, P. 1990. 'Tours de guet (watch-towers) et système de liaison optique sur le limes Tripolitanus.' *Limes* 14: 249–77

TROUSSET, P. 1992. 'La vie littorale et les ports dans la petite Syrte à l'époque romaine.' *115e Cong. Nat. Soc. Sav., Ve Coll. sur l'histoire et archéologie de l'Afrique du Nord.* Paris: 317–32.

UNESCO 1963 = *Recherches sur la zone aride XIX, Nomades et Nomadisme au Sahara.* Unesco Publications.

VAN BERCHEM, D. 1952. *L'armée de Diocletian et la réforme Constantinienne*. Paris.

VAN BERCHEM, D. 1977. 'Armée de frontière et armée de manoeuvre, alternative stratégique ou politique?' *Limes* 10: 541–3.

VAN NOSTRAND, J. J. 1925. *The Imperial domains of Africa Proconsularis. An epigraphical study*. University of California.

VATTIONI, F. 1981. 'La bilingue latine e neopunica di El Amrouni.' *Helicon* 20–21: 293–9.

VEEN, M. van der 1981. 'The Ghirza plant remains: Romano-Libyan agriculture in the Tripolitanian pre-desert.' In Barker and Jones 1981: 45–48.

VEEN, M. van der. 1985a. 'The UNESCO Libyan Valleys Survey X: Botanical evidence for ancient farming in the pre-desert.' *Lib Studs* 16: 15–28.

VEEN, M. van der. 1985b. 'Botanical remains.' In Brogan and Smith 1985: 308–11.

VEEN, M. van der. 1992. 'Garamantian agriculture: the plant remains from Zinchecra, Fezzan.' *Lib Studs* 237–39.

VERGERA-CAFFARELLI, E. 1960. 'Ghirza.' *Enciclopedia d'Arte Antica Classica*. Rome.

VINOGRADOV, A. R. 1973. 'The socio-political organisation of a Berber Taraf tribe: pre-protectorate Morocco.' In Gellner and Micaud 1973: 67–83.

VITA-FINZI, C. 1960. 'Post-Roman changes in the wadi Lebda.' In Willimot and Clarke 1960: 46–51.

VITA-FINZI, C. 1969. *The Mediterranean Valleys*. Cambridge.

VITA-FINZI, C. 1978. *Archaeological Sites in their Setting*. London.

VITA-FINZI, C. and Brogan, O. 1965. 'Roman dams on the wadi Megenin.' *LA* 2: 65–71.

VIVIEN DE SAINT-MARTIN, L. 1863. *Le nord d'Afrique dans l'antiquité grecque et romaine*. Paris.

VON CLAUSEWITZ, C. 1982. *On War*. London.

VONDERHEYDEN, M. 1927. *La Berbérie orientale sous les dynasties des Benoû'l-Arlab 800–909*. Paris.

WALDA, H. 1985. 'Provincial art in Roman Tripolitania.' In Buck and Mattingly 1985: 47–66.

WALDA, H. and Walker, S. 1984. 'The art and architecture of Lepcis Magna: marble origins by isotopic analysis.' *Lib Studs* 15: 81–92.

WALDA, H. and Walker, S. 1988. 'Isotopic analysis of marble from Lepcis Magna: revised interpretations.' *Lib Studs* 19: 55–9.

WALDA, H. and Walker, S. 1989. 'Ancient art and architecture in Tripolitania and Cyrenaica: new publications 1969–89.' *Lib Studs* 20: 107–15.

WARD, P. 1967. *Touring Libya. The Western Provinces*. London.

WARD, P. 1968a. *Apuleius on trial at Sabratha*. Cambridge.

WARD, P. 1968b. *Touring Libya. The Southern Provinces*. London.

WARD, P. 1969a. *Tripoli. Portrait of a city*. Cambridge.

WARD, P. 1969b. *Touring Libya. The Eastern Provinces*. London.

WARD, P. 1970. *Sabratha. A guide for visitors*. Cambridge.

WARD-PERKINS, J.B. 1948. 'Severan art and architecture at Leptis Magna.' *JRS* 38: 59–80.

WARD-PERKINS, J. B. 1950. 'Gasr el-Suk el'Oti: a desert settlement in central Tripolitania.' *Archaeology* 3: 25–30.

WARD-PERKINS, J.B. 1951. 'Tripolitania and the marble trade.' *JRS* 41: 89–104.

WARD-PERKINS, J. B. 1971. 'Pre-Roman elements in the architecture of Roman Tripolitania.' In Gadallah 1971:101–16.

WARD-PERKINS, J.B. 1982. 'Town planning in North Africa during the first two centuries of the empire.' *150 Jahr-Feier Deutsches Archaologisches Institut Rom* (Rom. Mitt. Erganzungsheft 25): 29–49.

WARD-PERKINS, J.B. 1993. *The Severan Buildings of Lepcis Magna* (ed. P. Kenrick, with G. D. B. Jones). London.

WARD-PERKINS, J. B. and Goodchild, R. G. 1949. 'The "limes Tripolitanus" in the light of recent discoveries.' *JRS* 39: 81–95 = Goodchild 1976a: 17–34.

WARD-PERKINS, J. B. and Goodchild, R. G. 1953. 'The Christian antiquities of Tripolitania.' *Archaeologia* 95: 1–83.

WARD-PERKINS, J. B., Little, J.H. and Mattingly, D.J. 1986. 'Town houses at Ptolemais.' *Lib Studs* 17: 109–53.

WARD-PERKINS, J. B. and Toynbee, J. M. C. 1949. 'The hunting baths at Lepcis Magna.' *Archaeologia* 93: 165–95.

WARMINGTON, B. H. 1954. *The North African provinces from Diocletian to the Vandal conquest*. Cambridge.

WARMINGTON, B. H. 1956. 'The career of Romanus "comes Africae".' *Byzantine Zeitschrift* 49: 55–64.

WARMINGTON, B.H. 1969. *Carthage* (2nd edn). London.

WARMINGTON, B. H. 1974. 'Frontier studies and the history of the Roman Empire: some desiderata.' *Limes* 9: 291–6.

WEBSTER, G. 1979. *The Roman Imperial Army of the first and second centuries A.D.* (2nd edn). London.

WELLES, C. B., Fink, R. O. and Gilliam, J. F. 1959. *The excavations at Dura Europos, Final Report V.l, The parchments and papyri*. New Haven.

WELSBY, D. 1983. 'The Roman fort at Gheriat el-Garbia.' In Jones and Barker 1983: 57–64.

WELSBY, D. 1988. 'The defences of the Roman forts at Bu Ngem and Gheriat el-Garbia.' In P. Bidwell, R. Miket and B. Ford (eds) *Portae cum turribus. Studies of Roman fort gates*. BAR S 206, Oxford: 63–82.

WELSBY, D. 1990. 'Observations on the defences of Roman forts in North Africa.' *Ant af* 26: 113–29.

WELSBY, D.A. 1991. 'ULVS XXIV: A late Roman and Byzantine church at Souk el Awty in the Tripolitanian pre-desert.' *Lib Studs* 22:61–80

WELSBY, D. 1992. 'ULVS XXV: the gsur and associated settlements in the Wadi Umm el Kharab: an architectural survey.' *Lib Studs* 23:73–99.

WENDORF, F. and Marks, A. E. 1975. *Problems in Prehistory: North Africa and the Levant*. Dallas.

WHEELER, M. 1954. *Beyond the Imperial frontiers*. London.

WHITTAKER, C.R. 1974. 'The western Phoenicians: colonisation and assimilation.' *Proc. Cambridge Phil. Soc.* n.s. 20: 58–79.

WHITTAKER, C. R. 1978a. 'Land and labour in North Africa.' *Klio* 60.2: 331–62.

WHITTAKER, C. R. 1978b. 'M. Benabou, La Résistance Africaine à la Romanisation.' *JRS* 68: 190–92.

WHITTAKER, C. R. 1978c. 'Carthaginian imperialism in the fifth and fourth centuries.' In P.D.A. Garnsey and C.R. Whittaker (eds) *Imperialism in the Ancient World*: 59–90.

WHITTAKER, C.R. 1989a. *Les frontières de l'empire romain*. Paris.

WHITTAKER, C.R. 1989b. 'Supplying the system: frontiers and beyond.' In J. Barrett, A. Fitzpatrick and L. McInnes, *Barbarians and Romans in North-west Europe*. BAR S 471, Oxford: 64–80

WHITTAKER, C.R. 1994. *Frontiers of the Roman Empire. A social and economic study*. Baltimore.

WILLIMOT, S. G. 1960. 'Soils of Jefara.' In Willimot and Clarke 1960: 26–45.

WILLIMOT, S. G. and Clarke, J. I. (eds) 1960. *Field Studies in Libya*. Department of Geography Research Papers 4, University of Durham.

WINKLER, A. 1910. 'La frontière entre la Tripolitaine et l'Afrique propre à l'époque romaine.' *RT* 17: 100–03.

WOOLF, G. 1992. 'Imperialism, empire and the integration of the Roman economy.' *World Archaeology* 23.3: 283–93.

WOOLMAN, D. S. 1969. *Rebels in the Rif. Abd el-Krim and the Rif rebellion*. London.

YORKE, R. A. 1967. 'Les ports engloutis de Tripolitaine et de Tunisie.' *Archéologia* 17 (July–August): 18–24.

YORKE, R.A. 1986. 'The harbour.' In Kenrick 1986: 242–5.

YORKE, R. A. et al. 1966. *Cambridge expedition to Sabratha 1966 Report* (privately circulated).

ZEVI, F. and Tchernia, A. 1969. 'Amphores de Byzacène au Bas-Empire.' *Ant af* 3: 173–214.

INDEX

Abd el-Hakam, Arab historian, 29, 71

Ad Amadum, 189; see also Dehibat

Ad Maiores, fort and *vicus*, 8, 137

Aedemon, moorish leader, 21

Aelius Lamia, L., proconsul Af., 52, 56, 71, 140

Aemilia Pudentilla, Oean millionaire
landed interests and other wealth, 143; marriage to
Apuleius, 53, 62, 123

Aemilianus, Donatist sympathiser, 211

Aemilius Aemilianus, soldier, 152

Aemilius Emeritus, decurion, 84-85

Aemilius Frontinus, L., Oean proconsul Asia, 59

Aethiopes, see Ethiopians

Africa Nova, post-Caesarean province, 19, 51

Africa Proconsularis, province, xiii, 1, 51, 55, 138-39, 158
as granary of Rome, 2, 138; as senatorial province,
51; legion transferred to legate, 52; Lepcitantians in
administration of, 57, 59; peoples of, 19; status of
late Roman governors, 172; Tetrarchic subdivision
and later history, xiii, 171-2, 181; Tripolitania as part
of, 1; urbanisation 134, 143, 160

Africa Vetus, early province, 3, 51

Africans, see Libyans

Agarlabas , see Henschir Margarine

Agisymba, sub-Saharan location, 72

Agma, road station? 64

agriculture
botanical evidence; 3, 35, 148-9, 151-2, 198; coast and
Gebel, 14-15, 76, 139-44; Garamantian agriculture,
35, 43; iconographic evidence, 143, 151, 198, 207;
mixed economy, 15, 47; modern 8; pre-desert, 15-16,
76, 138-40, 144-53; run-off and hydraulic technology,
11, 144, 147, 151; use of slaves, 143-4; see also, crops,
farms, oases, sedentarization, wadi farming.

Ain el-Auenia, see *Auru*

Ain Scerciara, see *Cercar*

Ain Wif, see *Thenadassa*

Ain Zara, cemetery, 123, 211

Akhaemeneis, Libyan tribe, 26, 31

Ala I Pannoniorum, 84

Albertini tablets, 215

Alele, Phazanian centre, 30, 43, 70

altars, see *Volubilis*

Amantes, Libyan tribe, 26, 31-2

Ammaedara (Haidra), fortress, 52, 70, 79

Ammon, deity, 33, 38-40, 133, 140, 168, 175, 212, 213;
oracles of, 33, 39

Ammonia (temples of Ammon), 33, 36, 39, 71, 168

amphitheatres and games, 119, 120, 127, 162, 181

amphorae, 153-5, 158-9
Dressel form 20, 153; exported to Pompeii, Ostia,
Rome, 153-4, 158-9; in Fezzan, 37, 74; on Monte
Testaccio, 153; Punic, 153; stamps on, 153-5;
Tripolitanian types, 153-4, 158-9; see also pottery

Ampsaga river, 19

Amr ibn el-Aasi, Arab general, 216

Anacutas, Libyan tribe, 26, 176

ancestor worship, 39, 207

ancient sources
on Tripolitania's geography and climate, 1-4; on
tribes 17-18, 20; problems with, 18-20

Anicius Faustus, Q., governor Numidia, 80, 92

animal displays (*venationes*), 3, 162

Annaeus Cornutus, L., Lepcitanian philosopher, 58

Anno Macer, Lepcitanian, 58

Annobal Tapapius Rufus, Lepcitanian, 58, 119, 161

Annobal, son of Masaucan, Libyan, 164-5

Antalas, Libyan chief, 39, 174

250